Integration-Ready Architecture and Design

Software Engineering with XML, Java, .NET, Wireless, Speech, and Knowledge Technologies

Jeff Zhuk
Internet Technology School, Inc.

Cambridge
University Press

PUBLISHED BY THE PRESS SYNDICATE OF THE UNIVERSITY OF CAMBRIDGE
The Pitt Building, Trumpington Street, Cambridge, United Kingdom

CAMBRIDGE UNIVERSITY PRESS
The Edinburgh Building, Cambridge CB2 2RU, UK
40 West 20th Street, New York, NY 10011-4211, USA
477 Williamstown Road, Port Melbourne, VIC 3207, Australia
Ruiz de Alarcón 13, 28014 Madrid, Spain
Dock House, The Waterfront, Cape Town 8001, South Africa

http://www.cambridge.org

First published 2004

Printed in the United States of America

Typefaces ITC Berkeley Oldstyle 10.75/13 pt. and ITC Franklin Gothic *System* $\LaTeX\ 2_\varepsilon$ [TB]

A catalog record for this book is available from the British Library.

Library of Congress Cataloging in Publication Data

Zhuk, Jeff.

Integration-ready architecture and design : software engineering with XML, Java, .NET, Wireless, speech, and knowledge technologies / Jeff Zhuk.

p. cm.

Includes bibliographical references and index.

ISBN 0-521-52583-7 (pb.)

1. Software engineering. 2. Expert systems (Computer science) I. Title.

QA76.758.Z48 2004
005.1 – dc22 2003065381

ISBN 0 521 52583 7 paperback

Contents

Preface

WHO SHOULD READ THIS BOOK?

Integration-Ready Architecture and Design strives for a union of theory and practice. Teaching the latest wired and wireless software technologies, the book is probably the first entry into "the next big thing," a new world of integrated knowledge and software engineering. Written by a software architect and experienced trainer, this book is for:

- **Software architects, designers, and developers**
- **Internet and wireless service providers**
- **IT managers and other IT professionals, as well as amateurs**
- **Subject matter experts** who will directly participate in a new development process of integrated software and knowledge engineering
- **Students and educators**, who will find up-to-date materials for the following courses:

1. Software Architecture,
2. Software Engineering,
3. Programming Concepts,
4. Information Technologies,
5. Smart Card and JavaCard Technologies,
6. Wireless Technologies,
7. J2ME and Wireless Messaging,
8. XML Technologies,
9. Speech Technologies,
10. Java Language and Technology,
11. C# and .Net Technology,
12. Integration Technologies,
13. Business Communications and Collaborative Engineering,
14. Web Technologies,
15. Introduction of Ontology, and
16. Integrated Software and Knowledge Engineering (introduced in the book)

- **Peers: students, instructors, consultants, and corporate team players** who might start using a peer-to-peer educational tool offered in the book as their entrance to the distributed knowledge marketplace
- **All of the above who want to know** how things work, should work, and *will* work in the IT world

Why Did I Write This Book?

Of course, I wanted to solve several global-scale problems. Divided by corporate barriers and working under "time-to-market" pressure, we often replicate data and services and produce software that is neither *soft* nor *friendly*. Working as fast as possible in this mode, we deliver products that lack flexibility and teamwork skill and are hardly ready for integration into new environments. These products strictly target user requirements—which become obsolete by the time the project ends. Producing "more of the same" and raising the number of product choices (instead of moving to new horizons), we actually increase entropy and slow down the progress of technology, which depends heavily on inventions, new usage, or new combinations of existing tools and methods.

The famous formula "write once" is not working *anywhere* today. One of the reasons is the absence of a mechanism capable of accepting, classifying, and providing meaningful information about new data or services created by knowledge producers.

We have not changed our way of writing software during the past twenty years.

We have not moved far from the UNIX operational environment (which was a big hit thirty years ago).

Our computers are much faster, but for the regular user, they are as stupid as they were forty years ago. We add power but we fail to add common sense to computers, we cannot help them learn, and we routinely lose professional knowledge gained by millions of knowledge workers.

Meanwhile, best practices in software and knowledge engineering are reaching the point of critical mass. By learning, understanding, and *integrating* them, we can turn things around. We might be able to improve the reliability of quickly changing environments by using distributed self-healing networks and knowledge base–powered application solutions.

We can finally stop rewriting traditional address book, scheduling, inventory, and order applications. We will shift our focus from ironing out all possible business cases in our design and code to creating flexible application mechanisms that allow us to change and introduce new business rules on the fly. Coming changes are similar to the transition from structural to object-oriented programming. We are going back to school.

How to Use This Book

I hope you find this book on your list of recommended reading or as "the best gift for yourself, your spouse, and your friends." Just buy two copies and let *them* figure out what to do with the book. In the worst case, it can be used for self-defense. It is almost as heavy as other good books.

If your gift list includes yourself, you might want to read this book in the bookstore first—at least some selected chapters, starting from the back.

For example, Chapter 10, about a JavaCard key that opens all doors, can be very handy the next time you lock your keys in your car. If this happens too often to you or your close relatives, you might find Chapter 11, on J2ME and wireless messaging, very practical.

Armed with the knowledge of wireless technologies from Chapters 8, 9, and 11, you can create your own communication service and finally stop switching from AT&T to Sprint and back to Verizon. Serve your friends and neighbors, compete with T-Mobile, and someday I'll be happy to buy your integrated "wireless portal communicator" product.

If you are a serious developer or plan to become one, you might prefer to start from the beginning and read all the way through. Search for long-term, secure, and exciting IT directions. Find out why all the pieces of the puzzle, as well as the glue, are almost equally important. Teach yourself to see every technology (component) as an object with three dimensions: what, why, and how. After reading the book, you might even become less serious and more efficient.

If you want to increase your business clientele from the 20% of the population who are fluent in current computer interfaces to the rest of us, including those who hate computers or cannot bear their stupidity—just go for it! Read Chapters 4, 5, 12, and 13, on speech and knowledge technologies, and create a natural user interface, a bridge from your business to humankind.

A professional hacker (whose average age is 15 but ranges from 6 to 66) might start with Appendix 3 ("Source Examples"). Find examples that can help to build collaborative and location-based services, screen/voice instant sharing and security monitoring, and speech and distributed knowledge alliance applications. Look there for spam killer hints to be ahead of the game.

If you just want to speak more languages, go to Appendix 1 ("Java and C#: The Saga of Siblings"). You can get two for the price of one, including the latest JDK1.5 language innovations.

If you would like to include XML in your repertoire, add Appendix 2 ("XML and Web Services"), which covers several dialects of the XML family.

Chapters 5 and 13 are not only for computer folks. The elusive category of "knowledge workers"—anyone who has gained knowledge and never had a chance to share—might be looking at the Promised Land. Subject matter experts (SME)—who used to talk to developers about *what* and *why*—can find in those chapters new ways to say *how*.

There is also a downloadable software product with this book. Students and educators can use the tool for collaborative work in team projects. The tool helps to connect students and instructors with educational knowledge resources. This can elevate the visibility and quality of student projects and transmit the best of them into industry contributions. The software can be handy in academic/corporate alliances.

What Is This Book About?

- The what's, why's, and how's on: J2EE, J2ME, .NET, JSAPI, JMS, JXTA, JMF, SALT, VoiceXML, WAP, 802.11, CDMA, GPRS, CycL, XML, and multiple XML-based technologies, including RDF, DAML, SOAP, WSDL, and UDDI. The book turns these abbreviations into understandable concepts and examples
- The distributed knowledge marketplace
- Collaborative engineering methods and technology

- XML and Web technology architecture, design, and code patterns
- Ontological (knowledge) engineering and natural user interface
- XML-based application scenarios that integrate dynamic user interface and traditional services with speech and knowledge technologies
- Unique recipes for creating integration-ready components across a wide range of client-server, multi-tier, and peer-to-peer distributed architectures for Internet and wireless service developers
- Innovative ideas, methods, and examples for building multidimensional worlds of enterprise applications
- Privilege-based access to corporate data and services, not only through PCs and workstations but also through multiple types of wired and wireless devices and personal digital assistants with seamless integration of wireless, Web, speech, and knowledge technologies
- A unified approach to architecture and design that allows for J2EE and .NET implementations with code examples in Java (most of the source code) and C# languages
- Integration of software and knowledge engineering in knowledge-driven architecture
- Union of theory and practice. As many of us do, I divide my professional time between the education (30%) and development (70%) worlds. Time sharing is not always the best option in real estate, but I hope it works for this book by providing more cross-connections between these parallel worlds. Like most parallel worlds, they have (almost) no intersections according to Euclidian geometry, but we can find many by moving into Riemann's space
- Questions and exercises, case study assignments, design and code samples, and even a learn-by-example self-training system that allows you to enter the distributed knowledge marketplace

Bridging the gap for a new generation of software applications, the book teaches a set of skills that are becoming extremely valuable today and that will certainly be in high demand tomorrow.

This book is designed to walk a reader through the peaks of current software, with a focus on foundations, concepts, specifications, and architecture. The hike then goes down to the valley of implementation, with detailed design examples and explanations, and finally flies to new horizons of software and knowledge technologies. There lies the happy ending, where software and knowledge engineering ride off into the sunset together.

Contributors

Many special thanks to the people who made direct contributions to this text:

Ben Zhuk—Cowrote a number of sections, edited the entire book for both content and style, and created all diagrams and illustrations (except those mentioned below). He was a sounding board for ideas throughout the writing process and was an invaluable resource. I am indebted to him, more than I can express, for his tireless efforts and the countless hours he put into this project.

Dmitry Semenov—Senior Software Architect who read the manuscript carefully and thoroughly. Dmitry's remarks and criticism helped me to clarify content and add significant parts to Chapters 3 and 13.

Olga Kaydanov, artist—Provided great design ideas and artistic inspiration for illustrations (http://artistandart.com).

Irina Zadov, artist—Illustrated Fig. I.1, Fig. I.2, Fig. I.5, and Fig. 1.4 (http://ucsu.colorado.edu/~zadovi).

Inna Vaisberg, designer—Illustrated Fig. 3.1 and Fig. A3.18 (http://javaschool.com/skills/Inna.Vaisberg.Portfolio.pdf).

My former students, talented software developers:
Masha Tishkov, who wrote and tested several XML parser methods in the Stringer.java source and helped to prepare the uploader package;

Slava Minukhin, who teamed up with me to write C# sources for Appendix 3: TextToSpeech.cs, SocketTTS.cs, Recognizer.cs;

Alex Krevenya, who helped write email- and spam-related sources for Appendix 3; and **Dina Malkina**, who wrote C++ sources for Chapter 12: ListeningClient.cpp and TalkingClient.cpp.

Thank you so much!

Acknowledgments

This is a great opportunity to say thank you to so many people without whom this book would be impossible. Thanks to my parents; if not for them, you might be holding a different book right now.

To my friends (many of them former students), who assisted and supported me with many essential steps in the book's production.

To Candi Hoxworth, IT Manager, who read most of the book and provided great suggestions on improving my American accent in it.

To Stuart Ambler, Mathematician and Software Architect, who reviewed and provided important feedback for Chapters 8, 10, and 12.

To Michael Merkulovich, Software Team Lead, who read and provided valuable suggestions for Chapter 6 and Appendix 1.

To Nina Zadov, Senior Software Engineer, who read and approved Chapter 7.

To Roman Zadov, Mathematician, who reviewed Chapter 5 (Ontology).

To Bryan Basham, Java Instructor, who reviewed a section (multipart/form upload) from Appendix 3.

To Linda Koepsell, Course Development Project Manager, who reviewed a section from Chapter 11 (J2ME).

To Jason Fish, Enterprise Learning, President, who invited me to teach for Java University at an international conference, where I met Lothlorien Homet from Cambridge University Press. Thank you Jason and Lothlorien, you got me started with this book.

To Cambridge University Press editors Lauren Cowles and Katherine Hew and TechBooks project manager Amanda Albert and copy editor Georgetta Kozlovski for their work and dedication.

To Cyc Corporation knowledge experts John De Oliveira, Steven Reed, and Dr. Doug Lenat, who taught me ontology and the Cyc Language and reviewed several sections from Chapters 5 and 13.

To my colleagues from the University of Phoenix, Mary A. Martin, Ph.D., Blair Smith, Stephen Trask, Adam Honea, Ph.D., and Carla Kuhlman, Ph.D., who reviewed sections from Chapter 2 (Software Architecture) and Notes for Educators.

To my colleagues from DeVry University, Ash Mahajan, Karl Zhang, Ph.D., and Mike Wasson, who reviewed the Preface and Introduction.

To Victor Kaptelinin, Ph.D., Umea University (Sweden), professor with whom I discussed multiple ideas for collaborative environments.

To Jay DiGiovanni, Director of Software Development, who reviewed and provided encouraging remarks on a section from Chapter 13.

To Vladimir Safonov, Ph.D., St. Petersburg University, Professor, who offered excellent suggestions for Chapter 2 (Software Architecture).

To Vlad Genin, Ph.D., Stanford University and University of Phoenix, Professor of Engineering, who gave me important notes on introductory sections.

To Robert Gathers, GN President, with whom I discussed the future of distributed networks and who reviewed several sections from Chapters 13 and 14.

To Rachel Levy, whose reviews of and ideas for the Introduction and Preface were inspired and right on-target.

To my children, Julie and Ben, for their moral support and phenomenal help during the entire process.

And finally, and most importantly, to my wife, Bronia, who makes everything in my life possible.

Introduction

One might think that the software industry is performing very well because it is armed with object-oriented approaches, Web services, Java and .NET technologies, and so forth. Unfortunately, this is not true.

There may be something wrong with the way we write programs. The process has not changed much during the past twenty years, except that applications and tools are getting bigger. Yet are they better and more scalable? Do they require any common sense? Can they be reused in different circumstances?

If these things were true, I do not think we would be rewriting the address book, schedule, order, and inventory applications over and over again instead of moving to new, untouched tasks. We would be able to accumulate the professional knowledge gained by millions of knowledge workers (everyone who manages information flow on a daily basis) instead of routinely losing it, as we do today. We would also not be facing the current IT crisis.

We could even have had more precise and direct access to the market's supply and demand, which would have reduced the glaring inefficiencies of the software marketplace of the 1990s. A big change is required to return investors' confidence to IT, and, hopefully, the change is coming.

Yes, technology can help economic stability if applied with precision. Sometimes I wonder why big companies are constantly growing bigger while small ones tend to disappear. Why do corporations prefer doing business with a few vendors, or often a single vendor, even when it is an expensive one? One of the reasons is that the integration of multiple vendors' products would be even more expensive.

Why Is Product Integration Such a Pain?

Products and services are currently designed to cover *predefined* tasks and work with *known* data.

Are they ready for *unknown* tasks and new data sources?
Are they ready for integration with other products and services?
Are they ready to be extended into the wireless world?

Figure I.1. Cooking Applications on Demand.

We think we know what is going on in our industry, but how close are we, really, to even asking the right questions?

Where can you look for information? Google.com is one answer. Where can you find any tangible product to buy? Ebay.com is a good solution. Can you find a service you need? This question is a bit harder, and the short answer is no, except for the technologies to register *Web services*, which we explore in following chapters. The ocean of industries and markets is filled with a myriad of services, but we notice only the brightest and loudest fish on the surface and have no equipment to help us swim the depths and explore this underwater universe.

If we somehow find a service, then we have a chance to take a closer look. We may subsequently find that it is not exactly what we *really* want.

Can we modify a product or service? Can we easily plug it into another service? Can I cook my application as easily as my lunch, from products and services selected right now for a single usage, as in Fig. I.1?

What does it mean to build *integration-ready* products?

Why and how do we use XML, Java, .NET, wireless, and speech technology components?

What is the next big thing? Is it about collaborative engineering, distributed knowledge marketplace, *knowledge-driven architecture*, or all of the above?

This book answers these questions, walks readers through the edge of current technologies, explains their fundamentals and interdependencies, helps to integrate the best practices of existing technologies into a new development paradigm, and provides an entrance into the world of knowledge alliances.

Examples, case studies, and the self-training application offered by this textbook arm students and instructors with ammunition for successful teamwork.

FIGURE I.2. A Mysterious Planet.

AN ILLUSTRATIVE PASSAGE FROM "BEN'S REAL AND DREAM MEMOIRS"

A hint: even if Ben were a real person (I doubt it) his stories are not necessarily real.

> *"If you are not a lucky person, you'd better get some skills." I suddenly appreciated this aphorism praising the advancement of knowledge as I rushed down the runway. I had just realized that, having failed to check the schedule, I was about to miss the last kicker-ship and now risked spending the night on the tiny planet known only as H.235.*
>
> *This was strictly forbidden by travel rules. H.235 was one of the infamous "black holes" rarely visited by tourists. There were rumors about strange forms of nightlife on the planet. No, this was not related to sex, but to unions of magicians, the legendary "global mind," and disappearing travelers. I tried to flag down a couple of H'sters, but they did not understand English.*

They immediately threw many extremely strange and incomprehensible words at me and then moved on when my face showed no understanding. I had always suspected that the people here spoke a different language, but I never expected it to go this far.

The street was now empty except for an old man coming my way. My memory struggled to find the right words, and a single phrase came out: "Sprechen sie Deutch?" This was the sole gem in my collection of foreign language knowledge.

The old man stopped and smiled while taking out his cell phone. My first thought was, "He is calling the police!" Then the second, "He is calling a gang!" The man spoke the strange language into the phone, repeating a word that sounded almost, but not quite, completely unlike the word Instructions. *Suddenly, he handed the phone to me.*

A voice from the phone spoke clear English. "This is the Common Brain help line. You are granted a guest level of permission to ask any question, except those related to H.235 security. Your question will be translated into our language. Please end your question with the words exit and translate."

I started asking rapid-fire questions. The phone worked like magic.

After the first question, the voice from the phone took a leading role. It navigated me through a question-and-answer session, helping me express my needs in system-specific terms. At the end of the session, the phone commanded: "Mister Ben, please pass the phone to the answering party."

The old man, whose name turned out to be Paul, played the role of the answering party. He listened to the phone's version of my queries and made strange sounds that came to me via the phone in perfect English. At the end of the call, Paul used his phone as a camera to photograph my smiling face.

The voice from the phone explained that I had missed the regular night shuttle, but could still make the special shuttle reserved for just such occasions. My picture was in the system now to allow me past the auto flight attendant. I was provided with precise directions over the phone, and at one point, a map was even displayed on the phone's screen.

I felt so happy I even tried to ask a couple of extra questions, but the only answer I received was "Questions about religion or sex cannot be answered, as they are related to H.235 security."

While on the way home in the shuttle, I thought about the Common Brain. Was it a high-tech company or a psychic organization? Or maybe both would be needed to help people understand each other?

Where was the catch? What technology was used? Could the old man have been a magician? I had heard the rumor that some magicians had access to a legendary "global mind." Why was there a special flight just for me? And why was this flight taking so long?

My eyes closed as a white fog slowly surrounded me.

Back to Reality: Mosaics of Technologies

That story sounds like science fiction, except for the final questions. These questions bring us back to reality, introducing *mosaics of technologies*.

Let us answer one question at a time. Was it technology or magic? Figure I.3 illustrates three related technologies that could be used today to make that science fiction story a reality.

Web technology is a respected parent: young, but mature. It has already raised a couple of very promising kids, and more are expected. A Web client or Hypertext Markup Language (HTML) browser talks directly to a Web server using HTML over the Hypertext Transfer Protocol (HTTP). HTML pages deliver text, graphics, and sound files over wired networks.

One of the Web's children is based on the wireless application protocol (WAP) and wireless markup language (WML). The small screen of a cellular phone serves as a destination for

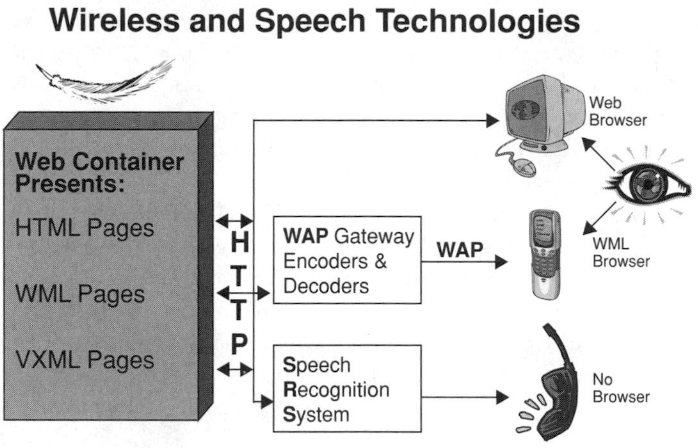

FIGURE I.3. Children of Web Technology.

WML pages. Not all wireless phones are capable of displaying WML pages; the phone must include a WML browser that provides this capability.

The other child of Web technology is based on a speech recognition system (SRS) and Voice Extensible Markup Language (VoiceXML or VXML) to deliver content to human beings in the most natural way possible. In all cases, the content is kept on the Web server or is generated dynamically by a Web container that includes a Web server and the software responsible for dynamic content generation.

In every case the content is presented by some kind of XML page, as XML is a common denominator for HTML, WML, and VXML. (See *http://w3.org* for a further description of this family.) SRS/VXML can be used for language translation. WAP/WML can be used for electronic document exchange: the photo ID that was created on the spot was sent to the server, and a map with directions was sent from the server back to the phone.

FROM CENTRALIZED COLLECTIONS TO INTEGRATION-READY SERVICES

Here is an interesting puzzle stated in a simple question. It looks like we are moving more and more resources to the server side. Is this the way technology is going? Will we face a huge service repository that continues to grow and collect more and more services?

Not necessarily. Another answer to our question is to improve the capacity for integration. This means that a service (in the simplest case, an application) might be made flexible enough to allow it easily to adapt to novel contexts. A library of services can be integrated on the fly and used on demand in real time and in a fashion transparent to the end user. For example, a wireless communication channel service, a map service, a shuttle-scheduling service, and a personal security authentication service might configure themselves to provide a new, integrated service to the end user, such as booking a flight.

This solution is more than a theoretical possibility. Businesses are already beginning to turn the focus of development from "more products in a package" to "friendly (easy to integrate and customize) products." Figure I.4 represents a multidimensional view of integration-ready services.

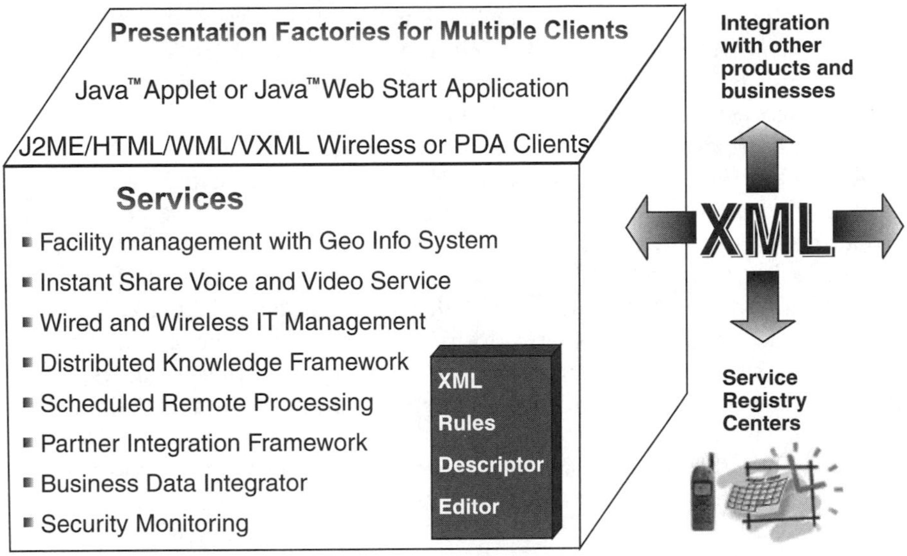

FIGURE I.4. Multidimensional Views of Enterprise Applications.

Perhaps you have heard about the "80/20" rule, which states that every service is focused on just the 20 percent of the possible scope that will produce 80 percent of the desired results.

This approach becomes even more beneficial when architecture, design, and development are done in such a manner that customization is an inexpensive process, when it is even possible to add or customize services without changing the core code.

What is important for corporate businesses that are selecting the right technologies?

System flexibility, the capacity to recapture business rules and structures, and readiness for integration with other products and systems are all rapidly becoming priorities. How can these goals be accomplished?

There are several methods that can be used for system integration. Java-specific integration techniques, such as JAIN (Java application program interfaces [APIs] for integrated network), introduce system integration. There is also a new world of Java-based Jini devices capable of promoting or announcing their skills/capabilities over the network. We consider these technologies and talk about a *unified service and data* integration approach.

This XML-based approach to integration interfaces defines system behavior as well as the data integration process. It paves the road for creating integration-ready services, defines unified integration protocols and policies, and helps to connect them into distributed business alliances.

Business clients access corporate repositories with multiple types of wired and wireless devices and personal digital assistants (PDAs). Corporate workstations still outnumber other devices, but this is changing rapidly.

We do not want to redevelop business services for every type of access. It is important to understand that we need only to build more ways to present/access the same content of enterprise data and services. This leads to one of the most important architecture rules: Separate business from presentation logics. This separation is very visible in Fig. I.4.

Presentation factories (software responsible for visual/audio depictions or presentations for different types of clients) allow us to reuse a set of framework services (e.g., facility management) **and** deliver service results properly formatted for multiple types of devices from corporate workstations to wireless phones or PDAs.

In the preceding example, common business problems are solved with several "core" frameworks. Each service was focused on just 20 percent of the possible scope that produced 80 percent of the results. Architecture, design, and development are accomplished in a manner that makes it possible to add or customize services without changing the core code.

This allows a business to transform into an e-business with the ability to connect to a global business alliance or distributed knowledge and service marketplace.

This marketplace instantly provides information on products, data, and services, along with their values (some services might be more valuable than others), allows multiple parties/systems to negotiate multiple forms of collaboration, and contains sufficiently flexible levels of access security.

Businesses will be able to leverage their existing application assets by making them available to others via Web service and distributed technologies. Business frameworks, presentation factories, Web service, and distributed technologies (and much more) are discussed further in separate chapters.

Software Architecture and Integration-Ready Systems

The past decade has moved software architecture into the center of system development. It has also provided many (perhaps too many) examples of inefficient "quick and dirty" solutions prompted by a lack of integration among the three worlds of what, why, and how.

The latest buzzwords, industry trends, and components have often been used without necessity and without understanding that they are beneficial in specific circumstances under specific requirements. At the same time, some projects have not benefited from new standards and technologies, simply because developers have not been aware of their existence or have not had enough skills to apply them.

The importance of developing integration-ready systems and components is another lesson we continue to learn from the past.

The book teaches the reader to understand design patterns and architectural styles, to be able to see multiple sides of a system through the prism of industry standards and specifications, to communicate this vision via multiple architectural views, and finally to transform this vision into design and code that can make the "write once" dream a reality.

Enterprise Service Components and Challenges

Wired and Wireless Telecommunications

Enterprise communications include telecommunication services as well as a variety of IT and data services.

Telecommunication services are competing for a limited market. (Though we called this market "unlimited" in the past, this clearly did not help matters much.) Telecommunication vendors offer new products and services that balance reliability, superiority of features, and price. Here is the client's usual question: "Will your new program work with my old one?" In this case, "I am not sure" is not the right answer.

FIGURE I.5. Phone Generations Hand in Hand.

There are "9-to-5" employees who work only in the office and use fixed telephony. There is also a growing community of telecommuters: mobile employees who, for example, work one day in the office and four on the road, and who use wireless telephony. Corporations have multibillion dollar investments in Legacy PBXs that run regular telephony. This is the best guarantee of their longevity. Voice over IP and wireless communications will have to find ways to coexist in the mixed-enterprise telecom environment. Interoperability and a smooth transition can be achieved with a unified approach to wired and wireless application architecture.

The increasing quantity and variety of wireless devices sets new challenges for companies competing for multiple markets that run multiple wireless technologies. The winners will be those wireless Internet providers (WISPs) and wireless application service providers (WASPs) who can offer reliable connections and content services and optimize development solutions with a unified approach across multiple client devices.

Wireless clients are truly mobile. Client environments, locations, connections, and other parameters can be changed more frequently and drastically than those of fixed-wired network clients. We have to develop smart location-based services for our PDAs, cars, and robots equipped with GPS (global positioning system). We will have to switch from centralized, fixed computing to *distributed self-healing networks* with *flexible service redistribution*. We'll deploy *knowledge base–powered* application solutions: quick and smart adjustments to client locations, connections, and overall environment changes (Fig. I.5).

Consolidation of Multiple Data Sources

Multiple data sources were historically created in multiple departments for different and often unrelated purposes. Company mergers and the process of building Web umbrellas for company services bring a new focus to an old task. Data consolidation is becoming one of the highest enterprise business priorities. Enterprise Web applications require data integration and consistency. Data integration is especially relevant to telecom applications, which by their nature must be connected to multiple enterprise data storages.

Data consolidation is an expensive, nontrivial process in which XML and Java technologies can play an essential role. In Chapter 6 we consider a unified approach to multiple data sources (Fig. I.6).

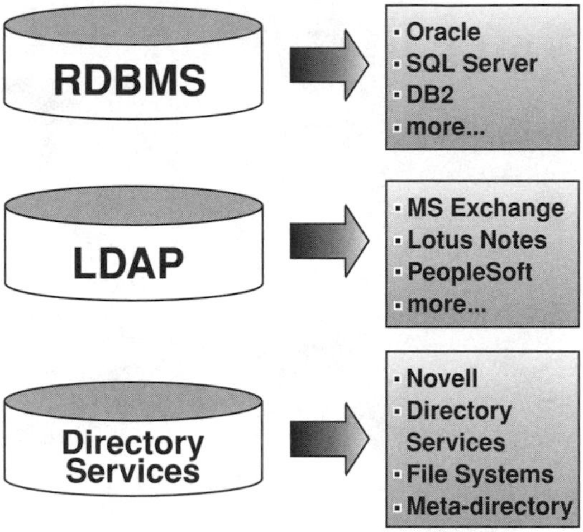

FIGURE I.6. Multiple Faces of Data Storage.

Natural User Interface and Knowledge Technologies

There are dependencies between the natural user interface and knowledge technologies. For example, current speech technologies are not quite ready to understand natural language speech initiated by a person. There are similar difficulties with machine translation from foreign languages. Can tasks like machine vision, speech recognition, and foreign language translation, which seem very different, have a common solution?

The first common denominator is easy to find: all these tasks belong to the field of data processing. The next move is to find common steps for all three activities. What do people do when they are engaged in image or speech recognition, when they translate text from Hebrew to English?

Can we build a computer program to perform similar steps? We know that data we usually keep in relational databases can hardly help us. What types of data are needed for the process?

Distributed yet connected, specific yet based on generic roots, different in themes yet non-conflicting: these are the qualities required for information to be inherently useful. Creating this quality data is extremely difficult; however, it has been proven possible.

We discuss architecture, design, and code samples that integrate knowledge technologies into enterprise applications and give the keys to a new breed of software—"softology," a mix of software and ontological engineering.

Because the knowledge engine is a new element that plays an important role in such architecture, I label it *knowledge-driven architecture*. It is very likely that this type of application will become the next big thing (after service-oriented architecture and event-driven architecture) in the near future.

This promising direction can raise the IQ level of our products; add more flexibility, intelligence, and common sense to applications; and even change the development paradigm by providing business experts with better tools that can eliminate several layers of the current development process.

Location-Based Services (Topology/Maps)

Topology data or geographical information systems (GIS) are necessary for mobile environments, facility management, military operations, and more.

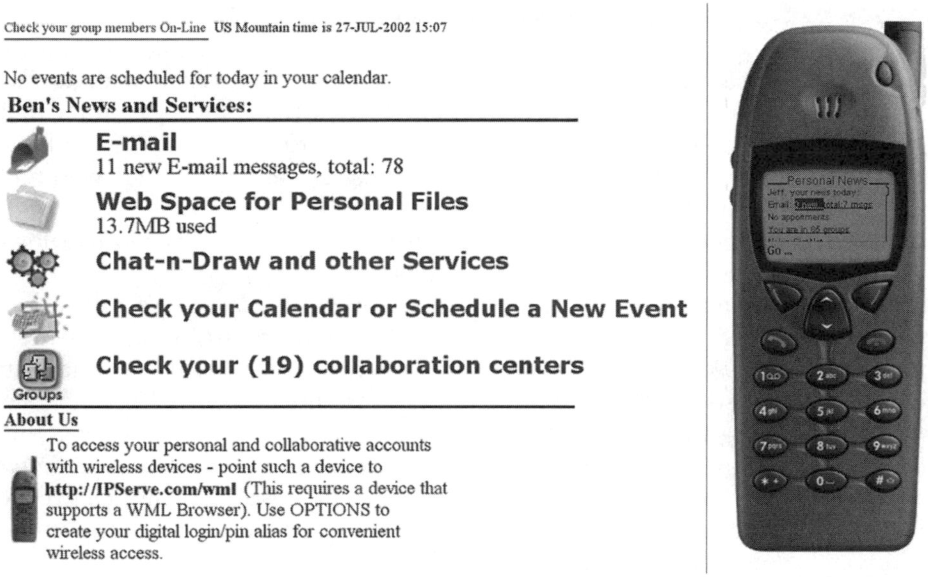
Check your group members On-Line US Mountain time is 27-JUL-2002 15:07
No events are scheduled for today in your calendar.
Ben's News and Services:
E-mail
11 new E-mail messages, total: 78
Web Space for Personal Files
13.7MB used
Chat-n-Draw and other Services
Check your Calendar or Schedule a New Event
Check your (19) collaboration centers
Groups
About Us
To access your personal and collaborative accounts with wireless devices - point such a device to http://IPServe.com/wml (This requires a device that supports a WML Browser). Use OPTIONS to create your digital login/pin alias for convenient wireless access.
Personal News
Go ...

FIGURE I.7. Integrated Wired and Wireless Portals.

In a very peaceful example, GIS can be used to locate things such as office equipment and to optimize sharing of resources such as books, computers, facsimile machines, copying machines, or microwaves, and services based on their locations.

Topology data also can be used by robot-based moving services to determine hallway widths and produce the best or perhaps only way to move an item.

IT Provisioning, Corporate Portals, and the Distributed Knowledge Marketplace

IT provisioning and collaboration technologies, which are often implemented with corporate portals, increase productivity and encourage the creation of a distributed knowledge and service marketplace. There, data as well as services can be measured and can represent a new currency.

People produce knowledge and services every day. Unfortunately, most of the knowledge gained by individuals is rarely shared. We have no direct access to this greatest treasure of humankind. Distributed knowledge technologies can improve the situation, drastically decreasing the time between a service's supply and the market's awareness of it, providing a more precise estimate of data and service usability values, and introducing a new marketplace where information and service contributions are rewarded according to their values.

Collaboration or openness must be supported by security mechanisms. Multiple security domains with multiple member roles and multilevel privilege-based access are a necessity to encourage data sharing and active teamwork. Collaboration is not just about corporate employees working at corporate workstations. Wireless devices using WAP or speech technology (phone) clients, as well as regular workstations, will also be looking to access the rich content of enterprise data and services. The full content can be made available via corporate workstations while team members with thin client devices use a subset of the data and services (Fig. I.7).

Integration of Software and Knowledge Engineering

There is a gap in the current development process between initial business input provided by business people and the final implementation. The current process requires multiple transformations to simplify the complex world of reality into low-level program functions and tables expressed with current programming languages. This gap is filled with multiple filters/layers and sometimes multiple teams.

The shift to service-oriented architecture together with recent advances in knowledge technologies has paved the way for a new development paradigm.

In the new development paradigm, knowledge technologies play an essential role in the development process. Business domain experts will be able to directly participate in the development agenda by writing business rules and application scenarios in a more "natural" language. This will also help to focus developers (currently distracted by technological details) on the business aspects of applications.

Some time ago, we thought of the C language as a language for application development, whereas Assembly was the language for system development. It is about time to move the current programming languages, such as C# and Java, to the system level and make applications that are driven by knowledge-based rules and scenarios.

Knowledge-driven architecture is not a dream but a reality.

Start with Good Design and Repeatable Process

There is always a temptation to jump ahead several steps. Sometimes this is possible, but it is never safe. (This is my experience, at least, as a former mountain climber and an inventor.) The plan for this book is to learn the best current development practices in the software industry, climb close to the top, and then see the horizon. We focus on Object-Oriented Programming (OOP) and we also look beyond. There are Aspect-Oriented Programming and Generative Programming directions. OOP is not the end of the story.

Current technologies have brought significant power to developers. These technologies can be successfully used to implement good design ideas. They can also be used to unsuccessfully implement bad ones. How do you start walking in the right direction before you can see the end of the road?

Enterprise applications are often complex enough to offer us this challenge. Building a robust development process and building a team capable of following this process are probably the most important tasks of development. Good teams produce good products. It is appropriate, then, to start Chapter 1 with a discussion of teamwork and development processes and then to move on to technology.

Notes for Educators: AMA Teaching Methods

The AMA teaching methods are Activate, Motivate, and Assess.

Activate

Interact with the group and solicit each student's contribution. Engage your students in *collaborative learning* (let them work in teams) and *collaborative teaching*—give the stage to your students so they can review the material and share their best practices. One learns twice while teaching! Reward the best contributors.

Motivate

Use all possible means to connect the course materials to the students' areas of expertise, thus increasing their motivation level. Motivation is the key to opening students' eyes and ears and unlocking their memories.

Assess

Facilitate a question-and-answer session, let students work in groups, and help them keep precise focus and timing.

Use the online assessment and evaluation forms periodically from the very beginning of the course.

This book provides a special section at the end of each chapter to reinforce the AMA methods.

The **Integrating Questions** are designed to help students build a thorough understanding of the relevance, relationships, and application of the content in the real world. To ensure that students can relate course theories to the workplace, illustrate points with examples drawn from your professional experience and the experiences of the students.

The **Case Study** serves as a guide for student assignments. The instructor can modify and personalize assignments based on instructor–student interactions and early assessments of a student's current and desired skills.

Recap Presentations and Midterm Assessments

Conduct two- or three-student recap presentations (ten to fifteen minutes each) starting with the second class. The content of each presentation is the student's work on the Case Study–based assignments. The presentations may serve as midterm assessments. They also increase students' motivation level and their understanding of the material (you learn twice while teaching).

Delivery Format for Assignments and Presentations

It is recommended to format assignments and presentations as illustrated white papers using, for example, Web pages, MS Word, PDF, or PowerPoint with notes. The content can be presented in three levels: definition (high level), functionality and applicability (middle level), and examples of implementations (low level). These three levels roughly map the "why," "what," and "how" of the selected subject. Students will enhance their ability to clearly express their ideas and will learn the art of publishing and presentation with text, images, diagrams, and code extracts.

Final Team Projects

Students may integrate selected parts of their weekly work assignments into team projects. This approach helps the student increase the quality of his or her work and consistently focus on the course materials.

Integration is not a copy-and-paste process. The team project allows students to exercise the downloadable software tool that comes with this book and helps them share their work with a distributed knowledge repository. The high visibility of a student's achievement adds to the perfection of her or his work and makes it possible to directly tie students' efforts to industry needs.

Chapter 1

Collaborative Engineering

Collaborative engineering is an important subject that is currently missing in schools, although some courses include a few of its aspects. I doubt I can cover it all at once, but I will try my best to *integrate* development technology and the development process under one roof, where integration-ready systems can be created.

Technology tends to fragment: to focus on pieces and omit the glue. The development philosophy that I associate with the terms of collaborative engineering helps keep a better balance between a narrow focus on particular components and their multiple connections to the rest of the world. The practice of collaborative engineering also assists in establishing a repeatable—yet flexible and constantly improving—development process. This is the foundation for integration-ready systems development.

What is collaborative engineering all about? It is about the development process in its organization, management, and methodology, integrated with innovative development technologies. I have had the privilege of teaching corporate developers and architects in the United States and overseas. Many times, I have had the amazing feeling that some of my brightest students, experienced developers, knew all the pieces of the puzzle and still could not start putting them together.

For example, almost every programmer knows one of the main design rules: Separate business from presentation logic. However, there are still more cases that break this rule than cases that follow it. One of the hardest questions is how to apply the rule properly.

Some developers believe that although theory is good, it is too costly for real life. This myth prevents many of them from developing the skills (in everyday practice) to quickly apply an existing design pattern or recognize a new one that will solve the problem "once and forever" and allow them to move on to other problems.

Guided by this myth, we win time and money on separate projects but miss the bigger picture, in which the industry pays a high price for overall inefficiency as well as data and service replication.

I think that by teaching separate pieces of the art and science of development, we omit the glue, the philosophy of programming that helps us find the right balance between "do it simply" and "do it once," which sometimes leads to beautiful solutions in which the two rules are not in conflict but are happily married.

Software is built from big and small blocks selected by architects and developers. In the top-to-bottom development pattern, the big blocks are selected first; the developers then try to fill the holes with the smaller blocks. During this process, they often find that the original direction of the design was wrong and there is a need for remodeling.

How can you start walking in the right direction before you can see the end of the road? Even some good developers cannot begin a project until they can see all the details involved. Unfortunately, the scope of enterprise applications and time limits rarely offer this luxury to developers.

The right answer is a development process that has a framework yet is flexible – a process that is understood, followed, and enhanced by developers.

At this point, some readers may be thinking that all this talk about a process is management's piece of the pie and not something developers need to worry about. Let's read further and reserve our judgment. We will see later how much the management style and the development process contribute to overall results.

Management Style as an Important Part of the Development Process: True Leaders versus "Pure" Managers

I do not even have time to read my own email reminders; of course I missed yours.
—From a management conversation (the terrible truth)

While working for multiple corporations as a developer or one of the key managers, I observed different management styles. In very generic terms, I would distinguish two major tendencies: "pure" management and true leadership. What is the difference between pure managers and real leaders? Some companies hire managers with little or no background in the field they are supposed to supervise. Their role is to provide and track plans and serve as a layer to smooth the edges among groups related to the plan.

However, project management is not just a Microsoft tool. It takes a leader to build a team, create a teamwork process, and promote best practices and collaborative technologies. It takes a leader to make decisions with creativity, not just through multiple-choice answers. Removing unnecessary layers and dealing with leaders instead of managers can greatly benefit projects, teams, and companies. I have learned this the hard way, working on multimillion dollar projects, consulting start-up companies, and teaching (and learning from) enterprise architects.

Shifting the weight of management toward developers enables those developers to grow and become leaders themselves. This approach focuses more on people than on current projects or tasks. It assumes (and this is the right assumption!) that the *main assets of a company are people*—and teams. The best teams produce the best products and services.

Workers (e.g., testers, developers, and system administrators) need to communicate and to translate to managers the essence of the work they are doing.

This takes minutes if a manager is a leader who knows the work. It takes hours for a pure manager who tries to learn a subject on the fly. The next time a worker wants to play a similar song with the manager, he or she has to start from the first music class—this note is called *A*, this is a *C sharp*—again and again. Even then, only a fraction of the information is retained.

Why? The orchestra conductor (the manager) is not a musician at all. (I know that many are, in a more literal sense.) There is no background where information can be stored. A pure manager often feels forced to choose between several opposing voices or lines in a document, and each voice or line sounds and looks the same as the others.

The management process often turns into a game for such a person, a game with the following rules:

- Use buzzwords, preferably generic (e.g., "stay focused!") or at least technological (e.g., "scalable solution!").
- Do not translate words into actions. Actions can be punished, because any action can be less than 100 percent safe, or incomplete, or not quick enough. Words are always right ("stay focused!").

A leader owns the solution that he or she created. *This ownership feeling is at the heart of the development of any creative process.* (I just read that again, and it looks like a line from Ayn Rand.) In this context, *ownership* means responsibility to make and foresee changes, fix problems, and answer all questions related to the solution.

Pure management removes ownership feelings, destroys creativity, and makes people "come and go." Every developer in the team is a leader who owns and has full responsibility for a specific area. Experienced developers with teamwork skills become the best managers or leaders.

On the opposite extreme of this spectrum is a leader who owns all the solutions, thus has a hard time delegating responsibilities. Such leadership can improve product quality in the short term (if this leader is the most experienced developer).

At the same time, this "babysitting" removes the ownership feelings of the others and prevents developers from growing on the job while making all the development tasks a sequential process funneling through a single leader-bottleneck. A leader should trust and delegate.

Product design and project management are interrelated. I recommend a practice in which team leaders are not only responsible for the part of the project delivered by their team, but also personally involved in that part's integration into the overall project. Leaders keep teams and projects together as orchestra conductors do with musicians and music.

Where is the border between a leader and a pure manager? We all have elements of both, in different proportions. We act as pure managers as soon as we start talking about things beyond our expertise without investing time and effort in learning the field.

Being in a position to issue orders makes the pure manager rather dangerous. Investing time in active learning is hard—but rewarding—and develops a leader.

"I have no time to even read my email" is a phrase from a Dilbert book. It is still a very popular line in the management drama. Another extreme is "I have done much more complicated projects before." Phrases like these are used to excuse a person from learning the specifics of a current task or project. Pure managers avoid specifics. This limits their participation in a development process in which generic frames are filled with specific details.

Development Methodologies: Capability Maturity Model and More

Some development organizations follow the Capability Maturity Model (CMM), some prefer ISO 9000 recommendations, and still others use Extreme Programming (XP) or Six Sigma methodology. None of these models suggests that it is an exhaustive recipe that covers all cases. The development process that fits your team and project is going to be built and enhanced by you. The process rules, or steps, should allow flexibility; they cannot be "final," in Java terminology.

An Extremely Brief Overview of CMM

The CMM [1] can be used as the basis for diagnosing an organization's software processes, establishing priorities, and acting on them. One of the most important goals of CMM (and of ISO 9000) is the capacity to measure success and reliability of software processes. Measurement results allow for process improvements. Process improvements lead to a maturity level increase. CMM recognizes five levels of maturity in a software development process. Each level comprises a set of process goals that, when satisfied, stabilize an important component of the software process.

1. *Initial*. The process is characterized as ad hoc and occasionally even chaotic. Few processes are defined, and success depends on individual effort and heroics. Delivery dates for projects of similar size are unpredictable and vary widely.
2. *Repeatable*. Basic project management processes are established to track cost, schedule, and functionality. The necessary process discipline is in place to repeat earlier successes on projects with similar applications.
3. *Defined*. The software process for both management and engineering activities is documented, standardized, and integrated into a standard software process for the organization. All projects use an approved, tailored version of the organization's standard software process for developing and maintaining software.
4. *Managed*. Detailed measures of the software process and product quality are collected. Both the software process and the products are quantitatively understood and controlled.
5. *Optimizing*. Continuous process improvement is enabled by quantitative feedback from the process and from piloting innovative ideas and technologies.

The International Organization for Standardization provides an ISO 9000 document that serves as a standard to certify processes and procedures. Whereas CMM focuses strictly on software development, ISO 9000 has a much broader scope: hardware, software, processed materials, and services. CMM provides many more details and measurement criteria.

The bottom line of both methods includes "document before acting," "plan and follow," or "say what you do, and do what you say."

Extreme Programming: Rules of the Game

Extreme Programming methodology gains more popularity every year. This section provides an overview of key XP concepts. (I can almost hear an impatient programmer's voice saying, "Another extremely brief overview? When are we going to see source code?")

Software development is not just about coding, as the art of painting is not just about the right paint selection. The heart of XP is a team of developers able and willing to communicate, plan, and design before coding. The team owns projects and processes and has fun planning and playing the project game by its own rules ("establish and follow"). A subset of XP rules is presented in Figs. 1.1 and 1.2. Does this look like XP?

Six Sigma

Six Sigma is another method that focuses on measurements of process capabilities and offers an integrated approach to shareholder value creation. Six Sigma suggests establishing seven to twelve measures in two areas: "critical to your business" (efficiency measures) and "critical to your client" (effectiveness measures). We select important measurement points that significantly contribute to overall business success.

Now we can consider an equation where business success depends on the measured functions. Some of them can serve as leading indicators that invite discussions such as "Why are these measures not moving in the right direction?" This enhances both discussions and critical thinking. Six Sigma helps to effectively break down complex processes into a matrix with multiple components and consistently works on component improvements.

Rational Unified Process

Rational Unified Process (RUP) is a method and a tool developed by Rational Company (currently a part of IBM, Inc.) that describes development as a four-phase process. In the *inception phase*, developers define the business outcome of the project. The *elaboration phase* considers basic technology and architecture. Developers deal with detailed design and source code in the *construction phase* and finally deploy the system in *the transition phase*. RUP offers software products that support developers as they walk through the phases.

Who implements the rules of the development process? People. This is the bottom line: You can select any methodology that fits your organization. Teams with their managers, leaders, and developers who understand and share the ideas of the methodology will make it work.

Distributed Collaborative Development

It is not an easy task to establish and follow a system, even for a single company. Can it work for a collaboration among several teams? Will this change the rules and the process?

Software communities working on common projects have recently suggested several answers to these questions. Two of the best examples are open source communities and the Java Community Process. However, there are still several factors that limit the success of collaborative engineering today.

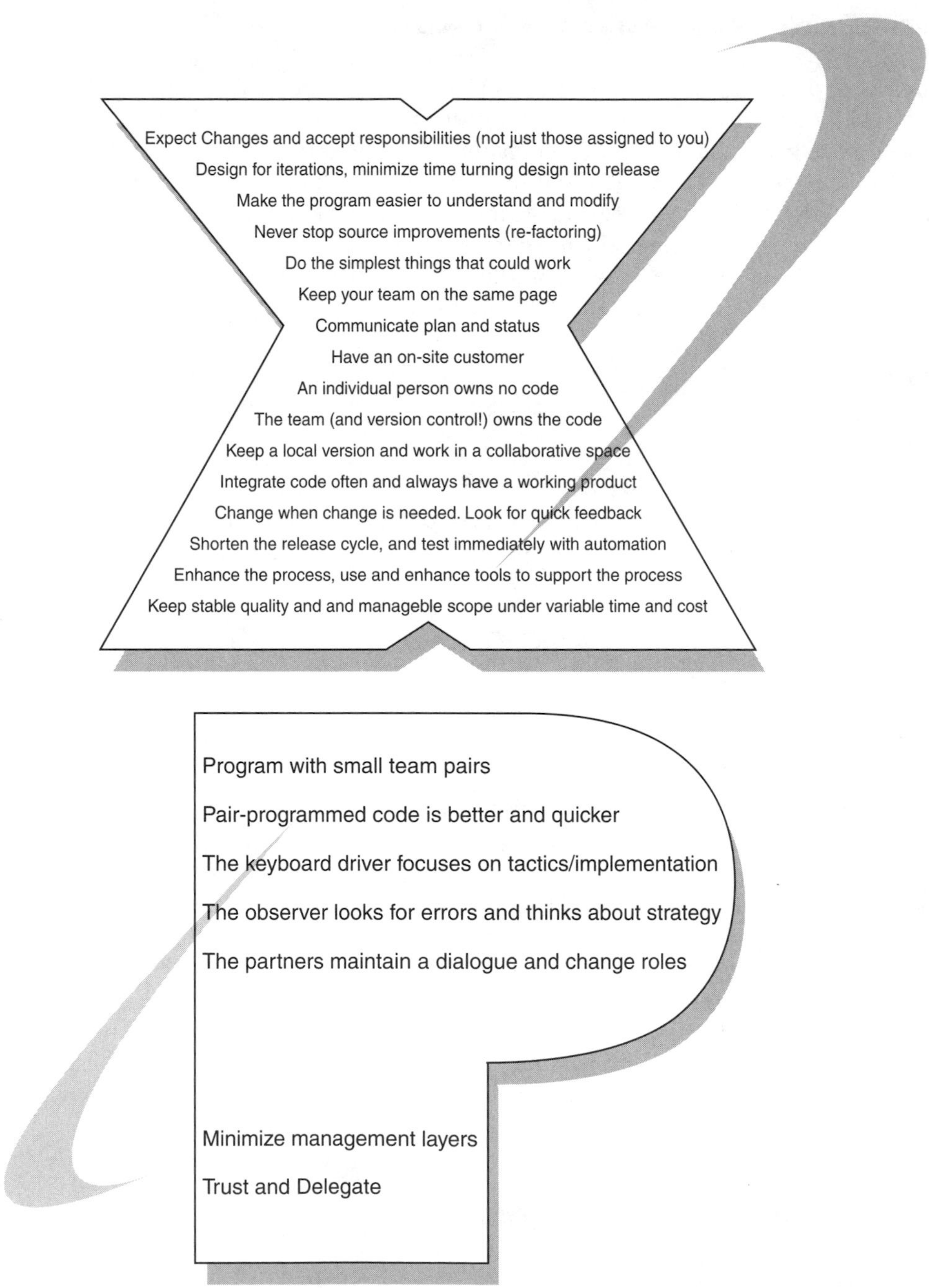
Expect Changes and accept responsibilities (not just those assigned to you)
Design for iterations, minimize time turning design into release
Make the program easier to understand and modify
Never stop source improvements (re-factoring)
Do the simplest things that could work
Keep your team on the same page
Communicate plan and status
Have an on-site customer
An individual person owns no code
The team (and version control!) owns the code
Keep a local version and work in a collaborative space
Integrate code often and always have a working product
Change when change is needed. Look for quick feedback
Shorten the release cycle, and test immediately with automation
Enhance the process, use and enhance tools to support the process
Keep stable quality and and manageble scope under variable time and cost
Program with small team pairs
Pair-programmed code is better and quicker
The keyboard driver focuses on tactics/implementation
The observer looks for errors and thinks about strategy
The partners maintain a dialogue and change roles
Minimize management layers
Trust and Delegate

Figure 1.1. The Rules of the Game (XP).

The motivation for sharing is very low, and there is no flexibility in establishing the rules of the game: security, roles, access, and so on. The value of the data to be shared or exchanged is unknown, and a contributor rarely gets her or his reward because the contribution itself is not accountable.

For more than a decade, I have worked with remote students and development groups in trying to overcome these limitations. I came up with several innovations, described in a corresponding patent application [2] as distributed active knowledge and process technologies (DKT). DKT supports the process of distributed development and helps to improve processes while enhancing technologies.

Distributed Knowledge Technologies

Existing on-line collaborative services allow users to share only a limited set of data types, usually restricted to messages and files, with the rare addition of a shared organizer or other similar service. This narrows collaborative actions to a small number of fields and introduces limitations on the scope of possible collaboration and data sharing. Though some users are satisfied with restricting their collaborative efforts to sharing files and sending group messages, such systems are often insufficient in scope to allow for efficient workflow in a real collaborative setting.

Existing services on the Internet also limit their collaborative structure to data objects and exclude processes. As a result, the large amounts of data that can accumulate in a group knowledge base cannot be mapped to better processing methods. As the number of data objects increases, it becomes more and more difficult to use the information contained in them to efficiently accomplish goals.

Current system structures do not permit users to collaboratively add objects of unknown data types and a service to process a particular type of data to best suit the goals of a group. They also prevent the creation and implementation of preprogrammed processes, services, or scenarios for distributed processing. This further limits collaborative efficiency.

Existing systems own and fully control their collaborative environments. This limits collaboration to a single system and does not permit systems to share data or other system elements. Data, process, and service sharing between systems belonging to different organizations is an even more complicated issue because there currently is no way for a system to determine and specify elements appropriate for free public sharing, elements that are to be shared on a pay-per-use basis, and elements that are to be exchanged for others of equal value.

Last, current online collaboration is limited by the unwillingness of users to share their data. Even in a collaborative setting, users rarely desire to make their data available to all members of their group, and they make adequate security a condition for sharing information.

The backbone of any online collaborative effort is security, and the current methods of assigning access privileges as a way to make specified data objects available to the appropriate viewers are inadequate.

Existing systems allow limited role-based privileges for all collaborative data. A common system has a limited number of privilege levels (in most cases, two). In such a system, if a user's profile defines her as an "administrator," she has read, write, and delete access to all group data.

If a user is defined as a "member," he can read and add messages but cannot edit or delete existing messages. This kind of system is limiting and does not encourage data sharing because it does not give users control over their data. Users cannot create new custom roles on the fly, cannot select who has certain kinds of access to the information they choose to share, and must provide the same level of access to all members within a privilege class.

The willingness of users to share is also limited by their knowledge of other elements inside and outside the user's system and of their values. It is important to know how valuable a particular service or data object is from a user's point of view. Current systems provide only the number of times a file has been downloaded and selected positive comments by current users. A new mechanism is needed to provide and update more meaningful usage and viewer response information inside the system and between systems.

DKT covers a need that exists for collaborative systems and permits increased flexibility in the types of data and services that can be shared. It allows data, processes, and services to be created and modified within the same collaborative framework and permits the mapping of appropriate data to these processes. DKT systems can notify interested parties on available objects, processes, and services and provide dynamic evaluation of data and services based on their usage.

DKT systems can negotiate several forms of collaboration and establish rules of access for internal members and outsiders (e.g., pay-per-use, and value-based exchange), using sufficiently flexible levels of data security to foster online collaboration. Sharing can be an enjoyable habit and an eye- and mind-opening experience (not a medical term).

This new mechanism to value data and services creates an environment of active participation in which each contribution is accountable. This accountability motivates contributors to enter this new marketplace, where knowledge and services play the role of virtual currency. There are many ways of transforming virtual currency to hard currency. What is the exact mechanism of this transition? Participants will find or invent a good one.

There are plenty of "how to" details and usage descriptions of DTK systems that might be too boring in the context of this book. They are very well explained in the DKT patent application published by the U.S. Patent and Trademark Office [2].

24 × 7 Distributed Development Practices

Especially important for an international development team with members distributed over the globe and working twenty-four hours a day, seven days a week, are "24×7" distributed development practices.

Is it possible to achieve coordination, understanding, and cooperation among multiple teams working in different time zones, speaking different languages, and living in different cultures? Can distributed development be cost effective and highly efficient at the same time?

Our virtual team was created as a side effect of several years of on-line training. It was a very attractive concept: to extend time and resources on a global scale. Learning the ABCs of important team member qualities/abilities and developing a core of "black belts" (in Six Sigma terms) for each team was, though very beneficial, quite a challenging task.

Collaborative technologies make the development process highly visible for every team member as well as for the management team. This visibility helps establish and reinforce teamwork rules. The system forces developers to provide daily and weekly plans and status reports that improve analysis and design quality. I say "forces" because the plan and status jobs are the least loved by developers. DKT makes them unavoidable habits. A notification engine working with the task management systems provides an action-reminder if a needed action has not yet been taken.

Global collaboration encourages open expertise exchange under a partnership umbrella. A very valuable benefit is that we can achieve much more working together than we can achieve separately. Network specialists from Hong Kong; a "Fifth Dimension" scientific group from Scandinavia; SZMA (oil and gas factory automation international integrators) engineers;

computer science researchers from St. Petersburg University and Institute of Information Technology in Russia; JavaSchool students and consultants.: these are some examples of teams collaborated in the distributed knowledge environment.

This book includes design and code samples and offers a tool that allows you to build your own system powered by a knowledge engine, support your own development process, establish your own rules of sharing, and, if you wish, connect to other systems and join in collaborative engineering.

Steps in the Process

What Is Your Development Mode: Proactive or Reactive?

We are coming back from the heights of management to the specific steps of the development process. Here is a quick quiz related to your organization's habits toward time distribution on a software project.

Which line (1, 2, or 3) represents the percentage of project time your organization allocates to analysis, design, code, and testing?

	Analysis	Design	Code	Testing
1.	40	30	20	10
2.	10	20	30	40
3.	25	25	25	25

There is no right or wrong answer to this quiz. Your selection sheds some light on your organization's development habits My experience shows that for bigger projects, shifting gears to line 1 helps to improve quality. However, for really small projects, number 3 works quite well. I have noticed that the second answer is often, though not always, associated with start-ups or organizations that are on the learning curve using "let-me-try-it" paths. (I hope I do not sound critical.)

Amazingly enough, all three ways can work very well for a team that uses one of them as part of a repeatable development process. Such a team usually understands where steps can start and stop and is able to recognize cases in which it makes sense to move along in the cycle. There is no single good answer. This is about your organization development style.

The object-oriented approach to application development is currently the leading approach in the software industry.

I will describe some basic steps of software application development with this approach; I have to add that the steps and their sequence can vary. I am sharing my experience, and I know that there is more than one good methodology, as there is more than one good solution to almost any problem. The most important thing is to have a system and consistently follow it: "Plan and follow" or "say what you do and do what you say."

Basic Development Roles

Developers (or a single developer for a small organization or a small project) play different development roles at major phases of the development process. System definition is usually performed by **system analysts**, **subject matter experts**, and **architects**. Architects and designers are responsible for system analysis and design. Developers participate in the implementation and deployment phases. **System developers** or service providers are different from **application developers**, who use provider services to create a higher-level system for end users. This separation is not always obvious. Service providers also have end users, but in most cases, their end users are application developers who can use their services.

It is possible that the deployment process requires **system integrators**. This role might disappear as more integration-ready products come out after this book is published. (I know you are smiling.)

Architects do not participate in the deployment process but are responsible for the deployment plan, which is usually expressed in the deployment diagram.

This is a very generic definition that can be customized to fit your development process specifics. For example, according to Sun Microsystems recommendations, Java 2 Enterprise Edition (J2EE)-based development involves the following roles:

- **Tool provider** (for example, Borland): provides development tools
- **Application component provider**: a generic name for Web component providers that develop Java server pages (JSPs), tag libraries, servlets, and related business classes located in the Web container; Enterprise Java Bean (EJB) developers; and Web page designers
- **Application assembler**: uses components developed by application component providers to assemble them into a J2EE application component
- **Deployer**: responsible for application deployment in a specific environment
- **J2EE product provider**: implements a J2EE product
- **System administrator**: provides the configuration and management of the system
- **Quality assurance (QA) engineer**: provides integrated testing.

Most of the development methods obligate developers to provide "unit testing" of the part delivered by the developer to a current system release. But system-level testing often requires a special environment that emulates production and special efforts.

The Role of the Software Architect

Software architecture is the highest level of a software system definition. A **software architect** is the one who actually provides this definition. The architect starts with user requirements and separates them into two categories: **functional requirements** that refer to system tasks and **nonfunctional requirements** that refer to system efficiency, scalability, flexibility, and other "-ilities." The architect participates (to some degree) in the analysis and design processes but does not go into implementation details; he or she focuses on the larger picture of the system instead.

It is important for the architect to negotiate with the client about the metrics (not just words) and priorities of requirements criteria. For example, the "must be scalable" requirement should come with some rough range numbers (e.g., expected number of users).

Basic Steps of the Development Process with an Object-Oriented Approach

The basic steps of the development process are shown in Fig. 1.3. **The rest of the chapter carefully moves over these steps.**

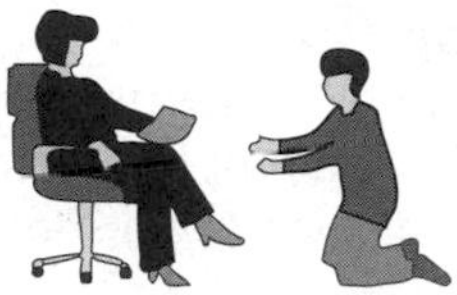

1. Capture User Requirements into a set of Use Cases

2. Play cards (CRC) to Recognize Classes

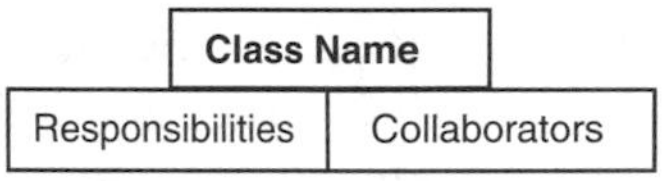

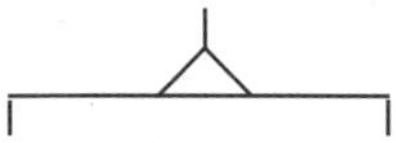

3. Form Object Model Diagram; define the relationships of the Classes

4. Architecture design: find playgrounds (tiers) for your objects

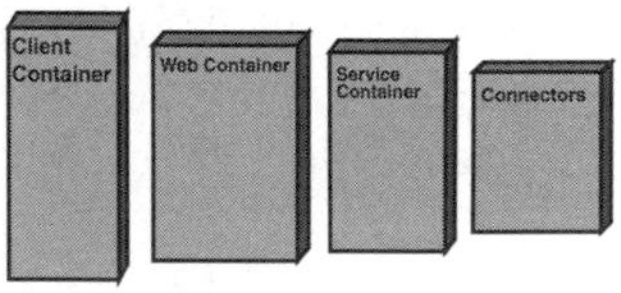

5. Recognize reusable services and shared data

6. Define the screens and user interface with Human–Computer Interface experts. Strive for consistency and simplicity.

7. Define the date and scope of the first deliverable, targeting to prove the basic concepts and to get feedback from the client on the very early stages of the development

8. Use Style Guidance while coding and review the code regularly (this also keeps the proper level of communication for a team).

9. Share the first results with domain experts. Make corrections and outline the plan to finish and fine-tune the project.

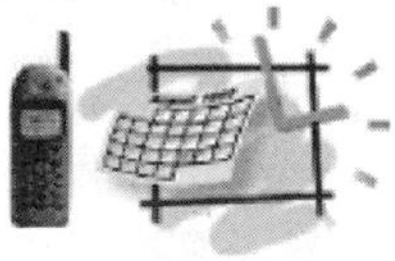

Employ technology to establish a proper level of documentation and communications in the team. Move from archives to an active repository of the shared parts of the project.

FIGURE 1.3. Basic Steps of the Development Process.

Start from User Requirements and Transit to Use Cases

Start with interviews of your clients, who are (hopefully) the domain experts. Your goal is to understand business rules and business user requirements. This is a proven way to smoothly come to an agreement with the customer and the users on what the system should do. The next step is the transition from user requirements to use cases.

Split an application into a set of use cases, or scenarios describing subtasks of the application. Yvar Jacobson's methodology is used to capture user requirements in a set of use cases [3]. Each use case describes a scenario, a flow of events initiated by an "actor."

An actor represents anything that interacts with the system. Written descriptions of use cases are complemented by process diagrams. This step is the first attempt to transition to objects from plain human language that describes "what to do" in terms of events and conditions. The user requirements record is a "no-objects" document that may be ten or ten hundred pages long. It provides a high-level definition of desired system functionality and can provide a list of conditional actions the system produces. The use cases diagram breaks this flow of words and events into subtasks or scenarios. Main objects or actors appear from the background and start playing their roles (at least on paper).

The following example of user requirements reflects one of the difficult situations that must be resolved by developers (almost a true story).

Black Holes, Inc., was a start-up company that targeted travelers by providing maps and directions to the least known and visited places, or "black holes." Unfortunately, the company did not meet annual revenue expectations. (The initial orders that looked so promising for investors were submitted by the company VP of marketing during his research work in the competing territory of the Bahamas.)

The board of directors took some measures to change the situation. It was decided to cut 75 percent of the development team staff (there used to be four of them) and introduce incentives to correlate each employee's paycheck to his or her actual work. The hourly workers' paychecks would depend on the number of hours worked. All the managers would continue to receive their salaries, but would get no bonuses while the company operated in the red. It was confirmed once again that the holes were extremely hard to sell. Therefore, the salespeople would be paid an hourly wage plus commission to stimulate hard work. Three new positions were opened to support the project: an IT director to improve the communication of management decisions over the network; a VP of travel arrangements to focus the development team on two new tasks (searching for "black holes" and optimizing travel routes); and an order administrator to support Web client registration and privileged access.

Of course, the changes had a serious impact on the "chess match" between the management and development groups (Fig. 1.4). It was over. Ben, who represented what was left of the development team, did not play chess. He took the silver (a trip to one of the "black holes") while the management team was awarded the gold. *The management team's spirits were extremely high, and the project started with the motto: "Each employee should be accountable. Failure is not an option."*

We can find the main actors and associated tasks/scenarios on the use cases diagram in Fig. 1.5. The Unified Modeling Language (UML) is a formal set of graphical notations that helps visually express object-oriented realities (models) of software applications. Note that actors are associated with objects and from a semantic point of view, are nouns, whereas scenarios introduce the desired functions with names that start with verbs.

FIGURE 1.4. "Team Players."

Object-Oriented (and/or Aspect-Oriented) Analysis—Make a Transition to Objects and Classes

From this point, we may concentrate on Use Case scenarios and then proceed to objects. After describing what needs to be done in terms of events, we start the transition to the object world; we now try to concentrate on data and pay less attention to the flow of events.

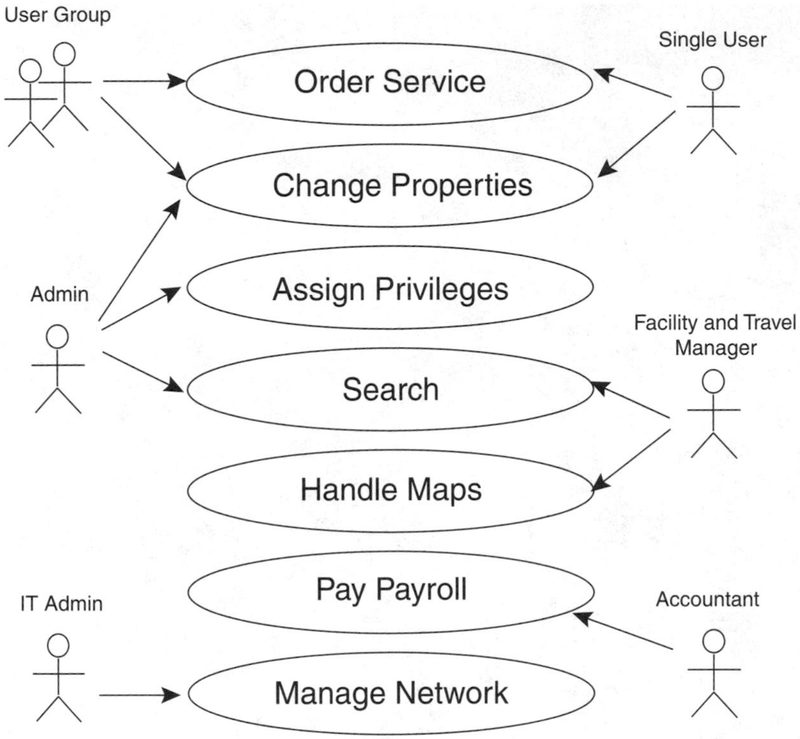

FIGURE 1.5. Use Cases.

It is definitely a different view of the user requirements; if you want, it is a different view of the world.

User requirements and scenarios usually describe a set of functions and a flow of actions produced. This approach represents a dynamic view of the application. It used to be the dominant approach supported by flow charts that showed structures of functions and conditions. This development practice was established in the 1970s as structural programming.

The programs started with the main routine that checked conditions and called the proper functions, which were easily visible on flow charts. Sources, such as the original flow charts, looked like this: "if THIS—call THAT; else, if THAT—call THIS" (Fig. 1.6). This style of programming was named "structural" because the main idea was to keep programs readable or "structured," keep functions or subroutines in separate files, and avoid the temptation to put all the code in the main routine.

Where are those beautiful days of program simplicity? I am afraid that time will never return. Software became increasingly sophisticated in the 1980s while trying to model more and more complicated tasks of the real world. The number of details associated with a single task exceeded the capacity of a single brain, and a new abstraction was born: the world of object-oriented concepts. These concepts shift our attention to static parts of the application. We learn to concentrate on data objects and model system behavior as the collaboration of these objects.

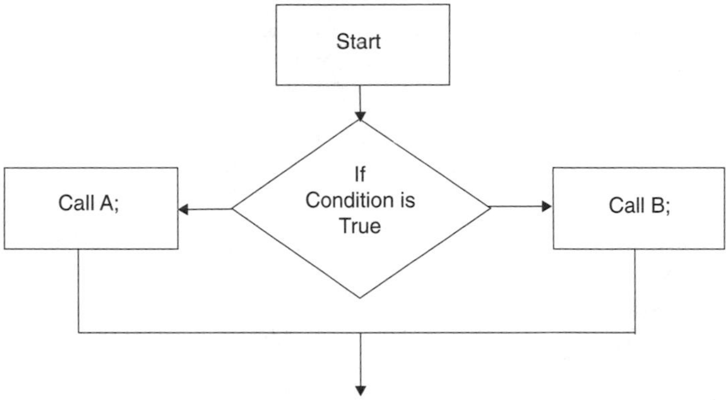

FIGURE 1.6. The Good Old Ways of Structural Programming.

Discussion about the static and dynamic view of the world started at more than 2,000 years ago:

> The world is a process that never stops. —Heracleitus, 540–480 BC, (the dynamic view of the world)
>
> The world is a composition of objects called atoms. —Democritus, 460–370 BC, the first object-oriented philosopher.

Here is your self-test: Who was right in this ancient debate?

1. Heracleitus
2. Democritus
3. Both of the above

(Hint: Both views, static and dynamic, are important and complementary.)

While transitioning to an object-oriented approach, we use the new abstraction "CLASS" to classify objects. An object is an instance of a class. How can we identify good objects—candidates for classes?

Look at the application through the client's eyes, forget about programmers' tricks, and concentrate on client objects. Look for repeatable objects, meaning those that are reusable in your application and complicated enough to deserve to be new data types. Look also for repeatable behaviors of these objects. If such objects can be grouped, a group or set of these objects can be considered a possible class.

The classes/responsibilities/collaborators, or CRC, approach can be used to identify classes. Any noun from a user interview or written business requirements can be considered a potential candidate for a class. Forget about implementation details for now.

A brief summary:

- Look at the application through the client's eyes.
- Classify objects.
- Ask basic questions:
  - What objects are involved?
  - What are the responsibilities of the objects involved?
  - What are helpers/collaborators of the objects involved?

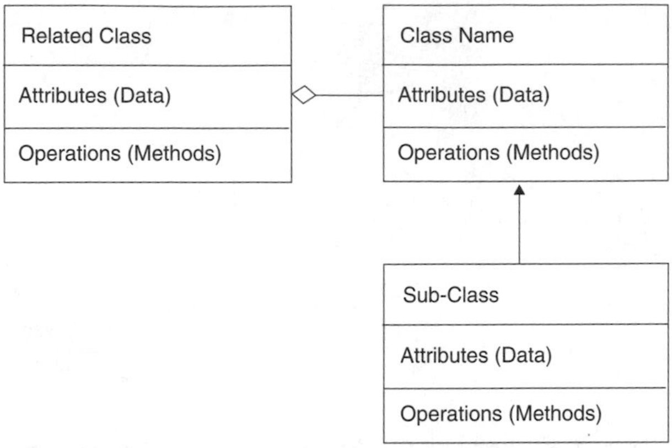

FIGURE 1.7. UML Notations to Describe Classes.

Classes allow us to encapsulate common object properties and behaviors. We can then hide implementation details beneath the surface of public methods or interfaces.

The main object-oriented concepts are encapsulation, inheritance, and polymorphism. The most important one is encapsulation. An object, according to this concept, is a self-contained set of data and functions or methods that operate on that data.

Each object represents a function, feature, or component of a larger system, much like a brick in a wall. The object contains all of the data concerning its function, along with a set of functions to access that data. The data is generally *private* to the object, but may be declared *public* if necessary. The "outside world" will access the data using the object's functions or methods.

Classes define the data (attributes) and the operations (methods) of the object. An object is said to be of a particular class. A class is like a blueprint, or a plan, for the object. It defines the data and functions to be included in the object. A class is similar to a structure but contains functions (methods) along with data. In Fig. 1.7, we see an example of the UML notations that define a class.

Use UML to Capture and Communicate Analysis Results

We use UML to show classes with their relationships in an object model diagram (OMD). If we want to declare a class that represents a person, we might use examples from C++ (Fig. 1.8) and Java (Fig. 1.9) class definitions.

Another important concept of object-oriented programming (OOP) is inheritance. Inheritance is actually an extension of the encapsulation concept. We can find an example of inheritance in the payroll scenario for the Unbelievable Holes start-up company: "The hourly worker paycheck depends on the number of hours worked. All managers receive their salary regardless of sales. Salespeople are paid an hourly rate, plus commission to stimulate hard work." We can clearly see three types of employees: hourly, salary (management), and sales.

When we look carefully into the set of scenarios in the use cases, we can see more actors, potential classes, related to the employee class. Both a single user and user groups can order services and change account properties. Single users and user groups have one thing in common: we call it an "Account" class.

We can also think about an employee as a potential user. Taking all this into account, we draw these classes, showing their inheritance relationships. The object model diagram

```
// Class CPPUser Example
class CPPUser {
    private:  // data
       char name[30];
    public:  // methods
       void setName(char* aName) {
            strncpy(name, aName;
        }
        char* getName( ) {
            return name;
        }
};  // ! semicolon at the end of class

//  Example of usage within another class:

// Define a CPPUser object
CPPUser user = new CPPUser();
//set name = "Peter" to the object
user->setName("Peter");
```

FIGURE 1.8

extraction presented in Fig. 1.10 is just one example of modeling. The same scenario can be modeled differently.

User requirements, not just imagination, should lead to the proper model selection. For example, in our example, the payroll task requires specific properties, such as the number of hours worked and the hourly rate for hourly employees. If the user requirements included item shipment to users, we would need to add a shipping address to the user properties, and so forth. There is often more than one good model for the task. If you have a choice, select the simplest one. It is very possible that later on, more details will be available and the model will be changed.

If your object model's bad—fix it, don't blame my dad
—*Ben Zhuk*, Web Genius, Inc., president, yet another object-oriented philosopher

Talk in Java and C++ about Employee in the Payroll Scenario

Figure 1.11 illustrates inheritance in the payroll scenario. Figure 1.12 actually delivers the same message in formal UML language.

Once a class is defined, it may be used as a model for other classes. This idea can be expressed using the C++ syntax *class Child : public Parent* or the Java syntax *class Child extends Parent*. The new *Child* class inherits all of the attributes and methods of the *Parent* class. Additional attributes and methods may then be added to the *Child* class without affecting the *Parent* class. The *Child* class is derived from the *Parent*.

```
//JavaUser Class Example
/**
 * The JavaUser class is an example of a Java class with data and
 * two methods
 */
public class JavaUser {
    // data
    private String name;
    // methods
/**
 * The setName() method assigns name
 * @param aName
 */
    public void setName(String aName) {
         name = aName;
    }
/**
 * getName() method returns the name
 * @return name
 */
    public String getName() {
        return name;
    }
} // There is no ";" at the end of class

// Example of usage within another class:

// Define a JavaUser object
JavaUser user = new JavaUser();
// set name = "Peter" to the object
user.setName("Peter");
```

FIGURE 1.9

Here is another example of inheritance that introduces the classes *Grandpa*, *Mom*, *Dad*, and *Me*, presented in Fig. 1.13 with code and pictures. Notice that the class *Dad* is derived from *Grandpa*. We will declare one more class now in Fig. 1.14.

The class *Me* will end up with Mom's mouth, Dad's eyes, and Grandpa's big ears, because the *Dad* class was derived from the *Grandpa* class. In this example, freckles are the attribute that exists only in the class *Me*. This example only deals with *data* inheritance; the same situation would occur with any methods (functions) that were contained in the base classes.

Note that the freckles (as well as the eyes in Java implementation) in the class *Me* are defined as *private*. These attributes will not be inherited by possible subclasses (or children) of the class *Me*. Protected or public access allows inheritance. At the same time, such access types open up objects and, in a way, break encapsulation. This is especially true for public access that exposes data to the outside world.

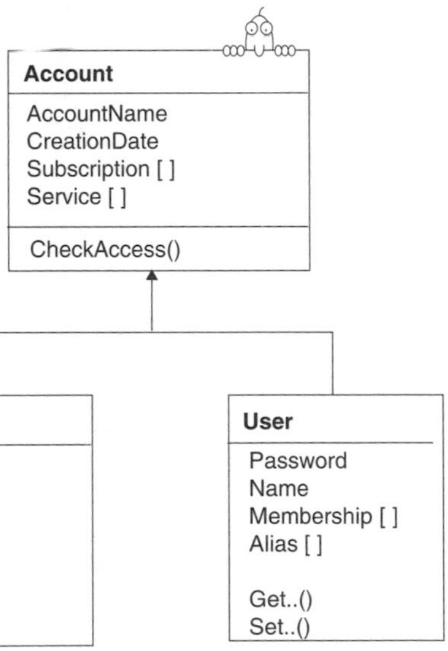

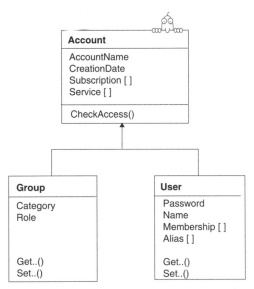

FIGURE 1.10. User and Group Accounts—Objects Model Diagram.

FIGURE 1.11. Inheritance: *Employee* and Potential Subclasses.

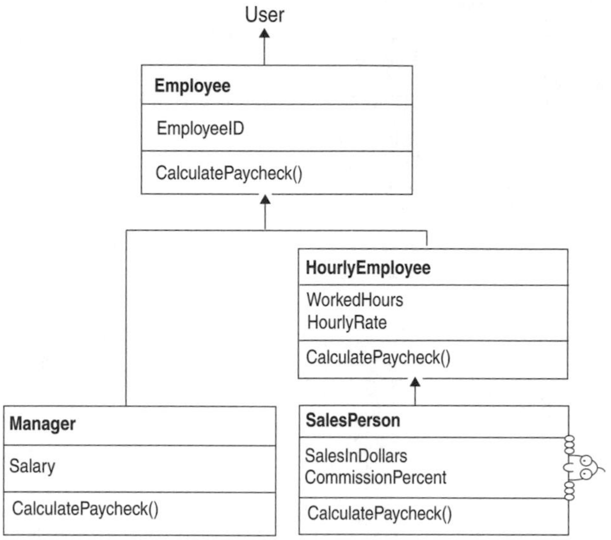
User
Employee
EmployeeID
CalculatePaycheck()
HourlyEmployee
WorkedHours
HourlyRate
CalculatePaycheck()
Manager
Salary
CalculatePaycheck()
SalesPerson
SalesInDollars
CommissionPercent
CalculatePaycheck()

FIGURE 1.12. *User, Employee*, and Subclasses—Object Model Diagram.

The basic rule of OOP is to keep data private while providing public methods to access the data. Inherited methods can be redefined (or reimplemented) in subclasses that create a platform for another OOP concept: polymorphism.

Polymorphism means the ability to take multiple forms. In OOP, this also refers to the ability of an object to refer at run-time to a type (or a class) of the object to select proper methods. You can design for polymorphism and benefit from its power.

If we wrote a procedural code for the payroll scenario, we would check on the type of employee and use different methods. Procedural code shows up with its clumsy "if-else" statements everywhere. For example, we would write here:

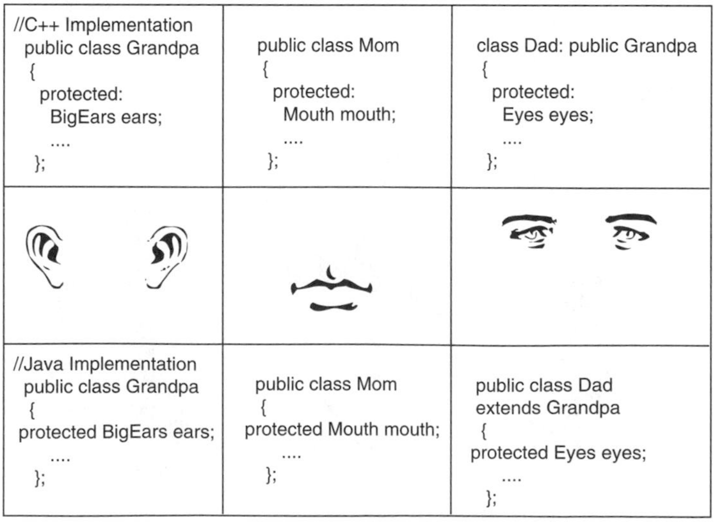
//C++ Implementation
public class Grandpa
{
protected:
BigEars ears;
....
};
public class Mom
{
protected:
Mouth mouth;
....
};
class Dad: public Grandpa
{
protected:
Eyes eyes;
....
};
//Java Implementation
public class Grandpa
{
protected BigEars ears;
....
};
public class Mom
{
protected Mouth mouth;
....
};
public class Dad
extends Grandpa
{
protected Eyes eyes;
....
};

FIGURE 1.13. Inheritance.

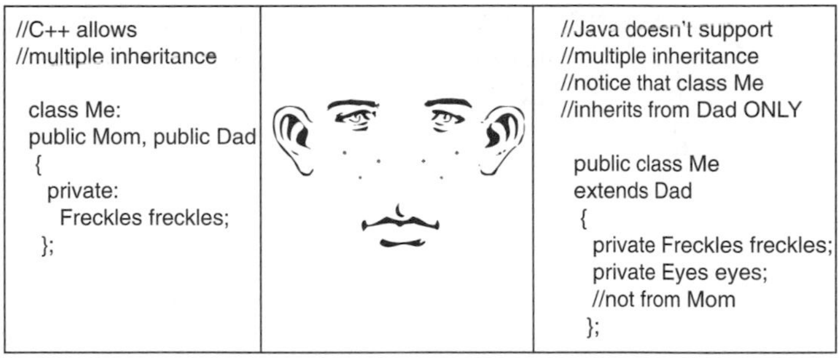
//C++ allows
//multiple inheritance
class Me:
public Mom, public Dad
{
private:
Freckles freckles;
};
//Java doesn't support
//multiple inheritance
//notice that class Me
//inherits from Dad ONLY
public class Me
extends Dad
{
private Freckles freckles;
private Eyes eyes;
//not from Mom
};

FIGURE 1.14. It Runs in the Family.

```
If(employeeType == 1) {// this is pure procedural code
    calculateManagerSalary();
} else if(employeeType == 2) {
    calculateHourlyCheck();
} else // etc., etc., etc.
In OOP we can write the same thing cleanly and easily:
// Get any Employee: Manager, Hourly, or Sales
  Employee employee = getEmployee();
// The system will use a proper method of Manager, or Hourly, or Sales
  employee.calculatePaycheck();
```

The proper *calculatePaycheck()* method will be picked by the system at run-time, depending on the object class type. This powerful feature does not come cheap. You need to do analysis upfront and design your classes with polymorphism in mind.

What does it mean to design for polymorphism? Create a base (parent) class, or an interface, and a set of derived classes, and teach them to behave. This means implementing polymorphic methods: methods with the same names and arguments that have different implementations for different classes. Then, just call one of the objects or instances of derived classes and say "object.doTheJob()."

You waste no time figuring out which object type is being called; no *if-else* is needed. The object knows about its own type and behaves accordingly. For example, given a base class *Employee*, we defined different *calculatePaycheck()* methods for derived classes, such as *Hourly*, *Manager*, and *Sales*. Now we can take any employee object from the list and provide the line: *employee.calculatePaycheck()*. No matter what type of employee is selected, a proper *calculatePaycheck()* method will apply to return the correct results. Any true OOP language offers polymorphism. (Even Visual Basic in its latest version offers polymorphism.)

LEARN BY EXAMPLE: COMPARE OOP AND PROCEDURAL PROGRAMMING

OOP is not easier than procedural code, especially at the beginning of your learning curve. It pays off later on.

Here is another example illustrated with C++ code. Imagine that you write an application related to factory workers and inventory items. When you write a procedural program, you make a flat set of procedures:

```
--setWorkerName(*name);
displayInventoryItemPrice();
```

It is relatively easy to oversee code for two objects. But when the number of objects grows, the increasing number of procedures makes the code almost unmanageable. In OOP, you create objects and encapsulate (hide inside the objects) their properties, and the methods that can manage these properties. Your procedures are now distributed in several classes that provide their behavior. Your main method that drives the application will immediately shrink from your big, flat procedural surface down to a set of objects that can be introduced and then start to *behave*. In the following example, you create the *Worker* class and the method *setName* and then the *InventoryItem* class and the method *displayPrice()*.

Now you are dealing with a much smaller number of objects than procedures. You can cut your main method from a fat *if-else* scenario into a couple of lines that introduce your objects. Your objects have methods and properties. They behave.

```
Worker *s=new Worker(); // create a worker object
s->setName("Jeff"); // set the name
InventoryItem *i=new InventoryItem();
   // create an InventoryItem object
i->setPrice("10");
i->displayPrice();
```

Yes, we produce more code overall, but this code is more understandable and manageable than procedural code, especially when the number of objects increases. Notice that we hide, or encapsulate, data (like price) and methods (like *setPrice* and *displayPrice*) into the *InventoryItem* class.

Below is another example. This time, we consider an inventory program where you can perform one of a set of operations, such as add, delete, or change, on inventory items. For simplicity, we offer these choices from a command line menu. Your main (testing) procedure can be outside of your other classes. The main class (or procedure) has a menu.

```
// main function shows the main program menu
int main()
{
InventoryMenu *menu = new InventoryMenu();
}
```

In the *InventoryMenu::InventoryMenu()* constructor, you display the menu and call methods from your menu that create (or take from a file, or take from a linked list in memory) your *InventoryItem* object. For example:

```
/**
* constructor-menu offers several choices and calls the proper method
* to operate on items
*/
InventoryMenu::InventoryMenu() { // constructor-menu
 cout << "Please select one of the operations below" << endl;
 cout << "Press 1 to add a new item to the inventory" << endl;
 // more choices
 cin >> choice;
  if(choice == 1) {
   addItem();
 } else {
  // more lines
 }
}// end of constructor
/**
* addItem() method creates a new item and calls its add() method
*/
InventoryMenu::addItem() {
  InventoryItem *item=new InventoryItem();
  item->add();
}
```

The *InventoryItem* object has the necessary properties (*itemName*, *price*) and does the necessary operations on these properties. The properties and methods are defined in the *InventoryItem* class. For example:

```
InventoryItem::add() {
// present main menu
cout << "Please enter item name:" << endl;
cin >> itemName;
cout << "Please enter item price:" << endl;
cin >> price;
cout << "Thank you" << endl;
}
```

OOP Has Its Limits

Does this mean that OOP solves all programming tasks and can treat all programming diseases? There is a temptation to say yes. But this would not be a true statement.

OOP brings an abstraction that can be overkill for some simple tasks. It works well on sizable projects with multiple objects spread over a huge surface of requirements. We group objects, finding common properties and behavior or concerns, and provide common implementations called *classes*. These implementations are based on a one-dimensional view of the common concerns most often related to a business domain.

We can broadly classify task requirements into core *module-level requirements* and *system-level requirements*. What if system-level requirements crosscut many core modules? For example, a typical enterprise application comprises crosscutting concerns such as authentication, logging, resource pooling, administration, performance, and storage management.

This multidimensional view of the application presents a real challenge to architects and designers. Current OOP-based implementation techniques tend to implement these requirements using one-dimensional methodologies, forcing implementation mapping for the requirements along a single dimension. That single dimension is often the core module-level implementation. The remaining requirements are tagged along this dominant dimension. In other words, the requirement space is an *n*-dimensional space, whereas the implementation space is one-dimensional.

Can you see the problem?

Several solutions for this problem already exist: *mix-in classes*, *design patterns*, *domain-specific solutions*, and *aspect-oriented programming* (AOP) [4]. AOP strives to cleanly implement individual concerns in a loosely coupled fashion and combines these implementations to form the final system. The module unit in AOP is called an *aspect*, similar to a class concept in OOP. We do not go to the horizons of AOP (at least not now), but it is good to know that they exist.

OOP is a proven way to create multiple abstractions—layers that filter complexity of application requirements down to simple functions and data tables. Unfortunately, almost every layer requires its own art of creation, and creating an application becomes a multistep project with a growing distance between initial ideas and actual implementations.

As you can see, OOP is not the end of the story. At the same time, it is a very essential part of almost any enterprise development today. (See Chapter 5 for a new development paradigm.)

UML Notations

Many programming languages support OOP concepts. There is also a graphical support provided by the UML. The UML helps communicate design ideas to developers. There are also some tools, such as Rational Rose, that are capable of generating code out of UML diagrams and notations. Figure 1.15 shows some examples of UML notations describing classes and their relationships.

To describe Classes in UML, we use three sections: Class Name, Attributes (data structure) and Operations (Methods)	Class Name: Attributes: Operations:
This notation is used to reflect the Class inheritance hierarchy, or the relationships between the base and derived classes	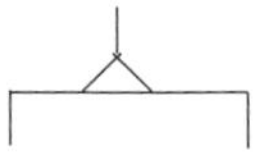
We use this notation when we want to outline associations between classes: One-to-one, or Many-to-one.	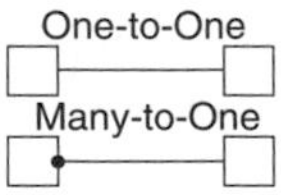 One-to-One Many-to-One
This notation is used to display class aggregation	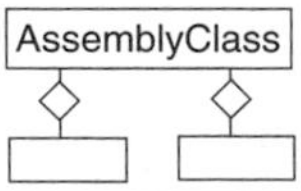 AssemblyClass

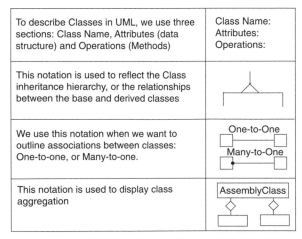

Figure 1.15. UML Notations to Express Relationships.

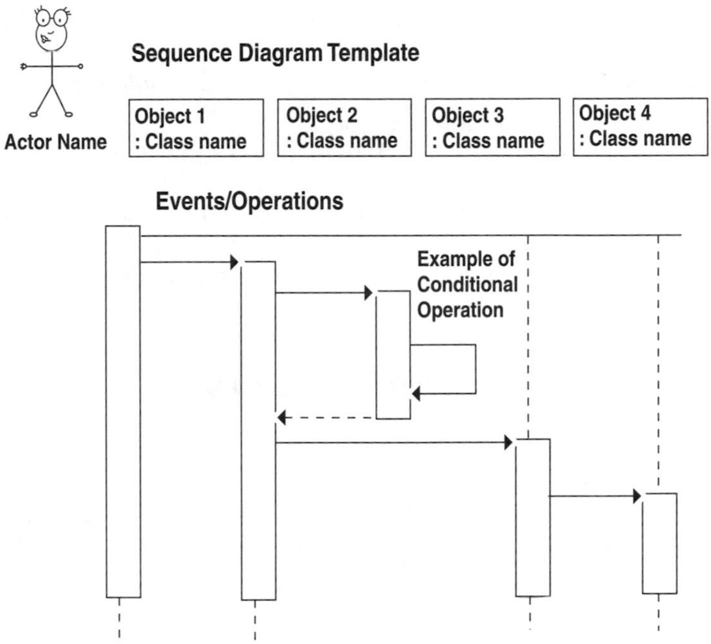

FIGURE 1.16. UML Notations to Express the Sequence of Events.

We already looked into an example of the OMD presented earlier. The OMD covers the static side of the design while the sequence diagram shows its dynamic side. Figure 1.16 presents the basic blocks we can find in almost any sequence diagram. The sequence diagram communicates the sequence of events and operations and participating objects. Figure 1.17

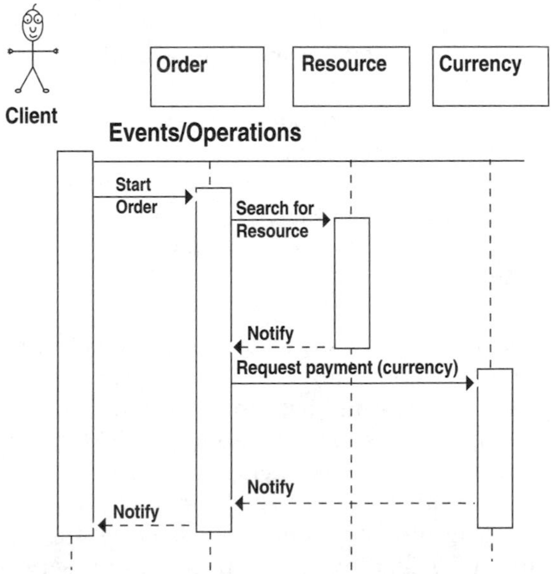

FIGURE 1.17. Service Order Sequence Diagram.

presents an example of a sequence diagram for the service order use case when the subject of the order is a physical item that can be located in stock.

The *OrderWindow* object sends an *initialize* message to the *Order* object, which in turn sends an *initialize* message to each *OrderLine* object.

The *OrderLine* object sends a message to the *Item* object to check the available stock. If the item is in stock, it is added to the *OrderLine*.

The *Item* object sends a message to itself to check the reorder point on the item and, if it needs be reordered, sends a message to the *ReorderItem* to reorder the item then returns to *OrderLine*. If the item is not in stock, the *OrderLine* object sends a message to the order, placing it on hold.

Example of Object-Oriented Analysis: Create an OMD for Document Services

Let us consider another type of service, one performed on business documents. When we work with files, for example, we perform file services. When we work with email messages, we request email services. We actually work with different applications built specifically for different types of documents. These applications have different visual interfaces and different sets of functions. The developers who created these applications began each time from user requirements limited by specific document types. Is this the right approach? Are there common features and properties for different documents, such as email messages and files? What is your answer?

Create the DocumentService Model

If you read the questions carefully, you can find the answer right there. The common word *documents* provides a base for common features and properties. Now we can look at this problem from a higher elevation and find more document types that can be modeled in the same way. We can think about forms, calendar and address book records, and linked articles in distributed knowledge bases.

By starting the design right from the beginning, we can save time on implementations for known documents, as well as bridges to new data types that may be unknown at this point. By consistently using the model design pattern, we can extract a conceptual part of the model into a base class or an interface. Let us discuss common features of different services. This discussion leads us to the *DocumentService* base class and the OMD for multiple types of data services presented in Fig. 1.18.

Data services work with documents or data elements. There are several operations that services perform on documents. We understand that operations can be very different, but again, we can look for common denominators. Generally speaking, every service *processes* documents. For some types of processing, data interpretation is needed. Let us add the *parseXML()* method to the base class. As I mentioned before, XML paves the way to unified services, and we will talk about this in more detail later. Specific services, such as a file manager or an email service, are subclasses derived from the *DocumentService* class.

The *DocumentService* class encapsulates common properties and behaviors of multiple document services. The subclasses that implement these specific services are much lighter now than they would be without this model. No repetition is necessary for common features implemented by the base *DocumentService* class.

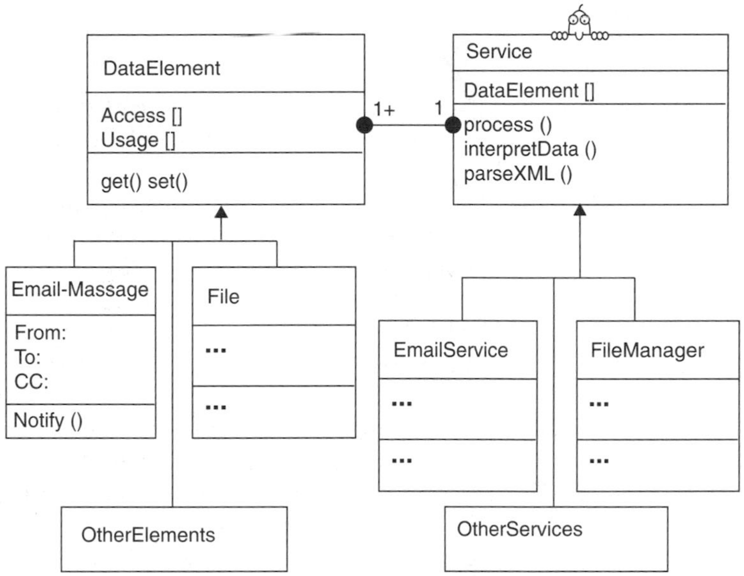

FIGURE 1.18. Document-Handling Services—Object Model Diagram.

Create the Document Model

A very similar model is created for multiple document types. The *DataElement* class represents the basic concept of a document. Every document type has its own data attributes. Common properties and operations can be found, based on an analysis of user requirements. Let us assume that data services are performed in a collaborative environment. In this case, documents can be grouped by security type to provide role-based access to them. For example, managers can access management-type documents, whereas administrators can access administration-type documents. Once we come to this conclusion, the security type becomes a common document property across all data types. We include this property and its associated methods in the *DataElement* class. This means that role-based access to different security type documents will be provided for files, email messages, and other known and unknown data types. Subclasses of the *DataElement*, such as *FileDocument*, *Email-Message*, and other data elements, inherit this ability without any extra code. Security values built into every data element provide for privilege-based secure data sharing.

A unified approach to handling multiple document types will lead to efficient reuse of functionality and (surprise!) to a consistent user interface throughout multiple document services. In Chapter 6, "Write Once," you can find a more extensive discussion of document handling applications with more design patterns and code samples.

Architecture Steps: Find Playground-Tiers for Your Objects

Divide each difficulty into as many parts as is feasible and necessary to resolve it.
—Rene Descartes (1596–1650)

What are the basic steps in architecture analysis?

- Define architecture goals and priorities.
- Decompose the system into presentation, services, data, and more layers.

- Define playground-tiers for application objects.
- Provide multiple architectural views

It is not necessary to finish your object-oriented analysis before starting to construct the architecture. On the contrary, these two processes work in parallel dimensions and have cross sections.

Enterprise applications in general are not single-user programs. The distributed computing nature of enterprise applications requires placing application objects on multiple tiers. It is possible that at this point, some objects can be redefined to avoid tight coupling and decrease network traffic.

Monolithic systems are easy to deploy but hard to change. Separating the presentation layer from the business logic is one of the most important design achievements.

We are going to undertake several steps of architectural analysis. We draw the lines between the presentation (client), business logic (server), and production layers (data and services) and find the right playgrounds (tiers) for application objects. At this point, you can expect some object redesign. This redesign can be related, for example, to the necessity to decrease the client object's dependency on server objects.

Before diving deep into the lake of architecture, let us take a high-level look. What is architecture? System architecture is a specialized view that focuses on a system's components and behaviors with no or minimum implementation details. Architects communicate this view in the form of design patterns, models, frameworks, and diagrams.

It is crucial to provide multiple architectural views. Look at any object from multiple sides and you can see more of it. Architectural views can be layered and can vary according to system specifics and viewer's goals:

- A set of Use Cases shows a **User's view** of the application.
- Object Model Diagram represents a **static structural view** of the system in the process of Object-Oriented Analysis.
- **Behavioral View** includes Sequence and Collaboration Diagrams
- Deployment Diagrams obviously communicate the way the application is going to be deployed or **Deployment View**.

For example, the deployment diagram will represent a solution for a problem we discussed before: what are the logical and physical tiers of the application? The art and science of architecture is to balance system capabilities, including performance, scalability, security, and other nonfunctional qualities in terms of the context of user requirements.

Unfortunately, it is not feasible to optimize all capabilities. For example, maximum performance can be achieved with minimum scalability and security. Architects need to define their architectural goals with clients and capture these nonfunctional capabilities with numbers and priorities as measurable items on the list of system requirements.

From Single-User to Client-Server and Multi-Tier Architecture Models

In the early stage of the design process, we try to identify containers for the functions we want to provide. We can describe these containers in terms of layers and tiers. A single-user

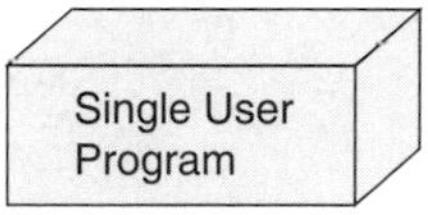

FIGURE 1.19. A Single-User Program—The Simplest Software Architecture.

program is an example of the simplest architecture (Fig. 1.19). It consists of a single tier—the process running the program.

Microsoft Paint can be considered an example of such a program. An IBM mainframe with old 3270 dumb terminals represents the next step to a multi-user system (Fig. 1.20). It is still a single-tier architecture. The programs run on a single tier—the IBM mainframe—while the terminals connected to the machine by long wires share no processing and justify their "dumb" alias.

A UNIX network can best represent the client–server architecture that was predominant in the 1980s. Client and server machines shared computer processing; in most cases, this sharing was provided by an X-windows operating system that separated presentation (keyboard, mouse, and display functionality) from computation, data storage, and networking, all of which were provided by a server/host computer (Fig. 1.21).

The client–server model failed to provide the necessary resources (e.g., database connections) to a growing number of clients. The work of servers was redistributed to business and data tiers. The business tier included connection pooling and other functions and mechanisms that provided scalability (Fig. 1.22).

Web technology brought another tier (or container) into the game. The Web container took responsibility for connectivity between multiple Web clients and services. The Web container includes a very efficient and inexpensive Web server (one of the best Web servers, Apache, is free) and/or an application server. The Web container and business processes can run on one server or be distributed on multiple machines.

The simplest glue that connects business processing with a Web server is the common gateway interface (CGI). The Web server intercepts client requests for program processing and sends them to executable programs. The program provides a necessary service—for example, retrieved or saved data—and in return generates a dynamic response in Hypertext Markup Language (HTML) format.

The Web server delivers this response back to the Web client, which is waiting for this response. The Web client, a Web browser running on a client machine, understands the HTML page and renders it into a context of text, graphics, and sound. The page regularly includes new links and/or forms that help the user navigate to more services.

The drawback of CGI technology, because of its simplicity, is that it has to create a new process for every client. When two clients request services—two programs—full-blown processes have to be created on the server. Ten clients hit the server, ten processes are

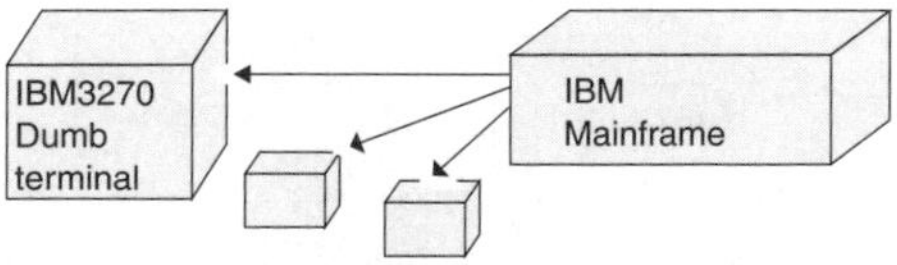

FIGURE 1.20. Multiple Users, Multiple Terminals, a Single Processor, and Time Sharing.

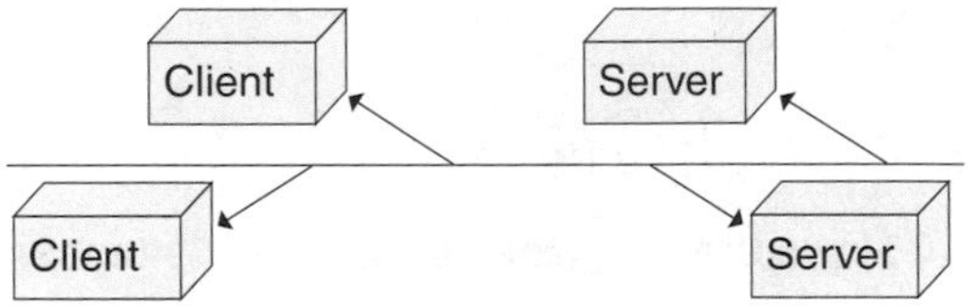

FIGURE 1.21. Client–Server.

created. A hundred clients hit the server—the server goes down. Simplicity and scalability are not always the best of friends.

Enterprise applications must serve thousands, sometimes millions, of clients. New technologies allow the Web server and business logic to be glued in such a way that every client request creates a new service thread on the server side. The thread is a very tiny process and much lighter than a regular one. This benefit multiplied a thousand times scales Web application capacity way up. One example of such an architecture is presented in Fig. 1.23. This example is based on J2EE components.

Tier 1. Client Container. Multiple types of clients request services via an *XML-based service application program interface (API)* using synchronous Hypertext Markup Transport Protocol (HTTP) or asynchronously using Java Message Service (JMS) or email with Simple Messaging Transport Protocol (SMTP) mechanisms.

Client types:

- Java Web Start or partner service application running on a corporate workstation (connects to Web container over HTTP or directly to JMS, JMail (SMTP), or application server in the service container using proper ports and protocols).
- Web (HTML) browser with or without a Java Applet (connects to the Web container over HTTP)
- Wireless devices, such as Smart Mobile Phone, personal digital assistant (PDA) with wireless application protocol (WAP), or iMODE-iApplix (a *defacto* standard established by NTT DoCoMo, a Japanese company).
- Wireless devices connected to the network with other radio frequency (RF) protocols, such as GSM, GPRS, 802.11 (WiFi), and Bluetooth.
- Operating environments for wireless devices range from WindowsCE and TabletPC (full Windows XP geared towards pen/voice interface) to PalmOS. These devices can run scaled down Java Virtual Machine versions, which are often presented under the single umbrella of the Java 2 Micro Edition (J2ME).
- Smart Cards, for example those based on JavaCard technology, secure personal identity features. Smart Cards require special devices—readers that used to be quite expensive in the past.

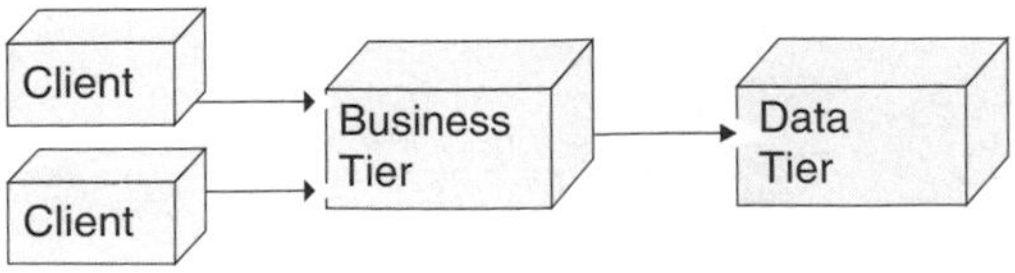

FIGURE 1.22. Multi-tier Architecture.

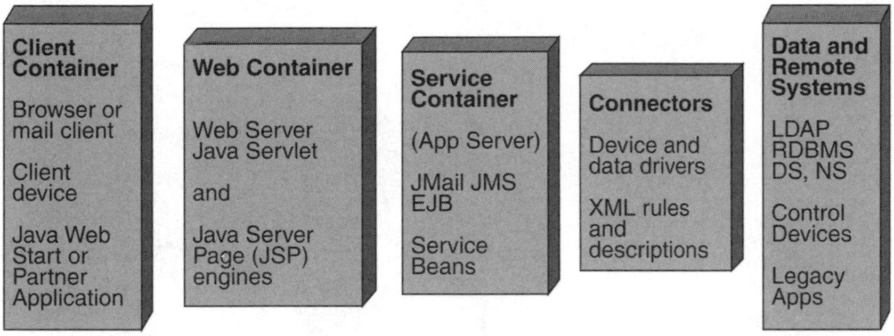

FIGURE 1.23. Example of the Architecture of a J2EE-Based Enterprise Web Application.

- Regular phones (connected to the Web container via a speech recognition system, for example one provided by Nuance.com)
- Email client programs (connect to JMail or SMTP server in the service container using SMTP)

Tier 2. Web Container. Web server, Java servlet, and JSP engines are glued into a single process in the Web container. The Java servlet engine is responsible for session tracking and request distribution, and JSPs provide a presentation layer back to the client.

Tier 3. Service Container. The service container can include generic services, such as Java Mail and JMS, and specific business services implemented with Java worker beans and classes. The services can be implemented as EJBs to gain the advantages of generic features like security and transaction monitoring provided by EJB vendors.

Tier 4. Connectors. This container includes the necessary software and hardware solutions that provide access from services to data and remote systems, legacy applications, and control devices. This book promotes a unified approach to data drivers and device controllers. Data drivers implement basic operations on data using Java Naming and Directory Interface (JNDI).

Data drivers are able to understand XML-based business rules and descriptors governing data access. The application business logic captured in the service container will never change, no matter what data source is used, whether Oracle RDBMS (relational database management system) or LDAP (Lightweight Directory Access Protocol). Device and system controllers implement a unified service model, which focuses on the interpretation function of controllers. The model considers the controller an interpreter with a set of possible input and output instructions. An important part of both models is an XML API and descriptors that capture system rules and behavior.

Tier 5. Data and Remote Systems. This container includes different types of data sources, legacy applications, production system terminals, remote systems, and devices controlled by the application or interacting with it. Data sources may include different types of RDBMS, LDAP, directory services, meta-directories, and so forth.

This example of multi-tiered architecture is one of many possible solutions. The architecture analysis will produce, among other design documents, a deployment diagram similar, or not very similar, to the one above. The deployment diagram will include more details. For example, we need to decide on communication protocols between tiers and provide

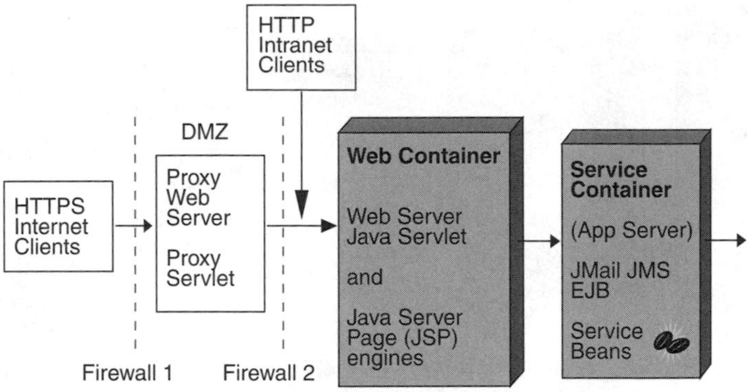

FIGURE 1.24. Demilitarized Zone (DMZ) in Web Applications.

security considerations. We need to consider client types expected by the application. The architectural solution will include presentation layers, or factories, for these types of clients. Choosing between thin and thick clients for a Web-based enterprise application is one of the more important architectural decisions.

The choices are related to your potential audience: for internal corporate clients, it is possible to control the Web browser type and version usage. This would allow, for example, reenforcing usage of the Java Plug-In for a Web browser to support the heavyweight Java Foundation Classes (JFC). Keep in mind that using JFC can easily add an extra megabyte or more to the applet size.

Java Web Start, a new client container, can deliver a full-blown Java application to your client over the Web and replace the Web browser as the most commonly used container. Unfortunately, Java Web Start-based applications will require significant resources on client machines. This can still work well for a selected group of Internet users. If your audience is the Internet population, it is a safe bet to use a Java applet supported by the major Web browsers, or to rely on HTML pages generated on the server side.

The user requirements might also include wireless access. Even if these requirements are not in place from the beginning, we can expect them to be in the future. We do not want to do extra work "just in case," and we do not need to. We can solve this problem by separating business logic from the presentation layer. Placing the right objects on the right tiers is the key to this solution.

Communication between client and server containers can be provided with any protocol supported by Java: RMI, TCP/IP Sockets, or HTTP. This is valid for Intranet applications. Enterprise applications that are open to Internet users provide a security zone called the "demilitarized zone" (DMZ), between Internet clients and business services (Fig. 1.24).

The DMZ is based on two firewalls. Internet users can access generic Internet services, including a Web proxy, located inside the DMZ. The proxy servlet will redirect client requests to the Web container behind the second firewall. It is useful to remember that only the HTTP protocol is free to fly over the corporate firewall by default. For other protocols, special agreements with the security folks must be in place.

There is no firm line between architecture and the design process. Architecture is a general view, whereas design considers more details. It is possible that developers will need to reconsider their architectural plan during detailed design considerations.

Basic Design Steps and Rules

A repeatable design process requires discipline as well organizational and technological reinforcement to follow basic design rules:

- Focus on reusability: recognize reusable services and shared data.
- Use design patterns.
- Distinguish the conceptual part from implementation details.
- Balance overhead.
- Document design before coding.

It takes time and effort to acquire healthy habits for a proper level of documentation and communication in a team. The right approach to documentation sharing is important. Documentation should not die in files that are released once; it should have a living and easily updateable nature.

This book describes collaborative engineering technology that encourages privilege-based data sharing and increases members' feeling of ownership and willingness to be proactive. This technology keeps the team "on the same page" and minimizes the need for long and often unproductive meetings.

Recognize Reusable Services and Shared Data

Look for reusability from two points of view: within an application and throughout a multiapplication environment. For example, security services or data-caching mechanisms are good candidates for reuse. I have heard a lot of complaints about security services that require users to enter different names and passwords for different applications within a single company.

Of course, users at these companies may be under a lot of stress to remember several passwords, and their performance may suffer. Obviously, developers at their organizations did not think much about reusability when creating different applications. (Of course, they might be under stress, too.)

Reusability can be achieved only by extra work done on a specific part of the project. Then this part can be reused multiple times, providing a tremendous payoff. Focus on the idea that functionality can be reused and data can be shared. Two types of shared data should be recognized: data shared by different functions performed by a single user and data shared between multiple users.

For example, a single user's data are shared between different layers or screens within the application. This kind of data can serve as a common interface and should be stored, cached, on a tier that is the most active in processing this data. Each user/client works with its own set of the client's shared data. One of the mechanisms for caching client data is presented by the session object in Java servlet.

Data shared by many users, such as statistics or short database tables, can be stored on a proper tier as a unique copy that can be accessed by all the users running this application. One of the mechanisms to provide such access can be offered by static data.

Components of the user interface, or widgets (e.g., data fields and buttons), can also be considered a source of reusability. It is preferable to dynamically change widget state from visible to invisible, from active to inactive, or to change the color or label name instead of removing and recreating the widget.

I have provided several examples of reuse. These examples do not necessarily work for all cases. The key is to recognize any cases of data sharing or function reuse and find the best implementation based on considerations that are more detailed. Well-documented design, as well as readable code with good, understandable comments, has more chances to be reused.

Use Design Patterns

Design patterns are known solutions for common problems. Design patterns give us a system of names and ideas for common problems. This system improves communication and understanding among developers. It is a great advantage to recognize a common problem to which a design pattern can be found. Take a known solution and implement it in your application. Use the name of the pattern to communicate to your team and to search for the best implementation. Several examples of design patterns are provided below.

Adapter—helps to reuse an object or method by adapting its interface to a more common one
Controller—controls client access and manages every request
Data access object (DAO)—encapsulates access to data, hiding its complexity from users
Dispatcher—controls client access and redirects or dispatches client requests to the proper party, which can be located on the same or a different tier
Façade—hides a functional complexity; DAO can be considered a specialized façade
Factory method—creates a family of related objects instantiated by subclasses
Abstract factory method—creates a family of families (adds a dimension to the factory method)
Model—logically represents (models) system states and functions
Observer—provides a mechanism (implementing an interface or abstract class) for event notification
Proxy—provides access to a remote target via an intermediate object
View—takes responsibility for the presentation layer
Model-view-controller (MVC)—separates business and presentation logic into three components named by design patterns listed above (this is an example of an architectural design pattern)

There are different types and levels of design patterns [5, 6]. For example, the MVC is the architectural level of design pattern, whereas the rest of the patterns from the list above are component level design patterns. The basic types are Behavior, Creational, Structural, and System design patterns. Names are extremely important in design patterns; they should be clear and descriptive. Throughout the book you'll find multiple examples of design patterns and their implementations. Let us take a brief look at an extract from the OMD (Fig. 1.25).

The factory method design pattern is used here to create a family of services. The benefit of such design is the ability to use the powerful mechanism of Java Reflection and load run-time services on demand. Look at the code needed to implement the solution.

```
// Retrieve parameters from the client request
String serviceName = request.getParameter("serviceName");
Hashtable parameters = new Hashtable();
// Load service at run-time
Service service = (Service) Class.forName(serviceName).newInstance();
// make it work!
boolean success = service.process(parameters);
```

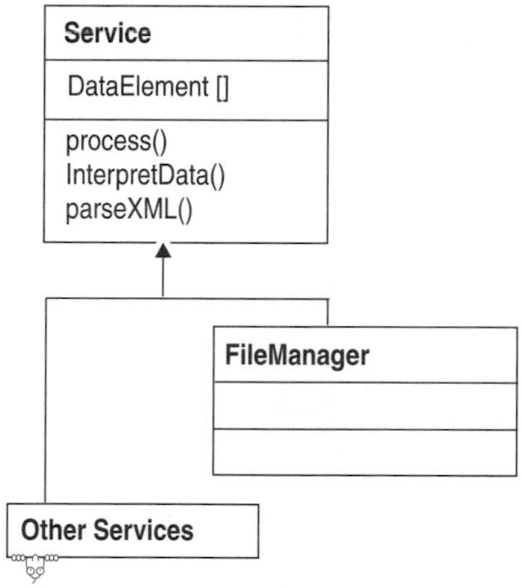

FIGURE 1.25. A Family of Services Created with the Factory Method Design Pattern.

The loaded class MUST extend the Service class and implement the *process* method that can expect necessary parameters as an input argument. This design allows us to create a new service object without knowing the service type upfront. Walking through the book we'll meet more design patterns and implementation examples.

Design: Strategic and Tactical Considerations

I separate the list (very subjectively) into strategy and tactical points.

Strategy Points

- Define and redefine major milestones.
- Do not "overdesign." Focus on the date and scope of the first deliverable step.
- Define milestones with the best precision possible at this point. It is OK that some details look fuzzy right now. Milestones will be redefined when you come closer and are able to see a sharper image.

Define basic concepts during the early stages of project development. Focus on and deliver the smallest possible portion of the project in the shortest possible time. Do not allow the temptation to "do everything right" to win and delay your first deliverable step.

Have you ever heard of projects being canceled?

- Time intervals between deliverables that are too long are often the reason. The client, being disconnected from the development process, is not "hot" about the project anymore and can sacrifice it for another one.
- Have an "on-site client," try to cultivate the feeling that your client is part of the development team, and carefully plan your first deliverable. This helps get early feedback from the client and makes sure that the *project is funded*. Early client involvement is sometimes crucial for a project's success.

Keep in mind that the object-oriented approach leads to a spiral development process. Each cycle gives developers more understanding and personal feeling about an application and about the new tools, software packages, and new environments that are often used with a new application.

The first visible milestone is a good point to review your approach. It may lead to reinventing the design. It is beneficial to make this cycle shorter. On the other hand, every milestone, including the first one, should deliver enough visibility to serve as a platform for milestone reviews.

Tactical Points

- Consider the user interface a priority.
- Code with style.
- Support teamwork.
- Use distributed technologies to capture and share development ideas.

The user interface (UI) is often an underestimated factor. The UI is one of the most important selling points of any product. An application's success or failure may depend on the UI.

There are many examples of good products that could not win market share, losing the UI battle despite their superior functionality. Client participation in UI design improves the chances of client acceptance. Define the screens and user interface with human-computer interface experts, people trained to balance simplicity, functionality, and efficiency. Learn from experts [7, 8] what information to collect when you talk to your future clients or observe a current process.

There are several general UI recommendations:

- Work with a client representative and UI experts.
- Set defaults for the most commonly used operations.
- Balance (with the client) between a multichoice and multistep (wizard) graphical user interface (GUI).
- Use role/audience-based GUI options.
- Provide clear options and messages/recommendations.
- Provide context sensitive on-line help.
- Extend the help system into a privilege-based reference for the maintenance team.

First of all, the UI (screens) should function to cover the user requirements. The UI can be tailored to its audience; a role-based UI can help accomplish this concept. The idea is to have fewer choices and easier wizard screens set for the non-tech audience while offering more sophisticated multiple-menu screens for the advanced client role/audience.

It takes time to learn the operations and situations most commonly experienced by a client. This knowledge can be used to provide the right "defaults" for the most common objects and operations. It is also important to take into account data dependency and to design the UI accordingly.

The screen should be understandable to those with minimal or no training. This also means context-sensitive on-line help provided by the developer. The on-line help system can be extended with information for the maintenance team and remote troubleshooting. Privilege-based on-line access to the help system keeps the administration and maintenance team, as well as end users, on the top of things as they are needed.

Code with Style and Conduct Code Reviews

- Agree on a common style.
- Do not use abbreviations.

- Capture the design in source code comments.
- Keep JavaDoc comment style and provide a clean API.
- Conduct code reviews.

Did you notice how close we came to coding?

A lot of C and C++ programmers think they write in the same language. They realize that this is not completely true when they read each other's source. Style differences make the code unreadable. Java programmers are luckier: the Java style guide was released almost the same time as Java itself. A common coding style is important for team communication.

JavaDoc style makes it possible to capture the essential part of the design in the code and make it available with the API. Use style guidelines while coding, and review the code regularly. This also keeps communication at the proper level for a team. Use commercially available applications that check compliance with a formal coding style.

Figure 1.26 helps illustrate several style points. The very first line indicates a class name. Package and import statements follow this line. A JavaDoc comment header provides the definition for a class. Understandable descriptions and examples of usage drastically improve reuse chances for this class. (This statement is based on the assumption that there is some function to be reused.) The next several lines present a method that illustrates the healthy habit of checking objects that have just been created or passed as parameters.

Such objects can be null and may cause run-time exceptions. A simple check in this example prevents the possibility of a Java Virtual Machine crash. This is equally valid for the case of an array of objects. Note the next condition in the same line. After checking that the object is not zero, we provide a condition to check the length of the array. Java performs conditional operations in the sequence specified by the rules: brackets, left-to-right, and so on. Never use try/catch for run-time exceptions. Correct logics should be in place to prevent such exceptions.

Code and design reviews help to communicate coding standards and best design and coding practices to team members. I do not recommend big parties for code reviews; two or three team members, including the author of the code that is going to be reviewed, can efficiently accomplish this task.

Start coding with comments/plans that you provide in your class and method headers. Perfect your comments to such a degree that you can create your design document based on these comments. The JavaDoc tool will extract your comments into a set of HTML documents that reflect your API. Reading these documents, you can see if your comments are self-sufficient. This is your design specification.

This document is an important part of your project, in addition to higher-level documents, and communicates to the other team members and outsiders the lowest level of your plan, without using actual code. Even nonprogrammers or programmers who write in a different language can read this document.

This is also a very clear plan that helps you code this part of the application. This will help you implement the rule "Say what you do, then do what you say." Think about what you want to do first, and capture your plan in your code headers.

Plan for a new class? Provide your plan in the class header; then start the code (or implement your plan). Plan for a new method? Provide your plan in the method header; then start the code (or implement your plan).

Do you want to communicate your plan to other team members or to your client? Your documentation serves this purpose. On the lowest level, it is your design specification,

```
// StyleExample
package its.examples;
import java.io.*;

/** A class implementing Java Style Example.
 * The purpose of the class is Ö
 * How to use this class: ...

Example:
<code>
    // code example

</code>

 * @version 0.1 September 10, 1996
 * @author Jeff.Zhuk@JavaSchool.com
 */

public class StyleExample extends ITShape {
     // class data members
     private Tree[] dataTree;

     // .. More data Ö

     // class methods with JavaDoc headers

     /** getDataTree(int iIndex)method returns one element of array
      * @param iIndex element index in the dataTree[] array
      * @return dataTree if available, return null in other cases
      */
      public Tree getDataTree(int iIndex) { // Check objects and
                                            // arrays!
           if(iIndex < 0 || dataTree == null ||
           dataTree.length < iIndex)  {
               return null;  // to prevent run-time exceptions!!!
           }
           return dataTree[iIndex];
      }
 } // end of StyleExample class
```

FIGURE 1.26

or program APIs, extracted from your code. Make your comments good enough for your audience. Your audience is not necessarily made up of programmers. Design specification is a communication document for your management, clients, partners, and others.

If you create your design specification as a separate document, this will not only double your work, but there will also always be a gap between the real code and your documentation.

Your comments are integral parts of the code, as your design and planning skills are integral parts of your development skills.

Use Technologies, Not Long Meetings, to Keep the Whole Team on the Same Page

Team communication is one of the most important keys in the development process. Some companies understand this as the undesired but unavoidable necessity of long and unproductive meetings.

Most people are not active during such meetings. Some even sleep through them, especially if slides are projected and the lights are off. Collaborative technologies help to keep teams literally "on the same page" without management meetings, motivate active participation, and force developers to document design and communicate development plans and status.

Later, we consider the distributed knowledge base system (DKB) as an example of collaborative technologies. Documents in the DKB are not dead files stored in archive folders. Documents are available on-line as a living and updateable repository with secure privilege-based access.

The system arranges a hierarchical structure and hypertext links (that we love so much on the Web) for multiple types of documents. It provides for multiple types of communication, from email to personal chat, from instant messages to group conferences with screen and voice sharing. Development is a complicated process; it requires and benefits from proper technology support.

Share Your First Results with a Client; Try to Make the Client a Part of Your Team

Armed with these rules and recommendations, we can pretend that we have finished the first step of the development process. What is next? Of course, we must now share this milestone with the client in a special demo (Fig. 1.27). Early client involvement often means early approval. Otherwise it is even more important to recapture the user's point of view.

Make corrections and outline the plan to finish the project and tune its performance. Tuning up performance does not necessarily mean redesigning. Multi-tier architecture, if properly designed, makes it possible to redistribute or partition services to optimize the load and to improve performance.

FIGURE 1.27. Make Your Client a Part of Your Team.

Java-based architecture is perfect for such a repartition. The following chapters are dedicated to a more precise view of design and coding with Java. We also take a look into the .NET world and give special consideration to XML, which acts in both worlds as a business flow and interoperability conductor.

The basic development steps provided above can't be considered a universal formula that fits any development organization. They just give you an idea of the necessary components of collaborative engineering that make development a repeatable success.

If we glue technology and process components together with the philosophy and practice of distributed instant knowledge services, we can increase development efficiency and maybe even improve the existing business model.

Instead of a Summary: How Direct Access to Products and Services Improves the Balance of Supply and Demand

The current crisis in telecommunications companies and IT overall reminds us about the waves of the free market. We felt great going up, but we did not like sinking down. The market is too loose, and the waves are too big. Some people believe that strong regulations (a la Europe) should frame the free market and help stability. I am not a politician, but I tend to fix the mechanical problems I see.

There is way too much distance between demand and the market's feeling for demand, between oversupply and the market's reaction. In April 2002, my friend filed an unemployment application on the Internet and pointed me to the government *job projections* page. The page bravely stated that computer jobs will double every year starting in the year 2000. The government agency made its projection based on the past and didn't take into account that after the positive wave (1992–1999), the IT market took a negative turn called a *recession* (seven good years, seven bad years?). There are direct lies, and then there are statistics. No, they are not the same, but they certainly do not reflect reality.

How can we increase the sensitivity of the market? Streamline access to industry products and customer requests. A global knowledge and service container can provide direct access to data and services, accelerate market awareness of product existence and consumer demands, improve the ongoing balance between supply and demand, and cut short the waves of the free market. In the meantime, collaborative engineering can improve the development process and increase overall productivity.

Integrating Questions

1. Which development methodology would work best at your workplace? Compare with other methodologies and explain your choice.
2. Describe the development life cycle and the role of a software architect at your workplace. Can you think about possible improvements?
3. Why is it important to know and understand concepts, standards, and specifications? Provide examples from your workplace.

Case Study (Exercises): Design Patterns

Present a white paper on any design pattern from the list below or beyond (a student makes this determination with the instructor during the class or on-line).

The white paper delivers the content in a presentable format: PowerPoint with notes, Web pages, MS Word, PDF, and so on. The content considers three levels of the topic: definition (high level), functionality and applicability (middle level), and an example of implementation (low level). These three levels roughly map the why, what, and how of the selected subject.

"Dress" the content (text) in an attractive presentation, with diagrams and code illustrations.

Suggested design patterns (a student can go beyond this list) are:

- Model-view-controller (MVC)
- Observer and messaging mechanisms
- Factory method and abstract factory method
- Data access object
- Proxy

References

1. Paulk, M., C. Weber, B. Curtis, M. Chrissis, et al. 1995. *The Capability Maturity Model Guidelines for Improving the Software Process*. Boston: Addison-Wesley.
2. Zhuk, Jeff. Distributed active knowledge and process base. Patent Pending. http://uspto.gov.
3. Jacobson, I., G. Booch, and J. Rumbaugh. 1999. *The Unified Software Development Process*. Reading, MA: Addison-Wesley.
4. Safonov, Vladimir, O. *Aspect.NET- a new approach to aspect oriented programming*. .NET Developers Journal, April 2003.
5. Gamma, Erich, Richard Helm, Ralph Johnson, and John Vlissides. 1994. *Design Patterns: Elements of Reusable Object-Oriented Software*. Boston: Addison-Wesley.
6. Stelting, Stephen and Olav Maasen. 2002. *Applied Java Patterns*. Palo Alto, CA: Sun Microsystems, Inc.
7. Hackos, JoAnn T. and Janice C. Redish. 1998. *User and Task Analysis for Interface Design*. New York: Wiley.
8. Kaptelinin, V. (2003) UMEA: Translating interaction histories into project contexts. In: Proceedings of the CHI'2003 Conference on Human Factors in Computing Systems (Ft. Lauderdale, Florida, April 5–10, 2003).

CHAPTER 2

Software Architecture and Integration Technologies

You have a better chance of finding a solution if you understand the problem.
—From teaching experience

SOFTWARE ARCHITECTURE—THE CENTER PLACE OF SOFTWARE DEVELOPMENT

Software architecture is the highest level of a software system definition that can include subsystems with their own architectures. The main question is how deep one should go into the nested abstractions to define software architecture. The general answer is to stop right before implementation details that can be considered "private" parts of the design. More visible and exposed "public" containers, components, and connectors of the system with their run-time behavior and relationships comprise software architecture.

Software architecture has its own worlds of "what," "why," and "how." The *what* world is mostly inhabited by industry standards, tools, and modules. The *how* world is about development process, design patterns, and architectural styles. The *why* world is a map between requirements criteria and the worlds of what and how. Design patterns [1, 2] and architectural styles [3] are very close by their nature but different in their scope and manners. Both are symbol names and concepts that describe approaches to common development problems.

Multiple architectural views work as light projectors helping us to see the systems from different sides by eyes of different parties interested in the product.

ARCHITECTURAL ELEMENTS, STYLES, VIEWS, AND LANGUAGES

Most of today's enterprise applications are built with **object-oriented architecture**, in which system components encapsulate data and behavior and communicate via messages.

Components, containers, and connectors are basic elements of the architecture.

A **component** (more specifically, an atomic component) is an architectural element that performs a distinguished function in a system.

A **container** is also a component, but there is a difference. A container can *contain* one or more components and provide some generic services for the insider components. For example, an Enterprise Java Bean (EJB) container can take responsibility for the well-being of insider EJBs, that is, their initiation and invocation, security and transactional mechanisms, and so on. This allows the EJBs to focus on their specific businesses.

Connectors provide communication among components that have no common interfaces.

Architecture Styles

If you travel through France, you will find buildings of every architectural style: monumental classics, early Gothic architecture, Renaissance, and others. In a similar way, software architecture has its own styles. Architectural style is a convenient symbol name that we use to describe some recognizable features of software system architectures.

For example, in **client–server** architecture, a server and a client (or often many clients) are two processes that communicate via a network. The client process usually requests a service; the server process is capable of providing services to a client or to multiple client systems.

The **layered client–server** adds more abstract mediator components to client–server architecture.

Tiered architecture is based on layered architecture, with essential structural differences between layer-tiers.

Contract-based architecture is aware of client–server interface specifications and often implements a protocol (see Chapter 14) that allows a service provider to advertise this interface as a contract between a client and a server. A client program, in its turn, can (dynamically) use this contract to request a service.

The **representational state transfer** (REST) architectural style focuses on the efficiency of client–server communications and minimizes networks by providing the caching mechanisms with dynamic component substitution. At the same time, REST architecture strives for component independence, trying to encapsulate event handling within the component. The goals of REST architecture style almost completely match the design goals of Web application.

Model-view-controller (MVC) is probably the most famous architectural style and architectural design pattern today and is applicable to any interactive application. MVC promotes one of the most important design rules that separate business and presentation logics. There are many variations on the MVC design pattern. The model part represents data and business logics, the view is responsible for presentation formats, and the controller controls the flow of information.

In Java 2 Enterprise Edition (J2EE)-based Web applications, the model is implemented in the service container as service beans and EJBs that communicate to data sources; the view is built with presentation factories that consist of Java server pages (JSPs), custom tag libraries, and/or server-side Java classes; and the controller is made up of a Java servlet and related helper beans or a more sophisticated StrutsAuthor. Please spell out at first mention: struts is not an abbreviation framework that provides an extensible development environment.

Service Browsers and Interaction Scenarios

The Model in most cases defines a fixed set of rules and services implemented with one or more programming languages and compiled into binary libraries. More sophisticated approach can consider a flexible Model that includes some fixed computing part and can also be changed dynamically.

Such flexible Model can learn new rules and services presented at run-time as XML descriptions-scenarios. The Model would include an interpreter that would transform these descriptions into services. This would provide a great flexibility for an application. We can call such interpreter as the Service Browser.

Scenarios can describe user interface and business information flow as a set of application behavior steps or acts of the scenarios. It is important to keep in mind that these Interaction Scenarios target not only user-program interactions but program–program interactions as well. The Service Browsers work not only for human beings as their target audience but also for partner applications that interact according to interaction scenarios. You can find more details and examples on this subject in following chapters, especially in the Chapters 7 and 13.

Data-flow architectures focus on a sequence of steps presented, for example, by a set of batch files or by a set of input and output streams of data and their transformations (pipe-and-filter style). The pipe-and-filter style usually represents a one-way data flow network [4].

Procedure-based architectures, such as call-back, remote procedure calls (RPCs), library-based application program interfaces (APIs), and Dynamic Link Libraries (DLLs), provide direct access to code modules using terms defined by these modules. This type of architecture not only gives programmers full control over someone else's code but also enforces tight coupling and restricts the code semantics.

Procedure-based architectures can be considered a subset of **synchronous** architectures. If we compare synchronous and **asynchronous** architectures, we find that synchronous architectures exhibit tight coupling, necessitating a wait for a response or communication handshake, and in most cases, any network problem will immediately result in the synchronous system failure. Overall, synchronous architectures place more demands on the application development and deployment.

Asynchronous applications make fewer demands on the development and deployment environment and can survive for some time without a network because their components are loosely coupled and more independent than those in synchronous applications. These qualities manifest the robust, scalable, and reliable solutions that we often find in messaging products, such as IBM Message Queue (MQ).

The trade-off is cost, which used to be much higher for asynchronous than for synchronous solutions. However, with new messaging technologies like Java Messaging Services (JMS) by Sun Microsystems and Microsoft Message Queue (MSMQ), the cost difference is decreasing and more applications will adapt the asynchronous style.

Service-oriented architecture (SOA) may be considered a modern representative of synchronous architecture. SOA allows developers to create standard interfaces **with relatively**

small sets of APIs and well-described message protocols between components and to build multicomponent applications with very little or no knowledge of the components' inner structure.

For example, Extensible Markup Language (XML) Web services can be defined with the Web Services Description Language (WSDL) and discovered with the Universal Description, Discovery, and Integration (UDDI) interfaces. The service messages are also standardized and use XML-based Simple Object Access Protocol (SOAP) over Hypertext Transfer Protocol (HTTP). SOA shifts some of the load of application development onto the system (service) level. Web service providers must add standard interfaces to any Web services. SOA applications consist of a set of component-services that work sequentially in a linear fashion similar to data-flow applications.

Event-driven architecture (EDA) can complement SOA applications to provide more efficient multithreaded performance when asynchronous events can act in parallel. Application business rules can distinguish events that require immediate handling from those that can wait or just be archived.

You can see that EDA leads to complex event processing (almost parallel processing). This is a new area for many application developers. Fortunately, message-oriented products help simplify the job by providing easy-to-use mechanisms to publish events and notify event handlers.

The other part of this puzzle is how to present business rules to the application. Encapsulated in code algorithms, they are inflexible and sometimes do not tell the whole truth. They rarely express business ideas in their original sense, but interpret them via programming language primitives.

The knowledge technologies described in this book may pass this work directly into the hands of business experts who will be able to use "almost natural" languages to share their vision (user requirements) with a knowledge base that would play a significant role in software architecture.

Observer Design Pattern and Publish/Subscribe Mechanisms

The key to programming EDA is an understanding of the **observer** design pattern that is very often used for user interface components but goes far beyond this original idea.

The observer object registers with the event **consumer** (or **subject**) object. The consumer—for example, a Web form—receives events (mouse clicks). The consumer (subject) notifies the observer about the events as they occur. The observer usually has some event-handling procedure that is triggered upon the notification. Note that not all events that happen to the consumer are interesting to the observer. While registered, the observer usually specifies the events that deserve notification.

The observer design pattern is implemented in messaging applications as the **publish/subscribe** mechanism. Users register or subscribe to specific topics (events) and are notified when a message is posted to these topics. We call these users *subscribers*. The same or other users register as *publishers*, and they have the privilege to publish messages to specified topics.

Messaging applications are loosely coupled and do not always require a network, which is especially important to wireless clients. Publishers can publish at any time convenient to them; subscribers can receive their notifications when the network is available. They do not have to wait for simultaneous connections and handshakes as they would in synchronous applications.

Shared Information (Collaborative) Systems

Collaborative systems provide multiple users with privilege-based access to centralized data and services (e.g., Yahoo.com and IPServe.com) or to distributed resources [e.g., peer-to-peer (P2P), JXTA, the Knowledge Connector training tool that comes with this book]. Sharing does not necessarily mean equal access, although many current systems provide equal sharing or distinguish among only two or three levels of privileges.

Distributed active knowledge base [5] architecture allows a collaborative system to dynamically build new communities, negotiate multiple forms of collaboration, and establish rules of access for internal members and outsiders (e.g., pay-per-use and value-based exchange) using sufficiently flexible levels of data security with multiple types of data and services that can be shared. The system notifies interested parties about available objects, processes, and services and provides dynamic valuation of data and services based on their usage.

Data-Centered Architectures (Databases, Oracle Application Server)

Data-centered architectures allow client programs to access a central data repository that in many cases is represented by a relational database. Clients never exchange data directly but instead use a central repository to pass messages. Oracle Application Server is a good example of a program that implements data-centered architecture.

Distributed, de-centralized (DECENT) architectures (e.g., Jini, JXTA, and GRID)

Software systems in which the components (subsystems or individual peers) have no agreement on simultaneous actions and can work independently, with no centralized control. These components can implement (optional) protocols that allow their coordination. You can find more details on Jini and JXTA distributed technologies in Chapter 14.

Data grid (GRID) architecture also strives for subsystem independence but emphasizes sharing resources and coordination protocols to negotiate and manage these resources. Big scientific projects that analyze human genetics (Genom) or compute planetary movements benefit today from GRID architecture.

Knowledge-driven architecture (KDA) is a software architecture type or style that integrates software and knowledge engineering. KDA allows developers to represent the application level (a business model and a business flow) of the architecture in "almost natural" terms of knowledge-base rules and application scenarios and provides a bridge/connector/interpreter to traditional services that represent a system level of the architecture.

The combination of a knowledge engine and traditional application services creates a new development paradigm and development roles. You can find more details on software and knowledge integration in Chapter 13.

Architectural Views

When we look at beautiful buildings or pieces of jewelry, we view them from several angles before selecting the best one or the one we enjoy most. System architecture (even though it is not always as beautiful) also deserves multiple views. Which architectural view is the most significant? It depends on the role of the viewer. Software architectural views can be provided with Unified Modeling Language (UML) documents. Following are several examples of architectural views and their related UML documents.

The **user's view** is a set of use cases of the application.
The object model diagram represents a **static structural view** of the system in the process of object-oriented analysis.
The **behavioral view** includes sequence and collaboration diagrams.
Deployment diagrams obviously represent the way the application is going to be deployed, or the **deployment view**.

The views provided above are only examples, not a fixed set. Architectural views can be layered and can vary according to system specifics and the viewer's goals. For example, the **functional view** describes components with their operations. The **interaction view** focuses on interfaces, connections, protocols, and other parameters. Connections between components, related component data, and processing operations are all important elements of architectural views. Views are not exclusive but complementary. A combination of architectural views can be used to formally describe software architecture with architecture description languages (ADLs).

Architecture Description Languages

As architecture becomes a focal theme in software development, a formal description of architecture is gaining more attention. ADL can provide features to model system architecture and define system specifications in terms of components, connectors, configurations, functional, and *nonfunctional* criteria and constraints.

For example, **UniCon** [6] focuses on two major architectural elements: components that represent operations and data and connectors that represent interactions between components. Components are defined by interfaces with a set of players, whereas connectors are defined by protocols with a set of player roles.

There is a set of distributed architecture description languages (DADLs) in which the main concepts are the conversation and the participants. These participants are distributed systems or agents that converse to each other according to conversation contracts and participant expectations.

For example, Rapide [7, 8] is an event-based language for defining and modeling concurrent and distributed system architectures, both hardware and software. Rapide includes events and their interrelationships in the interface definitions and describes system actions with asynchronous primitives (events).

"The formation of different languages and of distinct species, and the proofs that both have been developed through a gradual process, are curiously the same." That famous quote by Charles Darwin helped developers from Imperial College, UK, to name one of the first ADLs. The **Darwin** [9] ADL has been (successfully) used in many configurable distributed and parallel processing applications. Darwin syntax is similar to Interface Definition Language (IDL), which was introduced by Common Object Request Broker Architecture (CORBA). Darwin adds several specifics to common DADL features and provides interoperability with non-Darwin services and legacy applications.

PROGRAMMING STYLES

Procedural Programming

Procedural programming focuses on breaking applications into a sequential set of executable procedures or modules. These procedures or modules called each other and presented an application as a chain of highly dependable pieces. Although this approach is relatively simple and straight-forward it has a major drawback. A resulting application is cemented in the way that it is difficult or sometimes even impossible to change any part of the code without re-writing the whole application.

Object-Oriented Programming

Object-Oriented or Component-based approach has replaced procedural programming and became the most common approach to building software architecture today. Object-oriented approach works perfectly well on sizable projects with multiple objects spread over a huge surface of requirements.

We group objects, finding common properties and behavior or concerns, and provide common implementations called *classes*. These implementations are based on a single dimensional view of common concerns most often related to a business domain. We build components and containers that hold components and provide basic care about common component needs.

Aspect Oriented Programming

Aspect oriented programming (AOP) is based on the concepts of aspect and concern which might crosscut many components. Typical crosscutting concerns for enterprise application would be security concerns, like authentication and logging; resource and administration management, and etc. AOP is not a competitor but a complementary approach to object-oriented and structured programming. Looking from another point of view (I cannot stress more the power of multiple complementary views) AOP finds the missing parts of the desirable functionality across multiple components. AOP complements OOP providing more predictable and structural approach to developing large-scale systems. In this process aspects or concerns receive their own language and names. AOP supporters from the AOP/C-Sharp and AOP/Java worlds work on scientific and practical aspects of **aspects** to allow system developers to manipulate aspects in the process of system design in a similar way as they manage data: view, update, create, delete, and etc. [10, 11].

Generative Programming or "Pieceware" Engineering

Generative Programming is a whole new world where software can be evolved or generated from initial pieces. This "pieceware" engineering generates new pieces from existed ones. The process can include integration and adaptation and can be executed sequentially or recursively until generated software satisfy preset system requirements.

A compiler that generates binary code from a source can be considered an ancestor of Generative Programming. But today the initial pieces of "pieceware" engineering may not only be sources but also can represent themselves as models, requirements, test results, and so on. [12].

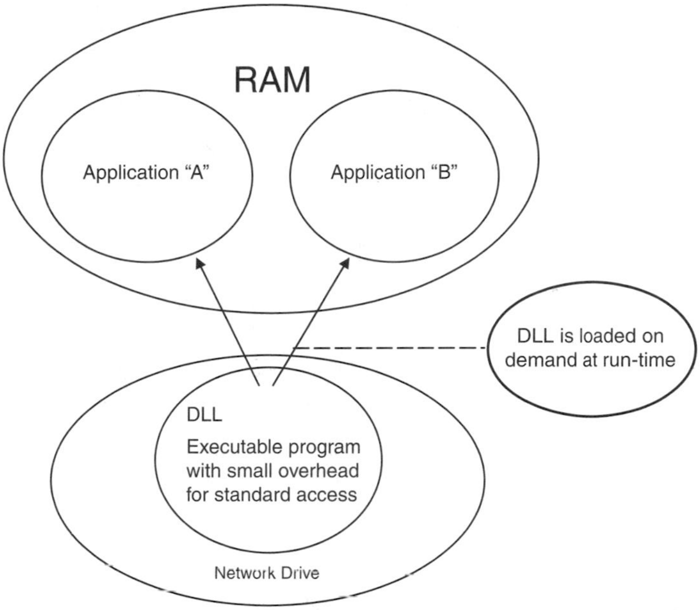

FIGURE 2.1. Multiple Applications Share a Single DLL.

INTEGRATION TECHNOLOGIES

Reusable Components: from DLLs and Up

The main ideas stated in this book can be implemented in multiple technologies. To illustrate the ideas with design and code examples, it is necessary to link them to specific technologies. This is the catch-22. You need to operate with visible images to describe invisible ones. This chapter introduces a sequence of integration technologies that make products reusable. The reuse simply opens more doors for products and multiplies their value.

Dynamic Link Libraries are one of earliest implementations for reusable components. A DLL is a collection of reusable programs that can be loaded on demand, at run-time, by a main program or an application. A DLL program is an executable file that has a .dll extension in most cases, but may also have another extension (for example ".exe" in the MS Windows environment). A DLL file can be shared by multiple applications. The important advantage to using DLL files is the saving of RAM space; DLL files are not loaded in memory until they are needed for execution. Figure 2.1 shows multiple applications that share one DLL. We can see that the DLL is loaded at run-time by application A or application B.

OBJECT LINKING AND EMBEDDING (OLE) AND ACTIVEX

The next step in creating reusable component technology was the Object Linking and Embedding (OLE) technology introduced by Microsoft Corporation. The OLE framework allowed us to link objects (compound documents) from different applications within the MS Windows environment. MS Word, for example, handles pictures by providing an internal link to MS Paint and other applications (Fig. 2.2).

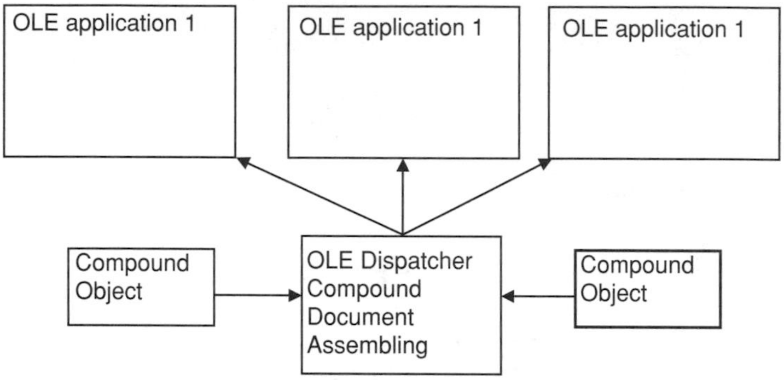

FIGURE 2.2. OLE Framework Allows Multiple Applications to Share Compound Documents.

Note that an alternative would be to duplicate MS Paint functionality in the MS Word program. This reuse did not come free. OLE technology required creating a very complicated overhead for every document-component. This overhead imbued components with OLE-compliant features. In addition, every Microsoft program was enhanced to understand this set of OLE features and function properly. This was a very expensive reworking.

The OLE specification went through multiple changes. The OLE, and later the OLE2, specification paved the road for an even more general concept, the Component Object Model (COM), followed by the Distributed Component Object Model (DCOM), with a new umbrella named *ActiveX*. The OLE-ActiveX evolution is presented in Fig. 2.3.

ActiveX components are self-sufficient programs or COM objects. These objects are most commonly stored with the .OCX extension, which stands for *OLE control*. ActiveX components are used and reused in the applications that serve as containers for such components.

Every component and every container in this game is built according to the rules of the game, or COM/ActiveX specifications. Some overhead built into every component allows an ActiveX application or an ActiveX tool to recognize the component's functionality and even to customize its appearance and behavior.

The UNIX world provided its own answer. The Object Management Group (OMG) established a set of standards targeting the same goals. The OpenDoc model was in a way similar (but different) to compound documents and OLE technology. The CORBA standard, with

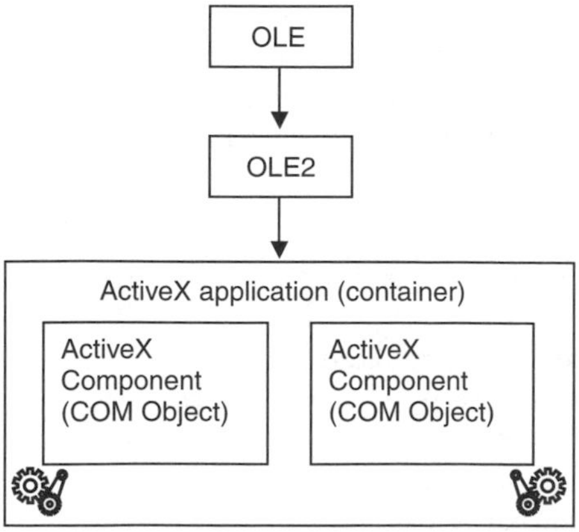

FIGURE 2.3. From OLE to Component Object Model (COM) and ActiveX.

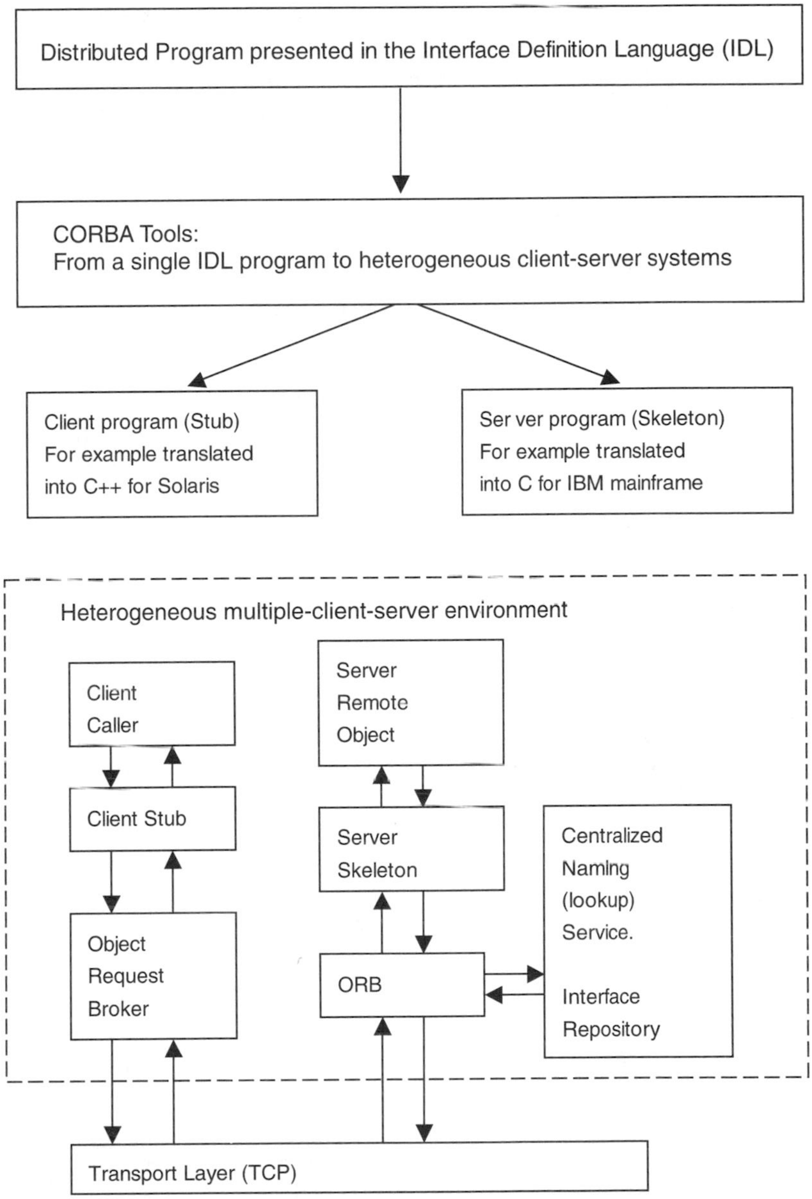

FIGURE 2.4. CORBA Handles Objects in a Heterogeneous Client-Server Environment.

its IDL, has solved the puzzle of distributed integration in a heterogeneous environment. Figure 2.4 presents some basic steps and elements of CORBA.

CORBA AND IDL

The IDL allows us to describe client–server communications, interfaces, and objects in a platform-independent way. CORBA vendors, such as Iona, Inc., and others, create tools that allow us to convert IDL programs into almost any existing programming language for any existing platform.

These tools separate the client parts of an application into programs called *stubs* or *proxies* and the server parts into programs called *skeletons*. The names reflect the fact that the real services are located on the server side (skeletons) and client programs include only stubs (proxies) with a very limited knowledge about the services or remote objects.

The client (application) makes a call to locate and start a remote service. This call goes through the client stub (proxy) and reaches the Object Request Broker (ORB).

The Object Request Broker consults with the centralized naming service about the remote service location. Every service object should be registered with the naming service. Remember that distributed architecture assumes that multiple servers are responsible for services.

The client has no clue about the service's location. The ORB gets directions from the centralized naming service and calls the remote skeleton that interacts with the remote service. The circle is closed; the client gets the service. Note that the client–server communications are based on the Internet Inter-ORB Protocol (IIOP), one more standard that contributes to the distributed integration solution.

MICROSOFT'S DISTRIBUTED COM ARCHITECTURE

Microsoft's Distributed COM (DCOM) architecture is presented in Fig. 2.5. This architecture is very similar to CORBA. Microsoft has also provided IDL to describe remote objects in a language-neutral form. Note that this IDL is different from the CORBA IDL. Client and server parts in the DCOM architecture are separated into client proxies and server stubs: note the terminology difference. CORBA server parts are called *skeletons*.

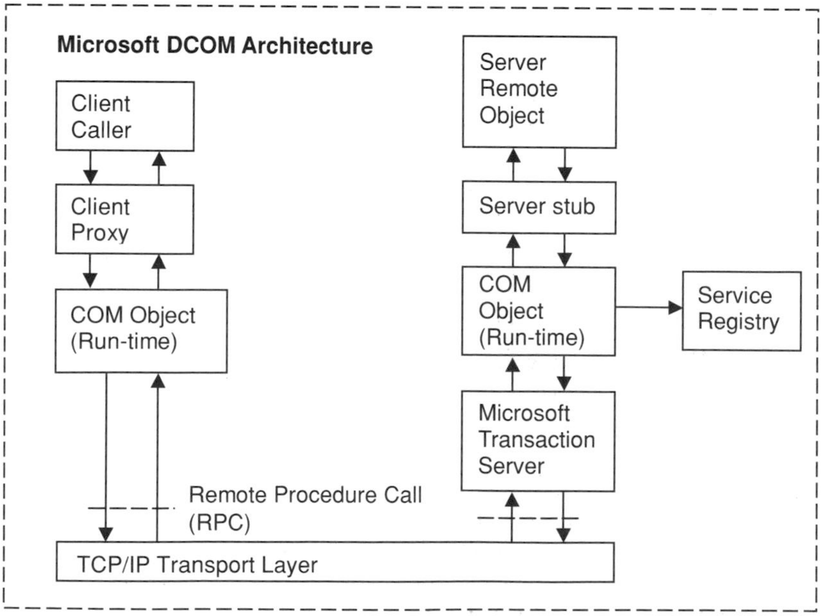

FIGURE 2.5. Microsoft Distributed COM (DCOM) Architecture.

The objects must be registered with the Registry. The Microsoft Transaction Server tracks running objects on the server side. DCOM uses the RPC service and the Transmission Control Protocol transport layer for client–server communications. DCOM was designed to serve on multiple platforms, but in reality, it is mostly used for Windows, with very rare exceptions (e.g., it was ported to UNIX by Software AG). It is impossible not to mention Java when we talk about integration technologies.

Starting with Chapter 3, Java and XML take the central place in this book. However, I do not want to jump to this technology abruptly. I am trying to move as smoothly as possible and to provide a high-level overview of multiple technologies.

Java Technology Architecture

Java offers many benefits: Java is cross-platform through Java Virtual Machine (JVM) support. Java has built-in security for the Internet and local networks. Java is the unique case in which a rich and well-supported out-of-the box package comes free. The Java Development Kit (JDK) includes multiple integrated libraries. The Java API comes with the JDK as easy-to-use on-line documentation that greatly enhances the usability of Java technology. All of these factors have created the momentum for Java to grow with unprecedented speed.

Let us look at the reusable component paradigm that Java offers.

Java Applet

The simplest Java component is a Java applet running in a Web browser container (Fig. 2.6). Any computer with a Web browser compliant with the Java license can easily reuse this applet client program. The applet program includes at least one Java class or file that extends the *java.applet.Applet* class provided in the JDK. This extension immediately enables the client program with wonderful network and media features. You can also see the "sandbox" security restrictions applied to a regular (unsigned) applet.

The applet cannot touch system resources (e.g., it cannot print to the local printer or create/delete a file on the local machine). The applet can only communicate to the single server from which it was loaded. In Chapter 3, we play with Java components and learn how to make them reusable and integration ready.

The Java Bean Architecture

Java offers new ways to create components and libraries that serve as building blocks for bigger applications. Java Beans are, in a way, similar to ActiveX controls. Conversely, it might be said that ActiveX controls mimic Java Beans. Java Beans require some overhead for the Java class. For example, every variable in the class must have its own get and set methods.

This overhead is part of the Java Beans standard that allows Java applications or tools to recognize a Java Bean's functionality and even customize its behavior. The overhead needed for Java Beans is much simpler than what is needed for ActiveX. You can write Java Beans by hand, whereas you need Microsoft tools to hide the complexity of ActiveX (you can read it as OLE2) control standards.

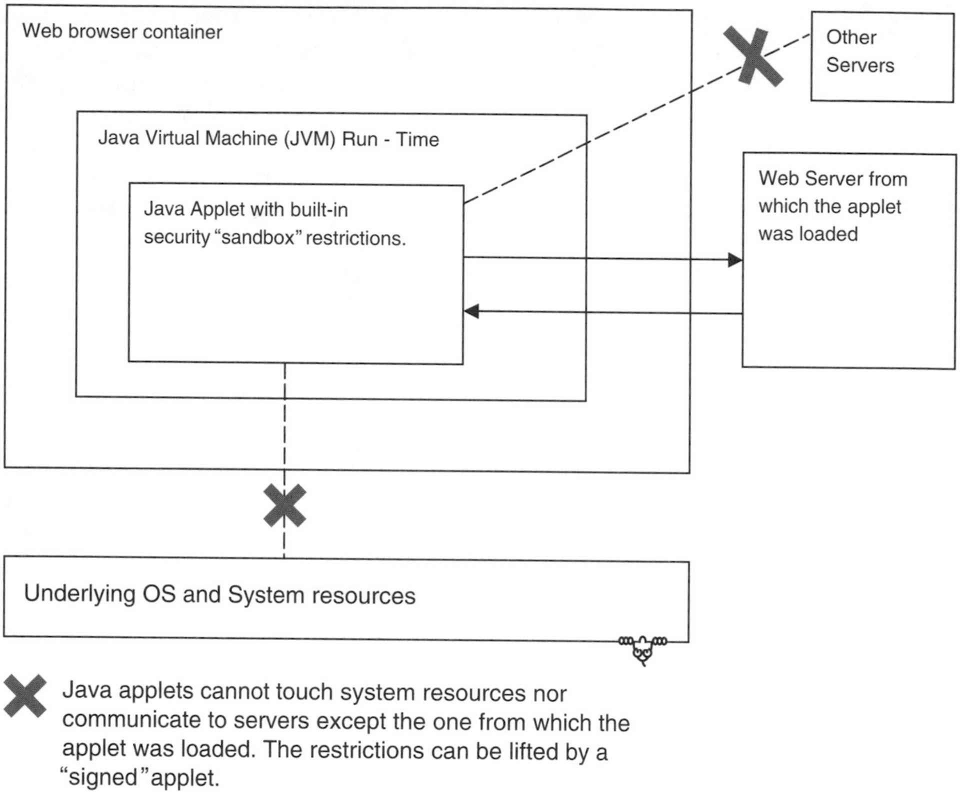

FIGURE 2.6. Java Applet Running in a Web Browser Container.

Java Beans are used mostly on the client side, although they can be used on the server side as well. J2EE platform standards provide rules for building application components and containers. The Enterprise Java Bean (EJB) is the only standard that specifically targets server components. Figure 2.7 shows Java Bean architecture.

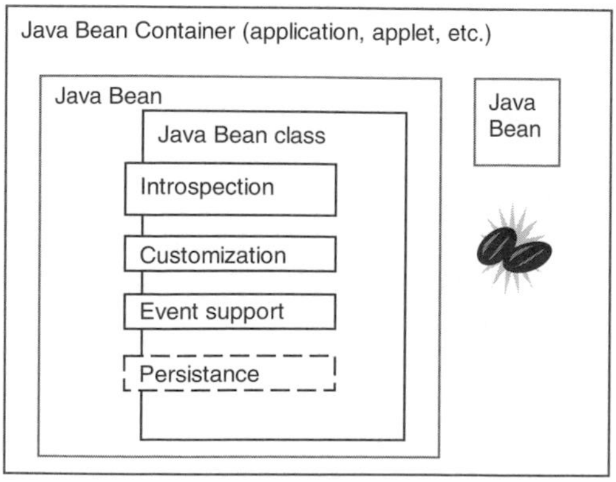

FIGURE 2.7. The Java Bean Architecture.

Java Bean specifications require common features that all beans share, such as support for introspection (see the java.reflection package). This helps application builder tools to understand a bean's properties and its functionality.

Java Beans also provide the possibility to alter their appearance and behavior. Other common features include support for events—a Java Bean can fire events as well as inform about events. Java Beans can also provide persistence; in other words, they are capable of saving and restoring their state. Java Beans are reusable components that run inside a bigger container.

J2EE Architecture

Five basic containers play important roles in enterprise multi-tier applications (Fig. 2.8); we discuss these in the context of J2EE architecture. Note that the client, Web, service, connector, and data containers can be also considered beyond the scope of Java technology. Any of these containers, however, can benefit from Java Bean-based components. The service container often includes a J2EE-complaint application server with EJB support. In this case, EJBs serve as basic bricks for building services.

A Web browser is an example of a client. Such a client container can run an applet with built-in Java Bean components. Another example of a client is a Java application. The application, as well as the applet that we just considered, could be built using Java Beans as parts. Several tools, such as Visual Age for Java and Forte for Java, allow you to quickly build client programs using Java Bean components.

The Web container is responsible for communication with multiple clients in Web-based applications. The J2EE platform architecture supports a Web container with Java servlet and JSP engines. The Java servlet serves as a dispatcher (see the "dispatcher pattern" in Chapter 1) that controls client access and redirects or dispatches client requests to the proper party that can be located on the same or different tier (container).

Java Server Pages

JSPs serve as views in a classical MVC pattern that separates business and presentation logic into three components. The JSP uses Java Beans as helpers or direct business solutions that can be located in the same Web container or in the server tier (container).

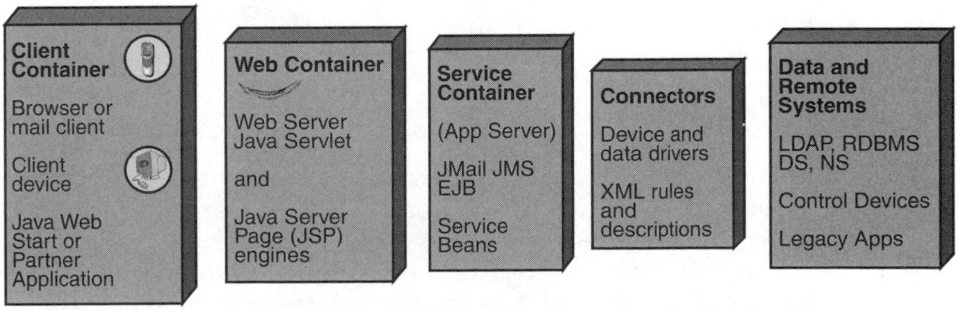

FIGURE 2.8. An Example of Enterprise Architecture with J2EE Containers.

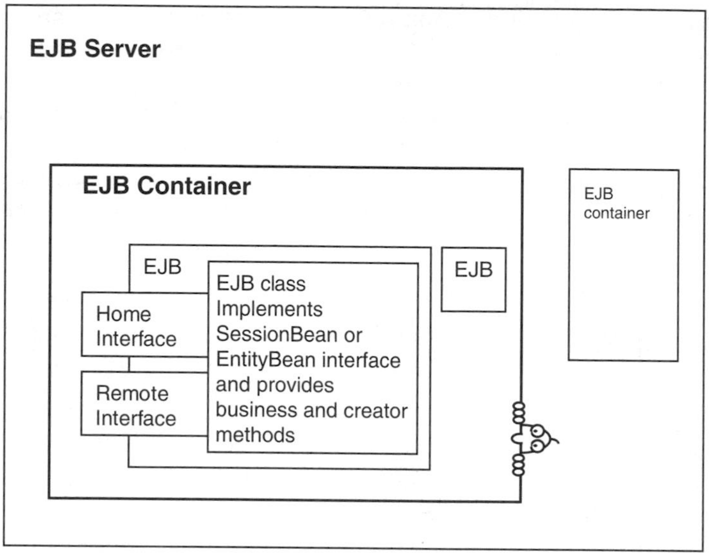

FIGURE 2.9. The Enterprise Java Bean Architecture.

What is a container and what is its function? Generally speaking, a container supports its components. Containers are able to locate and execute their components and can provide some support for their life cycle and generic needs, such as security. *The main idea is that the container takes care of common problems and leaves us (developers) tête-à-tête with our specific business tasks*. The J2EE platform specification requires containers to provide the APIs that application components use to access services. The specification also describes standard ways to extend J2EE services to non-J2EE application systems.

THE ENTERPRISE JAVA BEANS ARCHITECTURE

Similar to Java Bean architecture, an EJB component lives inside an EJB container (Fig. 2.9). An EJB server is an additional element that is necessary for EJB survival. EJB vendors that are based on the EJB specification, a single industry standard for server-side components and containers, produce EJB servers as well as EJB containers.

The vendors take care of common problems, trying to solve them on the level of containers. This helps application developers focus on specific business tasks that can be implemented in EJB components.

EJB COMPONENTS AND CONTAINERS

When we develop an EJB, we need to answer several design questions, such as: Do we want this server component to outlive a client session, or is its task to support the session?

If the EJB is directly responsible for a database connection and updates, we might want this component to live a long life. This component provides data persistence and must implement the EntityBean interface. If the EJB's task is to provide business logic for a client session, we might want this component to live just during the session.

This component must implement the SessionBean interface. The session bean component can be lightweight or stateless. This EJB only belongs to a client during a client call. The other alternative is a "stateful" EJB that saves its state and serves a client during the client's conversation or session. Stateless session beans do not remember their conversational state with the client. Any number of clients can use a particular stateless bean. A stateful session bean, on the other hand, belongs to a particular client for the client's session.

EJB Home and Remote Interfaces

The EJB container includes EJBHome and EJBObject classes that implement home and remote interfaces and wrap client requests to important generic services, such as transaction, memory, and security management. This container also provides the EJB instance with a context object. Developers use the home interface and Java Naming Directory Interface (JNDI) to locate EJB instances. Remote interface implementation is usually responsible for business methods and access to remote objects, for example, to connect a session bean to an entity bean that can be directly connected to a database. The Remote Method Invocation (RMI) architecture supports communications between EJBs that live on multipletiers.

Distributed computing in a Java-enabled world can be done with the Java RMI architecture. Yes! If all your objects are comfortable with Java, if they can live inside JVM on multiple platforms, you can simply write them all in Java then use the Java RMI architecture as shown in Fig. 2.10.

The Java RMI Architecture

The Java RMI architecture is similar to CORBA and much easier to implement. The RMI compiler (rmic) compiles Java source code that describes remote objects distributed on multiple tiers as client stub or proxy programs and server skeleton Java sources. Then, you can use the regular Java compiler (javac) to compile client and server sources into binary code that can run on any platform that has JVM support. The RMI client stub provides a proxy service to call a remote object. The RMI server skeleton calls a method on a remote server object. Remote objects must be registered with the RMI Registry. We start the RMI Registry Server (rmiregistry) before we start an RMI application.

The Java RMI uses the native Java Remote Method Protocol (JRMP) or IIOP if there is a need to include non-Java remote objects into the flow of distributed computing. The visible benefits of using the RMI architecture are natural Java benefits: simplicity (compared with CORBA or DCOM), built-in security, distributed garbage collection, and the ability to pass references and objects. RMI is able to automatically tunnel through HTTP if the RMI protocol is rejected by a firewall.

The Bridge from Java to CORBA Technology

What if we work in a heterogeneous environment, where some remote objects are written in Java and others in different languages? CORBA is the right solution to this puzzle. The java.idl package provides the direct bridge from Java to CORBA technology. You use IDL to Java (*idlj*) compiler to translate CORBA object interfaces written in IDL. The compiler will produce Java client stub and server skeleton classes that will be able to communicate with

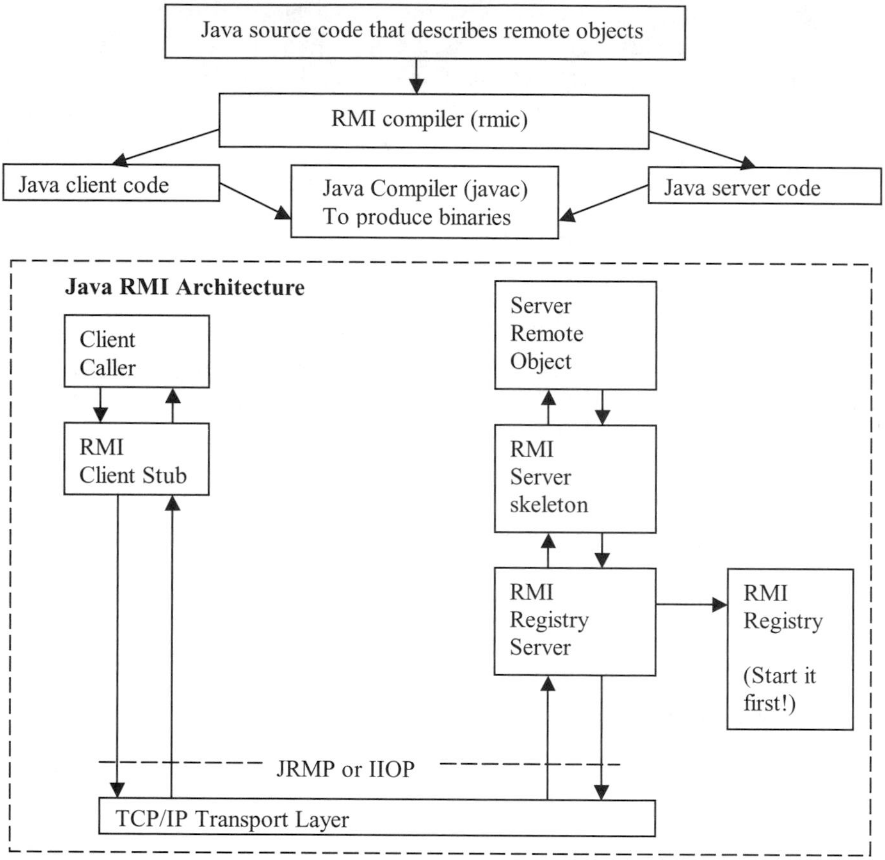

FIGURE 2.10. The Java RMI Architecture.

non-Java objects. Figure 2.11 shows Java-CORBA interoperability. Java and CORBA objects use the standard IIOP communication protocol.

From Components to Services

With the growing number of available components, the number of options of what to do with the components grows exponentially, and integration can easily become a nightmare. At this point, enterprise architects start partitioning such a multicomponent application with tiers and/or functions. The alternative approach is a *service-oriented* architecture.

Service-oriented architecture offers service hooks with relatively small sets of APIs and well described message protocols. Clients are completely left out of the implementation details and left in the world of business options. Let us distinguish pure business services (called vertical services) that represent business goals from underlying infrastructure or horizontal services. Figure 2.12 presents examples of vertical and horizontal services.

Vertical and Horizontal Services

Facility management, accounting, IT and network management, e-provisioning, and communications are all examples of vertical or business services. Horizontal services build the underlying infrastructure for every business service. Security, integration, and collaboration are examples of horizontal services. Distributed systems built with CORBA, DCOM, or RMI

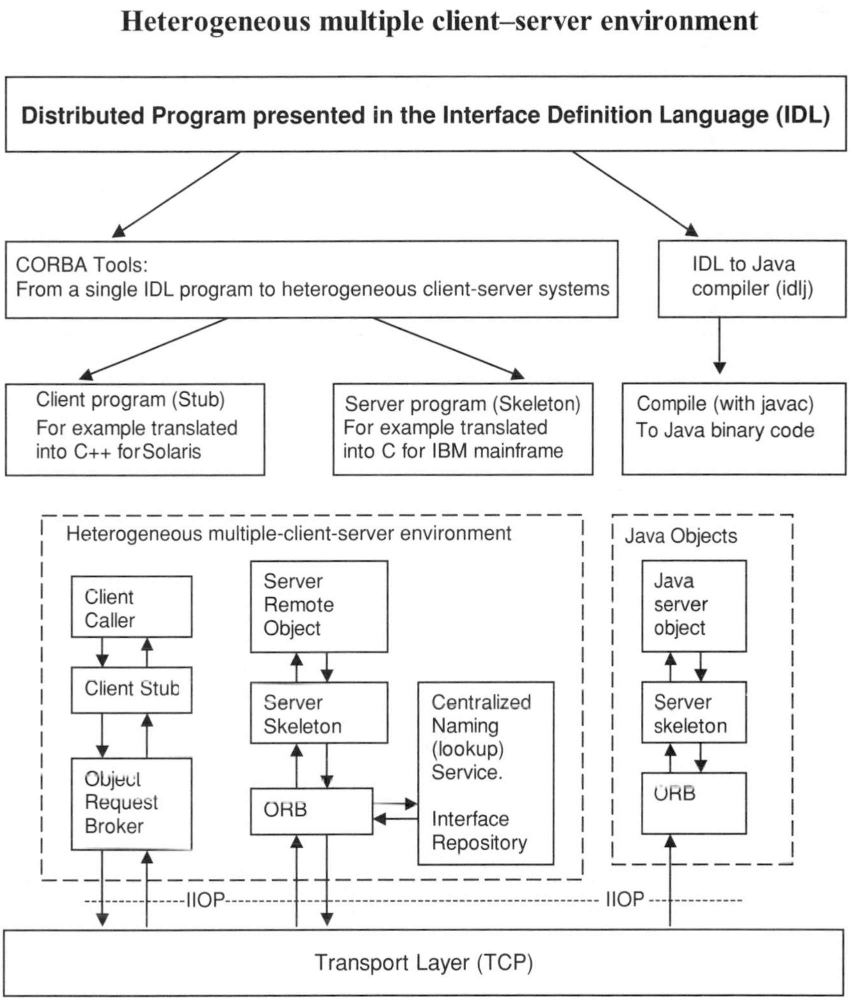

FIGURE 2.11. IIOP—a Common Communication Channel for the Java and CORBA Worlds.

architecture offer complex and proprietary APIs for their usage. These systems have been developed to solve integration tasks inside specific enterprise environments and hardly fit into the global collaboration picture. On the other side, Internet applications started with, and continue to use, text-based protocols.

Distributed systems that communicate over the Internet via HTTP are often called Web services. Today, in most cases, Web services work with Web browser clients. Such systems use Hypertext Markup Language (HTML) for client-server exchange. The clients send HTML forms and links to the server and receive back HTML (or Web) pages. Web browsers render these HTML pages into text, graphics, and sound.

XML WEB SERVICES

XML is the underlying language for inter-application exchange. The data recipient is not a human being armed with a browser, but an application. XML has become the language

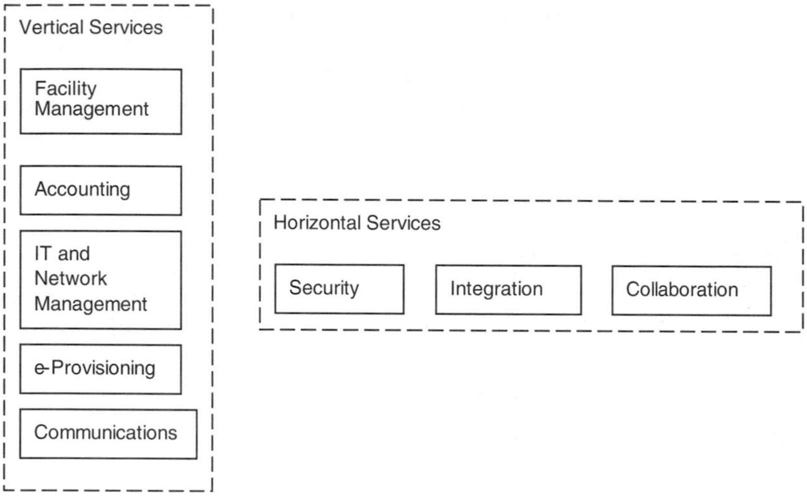

FIGURE 2.12. Vertical and Horizontal Services.

of Internet data exchange. It is used across platforms and operating systems. XML Web services talk XML over HTTP or HTTPS. They share data between applications and invoke the services of other applications.

What is XML and what makes it such a favorite in the integration field? XML appeared with a limited ambition—just to extend HTML with more tags. Every tag starts with "<" and must have the correct ending—"/>". The name of the tag is up to you, as is the data inside the tag.

Almost immediately after the creation of HTML, rules to capture any system of tags with DTD (data table definition) and the XML schema were created. Built-in language simplicity prompted tool vendors and independent developers to produce a set of products to parse and create XML data on the fly very quickly.

Unlimited language flexibility attracted developers in different areas to express their specific data with their own tag systems. The next step was very natural: "We all know how to deal with XML, let us try it with cross-platform, cross-business, and cross-industry conversations."

XML Web services use other XML-based standard protocols, including SOAP, WSDL, and UDDI. They are defined through public standards organizations such as the World Wide Web Consortium (W3C).

AN EXAMPLE OF AN XML-BASED SERVICE API

Before we can discover all the pieces related to XML, let us consider the small example of a service API provided with XML.

Multiple proprietary APIs describe multiple products. There are attempts to integrate these APIs under specific industry committees and standards. We have already considered several examples, such as CORBA, Java RMI, and ActiveX. We can add the Java Integrated Network APIs (JAIN) that target telephony and data network services, and there is a whole world of Jini (Java-based network devices and services technology). They all have had limited

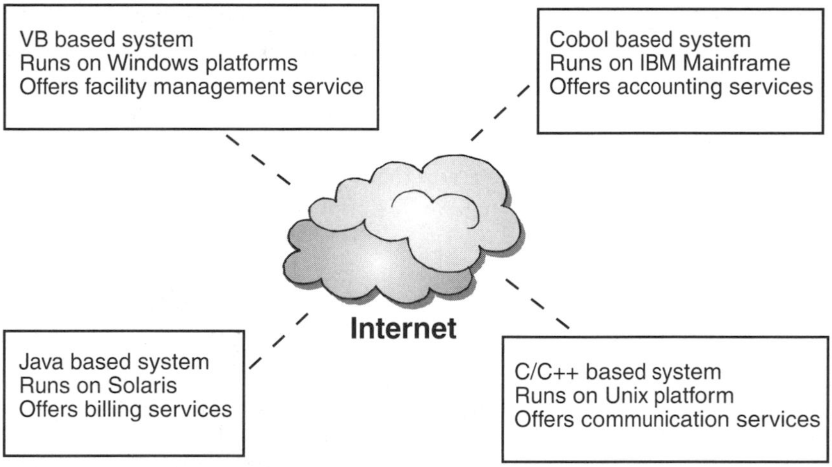

Unified Service API:

```
<ServiceRequest Service="..." Action="..." Type="..."  MessageID="..">
<Parameters>
.....Generic (security) and business specific parameters...
</Parameters>
</ServiceRequest>
```

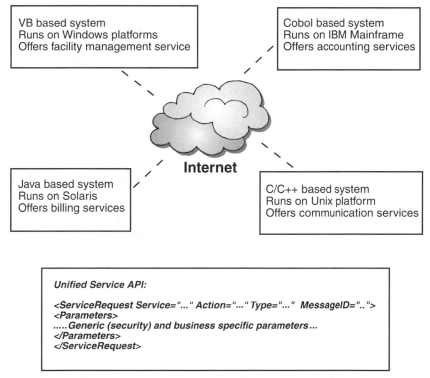

FIGURE 2.13. XML-Based Messages Provide Unified Service APIs for Multiple Systems.

success as integration strategies. The limitation is related to the fact that all these strategies are centered on some specific technologies.

The universal answer to this problem appears to be the XML that increasingly dominates interplatform and intersystem communications. The very first step in this direction is to provide an XML-based API to services (products) that you plan to offer. This API in no way leads to any specific implementation or technology. On the contrary, it can be implemented with any language and on any platform. Figure 2.13 presents an example of an XML-based API that can serve multiple services.

The service request includes required elements like Service, Action, Type, and MessageID. There is also an optional section of Parameters that includes security and specific business elements.

The *Service* is the direct pointer to the business service interface that should be invoked upon receiving this request. It is unique within the service provider's domain. We consider Java examples of implementation (beautifully clean and simple) and leave it to the reader to implement a similar strategy in other languages.

The *Action* identifies a process within a Service interface. The Action shall be unique within the Service interface in which it is defined.

The *Type* indicates the type of output (a presentation type) requested by a client device or a workstation. Examples of presentation types can be "HTML" for Web browser-based clients, "WML" for WAP (Wireless Application Protocol) devices, "VXML" for VoiceXML-based speech recognition system (SRS) clients, "Applet" for Java applet-based clients, "XML" for direct data exchange, and so on.

The *MessageID* is a unique identifier for the message that can be especially useful with asynchronous communications when the service's response should point to the initial service request. This is not always necessary for Web browser-based clients. A service request initiated by a Web browser will, in most cases, be immediately answered and served by a server. (It does happen that an immediate response is still a very slow one.)

A similar picture is valid for applications that wait for the service's response or communicate in a synchronous mode. Asynchronous communications are based on messaging systems such as IBM MQ or JMS.

The optional *Parameters* section provides the necessary security and business parameters. In the examples that follow, we refer to the *SessionID* as a single security parameter that supports user session tracking. Business parameters are specifically related to requested services.

For example, if Service = "Email" and Action = "New" implies creating a new email message, no parameters are needed for the server to respond with the Compose window screen. However, if Service = "Email" and Action = "Get" implies retrieving an email message, the server would expect some pointer to a specific message to retrieve. For example, it can be a parameter like EmailID = "1234." The important feature of this example of a service API is that knowledge about specific parameters lies inside specific services.

ebXML

Developers familiar with the ebXML standard can recognize some elements in the API example (see http://www.ebxml.org). Take into account that the ebXML is a very broad Message Service Specification targeting e-Business transactions. The ebXML standard addresses transport, routing, and packaging issues. The example above can be considered a scaled-down (to earth) version to describe a service API to any software product with a unified approach. We used this approach before the ebXML standard release and adapted some changes after the release.

Example of XML-Based Communications in J2EE Application

An example of an implementation based on the J2EE architecture with Java servlet and JSP support is presented in Fig. 2.14. A similar implementation can be accomplished with Microsoft Active Server Pages (ASP.Net) support.

A client request hits the Web container. The Java servlet plays the role of a request dispatcher. The Java servlet works with the generic helper service in parsing the client's XML request. This provides nonspecific service processing, such as creating and maintaining the

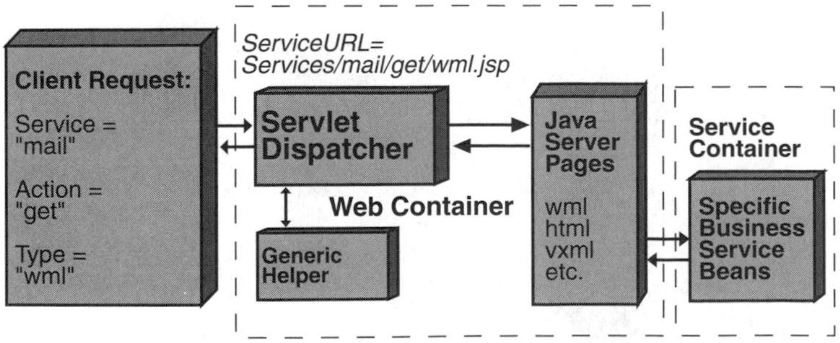

FIGURE 2.14. Translating an XML Service Request into a URL.

```
Unified Service API:

<ServiceRequest Service="..." Action="..." Type= "..." MessageID="..">
        <Parameters>
        .....Generic (security) and business specific parameters ...
        </Parameters>
</ServiceRequest>
```

```
// Servlet code responsible for dispatching a client request
// Forward the request to a proper service, action, and a presentation layer

// Use session attributes provided by the helper service to form the URL

String url = session.getAttribute("Service") +"/"+ session.getAttribute("Action") +
"/"+ session.getAttribute("Type") +".jsp";

// Use RequestDispatcher object to redirect the request to a proper service URL

RequestDispatcher dispatcher =
  getServletConfig().getServletContext().getRequestDispatcher(url);

dispatcher.forward (request, response);
```

FIGURE 2.15. The Java Servlet Code That Dispatches an XML Service Request.

session object and resolving security issues. The Java servlet then dispatches the client's request to the proper service JSP Uniform Resource Locator (URL). The URL is calculated based on the Service, Action, and Type attributes of the request.

An example of the code responsible for the creation of the URL and for forwarding the request is shown in Fig. 2.15. The Java servlet code responsible for dispatching a client request uses session attributes (Service, Action, and Type) to form the URL. Yes, they are the same attributes of the client request that the Java servlet and the generic helper retrieve from the XML request. The URL precisely points to a unique JSP responsible for this Service, that Action, and the Type of output (presentation layer) requested by the client. For example, if the Service is "mail," the Action is "get," and the Type is "wml," the resulting URL is /Services/mail/get/wml.jsp.

The first step is completed. A run time URL to the proper service JSP has been created.

The servlet then uses the *forward()* method of the *RequestDispatcher* object to redirect the client request to the proper service JSP.

Note that the service can be located on the same or even a different Web server.

This is the way toward load balancing, right? I have to note that if you plan to use multiple servers for your services, which is desired for enterprise services anyway, you need to modify the part of the code that is related to the RequestDispatcher object.

ADDITIONAL BENEFITS: ABILITY TO ADD OR CHANGE SERVICES AT RUN-TIME

What does it mean to introduce a new service for enterprise applications? In most cases, it means to stop a business process for a while. In many cases, it means that the existing "core code" will need to be changed; a new service invocation will be added, and so on.

None of these activities is needed if we stick with the architecture provided in the example above. A new service JSP with the supporting service beans can be uploaded to a running server. The JSP engine will recognize new JSPs that provide a new service and automatically compile them into "ready-to-go" code without any interruption of the ongoing business services.

No core code needs to be changed. The core code considered above *is ready* for the new service. The service will be served as soon as the request for the new service arrives from any client.

In the Java world, distributed client applications can be built and delivered with the Java Web Start mechanism. Java Web Start also allows automatic version upgrades.

We will consider client applications for multiple devices and clients in the following chapters.

How Can We Register a New Web Service?

A key benefit of the Web services is the ability to deliver integrated, interoperable solutions anywhere in the world. There is a specification for registering and requesting Web services—its name is *UDDI*. It is a free (no fee) public registry to publish and inquire about Web services. UDDI suggests registering three blocks of information: 1) contact information, including address and business identification, 2) category or description of the type of business, and 3) business services descriptions.

How Should We Describe Web Services?

WSDL is the recommended (although not required) service description format. WSDL describes services as ports, each of which has its own service type and a set of related operations. The language uses XML schema definitions (XSDs) to describe data exchange formats. A very simple example of the service type can be "Mail" with a set of operations like "New" (Compose), "Get" (Read), and so on.

Is There a Mechanism to Pack Both Data and Services into a Message?

SOAP is an XML-based messaging specification that provides the rules for packaging complex objects into XML messages and integrating services into applications. SOAP messages consist of an envelope and possible attachments. The envelope can include a header, source and destination data, and a body. The request header might contain security-related data that can be encrypted with the recipient's public key. The response header might verify that the transaction was secure and successful.

How Do Software Vendors Support Web Services?

Microsoft, IBM, and Sun Microsystems are the biggest players in this field. There is also a great deal of support coming from open source organizations, such as Apache.

Microsoft supports Web services with its .NET initiative, which goes far beyond the Web services . .NET is a new Microsoft platform architecture that focuses on the C# (C-Sharp) and Visual Basic programming languages, with additional support for other languages provided

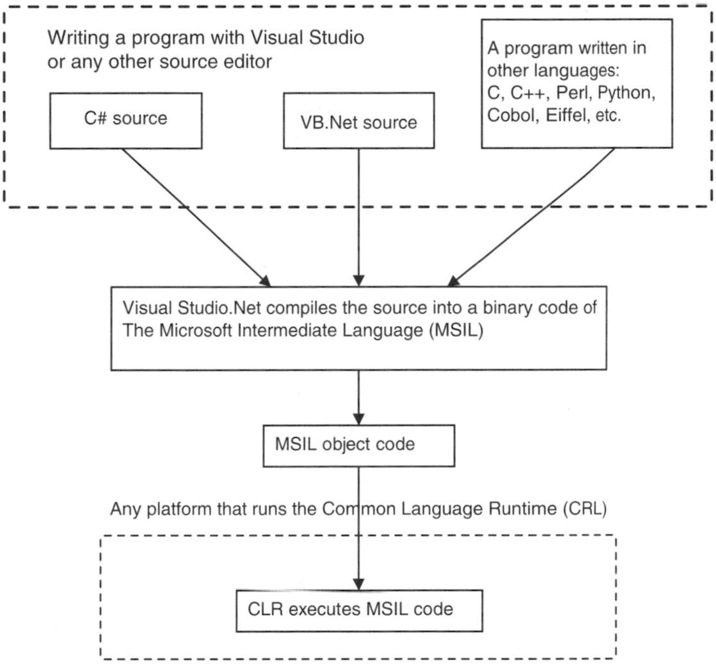

FIGURE 2.16. Microsoft .NET Technology Architecture.

by Microsoft Visual Studio. The list of alternative languages includes C, C++, Perl, Python, Cobol, and Eiffel.

Visual Studio.NET can compile any program from a language supported by the Studio to Microsoft Intermediate Language (MSIL) binary code. This binary code can be executed by a virtual machine called the Common Language Runtime (CLR).

The process of creating and using software in the .NET environment is represented in Fig. 2.16 . This process looks very familiar to Java developers; the original Java development steps are presented in Fig. 2.17 . Let us compare the two pictures. The MSIL object represents the original Java byte code concept, and the CLR plays the same role as the JVM that executes this code. The Java motto "write once (in Java) and run everywhere (where JVM can run)" is rephrased as "write once (in multiple languages) and run everywhere (where CLR can run)."

Microsoft's Visual Studio.NET and the Microsoft .NET framework support building, deploying, and running XML Web services with server products and also across multiple smart client devices. The .NET platform emphasizes client (distributed) applications named *User Experiences* that directly access Web services. These applications range from office types of programs to wireless phones and the Xbox (a game console). One of the important features of these applications is that they are able to automatically upgrade themselves as needed.

Assignment

Describe the relationships among DLL – OLE – ActiveX – COM – DCOM –.NET. What are the counterparts of these technologies in the UNIX world?

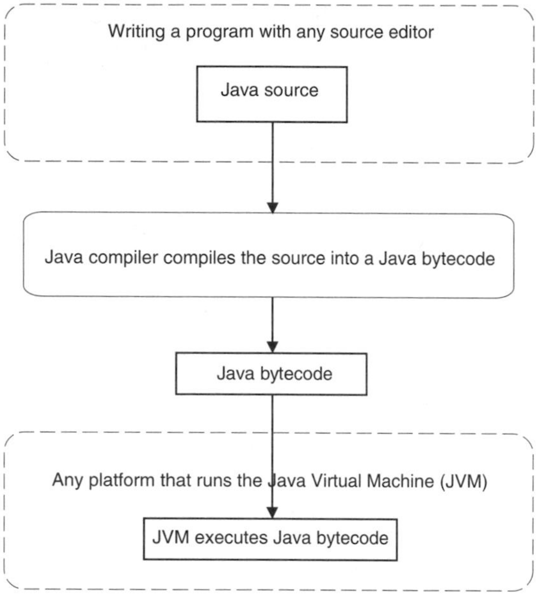

FIGURE 2.17. Java Technology Architecture.

SUMMARY

Pieces of software are becoming bigger in size and number. Integration technologies are extremely important to make sense of these pieces, helping us to reuse rather than rewrite applications. Integration technologies can be applied to products designed with integration in mind. Clean APIs and XML-ready services help with quick integration. XML Web services provide a standard way to create, describe, publish, and discover a service.

There is also fast-growing support for Web services from the .NET and Java communities. The Sun ONE (Open Net Environment) platform is based on J2EE architecture and heavily centered on the server side. Web service support is provided with several packages, such as the ones Java vendors pack together into convenient development tools like Forte for Java and Visual Age for Java.

Generic XML manipulation packages include:

- Document Object Model (DOM) or SAX (Simple API for XML) parsers
- JAX Pack with reference implementations of JAXP (Java API for XML Processing; can be used to process SOAP and WSDL), JAXB (XML binding), JAXM (XML messaging), JAXR (XML registries), and JAX-RPC (XML remote procedure calls)
- Web Services Pack with the Jakarta Tomcat servlet/JSP engine and JavaServer Faces.

For more information on the XML family and Web Services, see Appendix 2.

Knowledge-driven architecture (described later in this book) extends current technology trends, such as service-oriented architecture, event-driven architecture, and XML Web services, in their search for efficient ways of creating multipurpose ready-to-serve and ready-to-work-together products.

Integrating Questions

1. Can you describe any application with the REST style?
2. Can you describe any application with the DECENT style?
3. What requirements would force you to select event-driven over data-flow architecture and vice versa?
4. What are the benefits and disadvantages of library-based APIs compared with XML-based APIs? Please provide an example from your workplace (if applicable).
5. What are the benefits and disadvantages of .NET compared with Java technology? Please provide an example from your workplace (if applicable).

Case Study

Client-Server and Other Architecture Styles

Present a white paper on one or more architecture styles that you can associate with applications that run or have been developed in your workplace. Compare this (these) to some other styles, and explain if this style was the best choice.

The white paper should deliver the content in a presentable format: PowerPoint with notes, Web pages, MS Word, PDF, and so on. The content considers three levels of the topic: definition (high level), functionality and applicability (middle level), and an example of implementation (low level). These three levels roughly map the why, what, and how of the selected subject. It is recommended that you "dress" the content (text) in an attractive presentation with diagrams and code illustrations.

ASP.NET and Java STRUTS

Present a white paper on ASP.NET or Java STRUTS technology. Select one that you can associate with one of the applications that run or have been developed at your workplace. Explain why this is a good choice, or not such a good choice, for this application.

References

1. Alexander, C., S. Ishikawa, M. Silverstein, M. Jacobson, I. Fiksdahl-King, and S. Angel. 1977. *A Pattern Language*. New York: Oxford University Press.
2. Gamma, E., R. Helm, R. Johnson, and J. Vlissides. 1994. *Design Patterns: Elements of Reusable Object-Oriented Software*. Boston: Addison-Wesley.
3. Shaw, M., and D. Garlan. 1996. *Software Architecture: Perspectives on an Emerging Discipline*. Upper Saddle River, NJ: Prentice-Hall.
4. Andrews, G. 1991. "Paradigms for Process Interaction in Distributed Programs." *ACM ComputingSurveys* 23:49–90.
5. Zhuk, J., Distributed active knowledge and process base, Patent Pending, *http://uspto.gov*.
6. Zelesnik, G. 1996. *The UniCon Language Reference Manual*. Available at: *http://www-2.cs.cmu.edu/afs/cs/project/vit/www/unicon/reference-manual/Reference_Manual_1.html*.
7. The Stanford Rapide Project: *http://pavg.stanford.edu/rapide/language.html*.

8. Katiyar, D., D. Luckham, and J. Mitchell. 1994. "A Type System for Prototyping Languages." Presented at Proceedings of 21st ACM Symposium on Principles of Programming Languages, Portland, OR.
9. "Darwin, an Architectural Description Language." Imperial College, London. Available at: *http://www.dse.doc.ic.ac.uk/Software/Darwin.*
10. AOP/C#, St. Petersburg University, Russia, Prof. Vladimir O. Safonov, *http://user.rol.ru/~vsafonov/.*
11. AOP/Java, AspectJ, Xerox PARC, *http://aspectj.org.*
12. Generative Programming, *http://www.generative-programming.org/.*

CHAPTER 3

From a Specific Task to "Integration-Ready" Components

The whole is more than the sum of its parts.
—Aristotle

One of the challenges programmers face every day is creating reusable components with a minimum of overhead.

We will consider an example of a service component and a service container, as well as their design and code evolution from a specific to a very flexible solution.

This chapter starts with a single Java class, which then evolves into a visual component. Then, a service container takes the central place on the stage. The chapter teaches how to build a container that is reusable in a Java applet or an application (desktop) program. It provides a solution to one of the most difficult problems: how to make the service container extensible and ready for more services, including those unknown at this time.

This very first example demonstrates one of Java code's benefits. Imagine a small device, such as a wristwatch, with a built-in Java chip. A single text line in the middle of this small screen usually displays the current time. With wireless Internet connection we will enable this device to display weather, stock, traffic, news from friends and family, community or business information (delivered via Short Message Service), and turn it into a "**news watch**." Figure 3.1 illustrates this device that can be viewed as an extended wireless pager or scaled down wireless messenger described in the Chapter 11 (J2ME).

FIGURE 3.1. The News Watch Device.

We will start with a Java applet example that saves the real estate of a Web page by running multiple-line information in a small single-line space. Then we will walk through several transformations, creating reusable code and integration-ready multifunctional components. You can find more sources in Appendix 3 and/or on the Java School Web site.

In the following chapters, we will add interactive features and voice support that makes this small product even more attractive. At some point, we will view this news watch as the simplest client device in the world of distributed knowledge and collaborative services. The very first example presents a simple applet-component that plays its small role inside a Web browser-container. User requirements are easy enough for the component to play on its own, with only standard Web browser support.

Later on, we will add more components. Then, it will make sense to outsource some (generic) component activity to a container. A Web browser does not offer all the functionality we need, so we will create our own containers.

We would like to find a common approach to handling components. Java and C-Sharp offer beautiful ways for describing common behavior—via interfaces, abstract classes, and powerful reflection features.

But this was a jump ahead. Now let us come back and start from a very specific task, the first version of the user requirements.

USER REQUIREMENTS, VERSION 1: THE "NEWS WATCH" APPLET

Create an applet built into a Web page to display multiple-line information in a small single-line space. The information should move from left to right, at a predefined speed. The

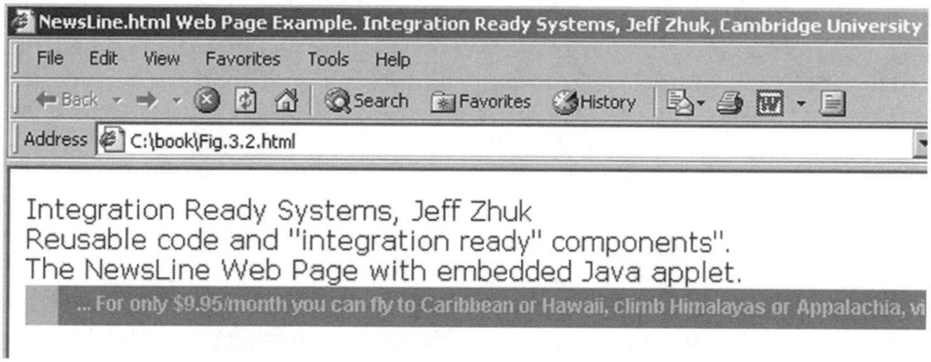

FIGURE 3.2. Screen Shot of the *News Watch* Applet.

information, as well as moving speed parameters, should be passed to the applet with HTML PARAM tags. Let's name the applet class as the "NewsLineApplet." A screen shot is provided in Fig. 3.2.

The Applet Starts with an HTML Page

The HTML source of the Web page is provided in Fig. 3.3.

Applet tags include:

```
applet code=com.its.client.NewsLineApplet archive=newsline.jar
```

```
<html>
<head>
<title>NewsLine.html Web Page Example. Integration-Ready Systems,
Cambridge University Press</title>
   </head>
   <body><center>
<!-- Provide a header for the web page -->
  <font face=verdana color=blue>Integration-Ready Systems, Jeff Zhuk<br>
  Cambridge University Press.<br>
  Java Applet Example: NewsLineApplet is embedded in the web page.</font>

<!-- an embedded applet -->
   <applet code=com.its.client.NewsLineApplet archive=newsline.jar
           width=400 height=24>
      <param name=news value="NewsLineApplet example.
Java source code and explanations are provided in the book
(Integration-Ready Systems) by Cambridge University Press.">
             <param name=shiftInPixels value=2>
             <param name=timeInMsec value=40>
   </applet>

<!-- the rest of the web page -->
     </center>
     </body>
</html>
```

FIGURE 3.3

These tags command the Web browser to download a file named *newsline.jar* from the same server and folder in which the Web page is located and then to find the class com.its.client.NewsLineApplet.class in the newsline.jar file. This class must derive from (extend) the java.applet.Applet class. There are also PARAM tags to pass speed and text parameters from the HTML page to the applet class.

```
param name="news" value="  ... Integration-Ready System ..."
param name="shiftInPixels" value="2"
param name="timeInMsec" value="40"
```

We can place this HTML page in our local folder and try to open it with any Web browser. Nothing much happens until we create, compile, compress (into a jar file), and place the file into the same folder. Until then, all we can see is the "ClassNotFound..." message in the Java Console window that we open under the View menu.

In a Web Browser's Hands

A Java applet appears on the scene (on a Web page) as soon as a browser reads the applet tag from the HTML page and loads the jar file from the server or a local folder. The browser will call the *init()* method when the applet is loaded for the first time. The browser will call the *start()* method of the applet immediately after the *init()* and also each time the page is reloaded.

So, *init()*, *start()*, and *stop()* methods are initiation and destruction points, control points of the browser-Java protocol. We will write some code in these methods, and the browser will execute this code at the proper time.

We will also write and discuss other methods that are specific to our task.

The browser is the main program that runs the show. It offers the frame in which the applet-panel will be displayed. The browser communicates system event messages to the Java Virtual Machine (JVM) that runs the applet, etc.

Note that JVM is a part of the browser itself, its original or third-party library. The browser securely contains the applet and keeps it out of streets inside the browser's sandbox. The browser exhibits typical "big brother" behavior that, in architecture terms, will be called a container.

Our plan is to investigate a single class's applet code and then slowly extend our requirements, discussing at each point what would be an efficient and yet scalable solution.

Writing an Applet

The Java source code is started in Fig. 3.4.

The *NewsLineApplet* class uses (the Java term is *import*) *java.applet.Applet* and classes from the *java.awt.** package, such as *java.awt.Font*, *java.awt.Canvas*, and *java.awt.Dimension*.

The *NewsLineApplet* class extends *Applet* and implements the *java.lang.Runnable* interface.

The *NewsLineApplet* creates a thread, which is responsible for moving the news line. The promise to implement the *Runnable* interface obligates a programmer to implement the *run()* method, a single method of the *Runnable* interface. Later, you will see that most actions occur with this method.

Note that in resource constrained systems, threads can be a prohibited luxury.

```
// NewsLineApplet

package com.its.client; // Internet Technology School, Inc. (ITS)

import java.applet.Applet;
import java.awt.*;

/**
 NewsLineApplet applet gets a message as a parameter and runs it
 with a predifined speed
 @author Jeff.Zhuk@JavaSchool.com
 */
public class NewsLineApplet
  extends Applet // this code will be invoked by a web browser
                 // that serves as an applet container
  implements Runnable // this code MUST implement run() method to
                      // run a thread with moving news line
    {
    public static boolean debug = true; // turns ondebug printing to
                                        // the console
    private int defaultSleepInterval = 40;
    // default time to sleep in msec that defines moving speed
    private int msec = defaultSleepInterval;
    private int defaultShiftInterval = 3; // the newsline is shifted 3
                                          // pixels left each run cycle
    private int shiftX=defaultShiftInterval;
    protected Thread thread;
    private String news = null;
    private int x=0, y=15; // NewsLine starting point
    private int offsetX=20; // offset of the NewsLine rectangle
                            // inside applet panel
    private Dimension dim = new Dimension(600,24);
    // size of the NewsLine rectangle
    private Font font = new Font("Ariel",Font.BOLD, 12);
    // font for drawing the news line
    private int lengthOfNewsLineInPixels;
    private Image newsLineImage = null; // offscreen image
    private boolean thread_stop  = false;
```

FIGURE 3.4

How to Avoid a Flicker Effect in the Moving Line

To achieve the impression of a moving line, we will periodically draw the news line using the drawString() method of the *awt.Graphics* class on the off-screen image located in *java.awt.Canvas*. Each time, the line will be drawn in the new position. The shift between positions and the time interval between the two drawings are two parameters that define the speed of the moving line.

In the beginning of the code, we define the default parameters and provide variables to store the parameters in the String and integer formats.

We define the Font that will be used to draw the news line and the off-screen Image where this line will be drawn. Using an off-screen Image helps to smooth the movement and avoid a flickering effect.

The browser on the client side will read the HTML page and download the applet. As soon as the browser finishes the download process, the *init()* method of the applet will be invoked by the browser.

Applet Life: The *init()*, *start()*, and *stop()* Methods

The source code for the *init()* method is provided in Fig. 3.5.

In the *init()* method, we read parameters from the Web page and try to replace default values with run-time parameters. The reason I say "try" is that two parameters must be

```
/**
 * init() method is called by a web browser when applet just started
 * The method uses applet.getParameter() method to read parameters from
 * html page
 * Then it creates the graphical user interface (GUI) with running news line
 **/
    public void init() {
        news = getParameter("news");
        String timeInMsec = getParameter("timeInMsec");
        if(timeInMsec != null) {
            try {
                msec = (new Integer(timeInMsec)). intValue();
            } catch (Exception e) {
                msec = defaultSleepInterval;
            }
        }
        String shiftInPixels = getParameter ("shiftInPixels");
        if(shiftInPixels != null) {
            try {
                shiftX = (new Integer(shiftInPixels)). intValue();
            } catch (Exception e) {
                shiftX = defaultShiftInterval;
            }
        }
if(debug)
System.out.println( "NewsLineApplet.init:msec=" + msec + " shiftX=" + shiftX
+ " news=" + news);

        setSize(dim);     // paint a gray panel for NewsLine
        setFont(font);
        FontMetrics fm = this.getFontMetrics(font);
        lengthOfNewsLineInPixels = fm.stringWidth(news);
        // calculate total NewsLine length
        x = dim.width - offsetX;
        thread = new Thread(this); // create a thread and start running
        thread.start();
    }
```

FIGURE 3.5

```
/**
 * This applet method will be called by a browser when web page is
 * changed
 * It is a good time to stop the thread
 */
    public void stop() {
        thread_stop = true;
    }
/**
 * This applet method will be called by a browser after init() or
 * when the web page is back
 * It is a good time to re-start the thread
 */
     public void start() {
        if(thread_stop == true){
             thread.start();
             thread_stop = false;
        }
    }
```

FIGURE 3.6

integers. If they are not integers, the program will pass control to the "catch" section that will intercept the Exception and keep the default speed values.

After reading the parameters, the program builds a graphical user interface (GUI), which provides size and visibility to the rectangle where the moving news line will be located.

The *init()* method then creates a thread responsible for drawing the news line and starts this thread. At this point, program control will be passed to the *run()* method. According to the Java application program interface (API), *thread.start()* is actually an invocation of the *run()* method.

Before I describe the *run()* method, let me say several words about two convenient applet methods: *start()* and *stop()*.

- The methods *start()* and *stop()* are provided in Fig. 3.6.
- The *stop()* method will be called by a browser when the Web page is changed.
- This a good place to provide instructions to stop the thread.
- The *start()* method will be called by a browser immediately after the *init()* method and also every time we return back to the original Web page after a page change.

This is a good place to provide instructions to restart the thread.

Who Runs the Show?

The *run()* method is provided in Fig. 3.7.

We find an indefinite *while(true)* loop in the *run()* method. It is a very common beginning of the thread's *run()* method. There is a *thread.sleep(msec)* line in the *while* loop that gives

```
/**
 * running a thread
 **/
    public void run() {
        while(!thread_stop) {
            try {
                thread.sleep(msec); // in msec, in this
                                    // example = 40 msec
            } catch (InterruptedException ie) {
                System.out.println("Clock.run:" + ie);
            }
            if(!isShowing()) {
                continue;  // wait till GUI is built
            }
            if(newsLineImage == null) { // create an off-screen
                                        // image to draw news line
                newsLineImage = createImage(dim.width-offsetX,
                dim.height);
                continue;
            }
            drawLineOffScreen(newsLineImage. getGraphics());
            // draw newsline image in memory
            repaint(); // place this image on the page
            x -= shiftX; // shift text left
            if( x < (0 - lengthOfNewsLineInPixels) ) { start new scan
                x = dim.width;
            }
        }
    }
```

FIGURE 3.7

up control to other threads for the time in milliseconds. When this time is over, this thread takes control of the program execution again.

Off-screen Graphics Are Smooth Graphics

The main purpose of the loop is to periodically redraw news line information, each time in the new (shifted left by several pixels) space. If we were to draw the string in the *paint()* method, the image on the screen would blink, showing a flickering effect created by multiple system threads that refresh the screen. The better strategy is to render the graphics in memory, then place the prepared image on the screen.

I just described the drawing "off-screen" image technique. We need to create an off-screen image first, then render our news line into this image.

We can create the off-screen image only after *this* component is completely drawn. Otherwise, such an attempt fails. The method *isShowing()* returns true if *this* component is visible on the screen. If drawing is not completed, the method returns false and the program skips the rest of the loop and continues with the next loop.

```
/**
 * drawLineOffScreen() method prepares graphics in memory
 * This preparation significantly saves painting time
 * @param g
 */
    public synchronized void drawLineOffScreen(Graphics g){
        if(g == null)
            return;
        // draw newsline
        g.setColor(Color.gray);
        g.fillRect(0,0,dim.width - offsetX, dim.height);
        g.setColor(Color.orange);
        g.drawString(news, x - offsetX, y);
    }
```

FIGURE 3.8

After the method *isShowing()* returns true, the program checks whether the off-screen image exists.

If the off-screen image does not exist, it will be created as a rectangle of predefined size. If the off-screen image exists, the program will draw the news line in this image, changing its position in every loop by *shiftX pixels*. This provides an impression of a moving line. Then, the *repaint()* method is called to schedule *update()* and *paint()* of the component.

The method *drawLineOffScreen()* presented in Fig. 3.8 prepares graphics in memory. This preparation significantly saves painting time.

Java Painting Habits: *update()* and *paint()*

The methods *update()* and *paint()* are presented in Fig. 3.9.

The *update()* method [together with the *paint()* method] is one of the JVM system methods. The standard *update()* method would clean the paint area before the *paint()* method's invocation.

As the *drawLineOffScreen()* method redraws the full off-screen image, there is no need for another cleaning process. We override the *update()* method to avoid the extra cleaning that would create the flickering effect.

The off-screen image filled with the news line is placed on the screen by the *paint()* method.

What If We Want to Change the Information Running in the *NewsLine* Applet?

The method *reset()*, presented in Fig. 3.10, answers this question and ends the class definition.

Done with the Single Applet Source Code? This Was Just the Beginning

We just finished a story about a single Java applet class.

```
/**
 * update() as well as paint() is one of JVM system methods
 * standard update() would clean paint area before calling paint()
 * drawLineOffScreen() method redraw full rectangle, so no need in
 * another cleaning process by overriding update() we avoid extra
 * cleaning that would create flickering effect
 * @param g
 */
   public void update(Graphics g) {
        paint(g);
   }
/**
 * paint() is called by JVM to refresh the screen
 * It will place the NewsLine image (prepared in memory) on the page
 * @param g
 */
   public void paint(Graphics g) {
        if(newsLineImage != null) {
             g.drawImage(newsLineImage, offsetX, 0, this);
        }
   }
```

FIGURE 3.9

The design provides us the flexibility to easily change information and speed parameters in the Web page without changing the Java code. What else can be done to make this code even more usable?

We can think about a bigger task, one in which a moving news line appears as one of the tasks to be done, one of the problems to be solved, one of the components of a bigger container.

```
/**
 * reset() method is to reset the news information
 * @param news
 */
   public void reset(String news) {
        x = dim.width;
        this.news = news;
        FontMetrics fm = this.getFontMetrics(font);
        lengthOfNewsLineInPixels = fm.stringWidth(news);
        // calculate total NewsLine length
   }
}
```

FIGURE 3.10

Let us create a component with a moving news line, a component that can be *reused inside any container*.

USER REQUIREMENTS, VERSION 2: THE REUSABLE *NEWSLINE* COMPONENT

Create a component to display multiple-line information in a small single-line space. The information should move from left to right, with a predefined speed. The news line information, as well as the moving speed values, should be passed as parameters to the component's methods.

The component can be used inside any container in a Java application or Java applet environment. Provide a single test class that can serve as a Java applet as well as a Java application with a container that includes the *NewsLine* component.

The starting part of the Java source code for the *NewsLine* component is presented in Fig. 3.11.

There are several changes in this source in comparison with the *NewsLineApplet* code.

The *NewsLineComponent* class extends *java.awt.Canvas* instead of *java.applet.Applet*.

There is also a new integer variable, "counter," that will be used to show the time it takes to create the GUI. You will find out that this process differs from the applet to the application.

NewsLineComponent() constructor code is presented in Fig. 3.12.

The constructor replaces the *init()* method in building the GUI of the component. The constructor takes three parameters. Two of them are responsible for speed values; the third is the news line information.

The *NewsLineComponent()* constructor's story is very similar to the *init()* method of the applet that we discussed above. The constructor will try to replace default values with run-time parameters. It will then build the GUI, create a thread responsible for drawing the news line, and start this thread.

The *stop()* and *start()* methods are not changed, except that they will be called by a container. The source code is presented in Fig. 3.13.

The source code for the *run()* method is presented in Fig. 3.14.

The new integer variable "counter" counts the time required for building the GUI (with the counter++ operation). This counter is then used to check the time needed to create the off-screen image.

When running this component program inside an applet or an application container, we can see that it takes different amounts of time for an application and an applet to complete the GUI.

The methods *drawLineOffScreen()*, *update()*, and *paint()* are presented in Fig. 3.15. These methods do not change.

Create a Reusable Applet/Application Container

The beginning of the Java source code for the Java applet-application container is provided in Fig. 3.16.

The *NewsLineContainer* class uses (imports) *java.applet.Applet* and *java.awt.Frame* classes.

The *NewsLineContainer* class extends the applet and can serve as an example of an applet container for the *NewsLineComponent*. It also has the *main()* method and can serve as an application container for the *NewsLineComponent*.

The properties of the container are dimension values and *NewsLineComponent*.

```
// NewsLineComponent

package com.its.client; // Internet Technology School, Inc. (ITS)

import java.awt.*;

/**
 NewsLineComponent gets a message as a parameter and runs it with a
 predefined speed
 @author Jeff.Zhuk@JavaSchool.com
 */
public class NewsLineComponent
  extends Canvas // The news line will be moving from left to right
                 // inside the canvas
  implements Runnable // this code MUST implement run() method to run
                      // a thread with moving news line
    {
    public static boolean debug = true; // turns on debug printing
                                        // to the console
    private int defaultSleepInterval = 40;
    // default time to sleep in msec that defines moving speed
    private int msec = defaultSleepInterval;
    private int defaultShiftInterval = 3;
    // the newsline is shifted 3 pixels left each run cycle
    private int shiftX=defaultShiftInterval;
    protected Thread thread;
    private String defaultNews = "NewsLineComponent example. " +
      "Java source code and explanations are provided by
      Jeff Zhuk in the book " +
      "\"Integration-Ready Systems\" by Cambridge University Press.";
    private String news = defaultNews;
    private int x=0, y=15;  // NewsLine starting point
    private int offsetX=20; // offset of the NewsLine
                            // rectangle inside a container
    private Dimension dim = new Dimension(600,24);
    // size of the NewsLine rectangle
    private Font font = new Font("Ariel",Font.BOLD, 12);
    private int lengthOfNewsLineInPixels;
    private Image newsLineImage = null;
    protected boolean thread_stop = false;
    private int counter = 0;
```

FIGURE 3.11

The Applet Portion of the Code

Applet methods *init()*, *stop()*, and *start()* are presented in Fig. 3.17.

The *init()* method gets *speed* and *news* parameters from the Web page then calls the *build()* method and passes these parameters to the method.

The *init()* method is called by a browser running the applet-container.

```
/**
 * The constractor
 * @param timeInMsec
 * @param shiftInPixels
 * @param news
 **/
    public NewsLineComponent(String timeInMsec, String
shiftInPixels,
    String news) {
        if(news != null) {
            this.news = news;
        }
        if(timeInMsec != null) {
            try {
                msec = (new Integer(timeInMsec)). intValue();
            } catch (Exception e) {
                msec = defaultSleepInterval;
            }
        }
        if(shiftInPixels != null) {
            try {
                shiftX = (new Integer(shiftInPixels)). intValue();
            } catch (Exception e) {
                shiftX = defaultShiftInterval;
            }
        }
if(debug)
System.out.println( "NewsLineComponent.init:msec=" + msec + "
shiftX=" + shiftX + " news=" + news);
        setSize(dim); // paint a gray panel for NewsLine
        setVisible(true);
        setFont(font);
        FontMetrics fm = this.getFontMetrics(font);
        lengthOfNewsLineInPixels = fm.stringWidth(news);
        // calculate total NewsLine length
        x = dim.width - offsetX;
        thread = new Thread(this); // create a thread and start
                                   // running
        thread.start();
    }
```

FIGURE 3.12

If we run an application-container, the *main()* method is called by the Java-executable module running on any operating system.

The *stop()* method is called by a browser when the Web page is changed.

This is a good time to stop the thread running in the *NewsLineComponent*.

```
/**
 * This method will be called by a container to stop the thread
 */
    public void stop() {
        thread_stop = true;
    }
/**
 * This method will be called by a container to start a thread
 */
     public void start() {
        if(thread_stop == true){
            thread.start();
            thread_stop = false;
        }
    }
```

FIGURE 3.13

The *start()* method is called by a browser after *init()*, or when the original Web page is back after being changed.

This is a good time to restart the thread running in the *NewsLineComponent*.

Build the GUI in the Reusable Portion of the Code

The *build()* method is presented in Fig. 3.18. The *build()* method is used by both the applet and the application container.

The method creates the *NewsLineComponent* object. The constructor of the *NewsLineComponent* object takes the necessary speed and news parameters.

Then, the *build()* method adds this component to the container, gives dimensions to the container, and makes it visible. This container can be a Panel or a Frame. It will be a Panel in the case of an applet-container, because an applet extends *java.awt.Panel*. This container will be a Frame created in the *main()* method of an application.

The *NewsLineComponen*t object gets everything it needs to live its life in a container. The story is over.

The Application Portion of the Code: the *main()* Method

The *main()* method of an application-container is presented in Fig. 3.19.

The *main()* method is the one the JVM will start when we run the application with the command line "java *com.its.client.NewsLineContainer*." In this case, the application will use some default values for speed and news parameters. We can also run this application with the following command line, which includes speed and news parameters:

```
java com.its.client.NewsLineContainer 20 2 test this application.
```

The *main()* method checks whether the required parameters are given and replaces default values with the parameters. Then, the *main()* method creates a *java.awt.Frame* that serves as a container for the *NewsLineComponent*. The method also creates the *NewsLineContainer*

```
/**
 * running a thread
 **/
    public void run() {
        while(!thread_stop) {
            try  {
                thread.sleep(msec);   // in msec, in this
                                      // example = 40 msec
            } catch (InterruptedException ie) {
                System.out.println("Clock.run:" + ie);
            }
            if(!isShowing()) { // first run cycle
                counter++;
            } else if(newsLineImage == null) {
                if(counter >= 0) {
if(debug)
System.out.println("NewsLineComponent.run.component drawing is
                    completed:counter=" + counter);
                    newsLineImage = createImage(dim.
                    width-offsetX, dim.height);
                    counter = 0;
                }
                counter--;
            }
            if(!isShowing() || newsLineImage == null) {
                continue;
            }
if(debug && counter != 0)  {
System.out.println("NewsLineComponent.run.off-screen image is
completed:Counter=" + counter);
counter = 0;
}
            drawLineOffScreen(newsLineImage. getGraphics());
            // draw newsline image in memory
            repaint(); // place this image on the page
            x -= shiftX; // shift text left
            if( x < 0 - lengthOfNewsLineInPixels ) { // start new scan
                x = dim.width;
            }
        }
    }
```

FIGURE 3.14

object and makes this object execute its *build()* method; it will also pass necessary parameters to the *build()* method.

Recall that the *build()* method creates the *NewsLineComponent* object. The *NewsLineContainer* object with built-in *NewsLineComponent* is then added to the *java.awt.Frame*. The *main()* method then sets the dimensions for the frame and makes it visible.

```
/**
 * drawLineOffScreen() method prepares graphics in memory
 * This preparation significantly saves painting time
 * @param g
 */
    public synchronized void drawLineOffScreen(Graphics g){
        if(g == null)
            return;
        // draw newsline
        g.setColor(Color.gray);
        g.fillRect(0,0,dim.width - offsetX, dim.height);
        g.setColor(Color.orange);
        g.drawString(news, x - offsetX, y);
    }
/**
 * update() as well as paint() is one of JVM system methods
 * standard update() would clean paint area before calling paint()
 * drawLineOffScreen() method redraw full rectangle, so no need in
 * another cleaning process by overriding update() we avoid extra
 * cleaning that would create flickering effect
 * @param g
 */
    public void update(Graphics g) {
        paint(g);
    }
/**
 * paint() is called by JVM to refresh the screen
 * It will place the NewsLine image (prepared in memory) on the page
 * @param g
 */
    public void paint(Graphics g) {
        if(newsLineImage != null) {
            g.drawImage(newsLineImage, offsetX, 0, this);
        }
    }
}
```

FIGURE 3.15

How Do We Make It All Work? Starting Points

The shell script (or batch file for Microsoft users) that simplifies the job of compiling these files is presented in Fig. 3.20. This script compiles the source code and creates a compressed jar file. This compressed jar file can be used by the Web page to decrease applet download time by about three times.

The Web page source code to run the *NewsLineContainer* applet is presented in Fig. 3.21. It is interesting to compare the performance of *NewsLineContainer* as an applet with its performance as an application.

```
// NewsLineContainer

package com.its.client; // Internet Technology School, Inc. (ITS)

import java.applet.Applet;
import java.awt.*;

/**
 * NewsLineContainer can be an applet or an application
 * The NewsLineContainer uses NewsLineComponent to run a news line
 * @author Jeff.Zhuk@JavaSchool.com
 */
public class NewsLineContainer
  extends Applet // this code will be invoked by a web browser that
                 // serves as an applet container
    {
    public static boolean debug = true;
    private int width = 700; // default container width
    private int height = 100; // default container height
    private NewsLineComponent newsLine;
    // component will be created with proper parameters
```

FIGURE 3.16

What Software Do You Need? Build Your Environment

Make sure you have JDK1.4 or JDK1.5 (in this case, it can be any version of JDK1.1 or higher) installed. You can test this by running "java –version" in your shell window (for MS Windows products, it is the MS DOS or Command Prompt window).

Create a folder named *src* (any other name is OK, too) in your home area (for MS Windows users, this could be the *C:\src* folder, for example). Then create the following hierarchy of folders (the names matter!): *src/com/its/client*. The full path in this case would be *c:/src/com/its/client/*.

Find the NewsLineComponent.java and NewsLineContainer.java source files in Appendix 3 (or in the on-line book support) and place these two source files in the "client" folder.

Copy the script file (Fig. 3.20) to the *src* folder, and copy the HTML file presented in Fig. 3.21 into the same *src* folder. Then run the shell script in the *src* folder to compile the sources. You are now ready to run the *NewsLineContainer* as an applet or as an application.

Test It Now

Open the Web page that you copied to the *src* folder with your Web browser, and look at the applet's performance. To see a Java Console with the program's debug messages, click on the Web browser's View menu and select the Java Console menu item. (You might need to set up your Web browser properly to show this menu item.)

```
/**
 * init() method is called by a web browser when  applet just
 * started The method uses applet.getParameter() method to read
 * parameters from html page Then it creates the graphical user
 * interface (GUI) with running news line
 **/
   public void init() {
        String timeInMsec = getParameter ("timeInMsec");
        String shiftInPixels = getParameter ("shiftInPixels");
        String news = getParameter("news");
        build(timeInMsec,shiftInPixels,news);
   }/**
 * This applet method will be called by a browser when web page is
 * changed It is a good time to stop the thread
 */
   public void stop() {
        newsLine.stop();
   }
/**
 * This applet method will be called by a browser after init() or
 * when the web page is back It is a good time to re-start the
 * thread
 */
    public void start() {
         newsLine.start();
   }
```

FIGURE 3.17

```
/**
 * build() method creates NewsLineComponent and places the
 * component into the current container
 * @param timeInMsec passed as a parameter from the web page or
 * from an application
 * @param shiftInPixels passed as a parameter from the web page or
 * from an application
 * @param news passed as a parameter from the web page or from an
 * application
 */
   public void build(String timeInMsec, String shiftInPixels,
   String news) {
        newsLine = new NewsLineComponent(timeInMsec,
        shiftInPixels,news);
        add(newsLine);
        setSize(width, height);
        setVisible(true);
   }
```

FIGURE 3.18

```
/**
 * main() method is to test NewsLineContainer as an application
 * @param args used as parameters: timeInMsec, shiftInPixels,news
 */
    public static void main(String[] args) {
        String timeInMsec = "40";    // default value
        String shiftInPixels = "3"; // default value
        String news = "default news content";
        if(args != null && args.length > 0) {
            timeInMsec = args[0];
            if(args.length > 1) {
                shiftInPixels = args[1];
            }
            // rest of parameters represents news line
            if(args.length > 2) {
                news = args[2];
                for(int i=3; i < args.length; i++) {
                    news += " " + args[i];
                }
            }
        }
        // create a frame replacing a frame of a web browser when
        // applet is running
        Frame f = new Frame();
        // create and show a container with newsLine
        // NewsLineContainer is a awt.Panel as Applet extends
        // awt.Panel
        NewsLineContainer newsLineContainer = new
        NewsLineContainer();
        newsLineContainer.build(timeInMsec, shiftInPixels, news);
        f.add(newsLineContainer);
        f.pack();
        f.setVisible(true);
    }
}
```

FIGURE 3.19

To run the same code as an application, you need to open your shell window, navigate to the *src* folder, and type

```
java com.its.client.NewsLineContainer.
```

In this case, the application will use some default values for speed and news parameters. You can also run this application with a command line that includes speed and news parameters.

```
java com.its.client.NewsLineContainer 30 2 test this application
```

We provided the number 30 as the time interval in milliseconds, the number 2 as the shift to the left with every 30-millisecond interval, and the sentence *test this application* as

```
javac com/its/client/NewsLineContainer.java
jar cf newsContainer.jar com/its/client/NewsLineContainer.class
com/its/client/NewsLineComponent.class
```

FIGURE 3.20

the news information to display in the *NewsLineComponent*. Watch your shell window for application messages, and compare these with the applet messages.

Now we can move on to the task of integrating the *NewsLineComponent* into a client-server environment. Here, the real fun begins.

USER REQUIREMENTS, VERSION 3: VIEW MULTIPLE WEB INFORMATION CHANNELS IN THE *NEWSLINE COMPONENT*

Feed the *NewsLineComponent* with information from the Web. Create a control component to help users select an informational channel. The control component will include several

```
<html>
<head>
<title>NewsLine Web Page. Integration-Ready Systems, Jeff
Zhuk</title>
    </head>
    <body>
    <!-- Provide a header for the web page -->
         <font face=verdana color=blue>Integration-Ready Systems,
         Jeff Zhuk <br>
         Reusable code and "integration-ready" components". <br>
         The NewsLine Web Page with embedded Java applet.</font>

<!-- an embedded applet -->
          <applet code=com.its.client.NewsLineContainer
          archive=newsContainer.jar width=600 height=24>
 <param name=news value="NewsLineComponent example.
Java source code and explanations are provided by Jeff Zhuk in his
book
\"Integration-Ready Systems\".">
             <param name=shiftInPixels value=2>
             <param name=timeInMsec value=40>
          </applet>

<!-- the rest of the web page -->

      </body>
</html>
```

FIGURE 3.21

FIGURE 3.22. Screen Shot of the *WebNewsContainer* with Multiple News Channels.

buttons, such as *W* for weather, *T* for traffic, *S* for stocks, *F* for friends and family, and *B* for business news.

Each button will point to a specific Web location, or Uniform Resource Locator (URL), responsible for the specific information feed. The user will be able to press a button and receive information from the selected channel into the *NewsLineComponent*. Keep in mind that if the *NewsLineComponent* is a part of an applet, all URLs must be limited to the same server in which the applet is located.

From the very beginning, let us think about the control component as a reusable one. We will add this component to the bottom of our *WebNewsContainer*. A screen shot is presented in Fig. 3.22 .

We would like to configure the buttons and their related URLs in a very flexible way. We might think about distributing the application or the applet to multiple clients. We can prepare a configuration file that will reside on our server.

This file will be downloaded by an applet or an application during the initiation time. This solution allows us to easily extend or update the configuration file and keep the client software untouched.

Architecture diagrams for the applet and the application are presented in Figs. 3.23 and 3.24, respectively.

In both cases, the client includes presentation components and relies on the server for services. It is also possible to provide a "fat" client that will not need server support. Such a client will include all the necessary presentation and service components. The architecture diagram is presented in Fig. 3.25.

Note that the applet always makes a connection to its own server. The server in its turn can connect to any of the Web servers providing feed information. The application can directly connect to any Web server information providers. Both the applet and the application will download the configuration file from the same server.

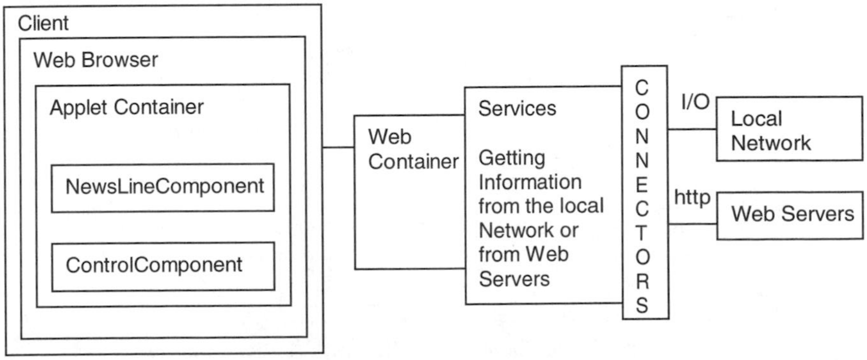

FIGURE 3.23. Thin Client Applet.

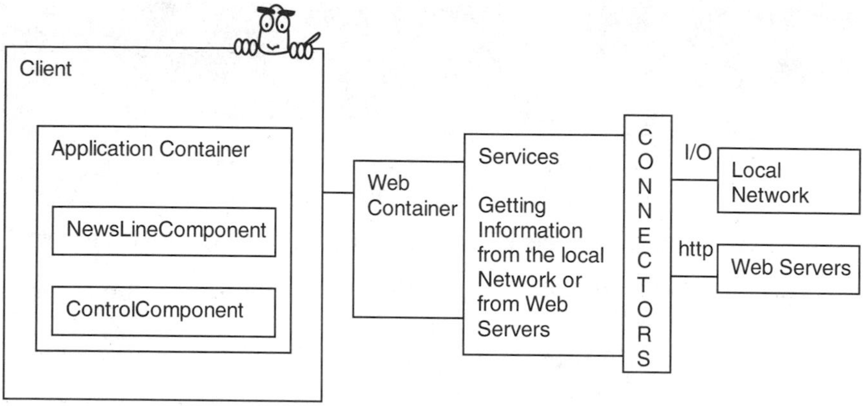

FIGURE 3.24. Thin Client Application.

The configuration file will evolve together with the sample sources. We can start with a very simple text-based configuration file. Every line of the file will include a button name and a related URL, separated by a comma. For example:

```
"Weather, http://ipserve.com/go/web/to/Weather".
```

The configuration file is presented in Fig. 3.26.

Later in this chapter, we describe more complex configuration goals and use XML-based ammunition to attack these goals.

Starting the *ControlComponent*

The source code for the *ControlComponent* starts in Fig. 3.27.

The *ControlComponent* extends *java.awt.Panel*. The Panel is the lightest container able to contain other components. The *ControlComponent* will contain a set of control buttons.

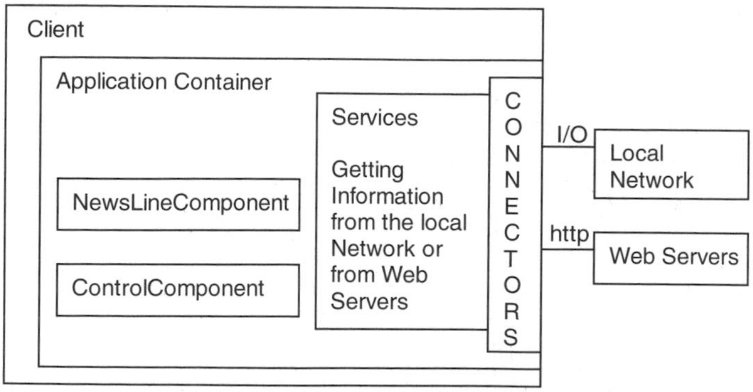

FIGURE 3.25. Thick Client Application with Its Own Services.

```
Business,http://ipserve.com/go/web/to/business
FriendsAndFamily,http://ipserve.com/go/web/to/friendsAndFamily
Stocks,http://ipserve.com/go/web/to/stocks
Traffic,http://ipserve.com/go/web/to/traffic
Weather,http://ipserve.com/go/web/to/weather
Config,config.txt
Help,Inline data: Available options are: B - Business news,
F - from Friends and Family, S - Stock;
T - Traffic, C - for configuration file, and W - for Weather
```

FIGURE 3.26

There is a need for a listener object for button events; the listener type for the *java.awt.Button* component is the *ActionListener*. The *ActionListener* interface requires the implementation of a single method. Note that in the *ControlComponent* class definition, we promised to implement the *ActionListener* interface. This means two things: we assigned the *ControlComponent* to play the role of the listener, and we promise to provide the *actionPerformed()* method in the body of the *ControlComponent* class.

We now define the array of control buttons. We will form the buttons at run-time based on the configuration file. The *awt.util.Hashtable* (which maps object-keys to object-values) will hold the button names and related URLs. The *Hashtable* will also be formed at run-time based on the configuration file.

We would like to distinguish a selected button from the rest of the crowd. Default and selected colors for background and foreground buttons will serve this purpose well. The *ControlComponent* class includes properties (like *buttonPressed* and *defaultBackground*) to facilitate this distinguished appearance.

Dispatching Events: Alternatives and Solutions

The *ServiceControl* object deserves special consideration. This object will help dispatch events from the *ControlComponent* to the *NewsLineComponent*. The observer-consumer design pattern for handling events in Java requires us to assign an observer object to listen for the events that happen with a consumer object.

The *ControlComponent* includes several buttons that play consumer object roles. We prepared the *ControlComponent* itself to play the observer role (see "implements *ActionListener*" in the class definition). We will directly assign the *ControlComponent* to listen for button events when we create buttons in the constructor in Fig. 3.28.

The *actionPerfomed()* method presented in Fig. 3.29 handles action events.

Every time a user presses a button on the *ControlComponent*, an action event occurs and the *actionPerformed()* method is executed. The *actionPerfomed()* method recognizes the selected button's name and finds the URL connected to this button, which leads to a proper information channel.

Then the *actionPerformed()* method forms a *Hashtable* of parameters and places the (user-selected) channel name and related URL there. The *service()* method presented in Fig. 3.30 is then called with the *Hashtable* of parameters.

```
// ControlComponent

package com.its.client; // Internet Technology School, Inc. (ITS)

import java.awt.*;
import java.awt.event.*;
import java.util.Hashtable;
import java.util.Vector;
import com.its.util.IOMaster;
import com.its.util.Stringer;

/**
 * ControlComponent class is to control information flow
 * @author Jeff.Zhuk@JavaSchool.com
 */
public class ControlComponent extends Panel implements ActionListener {
    public static boolean debug = true; // turns on debug printing

    private Button[] buttons; // will be defined run-time
    private Hashtable namesAndLetters = new Hashtable();
    // first letter = key, full name = object
    private Hashtable namesAndURLs = new Hashtable();
    // populated after reading the config file
    private Hashtable namesAndButtons = new Hashtable();
    // populated after reading the config file
    private ServiceController serviceController; // service dispatcher
    private Button buttonPressed; // currently selected control button
    private static final Color defaultBackground = Color.lightGray;
    private static final Color defaultForeground = Color.black;
    private static final Color selectedBackground = Color.black;
    private static final Color selectedForeground = Color.black;
```

FIGURE 3.27

The *service()* method retrieves information from the Web or the local network based on the URL passed to the method in the *Hashtable* of parameters. The *service()* method uses the *IOMaster.readFromTextFile()* utility to connect to the end point of the URL and get the information from the network.

We consider the *IOMaster.readFromTextFile()* utility as well as related methods in Appendix 3.

After reading the news, the *service()* method returns this information as a String object *value* inside the *Hashtable* with the *key* equal to "news."

The problem is how to pass this information to the *NewsLineComponent*. There are several implementation alternatives.

Let us consider each alternative along with brief "for" and "against" comments.

1. Pass the direct reference to the *NewsLineComponent* to the *ControlComponent*.

   Yes! This is the simplest solution.

   No. It couples the *ControlComponent* to the *NewsLineComponent* too tightly. We want to avoid such coupling. The *ControlComponent* can potentially be used with other components that may be similar but not exactly the same, such as the *NewsLineComponent*.

```
/**
 * the constructor reads the config file and creates a GUI (based on
 * the config file)
 * @param serviceController reference to dispatch service
 * provided by a container
 * @param urlToConfigFile
 */
    public ControlComponent(ServiceController
    serviceController, String urlToConfigFile) {
        this.serviceController  = serviceController;
        String controlConfig  = IOMaster.readTextFile
        (serviceController, urlToConfigFile);
        if(controlConfig  == null || controlConfig.
        startsWith("ERROR")) {
            return;
        }
        controlConfig  = Stringer.replace("\r\n","\n", controlConfig);
                         // to Unix ending the latest
                         // java.lang.String includes split method
        String[] lines  = Stringer.split("\n", controlConfig);

        if(lines ! = null) { // create array of buttons
            buttons  = new Button[lines.length];
}
for(int i =0; lines ! = null && i < lines.length; i++) {
        String[] splits  = Stringer.split(",", lines[i]);
        // split values: name and url
        if(splits  == null || splits.length < 2) {
            continue; // not sufficient line
        }
        // put into the namesAndURLs Hashtable a name
        // as a key and a URL as an object
        namesAndURLs.put(splits[0], splits[1]);
        // create a new button with the label as the first letter
        // of the name
        String firstLetter  = splits[0]. substring(0,1);
        namesAndLetters.put(firstLetter, splits[0]);
        // associate firstLetter with the full name
        buttons[i]  = new Button(firstLetter);
        // example: "w" - for weather add(buttons[i]);
        // put into the namesAndButtons Hashtable a name as
        // a key and a button as an object
        namesAndButtons.put(splits[0], buttons[i]);
        // the ControlComponent itself will listen to button events
        buttons[i].addActionListener(this);
      }
    }
```

FIGURE 3.28

```
/**
 * actionPerformed() method is to handle action events
 * In this case the method is called when a user presses any of control
 * buttons
 * @param actionEvent to be used to figure out which button was pressed
 */
    public void actionPerformed(ActionEvent actionEvent) {
        String command  = actionEvent. getActionCommand(); // first letter
        String name  = (String)namesAndLetters. get(command);
        String url  = namesAndURLs.get(name);
        Hashtable parameters  = new Hashtable();
        parameters.put(name, url);
        parameters  = service(parameters); // change information channel
        serviceController.dispatch(parameters);
        // dispatch information to the news line !
        // change control button appearance to highlight a selected button
        if(buttonPressed ! = null)
            buttonPressed.setForeground (defaultForeground);
            buttonPressed.setBackground (defaultBackground);
        }
        buttonPressed  = (Button)namesAndButtons. get(name);
        buttonPressed.setForeground (selectedForeground);
        buttonPressed.setBackground (selectedBackground);
    }
}   // end of the ControlComponent class
```

FIGURE 3.29

2. Pass the reference to the *WebNewsContainer* to the *ControlComponent*. The *WebNewsContainer* can use the already-existing reference to the *NewsLine Component*.

   Yes! This will enable the *WebNewsContainer* to direct not only the *NewsLineComponent* but other components that this container can control.
   No. Such a solution, even though it is better than the previous one, still restricts the *ControlComponent* to work with a very specific container, the *WebNewsContainer*.

3. Delegate the dispatcher role to a new object that will have a reference to the *WebNewsContainer*.

   Yes! This solution will decouple the *ControlComponent* from the *WebNews Container*.
   No. The solution will increase complexity by introducing another class. Unfortunately, the new class will be tightly coupled with the *WebNewsContainer*.

4. The most commonly used solution (which we will consider first) is close to the second one but is more elegant and generic. In this solution, we still connect a component to its container, but with a very light connection. Later on, we will discuss an even better alternative, but everything at its own time. Here are several steps to implement solution 4:

   4.1. Define an interface with a generic method that can be used for multiple purposes. The *ServiceController* interface with the *dispatch()* method is presented in Fig. 3.31.

```
/**
 * The service() method retrieves news data from a selected channel
 * (URL) or channels
 * @param parameters
 * @return parameters
 */
    public Hashtable service(Hashtable parameters) {
        String pattern  = "Inline data: ";
        // one or more Hashtable entries
        Enumeration keys  = parameters.keys();
        String newInformation  = "News: ";
        while(keys.hasMoreElements()) {
        // theoretically we could allow several key-channels at once
            String name  = (String)keys.nextElement();
            String url  = (String)parameters.get(name);
            // retrieve info
            newInformation + = name + " : ";
            if(url.startsWith(pattern) ) {
                newInformation + = url.substring (pattern.length());
            } else {
                String data  = IOMaster.readTextFile (container, url);
if(debug)
System.out.println("ControlComponent.service:data =" + data + "\nurl ="
+ url);
                if(data  == null) {
                    data  = "No " + name + " information found. ";
                }
                newInformation + = data;
            }
        }
        parameters.clear();
        parameters.put("news", newInformation);
        return parameters;
    }
```

FIGURE 3.30

4.2. Make the *ControlComponent* class constructor accept the *ServiceController* object as an argument.
4.3. Define the *WebNewsContainer* as a class that implements this generic interface, and pass a reference to this interface to the *ControlComponent* object.

Note that the *ControlComponent* has no *direct* coupling with the *WebNewsContainer*. The *ControlComponent* can work with a wide variety of containers or objects that implement the *ServiceController* interface. Yes, one of the possibilities is working with the *WebNewsContainer*. We use this possibility in the *build()* method of the *WebNewsContainer*.

Continue with the *ControlComponent* Class

The constructor of the *ControlComponent* was presented above in Fig. 3.28.

```
// ServiceController

package com.its.util; // Internet Technology School, Inc. (ITS)

import java.util.Hashtable;

/**
 * ServiceController must implement dispatch() method
 * @author Jeff.Zhuk@JavaSchool.com
 */
public interface ServiceController {
/**
 * The dispatch() method is defined to satisfy a wide variety of services
 * @param parameters
 * @return result an optional return value
 */
    public Hashtable dispatch(Hashtable parameters);
}
```

FIGURE 3.31

There are two arguments passed to the constructor: the *ServiceController* object and the URL to the configuration file. The *ServiceController* object, as we discussed before, will dispatch control events to the *NewsLineComponent* and change the information channel that provides news to the *NewsLineComponent*.

The URL to the configuration file is needed to retrieve names and related URLs to information channels from the file button.

We read the configuration file from the Internet or a local network with the *read()* method of the *com.its.util.IOMaster* class. We will consider this code in a later chapter.

Now, we mention only that the method is able to retrieve information from the Web as well as from a local file system. You can refresh your memory about the configuration file's structure by looking back at Fig. 3.26 .

The *IOMaster.read()* method returns the result of the reading as a single string. We split the string into separate lines. Then we split every line into two variables: a button name and a related URL.

Note that we use the *com.its.util.Stringer.split()* method, not the *split()* method of the *java.lang,String* class from the latest Java Development Kit (JDK). We understand that current Web browsers do not yet support this latest JDK unless they are provided with a plug-in.

We use the *namesAndURLs Hashtable* to keep button names and related URLs together. The names will serve as keys of the *Hashtable* to retrieve the value of the URLs. We create a new button on the fly and add an action listener object to every button. The *ControlComponent* itself serves as the action listener for all the buttons.

The Java keyword *this* that we passed as an argument to the *addActionListener()* method makes this component responsible for handling action events for every button. As we discussed before, the *ControlComponent* must implement the *actionPerformed()* method to be in compliance with action listener requirements and with the promise to implement *ActionListener* in the *ControlComponent* class definition.

Start the Integration Party: Put It All Together in the Container

The source code for the *WebNewsContainer* starts in Fig. 3.32 .

Like the *NewsLineContainer*, the *WebNewsContainer* is defined as an applet. The *WebNews-Container* implements the *ServiceController* interface and the *ActionListener* interface.

When introducing the *ServiceController* interface, we are looking into the future, where a system developer can use the extremely simple API of the interface without any exposure to all the specifics of code implementation. It is very possible that multiple containers similar to the *WebNewsContainer* are available at this point, each for its own specific area, and all these containers can be governed with the same simple API performing similar functions in different ways.

When we declare that the *WebNewsContainer* implements the *ServiceController* interface, this declaration must be supported later on in the code by the implementation of the methods that represent the *ServiceController* interface.

There are several properties that belong to the *WebNewsContainer*: it defines the container's dimensions, the *NewsLineComponent* object, and the *ControlComponent* object.

Figure 3.33 presents three applet methods. A Web browser that will run this applet version of the container will invoke these methods. The *init()* method collects initial data and calls the *build()* method that builds the GUI. The *stop()* and *start()* methods are called by a Web browser and serve to control the news line thread.

```
// WebNewsContainer

package com.its.client; // Internet Technology School, Inc. (ITS)

import java.applet.Applet;
import java.util.Vector;
import java.awt.*;

import com.its.util.IOMaster;
/**
 * WebNewsContainer can be an applet or an application
 * The WebNewsContainer uses NewsLineComponent to run a news line
 * @author Jeff.Zhuk@JavaSchool.com
 */
public class WebNewsContainer
  extends Applet // this code will be invoked by a web
                 // browser that serves as an applet container
  implements ServiceController // obligation to implement dispatch() method
    {
    public static boolean debug = true;
    private int width = 400; // default container width
    private int height = 200; // default container height
    private NewsLineComponent newsLine;
    // component will be created with proper parameters
    private ControlComponent controlComponent;
    // component will be created with proper parameters
```

FIGURE 3.32

```
/**
 * init() method is called by a web browser when applet just started
 * The method uses applet.getParameter() method to read parameters
 * from html page
 * Then it creates the graphical user interface (GUI) with running
 * news line
 **/
    public void init() {
        String urlToConfigFile = getParameter ("configFile");
        String timeInMsec = getParameter ("timeInMsec");
        String shiftInPixels = getParameter ("shiftInPixels");
        String news = getParameter("news");
        build(timeInMsec, shiftInPixels, news, urlToConfigFile);
    }
/**
 * This applet method will be called by a browser when web page is
 * changed
 * It is a good time to stop the thread
 */
    public void stop() {
        newsLine.stop();
    }
/**
 * This applet method will be called by a browser after init() or when
 * the web page is back
 * It is a good time to re-start the thread
 */
     public void start() {
         newsLine.start();
    }
```

FIGURE 3.33

Figure 3.34 presents a *build()* method that looks very similar to the *build()* method of the *NewsLineContainer*. There is a very important difference, though. In the *WebNewsContainer*, we create an additional component.

Note, that the *build()* method of the *WebNewsContainer* creates the *ControlComponent* object and passes *this* (the reference to the *WebNewsContainer* object itself) to the *ControlComponent* object constructor.

TheControlComponent object will change the initial information running in the *NewsLineComponent*. We pass two arguments to the *ControlComponent*'s constructor. The first argument is the *WebNewsContainer* itself.

Does this mean that the *WebNewsContainer* and the *ControlComponent* are tightly coupled? Fortunately, the answer is no. For the *ControlComponent*, the passed object is just one of the *ServiceController* implementations. (You can still see a slight coupling, which we will get rid of in the alternative solution.)

The *ControlComponent* is very open about its companions and will work with everyone who implements the *dispatch()* method. The other object we pass to the constructor is the URL of the configuration file. The *ControlComponent* builds itself based on this file description.

```
/**
 * build() method creates NewsLineComponent and places the component
 * into the current container
 * @param timeInMsec passed as a parameter from the web page or
 * from an application
 * @param shiftInPixels passed as a parameter from the web page or
 * from an application
 * @param news passed as a parameter from the web page or from an application
 * @param urlToConfigFile
 */
    public void build(String timeInMsec, String shiftInPixels, String news,
    String urlToConfigFile) {
        newsLine  = new NewsLineComponent (timeInMsec,shiftInPixels,news);
        setLayout(new BorderLayout());
        add("Center", newsLine);
        controlComponent  = new ControlComponent(this, urlToConfigFile);
        add("South", controlComponent);
        setSize(width, height);
        setVisible(true);
    }
```

FIGURE 3.34

Implement the Universal *dispatch()* Method in a Specific Way

The *dispatch()* method was defined in the *ServiceController* interface for multiple implementations. The interface definition tends to be universal. The interfaces are designed to serve as umbrellas for many possibilities. *Otherwise why would we need interfaces?*

When we implement an interface, however, we must be very specific. Figure 3.35 shows the implementation of the *dispatch()* method in the *WebNewsContainer* class.

```
/**
 * dispatch() method is to dispatch information from a specific channel
 * and reset the NewsLineComponent with this information
 * @param parameters
 * @return null not used in this implementation
 */
    public Hashtable dispatch(Hashtable parameters) {
        if(parameters  == null || parameters.size()  == 0)
        { // protect against NullPointer exceptions
            return null;
        }
        // reset the NewsLineComponent
        String news  = (String)parameters.get("news");
        newsLine.reset(news);
        return null;
    }
```

FIGURE 3.35

The implemented *dispatch*() method retrieves news information from the *Hashtable* of parameters passed from the *ControlComponent* class. This information is then passed further to the *reset*() method of the *NewsLineComponent*.

Add the *main()* Method and an Application Flavor to This Container

The *main*() method is very similar to the one from the *NewsLineContainer* class.

In the *main*() method we collect parameters passed in the command line or use the default versions.

Figure 3.36 demonstrates the *main*() method.

We create a frame, build the *WebNewsContainer* object (remember that it is a Panel, from a graphical point of view), and add this object to the frame. As we make the frame visible, the object begins its life, runs the initial information, and is ready to switch between informational channels as we use the control buttons.

Put It All Together!

Let us quickly compile and test the programs.

First of all, we need to put them in the right places. Down the road, we will look into XML and find the way to make this all automatic with a single XML-based configuration file. It is still important to understand the basic structure of the package. You might already have the folder named *src* that serves as our base.

Let us create a Web page to host the *WebNewsContainer* as an applet. Figure 3.37 contains this HTML code. We now place this HTML file in the *src* folder.

Our set of sources includes several files from the *com.its.client* package and two files from the *com.its.util* package. Java requires that sources live in folders named according to the package naming structure. Make sure that the *src* folder includes a *com* folder and the *com* folder includes an *its* folder.

There should be two folders in the *its* folder: *util* and *client*. Place the *WebNewsContainer.java, ControlComponent.java*, and *NewsLineComponent.java* files into the *client* folder. Then place the *IOMaster.java* and *Stringer.java* files into the *util* folder. (We will discuss the utility classes in the following chapter.) Let's create a script to compile sources and place it in the *src* folder. Figure 3.38 shows an example of the compilation script.

We then create a script that will run the program as an application (Fig. 3.39), and we place this script in the *src* folder.

Let us place the configuration file (see Fig. 3.26) in the *src* folder and name the file *config.txt*. We want to cover both the applet and application options with our test.

Run the test script to see the application perform. Then, open the Web page to look into the applet's performance. It works for me (this is the most common phrase you hear from a programmer in a conversation with a customer). I hope it works for you.

Integration-Ready Service Components and Extensible Service Containers

It looks like we have provided a flexible solution to the problem. Some development teams would finish their work right here and switch to a celebration party or to another project. However, there are questions it makes sense to ask before saying goodbye to this project.

```
/**
 * main() method is to test WebNewsContainer as an application
 * @param args used as parameters: timeInMsec, shiftInPixels, news,
 * urlToConfig
 */
    public static void main(String[] args) {
        String timeInMsec = "40";    // default value
        String shiftInPixels = "3"; // default value
        String news = "default news content";
        String urlToConfigFile = "config.txt";
        // example is presented on the Fig.3-6.5
        if(args != null && args.length > 0) {
            timeInMsec = args[0];
            if(args.length > 1) {
                shiftInPixels = args[1];
            }
            if(args.length > 2) {
                urlToConfigFile = args[2];
            }
         // rest of parameters represents news line
            if(args.length > 3) {
                news = args[3];
                for(int i=4; i < args.length; i++) {
                    news += " " + args[i];
                }
            }
        }
        // create a frame replacing a frame of a web browser when
        // applet is running Frame f = new Frame();
        // create and show a container with newsLine NewsLineContainer
        // is a awt.Panel as Applet extends awt.Panel
        WebNewsContainer webNewsContainer = new WebNewsContainer();
        webNewsContainer.build(timeInMsec,
        shiftInPixels, news, urlToConfigFile);
        f.add(webNewsContainer);
        f.pack();
        f.setVisible(true);
    }
}
```

FIGURE 3.36

Components still hold a pointer to the *ServiceController*, which represents a specific type of container. This is a restriction; components can only work with this type of container. It would be the right move to completely free components from any knowledge of a container, and even about a container type. The best proof of this freedom would be the ability to compile component classes without any container-related code.

```
<html>
<head>
<title>WebNewsContainer.html Web Page Example.
Integration-Ready Systems, Jeff Zhuk,
Cambridge University Press</title>
 </head>
 <body>
<!-- Provide a header for the web page -->
  <font face=verdana color=blue>Integration-Ready Systems, Jeff Zhuk<br>
  Reusable code and "integration-ready" components.<br>
  The NewsLine Web Page with embedded Java applet.</font>

<!-- an embedded applet -->
        <applet code=com.its.client. WebNewsContainer
        archive=webNewsContainer.jar
       width=400 height=60>
             <param name="news" value="...Integration-Ready Systems,
              Jeff Zhuk
     Cambridge University Press ...">
            <param name="shiftInPixels" value="2">
            <param name="timeInMsec" value="20">
            <param name="configFile" value="config.txt">
        </applet>

<!-- the rest of the web page -->

 </body>
</html>
```

FIGURE 3.37

What happens if we need to add another service to this container? Can we do this? What if we need to customize our component's properties and behaviors? Can we accomplish a hierarchy of parameters in our configuration file?

The answer to these real-life questions (based on the code provided above) is negative. The current design and code is not bad, but neither is it perfect. It is not extensible. Here

```
javac com/its/util/*.java
javac com/its/client/NewsLineComponent.java
javac com/its/client/ControlComponent.java
javac com/its/client/WebNewsContainer.java
jar cf webNewsContainer.jar com/its/util/*.class
com/its/client/WebNewsContainer.class
com/its/client/NewsLineComponent.class
com/its/client/ControlComponent.class
```

FIGURE 3.38

```
java com.its.client.WebNewsContainer 20 2 config.txt default
```

FIGURE 3.39

is the challenging task: to make components and the service container extensible and ready for more services, including those unknown at this time.

It is understandable that we cannot describe unknown services in the container code. So where is the place for service component definitions?

The best place for component definitions is in the configuration file, of course. It is also the most natural place for us to start building extensible solutions.

AN XML-BASED CONFIGURATION FILE

Why XML? To answer that question, we need to answer another one.

What Is XML [1]?

Extensible Markup Language was first invented to extend HTML with new tags that can be defined by customers. For example, HTML has tags such as "<table>" and "<font>." But for a human resources application, we would like to introduce new tags such as "<Last Name>" and "<Phone>."

XML can easily accomplish this and create a new (tag-based) language specifically for human resources applications. XML quickly became *the* language for creating business-oriented dialects, such as Wireless Markup Language (WML), which is used in wireless Web browsers; VoiceXML, which is used in speech recognition systems; and Enterprise Business XML (ebXML) [2], the language of business-to-business transactions.

It is very natural to use XML to provide extensible solutions. A variety of industry products, such as the Apache Web server [3], Tomcat JSP and servlet engine, J2EE, and .NET-based applications, describe application properties with XML-based configuration files such as web.xml and config.xml.

XML requires all tags to be closed. For example:

```
"<Last Name>Zhuk</Last Name>", or
"<Phone name="cell" value="123-456--7890"/>".
```

Both examples are "well-formed" cases of XML. Most HTML tags are also well-formed from an XML point of view, but not all. For example, *
*, or the break-line tag, is not well formed in XML, although it works well for Web browsers.

Generally speaking, Web browsers are forgiving and are not even strict about HTML rules. To the contrary, XML is strict and straightforward. Document type definitions (DTDs) and the XML Schema Definition [4] help vendors standardize XML handling.

This has encouraged many vendors to create powerful tools that handle XML, ranging from XML parsers based on Simple API for XML (SAX) [5] and Document Object Model (DOM) programming [6] to application generator products like Struts [7] and Cocoon [8], based on Extensible Stylesheet Language (XSL) [9] and Extensible Stylesheet Language Transformation (XSLT) [10] specifications. The World Wide Web Consortium (w3c.org) [11] governs most standards related to XML.

```
<html>
<head>
<title>WebNewsContainer.html Web Page Example.
Integration-Ready Systems, Jeff Zhuk,
Cambridge University Press</title>
       </head>
       <body>
<applet code=com.its.client.WebNewsContainer
archive=webNewsContainer.jar width=400 height=80>
<param name="configFile" value="config.xml">
</applet>

<!-- the rest of the web page -->

 </body>
</html>
```

FIGURE 3.40

An XML document *must be* well-formed; XML documents *can be* validated. We can provide special rules about XML document data structure in a special file called *DTD*. This makes sense if we expect multiple XML documents to be formed and validated against the specific data structure provided in the *DTD* file.

Almost every chapter of this book discusses and provides examples of XML, although the most concentrated bouquet of XML technologies can be found in Appendix 2.

Let us come back to our current task. Our decision to use an XML-based configuration file is pretty firm. We plan to provide all the necessary parameters in this file. The service container represented by the *WebNewsContainer* class will use this XML descriptor to build service components.

This approach will change some of the sources considered above. First of all, the Web page with an embedded applet will contain only one applet parameter with a URL that points to the configuration file. Figure 3.40 shows the HTML source of the page.

We are aware of at least two service components we want to build: the *NewsLineComponent* and the *ControlComponent*. Let us describe the parameters we need to build these components. Figure 3.41 shows what parameters are needed to build the *NewsLine Component*.

```
<!-- Hashtable key="com.its.client. NewsLineComponent" -->
<Component name="com.its.client.NewsLineComponent">
    <Parameter name="timeInMsec" value="40"/>
    <Parameter name="shiftInPixels" value="3"/>
    <Parameter name="news" value="Integration-ready
    service components and containers"/>
</Component>
```

FIGURE 3.41

START FROM THE PARAMETERS FOR A SINGLE COMPONENT

That was an easy start. We just transformed several parameters that we used in the *build()* method of the *NewsLineComponent* class to XML. Now is a good time to refactor or improve our design and code for this class.

Do we have more parameters that can be flexible and we would do better to provide in the configuration file? Sure we do!

For example, it makes sense to describe the width and height of the component, right? The component was placed on the top (north) of the container, but this can be changed. It makes sense to provide the location of the component inside the container. Figure 3.42 contains a bigger set of parameters for building the *NewsLineComponent*.

What else?

This was a question to you, my reader. I did not cover all the properties for a reason. I left something for you.

Exercise: Please provide your version of the set of parameters for building the *NewsLineComponent*.

It is not very difficult right now to repeat the same routine and create the set of parameters to build the *ControlComponent*. Figure 3.43 contains the set of parameters we think are sufficient to build the *ControlComponent*.

We provided component dimensions and its location in the parameters. There is also a line that points to the fact that the *ControlComponents* might have some controllable objects that can produce events.

The line in configuration file tells the container what type of event handler should be used and also provides the name of the class to handle these events. In this particular case, we decided that the *WebNewsContainer* itself will take full responsibility for event handling.

There is nothing wrong with assigning a special class to handle events. For example, we can think about an interactive version of the *NewsLineComponent*, which can be sensitive to a user's mouse clicks on the running news line. In this case, we could create a special class—for example, *NewsLineEventHandler*—to handle these events and point to this class in the configuration file.

```
<!-- Hashtable key="com.its.client.NewsLineComponent" -->
<Component name="com.its.client.NewsLineComponent">
    <parameter name="location" value="Center" />
    <parameter name="timeInMsec" value="40" />
    <parameter name="shiftInPixels" value="3" />
    <parameter name="news" value="Integration-ready
    service components and containers" />
    <parameter name="width" value="300" />
    <parameter name="height" value="24" />
</Component>
```

FIGURE 3.42

```
<!-- Hashtable key="build" (used in the container.build() method ) -->
 <build>
  <!-- Hashtable key="com.its.client.NewsLineComponent" -->
  <Component name="com.its.client.NewsLineComponent">
      <parameter name="location" value="Center" />
      <parameter name="timeInMsec" value="40" />
      <parameter name="shiftInPixels" value="3" />
      <parameter name="news" value="Integration-ready
      service components and containers" />
      <parameter name="width" value="300" />
      <parameter name="height" value="24" />
  </Component>
  <!-- Hashtable key="com.its.client.ControlComponent" -->
  <Component name="com.its.client.ControlComponent">
      <parameter name="location" value="South" />
      <parameter name="width" value="360" />
      <parameter name="height" value="50" />
      <parameter name="eventHandler" type="ActionListener"
      handler="com.its.client.WebNewsContainer" />
  </Component>
  <!-- more components -->
 </build>
```

FIGURE 3.43

Here is the line in the configuration file that we would add to the list of parameters for building the *NewsLineComponent*.

```
<Parameter name="eventHandler" type="MouseListener"
handler="NewsLineEventHandler" />
```

HOW WOULD WE USE XML-BASED PARAMETERS WHILE BUILDING COMPONENTS?

Take a look at the two sets of parameters in Figs. 3.42 and 3.43. The parameters in two sets have different names and different values. At the same time, both sets look awfully similar. Is there a pattern? Can it help us to build both components in a similar way? If so, can we create a generic *build()* method for all components? This would help us to build any number of components inside the container!

This might be too much of a leap. Let us do the next step slowly.

We need to provide information on control buttons and related actions. We pack this data into two XML elements. The *namesAndLetters* element contains button names and their abbreviations (the first letter). The *namesAndValues* element includes control button names and related URLs to retrieve data.

It is expected that the event handler (the *WebNewsContainer* was assigned to handle button events) will retrieve data from the URL associated with the pressed button. Figure 3.44 displays these two sets together.

```
<!-- abbreviations of commands -->
   <namesAndLetters>
      <abbreviation name="B" value="Business" />
      <abbreviation name="F" value="FriendsAndFamily" />
      <abbreviation name="S" value="Stocks" />
      <abbreviation name="T" value="Traffic" />
      <abbreviation name="W" value="Weather" />
      <abbreviation name="C" value="Config" />
      <abbreviation name="H" value="Help" />
   </namesAndLetters>
<!-- commands and related URLs -->
   <namesAndValues>
      <url name="Business" value="http://ipserve.com/go/web/to/
      // business" />
      <url name="FriendsAndFamily"value="
      http://ipserve.com/go/web/to/friendsAndFamily" />
      <url name="Stocks" value="http:
      // ipserve.com/go/web/to/stocks" />
      <url name="Traffic" value="http:
      // ipserve.com/go/web/to/traffic" />
      <url name="Weather" value="Weather" />
      <url name="Config" value="config.xml" />
      <url name="Help" value="Inline data: B-Business, F-Friends/
      Family, S-Stock, T-Traffic, C-Config, and W-Weather." />
   </namesAndValues>
```

FIGURE 3.44

We can clearly see that components have some common behavior, at least from the container's point of view. The container tends to treat them in a similar way.

How can we capitalize on these commonalities? We create the *ServiceComponent* interface that collects all common features for all current and future service components and allows a container to govern components through this interface.

Figure 3.45 demonstrates the *ServiceComponent* source. The *ServiceComponent* is the common base for all service components. The *ServiceComponent* interface includes several methods that must be implemented by service components.

The *build()* method that accepts a *Hashtable* of parameters is going to be responsible for constructing a component. The *service()* method also requires a *Hashtable* of parameters and is expected to provide some component services. The *getEventSources()* method returns a *Hashtable* of internal components—for example, buttons—that can be sources of events.

This method helps to free components from any knowledge of their container by moving the entire event-handling business to the container.

How can we do this if event sources—for example, control buttons—belong to the component?

Free Components from Any Knowledge of Their Container

Components will lose event-handling responsibilities and become even lighter. The container will supervise more generic functionality and will become a bit bigger, a move in the right

```
// ServiceComponent

package com.its.util; // Internet Technology School, Inc. (ITS)

import java.util.Hashtable;

/**
 * ServiceComponent interface
 * @author Jeff.Zhuk@JavaSchool.com
 */
 public interface ServiceComponent {
 /**
 * The build() method is to build a service component
 * @param container where this service component is located
 * @param parameters
 */
    public void build(Hashtable parameters);
 /**
 * The service() method is defined to satisfy a wide variety of services
 * @param parameters
 * @return result an optional return value
 */
    public Hashtable service(Hashtable parameters);
 /**
 * The getEventSources() method is defined to satisfy
 a wide variety of services
 * @return sources of events if any or null
 */
    public Hashtable getEventSources();
}
```

FIGURE 3.45

direction. Shift generic functions from multiple components to a container and give the components the luxury of focusing on component-specific business functions while the container takes care of common problems.

The hierarchy of service component classes enables us to create new service components that implement the *ServiceComponent* interface.

Now we can apply this advantage when building new service components.

Generally speaking, the process of creating a new object in Java is simple:

```
ClassName object = new ClassName();
```

All service components (even those of different classes) implement the same *ServiceComponent* interface. With this in mind, we rewrite the line above as:

```
ServiceComponent object = new SpecificServiceComponent();
```

The *SpecificServiceComponent* is one of the components that implement the *ServiceComponent* interface.

We already know that the configuration file can include definitions for several service components. How can we build new service component objects based on these definitions?

One alternative for creating different objects based on configuration file definitions can be the following code:

```
String specificServiceComponenClassName = parameters.get("className");
ServiceComponent object = null;
If(className.equals("specificServiceComponentClassName")) {
      object = new SpecificServiceComponentClassName();
} else if(className.equals("AnotherSpecificServiceComponent
ClassName")) {
      object = new AnotherSpecificServiceComponentClassName();
} else if(..........................
```

If you think this is good code, think again.

Whenever you see *if-else* "layers and stairs," look for code improvements. In our case, this is possible and even necessary.

A single line with the powerful *Class.forName()* Java method replaces multiple *if-else* cases when we need to create a new object, often one unknown at the time the code is written.

Here is the line:

```
ServiceComponent object = (ServiceComponent)
Class.forName(parameters.get("className")).newInstance();
```

Note that we need to *cast* the object to *(ServiceComponent)*. We also *must* frame this line with *try-catch* statements, as there is no guarantee that the class will be found to be the Java *ClassLoader*, which will result in the *ClassNotFoundException* being thrown.

Where will the *ClassLoader* look for a class to be loaded? In all the places (folders and archives) specified in the CLASSPATH environment variable.

The *WebNewsContainer* Class

That was a long introduction to code review. Figure 3.46 shows the beginning of the *WebNewsContainer* class. The declaration of the class promises to implement the *ActionListener* interface. There are a couple of new faces on the list of properties of the class. The *ServiceConnector* object will help us to invoke (almost) any methods on any service objects. We discuss the *ServiceConnector* class here and elaborate more in the following chapters.

Whether It's an Applet or an Application, the *WebNewsContainer* Will Perform the Same Duties According to Its XML Configuration

There will be a slight difference in networking, however. A Java applet can only communicate to its own server, whereas a Java application has no such restrictions and can access a local file system as well as the Internet.

The application flag helps us to easily distinguish and encapsulate this networking behavior into the *readTextFile()* method.

The *init()* method of the class provides access to an XML configuration file. The Web browser would invoke the *init()* method with no arguments if this class ran as a Java applet.

In this case, the *init()* method would intercept the URL to the configuration file as an applet "parameter" in the HTML page (Fig. 3.40). In the case of the Java application, the URL to the configuration file would be provided in the *main()* method of the *WebNewsComponent* class.

```
// WebNewsContainer

package com.its.client; // Internet Technology School, Inc. (ITS)

import java.lang.reflect.Method;
import java.applet.Applet;
import java.util.*;
import java.awt.*;
import java.awt.event.*
;
import com.its.util.IOMaster;
import com.its.util.Stringer;
import com.its.util.ServiceConnector;
import com.its.util.ServiceComponent;

/**
 * WebNewsContainer can be an applet or an application
 * The init() and configure() methods provide access to XML descriptor in
 * the configuration file
 * Uses Stringer.parse(xml) to interpret XML descriptor into a set of
 * (Hashtable) parameters
 * The build() method uses "build" config parameters to build multiple
 * service components and resize the container
 * The dispatch() method uses "dispatch" config parameters to dispatch
 * services
 * @author Jeff.Zhuk@JavaSchool.com
 */
public class WebNewsContainer
  extends Applet // this code can be invoked by a web browser that serves
                 //  as an applet container implements ActionListener
                 //  must implement actionPerformed() method
    {
    public static boolean debug = true;
    private int width = 400; // default width; replaced by a configuration
                             //  parameter
    private int height = 60; // default height; replaced by a configuration
                             //  parameter
    private ServiceConnector connector = new ServiceConnector();
    // component register and service connector
    private Hashtable parameters; // describing "build" and "dispatch"
                                  //  behavior
    private boolean application = false; // default is Applet mode
/**
 * init() method is called by a web browser when applet just started
 * The method uses applet.getParameter() method to read urlToConfigFile
 * parameter from the html page
 * Then it calls for configure(urlToConfigFile) method that reads the
 *  configuration file
 **/
    public void init() {
        String urlToConfigFile = getParameter("configFile");
        configure(urlToConfigFile);
    }
```

FIGURE 3.46

```
/**
 * configure(String url) method reads XML descriptor from the configuration
 * file
 * Then it calls for build() method that uses the descriptor to fill the
 * containier with components
 */
   public void configure(String urlToConfigFile) {
       String config = readTextFile(urlToConfigFile);
       if(config == null || config.startsWith("ERROR")) {
                  System.out.println("WebNewsContainer:urlToConfigFile=" +
                  urlToConfigFile + " info=" + config);
         return;
       }
       Hashtable parameters = Stringer.parse(config);
       parameters = (Hashtable)parameters.get("WebNewsContainer");
       build(parameters);
   }
/**
 * The readTextFile() method uses IOMaster to deliver data from the web
 * or from the file
 * The method checks for the application flag to use a proper delivery
 * method
 * @param url
 * @return data
 */
   public String readTextFile(String url) {
 if(application) {
       return IOMaster.readTextFile(url);
 }
 return IOMaster.readTextFile(this, url);
 }
```

FIGURE 3.46. (*cont.*)

The Java applet, as well as the Java application, calls the *configure()* method and passes this URL as an argument to the method. The *configure()* method in its turn calls the *readTextFile()* method, which uses the *IOMaster.readFromTextFile()* utility and passes the URL as an argument. The utility reads the configuration file and returns it as a Java String.

The *Stringer.parse(xml)* method then interprets any XML descriptors into a set of *Hashtable*-based parameters, and finally, the *build()* method uses the parameters to build multiple service components and resize the container.

The *Stringer.parse(xml)* method can be found in Appendix 3.

Describe Component Properties and Methods' Behavior!

Figure 3.47 contains the *build()* method of the *WebNewsContainer* class. This is where the magic happens.

The *build()* method accepts a *Hashtable* with at least several groups of parameters. The *build()* method extracts container dimensions and a group of parameters that describe the *build()* method's behavior and lists service components with their properties.

```
/**
 * build() method creates all service components according to a
 * configuration file descriptor
 * Then it adds component-services to the container
 * @param parameters
 */
    public void build(Hashtable parameters) {
        this.parameters = parameters;
        setLayout(new BorderLayout());
        try {
            // get width and height for the container
            width = Integer.parseInt( (String) parameters.get("width") );
            height = Integer.parseInt( (String) parameters.get("height") );
        } catch(Exception e) {
 System.out.println("WebNewsContainer.build:default.width=" + width + "
 heght=" + height);
            // do nothing; default width and height can be uused
        }
        // get all components to be build
        Hashtable buildParametersForAllComponents  =(Hashtable)
        parameters.get("build"); // name, Hashtable
        if(buildParametersForAllComponents == null) {
            // we are in trouble; something wrong with the config file
            System.out.println("ERROR!WebNewsContainer. build:Check
            configuration parameters. ");
            return;
        }
        Enumeration keys = buildParametersForAllComponents. keys();
        // component names
        while(keys.hasMoreElements()) {
            // every component has its name as the key and its Hashtable of
            //  parameters as the value
            String componentName = (String)
            keys.nextElement();
            try {
                // create a component
if(debug)
System.out.println("Create " + componentName);
                ServiceComponent component = (Service Component)
                Class.forName(componentName). newInstance();
                // store the component
                connector.registerObject(componentName, component);

                // add the component to the container
                Hashtable componentParameters = (Hashtable)
                buildParametersForAllComponents. get(componentName);
                String location = (String)componentParameters.
                get("location");
```

FIGURE 3.47

```
                add(location, (Component)component);
                // initialize the component
                component.build(parameters);
                // the component will extract necessary parameters

                // Check for possible sources of events
                Hashtable sources = component.getEventSources();
                if(sources != null) { // still work to do: assign event
                                      // handlers to event sources
                         assignEventHandlers(sources);
  }
            } catch(Exception e) {
                // try to survive without "not found" or troubled component
 if(debug)
 System.out.println("ERROR:" + e);
                continue;
            }
        }
        setSize(width, height);
        setVisible(true);
    }
```

Figure 3.47. *(cont.)*

The *build()* method expects a *Hashtable* with keys that contain service component names and values containing a nested *Hashtable* with the component parameters.

What if the configuration file is damaged or incomplete?

The width and height parameters are not so critical, and we can use defaults in the worst case; but we are in trouble if the whole *build* portion of the parameters disappears. Hopefully, there is a key that equals *build* in the big *Hashtable* of parameters and *parameters.get("build")* extracts this portion as a smaller *Hashtable* object.

Let us take a look again at Fig. 3.43, which describes service components.

There we find multiple component descriptions. Can we say "multiple" about two components? Every service component is described with a key that equals the class name of the service component and a value represented by a *Hashtable* object with component parameters.

The Container Knows Nothing about Component Specifics

The container only deals with the *ServiceComponent* interface.

The container creates service component objects and builds them in a unified way. All the program needs to do is to extract component names from parameters, then try to load a proper class and create a proper object of this class at run-time.

Here we can find a new appreciation for our design, because it allows us to act in a unified manner with all service components. After creating a service component object, the program registers the object with the *ServiceConnector*, invokes the *build()* method of this object, adds this object to a proper container location, and turns to another service component. Done!

Of course, every service component has its specific implementation of the *build()* method and knows what parameters to expect and what to do with them. We consider these (almost trivial) details in examples of the *build()* methods belonging to the *NewsLineComponent* and the *ControlComponent*.

After the *ServiceConnector* has registered the components, it is ready to invoke necessary methods on these service objects.

How Can We Assign Event Handlers to Potential Sources of Events?

At the end of the loop, we perform one more procedure: we check to determine whether the component needs event handling. This question is answered by the *getEventSources()* method of the service component that we are currently building. The *getEventSources()* is one of the interface methods that all service components must implement.

Remove Hard-Coded Behavior from the *dispatch()* Method

If the resulting answer is not null, the container will arrange event handling via the *assignEventHandlers()* method presented in Fig. 3.48.

The *assignEventHandlers()* method reads XML parameters describing a type and the class name of the event handler.

Here is an example of an XML element that describes event-handler characteristics:

```
    <parameter name="eventHandler" type="ActionListener"
handler="com.its.client.WebNewsContainer"/>
```

Now we need to find out what event sources are available at the specified component and provide a specified handler object for every such event source.

The code example provided in Fig. 3.48 is currently looking for several types of sources and related object handlers, and it can be extended with the help of the Java reflection package.

EVENT-HANDLING PROCEDURE

The configuration file in our example points to the container as an event-handler object. Expected events are related to the control buttons in our example. Each button is associated with some URL, and every click will change information displayed by the *NewsLineComponent*.

This part of the configuration file is presented in Fig. 3.49.

There are two XML elements described there: *namesAndLetters* and *namesAndValues*.

The *namesAndLetters* XML element relates button abbreviation labels to their names, whereas the *namesAndValues* XML element relates control names to their informational channels—URLs.

When one of the buttons is pressed, the *actionPerformed()* method of the container is executed. Figure 3.50 shows the *actionPerformed()* and *dispatch()* methods.

The *actionPerformed()* method uses both XML elements, *namesAndLetters* and *namesAndValues*, to get the proper channel and retrieve related information (using the internal *readTextFile()* method). The *actionPerformed()* method passes new information to the *dispatch()* method, which propagates this data to selected components.

The selected components and what they will do with this data are not defined in the *dispatch()* method. Surprised? We do not want to hard code this important information.

```
/*
 * The assignEventHandlers() method reads config parameters and uses
 * component event sources to assign handlers
 * @param sources
 */
public void assignEventHandlers(Hashtable sources) throws Exception {
   Hashtable eventHandler = (Hashtable) sources.get("eventHandler");
   String typeOfEventHandler = (String)eventHandler. get("type");
   String handlerClass = (String)eventHandler. get("handler");
   sources.remove("eventHandler");

   // Assign this container as the event handler
   String thisClassName = getClass().getName();

   // check if THIS class must be a handler
   boolean newHandlerNeeded = false;
   Object handlerObject = this; // THIS class is a handler by default
   if(!thisClassName.equals(handlerClass)) {
      newHandlerNeeded = true;
      if(typeOfEventHandler.equals("ActionListener")) {
        ActionListener handler = (ActionListener) Class.forName
        (handlerClass).newInstance();
         handlerObject = (ActionListener)handler;
   } else if(typeOfEventHandler.equals("MouseListener")) {
         handlerObject = (MouseListener) Class.forName
         (handlerClass).newInstance();
   }
}
for(Enumeration keys = sources.keys(); keys.hasMoreElements();) {
      String eventSourceName = (String) keys.nextElement();
      String[] typeAndName = Stringer.split(" ", eventSourceName);
                          // for example: "Button Traffic"
                          // The code example below can be extended
                          // with the help of reflection package
      if(typeAndName[0].equals("Button")) {
         Button source = (Button) sources.get(eventSourceName);
         source.addActionListener((ActionListener)handlerObject);
  } else if(typeAndName[0].equals("Panel")) {
     Panel source = (Panel) sources.get(eventSourceName);
     source.addMouseListener((MouseListener)handlerObject);
  }
 }
}
```

FIGURE 3.48

WHAT IS THE *DISPATCH*() METHOD FOR AND HOW DO WE DEFINE ITS FUNCTION?

I mentioned before that the XML descriptor in the configuration file contains definitions of the behavior (not just the properties!) for the *build*() method as well as the *dispatch*() method of the *WebNewsContainer*.

```
<!-- abbreviations of commands -->
 <namesAndLetters>
    <abbreviation name="B" value="Business" />
    <abbreviation name="F" value="FriendsAndFamily" />
    <abbreviation name="S" value="Stocks" />
    <abbreviation name="T" value="Traffic" />
    <abbreviation name="W" value="Weather" />
    <abbreviation name="C" value="Config" />
    <abbreviation name="H" value="Help" />
 </namesAndLetters>
<!-- commands and related URLs -->
 <namesAndValues>
    <url name="Business" value="http://ipserve.com/go/web/to/business" />
    <url name="FriendsAndFamily" value="http://ipserve.com/go/web/to/
    friendsAndFamily" />
    <url name="Stocks" value="http://ipserve.com/go/web/to/stocks"/>
    <url name="Traffic" value="http://ipserve.com/go/web/to/traffic" />
    <url name="Weather" value="Weather" />
    <url name="Config" value="config.xml" />
    <url name="Help" value="Inline data: B-Business, F-Friends/Family,
    S-Stock, T-Traffic, C-Config, and W-Weather." />
 </namesAndValues>
```

FIGURE 3.49

Remove Hard-Coded Behavior from the *dispatch()* Method

We do not want to hard code behavior anymore. As we allow multiple (and unknown) service components, we need to allow multiple (and unknown) dispatch actions. This can be provided with the "dispatch" portion of the configuration file (the second one).

Here is what we do with this portion as extracted from the main *Hashtable* of parameters. The dispatch *Hashtable* (like the "build" portion) contains keys that equal service components, as well as names and values that equal the names of service methods to be executed. The *dispatch()* method uses the *ServiceConnector* object to execute the proper methods on selected components. The *ServiceConnector* checks to determine whether the service component object was already registered, and if so, will reuse the component. If not, the *ServiceConnector* will try to create a new service component from scratch (using the *Class.forName()* method), then execute the proper method.

A complete example of the configuration file is shown in Fig. 3.51. The last portion of the configuration file includes a sequence of dispatched services.

The *dispatch()* method of the container reads and performs these instructions. First, it will invoke the *service()* method on the *ControlComponent* object. This method will use the name of a button pressed by a user to find the proper URL for the news channel and retrieve text from this URL.

Then, according to the configuration file, the second dispatched service will be executed. The *service()* method will be invoked on the *NewsLineComponent* object. This method will reset the *NewsLineComponent* with the new information.

We can add more service components and dispatch more services by extending the configuration file without changing the core code. For example, we can add a line that invokes

```
/**
* actionPerformed() method is to handle action events
* In this case the method is called when a user presses any of control buttons
* @param actionEvent to be used to figure out which button was pressed
*/
   public void actionPerformed(ActionEvent actionEvent) {
Hashtable namesAndLetters = (Hashtable) parameters.get("namesAndLetters");
Hashtable namesAndValues = (Hashtable) parameters.get("namesAndValues");
String command = actionEvent.getActionCommand(); // first letter
String name = (String)namesAndLetters.get(command);
String url = (String)namesAndValues.get(name);

String newInformation = url; // can be Inline data
Hashtable newsParameters = new Hashtable();
newsParameters.put(name, newInformation);

// read from the web/file if not inline data like HELP
if(!url.startsWith("Inline data:")) {
   newInformation = updateNews(newsParameters);
}
newsParameters.put(name, newInformation);
dispatch(newsParameters); // change information channel and provide
                          // specified services!
   }
/**
 * dispatch() method retrieves information from a specific channel
 * and invokes service methods on components according to the XML
 * parameters
 * @param newsParameters
 * @return dispatchParameters not used in this implementation
 */
   public Hashtable dispatch(Hashtable newsParameters) {
       // get all component names and related methods to dispatch services
       Hashtable dispatchParameters = (Hashtable) parameters.
       get("dispatch");
       Enumeration keys = dispatchParameters.keys();
       while(keys.hasMoreElements()) {
           String componentName = (String)keys.nextElement();
           String action = (String)dispatchParameters.get(componentName);

           // pass newsParameters to a selected method of a proper component
          connector.act(componentName, action, newsParameters);
       }
       return dispatchParameters;
   }
```

FIGURE 3.50

```
<?xml version = "1.0" encoding = "UTF-8"?>
 <WebNewsContainer width="400" height="200">
   <!-- abbreviations of commands -->
      <namesAndLetters>
         <abbreviation name="B" value="Business" />
         <abbreviation name="F" value="FriendsAndFamily" />
         <abbreviation name="S" value="Stocks" />
         <abbreviation name="T" value="Traffic" />
         <abbreviation name="W" value="Weather" />
         <abbreviation name="C" value="Config" />
         <abbreviation name="H" value="Help" />
      </namesAndLetters>
   <!-- commands and related URLs -->
      <namesAndValues>
         <url name="Business" value="http://ipserve.com/go/web/to/business"/>
         <url name="FriendsAndFamily" value="http://ipserve.com/go/web/to/
         friendsAndFamily" />
         <url name="Stocks" value="http://ipserve.com/go/web/to/stocks" />
         <url name="Traffic" value="http://ipserve.com/go/web/to/traffic" />
         <url name="Weather" value="Weather" />
         <url name="Config" value="config.xml" />
         <url name="Help" value="Inline data: B-Business, F-Friends/Family,
         S-Stock, T-Traffic, C-Config, and W-Weather." />
      </namesAndValues>
 <!-- Hashtable key="build" (used in the container.build()method ) -->
 <build>
  <!-- Hashtable key="com.its.client.NewsLineComponent" -->
  <Component name="com.its.client.NewsLineComponent">
      <parameter name="location" value="Center" />
      <parameter name="timeInMsec" value="40" />
      <parameter name="shiftInPixels" value="3" />
      <parameter name="news" value="Integration-ready service components
       and containers" />
      <parameter name="width" value="300" />
      <parameter name="height" value="24" />
  </Component>
  <!-- Hashtable key="com.its.client.ControlComponent" -->
  <Component name="com.its.client.ControlComponent">
      <parameter name="location" value="South" />
      <parameter name="width" value="360" />
      <parameter name="height" value="50" />
      <parameter name="eventHandler" type="ActionListener"
handler="com.its.client.WebNewsContainer" />
  </Component>
  <!-- more components -->
 </build>
 <!-- Hashtable key="dispatch" (used in the container.dispatch() method ) -->
 <dispatch>
  <Component name="com.its.client.ControlComponent" value="service" />
  <Component name="com.its.client.NewsLineComponent" value="service" />
 </dispatch>
</WebNewsContainer>
```

FIGURE 3.51

a service with voice support to the dispatch portion so that we can listen to the news. Chapter 4 considers voice support and demonstrates this extension.

Note the long component class names used in the configuration file. The names include the full paths to the classes (including all package names). This is not necessary, but it simplifies the work that the *ClassLoader* does when looking for classes. This is especially important in resource-limited environments like J2ME.

The *updateNews()* method is demonstrated in Fig. 3.52. This method uses the *readTextFile()* facilities to update information according to URL parameters.

Figure 3.53 provides an example of the *main()* method of the container as well as the *setApplication()* method that is used by the *main()* method.

In the *main()* method, we create a *WebNewsContainer* object and place it into a newly created frame. The *WebNewsContainer* is a *java.awt.Panel* type of object because it extends

```
/**
 * The updateNews() method retrieves news data from a selected channel
 * (URL) or channels
 * @param parameters
 * @return newInformation
 */
    public String updateNews(Hashtable parameters) {
        String pattern = "Inline data: ";
        // one or more Hashtable entries
        Enumeration keys = parameters.keys();

        String newInformation = "News: ";
        // there is only one news-channel associated with each control
        // button in the example
        while(keys.hasMoreElements()) { // theoretically we could allow
                                         // several key-channels at once
            String name = (String)keys.nextElement();
            String url = (String)parameters.get(name);

            // retrieve info
            newInformation += name + " : ";
            if(url.startsWith(pattern) ) {
                newInformation += url.substring(pattern.length());
            } else {
                String data = readTextFile(url);
                if(data == null || data.startsWith ("ERROR")) {
                    data = "No " + name + " information found.
                    Possible network problem.";
                }
                newInformation += data;
            }
        }
        return newInformation; // might be multiple news channels
    }
```

FIGURE 3.52

```
/**
 * The setApplication() method sets the application flag
 * @param flag
 */
    public void setApplication(boolean flag) {
     application = flag;
 }
/**
 * main() method is to test WebNewsContainer as an application
 * @param args used as a parameter for urlToConfig
 */
    public static void main(String[] args) {
        String urlToConfigFile = "config.xml"; // example is presented
        if(args != null && args.length > 0) {
            urlToConfigFile = args[0];
        }
        // create a frame replacing a frame of a web browser when applet
        // is running
        Frame f = new Frame();
        // create and show a container with newsLine
        // WebNewsContainer is a awt.Panel as Applet extends awt.Panel
        WebNewsContainer webNewsContainer = new WebNewsContainer();
        webNewsContainer.setApplication(true); // set the application flag
        webNewsContainer.configure(urlToConfigFile);
        f.add(webNewsContainer);
        f.setSize(400,100);
        f.setVisible(true);
    }
}
```

FIGURE 3.53

the *java.applet.Applet* that in its turn extends the *java.awt.Panel*. To clearly acknowledge that this is an application, we use the *setAppliaction()* method that sets the application flag to true.

As soon as we invoke the *configure()* method, the container reads the configuration file and starts to behave.

We hope it behaves well. Keep in mind that its behavior depends on the configuration file and service components.

Every service component is specific.

Now is the time to review service components.

Figure 3.54 contains the beginning of the *NewsLineComponent* class. The class implements the *ServiceComponent* and the *Runnable* interface. The beginning of the *NewsLineComponent* class defines default values that will (hopefully) be replaced at run-time by parameters from the configuration file. The *Hashtable namesAndValues* is ready to store these parameters (passed via the *build()* method).

When it comes to implementation of its *build()* and *service()* methods, every service component is very specific and knows exactly what parameters to expect and what to do with them. Figure 3.55 demonstrates the *build()* method of the *NewsLineComponent*.

```
// NewsLineComponent

package com.its.client; // Internet Technology School, Inc. (ITS)

import java.awt.*;
import java.util.*;
import com.its.util.ServiceComponent;

/**
 * NewsLineComponent gets a news line and runs it with a
 predefined speed
 * @author Jeff.Zhuk@JavaSchool.com
 */
public class NewsLineComponent
  extends Panel // The news line will be moving from left to right inside
                // the panel
  implements Runnable, // this code MUST implement run() method to run
                       // a thread with moving news line
  ServiceComponent // promise to implement build(),
                   // service(), and getEventSources() methods
    {
    public static boolean debug = true; // turns on debug printing to the console

    private int msec = 40; // default time to sleep in msec that defines
                           // moving speed
    private int shiftX = 3; // the newsline is shifted 3 pixels left each
                            //  run cycle
    private Thread thread;  // this thread with its run() method makes news moving
    private String news = "NewsLineComponent example.
    Integration-Ready Systems, " +
            "Jeff Zhuk, Cambridge University Press";
    private int x=0, y=15;  // NewsLine starting point
    private int offsetX=20; // offset of the NewsLine rectangle inside a container
    private int width = 300; // default width
    private int height = 24; // default height
    private Font font = new Font("Ariel",Font.BOLD, 12);
    private FontMetrics fm; // defined run-time based on the font properties
    private int lengthOfNewsLineInPixels; // calculated run-time based on
                                          // font metrics
    private Image newsLineImage = null; // off-screen image to draw newsline
    private boolean thread_stop = false;
    // this flag is checked in the loop of the run() method
    private int counter = 0;  // this counter is used to check performance
    private Hashtable parameters; // parameters from the configuration file

    public NewsLineComponent() {} // empty default constructor
```

FIGURE 3.54

The *build()* method stores the *Hashtable* of parameters. The *NewsLineComponent*, like other service components, has no specific knowledge, no coupling to the *WebNewsContainer*.

The same is true when we look from the opposite direction. The *WebNewsContainer* does not contain specific code that depends on service component internals. The container handles all service components in a unified way, because they are all *ServiceComponent* interfaces. This opens unlimited possibilities for integrating such service components into such containers.

```
/**
* the build() method builds a GUI (based on the config file)
* @param allParameters
*/
 public void build(Hashtable allParameters) {
 Hashtable buildParameters = (Hashtable) allParameters.get("build");
 if(buildParameters ==  null) {
          System.out.println("ERROR!NewsLineComponent.
          build:check parameters?!");
          return;
      }
// extract parameters that belong to the component
parameters = (Hashtable)buildParameters.get (getClass().getName());
      if(parameters == null) {
          System.out.println("ERROR!NewsLineComponent.
          build:check parameters?!");
          return;
      }
      // The NewsLineComponent potentially can have MouseListener type
      // event handler
      // The container will arrange event handling in this case
      // retrieve more parameters from the Hashtable
      try {
          news = (String) parameters.get("news");
          width = Integer.parseInt( (String) parameters.get("width"));
          height = Integer.parseInt( (String) parameters.get("height"));
          msec = Integer.parseInt( (String) parameters.get("timeInMsec"));
          shiftX = Integer.parseInt( (String) parameters.get
          ("shiftInPixels") );
      } catch (Exception e) {
          // do nothing; default parameters will be used instead
          // just print the exception message for troubleshooting
          System.out.println("Error!NewsLineComponent.build: " + e);
      }
      setSize(width, height);
      setVisible(true);
      setFont(font);
      fm = this.getFontMetrics(font);
      lengthOfNewsLineInPixels = fm.stringWidth(news); // calculate total
                                                        // NewsLine length
      x = width - offsetX;
      thread = new Thread(this);  // create a thread and start running
      thread.start();
   }
```

FIGURE 3.55

The *build()* method of the service component takes a *Hashtable* of parameters and extracts the specific parameters that it needs.

The traditional methods of the *NewsLineComponent* class are shown in Fig. 3.56. The methods *stop()*, *start()*, *run()*, *drawLineOffScreen()*, *update()*, *paint()*, and *reset()* have not changed since our previous version.

```
/**
* This method will be called by a container to stop the thread
 */
    public void stop() {
        thread_stop = true;
    }
/**
 * This method will be called by a container to start a thread
 */
     public void start() {
        if(thread_stop == true){
            thread.start();
            thread_stop = false;
        }
    }
/**
 * running a thread
 **/
    public void run() {
        while(!thread_stop) {
            try  {
                thread.sleep(msec);  // in msec, in this example = 40 msec
            } catch (InterruptedException ie) {
               System.out.println("Clock.run:" + ie);
            }
            if(!isShowing()) { // first run cycle
                counter++;
            } else if(newsLineImage == null) {
                if(counter >= 0) {
if(debug)
System.out.println("NewsLineComponent.run.component drawing is
completed:counter=" + counter);
                    newsLineImage = createImage(width-offsetX, height);
                    counter = 0;
                }
                counter--;
            }
            if(!isShowing() || newsLineImage == null) {
                continue;
            }
if(debug && counter != 0)  {
System.out.println("NewsLineComponent.run.off-screen image is
completed:Counter=" + counter);
counter = 0;
}
            drawLineOffScreen(newsLineImage. getGraphics());
            // draw newsline image in memory repaint();
            // place this image on the page x -= shiftX;
            // shift text left
            if( x < (0 - lengthOfNewsLineInPixels) ) {// start new scan
                x = width;
```

FIGURE 3.56

```
            }
        }
    }
 /**
  * drawLineOffScreen() method prepares graphics in memory
  * This preparation significantly saves painting time
  * @param g
  */
    public synchronized void drawLineOffScreen(Graphics g){
        if(g == null)
            return;
        // draw newsline
        g.setColor(Color.gray);
        g.fillRect(0,0, width - offsetX, height);
        g.setColor(Color.orange);
        g.drawString(news, x, y);
    }
 /**
  * update() as well as paint() is one of JVM system methods
  * standard update() would clean paint area before calling paint()
  * drawLineOffScreen() method redraw full rectangle, so no need in another
  * cleaning process
  * by overriding update() we avoid extra cleaning that would create
  * flickering effect
  * @param g
  */
    public void update(Graphics g) {
        paint(g);
    }
 /**
  * paint() is called by JVM to refresh the screen
  * It will place the NewsLine image (prepared in memory) on the page
  * @param g
  */
    public void paint(Graphics g) {
        if(newsLineImage != null) {
            g.drawImage(newsLineImage, offsetX, 0, this);
        }
    }
 /**
  * reset() method is to reset the news information
  * @param news
  */
    public void reset(String news) {
        x = width;
        this.news = news;
        FontMetrics fm = this.getFontMetrics(font);
        lengthOfNewsLineInPixels = fm.stringWidth(news);
        // calculate total NewsLine length
    }
```

FIGURE 3.56. ***(cont.)***

```
/**
 * service() method is to reset the news information
 * @param newsParameters
 * @return newsParameters
 */
    public Hashtable service(Hashtable newsParameters) {
     // a name of a button is a single key of the Hashtable
        Enumeration keys = newsParameters.keys();
        String name = (String)keys.nextElement();
        String newsData = (String)newsParameters.get(name);
        if(newsData != null) {
            reset(newsData);
        }
        return newsParameters;
    }
/**
 * The getEventSources() method is defined to return an array of
 * components, possible event sources
 * @return components or null
 */
    public Hashtable getEventSources() {
        Hashtable eventHandler = (Hashtable) parameters.get("eventHandler");
        if(eventHandler == null) {// no need to handle this component
              return null;
        }
        Hashtable sources = new Hashtable();
        sources.put("eventHandler", eventHandler);
        sources.put("Panel", this);
        return sources;
    }
} // end of the NewsLineComponent class
```

FIGURE 3.57

The *service()* and *getEventSources()* methods are demonstrated in Fig. 3.57. The *service()* method takes new information parameters and updates the running line facilities with this information. The *getEventSources()* method checks to determine whether the configuration file includes event-handler instructions for the *NewsLineComponent*. If it does, the method creates a *Hashtable* of parameters and fills it with configuration file instructions. Then the method puts *this* component object into the *Hashtable*, providing the *Panel* key for this object. This gives the container a hint that the source of events is the component itself, which is a *java.awt.Panel*. The *getEventSources()* method returns null if the configuration file has no instructions for event handling for the component. Otherwise, the method returns the *Hashtable* filled with the information described above.

PROVIDE THE POSSIBILITY OF INTERACTIVE COMPONENTS (EVENT HANDLING)

We envision (somewhere in the future) that the *NewsLineComponent* could behave interactively. For example, users will be able to click on the moving line, and there will be some event handler to interpret this action.

```
// ServiceComponentMouseListener

package com.its.util; // Internet Technology School, Inc. (ITS)

import java.awt.event.MouseAdapter;
import com.its.util.ServiceComponent;

/**
 * ServiceComponentMouseListener is to model mouse handler for service
 * components
 * @author Jeff.Zhuk@JavaSchool.com
 */
public class ServiceComponentMouseListener extends MouseAdapter {
    protected ServiceComponent component; // service container
/**
 * The init() method is to store a reference to a service component
 * @param component that is a source of events
 */
    public void init(ServiceComponent component) {
        this.component = component;
    }
}
```

FIGURE 3.58

We are not ready to code this handler right now. At the same time, we would like to make such extensions possible in the future without changing the *NewsLineComponent* code. The configuration file can potentially contain a key that prescribes adding an event-handler object to the *NewsLineComponent*. We can name this key *eventHandler* and provide additional parameters, such as a type (*MouseListener)* and a class name for the object handler.

This additional XML element, as presented below, will instruct the container to create a new object of the *ServiceComponentMouseListener* class and assign this object as an event handler.

```
    <parameter name="eventHandler" type="MouseListener"
handler="com.its.client.ServiceComponentMouseListener" />
```

At this point, we know nothing about the *ServiceComponentMouseListener* class. It does not exist yet! We still can provide valid code that will be able to deal with this future class when it is needed. The Model and Adapter design patterns help us here. Figure 3.58 presents a draft for this class.

Exercise: Eliminate hard coded parameters in the *NewsLineComponent* class. Add more parameters to the build portion of the configuration file related to the *NewsLineComponent* class.

Exercise: Provide another version of the *NewsLineComponent* class that uses more parameters from the configuration file.

```
// ControlComponent

package com.its.client;

import java.awt.*;
import java.awt.event.*;
import java.util.*;

import com.its.util.ServiceComponent;

/**
 * ControlComponent class is to control information flow
 */
public class ControlComponent extends Panel implements ServiceComponent {
    public static boolean debug = true; // turns on debug printing
    protected Hashtable namesAndLetters;
    // first letter = key, full name = object
    protected Hashtable namesAndButtons = new Hashtable();
    // populated after reading the config file
    protected Hashtable parameters; // shared with the container
    protected Button buttonPressed; // currently selected control button
    protected static final Color defaultBackground = Color.lightGray;
    protected static final Color defaultForeground = Color.black;
    protected static final Color selectedBackground =  Color.black;
    protected static final Color selectedForeground = Color.white;
    protected int width=300; // default
    protected int height=40; // default
```

FIGURE 3.59

THE *CONTROLCOMPONENT* CLASS DESCRIPTION

The beginning of the *ControlComponent* class is demonstrated in Fig. 3.59.

The *ControlComponent* (as well as the *NewsLineComponent)* class implements the *ServiceComponent* interface and extends the *java.awt.Panel.* The purpose of this class is to provide a user interface for user control over the applet or application functionality.

Did you notice that *protected* data are used, rather than *private* data?

There is a reason for this. This class can potentially serve as a base class for more control components like this. The *protected* data can be accessed by subclasses (even ones from different packages), whereas *private* access would prevent inheritance of this data.

Properties of this class include several *Hashtables* with key-value parameters, several colors, and a reference to the last pressed button. The pressed button changes its appearance, and when a new button is pressed, the last pressed button should be restored to its original appearance. This is the reason to keep this reference in place.

The *build()* method of this class is introduced in Fig. 3.60.

Like the *build()* method of the *NewsLineComponent*, the *build()* method of the *ControlComponent* extracts specific parameters needed for building this component from the *Hashtable* of parameters passed to the method.

```
/**
 * the build() method builds a GUI (based on the config file)
 * @param allParameters
 */
    public void build(Hashtable allParameters) {
        Hashtable buildParameters = (Hashtable) allParameters.get("build");
         if(buildParameters == null) {
             System.out.println("ERROR!ControlComponent.build:check
             parameters?!");
             return;
         }
         // extract parameters that belong to the component
         parameters = (Hashtable)buildParameters.get(getClass().getName());
         if(parameters == null) {
             System.out.println("ERROR!ControlComponent.build:check
             parameters?!");
             return;
         }
         namesAndLetters = (Hashtable) allParameters.get("namesAndLetters");
         if(namesAndLetters == null) {
             System.out.println("ERROR!ControlComponent.build:check
             parameters?!");
             return;
         }
         Enumeration keys = namesAndLetters.keys();
         while(keys.hasMoreElements()) {
             String keyName = (String) keys.nextElement();
             Button button = new Button(keyName); // example: "w" - for weather
             button.setBackground(defaultBackground);
             add(button);

             // put into the namesAndButtons Hashtable  a name as a key
             // and a button as an object
             namesAndButtons.put(keyName, button);
         }
         try {
             width = Integer.parseInt( (String) parameters.get("width") );
             height = Integer.parseInt( (String) parameters.get("height") );
         } catch (Exception e) {
             // do nothing; default parameters will be used instead
             // just print the exception message for troubleshooting
             System.out.println("Error!NewsLineComponent.build: " + e);
         }
         setBackground(Color.yellow);
         setSize(width, height);
         setVisible(true);
    }
```

FIGURE 3.60

```
/**
 * service() is to visually highlight a selected button
 * and restore appearance of the last pressed button
 * @param newsParameters of the currently pressed button
 */
 public Hashtable service(Hashtable newsParameters) {
     // a name of a button is a single key of the Hashtable
       Enumeration keys = newsParameters.keys();
       String name = (String)keys.nextElement();
       // change control button appearance to highlight a selected button
       if(buttonPressed != null) {
           buttonPressed.setForeground(defaultForeground);
           buttonPressed.setBackground(defaultBackground);
       }
       if(name != null) {
           buttonPressed = (Button)namesAndButtons.get(name);
           buttonPressed.setForeground(selectedForeground);
           buttonPressed.setBackground(selectedBackground);
       }
       return newsParameters;
   }
```

FIGURE 3.61

The *namesAndLetters Hashtable* is used to create a set of control buttons. While creating the buttons, we put every button into the *namesAndButtons Hashtable*, placing a button name as the key for the button object.

The *build()* method looks for the *namesAndLetters Hashtable* in the build section of the configuration file that points to the *ControlComponent*. If there are no specific instructions there, the *build()* method gets this XML element from the general container description (this is the case in our example).

Figure 3.61 contains the *service()* method. The *service()* method of the *ControlComponent* visually highlights a selected button and restores the appearance of the button that was last pressed.

The last fragment of the *ControlComponent* class is the *getEventSources()*, displayed in Fig. 3.62.

The *getEventSources()* method checks to determine whether the configuration file includes event-hander instructions for the *ControlComponent*. If so, the method creates a *Hashtable* of parameters and fills it with configuration instructions. Then the method places all the control buttons (one by one) into the *Hashtable*, providing a unique key for each button. The key name consists of the "Button" string followed by the name of a button. This gives the container a hint that the source of events is *java.awt.Button*.

The *getEventSources()* method returns null if the configuration file has no instructions for event handling for the component. Otherwise, the method returns the *Hashtable* filled with the information described above.

```
/**
 * The getEventSources() method is defined to return an array of
 * components, possible event sources
 * @return sources or null
 */
    public Hashtable getEventSources() {
        Hashtable eventHandler = (Hashtable)
        parameters.get("eventHandler");
        if(eventHandler == null) {// no need to handle this component
            return null;
 }
 Hashtable sources = new Hashtable();
 sources.put("eventHandler", eventHandler);
 Button[] components = new Button[namesAndButtons.size()];
 Enumeration keys = namesAndButtons.keys();
 for(int i=0; keys.hasMoreElements(); i++) {
            String keyName = (String) keys.nextElement();
            // include source type="Button" and name, for example,
            // "Business"
            sources.put("Button " + keyName, (Button)
            namesAndButtons.get(keyName));
 }
 return sources;
 }
}   // end of the ControlComponent class
```

FIGURE 3.62

REUSE, NOT ABUSE

Can reuse become unnecessary overhead? Yes, it does happen. Some developers (especially beginners) tend to create *every* new class or method using an existing library. This tendency can easily become abusive.

Imagine that you buy a cup. The cup appears to be a great fit for the cup holder in your car. You use this cup in your car most of the time, so it becomes your "car cup."

Then your current project makes you stay long hours at the office, and you feel the need for coffee more and more. A beginner would tend to reuse her or his car cup, even if it is not very convenient. Experienced developers can evaluate the situation and usually make a better decision: in this case, buying a second cup. This frees their hands and minds from unnecessary hassles.

SUMMARY

In this chapter, we created a service container that does not know much about its service components. We also created service components that do not know about their container.

We used design patterns (most importantly, the Model pattern) to teach the container and the components to behave. We created a multilevel XML-based configuration file that describes how to build service components and how to dispatch their services. This is an example of a small integration-ready extensible system with configurable properties and behavior.

We used interfaces (as implemented in the Java and C- languages) to minimize exposed implementation details and the complexity of object interactions.

The Model, Adapter, Container, and Component concepts helped us to make design decisions concerning generalization and customization issues.

We moved from a common denominator container, such as a Web browser, to a more specialized (but still generic enough) application container.

We performed analysis to distinguish between common and custom features and extracted all custom information from the source code into a configuration file. (XML is just an implementation choice, and it is a good one!)

We strived to achieve code stability and reusability: we can easily change the environment, appearance, and even behavior without changing a line of code.

The application gained a great deal of flexibility, becoming an integration-ready system. This is not the end of the story, just the beginning.

Integrating Questions

1. Container: Please briefly describe your conceptual understanding of a container and provide two or three examples of software that plays a container role.
2. Configuration—the file holding all customization information; XML is just an implementation choice: Provide an example of a configuration file (four or five lines) in XML.
3. Component: What are the features that make it integration-ready? If someone gives us a Java class, how do we know that it can be used in the container? Try to define a criteria set.
4. HTML page that shows the container: What are the minimal requirements for a browser to adequately show this page?

Case Study

1. Rewrite the *service()* method of the *ControlComponent* to provide a different appearance for the selected button.
2. Include parameters that would govern the selected button's appearance in the configuration file, and rewrite the *service()* method accordingly.
3. Rewrite the *NewsLineComponent* to scroll information vertically line by line (currently, the component scrolls news horizontally). Have three to four lines visible at a time. Make sure that the number of lines and font size are configurable.
4. Modify the *NewsLineComponent* and XML configuration file to make this feature (horizontal or vertical scroll) consfigurable.
5. Describe another "reuse, not abuse" example (this time with code) from your workplace.
6. Select one of the XML references below, then research and share its current status with your peers.
7. Add at least one more XML reference to the references below; research and share its current status with your peers.

References

1. XML specification: *http://www.w3c.org/XML*.
2. Enterprise Business XML: *http://ebxml.org*.
3. Apache XML pages: *http://xml.apache.org*.
4. XML Schema specification: *http://www.w3c.org/XML/Schema*.
5. SAX specification: *http://megginson.com/SAX*.
6. DOM specification: *http://w3c.org/TR/DOM-Level-2-Core*.
7. The Apache Struts Web application framework: *http://jakarta.apache.org/struts/*.
8. Apache Cocoon project: *http://?http://xml.apache.org/cocoon/*.
9. XSL specification: *http://w3c.org/TR/XSL*.
10. XSLT specification: *http://w3c.org/TR/xslt.html*.
11. World Wide Web Consortium (W3C): *http://w3c.org*.

CHAPTER 4

Integration with Voice

I have no words, my voice is my sword.
—William Shakespeare, *Macbeth*

Why voice? Business communication is mostly about paperless paperwork, right? Computer workers like you and I stare intently at the computer screen for long hours, and by the end of the day are ready to kill the computer.

"A picture is better than a thousand words" applies only when it is not a picture of a thousand words that we read on our computer screens every day. Voice components bring some relief to our eyes and allow us to listen to text pages and even to talk back. (We talk more about speech recognition systems in Chapter 12.)

This chapter is about integration with voice components based on free, downloadable Java libraries. Voice components make even more sense in devices with small screens, or no screens at all.

The news watch is an example in which the voice component would be highly appreciated. Imagine a talking watch that delivers the news. Someone could use the screen option in a crowded place and the voice option in a better environment—for example, outdoors.

We add a voice component to the news watch at the end of this chapter. Right now, we take a closer look at synthesis technology.

What Is the Base for Creating a Voice Component?

The free text-to-speech (*FreeTTS*) library was built by the Speech Integration Group of Sun Microsystems Laboratories as the first, though not complete, implementation of the Java speech application program interface (JSAPI) [1]. The JSAPI is the real base for voice components built in Java.

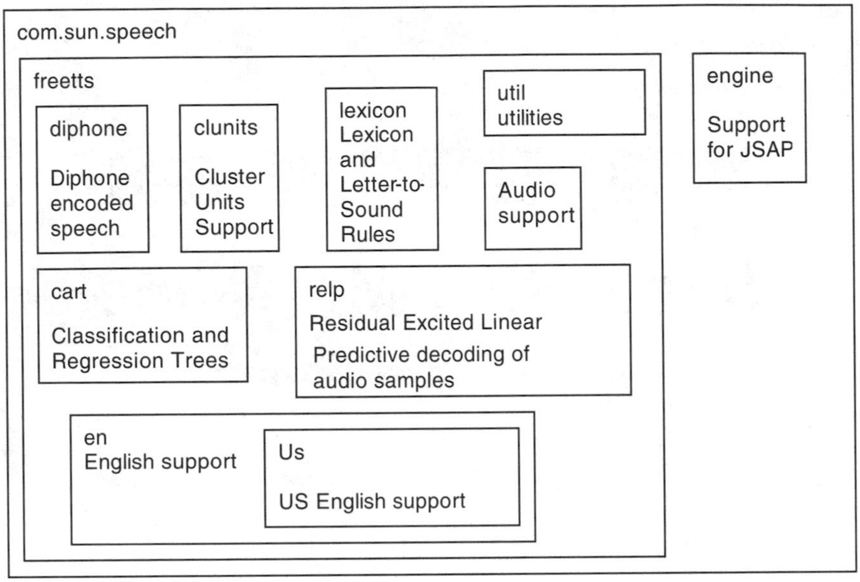

FIGURE 4.1. Free TTS Packages.

FreeTTS is based on both the Festival Speech Synthesis System [2] from the University of Edinburgh and the Flite Speech Synthesizer [3] from Carnegie Mellon University (CMU).

Festival is a general multilingual speech synthesis system written in C++ at the Centre for Speech Technology Research (CSTR) at the University of Edinburgh. Festival supports English (British and American), Spanish, and Welsh text to speech and offers an environment for development and research of speech synthesis techniques.

Flite (Festival-lite) is a small, fast run-time synthesis engine developed at CMU. Designed as an alternative synthesis engine to Festival, Flite targets embedded systems, personal digital assistants (PDAs), and smaller architectures. Figure 4.1 presents the *FreeTTS* packages as a tree inside the *com.sun.speech* package. The "*FreeTTS* Programmer's Guide" by Sun Microsystems [4] describes *FreeTTS* as two major packages: *com.sun.speech.engine* and *com.sun.speech.freetts*. The *com.sun.speech.engine* package contains support for JSAPI 1.0.

- ***com.sun.speech.engine***. This package contains support for JSAPI 1.0. Its main contents are:
- ***com.sun.speech.engine*** provides a partial support for the *javax.speech* package for JSAPI 1.0.
- ***com.sun.speech.engine.synthesis*** provides a Java Speech Markup Language (JSML) 0.6 parser as well as partial support of interfaces in the *javax.speech.synthesis* package for JSAPI 1.0.
- ***com.sun.speech.engine.synthesis.text*** provides a sample text-output-only synthesizer support that doesn't make any noise.

FreeTTS* implementation**. This package delivers real sound. *FreeTTS* synthesis engine implementation can be found in the ***com.sun.speech. freetts package and its branches.

- ***com.sun.speech.freetts.jsapi*** provides the JSAPI glue code for *FreeTTS*. The *com.sun.speech.freetts* package is broken down further into sets of subpackages as follows:

- *com.sun.speech.freetts* contains high-level interfaces and classes for *FreeTTS*. Much nonlanguage and voice-dependent code can be found here.
- *com.sun.speech.freetts.diphone* provides support for diphone-encoded speech.
- *com.sun.speech.freetts.clunits* provides support for cluster unit-encoded speech.
- *com.sun.speech.freetts.lexicon* provides definition and implementation of the lexicon and letter-to-sound rules.
- *com.sun.speech.freetts.util* provides a set of tools and utilities.
- *com.sun.speech.freetts.audio* provides audio output support.
- *com.sun.speech.freetts.cart* provides interface and implementations of several classification and regression trees (CARTs).
- *com.sun.speech.freetts.relp* provides support for residual excited linear predictive (RELP) decoding of audio samples.
- *com.sun.speech.freetts.en* contains English-specific code.
- *com.sun.speech.freetts.en.us* contains U.S. English-specific code.

Here are the main*FreeTTS* objects that work together to perform speech synthesis:

- *com.sun.speech.freetts.FreeTTSSpeakable* is an interface. Anything that is a source of text that needs to be spoken with *FreeTTS* is first converted into a *FreeTTSSpeakable*. One implementation of this interface is *FreeTTSSpeakableImpl*. This implementation will wrap the most common input forms (a String, an *InputStream*, or a JSML XML document) as a *FreeTTSSpeakable*. A *FreeTTSSpeakable* is given to a Voice to be spoken.
- **com.sun.speech.freetts.Voice** is the central processing point for *FreeTTS*. The Voice takes as input a *FreeTTS*Speakable, translates the text associated with the *FreeTTSSpeakable* into speech, and generates audio output corresponding to that speech.

The Voice is the primary customization point for *FreeTTS*. Extending the Voice can perform all language, speaker, and algorithm customizations. A Voice will accept a *FreeTTS*Speakable via the *Voice.speak* method and process it by converting a *FreeTTS*Speakable into a series of Utterances. The rules for breaking a *FreeTTS*Speakable into an Utterance are generally language dependent. For instance, an English Voice may chose to break a *FreeTTS*Speakable into Utterances based on sentence breaks.

As the Voice generates each Utterance, a series of *UtteranceProcessors* processes the Utterance. Each Voice defines its own set of *UtteranceProcessors*.

This Is the Primary Method of Customizing Voice Behavior

For instance, to change how units are joined together during the synthesis process, a Voice would simply supply a new *UtteranceProcessor* that implements the new algorithm.

Typically, each *UtteranceProcessor* will run in turn, annotating or modifying the Utterance with information. For instance, a "Phrasing" *UtteranceProcessor* may insert phrase marks into an Utterance that indicate where a spoken phrase begins. The Utterance and *Utterance-Processors* are described in more detail below.

Once all Utterance processing has been applied, the Voice sends the Utterance to the *AudioOutput UtteranceProcessor*. The *AudioOutput* processor may run in a separate thread to allow Utterance processing to overlap with audio output, ensuring the lowest sound latency possible.

com.sun.speech.freetts.Utterance

The Utterance is the central processing target in *FreeTTS*. A *FreeTTSSpeakable* is broken up into one or more Utterances, processed by a series of *UtteranceProcessors*, and finally output as audio. An Utterance consists of a set of Relations and a set of features called *FeatureSets*.

com.sun.speech.freetts.FeatureSet

A *FeatureSet* is simply a name/value pair. An Utterance can contain an arbitrary number of *FeatureSets*. *FeatureSets* are typically used to maintain global Utterance information such as volume, pitch, and speaking rate.

com.su.speech.freetts.Relation

A Relation is a named list of Items. An Utterance can hold an arbitrary number of Relations. A typical *UtteranceProcessor* may iterate through one Relation and create a new Relation.

For instance, a word normalization *UtteranceProcessor* could iterate through a token Relation and generate a word Relation based on token-to-word rules. A detailed description of the Utterance processing and how it affects the Relations in an Utterance is described below.

com.sun.speech.freetts.Item

A Relation is a list of Item objects. An Item contains a set of Features (as described previously, *FeatureSets* are merely name/value pairs). An Item can have a list of daughter Items as well. Items in a Relation are linked to Items in the same and other Relations.

For instance, the words in a word Relation are linked back to the corresponding tokens in the token Relation. Similarly, a word in a word Relation is linked to the previous and next words in the word Relation. This gives an *UtteranceProcessor* the capability of easily traversing from one Item to another.

com.sun.speech.freetts.UtteranceProcessor

An *UtteranceProcessor* is any object that implements the *UtteranceProcessor* interface. An *UtteranceProcessor* takes as input an Utterance and performs some operation on the Utterance.

How Does Speech Synthesis Work?

The *CMUVoice* describes the general processing required for an English voice without specifying how unit selection and concatenation are performed. Subclasses of the *CMUVoice* (*CMUDiphoneVoice* and *CMUClusterUnitVoice*) provide this specialization. In this section, we describe the processing performed by the *CMUDiphoneVoice*.

Processing starts with the speak method of the *com.sun.speech.freetts.Voice* object. The speak method performs the following tasks or phases of the voice synthesis:

- Tokenization
- *TokenToWords*
- *PartOfSpeechTagger*
- *Phraser*
- *Segmenter*
- *PauseGenerator*
- *Intonator*
- *PostLexicalAnalyzer*
- *Durator*

- *ContourGenerator*
- *UnitSelector*
- *PitchMarkGenerator*
- *UnitConcatenator*

Tokenization

In this step, the Voice uses the *Tokenizer* as returned from the *getTokenizer* method to break a *FreeTTSSpeakable* object into a series of Utterances.

Typically, tokenization is language specific, so each Voice needs to specify which *Tokenizer* is to be used by overriding the *getTokenizer* method.

The CMUDiphoneVoice uses the *com.sun.speech.freetts.en.TokenizerImpl* Tokenizer, which is designed to parse and tokenize the English language. A *Tokenizer* breaks an input stream of text into a series of Tokens defined by the *com.sun.speech.freetts.Token* class.

Typically, a Token represents a single word in the input stream. Additionally, a Token will include such information as the surrounding punctuation and white space and the position of the token in the input stream.

The English *Tokenizer (com.sun.speech.freetts.en.TokenizerImpl)* relies on a set of symbols being defined that specify what characters are to be considered white space and punctuation.

The *Tokenizer* defines a method called *isBreak*, which is used to determine when the input stream should be broken and a new Utterance generated. For example, the English *Tokenizer* has a set of rules to detect the end of a sentence. If the current Token should start a new sentence, the English *Tokenizer isBreak* method returns true.

A higher-level *Tokenizer*, *FreeTTSSpeakableTokenizer,* repeatedly calls the English *Tokenizer* and places each Token into a list. When the *Tokenizer isBreak* method indicates that a sentence break has occurred, the Voice creates a new Utterance with the current list of Tokens. The process of generating and processing Utterances continues until no more Tokens remain in the input.

Utterance Processing

A Voice maintains a list of *UtteranceProcessors*. Each Utterance generated by the tokenization step is run through the *UtteranceProcessors* for the Voice. Each processor receives as input the Utterance that is being processed.

The *UtteranceProcessor* may add new Relations to the Utterance, add new Items to Relations, or add new *FeatureSets* to Items or to the Utterance itself. Oftentimes, a series of *UtteranceProcessors* are tightly coupled; one *UtteranceProcessor* may add a Relation to an Utterance that is used by the *next*.

CMUVoice sets up most of the *UtteranceProcessors* used by *CMUDiphoneVoice*. *CMUVoice* provides a number of *getXXX* methods that return an *UtteranceProcessor*, such as *getUnitSelector* and *getUnitConcatenator*.

Subclasses of *CMUVoice* override these *getXXX* methods to customize the processing. For instance, the *CMUDiphoneVoice* overrides *getUnitSelector* to return a *DiphoneUnitsSelector*.

TokenToWords

The *TokenToWords UtteranceProcessor* creates a word Relation from the Token Relation by iterating through the Token Relation Item list and creating one or more words for each Token.

For most Tokens, there is a one-to-one relationship between words and Tokens. In that case, a single word Item is generated for each Token Item. Other Tokens, such as "2003," generate multiple words: "two thousand three." Each word is created as an Item and added to the word Relation. Additionally, each word Item is added as a daughter to the corresponding Token in the Token Relation.

Phraser

The *Phraser* processor creates a phrase Relation in the Utterance. The phrase Relation represents how the Utterance is to be broken into phrases when spoken. The phrase Relation consists of an Item marking the beginning of each phrase in the Utterance. This phrase Item has as its daughters the list of words that are part of the phrase.

The *Phraser* builds the phrase Relation by iterating through the word Relation created by the *TokenToWords* processor. The *Phraser* uses a phrasing CART to determine where the phrase breaks occur and creates the phrase Items accordingly.

Segmenter

The Segmenter is one of the more complex UtteranceProcessors. It is responsible for determining where syllable breaks occur in the Utterance. It organizes this information in several new Relations in the Utterance.

The *Segmenter* uses the Lexicon and the *LetterToSound* interfaces and implementations that provide the phone list for words. The *Segmenter* performs the following steps for each word in the Utterance:

- Retrieves the phones that are associated with the word and iterates through each phone of the word, adding the phone to a Relation called "Segment."
- Notes the syllable break points in a Relation called "Syllable" and marks the stressed syllable in the phone.

The *Segmenter* adds three new Relations to the Utterance that denotes the syllable structure and units for the Utterance.

PauseGenerator

The *PauseGenerator* inserts a pause at the beginning of the segment list, thus all Utterances start with a pause. It then iterates through the phrase Relation set up by the *Phraser* and inserts a pause before the first segment of each phrase.

Intonator

The *Intonator* processor adds *accent* and *endtone* features to the syllable Relation of Utterances.

This processor relies on the generic interface for CARTs: an accent CART and a tone CART. This processor iterates through each syllable in the syllable relation, applies each CART to the syllable, and sets the *accent* and *endtone* features of the Item based on the results of the CART processing.

PostLexicalAnalyzer

The *CMUDiphoneVoice* provides a *PostLexicalAnalyzer* that performs two fixes:

Fix*ah*. The *CMUDiphoneVoice* uses the CMU Lexicon that contains a number of words that reference the "*ah*" diphone. The *CMUDiphoneVoice* PostLexicalAnalyzer iterates through all phones in the segment Relation and replaces "*ah*" with "*aa*" diphones.

Fix apostrophe-s. This step looks for words associated with the segments that contain an apostrophe-s. The processor then inserts a *schwa* phoneme in certain cases.

Durator

The *Durator* adds end times to each Segment. The *Durator* uses a CART to look up the statistical average duration and standard deviation for each phone and calculates an exact duration based on the CART-derived adjustment. Each unit is finally tagged with an *"end"* attribute that indicates the time, in seconds, at which the unit should be completed.

ContourGenerator

The *ContourGenerator* adds target Relation with frequency and timing data, calculates the fundamental frequency (F0) curve for an Utterance, and uses a file of feature model terms. For example, *CMUDiphoneVoice* uses *com/sun/speech/freetts/ en/us/f0_lr_terms.txt*.

The file consists of several columns with the feature name, starting point, midpoint, and ending point for the term (in terms of relative frequency deltas) and the *ToBI* (tones and break indices) label.

UnitSelector

The *UnitSelector* creates a "unit" Relation in the Utterance. This Relation contains Items that represent the diphones(two adjacent phone names) for the unit. The *UnitSelector* adds diphones along with its timing information to the unit Relation.

PitchMarkGenerator

The *PitchMarkGenerator* adds the *LPCResult* object with stored *pitch marks* to the Utterance. Iterating through the target Relation generates the pitch marks by calculating a slope based on the desired time and F0 values for each Item in the target Relation. The resulting slope is used to calculate a series of target times for each pitch mark. These target times are stored in an *LPCResult* object that is added to the Utterance.

UnitConcatenator

The *UnitConcatenator* processor collects and concatenates the sample data. For each Item in the unit Relation (recall this was the set of diphones), the *UnitConcatenator* extracts the unit sample data from the unit based on the target times as stored in the *LPC Result*.

Lexicon and Letter-to-Sound Rules

The Lexicon maps words to their pronunciations. *FreeTTS* provides a generic lexicon interface *(com.sun.speech.freetts.lexicon)* and a specific implementation *(com.sun.speech.freetts.en.us.CMULexicon)* that provides an English language lexicon based on CMU data. The Lexicon determines the pronunciation of a word via the *Lexicon.getPhones(word)* method. It also provides the ability to add new words to the Lexicon.

The *CMULexicon* is an implementation of the Lexicon interface and contains more than 60,000 pronunciations. If a word cannot be found, the Letter-to-Sound (LTS) rules are used to convert the words into phones.

To conserve space, the *CMULexicon* has been stripped of all words that can be recreated using the LTS rules. The 60,000 pronunciations in the Lexicon can be considered exceptions to the rule.

The Lexicon data are represented in two forms: text and binary. The binary form loads much quicker than the text form and is the form generally used by *FreeTTS*. *FreeTTS* provides a method of generating the binary form of the Lexicon from the text form of the Lexicon.

Letter-to-Sound Rules

LTS rules generate a phone sequence for words that are not in the Lexicon. The LTS rules are a simple state machine, with one entry point for each letter of the alphabet.

The state machine consists of a large list of entries. There are two types of entries: a State and a Phone. A State entry contains a decision and the indices of two other entries. The first of these two indices represents where to go if the decision is true, and the second represents where to go if the decision is false. A Phone entry is the final state of the decision tree and contains the phone that should be returned.

Unit Selection

The current methods of the unit selection implemented in *FreeTTS* are diphone and cluster unit selection. Note that the unit selection is independent of the wave synthesis.

The diphone unit selection is very simple: it combines each adjacent phoneme into a pair separated by a (-). These pairs are used to look up entries in the diphone database.

The cluster unit selection works on one unit at a time, and there can be more than one instance of a unit per database. The first step in cluster unit selection determines the unit type for each unit in the Utterance. The next step is to select the best unit instance using a Viterbi algorithm wherein the cost is based on the MEL cepstrum (pronounced "kepstrum") distance between candidates. Viterbi algorithm is based on Hidden Markov Models (HMM). The algorithm looks at an observation sequence (diphone units) and tries to determine the most likely sequence of underlying hidden states that generated this observation sequence. Originally invented for characterizing the seismic echoes, cepstrum is now used for representing the human voice and musical signals by taking the Fourier transform of the decibel spectrum. Mel-cepstrum is first transformed using the Mel Frequency bands.

How Are Voice Components Coded?

First, let us plan what we want to accomplish with this component. No design without a specification, no code without design.

We outline our plan as user requirements.

The voice component will have a voice on-off control and will be able to convert text-to-speech. The single control button will indicate "on" status when it is pressed down and "off" status when it is up. Every click on the button will switch the status. The voice component should serve as an additional service component in the *WebNewsContainer*. While the *NewsLineComponent* visualizes news data, the voice component speaks the news.

With this in mind, it is time to start designing. One idea that can accelerate code delivery is that the *ControlComponent* and the *VoiceComponent* have many things in common. The *VoiceComponent* has control buttons (just one for now, but it could have more later on).

It is now amazingly easy to program this button. All we need is an additional XML element in the configuration file. We define the button in the *namesAndLetters* element that is included in the description of the voice component in the "build" part of the configuration file.

The *VoiceComponent* is a part of the service container as well as the *ControlComponent*. The container handles action events and calls the *dispatch()* method of the container that in its turn dispatches the necessary actions to selected components according to the configuration file.

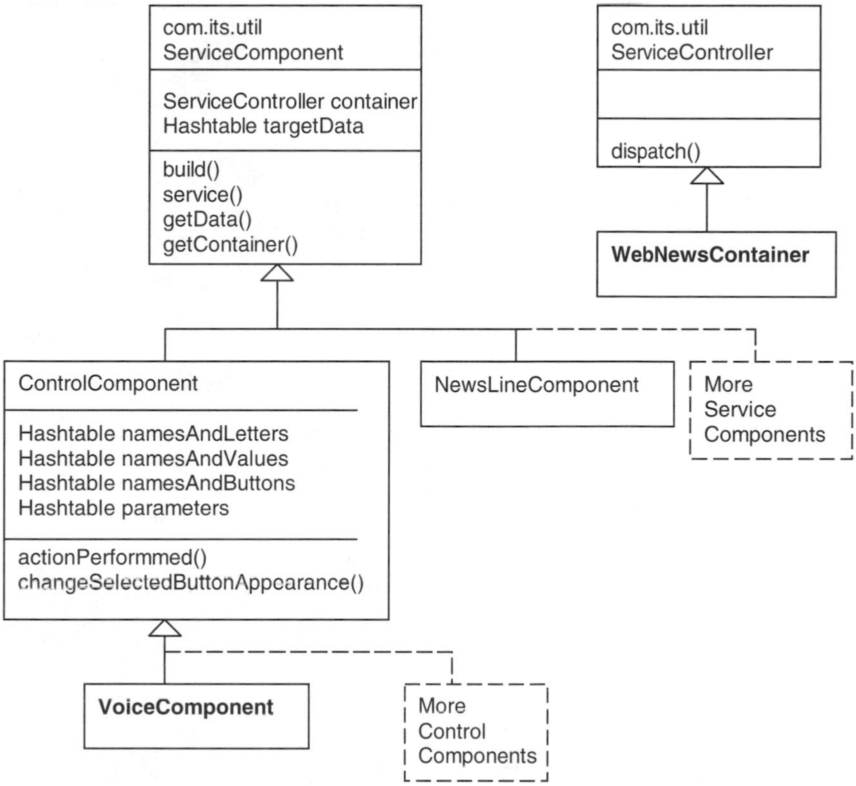

FIGURE 4.2. Adding the Voice Component to the News Watch Services.

To take advantage of these similarities we can duplicate (copy/paste) code from the *ControlComponent* to the *VoiceComponent*.

Do not do this, please! Copy/paste is not reuse.

The right thing to do is to define the *VoiceComponent* as a subclass of the *ControlComponent*. Luckily, we made all properties of the *ControlComponent* **protected**. That means that the *VoiceComponent* naturally inherits these properties. The object model diagram for service components is shown in Fig. 4.2. Figure 4.3 starts the *VoiceComponent* source code.

In the import section, we find several important libraries that enable this component to talk. Make sure that these libraries find the way to your machine and to the CLASSPATH environment variable.

The *VoiceComponent* extends the *ControlComponent*. This immediately solves the problem of building this component. The *build()* method is inherited from the *ControlComponent* and works perfectly for the *VoiceComponent* subclass. We create a Voice object in the beginning of the class with a single line:

```
private Voice talker = new CMUDiphoneVoice();
```

The talker is an object of the *com.sun.speech.freetts.en.us.CMUDiphoneVoice* class. Remember that there is the base class, *CMUVoice*, and its two subclasses, *CMUDiphoneVoice* and

```
package com.its.client;  // Internet Technology School

import java.util.*;
import com.its.client.ControlComponent;

import com.sun.speech.freetts.Voice;
import com.sun.speech.freetts.audio.JavaClipAudioPlayer;
import com.sun.speech.freetts.en.us.CMULexicon;
import com.sun.speech.freetts.en.us.CMUDiphoneVoice;

/**
 * The VoiceComponent class has voice "on-off" control button
 * The class has capability to convert text-to-speech
 * The service() method makes the conversion and produces sound
 * if the control button status is "ON"
 * The VoiceComponent object can serve in the service container.
 * @author Jeff.Zhuk@JavaSchool.com
 */
public class VoiceComponent extends ControlComponent {
    private Voice talker = new CMUDiphoneVoice();
    private voiceStatus = false; // default - silence

    public VoiceComponent() {
        talker.setLexicon(new CMULexicon());
        talker.setAudioPlayer(new JavaClipAudioPlayer());
        talker.load();
    }
```

FIGURE 4.3

CMUClusterUnitVoice. We use the *CMUDiphoneVoice* class to create the *talker* object in the data section of the *VoiceComponent* class.

The constructor of the *VoiceComponent* class provides the necessary settings for the talker object.

```
talker.setLexicon(new CMULexicon());
talker.setAudioPlayer(new JavaClipAudioPlayer());
talker.load();
```

It sets the lexicon, creating a *CMULexicon* object on the fly, sets the audio player by creating a *JavaClipAudioPlayer* object on the fly, and finally invokes the *load()* method. It loads the lexicon and the audio output handler and creates an audio output thread, if one has not already been created. It then calls the *loader()* method to load voice-specific data, which include utterance processors.

There is no code for building component in the *VoiceComponent* class; the *build()* method, reused from the *ControlComponent*, does the job.

Note that this time, the *build()* method finds button descriptions in the build section specifically provided for the *VoiceComponent*. Here is the code extract from the *build()* method of the *ControlComponent*:

```
public void build(Hashtable allParameters) {
   Hashtable buildParameters = (Hashtable)
   allParameters.get("build");
   .... More code ...
   // extract parameters that belong to the component
   parameters = (Hashtable)buildParameters.get(getClass().getName());
   // try to get button descriptions specific for this component
   namesAndLetters = (Hashtable)parameters.get("namesAndLetters");
   if(namesAndLetters == null) {
      // in this case get them from the container definition
      namesAndLetters =
      (Hashtable)allParameters.get("namesAndLetters");
   }
   .... More code ...
```

Here is the extract from the configuration file:

```
<build>
   .................. Component definitions .... .
   <Component name="com.its.client.VoiceComponent">
      <parameter name="location" value="East"/>
      <parameter name="width" value="20"/>
      <parameter name="height" value="15"/>
      <namesAndLetters>
         <abbreviation name="V" value="Voice"/>
      </namesAndLetters>
      <parameter name="eventHandler" type="ActionListener"
                 handler="com.its.client.WebNewsContainer" />
   </Component>
...... Other component definitions .... .
</build>
```

The *build()* method will create a component of size 20×15 with a single button. The container will place this component on the east side. You remember that the event-handling mechanism is located in the container class.

Figure 4.4 displays the *actionPerformed()* method of the *WebNewsContainer*. The *actionPerformed()* method starts with looking for the source of the trouble and asking, "Who just woke me up?" The very first line retrieves the name of the pressed button. According to our design specification, this is currently a single button, although this can be easily changed depending on the configuration file. If the same button was selected over and over again (as in the case of our design), each selection would change the button's status from "on" to "off" and back. This is all that the *actionPerformed()* method does. It changes the status of the selected button.

```
/** Code extract from the WebNewsContainer class
 * actionPerformed() method is to handle action events
 * In this case the method is called when a user presses
 * any of control buttons
 * @param actionEvent to be used to figure out which
 * button was pressed
 */
public void actionPerformed(ActionEvent actionEvent) {
    Hashtable namesAndLetters = (Hashtable)
    parameters.get("namesAndLetters");
    Hashtable namesAndValues = (Hashtable)
    parameters.get("namesAndValues");
    String command = actionEvent.getActionCommand();
    // first letter
    String name = (String)namesAndLetters.get(command);
    String url = (String)namesAndValues.get(name);

    String newInformation = url; // can be Inline data
    Hashtable newsParameters = new Hashtable();
    newsParameters.put(name, newInformation);

    // read from the web/file if not inline data like HELP
    if(!url.startsWith("Inline data:")) {
        newInformation = updateNews(newsParameters);
   }
    newsParameters.put(name, newInformation);
    dispatch(newsParameters);
    // change information channel and provide specified services!
}
```

FIGURE 4.4

The *actionPerformed*() method calls the *dispatch*() method of the container to dispatch new information to components according to XML instructions.

Here is another extract from the configuration file with the new XML element in the dispatch section:

```
<Component name="com.its.client.VoiceComponent" value="service"/>
```

The *service*() method (Fig. 4.5) performs one of two functions, depending on the button pressed. If the Voice button is pressed, the *service*() method switches the voice status from "on" to "off" and back. If any other button is pressed, the *service*() method checks the voice status, and if the status is "on," the *service*() method retrieves news information from the *Hashtable* of parameters and passes the news to the *speak*() method of the talker object. Now we can hear the voice talking. If the voice status is "off," the method silently returns control back to the calling function without much talk or any other service.

```
  /**
  * service() method provides voice support for information inside
  * Hashtable "targetData"
  * @param parameters with data to speak
  * @return parameters
  */
public Hashtable service(Hashtable newsParameters) {
    // a name of a button is a single key of the Hashtable of parameters
    Enumeration keys = newsParameters.keys();
    String name = (String)keys.nextElement();

    // get a name of the component button
    keys = namesAndButton.keys();
    String componentButtonName = (String)keys.nextElement();

    // check if this is the Voice button pressed
    if(name != null && name.equals(componentButtonName)) {
        // change control button appearance to highlight a selected button
        // if it was ON - turn it OFF
        if(buttonPressed != null && voiceStatus) {
            buttonPressed.setForeground(defaultForeground);
            buttonPressed.setBackground(defaultBackground);
            voiceStatus = false;
        } else if(!voiceStatus) {
            buttonPressed = (Button)namesAndButtons.get(name);
            buttonPressed.setForeground(selectedForeground);
            buttonPressed.setBackground(selectedBackground);
            voiceStatus = true;
        }
        return parameters;
    }
    // for any other button
    if(!voiceStatus) { // "OFF"
        return parameters; // do not speak out
    }
    // get news and speak
    String news = (String)newsParameters.get(name);
    talker.speak(news);
    return parameters;
}
```

FIGURE 4.5

Figure 4.6 demonstrates the configuration file with additional lines that craft the miracle of seamlessly integrating this new *VoiceComponent* into our existing service container. We need no Java code to be changed or added, just several lines in the configuration file.

We added the *VoiceComponent* set of parameters into the "build" section of the XML descriptor. We also added a line to the dispatch section. This line teaches the *dispatch()* method of the *WebNewsContainer* to invoke the *service()* method of the *VoiceComponent*.

```
<?xml version = "1.0" encoding = "UTF-8"?>
<WebNewsContainer width="400" height="200">
   <!-- abbreviations of commands -->
      <namesAndLetters>
         <abbreviation name="B" value="Business" />
         <abbreviation name="F" value="FriendsAndFamily" />
         <abbreviation name="S" value="Stocks" />
         <abbreviation name="T" value="Traffic" />
         <abbreviation name="W" value="Weather" />
         <abbreviation name="C" value="Config" />
         <abbreviation name="H" value="Help" />
      </namesAndLetters>
   <!-- commands and related URLs -->
      <namesAndValues>
         <url name="Business" value="http://ipserve.com/go/web/
         to/business" />
         <url name="FriendsAndFamily" value=
         "http://ipserve.com/go/web/to/friendsAndFamily" />
         <url name="Stocks" value="http://ipserve.com/go/web/
         to/stocks" />
         <url name="Traffic" value="http://ipserve.com/go/web/
         to/traffic" />
         <url name="Weather" value="Weather" />
         <url name="Config" value="config.xml" />
         <url name="Help" value="Inline data: B-Business,
         F-Friends/Family, S-Stock, T-Traffic, C-Config, and
         W-Weather." />
      </namesAndValues>
  <!-- Hashtable key="build" (used in the container.build() method ) -->
  <build>
   <!-- Hashtable key="com.its.client.NewsLineComponent" -->
   <Component name="com.its.client.NewsLineComponent">
       <parameter name="location" value="Center" />
       <parameter name="timeInMsec" value="40" />
       <parameter name="shiftInPixels" value="3" />
       <parameter name="news" value="Integration-ready service
       components and containers" />
       <parameter name="width" value="300" />
       <parameter name="height" value="24" />
   </Component>
   <!-- Hashtable key="com.its.client.ControlComponent" -->
   <Component name="com.its.client.ControlComponent">
       <parameter name="location" value="South" />
       <parameter name="width" value="360" />
       <parameter name="height" value="50" />
       <parameter name="eventHandler" type="ActionListener"
       handler="com.its.client.WebNewsContainer" />
   </Component>
```

FIGURE 4.6

```
    <!-- Hashtable key="com.its.client.VoiceComponent" -->
    <Component name="com.its.client.VoiceComponent">
        <parameter name="location" value="East "/>
        <parameter name=â€ width â€ value=â€ 20â€ />
        <parameter name=â€ height â€ value=â€ 15â€ />

        <namesAndLetters>
            <abbreviation name="V" value="Voice" />
        </namesAndLetters>
        <parameter name="eventHandler" type="ActionListener"
        handler="com.its.client.WebNewsContainer" />
    </Component>
    <!-- more components -->
   </build>
   <!-- Hashtable key="dispatch" (used in the
   container.dispatch() method ) -->
   <dispatch>
    <Component name="com.its.client.ControlComponent" value="service" />
    <Component name="com.its.client.NewsLineComponent" value="service" />
    <Component name="com.its.client.VoiceComponent" value="service"/>
   </dispatch>
  </WebNewsContainer>
```

FIGURE 4.6. *(cont.)*

Did we forget about the *getEventSources()* method? No. The *getEventSources()* method is a complete reuse (not a rewrite!) from the *ControlComponent*. The *getEventSources()* method will return the *Hashtable* with the single Voice button as the source of events.

There is one more method in the *VoiceComponent*. The *main()* method (Fig. 4.7)—the final method—serves as the unit test for the voice portion of the component. This is the right thing to do: test just this new component before testing the new integrated solution.

The *main()* method can test the *VoiceComponent* without any container just to prove that voice is really coming. It can take optional arguments, interpreting arguments as words and concatenating them into a string-sentence.

The *main()* method creates a talker object and makes it talk via the *speak()* method. The default test string or the string created from passed arguments serves as an input to the *speak()* method. The *main()* method tests only the voice part of the class. This is the only part of the component that is completely new for us, and we want to be sure it is working.

I want to highlight the fact that the Voice object we use in the example is a very specific one. It is the *CMUDiphoneVoice* object type. This is just one of the possible types of voices we can produce. Figure 4.8 shows the hierarchy diagram of the voices.

The *com.sun.speech.freetts.Voice* class sits on top of the hierarchy. This class performs text-to-speech conversion using a series of *UtteranceProcessor(s)*. It is the main conduit to the *FreeTTS* speech synthesizer.

The Voice class invokes the method *speak()* to produce sound. The *speak()* method accepts as an input argument ASCII text, a JSML document, an *InputStream*, or a *FreeTTSSpeakable* object. Before a Voice can perform TTS conversion, it must have a Lexicon, from which it gets the vocabulary, and an *AudioPlayer*, to which it sends the synthesized output.

```
/**
 * The main() method tests only the voice part of the class
 * @param args optional words to speak can be passed to the method
 */
    public static void main(String[] args) {
        String speech = "test. 1,2,3, how are you?";
        if(args.length > 0) {
            speech = "";
            for(int i=0; i<args.length; i++) {
                speech += " " + args[i];
            }
        }
        Voice talker = new CMUDiphoneVoice();
        talker.speak(speech);
    }
}   // The end of the VoiceComponent class
```

FIGURE 4.7

The Voice class currently has two subclasses. The *com.sun.speech.freetts.en.us. CMU-Voice* class provides generic *CMU-Voice* support. The second subclass, *com.sun.speech.freetts.en.us.SimpleVoice*, provides a nonfunctional voice used for testing purposes. The *CMU-Voice* class, in turn, has two subclasses.

The *com.sun.speech.freetts.en.us.CMUClusterUnitVoice* defines a limited domain synthesis voice that specializes in telling the time (with an English accent) and has an even more specialized *com.sun.speech.freetts.en.us.CMUTimeAWBVoice* subclass.

The second subclass of the *CMUVoice* class is the *com.sun.speech.freetts.en.us. CMUDiphoneVoice* class that defines an unlimited-domain diphone synthesis-based voice. The *CMUDiphoneVoice* class is the most interesting to us, because we actually use an object of this class in the *VoiceComponent* example.

SUMMARY

In this chapter, we learned the basic principles of programming voice-enabled applications with Java, based on the JSAPI. We created the *VoiceComponent* and seamlessly added this component to our existing service components. We did not change any sources except the configuration file with the XML-based descriptor.

We have not talked about speech recognition systems yet. We discuss this topic at length in Chapter 12.

Integrating Questions

1. Are you aware of any standards in the area of speech technology? Which ones?
2. What is the basic mechanism of Text-to-Speech conversion?
3. What are Tokens, Utterances, and Lexicons?

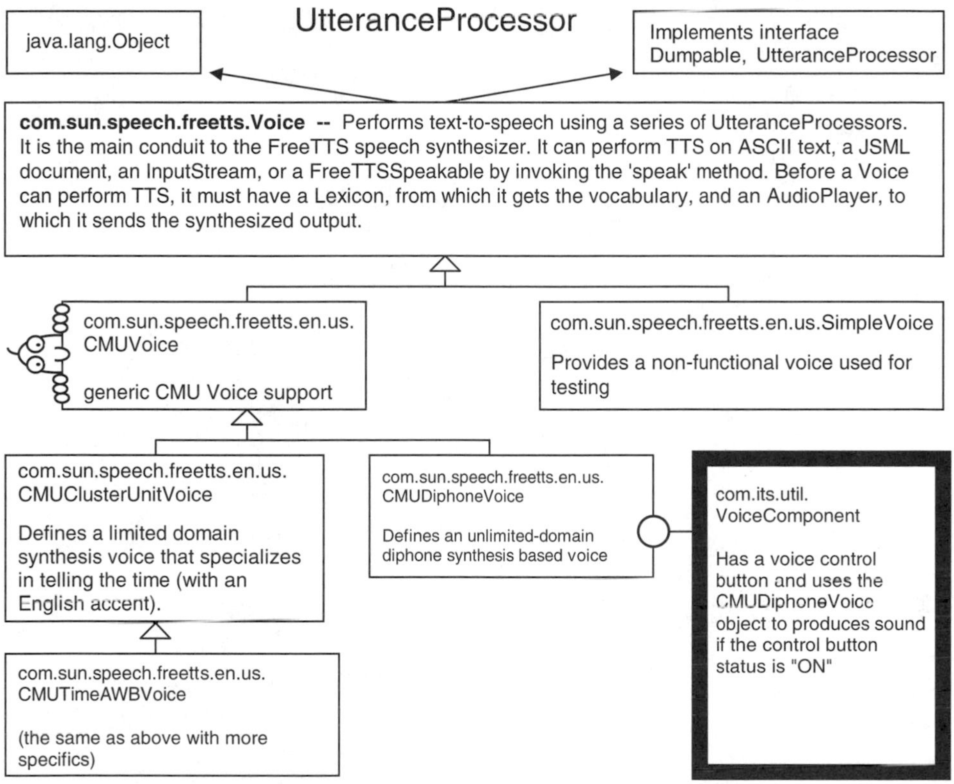

FIGURE 4.8. Hierarchy Diagram of the Free TTS Voices.

Case Study

1. Rewrite the *actionPerformed()* method of the *VoiceComponent* to turn the sound on or off immediately after the control button is pressed. (Currently, this only takes effect after switching news channels.) Hint: look into the *actionPerformed()* method of the *ControlComponent*, and recollect what the main mechanism of dispatching services is.
2. Research mechanisms of creating different voices with *FreeTTS*, and share the results with your peers.
3. Write two additional methods for the *VoiceComponent:s boyTalk()* and *girlTalk()*. These two methods will implement two different voices.
4. Research mechanisms and the current status of creating non-English lexicons, and share the results with your peers.
5. Describe an application at your workplace that can benefit from Text-to-Speech technology.

REFERENCES

1. Java Speech API (JSAPI)
   http://java.sun.com/products/java-media/speech/.

2. The Festival Speech Synthesis System, University of Edinburgh, UK: *http://www.cstr.ed.ac.uk/projects/festival/*.
3. The Flite Speech Synthesizer, Carnegie Mellon University: *http://www.speech.cs.cmu.edu/flite/*.
4. *FreeTTS* Programmer's Guide: *http://freetts.sourceforge.net/docs/ProgrammerGuide.html*.

CHAPTER 5

An Introduction to Knowledge Technologies

Knowledge is power. (Ipsa Scientia Potestas Est)
—**Sir Francis Bacon (1561–1626), Meditations**

Ontology is a controlled, hierarchical vocabulary for describing a knowledge system or knowledge-handling methods.

This chapter is an introduction to a development paradigm in which software and knowledge engineering are integrated. As always happens on the other side of an economic crisis, a new set of skills will be required. A growing number of developers will actively use the knowledge technologies reviewed in this chapter.

The chapter starts by talking about fundamental standards that currently bridge ontology and engineering: the Resource Description Framework (RDF), the Semantic Web language DAML+OIL (DARPA Agent Markup Language + Ontology Inference Layer), Topic Maps concepts, and their XML Topic Maps (XTM) standard knowledge exchange format.

We'll continue with a brief overview of data-mining methods with coming Java support and eventually discuss the challenging topic of *generic* knowledge, not just knowledge of a specific business domain, expressed in natural language. The final part of the chapter describes OpenCyc, probably the most exciting knowledge instrument today, and provides examples of using the CycL language and OpenCyc engine in distributed knowledge systems.

I hope this chapter does not take you, my reader, by surprise. Integration-ready systems and collaborative engineering *need* and *help create* knowledge technologies, which create a very healthy cycle.

A customer with a computer and computer skills is still the main target for computerized services today.

Even when searching Google.com for a specific topic, you need to know the specific terms of the industry this topic belongs to. This requirement prevents or hinders information exchange between different knowledge domains.

The computer-illiterate part of the population is almost completely excluded from the computerized service client base. There also are people with disabilities who are prevented from using computers in a general manner.

In addition, there is a "gray area" of the population who have limited computer skills but no desire to use these skills. These individuals have learned from their experience that computers are too stupid and cannot serve them well in their specific fields today. Service providers have a great reason to employ knowledge technologies and drastically increase clientele for their services.

Knowledge technologies help to create a bridge from natural language to a specific service request. For example, the Semantic Web is the representation of data on the World Wide Web based on the RDF. The previous chapter brought up the topic of voice synthesis. Naturally, this leads to speech recognition systems (SRSs). SRSs are extremely narrow in their business domains today. Current SRSs lack general knowledge representation; they direct customers into the "select one of the options" routine.

There are many methods for representing knowledge, including written documents, text files, and databases. Below, I review a few technologies used in this vast area: The Semantic Web (an umbrella for many other technologies), XML, RDF, Topic Maps, frames and slots methods, the CycL language, and others.

> The Semantic Web is a vision for the future of the Web, in which information is given explicit meaning, making it easier for machines to automatically process and integrate information available on the Web. The Semantic Web will build on XML's ability to define customized tagging schemes and RDF's flexible approach to representing data. The next element required for the Semantic Web is a Web ontology language, which can formally describe the semantics of classes and properties, used in Web documents. In order for machines to perform useful reasoning tasks on these documents, the language must go beyond the basic semantics of RDF Schema. [1]

Ontology

Knowledge-handling methods and terms are often called *ontology*. Ontology formally defines a common set of terms that are used to describe and represent a domain of knowledge. Automated tools to power advanced services related to knowledge management can use ontology (knowledge-handling methods and terms). Ontology is critical for applications that want to search across or merge information from diverse communities.

Ontology can provide terminology for describing content with *rules or assertions and inferences* that define *terms using other terms*. Good search engines include some ontology definitions provided for specific business areas. We can call them *specific ontologies*.

For example, a specific ontology can be created to define group memberships. This ontology might include terms such as *user*, *group*, *member*, and *role*. This ontology could also include definitions such as *groups have members*, and *every group member has a role*.

A search system that uses such ontology would take initial key data entered by a user and look for additional data required by the rules. Such a system can obtain search results superior to conventional search systems. Of course, this superiority relies on additional data provided with content annotations. Content providers must be in the game.

It is important that ontologies are publicly available and different data sources can commit to the same ontology for shared meaning. In addition, ontologies should be able to extend other ontologies in order to provide additional definitions.

XML document type definitions (DTDs) and XML Schemas are sufficient for exchanging data between parties who have detailed agreements, specifications, and an existing and stable vocabulary. At the same time, they have no semantic mechanisms to understand changing or new XML vocabularies.

RDF and RDF Schema

RDF and RDF Schema [2] begin to approach this problem by allowing simple semantics to be associated with terms. With RDF Schema, one can define classes that may have multiple subclasses and superclasses; one can also define properties, which may have subproperties, domains, and ranges. In this sense, RDF Schema is a simple ontology language.

However, in order to achieve interoperation between numerous, autonomously developed and managed schemas, richer semantics are needed. There is a need for instruments capable of sharing the knowledge across the boundaries of notation, grammar, knowledge domains, and natural language.

In RDF, each schema has its own namespace identified by a Uniform Resource Identifier (URI).

The URI identifies any content presented by text, an image, or a sound file. A typical example of a URI is *http://IPServe.com*.

Each term in the RDF Schema is identified by combining the schema's URI with the term's ID. Any resource that uses this URI references the term as defined in that schema.

However, RDF is unclear on the definition of a term that has partial definitions in multiple schemas. The specification appears to assume that the definition is the union of all descriptions that use the same identifier, regardless of source.

DAML+OIL: A Semantic Markup Language for Web Resources

DAML [3] was created as part of a research program started in August 2000 by the Defense Advanced Research Projects Agency (DARPA), a U.S. governmental organization. OIL is an initiative funded by the European Union Programme for Information Society Technologies as part of its reasearch projects.

The marriage of DAML and OIL produced a semantic markup language for Web resources. The language is based on RDF and RDF Schema. DAML+OIL extends RDF capabilities with richer modeling primitives.

A few words about RDF. An RDF document is a collection of assertions that typically begins with the tag *<rdf:RDF* and several obligatory RDF declarations that refer document prefixes (e.g., *xsd:*) to existing specifications. Each topmost RDF element is the subject of a sentence. The next level of enclosed elements represent verb/object pairs for this sentence.

For example:

```
<Class ID="GroupAccount">
  <subClassOf resource="#Account"/>
</Class>
```

This means that the *GroupAccount* class is a subclass of the *Account* class.

The DAML example provided below is in effect an RDF document that includes DAML extensions. DAML extensions are easily recognizable because they have *<daml*: prefixes. The example begins with an RDF start tag including several namespace declarations:

```
<rdf:RDF
      xmlns:rdf ="http://www.w3.org/1999/02/22-rdf-syntax-ns#"
      xmlns:rdfs="http://www.w3.org/2000/01/rdf-schema#"
      xmlns:xsd ="http://www.w3.org/2000/10/XMLSchema#"
      xmlns:daml="http://www.w3.org/2001/10/daml+oil#"
      xmlns:dex ="http://www.w3.org/TR/2001/NOTE-daml+
      oil walkthru-20011218/daml+oil-ex#"
      xmlns:exd ="http://www.w3.org/TR/2001/NOTE-daml+oil-
      walkthru-20011218/daml+oil-ex-dt#"
      xmlns ="http://www.w3.org/TR/2001/NOTE-daml+oil-
      walkthru-20011218/daml+oil-ex#"
>
```

XML namespace declarations (the *xmlns* above) relate prefixes to their specifications. Therefore, in this document, the *rdf*: prefix should be understood as a reference to *http://www.w3.org/1999/02/22-rdf-syntax-ns#*. This is a conventional RDF declaration appearing at the beginning of almost every RDF document.

The second and third declarations make similar statements about *rdfs*: and *xsd*: prefixes that refer to the RDF Schema and XML Schema datatype namespaces.

The following declarations provide references for *daml*:, *dex*:, and *exd*: prefixes. These again are conventional DAML+OIL declarations.

The final declaration states that unprefixed elements refer to *http://www.w3.org/TR/2001/NOTE-daml+oil-walkthru-20011218/daml+oil-ex#* that is, the location of this document itself.

After these initial declarations, we can indicate that this RDF document *is* an ontology.

```
<daml:Ontology rdf:about="Collaborative Engineering">
```

Before we can describe our topic, we need to define some basic types. DAML, like object-oriented languages, does this by giving a name for a class.

```
<daml:Class rdf:ID="Account">
```

This assertion tells us that there is a class named *Account*. It is possible for others to refer to the definition of *Account* that we give here.

```
<rdfs:label>Account</rdfs:label>
<rdfs:comment>
  This class of Accounts provides a base for User and Group Accounts.
</rdfs:comment>
</daml:Class>
```

We introduced a label for graphical representations of RDF, as well as a comment, and we closed the class definition.

There are two types of accounts, Group and User.

```
<daml:Class rdf:ID="GroupAccount">
  <rdfs:subClassOf rdf:resource="#Account"/>
</daml:Class>
```

The *subClassOf* element indicates that its subject — *GroupAccount*—is a subclass of its object—the resource identified by *#Account*.

```
<daml:Class rdf:ID="UserAccount">
  <rdfs:subClassOf rdf:resource="#Account"/#
  <daml:disjointWith rdf:resource="#GroupAccount"/>
</daml:Class>
```

The *disjointWith* element is a DAML extension of *rdfs*. This element tells us that no object can be both a *UserAccount* and *GroupAccount* in this ontology.

We can define DAML+OIL properties that relate objects to other objects or those that relate objects to datatype values.

We define the *hasGroupMembership* relation that will be used to connect a User to Group accounts.

```
<daml:ObjectProperty rdf:ID="hasGroupMembership">
```

Then we say that *hasGroupMembership* is a property that applies to *UserAccount*.

```
<rdfs:domain rdf:resource="#UserAccount"/>
```

Like the domain, we also declare the range of the *hasGroupMembership* relation. Below, we define that the value of the *hasGroupMembership* property can only be *GroupAccount*.

```
<rdfs:range rdf:resource="#GroupAccount"/>
```

We then close the *ObjectProperty* tag.

```
</daml:ObjectProperty>
```

Above, we effectively declared that every user could have memberships in one or more groups.

In a similar way, we can define *DatatypeProperty*.

The more sophisticated example below defines some restrictions on *GroupAccount*. For objects that have the type *GroupAccount* (subclasses), we provide property constraints. We not only specify a maximum, minimum, or precise number of values for that property, but also enforce the type that these property values must have:

```
<daml:Class rdf:about="#GroupAccount">
   <rdfs:comment>
```

Only one administrator is allowed in the group, and it must be a group member.

```
</rdfs:comment>
<rdfs:subClassOf>
   <daml):Restriction DAML:maxCardinalityQ="1">
     <daml):onProperty rdf):resource="#hasAdministrator"/>
     <daml:hasClassQ rdf:resource="#GroupMember"/>
   </daml/:Restriction>
 </rdfs:subClassOf>
</daml:Class>
```

This states that a *GroupAccount* may have at most one administrator that is a *GroupMember*. After we define some basic types, we can create objects of these types.

```
<UserAccount rdf:ID="Alex.Nozik">
  <loginName>alex.nozik</loginName>
</UserAccount>
```

Finally, we end the document with the *rdf:RDF* closing element.

```
</rdf:RDF>
```

We can see that the RDF-based approach is very scalable and can be applied to many knowledge areas. At the same time, however, it is not rich enough to deal with natural language flexibility

Topic Maps

Topic Maps is the ISO 13250 standard that defines a model and interchange syntax for knowledge representation with topics, occurrences of topics, and relationships—"associations"—between topics. Topic Maps can be compared to the "GPS (Global Positioning System) of the information universe," a base technology for knowledge representation and knowledge management.

Topic Maps modeling started in 1991 with the initial goal of merging information. The idea was to find a formal way for capturing information models. The scope was later broadened to multiple applications providing access to information based on a model of the knowledge it contains.

The key concepts of Topic Maps modeling are:

- Topic (and topic type)
- Occurrence of the topic (and occurrence role)
- Association of the topic (and association type)
- Scope of the topic

A topic can be any "thing" whatsoever—a person, an entity, a concept, really anything—regardless of whether it exists.

The term *topic* refers to the element in the Topic Map document. Topic types represent a typical class–instance relationship. Topic types are themselves defined as topics. For example, in software documentation, they might be functions, variables, objects, or methods.

Topics have three kinds of characteristics: names, occurrences, and roles in associations. There are base names (required), display names (optional), and sort names (optional). A topic may be linked to one or more information resources, called *occurrences* of the topic. An article about the topic and a picture related to the topic are examples of occurrences.

Occurrences may be of different types—for example, "file," "monograph," "article," "illustration,"—generally supported in the standard by the concept of the *occurrence role*.

A topic *association* asserts a relationship between two or more topics. For example:

- "The Sun Educational Services (SES) headquarters are *located in* Broomfield, Colorado."
- "Java Distributed Computing (book) was *written by* Jim Farley."
- "Alexander Pushkin was *born in* Russia."

Association types, such as *located in*, *written by*, and *born in*, define relationships between topics. Topics can play different, or the same, roles in these relationships. For example, A and B have the same role in the association "A *works with* B." However, they play different roles in the "A was *rescued by* B" association.

Scope is another characteristic of topics that limits their applicability. The same topic can be considered under different circumstances, or in a different scope. For example, when we refer to Washington, we always provide a scope for this topic. It can be a president of the U.S., a state, or Washington, D.C.

We have now considered the main characteristics assigned to topics: names, occurrences or resources, and association roles.

Topic Map representation is defined by the XTM specifications [4].

Is there any code around that supports some concepts of Topic Maps? There are several companies and open source projects [5] working in this direction. Every project has its own model that maps Topic Map concepts to its software and supports these concepts. All models are different but still have many common features. I have tried to summarize these models in a simplified version that reflects the mainstream approach to Topic Map object-oriented modeling. Figure 5.1 displays this "averaged" version of an object model diagram that represents Topic Map concepts in most current projects.

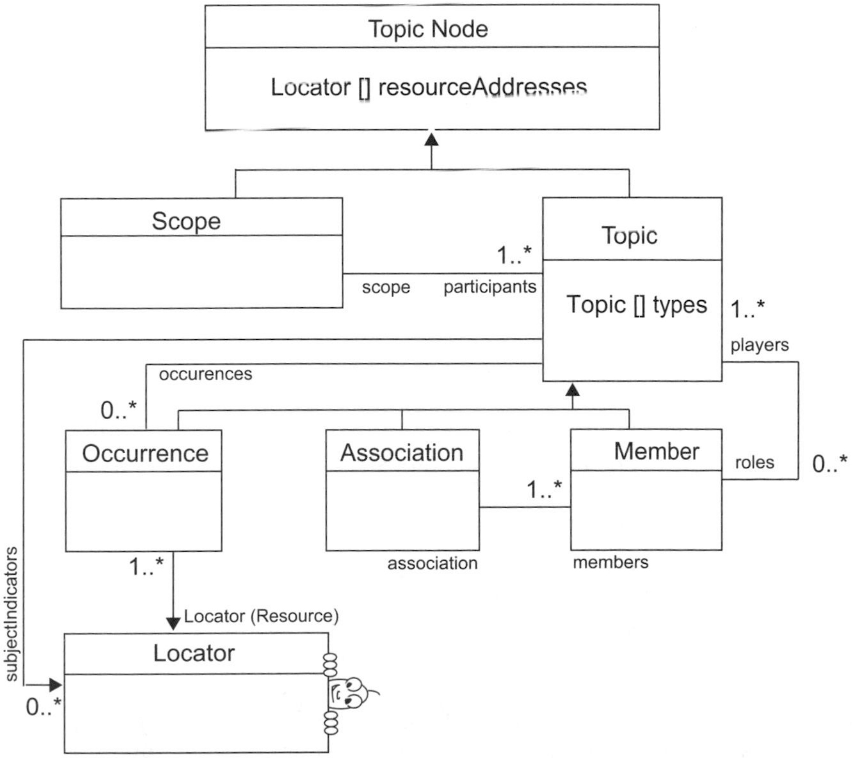

FIGURE 5.1. An "Averaged" OMD Version of Topic Maps Concepts.

One of the Java implementations of Topic Maps can be found in the Topic Maps 4 Java open source project [5]. An early version of this project released around 100 classes that support handling Topic Maps.

After reviewing different models, I suggest that all Topic Map objects behave in a very similar manner and can be represented with a typed collection of objects. The *com.its.base.DataElement* class is the base for this collection, and the *com.its.base.TMService* class is able to handle the whole collection.

Object-oriented programming (OOP) enforces strong typing in OOP languages. Some developers tend to create a new class for any new data structure. This expensive practice works OK on corporate workstations; however, it quickly fails under small-device constraints. Server-side development has been steadily growing during the past decade. I expect this decade will show increasing demand for client applications for numerous devices. The typed-object approach leads to an economic programming model. This does not mean that we must deviate from OOP, we just want to be more selective in creating new classes. Object behavior is an important criterion in this choice.

The *com.its.base.DataElement* class will be considered with several different services later in this book. This class has built-in properties to provide security access and data evaluation and generic support for business attributes and associated objects.

Figure 5.2 displays an object model diagram that represents Topic Maps with the typed-object approach.

Products that support XTM deliver (and are capable of reading) files with exactly the same standard format, regardless of the chosen object model and implementation details. Here is an extract of an XTM file:

```
<?xml version="1.0" encoding="ISO-8859-1"?>
<topicMap id="global knowledge container">
  <topic id="Services">
   <baseName>Training</baseName>
   <occurrence>
    <topicRef xlink:href="http://JavaSchool.com"/>
   </occurrence>
 </topic>
 ...
 </topicMap>
```

I provide more details on this subject in Appendix 3, with a set of classes that transforms XTM files to and from the internal representation based on the model described above.

Knowledge management is different from information management because knowledge assumes more than just having information about a subject. Topic Maps may be considered the standard for knowledge classification, codification, and formalization.

Topic Maps and the associated syntax of XTM can represent both human knowledge and the structural relations within elements of that knowledge. Topic Maps are capable of providing the interchange of such information across the boundaries of knowledge domains. To accomplish such interchange, this technology relies on the availability of a set of rules capable of expressing the reasoning needed for knowledge classification.

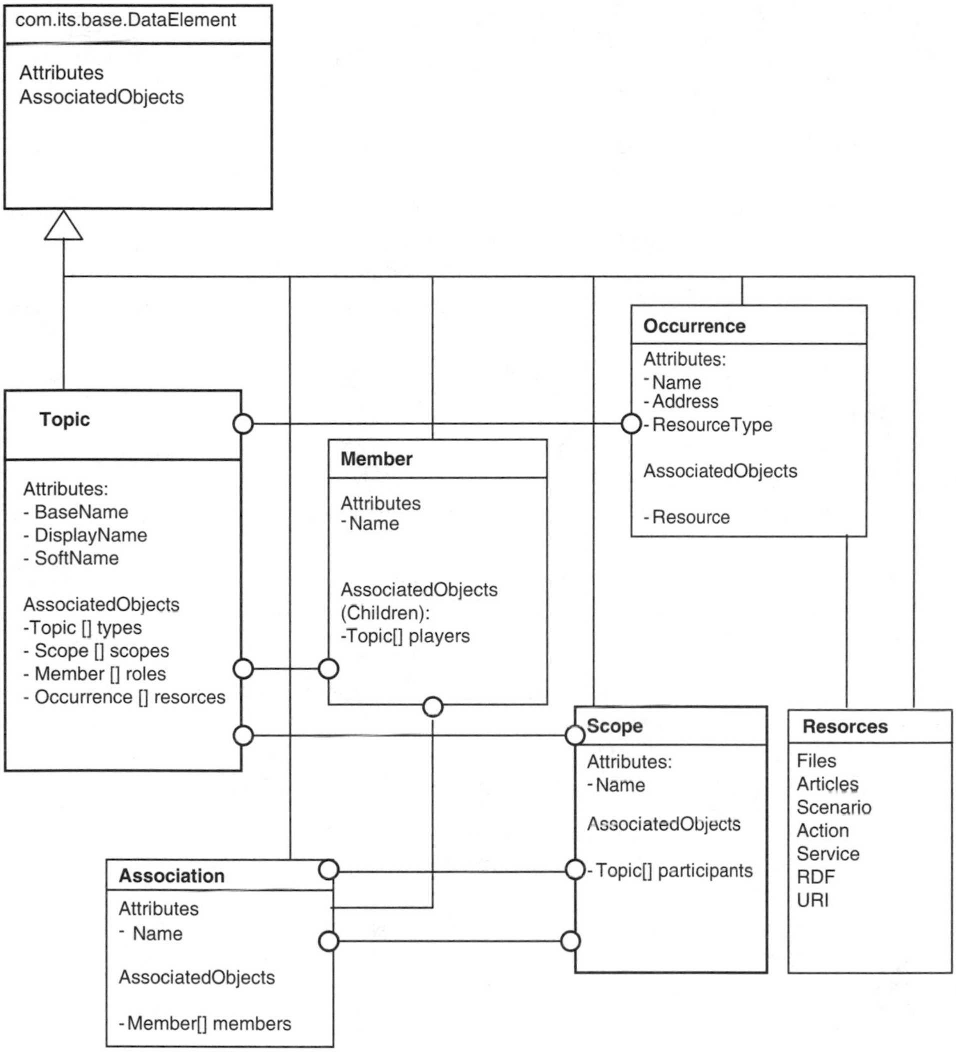

FIGURE 5.2. Topic Maps Implementation with the Typed Object Approach.

Do we become a bit smarter by getting more data? Yes and no. We would appreciate information much more if it helped us predict market behavior, prevent fraud, or explain the cause of cancer or the reason for the disease called *aging*.

About 20 years ago, I had the privilege of working with a very talented, world-famous gerontologist, Dr. Tamara Dubina. At the time, she was researching a new concept of biological age. Her work related health indicators to this new concept, thus giving different perspectives on people's aging process. (I helped with the math model and programming, using non-linear regression methods.) [6]

Tamara collected a tremendous amount of data during this research. There was a common feeling that the volume of information did not make retrieving knowledge easier. Creating a model that could describe this data was not a trivial task. At the same time, the data were priceless for testing the model. That was a typical data mining process: analysis—model—test.

DATA-MINING PROCESS AND METHODS

Statistics help with data analysis and give us a more focused view on the past. *Data mining* methods look for patterns hidden in multiple data records and help build a model that can actually provide some insight into the future. For example, MatchLogics, Inc., one of the early Internet successes, used data mining to understand Internet users and offer them the right products.

The data mining process consists of several steps.

1. Collecting data.
2. Sorting and filtering data for modeling.
3. Building a model.
4. Testing the model on another set of data. Testing the model on the same data (which we used to create the model) proves nothing.
5. Tuning/fixing/redoing the model, based on the test results; then return to step 4 or (if the test shows great results) move on to step 6.
6. Applying the model to real data and looking into the future.

Some models change rarely, some often. Most day traders, for example, may not have enough time to create a working model.

One of the specifications provided in the data mining area belongs to the Java community. Java Specification Request (JSR) 73 [7] identifies the main specification objectives:

1. Provide access to data mining systems in a vendor-neutral manner.
2. Make it accessible to non-data-mining experts.
3. Provide a set of functions and algorithms.
4. Target the J2EE platform with consistent interface to
   JCX—Connector Architecture (JSR 16);
   JMI—Metadata Interface (JSR 40); and
   JOLAP—Online Analytical Processing (JSR 69).
5. Provide compatibility with existing data-mining standards:
   CWM DM—Common Warehouse Metadata;
   PMML—Predictive Model Markup Language;
   SQL/MM for DM—ISO SQL (structured query language) standard.

An application programming interface (API) with supported Java class implementations will glue client applications to the data-mining engine and metadata repository.

The main data-mining methods start with data classification and approximation functions and continue with association rule discovery and attribute importance evaluation. Data-mining software captures high-level specifications for model building. The software must be able to specify the algorithm of data approximation (or regression) using association rules, a decision tree, or another specific model. The target client can be an expert or a novice user.

How does software help produce a model from mostly numeric data? There are several typical operations: Connect to a data set. Map physical data to logical data (a set of logical

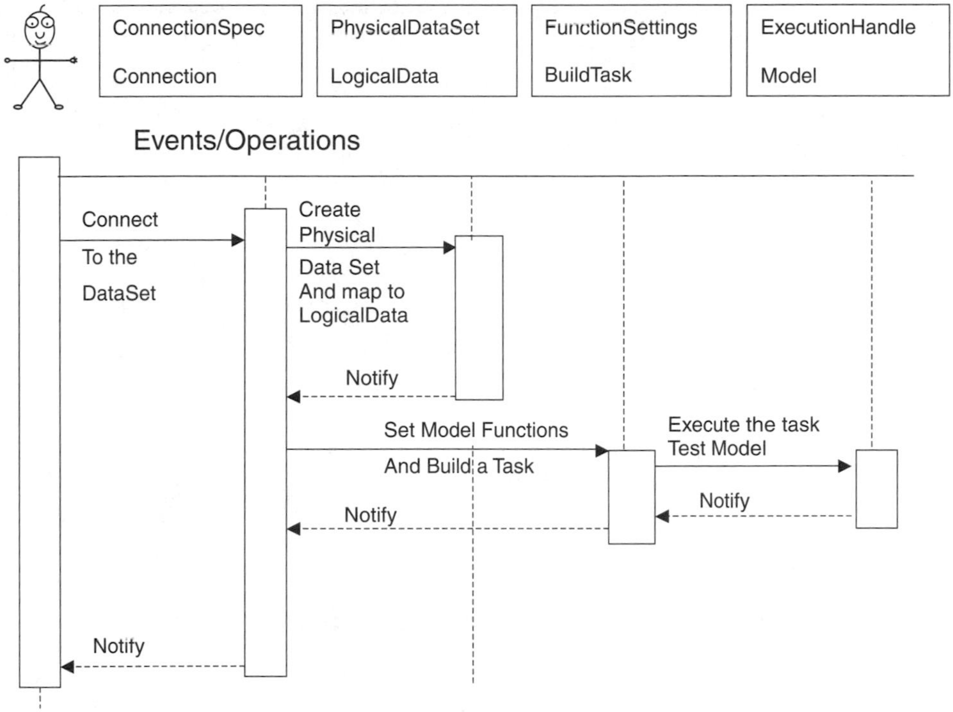

FIGURE 5.3. Data Mining: Build, Test, and Apply the Model—Sequence Diagram Example.

attributes used as input to model building). Set functions for a future model. Build, test, and apply the model. Figure 5.3 shows the sequence diagram, and Fig. 5.4 provides an example with several lines of code using *javax.datamining package* classes.

Be aware that the *javax.datamining* package is not released at this time, and the final release version may have some syntax differences. Data-mining methods expressed in object-oriented language help us understand numbers, build models, and predict future numbers.

Probably the most difficult task is to understand people and natural language and to retrieve knowledge from textual and spoken information. This is different from a search for textual information. I will review the method of frames and slots that is currently used in the Dialog Manager (Speech Recognition) product to parse natural language. Then, I would like to introduce you to the CycL language, which from my point of view, is the most powerful instrument created for building a bridge between computers and natural language.

Following are a few techniques that are currently dealing with natural language.

FRAMES AND SLOTS

Frames and slots are very convenient for representing *domain* information. A frame has a name and a set of slots. Each slot is a concept hierarchy with the slot name as the root. For example, CU Communicator with its Dialog Manager [8] engine is a product based on the frames-and-slots method that offers a library of functions (parsers) for manipulating frames.

```
import javax.datamining.*;

// connect to the DataSet1
 ConnectionSpec connectionSpec =
connectionFactory.createConnectionSpec("DataSet1", "Mark", "pswd");

Connection dataSetConnection =
connectionFactory.getConnection (connectionSpec);

// Create PhysicalDataSet
PhysicalDataSet dataSet = new PhysicalDataSet
("http://JavaSchool.com");
dataSet.getMetadata();

// Create LogicalData and map to Physical data
LogicalData logicalData = new LogicalData(dataSet);

// Set Model Functions
FunctionSettings modelSetting =
new ClassificationSettings (logicalData, "servicePrice");

// Build the task, execute the task, test model
BuildTask testModelTask = new BuildTask(dataSet,
modelSettings,"trainingModel");
dataSetConnection.addObject ("testModel", buildTask);
dataSetConnection.save();

ExecutionHandle testing = dataSetConnection.execute(testModelTask);
testing.waitForCompletion ();

Model model = (Model) dataSetConnection.getObject ("testedModel");
```

FIGURE 5.4

Information is extracted from parses into frames and is stored in frames directly by the Dialog Manager. Here is an example:

```
Frame: System_Groups
[Group1]
[Roles]
[Role1]
[RoleN]
[Available_Services]
[Service1]
[ServiceN]
;
```

The application developer creates a task file, which is similar to a frames file for the parser. The task file contains:

- The definition of the system ontology
- Templates for prompting for information
- Templates for verifying information
- Templates for generating SQL queries

Dialog Manager offers a set of standard canonical functions for dates, times, and numbers.

When Dialog Manager receives a parse, it calls the function *extract_values()* to extract information from the parse into frames. The *extract_values()* function scans the parse for any token names that are in the canonical function table. When it finds a token in the table, it calls the function associated with the token, passing it to a pointer to the input string, starting at the token. The function rewrites the input string starting at that point.

After information is extracted and merged into the context, the function *action_switch()* is called to determine the next system action. This function examines the context and takes an action based on a prespecified order of priorities.

The frames-and-slots method, as well as the products (like Dialog Manager) that are based on this method, have their advantages and limitations. The method is relatively simple and works OK in a single domain, but it is hard to extend across domain borders to the level of generic knowledge.

Systems based on this method currently have a good business standing, as they are early in the speech recognition market. The proprietary technology (with no mainstream standards) used in most frames-based systems locks current clients into a single-vendor schema. It also limits knowledge-base development by current client business domains with very modest growth of generic knowledge data. This may discourage many customers as competition from VoiceXML-based systems (e.g., BeVocal, Nuance, SpeechWorks, and Tellme) grows and XTM-based data become available to the public.

THE CYCL LANGUAGE

The CycL language has been in development by Cycorp for almost two decades, but only recently has it been made available to the public in the OpenCyc project [9]. I would like to thank the ontology experts from Cycorp who helped me by providing their insight into this new and exciting technology: Jen Headley, Doug Lanet, John De Oliveira, Steve Reed, Keith Goolsbey, Jon Curtis, Michael Witbrock, Roland Reagan, Kevin Knight, Douglas Foxvog, and Tony Brusseau.

The advantage that the Cyc method has over methods considered earlier is that Cyc has a language that is capable of expressing knowledge: CycL. In CycL, the meanings of statements and inferential connections between statements are encoded in a way that is accessible to a machine.

Presently, natural languages are virtually meaningless to machines. I can say, "All system users have at least one login. All system users are people. Hal is a system user." From these sentences, a *person* can infer that Hal has a login, but a *machine* cannot, at least not until a machine can understand English sentences using some common sense.

In the formal language Cyc uses, inference is reduced to a matter of symbol manipulation, something that a machine can do. When an argument is written in CycL, its meaning is encoded in the shape, or symbolic structure, of the assertions it contains. Determining whether an argument is valid can be achieved by checking for certain simple physical patterns in the CycL sentence representing its premises and conclusions. One issue in the choice of representations is expressiveness.

It is impossible to express the complicated realities of life with programming language primitives. Yet, somehow we do this every day. We create multiple abstractions—filters that finally break down the complexity—and often disconnect the final product from our initial ideas. Natural language would be ideal, but not for machines that cannot tolerate conflicts created by the language. An "almost natural" language like CycL is a better choice. It allows great flexibility in creating new expressions while preserving nonconflicting rules and data.

Yes, we want a great deal of expressiveness. We would like to create a kind of ideal comprehensive system. Does this mean we should use natural language for such a system?

The expressiveness of natural language, though, goes beyond the minimum of complexity we would like to introduce for this task. The expressiveness of natural language also gives rise to special problems if one wants not only to store, but also to reason with, the represented knowledge. Logic-based representation, in contrast, gives us enough expressiveness, and facilitates the reasoning as well.

Natural language is obviously very expressive, too expressive to be formalized for the machine. Consider the following sentences.

Jeff's failure resulted from his error.
Jeff's error caused his failure.
Jeff's failure was a consequence of his mistake.
Jeff's mistake occurred before his failure.

Each of these sentences means roughly the same thing, and each implies that Jeff's error occurred before his failure. If we want to represent that implication, do we write a rule for every natural language expression that could possibly express this point?

CycL is a logic-based language that offers a simplified, more efficient approach. First, we identify the common concepts—for example, the relation "error caused failure." This is a very common relationship for English sentences. Then, we formulate rules about those common concepts. For example, "if error caused failure, then error temporally precedes failure."

Another issue in the choice of a knowledge representation language is ambiguity. Natural language is highly ambiguous. For example, if we say, "Steve is running fast," we don't know whether Steve is changing location, operating a piece of machinery, or running as a candidate for office. On the other hand, with a logical representation, we can precisely define the concepts we use. We can, for example, define a distinct concept corresponding to each of these three senses of "running." This allows us to place the appropriate rules on their respective concepts, whereas they could not all be placed on the one ambiguous word.

Cyc Technology: Current Status and Projections

The CycL language is probably the most advanced instrument for general knowledge capture and processing. After almost two decades of development sponsored by the U.S. government, IBM, and others, Cycorp is opening the language, sources (partially), and knowledge base (partially) to the public in the OpenCyc project. This opening is increasing the number of current Cyc clients, accelerating Cyc technology development, and providing the potential for rapid growth of the Cyc-based generic knowledge base.

Cyc technology is not yet a standard. However, the bridge from Cyc to XTM delivers the promise of a standardized interchange of such information across the boundaries of knowledge domains, computer notation, and even natural language.

Today, Cyc is the best technology for building a generic knowledge-based product that provides a bridge for non-computer-literate users to talk to computer services. Cyc itself is not a speech recognition system; another layer must be provided to include Cyc in such systems. This additional layer can be made with mainstream technologies (based on SALT [Speech Application Language Tags], VoiceXML, or Java Speech API standards) integrated with knowledge services. Such integration can occur in the XML-based scenarios we will discuss a bit later. Figure 5.5 illustrates relationships between knowledge, XML, and speech technologies.

What Is CycL? How Hard Is It to Learn and Use This Promising Language?

First, Cyc is very different from frame-and-slot systems, in which creating new rules and vocabulary would be considered expensive. Cyc encourages the expression of complex problems and ideas using more vocabulary and simple rules.

In CycL:

- Creating collections is not hard and is relatively inexpensive.
- Creating functions is not expensive.
- Creating predicates is easy and cheap.
- Adding new vocabulary and microtheories is *not* expensive.

The Cyc language consists of:

- Constants—*#$Login*, *#$GroupMembers*; denote individuals or collections.
- Predicates—*#$likesAsFriend, #$bordersOn, #$objectHasColor, #$isa*
- Logical connectives—*#$and*, *#$or*, *#$not*
- Quantifiers—*#$implies*, *#$forAll*, *#$thereExists*
- Sentences—*#$isa*, *#$Simon.Roberts*, *#$SystemUser*; form assertions or queries. The assertion in this example says that *Simon.Roberts* is an instance of *SystemUser* collection.
- Denotational functions—*#$LoginFn Simon.Roberts*; relations that can be applied to some arguments to pick out something new. For example, we can interpret the formula
- *#$password (#$LoginFn #$Simon.Roberts) #$cessna172* as "The password in the login function for Simon Roberts is cessna172."
- Microtheories—*#$HumanActivitiesMt, #$OrganizationMt, #$JavaSchoolMt*; bundle assertions together based on time, space, or anything else that can help in knowledge organization.

Is CycL Flexible Enough to Express Complicated Logic? Can We Build Efficient Systems Based on the Language?

I would like to try to resolve these questions, which also troubled me when I started with CycL.

Is this language flexible and extensible enough to express complicated logic related to natural language? If so, can this language be efficient? Does it have validation mechanisms?

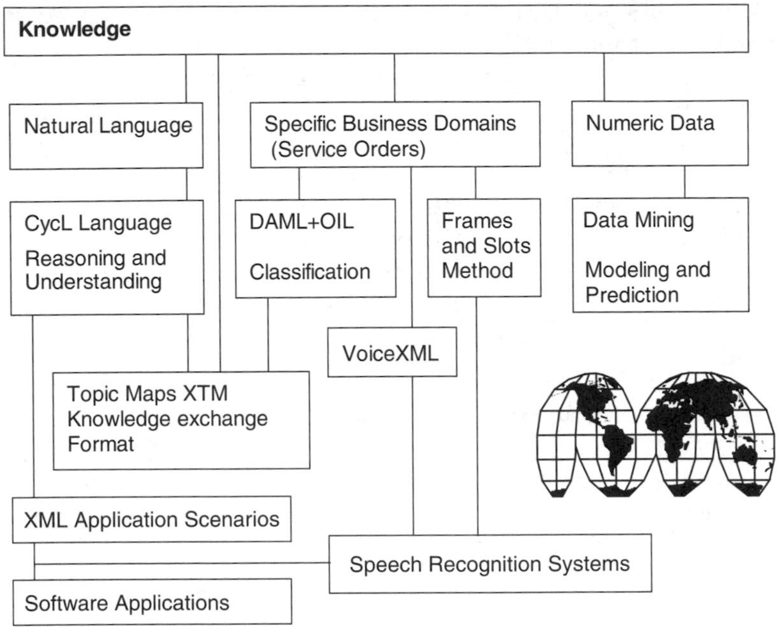

Examples:

Cycl Language

```
(genls PublicAccess AccessType)
(genls ForGroupMembers AccessType)

(implies
 (and
  (isa ?READ Access)
   (performedBy ?READ ?USER)
   (performedOn ?READ ?OBJECT)
   (hasAccessType ?OBJECT ForGroupMembers))
 (isa ?USER GroupMember))
```

XTM example

```
<?xml version="1.0" encoding="ISO-8859-1"?>
<topicMap id="global knowledge container">
 <topic id="Data and Services">
  <baseName>Training</baseName>
  <occurrence>
   <topicRef xlink:href="http://JavaSchool.com"/>
  </occurrence>
 </topic>
...
</topicMap>
```

DAML+OIL

```
<rdf:RDF xmlns:rdf ="http://www.w3.org...
...
<daml:Ontology rdf:about="System Users">
<daml:Class rdf:ID="UserAccount">
 <rdfs:subClassOf rdf:resource="#Account"/>
 <daml:disjointWith rdf:resource="#GroupAccount"/>
</daml:Class>
...
</rdf>
```

Voice XML

```
...
<prompt>
 <audio>
  Please select one of the following service options:
  1 - Check messages
  ....
 </audio>
</prompt>
<nomatch>
 <audio>
  Sorry, I didn't understand that.
 </audio>
 <reprompt/>
</nomatch>
...
```

FIGURE 5.5. Knowledge, XML, and Speech Connections.

(Natural language does not have validation rules, which is one of the reasons it is not suitable for computers.)

Working with CycL, I found positive answers to both of the questions above. Let us start with CycL validation mechanics.

CycL allows (but does not require) us to specify the number and types of arguments for any sentence type. This is very similar to regular programming languages so loved by computers.

How does Cyc deal with possible contradictions between existing and new knowledge? It is not feasible for Cyc to reconsider every assertion in its knowledge base every time we add new data. Cyc's truth maintenance system (TMS) and its argumentation method help Cyc deal with this issue. (I will talk more about TMS later.)

Here is an example of how CycL establishes rules for creating expressions. It is very important (especially for a machine) that there are rules and that every expression can be validated against these rules. Let us say we want to create a new predicate.

There are a couple of important features that every predicate and function has. The first is *arity*. Arity has to do with how many arguments a predicate or function requires, in other words, how many arguments to which you have to apply the function at a given time to result in a meaningful sentence or term.

The second feature is the notion of *argument type*, which has to do with what types of things a predicate or function requires as a particular argument.

Arity is the number of argument places a predicate or function has. It is expressed in CycL in two ways:

1. The predicate *#$arity*

```
(#$arity #$GroupFn 1)
(#$arity #$loginPassword 2)
```

2. The collections

```
#$UnaryPredicate, #$UnaryFunction, #$BinaryPredicate, #$BinaryFunction,
etc.
(#$isa #$GroupFn #$UnaryFunction)
(#$isa #$loginPassword #$BinaryPredicate)
```

Arity, as you know, refers to the number of argument places that a particular predicate or function has. There are two ways to express the arity of a particular predicate or function in the CycL language.

First, we have a predicate, *#$arity*, which you can apply to any relation—in other words, any predicate or function—in conjunction with a numeric value to denote how many arguments that relation accepts. For example, *(#$arity #$GroupFn 1)* denotes that the *#$GroupFn* function accepts only one argument. The *#$loginPassword* predicate has an arity of two; thus it takes two arguments at a time.

Most relations in CycL have low arities (a low number of arguments); in fact, most have just one or two as their arity. *Remember that Cyc encourages simplicity!* Some relations take three or four arguments, a few take five arguments, and a very small number take more than five arguments. Seven is probably the highest arity used, although in principle, arity could be any number. Try to keep them on the low side.

Yet, there are few instances of *#$UnaryPredicate* in CycL.

Instead, unary properties are usually represented either as *#$Collections* or *#$Attribute-Values*. For example, see the *#$TeamLeader* collection below:

```
(#$isa #$JeffZhuk #$TeamLeader)
```

This is the recommended way, rather than the new predicate *#$teamLeader*, as in the assertion below:

```
(#$teamLeader #$JeffZhuk)
```

There are a lot of unary functions, but very few unary predicates. The reason for this has to do with the Cyc inference engine and certain facts about how it works most efficiently. There are alternative ways to express what you might think of intuitively as a unary property.

I mentioned before that Cyc has its own way to maintain logical data consistency. Let us say we want to add an argument to an existing assertion. This action would immediately trigger the TMS's argumentation on this assertion. If this assertion changes its value from true to false or otherwise, Cyc looks at all the assertions supported by the newly changed assertion.

The TMS does not add new deductions or assertions, it only changes or removes them. The changing is done in such a way that infinite oscillation is impossible. If the change removes the last argument from an assertion, the assertion now has a truth-value of "unknown" and is removed from the knowledge base.

For example, someone removes the assertion "JeffZhuk is a person." The TMS will trigger an investigation of other assertions that are based on the one just removed. All found related rules will be removed. For example, the rule "spouse of JeffZhuk is Bronia" will be removed if TMS maintains the rule that only a person can have a "spouse."

What Is the Basic Structure of the Cyc Knowledge Base?

The knowledge base comprises a massive taxonomy of concepts and specifically defined relationships that describe how those concepts are related.

The context of the knowledge is arranged by degrees of generality, with a small layer of abstract generalizations at the top and a large layer of real-world facts at the bottom.

A very powerful and simple CycL constant helps to create unlimited hierarchies. To express that one collection is subsumed by another, we use the CycL constant *#$genls*. A formula of the form below means that every instance of the first collection, *GroupMember*, is also an instance of the second collection, *SystemUser*.

```
(#$genls #$GroupMember #$SystemUser)
```

In other words, *SystemUser* is a generalization of *GroupMember*.

Most abstract concepts belong to the highest layers of Cyc knowledge base hierarchy. Real and specific concepts and facts belong to lower levels of Cyc knowledge base structure.

We can roughly separate the Cyc knowledge base into four layers.

1. The upper ontology—abstract layer
2. Core theories
3. Domain-specific theories
4. Ground-level facts

The highest, abstract layer is called the *upper ontology*. The upper ontology layer does not say much about the world at all. It represents very general relations among very general concepts. For example, it contains assertions to the effect that every event is a temporal thing, every temporal thing is an individual, and every individual is a thing. "Thing" is Cyc's most general concept. Everything whatsoever is an instance of "thing."

The next knowledge base layer is called *core theories*. Thies layer contains several core theories that represent general facts about space, time, and causality. These are the theories that are essential to almost all commonsense reasoning.

Domain-specific theories are more specific than core theories. These theories apply to special areas of interest, such as group security policies, the service request structure, sentence types, and dialog management rules. These are the theories that make Cyc particularly useful, but they are not necessary for commonsense reasoning.

The final layer contains what is sometimes called *ground-level facts*. These are statements about particular individuals in the world. For example, "Kathy started a session" is a specific statement about one person. Generalizations would not go here; they would go in a higher layer. Anything you can imagine as a fact or a headline in a newspaper (the two are not the same, of course) would probably go in ground-level facts.

What Is the Syntax of CycL? Constants and Predicates

CycL tries to model the world in terms that most people know and understand. Its constants are the "vocabulary words" that represent collections of concepts.

For example, *#$ComputerService* represents the set of all computer services, or *#$ServiceAction* represents all possible actions provided by a service. Each constant has its own data structure in the knowledge base. The data structure includes (besides the constant itself) the assertions (statements) that describe this constant.

Imagine that we want to express an idea that email belongs to computer services. We tell CycL:

```
(#$isa #$Email #$ComputerServices)
```

We read this sentence as, "Email is an instance of computer services."

What is *#$isa* in this sentence? In knowledge terms, it is a predicate. Predicates establish relationships between objects. Other predicate examples are *hasFriends* and *accessType*. We form sentences by applying predicates to some arguments. For example:

```
(#$isa #$VoiceTechnology #$TrainingCourse)
```

In this sentence, the predicate *#$isa*, which means, "is an instance of," is applied to the arguments *#$VoiceTechnology*, which relate *VoiceTechnology* to *#$TrainingCourse*, which denotes the collection of all training courses. The resulting sentence says that *VoiceTechnology* is an instance of a training course.

CycL Has Functions

Here is a definition for the function *#$MemberRoleFn*:

```
(#$arity #$MemberRoleFn 2)
(#$arg1Isa #$MemberRoleFn #$User)
(#$arg2Isa #$MemberRoleFn #$Group)
(#$resultIsa #$MemberRoleFn #$GroupRole)
```

We read this function definition as "the *MemberRoleFn* function has two parameters: user and group." The function returns a specific role that the user plays in the specified group.

Functions differ from predicates. Functions return a Cyc term as a result. Accordingly, function definitions describe not only the number and types of arguments (e.g., predicate definitions) but must also describe the type of the result to be returned using the predicate *#$resultIsa*.

Functions with fixed arity are similar to predicates in that the definition of the function must specify the type of each argument using the predicates *#$arg1Isa*, *#$arg2Isa*, and so forth.

Functions without fixed arity are defined using the predicate *#$argsIsa*, which specifies a single type of which every argument must be an instance.

Use Variables and Logical Connectives to Create New Rules

CycL has variables. Variable names begin with a question mark and are written in capital letters: ("?OBJECT") or ("?X").

Creating rules in CycL is easy. I will do it right now with the *#$implies* keyword.

```
(#$implies
 (#$and
   (#$hasMembershipIn ?USER ?GROUP)
   (#$hasRole ?USER ?GROUP #$Admin)
   (#$hasPrivilege ?USER ?GROUP #$ChangeMemberRoles)))
```

This rule says that if a user has membership in a group and the user has the role of an administrator in this group, the user has the privilege of changing member roles in this group. Creating rules in Cyc is *not* expensive.

#$implies, *#$and* as well as *#$or*, and *#$not* are the most important logical connectives in CycL.

Assertions and Microtheories

After a new sentence is successfully inserted (or asserted) into the Cyc knowledge base, it is stored as an assertion. Every assertion belongs to one or several microtheories.

A grouping mechanism that is an improvement over functions is offered by CycL microtheories.

Microtheories offer an assertion grouping mechanism.

A microtheory provides an umbrella over several assertions. Microtheories enable better knowledge base building together with better and more scalable inference.

Microtheories focus development of the Cyc knowledge base and enable shorter and simpler assertions.

Under a microtheory umbrella, we can provide a set of short assertions instead of a single complicated one.

Here is an example:

Mt: DataAccessMt

#$isa	*#$Read*	*#$AccessType*
#$performedBy	*#$Read*	*#$AlexNozik*
#$performedAt	*#$Read*	*#$08/07/2002-23:30:56*

In this example, *Mt: DataAccessMt* is a common name (umbrella) over several assertions.

Microtheories also allow us to cope with global inconsistency in the knowledge base. In building a knowledge base of this scale and covering different points of view, different times and places, different theories, and different topics, some inconsistency is inevitable. Inconsistencies, however, can make accurate reasoning impossible. Using microtheories, we can isolate terse assertions like the one above from others with which they might be inconsistent, and reason within consistent bundles.

We can allow inference to focus on the most relevant assertions and those that share the current assumptions.

Can Cyc Understand the Concept of "Events"?

Yes. CycL has a collection of Events.

Events are represented as individuals that:

- Have components (are not empty in space or time)
- Are situations
- Have temporal extent
- Are dynamic

Events are classified in Cyc collections such as those below:

`#$Reading, #$SalesActivity, #$Communicating, etc.`

Events in Cyc belong to a collection called *#$Event*. Events have components or stretches of space or time. Events have temporal extent: they occur over time. Events are also dynamic: they can change over time. They are also *situations*. The situation can be any configuration or arrangement, such as a set of objects, a specific place, or a specific time.

This is really just the tip of the iceberg. There are many more specializations of *#$Event*. The *#$Information-TransferEvent* collection can be very useful in describing computer system tasks. The *#$Information-TransferEvent* collection has specializations, such as *#$Communicating* and *#$Reading*.

Why do we reify (store) individual events (instances of *#$Event*) in Cyc? If our knowledge about an event changes, having a reified (stored) data structure to represent the event enables us to add information or alter the representation in Cyc very easily.

Events are related to each other in the *#$genls* hierarchy. We can use that hierarchy to inherit knowledge downward from the more general types of events to the more specialized types of events.

For instance, if we have the general event collection *#$UserSessionEvent* and we state that this collection consists of *#$UserSessionInput* and *#$SystemSessionResponse*, Cyc will know that this is also true of specializations of *#$UserSessionEvent*, such as *#$ToddGreanierSessionEvent* or *#$ToddGreanierSessionInput*.

How Do We Attach Events to the Things Involved?

Many things can be components of events. Events can have performers, and there can be devices that performers use during the events. Events can have subevents, or substages. Events can occur at places, and those places are somehow involved in the events.

Events take place at certain times, and times of events are also somehow involved in events (we have special predicates to relate times to events). We state how components of events are involved in events with *role predicates*—predicates that are instances of the collection *#$Role*.

In CycL we use special predicates called *roles* to relate reified events to their components. There is a lot of knowledge built into the construction of role predicates to help Cyc understand how these roles function to relate components of events to reified events.

Roles have a hierarchy that extends Cyc's ability to reason about the components—the participants and subparts—of events. Roles are specialized predicates developed for relating components of events to events. There are two general specializations of the collection *#$Role*: *#$ActorSlot* and *#$Sub-ProcessSlot*. Roles are arranged in a predicate hierarchy based on *#$genlPreds*. The top node of the hierarchy is *#$actors*. Every instance of *#$Role* is a specialization of *#$actors*.

These CycL examples show the roles in the conversational events during a user session:

```
(#$performedBy #$Reading003 #$MashaTishkov)
```

MashaTishkov performs *Reading003*.

```
(#$informationRequested #$Reading003 #$ListOfUsers)
```

The information requested in *Reading003* is the *ListOfUsers*.

Here is an example of a CycL rule that captures general knowledge about roles, including knowledge about the kinds of things that are related by certain roles.

```
(#$implies
 (#$and
   (#$isa ?READ #$Reading)
    (#$informationOrigin ?READ ?OBJECT))
 (#$isa ?OBJECT #$TextualMaterial))
(#$implies
 (#$and
   (#$isa ?READ #$Reading)
    (#$performedBy ?READ ?USER)
   (#$hasSecurityType ?OBJECT #$GroupMembersOnly))
(#$isa ?USER #$GroupMember))
```

The first one says, "In every instance of *#$Reading* that has a source, that information source is textual material." A separate assertion should tell us that every instance of *#$Reading* does have an information source. In other words, "Whenever someone reads, they read text."

The next one says, "Any reading event done on an object with security type restricted to group members only must be done by a person who is a group member."

By the way, we do not always need to write the strange CycL-ish characters #$. Cyc can add them for us internally. Therefore, the example below is as valid as the example above.

```
(implies
  (and
   (isa ?READ Reading)
    (performedBy ?READ ?USER)
   (hasSecurityType ?OBJECT GroupMembers))
(isa ?USER GroupMember))
```

All these examples demonstrate CycL's unmatched capability of expressing knowledge. What can we do with CycL today?

Cyc Answers Questions

We can ask Cyc questions by creating three types of queries:

1. Ask—general-purpose query
2. Prove—conditional query
3. Query—either of the above

For example, we can have a query in the microtheory *2003ScheduleMt*

```
(groupMember XML-TrainingClass ?WHO)
```

This query is a request to generate a set of names from the list *XML-TrainingClass* according to the *2003ScheduleMt*.

An example of an answer is provided below:

```
((?WHO . ScottDennison))
...
...
```

These small examples may lead you to the wrong conclusion that we can do these same basic operations with almost any database. This is not exactly true. The difference will be more visible when you try to express more complicated problems, with many factors that must be taken into consideration, in multidimensional criteria space.

The core CycL algorithm treats the inference problem as a search through proof-space for a satisfactory resolution of a particular query. Each inference step in the search is a single supporting formula in the eventual proof. We would appreciate the very rich expressiviness of CycL and power of the core CycL inference engine algorithm when dealing with such problems.

How to Begin with OpenCyc

If you do not have Java 2 installed on your machine, please install it now. Then download the latest version of OpenCyc from *www.opencyc.org*, uncompress it, and follow the instructions in the readme file.

I provide an example for a Linux system, just to demonstrate how easy it is to start.

```
tar xvfz opencyc-version.tgz
cd opencyc-version/scripts/linux
./run-cyc.sh
```

At this point, the OpenCyc server is up and running. You can enter expressions from the command line or access the OpenCyc Web server running on your machine with your local browser.

The URL is *http://localhost:3602/cgi-bin/cyccgi/cg?cb-start*.

Good luck browsing OpenCyc using the *Guest* or *CycAdministrator* account.

How to Include OpenCyc in the Bigger Picture of Your Distributed System

OpenCyc has several communication options. We already looked into the simplest options that provide access to OpenCyc directly from the command line or via a Web browser. These options are helpful in exploring Cyc's behavior. To include the OpenCyc server into your business network, use one of the following options:

- Peer-to-peer JXTA interface (find more details on JXTA implementation in the Chapter 14)
- Direct TCP/IP socket communications with *org.opencyc.api.CycConnection*
- Remote TCP/IP communications via *org.opencyc.api.CycRemoteConnection* class with powerful methods like *converse(message)* and *getTrace()*.

A few words about the JXTA project: JXTA is not an abbreviation. The name was picked up by Sun Microsystems from the word *juxtapose*, which means to put things next to each other. The JXTA project is Sun Microsystems' peer-to-peer technology initiative supported by Java communities. The Chapter 14 takes a close look on Distributed Life in the JXTA and Jini Communities and specifically discusses distributed knowledge node implementation.

Socket communications include chat options supported by the *org.opencyc.chat* and *org.opencyc.conversation* packages. The chat is in the form of a text conversation. The chat participants send and receive asynchronous messages. This *org.opencyc.conversation.interpreter* class models the chat interaction with nested finite state machine stacks and supports mixed initiative with a dictionary of stacks, one of which is active and the rest suspended.

Find out about TCP/IP ports in the distributed file *init/parameters.lisp*.

We can look at the knowledge engine not only as a smart database, but also as a possible service brain that can add some smartness to our services. Naturally, this would require some interaction between existing services and the knowledge engine. An example might be XML-based APIs that allow user programs to request knowledge engine services.

We also want to enable the knowledge engine to directly invoke existing services. What we actually need is two-way XML-based communications from a user program to OpenCyc and back.

Let us start building a service-knowledge bridge that would greatly complement existing OpenCyc APIs.

We start with the *ServiceConnector* class presented in Fig. 5.6.

The *ServiceConnector* class invokes any service and can download additional service classes at run-time if necessary. The *ServiceConnector* class uses the service name to obtain a needed instance of a service class and invokes a selected method parameter on this currently acting object. The *ServiceConnector* class can be considered an actor that can actually play multiple (object) roles.

Two of the most important methods of the class are *act()* and *registerObject()*.

The *act()* method is responsible for invoking the proper method on the proper service object. The *registerObject()* method stores service objects in the table of services and helps to reuse the same service object for many method invocations.

Remember that service objects live their own lives and keep their states, which can have an important influence on invoked service behavior. The *KnowledgeService* class (Fig. 5.7) represents one of many services that can be invoked by the *ServiceConnector*.

```
package com.its.util;

import java.lang.reflect.Method;
import java.util.Hashtable;

/**
 * The ServiceConnector class invokes a selected method on a selected
 * class instance
 * The ServiceConnector can actually play not only its own (object)
 * role
 * As a good actor it can also play objects of any (existing) type
 * If necessary the ServiceConnector loads a new class at run-time
 * The ServiceConnector has a registry where it keeps (and reuses) all
 * actors
 * @author Jeff.Zhuk@JavaSchool.com
 */
public class ServiceConnector {
    protected Object[] parameters;
    protected Object result;
    protected Method method;
    protected Object actingObject;
    protected Class actingClass = getClass();
    protected String actingClassName = actingClass.getName();
    protected String defaultServiceName;
    protected Hashtable actingObjects = new Hashtable();
    // repository of objects
    public ServiceConnector() {};
/**
 * The constructor creates an object of a requested class
 * It a requested class name is "ServiceConnector" there is nothing
 * to do
 * In this case the actingObject is "this"
 * @param className
 */
    public ServiceConnector(String className) {
        // include package name in the className to increase efficiency
        defaultServiceName = className;
    }
/**
 * The act() method provides a unified way to find a requested method
 * and invokes the method on previously defined object.
 * There is a different version of the method for J2ME implementation
 * @param methodName
 * @param parameters
 * @return result
 */
    public Object act(String methodName, Object[] parameters) {
        return act(actingClassName, methodName, parameters);
    }
```

FIGURE 5.6

```
/**
 * The act() method provides a unified way to find a requested method
 * and invokes the method on previously defined object.
 * This version is a convenience method for a common case when
 * parameters passed via a hash table
 * @param className
 * @param methodName
 * @param table of parameters
 * @return result
 */
   public Object act(String className, String methodName, Hashtable
   table) {
       Object[] objects = new Object[1];
       objects[0] = table;
       return act(actingClassName, methodName, objects);
   }
   public Object act(String className, String methodName, Object[]
   parameters) {
        try{
           changeActingClass(className);
           // change acting class if necessary, or leave as is
           Class[] classes = null;
           if(parameters != null) {
               classes = new Class[parameters.length];
               for(int i=0; i<parameters.length; i++) {
                   classes[i] = parameters[i].getClass();
               }
           }
           method = actingClass.getMethod(methodName, classes);
       } catch (Exception e) {
           return ("ERROR:ServiceConnector.cannot find the
           method:actingClass=" +
             actingClass + " methodName=" + methodName + "
             parameters=" +
             parameters + " e=" +e);
       }
       try{
           result = method.invoke(actingObject, parameters);
       } catch (Exception e) {
           return ("ERROR:" + e + " @ServiceConnector->" +
             actingClassName + "." + methodName);
       }
       return result;
   }
/**
 * changeActingClass() instantiate a new object of a new acting
 * class if necessary
 * @param className
 */
```

FIGURE 5.6. ***(cont.)***

```
    public void changeActingClass(String className) throws
    Exception {
        if(className == null) {
            className = defaultServiceName;
        }
        if(!className.equals(actingClassName)) {
        // load the class and instantiate the object
            if(actingObjects.get(className) == null) {
                actingClass = Class.forName(className);
                actingObject = actingClass.newInstance();
                actingObjects.put(className, actingObject);
            } else { // use existing object
                actingObject = actingObjects.get(className);
                actingClass = actingObject.getClass();
            }
        }
        actingClassName = className;
    }
/**
 * registerClass() register objects in the Hashtable actingObjects
 * @param className
 * @param object
 */
    public void registerObject(String className, Object object) {
        if(actingObjects.get(className) == null) {
            actingObjects.put(className, object);
        }
    }
}
```

FIGURE 5.6. *(cont.)*

There are no dependencies between the *ServiceConnector* and services in the J2SE (standard) environment. If the application operates in J2ME, any services implemented are known to the *ServiceConnector* interface. This compensates for the absence of a reflection package in J2ME. (See Chapter 11 for more details and examples.)

The *KnowledgeService* serves as a wrapper around the *org.cyc.api.CycAccess* methods. The *KnowledgeService* class uses the *org.cyc.api.CycAccess* class to communicate to the Cyc engine over TCP/IP sockets. The constructor of the *KnowledgeService* initiates access to the knowledge engine and prepares Cyc to talk. The wrapper helps to simplify and unify access to Cyc via XML-based descriptions translated into hash tables.

The user can request a set of actions directly asking for *"service=\"className\"* *"with "action=\"methodName\"* ". The user can also request service instructions from the knowledge engine via the *getInstructions()* method.

The *getInstructions()* method provides for the possibility of a scripted dialog between a user program and the knowledge engine. The set of instructions (script) can be stored in-line in the knowledge base, or the knowledge engine can point to a file with instructions.

```
package org.opencyc.connector;

import java.io.*;
import java.net.*;
import java.util.*;

import org.opencyc.api.*;
import org.opencyc.cycobject.*;
import org.opencyc.util.*;

/**
 * The KnowledgeService class uses CycAccess to communicate to Cyc
 * engine over TCP/IP sockets.
 * The constructor opens standard input stream and prepares Cyc to talk.
 * User can request a set of actions via the getIstructions() method
 * The getInstructions() method provides a possibility for a scripted
 * dialog
 * between a user program and Cyc.
 * This dialog between a user (person) and Cyc can be arranged using
 * XML based scenarios
 * The main() method creates the KnowledgeService object and passes
 * initial instructions.
 * A user can always exit the program by typing "Quit".
 *
 * @author Jeff.Zhuk@JavaSchool.com
 */
public class KnowledgeService {
    public static boolean debug=false;
    protected CycAccess cycAccess;
    private String sessionWorldName, savedWorldName; // init values
    //////////////////////////////////////
    private String[] worldSystemMts;   // for future world integration
    private Hashtable worldMts = new Hashtable(); // mts created by user
    private Hashtable worldObjects = new Hashtable();
    // objects created by user
    private String report = "";
    public boolean connected = false;
    public KnowledgeService() {};

    /**
     * The constructor calls initCycAccess() method to start TCP/IP
     * session with Cyc and
     * opens standard input stream to accept user's input.
     * The constructor also sets initial actingObject to this and
     * makes request to Cyc
     * for initial instructions
     * @param savedWorldName filename for Cyc world
     * @param systemName
     * @param directSystemInput is true for keyboard handling in shell
     * testing
     */
    public KnowledgeService(String savedWorldName, String sessionWorldName)
{
```

FIGURE 5.7

```
        // set initial actingObject to this
        this.savedWorldName = savedWorldName;
        this.sessionWorldName = sessionWorldName;
    }
    /**
     * The getWorldMts() returns worldMts
     * @return worldMts
     */
    public Hashtable getWorldMts() {
        return worldMts;
    }
   /**
     * The getWorldObjects() returns worldObjects
     * @return worldObjects
     */
    public Hashtable getWorldObjects() {
        return worldObjects;
    }
    /**
     * The initComponents() method is to connect to Cyc
     */
    public void initComponents() {
        if(connected) {
            return;
        }
        try {
            // start TCP/IP session with Cyc
            cycAccess = new CycAccess();
            cycAccess.traceOn();
            connected = true;
        } catch(Exception e) {
            connected = false;  // it is false anyway
        }
    }
    /**
     * prepare and pass parameters to a proper method of the
     * cycAccess object
     * @param parameters
     * @return response
     */
    public String converse(Hashtable parameters) throws Exception {
        String msg = (String)parameters.get("msg");
        cycAccess.converseVoid(msg);
        return (msg + "-Done");
    }
    /**
     * prepare and pass parameters to a proper method of the
     * cycAccess object
     * @param constant
     * @return response
     */
    public String createNewPermanent(Hashtable parameters) throws
    Exception {
```

FIGURE 5.7. *(cont.)*

```
        String constant = (String)parameters.get("msg");
        String result =
        cycAccess.createNewPermanent(constant).toString();
        worldObjects.put(constant, new Hashtable());
        return result;
    }
     /**
     * Create a microtheory MT, with a comment, isa and array of genlMts
     * @param constant
     * @return response
     */
    public String createMicrotheory(Hashtable parameters) throws
    Exception {
        String comment = (String)parameters.get("msg");
        String mtName = (String)parameters.get("Mt");

        mtName = Stringer.beginWithUpperCase(mtName);
        String isaMtName = (String)parameters.get("isa");
        String genlMtsString = (String)parameters.get("genlMts");
        ArrayList genlMts = new ArrayList();
        if(genlMtsString != null) {
          String[] strings = Stringer.split(",",genlMtsString);
          for(int i=0; strings != null && i<strings.length; i++) {
                genlMts.add(strings[i]);
             }
        }
        String result = cycAccess.createMicrotheory(mtName,
        comment, isaMtName, genlMts).toString();
        worldMts.put(mtName, new Hashtable());
        return result;
    }

    /**
     * Remove (kill) a constant
     * @param parameters
     */
    public String killConstant(Hashtable parameters) throws
    Exception {
        String constant = (String)parameters.get("constant");
        CycConstant cycConstant =
        cycAccess.getConstantByName(constant);
        cycAccess.kill(cycConstant);
        if(worldObjects.containsKey(constant)) {
            worldObjects.remove(constant);
        } else if(worldMts.containsKey(constant)) {
            worldMts.remove(constant);
        }
        return ("OK");
    }
    /**
     * prepare and pass parameters to a proper method of the cycAccess
     * object
```

FIGURE 5.7. *(cont.)*

```
 * @param parameters
 * @return response
 */
public String getKnownConstantByName(Hashtable parameters)
throws Exception {
    String constant = (String)parameters.get("msg");
    return cycAccess.getKnownConstantByName
    (constant).toString();
}
/** The isExistingConstant() method checks for the constant in the KB
 * @param parameters
 * @return true if exists
 */
public boolean isExistingConstant(String constant) throws
Exception {
    initComponents(); // check if connected
    Integer id = cycAccess.getConstantId(constant);
    if(id == null) {
        return false;
    }
    return true;
}
/** The assertGAF() method
 * It is often described as assert, but must be different from
 * the Java keyword "assert" that appeared in JDK 1.4
 * They prepare and pass parameters to assertGaf() method of the
 * cycAccess object
 * expected parameters: Mt="MyMt" msg="(#$likesAsFriend
 * #$BillClinton #$AlbertGore)"
 * @param parameters
 * @return response
 */
public String assertGAF(Hashtable parameters) throws Exception {
    String msg = (String)parameters.get("msg");
    String mtName = (String)parameters.get("Mt");
    if(mtName == null) {
        mtName = savedWorldName; // mainMT
    }
    CycFort mt = cycAccess.getKnownConstantByName(mtName);
    // "PeopleDataMt"
    CycList gaf = cycAccess.makeCycList(msg);
    cycAccess.assertGaf(gaf, mt);
    return "OK";
}

/**
 * prepare and pass parameters to unassertGaf() method of the
 * cycAccess object
 * expected parameters: Mt="MyMt" msg="(#$likesAsFriend
 * #$BillClinton #$AlbertGore)"
 * @param parameters
 * @return response
 */
```

FIGURE 5.7. *(cont.)*

```
public String unassertGAF(Hashtable parameters) throws
Exception {
    String msg = (String)parameters.get("msg");
    String mtName = (String)parameters.get("Mt");
    if(mtName == null) {
        mtName = savedWorldName; // mainMT
    }
    CycFort mt = cycAccess.getKnownConstantByName(mtName);
    // "PeopleDataMt"
    CycList gaf = cycAccess.makeCycList(msg);
    //"(#$likesAsFriend #$BillClinton #$AlbertGore)");
    cycAccess.unassertGaf(gaf, mt);
    return "OK: deleting " + msg;
}
/**
 * saves Cyc data into a file and calls the exit() method to
 * close Cyc connection
 * @param world filename
 * @return response
 */
public String close(String world) {
    if(world == null) {
        world = sessionWorldName;
    }
    if(cycAccess == null) {
        return "ERROR: lost KB connection";
    }
    try {
        write(world);
        cycAccess.converseVoid("(exit)");
        cycAccess.close();
    } catch(Exception e) {
        return ("ERROR: saving world=" + e);
    }
    return ("Good bye");
}
/**
 * saves Cyc data into a file
 * @param world filename
 * @return response
 */
public String write(String world) throws Exception {
    if(world == null) {
        world = sessionWorldName;
    }
    String writeWorld = "(write-image \"world/" + world + "\")";
    if(cycAccess == null) {
        return "ERROR: lost KB connection";
    }
    cycAccess.converseVoid(writeWorld);
    return ("OK");
}
```

FIGURE 5.7. *(cont.)*

```
/**
 * The getInstructions() method gets comments from the Cyc
 * and passes to the askUser() method for interpretation
 * getInstructions() method does its own interpretation of a command
 * @param parameters for example "CycUsersMt InitCommand" or
 * "CycUsersMt NewUser"
 * @return response
 */
   public String getInstructions(Hashtable parameters) throws Exception {
       // for example "LoginCommand"
       // this constant should have the "instructionSet" predicate
       String msg = (String)parameters.get("msg");
       String filename = (String)parameters.get("file");
       if(filename != null) {
           return IOMaster.readTextFile(filename);
       } else { // create query with variable="INSTRUCTIONS
           parameters.put("variable", "INSTRUCTIONS");
           if(msg.startsWith("(") && msg.endsWith(")") ) { // ready msg
               parameters.put("msg",msg);
           } else {
               parameters.put("msg","(#$instructionSet #$" + msg +
               " ?INSTRUCTIONS)");
           }
           return query(parameters);
       }
   }
}   // end of KnowledgeService class
```

FIGURE 5.7. *(cont.)*

More complete source code for the *KnowledgeService* (and related classes described below) can be found in Chapter 13 and Appendix 3.

Here is a separate example of a request to the Cyc knowledge engine to create a constant, insert (assert) assertion, query, and so forth.

```
<act name="service1"
  service="KnowledgeService" action="createNewPermanent"
  constant="JeffZhuk" />
```

You can also include a request for your own (non-Cyc) service in the script.

In this case, all parameters that follow the action name will be passed as a single string to your method in your class.

A general recommendation is to pass key-value pairs to your method in a single string and provide the parameter interpretations inside your method.

For example:

```
<act name="service1"
 service="Mail" action="send" from="Jeff.Zhuk@JavaSchool.com"
 to="reed@cyc.com" subject="test" body="testing mail service" />
```

The actual communication API between Cyc and Java is still evolving. The basic Cyc-Java dialog and service operations described above are dressed into XML tags. An external user program can send XML-based instructions to the *KnowledgeService*.

The Cyc response to the *KnowledgeService* is also XML formatted. The *KnowledgeService* can work with a simple dialog manager (in this example, it is the *ScenarioPlayer* class) that implements the scenario interface (Fig. 5.8).

The scenario interface includes several methods that provide screens to the user and accept user input. The *prompt()* method, for example, supports a prearranged dialog between a user and the *KnowledgeService* and helps to retrieve necessary data from a user with XML-based dialog scenarios.

An example of an XML-based dialog scenario is provided in Fig. 5.9.

The dialog scenario in this example includes a set of questions that help a user introduce a new fact to the knowledge engine.

The *prompt()* method (implemented in a subclass—for example, the *ScenarioPlayer*) translates a multiline message passed as an argument into a set of questions for a user. The method stores user answers and uses them according to the instructions in the message.

The instructions can prompt a user for questions or refer to user services or to *KnowledgeService* methods. The *prompt()* method can replace script variables at run-time with the user's answers.

The *prompt()* method reads an XML-based dialog scenario with prearranged questions and consecutive service actions that may follow such questions.

The XML-based dialog scenario usually includes a set (or several sets) of question sequences.

Here is an example of a question that might be repeated, because some of us have more than one favorite rock band.

```
<prompt name="1" variable="REQUESTED-SUBJECT"
service="UserAVI" action="prompt"
msg="What do you want to know?" />
```

This XML description invokes the *prompt()* method on a service object of the *UserAVI* (audio-video interface) class.

The service selects a proper presentation layer to show or to speak out the question to a user.

The user's answer is stored under the variable name *REQUESTED-SUBJECT* and is used in the following instruction of this scenario.

```
<act name="2" service="KnowledgeService" action="query"
msg="(?X #$REQUESTED-SUBJECT ?Y)" />
```

This instruction queries Cyc for a requested subject and translates the knowledge engine's response into the proper presentation format.

Here is a bigger example of a set of questions about your lovely rock band. The answers will be stored in Cyc under a name

```
"LOGIN-NAME" + "FavoriteBand"
```

in the microtheory (that we create at run-time) with the name

```
"LOGIN-NAME" + "HobbiesMt"
```

```
// Scenario
package com.its.connector;

import java.awt.*;
/*
 * The Scenario includes several methods that provide user screen
 * and accept user input.
 * The prompt() method, for example,
 * supports pre-arranged dialog between a user and the
 * KnowledgeServiceConnector,
 * and helps to retrieve necessary data from user with XML based
 * dialog scenarios
 * @author Jeff.Zhuk@JavaSchool.com, Internet Technology School (ITS)
 */
public interface Scenario {
/**
 * The prompt() method will translate a multi-line message passed as
 * an argument
 * into a set of questions for a user.
 * The method will store user answers and use them according to
 * instructions in the message.
 * The instructions most likely will refer to
 * KnowledgeServiceConnector methods
 * The prompt method will be able to replace script variables with
 * user's answers

 * Example of XML based dialog scenario:

<dialogScenario service="org.opencyc.connector.UserCycDialog"
action="prompt">
 <setOfQuestions name="newTopic">
   <store name=variable1" variable="_$newObject" unique="true"
       msg="Please provide a unique name for your topic." />

   <serviceRequest service=
   "org.opencyc.connector.KnowledgeServiceConnector"
       action="createConstant" msg="_$newObject" />
 </setOfQuestions>
</dialogScenario>

 * The Scenario includes several methods that provide user prompt
 * and accept user input.
 * The prompt() method, for example,
 * supports pre-arranged dialog between a user and the
 * KnowledgeServiceConnector,
 * and helps to retrieve necessary data from a user.
 * The prompt() method reads an XML based dialog scenario with
 * pre-arranged questions
 * and consequtive service-actions that can follow such questions.
 * The XML based dialog scenario usually include set of questions
 * sequences.
```

FIGURE 5.8

```
<setOfQuestions name="setOne" />
or
<setOfQuestions name="setTwo" repeated="true" />

 * The set of instructions (script) can be stored in-line in Cyc or
 * Cyc will point to a file with instructions
 * Instructions can include following keywords (tags):
 - setOfQuestions - follow with questions to user and instructions
   on what to do with user's answers.
 - <setOfQuestions name="aName" repeated="true"
   useSectionName="_$sectionName"
   same for a group of repeatable answers;
   this will also instruct Cyc to establish a new constant-section
   to store multiple objects-answers
 - <store name="_$emailAddress" unique="true" msg="What is your email?" />
 - user's answer will be stored under the section name and
   this name can be used to create Cyc constants and make related
   assertions

   Example of a set of repeatable questions about your lovely rock band.
   The answers will be stored under an umbrella named with
   "[yourLoginName]" + "FavoriteBands"
   The login name will be supplied at runtime.
   Note that "Rock band you like:" is actual output by Cyc for the
   user that invites her/him for the first answer
   There are several assertions we do after the answer using methods
   "createConstant" and "assert" of the KnowledgeServiceConnector class
   Most of KnowledgeServiceConnector methods are wrapper to
   CycAccess class methods that translate text input into a proper
   set of parameters.
   Theoretically we could use any other actions and invoke other
   methods on other classes.

<setOfQuestions name="aName" repeated="true"
 useSectionName="_$loginNameFavoriteBands" />
<store name="_$emailAddress" unique="true" msg="What is your
 favorite rock band?" />
<ServiceRequest name="service1" service="KnowledgeServiceConnector"
    action="createConstant" msg="_$loginNameFavoriteBands" />
<ServiceRequest name="service2" service="KnowledgeServiceConnector"
 action="assert"
    Mt="_$loginNameHobbiesMt msg="(#$isa #$_$loginNameFavoriteBands
    #$AttributeValue)" />
<ServiceRequest name="service3" service="KnowledgeServiceConnector"
 action="assert"
    Mt="_$loginNameHobbiesMt"
    msg="(#$hasAttributes #$_$loginName
    #$_$loginNameFavoriteBands)" />
<ServiceRequest name="service4" service="KnowledgeServiceConnector"
 action="assert"
```

FIGURE 5.8. *(cont.)*

```
    Mt="_$loginNameHobbiesMt msg="(#$isa #$_$loginNameFavoriteBands
    #$InterestArea)" />
<ServiceRequest name="service5" service="KnowledgeServiceConnector"
action="assert"
    Mt="_$loginNameHobbiesMt msg=
    "(#$hobbies #$_$loginNameFavoriteBands \"_$rockBand\")" />?>

This set of questions is marked with "repeated" flag.
This means that this set of questions can be repeated
if some of us know more than one rock band - till a user presses the ENTER
key with no data entered.

The Dialog scenario can also include:
- request to Cyc to create a constant, make assertion, query data, etc.

- request to your own service.
  In this case all parameters that follow action name will be passed
  as a single String to your method in your class
  General recommendation is to pass key-value pairs to your method
  in a single string and interpret inside your method
  Example:
  <ServiceRequest name="aName" service="Mail" action="send"
   from="Jeff.Zhuk@JavaSchool.com" to="reed@cyc.com" subject="test"
   body="testing mail service ... etc. " />
*/
   public boolean prompt(String message) throws Exception;
/**
 * interpretInput() method checks user input against expected answers
 * expected answers should be embedded into Cyc (previous) response
 * @param inputLine
 * @return true if success or false to pass interpretation to
 * another Dialog Manager
 */
    public boolean interpretInput(String s);
}
```

FIGURE 5.8. ***(cont.)***

The login name is supplied at run-time as a parameter to the scenario.

Note that "What is your favorite rock band?" is the actual prompt for the user to provide the first answer. There are several assertions we make after the answer using "*createNewPermanent*" and "*assert*" methods of the *KnowledgeService* class.

Note that because JDK 1.4 supports *assert* as a new keyword, the real method name for *knowledge assertion* must be different—it is *assertGAF*. A mechanism of aliases implemented in the *ScenarioPlayer* treats such names properly.

```
<prompt name="1" variable="FAVORITE-BAND-ANSWER"
service="UserAVI" action="prompt"
msg="What is your favorite rock band?" />
<Act name="2" service="KnowledgeService"
   action="createMicrotheory"
```

```
<?xml version = "1.0" encoding = "UTF-8"?>
<dialogScenario service="org.opencyc.connector.UserCycDialog"
 action="askUser">
 <setOfQuestions name="newTopic">
   <store name="_$newObject" unique="true"
       msg="Please provide a unique name for your topic." />

   <serviceRequest name="service1"
       service="org.opencyc.connector.KnowledgeServiceConnector"
       action="createConstant" msg="_$newObject" />

   <store name="variable1" variable="_$yourMt"
    createIfUnique="true"
       msg="Please provide a microtheory (scope) name for your topic.
       Traditionally such names end with Mt. For example
       HumanSocialLifeMt.
       If this is not an existing name the system will create a
       new microtheory for you." />

   <store name="variable2" variable="_$isExistingObject" unique="false"
       msg="Please relate your new topic to some existing object.
       Enter an existing topic name that can serve as a parent
       to your new topic.
       You actually provide a TYPE for your new object: Event,
       Person, Animal, etc.
       You can always come back and edit this assertion as well as
       add more types and assertions to this topic." />

   <serviceRequest name="service2"
       service="org.opencyc.connector.KnowledgeServiceConnector"
       action="assert"
       msg="_$yourMt (#$isa #$_$newObject
       #$_$isExistingObject)" />
  </setOfQuestions>

</dialogScenario>
```

FIGURE 5.9

```
Mt="LOGIN-NAMEHobbiesMt"
msg="Personal interest areas of LOGIN-NAME" />
<Act name="3" service="KnowledgeService"
   action="createNewPermanent" msg="LOGIN-NAMEFavoriteBand" />
<Act name="4">
service="KnowledgeService" action="assert"
    Mt="LOGIN-NAMEHobbiesMt"
    msg="(#$isa #$LOGIN-NAMEFavoriteBand
    #$AttributeValue)" />
<Act name="5" service="KnowledgeService" action="assert"
   Mt="LOGIN-NAMEHobbiesMt"
   msg="(#$hasAttributes #$LOGIN-NAME
```

```
    #$LOGIN-NAMEFavoriteBand)" />
<Act name="6" service="KnowledgeService" action="assert"
    Mt="LOGIN-NAMEHobbiesMt
msg="(#$isa #$LOGIN-NAMEFavoriteBand #$InterestArea)" />
"Act name="7" service="KnowledgeService" action="assert"
    Mt="LOGIN-NAMEHobbiesMt
msg="(#$hobbies #$LOGIN-NAMEFavoriteBand \" FAVORITE-BAND-ANSWER \")"
/>
```

The dialog scenario includes a prompt to the user and a request for knowledge services or regular services such as email. For example:

```
<Act name="1" service="EMailClient" action="send"
  from="Jeff.Zhuk@JavaSchool.com"
  to="reed@cyc.com" subject="test"
  body="testing mail service ... etc. " />
```

While you read these lines, Cyc may be able to provide responses to external programs using custom format options suitable to your business model.

The current version of the program, available from OpenCyc.org, may include some changes that strive to provide a standard way of connecting the world of services written in Java, or other languages, to the world of knowledge.

OpenCyc in the Knowledge-Driven Architecture

I started the chapter with very pragmatic reasoning, arguing for the learning and use of knowledge technologies by service providers. With these technologies, service providers increase their capacities and client base and, accordingly, their profit. From my point of view, there is an even more important change that knowledge technologies help to achieve: they elevate everyday work effectiveness.

The famous formula "write once" is not working *anywhere* today, for several reasons. One is the absence of a mechanism capable of accepting, classifying, and providing meaningful information about new data or services created by knowledge producers. We are all knowledge producers, but we almost never share what we produce with the rest of the world.

Imagine a global knowledge and service container in which everyone can *easily* find and access data and services and can contribute and be rewarded for their contributions. (Want more details on the reward policy? Look further in the book.) We would greatly reduce work replication and redundancy, and drastically increase efficiency.

Distributed knowledge systems with the Cyc engine can make this dream come true.

Existing and upcoming Cyc tools and related products multiply the powerful features of the CycL language. Cyc-NL, the natural language processing system associated with the Cyc knowledge base brings closer the possibility of using Cyc in SRSs. Distributed knowledge systems with built-in speech recognition would help the average person, not just the computer geek, to participate in computerized knowledge and service consumption and contribution.

The architecture of a distributed knowledge system with the OpenCyc engine is displayed in Fig. 5.10. The OpenCyc and the Cyc-NL interpreter are connected to presentation layers to simplify human access to data and services.

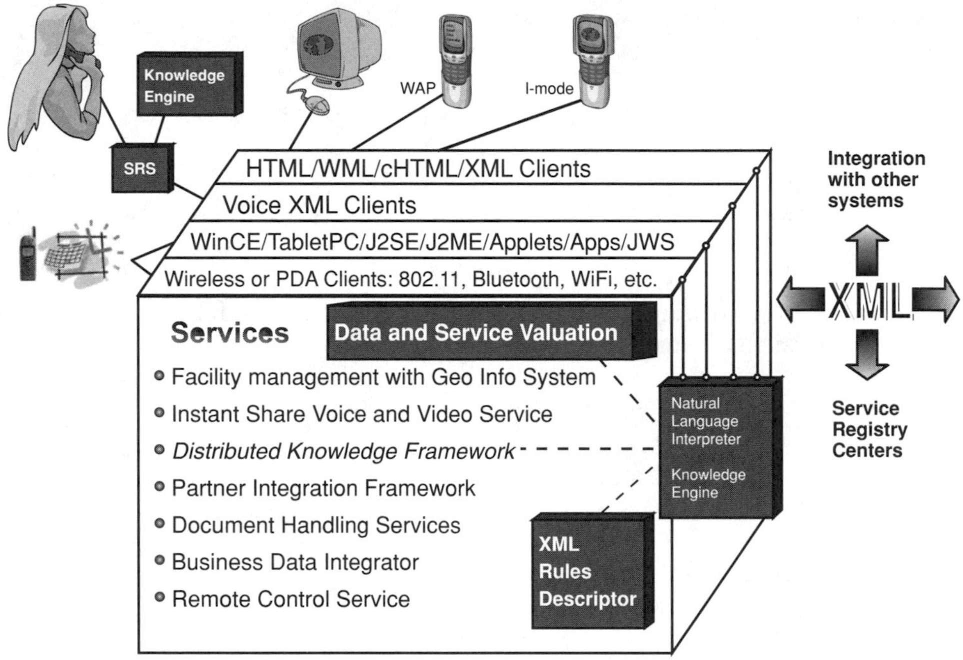

FIGURE 5.10. Enterprise Application Services Powered by Knowledge Technologies.

Some Intriguing Questions

How does the Cyc-NL interpreter work? Can we plug natural language parsers directly into an SRS? How can we use Cyc for software development, the details of knowledge to service integration, and other tasks? For the answers, we require another chapter.

This is just the beginning of a new development paradigm we can call *Software+Ontology=Softology*. Figures 5.11 and 5.12 illustrate current and new approaches to software engineering.

Current development process includes multiple teams providing multiple transformations of complexity of original business ideas into simplicity of programming functions and data tables. Business ideas can be easily lost or diluted on the way.

In the new development world, multiple layer-filters that separate business ideas from their implementations will disappear and business experts or SMEs (subject matter experts) will directly participate in the design process, working with "softology" engineers in a knowledge engine–powered environment.

SUMMARY

This chapter taught skills that are becoming increasingly important in the new spiral of software and business development. You learned about ontology, or knowledge-handling methods, but the subject is too broad for a complete overview. This chapter focused on standards established by the World Wide Web Consortium (W3C.org), such as RDF,

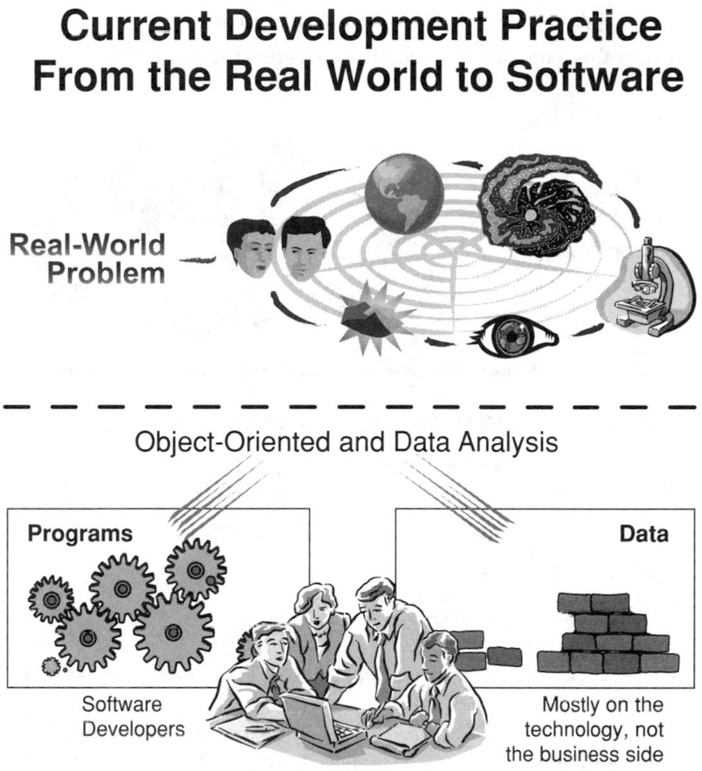

FIGURE 5.11. The Current Development Process.

DAML+OIL, Topic Maps, and XTM, and open (not proprietary) technologies, such as OpenCyc, that have great potential for the whole industry and can be immediately used in distributed knowledge systems that help connect people and organizations into knowledge federations.

Integrating Questions

1. What is the Semantic Web?
2. What are the main technology roles and targets of RDF and DAML+OIL?
3. Which of the knowledge technologies described in this chapter are applicable to your workplace?

Case Study

1. Create a DAML+OIL file describing email service with *Compose* and *GetMail* abilities.
2. Create an XTM file describing a hierarchy of groups of computer users and members of the groups.
3. Create a CycL microtheory describing a user's profile, and provide a query that requests a user's profile with the user's login name.

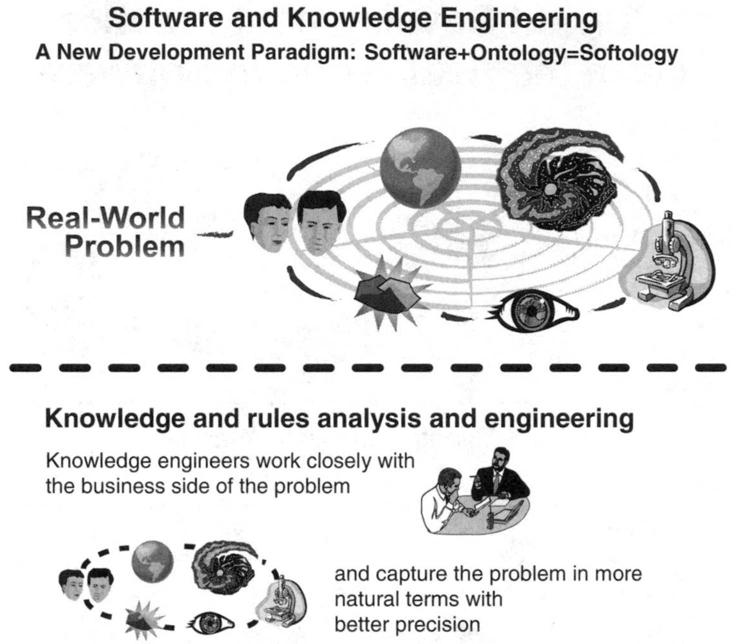
Software and Knowledge Engineering
A New Development Paradigm: Software+Ontology=Softology
Real-World Problem
Knowledge and rules analysis and engineering
Knowledge engineers work closely with the business side of the problem
and capture the problem in more natural terms with better precision

FIGURE 5.12. Software + Ontology: A New Development Paradigm.

4. (Advanced). Consider the Java source in Fig. 5.6. Suggest additional Cyc keywords that can be added to the *talkToCyc()* method. Change the code that would allow you to extend this method's vocabulary at run-time.
5. Describe several related facts or rules related to your workplace: first in plain English (try to limit yourself to three to five lines) and then in CycL language.
6. Describe as Topic Maps several facts or rules related to your workplace.

REFERENCES

1. Semantic Web:
   http://www.w3.org/2001/sw/.
2. Resource Description Framework (RDF) Model and Syntax Specification:
   http://www.w3.org/TR/1999/REC-rdf-syntax-19990222/.
3. DAML+OIL reference description:
   http://www.w3.org/TR/daml+oil-reference.
4. XML Topic Maps (XTM) 1.0:
   http://www.topicmaps.org/xtm/1.0/.
5. Open Source Project, Topic Maps 4 Java:
   http://tm4j.org.
6. Dubina, T. L, A. Y. Mints, and E. V. Zhuk. 1984. "Biological Age and Its Estimation." Experimental Gerontology 19:133–143.

7. JSR 73, Data Mining API Specifications
http://www.jcp.org/en/jsr/detail?id=73.
8. CU Communicator, Dialog Manager:
http://communicator.colorado.edu/.
9. Cycorp, common-sense knowledge base and inference engine:
http://www.cyc.com.

CHAPTER 6

Write Once

But the raven still beguiling all my sad soul into smiling,
Straight I wheeled a cushioned seat in front of bird and bust and door
Then, upon the velvet sinking, I betook myself to linking
Fancy unto fancy, thinking what this ominous bird of yore—
What this grim, ungainly, gaunt, and ominous bird of yore
Meant in croaking 'Nevermore.'

—Edgar Allan Poe, The Raven, 1845 (one of the earliest works on the subject)

"Write once and run everywhere" is one of the most important promises made by Java technology. Java Virtual Machines running on different platforms support this promise. With Microsoft's .NET initiative also you can write a program in C, C++, C#, Visual Basic, Perl, and so on. Then you can convert the program (with Visual Studio .NET) into the Microsoft intermediate language (MSIL) binary code that can be executed on any Windows platform by a virtual machine called the Common Language Runtime (CLR).

Unfortunately, the problem has many sides, and no technology by itself can help in every direction. Again, this is about the right development process coupled with the right technologies. What are the factors, other than language and compatibility problems, that prevent us from writing once?

When we try to use an existing service or application with a new environment, we find out that it does not fit. When business requires change and we want to adapt an existing product to that change, we find that there are no adaptation mechanisms in place. We realize that the basic properties, methods, and operations of the application are too specific to and too tight with the existing environment. The product has to be redone, often from scratch.

In this chapter, I provide three examples along with a problem analysis and some solutions. These examples are taken from three different areas: data storage in a business application, controllers in control systems, and document-handling services. In spite of the diversity in area and multiplicity of initial problems, we can derive some common features from these three solutions that may be considered generically applicable to areas other than the three presented.

Multiple Types of Data Storage

A Start-up Story

A start-up company developed a new software product that used a file system to store data for its services. It worked fine for the first client but the second client required data to be stored in their LDAP (Lightweight Directory Access Protocol) system.

The company hired an LDAP specialist, a programmer who quickly modified the product sources. He inserted a Boolean flag to indicate a type of data storage (files or LDAP) and added (to every place related to data saving) special "if-else" cases with code branches responsible for this or that persistence type. This quick and dirty solution increased application source and product complexity and provided job security to the LDAP professional.

The third client had an internal policy stating that all data must be stored in the company relational database, which happened to be an Oracle product. The start-up company grew by two more people: an Oracle DBA (database administrator) and an Oracle developer. The Boolean flag was lowered and replaced with fat variables, and the application code grew with more "if-else" branches.

The data storage team started a discussion about breaking the product into versions according to data storage types. The Oracle team suggested "simplifying" their version by using the Oracle Application Server (OAS) as the application core. They insisted that "The OAS has tools to reflect client data structure and make Oracle-based products more efficient."

Each new potential client had a different view or setup for data storage. The list of required storage solutions grew fatter with names such as Novell Directory Services, Lotus Notes, SAP, Meta-Directory, DB2, MS SQL Server, and others.

Under "time-to-market" pressure, the company expanded its quick and dirty architectural solution for two potential clients, but the extension came with a price. The product had lost its stability and required more testing and maintenance efforts. Every release required more development time as application changes were multiplied by the number of data storage types. The company grew by adding release and quality assurance (QA) managers and two QA engineers.

Meanwhile, the second and (especially) the third clients provided troubling feedback indicating that product data did not integrate well with existing client data structures. The start-up company was forced to invest time in learning client data and fighting the battle over data models on the clients' territories.

At this point, the company found itself in the position of trying to sell its new product while spending its time and money on data storage issues.

My reader, you are more than welcome to provide your own ending to this story.

How was it that data storage became the center point of the application? Would it be possible to start with a better architecture from the beginning? Yes, this is once again an illustration of the importance of process and technology integration.

A Unified Way to All Data Sources

First, let us find the right abstractions to easily bring multiple databases and different types of data storage under one umbrella. Why do we need data and what are the data functions we use?

Sure, we call these functions different names in different storage systems. We use *select* in SQL (Structured Query Language) for RDBMS (relational database management systems) and *read* in file system and other operations. We can abstract this operation for all data storage types as the *get* operation. You get the idea: we only need several data functions, such as *get, update, delete*, and *insert*.

That is all we need for a unified data storage object. Can we abstract all data sources under a single umbrella that expresses the idea of a unified data storage object?

This door is already half-open. Java Naming and Directory Interface (JNDI), Java Data Objects (JDO), or ActiveX Data Objects can serve as a high-level interface to all kinds of data. I will describe a JNDI-based solution performed in the Java world.

The starting point can be the *DataSource* interface that presents a unified data object as a factory for connections to the physical data. The *DataSource* interface is *typically* implemented by a driver vendor and registered with a naming service based on the JNDI application program interface (API).

The basic implementation produces a standard *java.sql.Connection* object that will automatically participate in connection pooling. This implementation targets relational databases and counts on specific JDBC (Java Database Connectivity) classes and methods working with the *Connection* object.

A *DataSource* object has properties that can be modified when necessary, but any application code accessing that data storage does not need to be changed.

Our task is to extend this abstraction even further, including different (from RDBMS) data storage systems under the JNDI umbrella. In effect, we must create an abstract class that implements the *DataSource* interface and includes the abstract method *open()* that returns a *com.its.data.DataConnector* object.

Figure 6.1 displays three sets of data connectors under the JNDI umbrella. The data connectors encapsulate the specifics of different data storage types and adapt their different APIs into a unified set of methods.

For example, the *open()* method means completely different things for different data storage types. In the case of a relational database, the *open()* method is implemented as the *getConnection()* method that returns a *java.sql.Connection* object.

In Fig. 6.1, you can see that the RDBMS data connector (besides being a subclass of the *com.its.data.DataConnector*) also implements the *java.sql.Connector* interface and bridges JDBC objects.

The *DataConnector* abstract class has abstract methods, such as *get(), update(), delete()*, and *insert()*. The nicest thing about this abstract class is that its subclasses can represent multiple data storages from RDBMS to LDAP and file systems.

This way, the data connectors encapsulate specifics of different data storages and adapt their different APIs into a unified set of methods.

The *com.its.data.DataConnector* abstract class also includes the *XMLdescriptor* property and the *parseXML()* method. Why do we need the *XMLdescriptor* and what do we plan to do with the *parseXML()* method? The *XMLdescriptor* allows the data owner, a developer or a data administrator, to express the data structure and business rules related to these data.

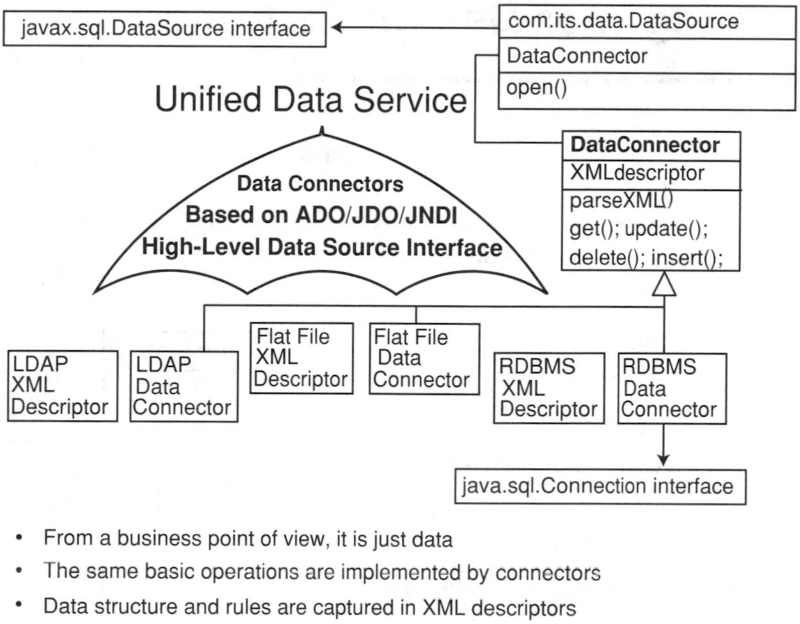

FIGURE 6.1. Unified Data Service.

At this point, we have unified data operations. The next problem is related to differences in data structure and business rules (i.e., behavior, usually embedded in the code).

To this data storage unification, we can add an important detail about data structure and the related business rules that can simplify the integration of multiple databases. Unified connectivity and data handling solve only one puzzle of corporate data integration. Every data storage system has its own specific structure, data relationships, and business rules defining data change.

Here is a list of potential problems related to enterprise data consolidation.

1. Multiple types of data sources (storages) are used: from relational databases and Lightweight Directory Access Protocol LDAP) to file system and directory services.
2. Every data source is surrounded by its own data handling applications, its own developers with specific data type knowledge.
3. Data sources are inconsistent, incomplete, and "dirty" (factually wrong).
4. Data are not synchronized; they might contain outdated and never-used information, but no statistics on actual usage to address this.
5. Data from different sources cannot be synchronized without extensive manual tuning.
6. There are some verbal or written rules that the data are supposed to follow, but the rules are not fully enforced.

Data analysis is a time-consuming, manual process that takes tremendous resources; there is no standard way established to describe data rules and structure.

There is no common model or standard that prescribes data structure and behavior for different data storages throughout the industry. The enormous task of mapping client data to product data fields takes a vast amount of time and money. The *XMLdescriptor* is a great

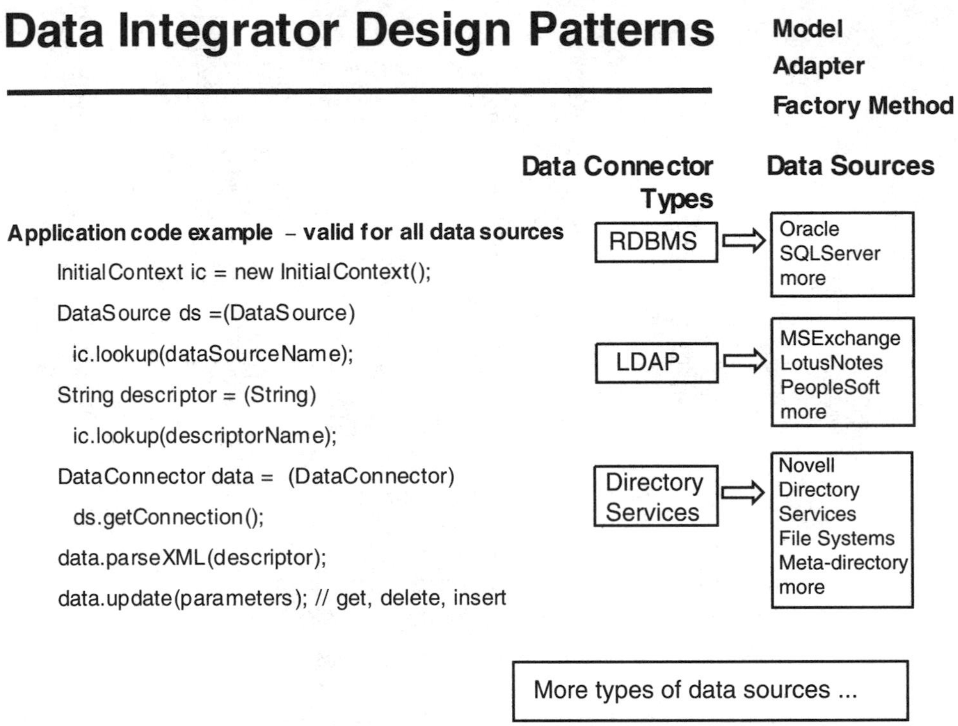

FIGURE 6.2. Data Integrator Design Patterns.

place to express the complexity of data structures and business rules, and XML is the perfect language for such expressions. The *parseXML()* method reads these expressions, teaching the *DataConnector* object to behave.

If the data structure or business rules change (and this happens a lot), the change will be reflected in the *XMLdescriptor* without any application code changes.

Figure 6.2 shows how the three basic types of data implemented with unified data connectors (files, LDAP, and RDBMS) cover multiple relational databases and numerous cases of specific data storages.

The Java code extracted from an application, for example, will never be changed, even if the application switches data storage from a file system to an MS SQL Server overnight. The JNDI property file will change its own portion associated with the *dataSourceName* variable that identifies the data source, object type, and location.

Data Integrator Design Patterns

This solution can be called the *Data Integrator*. Several design patterns are actively used here:

- *The model*—We model several subclasses after the *DataService* class.
- *The adapter*—We create a set of unified methods to adapt different APIs of different data source types.
- *The factory method*—We create a data service of a family of related objects, data services, instantiated by subclasses.

The solution does not come cheap. However, it still costs next to nothing compared with the cost of data and application stability. This layer of unified data connectors and data services (yes, it is an extra layer) takes care of sudden changes, merges, and integrations.

Today, product provider companies spend three to nine months rolling out their product into a client's data structures. The more client systems interact with the product, the more time is required for the integration. Sometimes a new full-blown application has to be developed to take over a bigger data structure. The data integration pattern and principles described above (if implemented) can save millions of dollars, improve work efficiency, and restore the write-once concept.

Control Systems and Controllers

There is a variety of hardware and software solutions related to control systems and controllers. These solutions, unfortunately, are very different, which makes the integration of two or more control systems a challenging task.

Why would we need such integration?

To answer that question, I provide an example from the telecommunications industry.

We often see wireless phones and Voice over IP systems working together with good old analog phones.

Legacy systems, which still dominate the mixed telecom environment, are slowly giving up more space to Voice over IP switches and wireless communications. All three types of systems are actually control systems with their own system controllers that are often connected to the application level of control systems.

The newcomers (Voice over IP and wireless switches) are slowly catching up to the amazing number of features provided by legacy systems. Integrating several telecom systems and providing for their smooth interoperability is a high-priority task. Every telecom vendor implements system controllers in its own way, which does not make the integration task easier.

Another example is from the world of robots. Hierarchical systems of controllers have to work together to execute smaller tasks under larger task umbrellas. When a robot gets the command "find shoes," it will translate this command into several middle-level controllers. It will pass a series of commands to its long-term memory: "retrieve shoes pattern"; "recollect last attempt to locate this pattern and if it was a success"; if so, retrieve longitude and latitude of the location." At the same time (we are talking about a multithreaded environment, right?), the robot will send commands—"move around" and "look around for the pattern"—to its mechanical and vision systems to initiate high activity.

Meanwhile, the robot will also set up a timeout for its reporting system to come back on time with the report: "The task is completed. Not found."

Middle-level controllers will translate their tasks to the next level's subsystems. For example, the mechanical system will activate its GPS controller to calculate the proper direction based on its current location, longitude and latitude numbers of the last success, and other parameters.

Let us look at control systems in a very generic way. Can we really generalize and abstract common features to build a unified system controller? I do not want to upset you, but I am not going to come up with an abstraction that covers 100% of the control system cases. You know (and I know, too) that this would be a far too expensive proposition. Let us spend

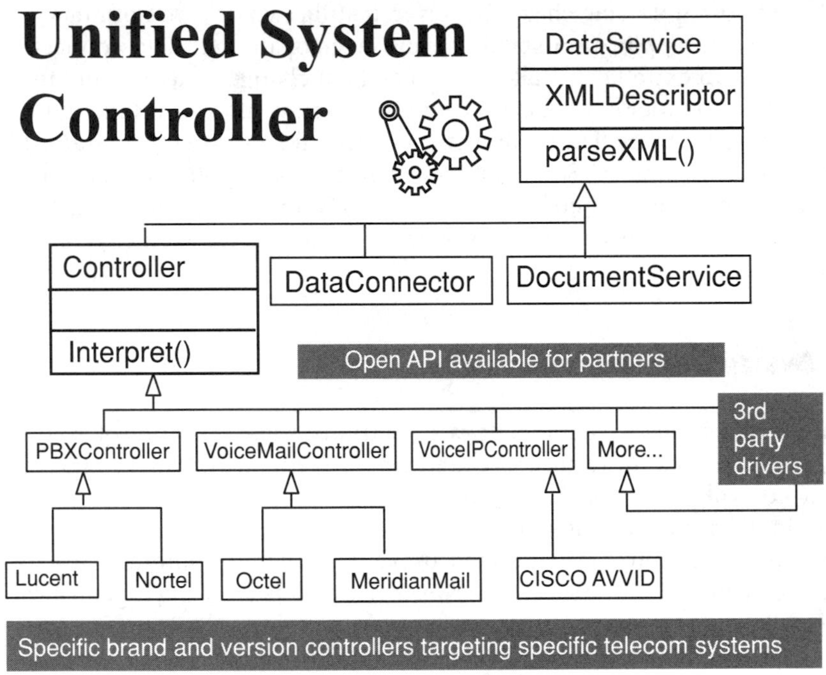

A single Java chip can serve as a universal controller.
XML Descriptor loaded at run - time defines controller behavior.

FIGURE 6.3. Unified System Controller.

only a fraction of the time and resources and still cover many cases. This is the 80/20 rule in action. With this in mind, let us return to general ideas about controllers.

A **control system**, generally speaking, consists of at least two subsystems: a **controller** subsystem and a **controlled** subsystem. The controller knows the control goals and criteria and translates this knowledge into behavior instructions for the controlled subsystem. In the hierarchical structure of real-time control systems, the controller receives the goals and criteria from the upper "management" level of the control system as its run-time input and interprets the input into a proper set of instructions to send down to the controlled subsystem.

Note that interpretation is the main function of the controller.

Figure 6.3 shows a hierarchy of system controllers. You can find the *interpret()* method right there. This method is really the heart of the *Controller* class. The *Controller* class also inherits the *XMLdescriptor* property and the *parseXML()* method from the *DataService* abstract class. What role does the XML descriptor play in the *Controller* class?

Remember that the main difference between controllers is the way they behave. The manner of the interpretation of upper-level instructions, goals, and criteria, and the feedback from the controlled system into output instructions, defines a controlled system's behavior.

A typical implementation places the controller behavior into software code as well as hardware specifics, which is what makes controllers so different.

We made the first step in the right direction when we abstracted behavior into the *interpret()* method. The next step is to describe the rules of the behavior in the XML descriptor instead of source code or hardware specifics. Let us think about the XML descriptor as a table or rules prescribing specific output upon receiving specific input.

In the Robot's World

The example from the robot's world is illustrated in Figs. 6.4 and 6.5.

In Fig. 6.4, the main controller (C1) issues a sequence of service requests to the next control level. Some parameters in these requests are found at run-time. For example, the long-term memory subsystem (C1.LM) retrieves an image pattern, and the vision subsystem (C1.VI) uses this pattern to locate the subject.

The parseXML() method implemented in the *Controller* class works together with the *interpret()* method. The *parseXML()* method is able to read these XML definitions and transform them into structures helpful to the interpretation process. Figure 6.5 displays an example of input and output instructions coming in and out of the main controller, C1, to the next level of the control system.

Now we see the exciting possibility to create a unified controller that will load the XML descriptor on initiation and learn behavior rules. This unified controller can be built as a single Java chip that implements the *parseXML()* and *interpret()* methods and is initialized by the XML descriptor at run-time.

This unified solution will work on multiple levels of a system control hierarchy using different XML descriptors. I must repeat that this solution does not cover 100% of the controllers; but it *is* applicable in many cases.

Figures 6.6 and 6.7 provide another example of the service request interpretation for a messaging system.

Control in the Messaging System

This service request is related to the *Get Mail* operation.

The high-level controller (HLC) translates this request down to its middle-level controllers (MLCs). This request is interpreted into a sequence of commands to the "HLC.MLC1" message controller:

1. Get IP address of the host machine and the port that supports this user.
2. Connect to the host and port (using data from the previous request).
3. Retrieve a list of mail messages (using existing connection).

Figure 6.7 displays the input service request coming to the HLC and output stream of commands generated by the controller toward the MLC, HLC.MLC1.

Alternative integration solutions such as JAIN (Java API for Integrated Network), Sun's JDMK (Java Dynamic Management Kit), and Microsoft DCOM (Distributed Component Object Model) focus on specific technologies based on Java or COM objects, whereas the unified controller solution avoids technology and implementation specifics.

The unified controller solution has several essential characteristics:

- They have an XML-based API, meaning they can talk and be understood by other controller products (that follow this design), regardless of their hardware and software platforms.
- Their behavior is encapsulated in the XML descriptor instead of in software code, firmware, or hardware solutions.
- They implement *parseXML()* and *interpret()* methods that work with the XML descriptor.

```
<?xml version="1.0" encoding="UTF-8" ?>
<!-- Simplified example of service request interpretation -->

<InterpretationScenario>

<!-- From the robot's world: Request Locator service at Control System
C1-->
  <ServiceRequest Destination="C1" Service="Locator" Action="Get">
   <Parameters>
     <User name="[userName]"/>
     <Subject name="[subjectToGet]"/>
   </Parameters>
  </ServiceRequest>

<!-- Interpretation for the next level of controllers.
 Activate 4 subsystems on the next control level:
  long-term memory=C1.LM
  mechanical=C1.ME
  vision=C1.VI
  report=C1.RE
-->
<!-- The service will return the last image associated with the subject
-->
  <ServiceRequest Destination="C1.LM" Service="Image" Action="Get">
    <Parameters>
       <Subject name="[subjectToGet]"/>
    </Parameters>
  </ServiceRequest>

<!-- The service will return the details of the last operation of this
sort -->
  <ServiceRequest Destination="C1.LM" Service="OperationReports"
  Action="Get">
   <Parameters>
    <Operation name="[operationName]"/>
    <Subject name="[subjectToGet]"/>
    <OperationID name="Last"/>
    <DetailsRequired>
         <Detail name="Success Level" />
         <Detail name="Subject location" />
     </DetailsRequired>
   </Parameters>
  </ServiceRequest>
<!-- The service will move robot around -->
  <ServiceRequest Destination="C1.ME" Service="Moving" Action="Move">
   <Parameters>
    <Movement Type="spiral" Radius="1 ft"/>
    <StartTime name="now"/>
```

Figure 6.4

```
      <Timeout name="[operation timeout]"/>
     </Parameters>
    </ServiceRequest>

  <!-- The service will try to locate the pattern retrieved by
  C1.LM -->
    <ServiceRequest Destination="C1.VI" Service="Vision"
    Action="Locate">
     <Parameters>
        <Pattern name="[$image.by.C1.LM]"/>
     </Parameters>
    </ServiceRequest>

  <!-- The service will setup timeout for the report -->
    <ServiceRequest Destination="C1.RE" Service="Reports"
    Action="Produce">
     <Parameters>
         <Operation name="[operationName]"/>
         <Timeout name="[timeout]"/>
         <Report name="[$operationResult.by.C1.VI]"/>
     </Parameters>
    </ServiceRequest>
  </InterpretationScenario>
```

FIGURE 6.4. (*cont.*)

Corporations allocate tremendous budgets to provision access to the multiple levels of corporate infrastructure.

The unified controller solution increases the efficiency and interoperability of control systems, promising savings in this area.

DOCUMENT-HANDLING SERVICES

Different applications handle different document types. This is a common practice. An email client program, such as Eudora, deals with email messages; a file management program handles files; and so on. Open Office and Microsoft Office work with many document types. Both packages consist of several loosely connected applications, and each application is responsible for a particular type of document.

Is it possible to eliminate the unnecessary complexity of operations, decrease the number of applications involved in handling documents, increase efficiency, and provide headway for a variety of small devices capable of working with all these documents? It sounds like a long question that may require a long answer.

From the Robot's World

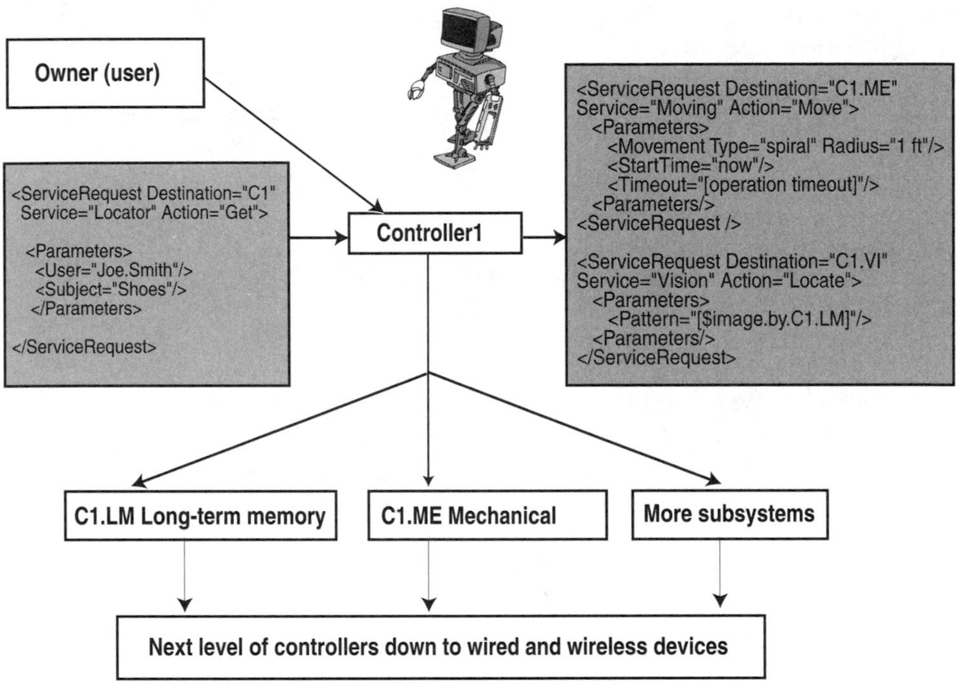

FIGURE 6.5. Robot System Controllers.

Let us start a chain of abstractions as we already did for business data and control systems. While creating abstractions, we may notice interesting details and similarities and eventually find the roots of the problem.

Email messages, files, articles, order forms, address books, and calendar records are documents. Each document type has its own format and a set of **attributes**. An address book includes records such as Name and Phone number. Email messages include such fields as To, From, Subject, and Date. The document (text as well as nontext) format can be also described with these attributes.

Let us recollect commonalities: documents have document attributes.

Now let us think about handling the documents. Services handling the documents display a list of these documents and must be able to pull a selected document out of its location.

Distinguish Data from Reference Information

There are more commonalities: All documents can be presented as lists of reference records. All reference records include selected (but not all) attributes of documents and pointers to document locations.

Figure 6.8 displays the object model diagram for unified document services.

The *DataReference* and *DataObject* classes are examples of an implementation that can be used for unified document-handling services.

The *DataReference* Java class represents a reference record with an array of selected document attributes. The *DataReference* object provides knowledge about an object,

```
<?xml version="1.0" encoding="UTF-8" ?>
<InterpretationScenario>

<!-- Simplified example of service request interpretation -->
<!-- The service will deliver messages for a specified user -->
<ServiceRequest Destination="HLC" Service="Mail" Action="Get">
  <Parameters>
    <User name="Joe Smith"/>
  </Parameters>
</ServiceRequest>

<!-- Interpretation for messaging subsystem.
   This request is interpreted into a sequence of commands
   to the next level "HLC.MLC1" message controller
   1. Get IP address of the host machine and the port that
      supports this user
   2. Connect to the host and port
   3. Retrieve a list of mail messages
-->
<!-- Get IP address of the host machine and the port that supports this
user -->
<ServiceRequest Destination="HLC.MLC1" Service="Locator" Action="Get">
    <Parameters>
        <User name="Joe Smith"/>
    </Parameters>
</ServiceRequest>

<!-- Connect to the host and port returned by a previous request -->
<ServiceRequest Destination="HLC.MLC1" Service="Connector"
  Action="Connect">
    <Parameters>
        <NetAddress name="12.34.56.78"/>
        <port name="9876"/>
    </Parameters>
</ServiceRequest>

<!-- Retrieve a list of mail messages -->
<ServiceRequest Destination="HLC.MLC1" Service="Mail" Action="Get">
    <Parameters>
        <User name="joe.smith"/>
        <Psw name="***********"/>
    </Parameters>
</ServiceRequest>
</InterpretationScenario>
```

FIGURE 6.6

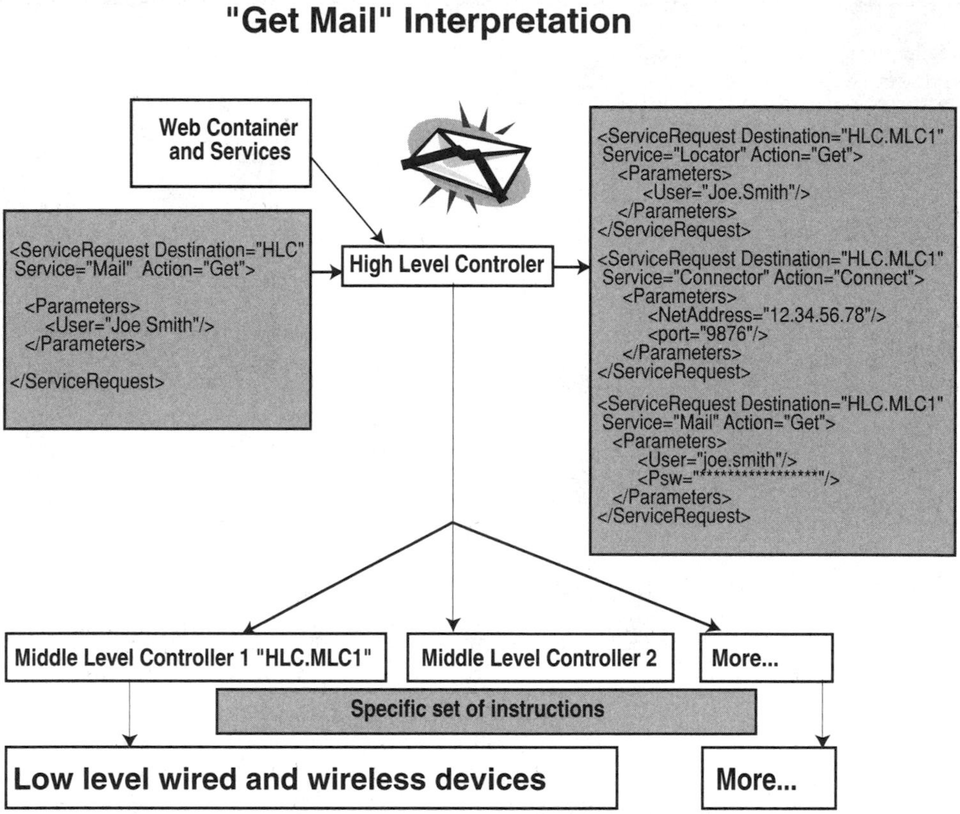

Figure 6.7. "Get Mail" Interpretation.

but not the object itself. To illustrate this concept, let us look at a great search engine, *http://www.google.com*. The search engine owns only reference records that include some information about real objects and point to real objects.

The *DataObject* class represents document objects that may be stored on this or other servers and may require special services to work with them. The *DataObject* may have more specific subclasses, such as *Email-Message, FileDocument*, and *DBRecord*, that represent specific properties and behaviors of specific document types.

> Each *DataReference* record is a snapshot of a corresponding *DataObject*. The *DataReference* records can be viewed as implementation of the Snapshot (or Memento) design pattern. Programs can access or send light document references to represent heavy document objects. This will protect original objects especially in the case when multiple programs compete for object access.
>
> You can find an example of such competition for a single email document between POP3 and SMTP programs in the Appendix 3, Spam Killer and Mail Server Enhancement section.

The *ReferenceService* handles the list of reference records. The *DocumentService* class unites all typical document-handling functions with a unified service API.

Specific services can extend the *DocumentService* class to provide very specific (nontypical) service functions. When a user selects a document from the list of reference records,

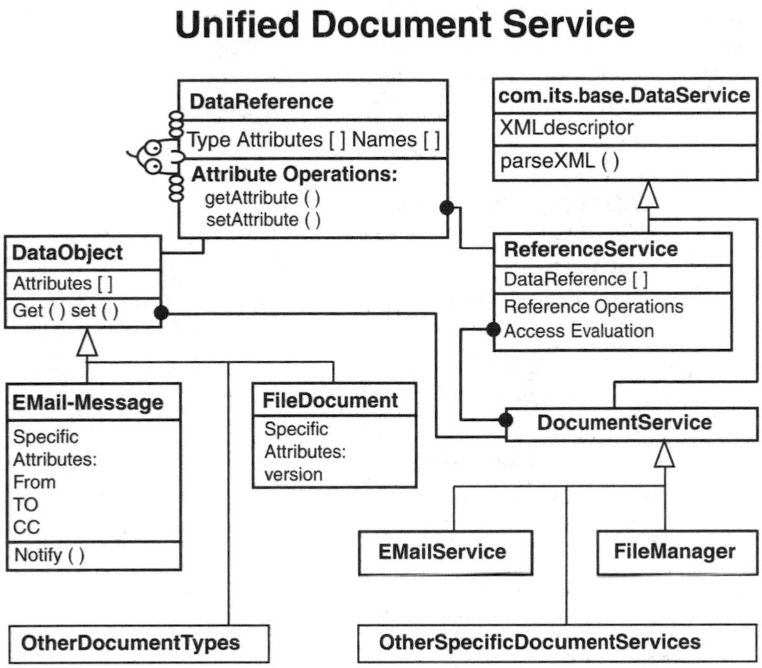

FIGURE 6.8. Object Model Diagram of Document Handling.

a *ReferenceService* object points to the proper *DocumentService* to handle the selected document.

The *DocumentService* and its subclasses can be implemented with existing third-party solutions. A library of objects based on the OpenOffice.org [1] project is a good example of an implementation of the *DocumentService* class and its subclasses for a rich client.

The rich client can afford to run the *OpenOffice* process. The *ReferenceService* class can use *OpenOffice* functions with the Universal Network Objects (UNO) API to create, convert, or edit a document of almost any formatted type directly or (better) via the *OpenOfficeAdapter*, a subclass of the *DocumentService*.

All *DataReference* objects have attributes. There are generic attributes used for the generic purposes of handling all types of documents and specific attributes that make sense only for specific data types.

Generic attributes help us solve common problems for all data types. For example, one generic attribute is *access scope*. This attribute can be used to provide secure, privilege-based access to all documents with all document-handling services. We also want to evaluate document usage and provide a usage-based score or "value" to all documents with the *value* attribute.

Documents often have hierarchical structures, and the reference records presented by the *DataReference* must support this feature.

Every record should have a unique ID and may have the parent ID attribute to enable document handling.

More generic attributes can be added to reference records.

The *type* attribute can be used to differentiate document types. It is possible to refer to a document type from another document type in the reference records. The *type* attribute is very handy in this case. The *type* attribute also gives hints to the *ReferenceService* on how to handle this type of document.

The *ReferenceService* class that handles all references uses the *type* attribute to load specific attribute names and specific behavior (if any) associated with the specific document type.

XML Descriptor and Document Services

This information (specific names and behavior) is provided with the XML descriptor and is parsed by the *parseXML()* method.

The *ReferenceService* and *DocumentService* derive from the *com.its.base. DataService* abstract class and inherit the *XMLdescriptor* property and the *parseXML()* method from the base class. The *ReferenceService* and *DocumentService* classes implement the *parseXML()* method. The primary goal of the implementation is to create, for any specific document type (described in the XML descriptor), an array of its attribute names and, if necessary, the presentation layer specifics (behavior structure) that are convenient for handling this type of document. The *ReferenceService* class works with the XML description of the reference record, whereas the *DocumentService* class works with the XML description of the data object itself.

The *ReferenceService* class represents a list of references that point to data objects. The *DocumentService* includes methods that handle these documents. The *ReferenceService* also has access evaluation methods.

Figure 6.9 illustrates privilege-based access with a version of an object model diagram. The diagram can be implemented with a set of Java classes and RDBMS support or as an algorithm provided by a knowledge engine and supported by a knowledge base.

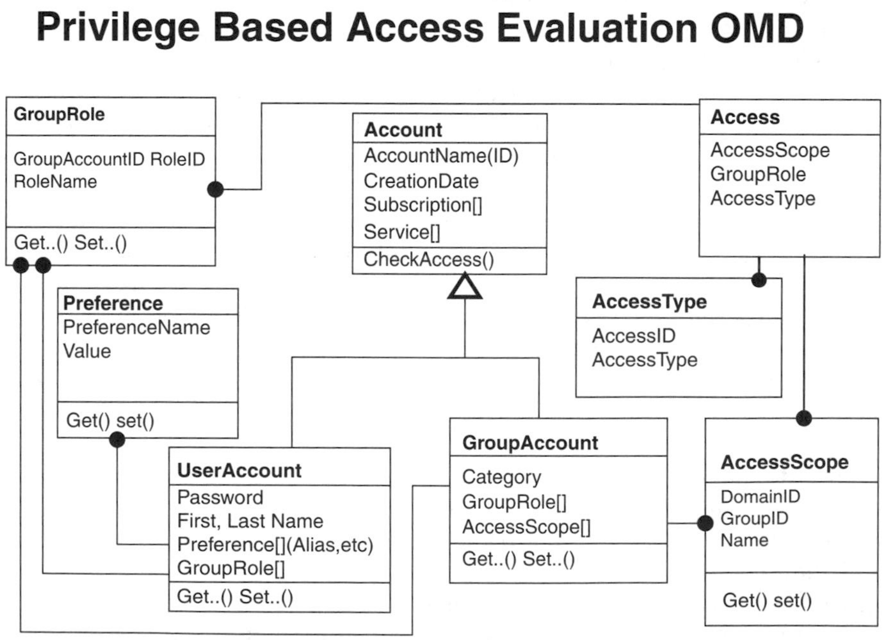

FIGURE 6.9. Object Model Diagram of Privilege-Based Access Evaluation.

The *DataReference* class represents a single reference record that includes some specific document fields and can point to a document location. It is possible for all document fields to be represented "in-line" in the reference record. It is also possible for the reference record to represent only selected fields. A file or database record keeps all the information about the document.

The *DataReference* class has a set of attributes consisting of generic attributes such as *document ID*, *document type*, and *access scope*. We use generic attributes as reference pointers and call them *references*. Generic attributes or references represent the main document features. For example, we use references when we display a list of documents and do not want to expose all the document details. For a particular type of document, there are also specific attributes. The XML descriptor holds definitions for every data type.

The *ReferenceService* can introduce a new data type.

Such an introduction populates a new XML record in the XML description. The type definitions include a list of attribute names specific to a document type and rules that define how to display these attributes. Some additional information may be included to define a specific behavior for the *DocumentService* class when handling a specific document type. For example, a particular type of document can have a specific validation rule.

The XML descriptor for a specific type of document may also include a new definition for the set of generic attributes or references. The definition, if present, overrides the default generic, set definition.

An extract of the XML descriptor example for several document types is shown in Fig. 6.10. The XML descriptor defines a set of generic attributes or references at the beginning. For every document type, a set of reference definitions map generic attribute names to specific names for the document type, for instance, on a list of scheduled events or email messages. Every document type definition also includes a set of specific attributes that build this document structure.

A code extract from the *DataReference* class is included in Fig. 6.11. The two methods presented in this code can get, or set, any generic or specific attribute in the selected record. The methods use the static hash table *attributeNames*, which is filled with names of attributes, keys, and related indexes. The methods use indexes to access proper attribute values in the array of attributes. The *ReferenceService* creates this hash table, as well as several other hash tables, at its initiation while parsing the XML descriptor.

The *ReferenceService* class will load the XML descriptor at initiation time. The set of XML definitions will be transformed into a set of hash tables with keys and values. I hope you recognize the same pattern that we provided in Chapter 3, in which we built multiple service components with an XML descriptor with configurable properties and behavior.

The reference map in the type description shows what fields should be displayed on the list of schedule records and what the displayed names for these fields are. For example, when a user requests a schedule, the *ReferenceService* class will read the calendar reference records and display three columns for every event: "Scheduled by," "Starts," and "Subject." Every reference record includes generic attributes plus the additional *Starts* attribute that, for example, provides information about the event's starting date and time.

The set of attributes in the XML descriptor defines a document along with its structure and helps to load and display the document. This example assumes that when we need to display a whole document, we display all document fields in some default manner.

A presentation model of the document may be different from the document structure. For example, we may not want to display some fields, or we may want to display them with a

```
<?xml version="1.0" encoding="UTF-8" ?>
<DataTypes>
<References>
    <!-- Generic Attributes -->
    <Reference name="documentID" value="hidden"/>
    <!-- unique ID -->
    <Reference name="parentID" value="hidden"/>
    <!-- can be array: link-copy creates another parent -->
    <Reference name="documentType" value="hidden"/>
    <!-- example: calendar, form, article -->
    <Reference name="location" value="hidden"/>
    <Reference name="accessScope" value="hidden"/>
    <!-- used by Access matrix and methods -->
    <Reference name="Order" value="optionalDisplayed"/>
    <!-- sequential number on the page -->
    <Reference name="Author" value="optionalDisplayed"/>
    <!-- or a sender, a receiver, etc. -->
    <Reference name="LastUpdate" value="optionalDisplayed"/>
    <!-- last time of access -->
    <Reference name="Subject" value="optionalDisplayed"/>
    <!-- Title or filename -->
    <Reference name="Value" value="optionalDisplayed"/>
    <!-- Value of the document based on document usage -->
</References>

<Type name="calendar">
    <ReferenceMap>
    <!-- Display these fields on the list of events -->
     <Reference name="Author" value="Scheduled by"/>
        <Reference name="Starts" value="Starts"/>
        <Reference name="Subject" value="Subject"/>
    </ReferenceMap>

    <Attributes>
        <Attribute name="Starts"/>
        <Attribute name="Subject"/>
        <Attribute name="Event lasts"/>
        <Attribute name="Send reminder to"/>
        <Attribute name="Hours before the event"/>
        <Attribute name="Description"/>
        <!-- Brief in-line description -->
    </Attributes>
</Type>
<Type name="email">
    <ReferenceMap>
      <!-- Display these fields on the list of mail messages -->
        <Reference name="Author" value="Sender"/>
```

FIGURE 6.10

```
            <!-- or Receiver for the Sent Messages folder -->
            <Reference name="Author"
            parentName="SentMessages" value="Receiver"/>
            <Reference name="CreationTime"  value="Date"/>
            <Reference name="Subject" value="Subject"/>
        </ReferenceMap>
        <Attributes>
     <Attribute name="From"/>
            <Attribute name="Date"/>
            <Attribute name="TO"/>
            <Attribute name="CC"/>
            <Attribute name="BCC"/>
            <Attribute name="Subject"/>
            <Attribute name="Priority"/>
            <Attribute name="NotificationToSender"/>
            <Attribute name="Attachments"/>
            <!-- can be an array of files -->
            <Attribute name="Body"/>
        </Attributes>
    </Type>
    </DataTypes>
```

FIGURE 6.10. (*cont.*)

different font and color. In this case, a **presentation definition** would be added to the XML descriptor, providing distinguished presentation forms.

I provided a very simple example of the XML descriptor. This example may be extended with a set of controls and a corresponding behavior for a specific document type. The XML descriptor may also include a set of validation rules for a specific document type.

Examples of validation rules provided with document type definition (DTD) and XML files are shown in Figs. 6.12 and 6.13.

In the DTD file (Fig. 6.12), we specify that every field should be marked for validation with one of the required stamps: "*notEmpty* | *charSet* | number | *notEmptyAndCharSet* | *notEmptyAndNumber* | *noCheckRequired.*"

In the XML file that establishes rules for validation (Fig. 6.13), we find that all fields but one require some checking. The core program includes the *TextValidator* class, (Fig. 6.14), which is able to interpret rules from the XML descriptor.

The *TextValidator* class includes several validation methods and the main (test) method that illustrates how validation rules prescribed by the XML descriptor will be re-enforced. The *main()* method of the *TextValidator* class uses the *ServiceConnector* class, with its powerful *act()* method, to obtain an object of the proper class and invoke a method on this object.

The *ServiceConnector* code is displayed in Fig. 6.15. The *ServiceConnector* class uses the *java.reflection.Method* mechanism to invoke a specified method on a specified class. The *ServiceConnector* instantiates an object of a class according to the parameter passed to the

```
// DataReference

package com.its.base;

import java.util.*;

/**
 * DataReference represents a reference record for one
 * document instance
 * or the document itself with its attributes
 */

public class DataReference {
    // The Hashtable attributeNames is filled in
    // at initiation time after reading the XML descriptor
    private static Hashtable attributeNames;
    // key=attributeName (String) value=NameIndex (Integer)
    private String[] attributes;
    // reference values or attribute values

    public String getAttribute(String attributeName) {
        Integer integerIndex =
        (Integer)attributeNames.get(attributeName);
        int index = integerIndex.intValue();
        if(attributes == null || attributes.lenth <= index) {
            return null;
        }
        return attributes[index];
    }
    public void setAttribute(String attributeName,
    String attributeValue) {
        Integer integerIndex =
        (Integer)attributeNames.get(attributeName);
        int index = integerIndex.intValue();
        if(attributes == null || attributes.lenth <= index) {
            return;
        }
        attributes[index] = attributeValue;
    }
    // convenience methods
    public String getID() {
        return attributes[0];
    }
    public void setID(String id) {
        attributes[0] = id;
    }
```

FIGURE 6.11

```
        public String getParentID() {
            return attributes[1];
        }

        public void setID(String id) {
            attributes[1] = id;
        }

        public Hashtable getAttributeNames() {
            return attributeNames;
        }
        // more code
    }
```

Figure 6.11. (*cont.*)

constructor. Then, the *ServiceConnector* uses its powerful *act()* method to invoke a specified method on a selected object.

Yes, the *act()* method of the *ServiceConnector* class can actually play a role other than its own (object) role. The *ServiceConnector* class can work with objects of any existing class type specified in the constructor parameter. The *act()* method of this class provides a unified way to find a requested method and invoke the method on a previously defined object.

What Does the ReferenceService *Do with Attributes of the* DataReference?

The *ReferenceService* class uses generic attributes such as *documentID* and *parentID* for its document handling. For example, the *ReferenceService* uses the attribute *parentID* to display a hierarchy of parents (folders) to which this document belongs. The *LastUpdate* attribute is used to indicate if this document is "new" for a user. If a user did not open the document after it was created or modified, this document will be considered new for this user.

The *ReferenceService* uses the *AccessScope* attribute to validate a user's access to the document based on the access matrix and privilege-based rules. We will consider the access matrix and access rules in later chapters.

In Chapter 7, we consider client–server communications and service partitioning for thin and thick clients. Services that we described above can process documents on the client side for thick clients. Thin clients can receive HTML-, Wireless Markup Language (WML)-, or XML-based screen definitions produced on the server side with these document-handling services. Solutions range from different client participation through data validation to full document processing, with or without *OpenOffice* invocation.

Note that a single *DataReference* class and a single *ReferenceService* class handle multiple types of documents. We encapsulated specific attribute names and behaviors for different document types in the XML descriptor.

We were able to abstract common document features and common document handling in basic classes, instead of creating a new application with a new set of classes for another

```
<?xml version="1.0" encoding="UTF-8"?>
<!ELEMENT Field (#PCDATA)>
<!ELEMENT ValidateFields (Field)*>
<!ELEMENT Rules (ValidateFields)>
<!ATTLIST Field
    name CDATA #REQUIRED
    check (notEmpty | charSet | number | notEmptyAndCharSet |
notEmptyAndNumber | noCheckRequired) #IMPLIED
>
```

FIGURE 6.12

document type. The XML descriptor and the *parseXML()* method served us well in this case, as they did in previous cases with business data integration and controllers.

SUMMARY

I would like to put the main points of the unified service approach under one umbrella.

- Recognize and implement commonalities in a core piece of code.
- Recognize and express differences (structures and behavior) in the XML descriptor.
- Implement the method that interprets the XML descriptor—for example, the *parseXML()*—so that specific attributes and behavior extracted from the XML descriptor can extend core structures and behavior at run-time.

One, two, three, and BINGO! We have a product that works anywhere. Of course, something that looks easy to you might seem difficult to somebody else.

Can the art of this design be more formalized? How can we find the right balance between common and disparate features? How can we best express differences, in structure and behavior, in the XML descriptor? Is it possible to look for a standard way of producing rules?

```
<?xml version="1.0" encoding="UTF-8"?>
<!DOCTYPE Rules SYSTEM "./Fig.6-12.dtd">
<Rules>
 <ValidateFields>
      <Field name="User" check="notEmptyAndCharSet"/>
      <Field name="AreaCode"
      check="notEmptyAndNumber"/>
      <Field name="PhoneNumber"
      check="notEmptyAndNumber"/>
      <Field name="Email" check="noCheckRequired"/>
 </ValidateFields>
</Rules>
```

FIGURE 6.13

```
package com.its.util;
// file location is "com/its/util/Actor.java"

import java.lang.reflect.Method;

/**
 * The Actor class invokes a selected method on a selected class
 * Yes, the actor can actually play not only own (object) role
 * It can also play objects of any (existing) type
 * Actor class itself has several methods
 * The methods serve as examples of validation operations
 * selected run-time
 * @author Jeff.Zhuk@JavaSchool.com
 */
public class Actor {
    private Object[] parameters;
    private Object result;
    private Method method;
    private Object actingObject;
    private Class actingClass = getClass();
    private String actingClassName =
    actingClass.getName();

/**
 * The constructor creates an object of a requested class
 * It a requested class name is "Actor" there is nothing to do
 * In this case the actingObject is "this"
 */
    public Actor(String className) {
        System.out.println("Actor:className=" + className
        + " actingClassName=" + actingClassName);
        // include package name in the className to increase efficiency
        try{
            if(className.equals(actingClassName) ) {
                actingObject = this;
            } else { // load the class and instantiate the object
                actingClass = Class.forName(className);
                actingObject = actingClass.newInstance();
            }
        } catch (Exception e) {
            System.out.println("ERROR:Actor:" + e);
            System.exit(0);
        }
    }
/**
 * The act() method provides a unified way to find a requested
 * method
 * and invoke the method on previously defined object
 * @param methodName
```

FIGURE 6.14

```
 * @param parameters
 * @return result
 */
   public Object act(String methodName, Object[] parameters) {
       try{
           Class[] classes = null;
           if(parameters != null) {
               classes = new Class[parameters.length];
               for(int i=0; i<parameters.length; i++) {
                   classes[i] =
                   parameters[i].getClass();
               }
           }
           method = actingClass.getMethod(methodName,
           classes);
       } catch (Exception e) {
           return ("ERROR:Actor.cannot find the
           method:actingClass=" +
             actingClass + " methodName=" + methodName +
             " parameters=" + parameters + " e=" +e);
       }
       try{
           result = method.invoke(actingObject,
           parameters);
       } catch (Exception e) {
           return ("ERROR:Actor.cannot execute the method:" + e);
       }
       return result;
   }
/**
 * The charSet() method is an example of validation
 * The validation depends on a specific set of characters
 * @param value for validation
 * @param chars valid set of characters
 * @return result of validation
 */
   public String charSet(String value, char[] chars) {
       // empty is OK
       if(value == null || chars == null) {
           return "OK";
       }
       // check against specific set of characters
       char[] origChars = new char[value.length()];
       value.getChars(0, value.length(), origChars, 0);
       for(int i=0; i < value.length(); i++) {
           boolean valid = false;
           for(int j=0; j < chars.length  !valid; j++) {
               if(origChars[i] == chars[j]) {
                   valid = true; // valid
               }
           }
```

FIGURE 6.14. *(cont.)*

```
            if(!valid) {
                return ("Not a Valid character:\'" +
                origChars[i] + "\'");
            }
        }
        return ("OK"); // if valid
    }
/**
 * The notEmpty() method is another example of validation
 * It checks if value passed to the method is not empty
 * @param value for validation
 * @return result of validation: "OK" if not empty or
 * error message if empty
 */
    public String notEmpty(String value) {
        // the method validates first element of the array of
parameters
        if(value == null) {
            return ("Not Valid: cannot be empty");
        }
        // trim() returns a copy of the string, with
        // leading and trailing whitespace omitted.
           value = value.trim(); // check if not spaces
        if(value == null || value.length() == 0) {
            return ("Not Valid: cannot be empty");
        }
        return "OK";
    }
/**
 * The notEmptyAndCharSet() method is another example of validation
 * It checks if value passed to the method is not empty
 * Then it checks if a proper set of characters is used
 * The method re-uses notEmpty() and charSet() methods
 * @param value for validation
 * @param chars valid characters
 * @return result of validation: "OK" or error message
 */
    public String notEmptyAndCharSet(String value, char[]  chars) {
        String result = notEmpty(value);
        if(result.equals("OK")) {
            return charSet(value, chars);
        }
        return result;
    }
/**
 * The noCheckRequired() method is another example of
 * validation
 * @param value for validation
 * @return result of validation: always "OK"
 */
```

FIGURE 6.14. ***(cont.)***

```
    public String noCheckRequired(String value) {
        return "OK";
    }
    // more validation methods like ifNumber, etc.
/**
 * The main() method tests the class and its methods
 * If no arguments passed in the command line -
 * The method will create the Actor object and invoke
 * notEmpty() method
 * If 4 arguments are provided the arguments are treated as
 * className, methodName, first parameter, second parameter
 * The test is not universal, it only invokes validation
 * methods
 * Although the Actor class and act() method are universal
 * Actor and act() are able to play all roles on all classes
 */
    public static void main(String[] args) {
        // test the class and one validation method

        // prepare an array of parameters
        String value = "Value for validation";
        String origCharSet = "Value";
        String methodName = "charSet";
        String className = "Actor";
        if(args != null  args.length == 4) {
        // take args as parameters
            className = args[0];
            methodName = args[1];
            value = args[2];
            origCharSet = args[3];
        }
        Actor action = new Actor(className);
        char[] chars = new char[origCharSet.length()];
        origCharSet.getChars(0, origCharSet.length(), chars, 0);
        Object[] parameters = {value, chars};
        String result = (String)action.act(methodName, parameters);
        System.out.println("Actor.main.validation
        result=" + result);
        if(args == null || args.length != 4) {
            System.out.println("\nTest with
            parameters:\n" +
            "java Actor className methodName valueString
            validCharactersString");
        }
        System.exit(0);
    }

}
```

FIGURE 6.14. ***(cont.)***

```
// ServiceConnector

import java.lang.reflect.Method;

/**
 * The ServiceConnector class invokes a selected method on a
 * selected class
 * It instantiates an object of a class according to the
 * parameter passed to the constructor
 * Then the ServiceConnector uses its powerful act() method
 * to invoke a method on a selected object
 * Yes, the ServiceConnector can actually play not only own
 * (object) role
 * It can also play objects of any (existing) type
 * @author Jeff.Zhuk@JavaSchool.com
 */
public class ServiceConnector {
    private Object[] parameters;
    private Object result;
    private Method method;
    private Object actingObject;
    private Class actingClass = getClass();
    private String actingClassName = actingClass.getName();

/**
 * The constructor creates an object of a requested class
 * It a requested class name is "ServiceConnector" there is
 * nothing to do
 * In this case the actingObject is "this"
 */
    public ServiceConnector(String className) {
        System.out.println("ServiceConnector:className=" +
        className +
          " actingClassName=" + actingClassName);
        // include package name in the className to increase
        // efficiency
        try{
            if(className.equals(actingClassName) ) {
                actingObject = this;
            } else { // load the class and instantiate the object
                actingClass = Class.forName(className);
                actingObject = actingClass.newInstance();
            }
        } catch (Exception e) {
            System.out.println("ERROR:ServiceConnector:" +
            e);
            System.exit(0);
        }
    }
```

FIGURE 6.15

```
/**
 * The act() method provides a unified way to find a
 * requested method
 * and invoke the method on previously defined object
 * @param methodName
 * @param parameters
 * @return result
 */
    public Object act(String methodName, Object[]
    parameters) {
        try{
            Class[] classes = null;
            if(parameters != null) {
                classes = new Class[parameters.length];
                for(int i=0; i<parameters.length; i++) {
                    classes[i] = parameters[i].getClass();
                }
            }
            method = actingClass.getMethod(methodName,
            classes);
        } catch (Exception e) {
            return ("ERROR:ServiceConnector.cannot find the
            method:actingClass=" +
              actingClass + " methodName=" + methodName +
              " parameters=" +
              parameters + " e=" +e);
        }
        try{
            result = method.invoke(actingObject,
            parameters);
        } catch (Exception e) {
            return ("ERROR:ServiceConnector.cannot execute
            the method:" + e);
        }
        return result;
    }
}
```

FIGURE 6.15. ***(cont.)***

Are these rules "final" (sounds scary to me), or it is possible to do some rule adjustments at run-time?

Can knowledge technology help smart brains struggle less and still win this battle? Answering questions with questions can work this time, right? This bridge to the knowledge technology chapter gives some hope to lazy programmers (myself included) who want to use their brains only after all their tools are exhausted.

What I plan to do next (after this book) is to employ a knowledge engine to help in this process. For example, the OpenCyc [2] engine (considered in the previous chapter) and its CycL language may be used to formalize concepts expressed in this chapter. OpenCyc also allows us to build rules to translate structures and behavior instructions into XML descriptors and to move even further to **adaptive behavior patterns** in which real feedback from the field produces rule changes and updates the XML descriptor.

The typed collection of objects discussed above leads to a very simple and economic implementation that can be reused, even for J2ME (Java 2 Micro Edition) and other small devices. The sophisticated and heavy parts of services shift to the server part and may be powered by a knowledge engine that generates XML descriptors and takes responsibility for overall system behavior.

There is also significant network savings in client–server communications. For example, the *DataReference* objects will only send their attribute values over the network because both the server and client sides are aware of the attribute names via the XML descriptor.

The same is valid for networking related to events, screens, and behavior. The XML descriptor may include economical descriptions of events, screens (user interface), and behavior that can be sent over the network and understood on both sides because of the XML descriptor's definitions. You will find more on client–server communications and user interfaces in the following chapters.

Integrating Questions

1. What does the expression *write once* mean?
2. What are the common steps that help you write applications once?

Case Study

1. Create an XML descriptor with an order form definition.
   (A server will send only the name of this definition to a client, and the client will show the appropriate screen.)
2. Create a set of XML definitions for different order forms.
3. Create an XML definition for a "Compose Email" screen.
4. (Advanced) Create a Java program capable of generating the screens based on the definitions. (See Chapter and Appendix 3 for help.)
5. Describe an application at your workplace that can benefit from the write-once approach.

References

1. Open Office: *http://openoffice.org*.
2. OpenCyc: *http://opencyc.org*.

CHAPTER 7

The New Generation of Client–Server Software

Divide and rule, a sound motto. Unite and lead, a better one.
—Johann Wolfgang von Goethe (1749–1832)

This chapter is about existing and upcoming client–server paradigms in communications, the distribution of computing power, and effective programming with reusable code that can be run on both sides of the client–server pair.

The past decade of client–server development turned to the server part of this happily married couple. The biggest software giants are in a hurry to translate desktop applications into Web services leased or sold on a pay-per-use basis.

This work, begun several years ago, was based on several assumptions:

1. Client networks will improve/upgrade faster and more cheaply than client computers.
2. HTTP-based Web technology will be able to provide all or most of the requested services.
3. Centralized data and services will benefit clients and service providers.

Unfortunately, not all of these assumptions happen to be true.

1. Computers and PDAs are much more capable *and* cheap today than they were several years ago, whereas digital subscriber line (DSL) and cable modems are still the same price, with no miracles to show for it.
2. One of the biggest requests for Internet services, streaming data, requires protocols other than HTTP and lies outside of Web technology. (This is just one example; applications with asynchronous natures are also not comfortable with HTTP limitations.)

3. Groups of clients are unhappy with the centralized service concept. For security reasons, they prefer peer-to-peer or similar communications.
4. Distributed computing and distributed knowledge architecture (hopefully, we are moving in this direction, aren't we?) is different from Web services architecture.

Having said that, I want to emphasize that Web services are still a very important segment of the software market. The most important and exciting part of Web services is their standards, which are recognized by the entire software industry.
There is a standard language to describe services. **WSDL** (Web Services Description Language) provides XML-based descriptions for a Web service's technical specifications.

There is a standard way to register Web services. A consortium of more than 200 companies is developing (as a work in progress) the **UDDI** (Universal Description, Discovery, and Integration) business registry. There is a standard way to exchange data, messages, and instructions over Web services. **SOAP** (Simple Object Access Protocol) presents complex objects as XML messages and enables an RPC (remote procedure call) layer. **SOAP Messages with Attachments** add multiple XML document exchange with non-XML attachments.

This may be the first time ever that technical standards have been introduced on a service level. The list of vendors that support Web service standards with their implementations includes, but is not limited to, IBM, Microsoft, Sun Microsystems, and Hewlett-Packard. Standards enable many companies to create tools and packages and build Web services. Naturally, the biggest group benefiting from the standards is Web service customers.

Web services technology is the front door for current clients—until new front doors become available. Object-oriented concepts include "private" and "public" methods. Let us extend this concept to services. Private services are designed for efficiency, for specific groups and controlled environments, most often inside corporate networks. Public services are not necessarily the most efficient but are easily *accessible, understandable*, and *standardized*. Today, we translate easy accessibility as Web technology, or HTTP communications over port 80. Port 80 is often a single open port on a corporate firewall machine. We translate the *understandable* part as readable, XML-based messages. The WSDL, UDDI, and SOAP Web service standards, all based on XML, are the rare ones that are accepted at a high service level by the whole industry.

Figure 7.1 shows an architecture in which users come through the front door of Web services to get access to other doors.

The current decade promises to shift the balance from server to client applications. The demand for new applications comes from new **client devices**. Small wireless devices, smart cards, and PDAs are becoming increasingly capable each day. They require us to reprogram old tasks, such as digital maps, and bring new and exciting features that have never been programmed before. The range of client types and capacities is rapidly growing.

The old PC-based client is able to play many server roles today. Low-end client devices, such as digital pagers, limited by memory and CPU constraints, struggle to deliver new, meaningful functionality to their users. Most new devices fall somewhere in between pure client and server types; some offer new features that combine multimedia with information flow.

This growing variety of client types leads to a bigger fragmentation of client–server solutions. Data, business, and presentation logics distribution, as well as communication activity between clients and servers, depends on many factors, which will be considered below.

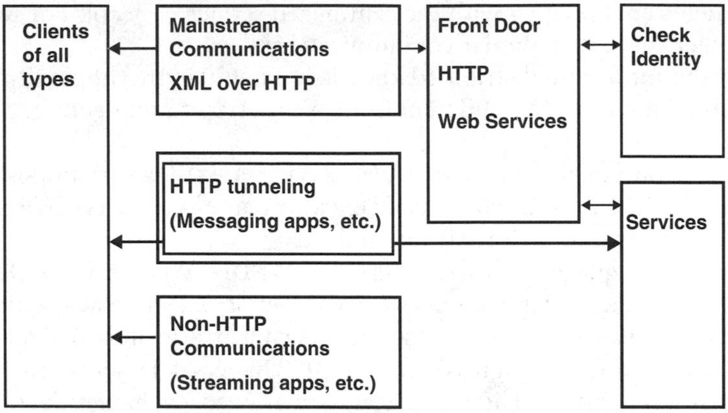

FIGURE 7.1. Client-Server Communications.

An important factor that I consistently bring to the reader's attention is building flexible, reusable, integration-ready systems that may cost a bit more in the short term, but pay off by drastically increasing overall productivity in the long run.

Figure 7.2 presents the simplest view of the client–server interaction. The client requests the *Mail* service with the *Get* action and indicates *WML* as the requested format type. The server dispatches this request to a proper service that retrieves email for this user and provides properly formatted output.

Let us consider the internal details of client functionality.

1. The client program must be able to present information to a user. The presentation may include video, audio, forms, and so on.
2. The client program must be able to collect information from a user.
3. The client program can collaborate with the server in processing information.
4. The client program may be able to complete some services without server connections and keep some data locally.

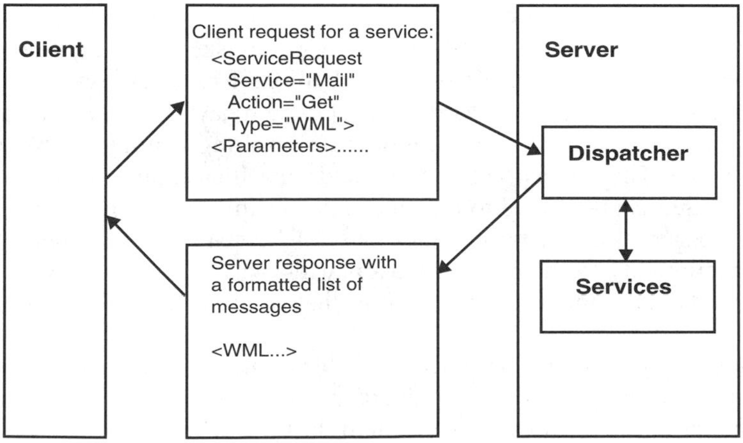

FIGURE 7.2. XML-Based Messaging.

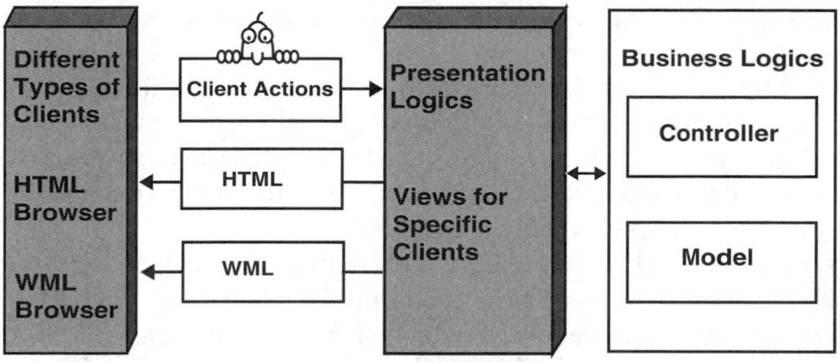

FIGURE 7.3. A Web Application with WML and HTML Clients.

WHAT ARE THE BEST WAYS TO PROVIDE CLIENT FUNCTIONALITY?

First, we realize that there is more than just one way. The second important observation is that we are probably not alone in the search for better ways to make client programs. This observation leads us directly to design patterns: known solutions for common problems.

The model-view-controller (MVC) architectural pattern describes the idea of separating applications into three functional parts to increase the flexibility and maintainability of the system.

Imagine a service, such as an email reader, that can be accessed from a regular Web browser's HTML page or from a Wireless Markup Language (WML) browser embedded in a wireless phone.

Figure 7.3 displays an example of MVC design pattern implementation.

Business logics represented by the **model** and the **controller** work with different presentation layers, or **views**: one for HTML and another for WML browsers.

A special category of design patterns describes specific ways of partitioning applications and combining their components. Some structural design patterns are Composite, Composite View, Façade, Decorator, Flyweight, and Value Object Assembler (VOA).

The **Composite** design pattern suggests a unified interface for a complex hierarchical structure as well as for every element in this structure. The **Composite View** pattern describes a view as a set of reusable views. Every screen is created as a composition of reusable components.

The **Façade** pattern suggests an additional layer that can simplify the interface to a complex product.

The **Decorator** design pattern, also known as **Wrapper**, allows us to add or build new object properties and behaviors on the fly, in a way that is transparent to the user.

The **Flyweight** pattern reduces the number of objects by sharing some objects and using specific context information to determine their function.

The **VOA** pattern suggests collecting data from multiple screens into a single object *(valueObject)* for a single client-server transaction.

A great example of a client program that uses some of these design patterns is a Web browser.

Every element of any screen, as well as the screen itself, is described with a unified interface: HTML in the case of a regular Web browser or WML in the case of a Web browser embedded in wireless phones.

Every screen is presented as a composite view of reusable components, such as buttons, text fields, and tables.

With all due respect to Web browsers, I have to admit their limitations. Issues exist with each browser's implementations and their compatibilities, but I want to focus on major problems. The crucial fact is that browsers are good for simple and mostly "static" applications and cannot fit into the new world of data-intensive applications with dynamic, sophisticated graphics and multiple communication channels.

Web browsers understand only HTML, which represents a very limited set of graphics primitives. Web browsers speak only one communication language via HTTP.

Web browsers have no infrastructure to add custom functionality.

Java applets significantly extend Web graphics, but playing in a sandbox is not always fun. Java applet restrictions limit their participation in distributed computing, or turn Java into a fat client—a signed applet or a stand-alone application.

We can find Web browserlike programs on devices other than PCs, such as wireless phones and PDAs.

HTML or WML browsers are universally known client programs, but they are limited by a set of HTML or WML tags (keywords).

How do we extend the functionality of a client program while striving for a unified solution?

I focus on examples that fit the integration-ready system paradigm. Client programs can be implemented with one technology (for example, Sun's Java technology), can work with a server based on another technology (for example, Microsoft.NET technology), and can work in other ways (for example, a Microsoft.NET client working with Sun's Java server).

What makes this possible? The text-based protocol, or application program interface (API) expressed with HTML, WML, or XML instructions. We are moving from HTML and WML browsers to the XML browser, capable of changing and loading extra functionality at run-time.

Thin Clients

The Thinlet [1] client program implements the Flyweight pattern in its extreme form. Thinlet shares all reusable components inside a single Java object. The interface to this object is provided as an XML descriptor, very similar to the HTML format. The XML descriptor may be passed as a parameter to this object or loaded via the network from the server.

Thinlet creates a multipurpose graphical user interface (GUI), such as a Web browser, with a very small footprint. Thinlet's size is below 30 KB, which makes this single-class GUI engine an attractive option for wireless phones, PDAs, and other implementations in which memory size is extremely limited. Thinlet can be compiled for the MIDP (Mobile Information Device Profile) version of the J2ME (Java 2 Micro Edition) virtual machine that runs on PDAs from Palm, Sharp, and some Nokia phones.

The GUI supports dialogs and menus, list/tree/table selection and modification, resize, reorder, sort columns, and other applications. This open source program provides convenient hooks in the code to add business logics and run it as an applet or as an application.

The Droplets [2] solution uses the same design patterns and introduces a multipurpose GUI on the client side driven by XML instructions from the server side. The Droplets client is a system-dependent executable program; it is not a Java binary object, which needs the

Java Virtual Machine. The program is downloaded at the very first session and is invisible to the user.

Droplets has a generic, an Abstract Window Toolkit- (AWT) style user interface. All application logics reside on the server side. The server provides the necessary XML instructions to update the client screen. The client and server have a permanent connection from the beginning of the session. The client sends user actions over the Internet and receives screen instructions from the server much like any Web browser.

Droplets has important bandwidth advantages over Web browsers. The Droplets protocol is faster because it does not require reconnection for every client action, as browsers do. Its protocol is less network intensive because it only passes screen changes to the client, whereas browsers always receive full pages from the server. The lightweight protocol boosts Droplets' client performance.

The Droplets server also takes care of invisible client version updates and simplifies administration issues. In some cases, permanent socket connections are not an option for security reasons. If necessary, Droplets allows for HTTP tunneling, a built-in feature that is transparent to application programmers.

Another thin client example is Ultra Light Client (ULC), by Canoo Engineering AG, which targets business-to-business applications as well as those run by application service providers (ASPs) [3].

ULC provides a comprehensive set of components for the development and deployment of thin client applications. It follows a proven approach of partitioning functionality between client and server—with a presentation engine on the client and the entire remainder of the application on the server. The presentation engine is application independent, is small, and can be run as an applet via Java Web Start or as a stand-alone application. Development is carried out exclusively with Java on the server side using the ULC framework. ULC components are tailored for thin clients and based on standards such as Java and Swing and protocols such as HTTP, HTTPS, Internet Inter-ORB Protocol, or Remote Method Invocation.

Figure 7.4 demonstrates client programs that serve strictly as terminals. The programs create screens according to server instructions and hit the server on every client action.

The clients presented above have limitations.
They cannot survive even a short time without a server connection.
In addition, clients have a limited set of visual components and their combinations, with little chance to expand.

This is the price paid for a client's small footprint, fast download, and clear separation of view, business model, and controller in the MVC design pattern.

Making Thin Clients Smarter—and Fatter

We plan to move on to the rich client paradise later on. Before doing this, let us consider ways to make thin clients smarter and maybe a bit fatter.
These are the goals:

1. Increase client independence.
2. Decrease the number of network trips.
3. Improve the user's perception of data processing.

We are going to add some business logics to the client side. The client will take its share of data processing, which will help the server side work with multiple clients. This extension of

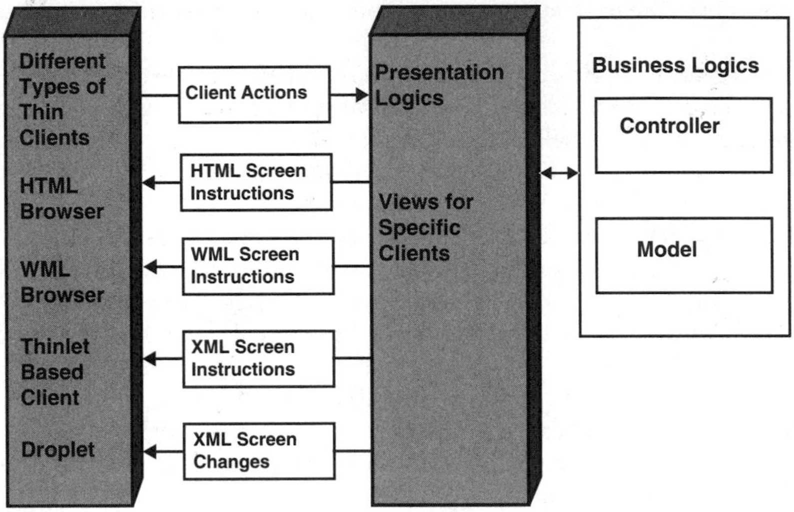

FIGURE 7.4. A Web Application with Multiple Thin Clients.

client functionality can easily make a very specific client able to serve a very specific business need, but that is the last thing we want to do. We want to start with generic functionality that can serve multiple businesses.

What are these generic client tasks?

The best place to start, once again, is with design patterns.

Figure 7.5 illustrates the VOA pattern applied to client-server communications.

The VOA pattern suggests collecting data from multiple screens into a single value object for a single client–server transaction. We can add to this suggestion the idea that collected data can be validated against some rules on the client side. For example, some fields entered by a user must be integer numbers, and some cannot be blank. It would make the user happier to receive an immediate warning of omitted or misspelled fields before the data flies to the server and a "Please reenter" message comes back.

Figure 7.6 illustrates the Aggregate Entity (AE) pattern applied to client–server communications. The AE pattern wraps a number of related, fine-grained, persistent objects into a single entity representing a structured organization containing those objects. The data tree in Windows Explorer is a good illustration of this pattern. Using the AE pattern in the

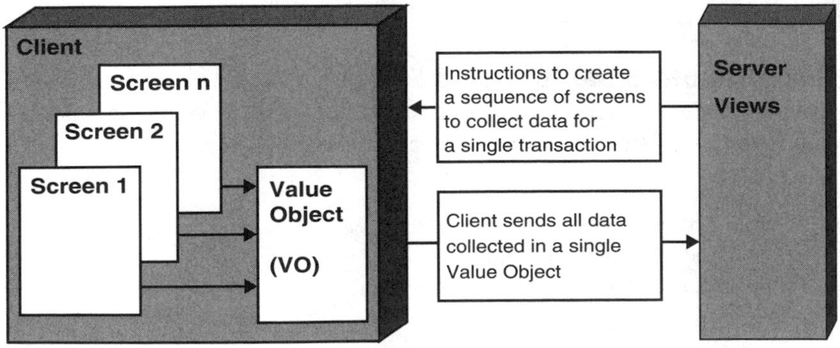

FIGURE 7.5. The Value Object Assembler in Client-Server Communications.

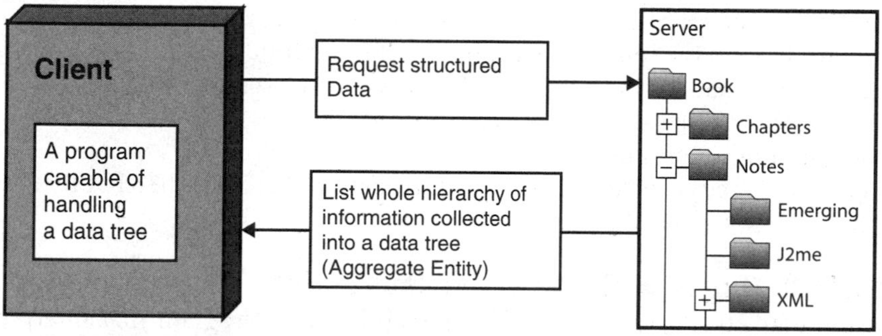

FIGURE 7.6. The Aggregate Entity Design Pattern in Client-Server Communications.

client–server environment can significantly decrease the number of network trips to the server and back.

Imagine that you are searching for a file located on the server side over the Internet. Your client program displays a folder at a time, and you are amazed to find more folders inside. Without an additional program that implements the AE pattern, each time a user selects a new folder, the client program sends a request to the server.

The server sends a list of files in the folder back to the client program. The AE pattern implementation on the server side allows the server to collect the whole file system hierarchy into a single structured object list. The server sends this list of files and folders to the client.

The client also implements the AE pattern with a function that can handle this list hierarchy without server support. The function, for example, is capable of showing data trees and their branches, and requests only the server's help when a user selects a file to load from the server.

Remember that our AE in this case is just a list of names of files and folders; there is no file content in the list. This makes the AE relatively small.

The AE is not limited to the file system example; it can help represent any hierarchical structure, such as an organization with departments and jobs or a map location with final intersections and addresses.

There may be cases in which the hierarchy of names exceeds client capacity. In this case, I recommend enhancing the AE pattern with additional parameters that the client program sends to the server in the service request (Fig. 7.7). These parameters give the server an idea about the client's capacity. The server then calculates the number of levels of hierarchy that will be included in the data tree to fit client abilities.

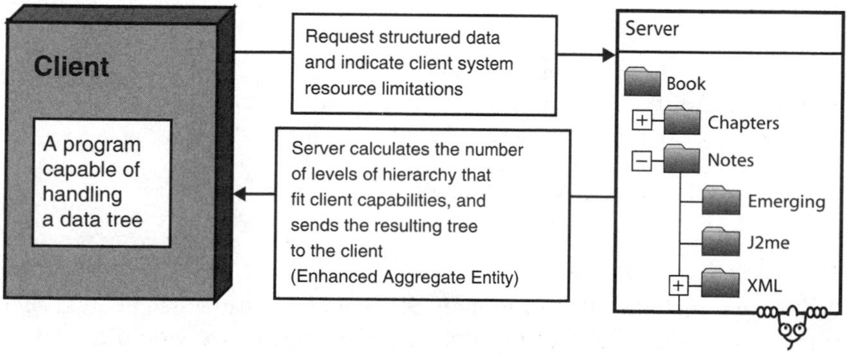

FIGURE 7.7. The Enhanced Aggregate Entity Pattern.

We can extend our set of screen instructions with the sequence of screens, provide validation rules and point to methods that can execute this functionality. Such extensions can be provided with JavaScript built into HTML pages; WML script; multiple WML cards in a single WML deck, with Java applet or ActiveX controls built in to the Web page, extended Thinlet code, and other programs.

We realize that these extensions make the thin client richer and fatter, but there are several techniques that smooth out the effect of the client getting fat.

Extend HTML Pages with Reusable JavaScript

The most popular client program today is a Web browser program that interprets *HTML* pages into nice looking words and graphics, shy sound-clips, and even beautiful songs. Most browsers support Java Script that dynamites HTML pages, in other words makes them dynamic (DHTML).

JavaScript is a very natural extension of HTML pages. Built-in an HTML page Java Script tends to be specific for the page. On the same token it sounds very natural that Java Script is reloaded each time when a new Web page is loaded. It looks like Java Script by its nature is not a good fit for reuse. Can we go against the lazy nature and add some reusable functionality with JavaScript? For example, we can add several functions that can validate form fields. The functions can check on a valid set of characters, a valid type of data (e.g., numeral and date), or a blank field.

Can we escape the necessity to send the same JavaScript functions with every page provided by the server? Yes, we can, and if the target is not a single Web page but a Web site—we should.

We'll start with an example of the simplest *validate*() function embedded directly in the Search page. The function is not only embedded in the page it is hard coded with the specific values like "search" and "search_criteria," the form and text field names.

```
<html><head><title> Simplest Validate Example</title>
<script language="JavaScript">
function validate() {// not a reusable function
 if(document.search.searchcriteria.value == "") {
     alert('Fill in searchcriteria');
     return false;
}
return true;
}
</script>
</head><body>
<form name="search" action=
"http://javaschool.com/search.get.html.jsp" method="post">
<input type=="text" name="searchcriteria" size=50>
<input type="button" value="Go" onClick="if
 (validate(document.search)) submit()">
</form>
</body></html>
```

This Web page includes the form named "search" with a single text field named "search_criteria" and the "Go" button. Pressing this button we would submit the search criteria to the server program "*http://javaschool.com/search.get.html.jsp*" provided with the action element of the form. But we want to validate the search criteria field first. So, we marked the "Go" button with the "button" type a(instead of the "submit" type) and we added the "*onclick*" element (we can spell it as *onClick* too, HTML is not case sensitive). The "onclick" element calls the Java Script *validate*() function and if the function returns *true*, submits the search criteria to the server. The validate() function checks if the search criteria field is empty, issues the alert, and, if so, returns *false* blocking the submission.

This function is not reusable. This means that the next time you'll need to validate text fields you need to write another function.

But this is not what we want. As soon as we found out what needs to be done we would like to use this knowledge for many cases. We need to solve three problems: one is to enhance the function, so it can check empty fields in any form; two is to add this function to some file that can serve us as a library; and finally three is to load this library once to serve multiple changeable pages. All these jobs are doable.

Reusable JavaScript code (e.g., validation functions) can be collected into a file, which will be loaded only once. This JavaScript source can be kept in a parent HTML source and used from multiple child sources. The parent HTML source usually describes a frameset with its frames. The frames display the Web content and reuse JavaScript code from the parent frameset page. Note that even when we display one-frame content, we still use the frameset page as a parent to keep reusable code and session variables. An additional benefit is that with the proper Web server settings, this code, as well as session variables in the JavaScript file, can be hidden from Web users.

An example of a parent frameset with an embedded JavaScript file is shown in Fig. 7.8. The frameset (parent) page refers to the JavaScript file *its.util.js* and describes a frameset with a single visible frame.

The *its.util.js* file with reusable JavaScript utilities is loaded onto the client browser once and will be kept by the parent HTML source to serve multiple HTML pages provided in the child frames. This example shows that one frame is blank by default and another frame is currently assigned to the */go/search.get.html.jsp* Java server page. The URL reflects the service name *search*, the action name *get*, and the presentation form, which happens to be *html*, which means that the server's presentation factory will return service results in the HTML format.

```
<html><head><title>Frameset with JS</title>
<SCRIPT LANGUAGE="JavaScript" src="its.util.js"></script>
</head>
<frameset FRAMEBORDER=0 FRAMESPACING=0 BORDER=0 cols="0,*">
    <frame name="fake" src="blank.html" scrolling=no
     marginheight=0 marginwidth=0 noresize>
    <frame name="main" src="search.form.html"
     marginheight=6 marginwidth=6 scrolling="auto">
</frameset>
</HTML>
```

FIGURE 7.8

Figure 7.9 shows an extract of the JavaScript file *its.util.js* that can include some user-session variables and provide reusable utility functions for encryption, validation, and other tasks.

It is recommended to refer to *its.util.js* file in the frameset. American Disability Act does not recommend using multiple visible frames. So we keep a single visible frame and use the frameset only to "parent" this frame. In the frameset code provided in Fig. 7.8 you find a reference to this small java script library. The frameset is loaded once as well as the script and serve multiple pages that will replace each other in a single frame.

Then the frame page will call Java Script functions using the "parent" keyword. For example, the form below can be a part of the *search.main.html* page visible in the single frame. The form will be tested by the validate function and will be submitted only if the validate function returns true.

```
<html><head><title>Prevent empty fields. Use JS in the
framset</title></head><body>
<form name="search" action=
"http://javaschool.com/search.get.html.jsp" method="post">
<input type="text" name="searchcriteria" size=50>
<input type="button" value="Go"
onClick="if(parent.validate(document.search)) submit()">
</form></body></html>
```

The *validate*() function is ready to check all text elements in a form. It returns true if no empty fields are found and allows the form submission. If there are empty fields the function provides the alert with the names of empty fields and returns false. There is no submission in this case.

The session related functions help to keep session values in the frameset. The session values are stored after user's authentication and then can be used during the session to confirm the user's identity. It is very easy to use *cookies* to store session related values directly on the user's machine.

The following Java Script lines write and read data to and from *cookies*.

```
// read cookie into variable cookieText
var cookieText = document.cookie;
//----------------
// prepare cookie in the var cookieText and write the cookie
// file
document.cookie = cookieText;
```

A cookie, a small amount of information that Web browser can save on a local machine is commonly used for session management. Saved on a client machine and later sent back to the server cookies can uniquely identify a user. In spite of this common usage some users consider cookies as a potential security hole and set their Web browser option that prevents cookies. This is a very good reason to keep session values on the server side or/and in the frameset as shown above.

There are two functions that might be helpful to encrypt messages, like password, etc, transferred over the Internet. The *encryptWithKey*() function replaces each character in the message with another character from the KEY-string using a sequential counter as the shift between the character position in the KEY and its replacement.

```
// its.util.js - reusable JavaScript by Internet Technology
// School, Inc.

// get user session variables
var userLoginName, sessionID;
function setUserSessionData(userLoginName, sessionID) {
    this.userLoginName = userLoginName;
    this.sessionID = SessionId;
}
function getUserLoginName() {
    return useLoginNamel;
}
function getSessionID() {
    return sessionID;
}
// encrypt message
function encrypt(message) {
    var encrypted = "";
    // algorithm that makes message encrypted
    return encrypted;

}
// validate text against a pre-defined set of characters
// function charSet(text)
    var set =  '0123456789abcdefghijklmnopqrstuvwxyzABCDE
    FGHIJKLMNOPQRSTUVWXYZ -_.:/"\\';
    return charSet(text, set); // see below
}
// validate text against a set of characters passed to the function
function charSet(text, set)
{
    var i, ch;
    if (text.length == 0 || set.length == 0) {
    // empty field or empty set
        return false;
    }
    // check for every character in the text
    for (i=0; i < text.length; i++) {
        ch = text.charAt(i);
        // try to find the character in the set
        if (set.indexOf(ch) == -1) {
            return false;
        }
    }
    // all characters are valid!
   return true;
}
```

FIGURE 7.9

```
<!-- Example of the usage of the validation function from the
parent page -->
<html><head><title>Test text field using JS in the frameset</title>
</head><body>
<FORM method="POST" name="info" action="server/program"
    onSubmit="return parent.checkText
    (document.info.importantTextField.value);">
<input type="text" name="importantTextField" size=20>
<input type=submit value="Submit">
</FORM></body></html>
```

FIGURE 7.10

The *encryptWithTwoKeys*() function is the cipher that replaces each character in the message with another character from the KEY1-string using the index found in the KEY2-string for this character.

The *checkText*() function validates text against a set of characters. The function issues an alert and returns false if an unspecified character found in the tested message.

Java Script functions and libraries make client behavior more independent of the server. For example, validation functions can provide immediate feedback to users if corrections are needed, without calling the server.

Figure 7.10 presents several lines of HTML code to illustrate validation of a text field on the client side with a reusable JavaScript function called from the parent page. This is a "classic HTML" example of giving the client some limited independence with JavaScript utilities and saving network bandwidth by placing reusable utilities in the invisible parent frame. Note, that we can use "onSubmit" function in the form element that prevents submission if the Java Script function "checkText" that we called from the parent-frameset returns false.

JavaScript extensions are limited by several factors. JavaScript is not scalable. Web browsers still have some disagreement with JavaScript compatibility. Web technology is not the single, nor always the best answer for all services. Current browsers bring their limitations with their convenience. HTML and WML browsers are limited by their predefined set of operations specified by the HTML or WML tags. They are still great programs in our *fixed computing* world. Fixed functionality is essential part of current programming paradigm. Fixed functionality enforces fixed roles of multiple participants in the computing process.

In the next sections we add more smartness to our programs and review an XML browser (or a service browser) that can relax fixed computing rules.

XML browser program can be considered as an example of flexible computing. XML is not limited by predefined tags but allows creating new languages. In a similar way XML browser can load new interpretation rules and interpret new XML scenarios as new services.

Add Smarts to Thin Clients

We now consider a wider spectrum of reusable client programs. Our goal is to add business logics to thin nonbrowser clients. Reusable thin clients such as Thinlet and Droplets are very similar to Web browser programs. These programs represent different sets of reusable widgets and can combine them into user screens by following server instructions. The instructions or APIs to these clients are based on XML.

The simplest way to extend client independence is to move a part of the specific business logics from the server side to the client. We still want to preserve client reusability. We do not want to create specific clients for every business case.

To achieve this goal, we first do our homework. From the business logics, we extract client parts that can be reused for multiple clients. We extend a client program—for example, Thinlet—with more reusable classes and methods.

Scenario for Multiple Object Roles and Actions

We add the *ClientScenarioPlayer* class, which can serve as the base for our XML browser. The *ClientScenarioPlayer* will play scenarios with multiple objects and invoke any method of any object according to instructions that specify objects and methods by name.

The *ClientScenarioPlayer* class is an example of the Chain of Responsibility design pattern, a behavior pattern that instructs the system on handling messages on a specific level or with a specific object. *ClientScenarioPlayer* establishes a chain of responsibility within a system and includes instructions on where user actions should be handled.

Figure 7.11 displays the *ClientScenarioPlayer* class with *init()* and *act()* methods. The *init()* method initializes a scenario name. The *act()* method uses the *ServiceConnector* class to instantiate an object and invoke the proper method according to XML instructions. The *act()* method returns a result object for future analysis.

For example, we use the *TextValidator* class with several validation methods.

Figure 7.12 illustrates text validation with the *TextValidator* class, according to the XML descriptor displayed in Fig. 7.13.

The *charSet()* method checks if all characters in the text field belong to a predefined set of characters. The value of the text field, as well as the character set, is passed as arguments to the *charSet()* method. The method returns "OK" or a specific error message that pinpoints a problem.

The *notEmpty()* method works in a similar way to solve an even simpler task. The method returns "OK" or a specific error message that pinpoints a problem.

There are more validation methods in the class; and even more methods may be added.

The screen described above is a simple dialog requesting a user's name and gender. The XML syntax is very close to HTML extended with several tags. This is a very natural likeness because the client program we are discussing is very similar to its big brother—the browser.

The XML parser reads an XML descriptor and translates the descriptor content into proper objects of the *ClientScenarioPlayer* class.

MULTIPLE SCENARIOS

Let us say we want to collect data from more than one screen on the client side and send all this data in a single network trip to a server for a meaningful transaction.

Here is an example. A product distribution company designed a set of screens that offer products. The marketing department of the company did a survey that revealed men and women can have quite different interests. This discovery was a driving force behind the Web design. The very first screen asks the user his or her name and gender. The next screen, personalized with the user's name, offers a set of products based on that user's gender.

```
package com.its.connector;

import java.util.*;
import com.its.util.IOMaster; // i/o and http connections
import com.its.util.Stringer;
// string manipulations and simple xml parsing

/**
 * The ClientScenarioPlayer class invokes a selected
 * method on a selected class
 * Yes, the ClientScenarioPlayer can actually play not
 * only with its own (object) methods
 * It can also play objects of any (existing) type
 * The ClientScenarioPlayer class uses ServiceConnector
 * object to create an actor object and play its role
 * @author Jeff.Zhuk@JavaSchool.com
 */

/**
 * ClientScenarioPlayer is able to read XML scenarios
 * and play their acts.
 */
 public class ClientScenarioPlayer implements Scenario {
    public static boolean debug = true;

    private ServiceConnector connector = new
    ServiceConnector();
    private Hashtable scenarios;
    // a set of scenarios (can be a tree) to choose for the
    // next step
    private Hashtable nextStepRules;
    // rules to choose the next scenario
    private Hashtable results;    // result name-values
    private static Hashtable voa;
    // Value Object Assembler collects data from multimple
    // screen for a single transaction
    private String scenarioName;
    // current ClientScenarioPlayer name, for example "main"
    private static String fullScenarioName = "";
    // concatenated from consequtive ClientScenarioPlayer
    // names: "main.MenProducts"

/**
 * The init() method creates an object of a requested class
 * If a requested class name is "Scenario" there is nothing to do
 * In this case the actingObject is "this"
 */
    public void init() {
        init(scenarioName);
    }
```

FIGURE 7.11

```
/**
 * The init() method creates an object of a requested class
 * If a requested class name is "Scenario" there is nothing to do
 * In this case the actingObject is "this"
 * @param scenarioName
 */
    public void init(String scenarioName) {
if(debug)
System.out.println("Scenario.init:scenarioName=" + scenarioName);
        this.scenarioName = scenarioName;
    }
/**
 * The act() method provides a unified way to find a
 * requested method
 * and invoke the method on previously defined object
 * @param className
 * @param methodName
 * @param parameters
 */
    public Object act(String className, String
    methodName, Object[] parameters) {
        try{
            if(className != null) {
            // keep previous class if null
            connector.changeActingClass(className);
            }
            return connector.act(methodName, parameters);
        } catch (Exception e) {
            System.out.println("ERROR:Scenario:cannot
          play service " + className + " action= " +
          methodName + " e= " + e);
        }
        return null;
    }
    // more methods ...
}
```

FIGURE 7.11. ***(cont.)***

To support nested scenarios, we extend the *ClientScenarioPlayer* class with additional properties and methods.

Figure 7.14 displays more of source code for the *ClientScenarioPlayer* class.

In the *setScenarios*() method we parse XML scenario descriptions only to transform it into the *Hashtable scenarios* with a set of scenarios-objects. Every key in the Hashtable is a name for an associated scenario-object.

There are several more objects from Fig. 7.11 that we actively use in the code above. The *Hashtable results* collects results of multiple user entries in one scenario.

```
// TextValidator
package com.its.util;
// file location is "com/its/util/TextValidator.java"

/**
 * The TextValidator class includes several methods for text
 * validation
 */
public class TextValidator {

/**
 * The charSet() method is an example of validation
 * The validation depends on a specific set of characters
 * @param value for validation
 * @param chars valid set of characters
 * @return result of validation
 */
    public String charSet(String value, String set) {
        if(value == null || chars == null) {
            return "OK";
        }
        // get array of characters that represent the
        // validation set
        char[] chars = null;
        set.getChars(0, set.length(), chars, 0);
        return(charSet(value, chars);
    }
    public String charSet(String value, char[] chars) {
        // empty is OK
        if(value == null || chars == null) {
            return "OK";
        }
        // check against specific set of characters
        char[] origChars =  new char[value.length()];
        value.getChars(0, value.length(), origChars, 0);
        for(int i=0; i < value.length(); i++) {
            boolean valid = false;
            for(int j=0; j < chars.length && !valid;
            j++) {
                if(origChars[i] == chars[j]) {
                    valid = true; // valid
                }
            }
            if(!valid) {
                return ("Not a Valid character:\'" +
                origChars[i] + "\'");
            }
        }
        return ("OK"); // if valid
    }
```

FIGURE 7.12

```
/**
 * The notEmpty() method is another example of validation
 * It checks if value passed to the method is not empty
 * @param value for validation
 * @return result of validation: "OK" if not empty or
 * error message if empty
 */
    public String notEmpty(String value) {
        // the method validates first element of the array
        // of parameters
        if(value == null) {
            return ("Not Valid: cannot be empty");
        }
        // trim() returns a copy of the string, with leading
        // and trailing whitespace omitted.
        value = value.trim(); // check if not spaces
        if(value == null || value.length() == 0) {
            return ("Not Valid: cannot be empty");
        }
        return "OK";
    }
/**
 * The notEmptyAndCharSet() method is another example of validation
 * It checks if value passed to the method is not empty
 * Then it checks if a proper set of characters is used
 * The method re-uses notEmpty() and charSet() methods
 * @param value for validation
 * @param chars valid characters
 * @return result of validation: "OK" or error message
 */
    public String notEmptyAndCharSet(String value,
    char[] chars) {
        String result = notEmpty(value);
        if(result.equals("OK")) {
            return charSet(value, chars);
        }
        return result;
    }
/**
 * The noCheckRequired() method is another example of
 * validation
 * @param value for validation
 * @return result of validation: always "OK"
 */
    public String noCheckRequired(String value) {
        return "OK";
    }
    // more validation methods like ifNumber, etc.}
```

FIGURE 7.12. ***(cont.)***

```
<dialog gap="4" top="2" left="2">
  <label text="Name:" />
  <textfield name="userName" columns="5"
  TextValidator="notEmpty" />

  <label text="Gender:" />
  <combobox name="selection" selected="2"
  editable="false" valign="center"
  action="setSelection">
      <choice text="F" />
      <choice text="M" />
 </combobox>

 <button text="Submit" action="submit" />
</dialog>
```

FIGURE 7.13

The *Hashtable nextStepRules* associates the result values of the current scenario with the scenarios to follow.

The protocol is limited to several key names: "default" (to point to the scenario played if no expected results happen) and "submit" (the instruction to send the necessary data to a server and thus finish a current set of possibly nested scenarios played on the client side). The "service" and "action" (internal) keywords specify client requests to the server, so the server knows exactly what service and what action the client requested. The String *scenarioName*, as well as the static String *fullScenarioName*, help identify scenario result variables stored in the *Hashtable valueObject*. The static *Hashtable valueObject* serves as a single object assembled for multiple screen-scenarios.

The *valueObject* stores a user's entries and scenario results according to the *nextStepRules* instructions. The variables stored in the *valueObject Hashtable* receive name keys created by concatenating the sequence of screen names and a user's entry field name. For example, the user name "Little Prince" will be stored with the key name *main.name* and the value *Little Prince*.

A product called "Shaver" selected by a user from the *MenProducts* scenario will be stored with the key name *main.MenProducts.product* and the value *Shaver*. As you can see, the static String *fullScenarioName* is concatenated from consecutive scenario names.

The *doNextStep()* method looks into the *Hashtable nextStepRules* to select and play the next scenario. A set of nested scenarios ends with a scenario in which the *nextStepRules* points to the *submit* action. The *doNextStep()* method also collects result values marked with *putToValueObject* into a static *valueObject*.

If no scenario is scheduled next but the *methodName* is provided instead, this method will be invoked with the current acting object. This is done by simply exercising the *play()* method at the end of the loop in the *doNextStep()* method. In most cases, the *submit()* method will be provided with the *methodName* to finish a multiple screen-scenario transaction.

The *submit* action is defined by the server destination and data that will be sent to the destination. The *submit()* method translates the static *valueObject* data to XML

```
/**
 * setScenarios() method is to init scenarios-children of
 * the current scenario
 * @param xmlScenarioDescription
 */
    public void setScenario(String xmlScenarioDescription) {
        scenarios = Stringer.parseXML (xmlScenarioDescription);
    }
/**
 * setNextStepRules() method is to init rules to select
 * the next scenario
 * @param nextStepRules
 */
    public void setNextStepRules(Hashtable nextStepRules) {
        this.nextStepRules = nextStepRules;
    }
/**
 * The doNextStep() method looks into the
 * nextStepRules to choose one of scenarios
 */
    public void doNextStep() {
        // get fullScenarioName
        fullScenarioName += "." + scenarioName;
        // example: "main.MenProducts"
        // look for current scenario results
        Enumeration resultNames = nextStepRules.keys();
        // check if the nextStepRules define next method to execute
        // in most cases it would be "submit()" method
        // to send stored (ValueObjectAssembler) data
        String methodName = (String) nextStepRules.get
        ("action"); // can be null
        String className = (String) nextStepRules.
        get("service"); // can be null
        Object[] parameters = (Object[])
        nextStepRules.
        get("parameters"); // null in most cases
        // check result values, save to valueObject
        // results marked as "putToValueObject", check
        // for related scenario
        boolean done = false;
        while(!done && resultNames.hasMoreElements()) {
            // look for expected result values
            String resultName = (String)
            resultNames.nextElement();
            // find actual result value
```

FIGURE 7.14

```
            String resultValue = (String)results.
            get(resultName);
            // get all possible result values associated
            // with next step scenarios
            Hashtable values = (Hashtable)
            nextStepRules.get(resultName);
            // check if the result value should be
            // stored in the Value Object Assembler (VOA)
            String putToValueObjectFlag =
            (String)values.get("putToValueObject");
            if(putToValueObjectFlag != null &&
            putToValueObjectFlag.equals("true") ) {
                // stored is a private static object - a
                // single object for multiple scenarios
                stored.put(fullScenarioName + "." +
                resultName, resultValue);
            }
            if(methodName != null) {
            // no need to look into possible scenarios continue;
            }
            // get default scenario name (can be null,
            if not provided, by a scenarist)
            String scenarioName = (String)values.
            get("default");
            // check if actual result value is expected
            if(values.containsKey(resultValue) ) {
                // get associated scenario name
                scenarioName = (String)
                values.get(resultValue);
            }
            if(scenarioName == null) {
                continue;
                // nothing to play, try other result values,
                // probably do nothing
            }
            Scenario s = (Scenario) scenarios.get
            (scenarioName);
            s.doNextStep(); // recursive scenario
            done=true;
        }
        if(methodName != null) {
            play(className, methodName, parameters);
        }
    }
  /**
   * submit() method sends collected stored
   (ValueObjectAssembler) data to the predefined server
   destination.
```

FIGURE 7.14. *(cont.)*

```
  */
    public void submit() {
        // get important info from the current nextStepRules
        String destination = (String)nextStepRules.
        get("destination");
        String service = (String)nextStepRules.get("service");
        String action = (String)nextStepRules.get("action");
        // put service and action into the VOA
        stored.put("service", service);
        stored.put("action", action);
        // translate stored toXML
        String xmlData = Stringer.toXML(stored);
        // send data to server using HTTP or other
        // protocols from IOMaster
        try { // submit with multipart/form-data
                // protocol implemented in IOMaster
            IOMaster inOut = new IOMaster
            ("urlToServlet");
            // http://urlToServer/CGI.or.ServletProgram
            inOut.addParameterToForm("valueObject", xmlData);
            inOut.post();
            // makes connection, send data, returns response
        } catch(Exception e) {
            System.out.println("Scenario.submit:ERROR e=" + e);
        }
        // cleaning
        stored = new Hashtable();
        fullScenarioName = "";
    }
}
```

FIGURE 7.14. ***(cont.)***

and sends the XML stream to the server. The *submit()* method uses destination information defined in the *nextStepRules* object.

After this major accomplishment, the *submit()* method does some cleanup to get the client ready for data and new instructions from the server side. The *valueObject* is renewed by a new *Hashtable()* statement, and the static String *fullScenarioName* is blank again, as it was at the beginning of the transaction.

SYNCHRONOUS OR ASYNCHRONOUS CLIENT–SERVER COMMUNICATION

Client–server communication can be synchronous or asynchronous. The *submit()* method can use the *HTTPConnection* object or TCP/IP sockets. In both cases, some *java.io.OutputStream* may be used to send the object and some *java.io.InputStream* to get a response from the server. This is an example of synchronous communication.

A client program can also post (publish) a message to a server's message box without waiting for the server's response. The server can run Java Message Service (JMS), which picks up the message at the server's convenience, invokes the proper business services, and publishes the results to a client message box.

A client program can play the role of a JMS client and pick up the message if the message topic matches the client's subscription. This is an example of asynchronous communication, which is based on messages, topics, subscribers, and publishers. Clients and server(s) can subscribe to their topics of interest and publish message objects to these and other topics.

The regular method for JMS communications is a set of TCP/IP sockets, although JMS implementations may have several protocols available for a user's selection, including User Datagram Protocol and HTTP.

The *submit()* method can use *service* and *action* attributes to calculate a unique URL for an HTTP connection. For example, the URL may consist of an initial destination variable and additional service and action attributes.

```
String url = destination + "/" + service + "/" +
action + "/" + clientType + ".jsp";
```

The *submit()* method can also use a single URL based on the destination string and pass *service* and *action* parameters to the server dispatching mechanism. A Java servlet may play the role of dispatcher in this case.

A client program can use the asynchronous mechanism based, for example, on JMS. In this case, *service, action*, and *username* values can be used to define a topic and a selector of the message. The *valueObject* would be published by the *submit()* method to this topic.

The actual communication protocol can be selected at deployment or even at run-time via parameters passed from the server. The application developer should not be concerned with the protocol, and application code should not be tied to the method of communication.

Example of XML Multiple-Screen Scenario

An example of a multiple-screen scenario is shown in Fig. 7.15. Every scenario has a name, pointers to a class, and a method that should be invoked with the scenario. The scenario may also point to a screen definition. In this example, the class name is *UIMaster* (this can be an extended Thinlet, for example) and the *methodName* is *parseXML*. The screen definition name is *dialog*.

The screen description itself can be found inside the scenario as well as in the "next step" rules. The rules describe which user entries (results) should be put into the VOA and what scenario follows the current scenario.

The example provided in Fig. 7.15 shows two nested scenarios inside the top *main* scenario. The top scenario offers a screen to enter a user's name and gender. One of the second-layer scenarios will be played next, based on the user's gender selection.

```
<Scenario name="main" className="UIMaster" methodName="parseXML"
description="dialog">

 <dialog gap="4" top="2" left="2">
     <label text="Name:" />
     <textfield name="userName" columns="5">
          <validation className="TextValidator"
          <methodName="notEmpty" />
  </textfield>

     <label text="Gender:" />
     <combobox name="selection" selected="2"
     editable="false" valign="center" action="setSelection">
          <choice text="F" />
          <choice text="M" />
     </combobox>

     <button text="Submit" action="doNextStep" />
 </dialog>
 <NextStepRules>
 <ResultNames>
      <ResultName name="name" putToVOA="true"/>
               <ResultName name="selection" putToVOA="true">
               <ResultValue value="F" scenario="GirlStuff"/>
                   <ResultValue value="M"
               scenario="MenProducts"/>
      </ResultName>
 </ResultNames>
 </NextStepRules>

 <Scenario name="GirlStuff" className="UIMaster"
 methodName="parseXML" description="dialog">
 <!-- screen description for a catalog of products can
  be inserted here -->

 <NextStepRules methodName="submit"
 destination="http://ipserve.com/go/private.ip"
 service="product" action="getDetails"/>
   <ResultNames>
         <ResultName name="product" putToVOA="true"/>
   </ResultNames>
 </NextStepRules>

</Scenario>
 <Scenario name="MenProducts" className="UIMaster"
 methodName="parseXML" description="dialog">

 <!-- screen description for a catalog of products can be
 inserted here -->
```

FIGURE 7.15

```
<NextStepRules methodName="submit"
destination="http://ipserve.com/go/private.ip"
service="product" action="getDetails"/>
  <ResultNames>
          <ResultName name="product" putToVOA="true"/>
  </ResultNames>
</NextStepRules>

</Scenario>

</Scenario>
```

Figure 7.15. *(cont.)*

The *nextStepRules* built into the *main* scenario give the program a hint about expected entries: *name* for a user's name and *selection* for a user's gender. The *nextStepRules* instruct a program to put both entries into the *valueObject* (VOA) *Hashtable* object. The *nextStepRules* indicate expected values of the *selection* entry. The rules specify that in the case of selected gender *F*, the next scenario to play is *GirlStuff*, and in the case of selected gender *M*, the next scenario to play is *MenProducts*. Both scenarios would consist of presubmitted catalog pages for the user's product selection.

Immediately after the *nextStepRules*, we can see both the *GirlStuff* and *MenProducts* scenarios. Scenarios include some product descriptions (I only provided comments, you are welcome to fill in the blanks) and the *nextStepRules*. The *nextStepRules* point to the *submit()* *methodName* and indicate that the selected product should be added to the static *Hashtable* *valueObject* that collects all the variables for a single client–server transaction. The *submit()* method described above executes this transaction.

The Client Wants to Play New Games

How can we add new features to a client program?

We can think about refreshing some screens with new widgets, and we want the program to add some new behavior tricks. This means new class services on the client side.

We can add to the server side new classes that support new features and provide new instructions that refer to these classes. Of course, the client program is going to be puzzled at first, because it will not find those classes locally.

Such classes, not found locally, will be loaded from the server dynamically. It is important for client performance to keep this type of unexpected upgrade to a minimum. Looking for a new class over the network on the server side can be noticeably slow for the poor person sitting in front of the screen.

A better way to perform a version upgrade is through a silent upgrade. The best time for that is when your client is not using the application and is still connected; the next-to-best time is while the user is entering fields in a multiple entry form, editing a document, or performing similar tasks.

By starting this discussion, we have slid down to an even bigger discussion about client program administration.

As soon as we landed software on a user's machine, we assumed administration responsibilities. On our plate now are version upgrades, remote diagnostics, usage statistics, recovery mechanisms, and so on. All these issues require a bit of code on the client and server sides.

The Client Claims Independence

We are not always lucky with Internet connections and would like to be able to do some work without being connected. This sounds like a tough call, especially for a thin client. However, let us take a closer look, and we will see what we can do.

For example, let us say we have prepared some document or even just a short message, and when we send the message, we realize that no connection is available. We would be very upset if the message or the document disappeared.

We should be able to save files locally. If this situation involves a Java applet client, a signed applet could do the job. All J2ME level PDAs and devices can save these types of files, so the client can locally review such files or documents, edit them, and send them out when the network is restored.

Besides server services, we can provide a client program, including a thin client, with some limited local services. For example, we can review our schedule and have a schedule program play reminders for us. We can use an address book, view old messages, and prepare new ones, all locally.

Web browsers and mail client programs (especially MS Outlook) are great examples of network programs that started the race for independence from the server.

An important and frequently used service is geographical map rendering. This information is fairly stable: unlike stock prices, maps are not going to be changed every minute. This gives us a good opportunity to store these data on a compact medium connected to your local client (PC, PDA, wireless phone).

Then, a program reads the original files from the storage device, and another part of the program renders the data on the user's screen. Appendix 3 provides examples of reading maps with vector graphics provided in data exchange format (DXF) and Shapes files. By switching your program to text-to-speech mode, you can get directions to your destination.

A traffic jam is the perfect opportunity for you to tune your radio to your PDA's broadcast wavelength, listen to your wireless news, and dictate your response messages. I hope this kind of radio, with a good microphone at the steering wheel, has already been installed in your car by the time you read these lines.

Your semi-independent PDA client can play messages and record your response object even when disconnected from a server. When a connection to the server is available, it will intelligently collect news and send your recorded responses to the server. Does this remind you of the MS Outlook interaction model?

We briefly considered text-to-speech software in Chapter 4, and we plan to look at speech recognition software a bit later. This is typical client software, not because of the software size—it is still big—but because of the nature of the service. There is no information to distribute and share in the speech service (we are not talking about conferences and talk shows here); the service belongs to a single user, and the user tends to customize the service.

Client independence gained with the features described above has its limits. Let us say that a client program can create, massage, and generally own a set of objects. The user still wants to distribute some of these objects to other users and/or keep them safe on the server side to protect them from becoming lost on the client. The user also wants to request "server" services on these objects.

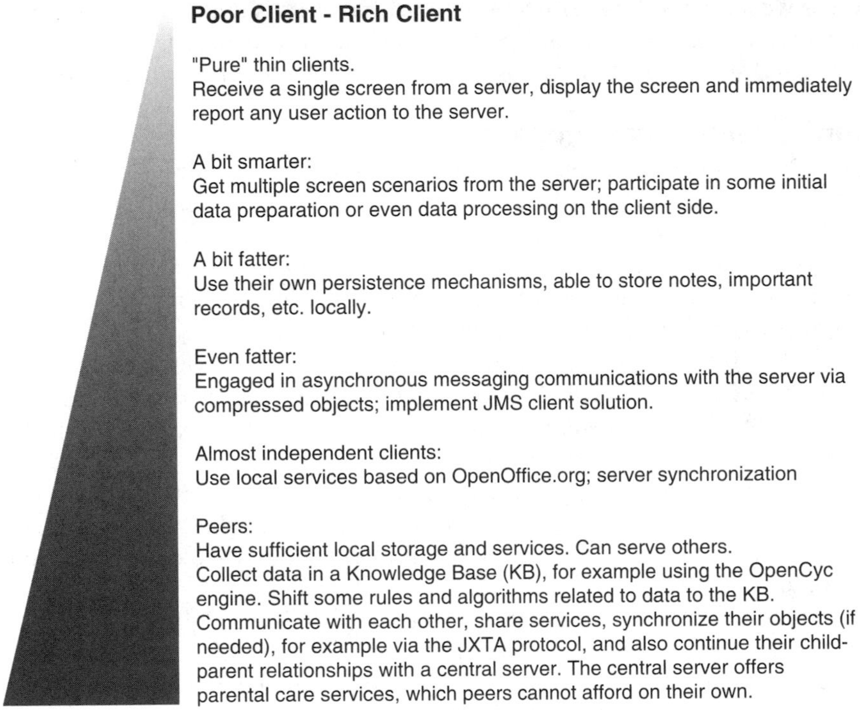

Poor Client - Rich Client
"Pure" thin clients.
Receive a single screen from a server, display the screen and immediately report any user action to the server.
A bit smarter:
Get multiple screen scenarios from the server; participate in some initial data preparation or even data processing on the client side.
A bit fatter:
Use their own persistence mechanisms, able to store notes, important records, etc. locally.
Even fatter:
Engaged in asynchronous messaging communications with the server via compressed objects; implement JMS client solution.
Almost independent clients:
Use local services based on OpenOffice.org; server synchronization
Peers:
Have sufficient local storage and services. Can serve others.
Collect data in a Knowledge Base (KB), for example using the OpenCyc engine. Shift some rules and algorithms related to data to the KB.
Communicate with each other, share services, synchronize their objects (if needed), for example via the JXTA protocol, and also continue their child-parent relationships with a central server. The central server offers parental care services, which peers cannot afford on their own.

FIGURE 7.16. Poor Client—Rich Client.

This means that a client program will use any opportunity to send data to the server. If we collect data into a *valueObject* and send data in a compressed form to and from the server, we save a lot of network traffic and get an even better score on client independence. The *Java.util.zip* package is conveniently available on the J2SE, but not the J2ME, platform. Client device capacity is the major factor influencing decisions on how much of which parts of the business logics can be delegated to the client side to raise the flag of client independence. Figure 7.16 presents several client solutions, from "pure" thin clients to rich, independent peers.

Pure thin clients represent only the view portion of the MVC paradigm. These clients are able to receive one screen at a time from a server, display this screen to a user, and then report any user action back to the server and wait for new screen instructions.

Smarter clients can be engaged in multiple-screen scenarios. They may participate in some initial data preparation, or even processing.

The next line of clients can have their own persistence mechanisms and may be able to store notes, important records, and other information locally. Such clients engage in asynchronous messaging communications with the server via compressed objects. Implemented as JMS clients, some use essential local services based on an environment such as OpenOffice.org. They invoke the proper services to create or edit many types of documents and messages locally. A silent synchronization service sends these messages in a single compressed object to the server side when a connection is available and receives server objects to which the client has a subscription.

A rich client can be even more independent and can cross the pure client line. Such clients have their own services—we will call them "peers." The peers can include sufficient storage,

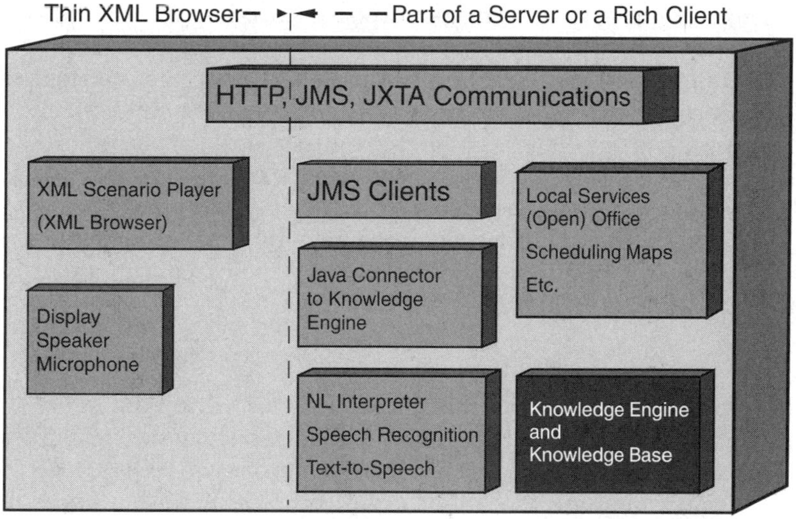

FIGURE 7.17. Flexible Client–Server Computing Allows Clients to Grow.

not necessarily a database, to support their independence. There are groups of users whose everyday work is to produce knowledge. Such users often collect information about objects or reference records, not objects themselves. This is very similar to the google.com view of the world.

The most natural way to collect knowledge is in a knowledge base—for example, using the OpenCyc engine and knowledge base. Working with a knowledge base instead of an RDBMS opens a new programming paradigm. We can shift some rules and algorithms related to data to the knowledge base. Figure 7.17 illustrates a unified approach to a range of client types, from a thin client that implements an XML browser with scenario support to a thick client-peer that adds powerful features that would otherwise be on the server side.

The number of services on the client side can grow if the client device capacity allows. The thinnest client consists of an XML browser and scenario services. The XML browser works with a flexible set of display primitives (tags) and includes the full initial set of functions.

There is still a big difference between orthodox (HTML/WML/cHTML [compact HTML]) browsers and the XML browser: the XML browser can change its tags and functionality at run-time.

The scenario service helps change the flow of client–server communication from a single screen or a single action to several behaviors provided within a scenario. The server can send multiple screens and related algorithms-instructions or "acts of the play" to the client.

The scenario service uses the power of Java Reflection to play some actions—services that are loaded at run-time if necessary.

There are other services that can be shifted to the client, or outsourced to the server side: asynchronous messaging (JMS client), teamwork productivity (OpenOffice), natural language interpretation and speech recognition, a knowledge engine, and specific business services.

This architecture allows a client to grow from a thin client into a rich client-peer able to live an independent life; it helps create self-forming and self-healing networks. This quality is especially important for wireless LANs (local-area networks) with floating connectivity.

The knowledge engine may serve many purposes, including the optimization of client–server scenarios.

Peers can communicate to each other, share some services, synchronize their objects (if needed)—for example, via the JXTA protocol—and continue their child–parent relationships with a central server. Of course, these children are grown-ups; they do not need instructions every minute. The central server offers some parental care services that peers still cannot afford on their own. One of these services is global object lookup and backup.

What is **JXTA**? It is not an abbreviation; the name of this open source initiative is derived from the word *juxtaposed*. In the case of JXTA, the juxtaposed entities are network devices and computers. We discuss JXTA further in Chapter 14.

Client Types

We can explore client types in a three-dimensional space, as displayed in Fig. 7.18.

One dimension shows client presentation types limited by their device profiles. In the Java world, we talk about J2SE, PersonalJava, and J2ME platforms with MIDP, CLDC (Connected Limited Device Configuration), and other device profiles. If we narrow it down to just Windows platforms, we have Windows Forms. Should we decide, for some reason, to deal with Linux only, we would look into Java-GNOME and other environments. GNOME is a free GUI program designed to work on all UNIX-like operating systems. GNOME stands for GNU Network Object Model Environment and consists of a set of graphical widgets and desktop applications.

The second dimension considers client communication types, such as synchronous, asynchronous, centric, and peer-to-peer and the protocols used.

The third dimension is defined by client participation in distributed data processing, specializations, and locally offered features. An example of such clients is gaming facilities; another client may be more business or travel oriented.

The richest and fastest presentation layer can be provided with an API that directly calls low-level native functions. Windows Forms [4] is one of the richest sets of GUI libraries. It targets only Microsoft Windows platforms, as do most other Microsoft products and APIs.

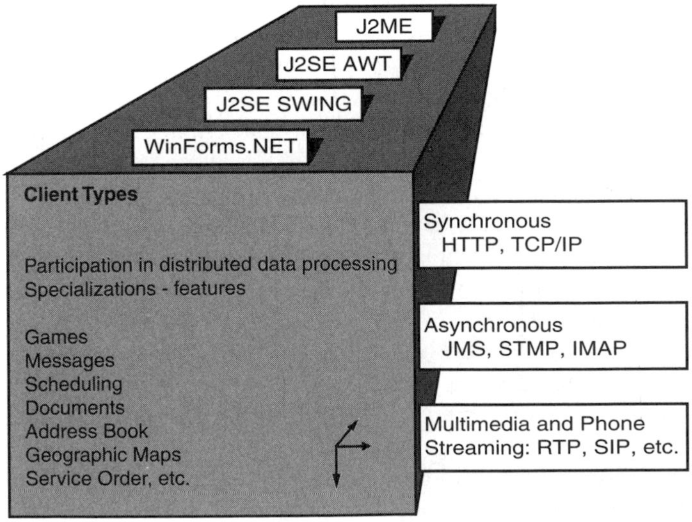

FIGURE 7.18. A Three-Dimensional View of Client Facilities.

Windows Forms is similar to the native Windows API but is more powerful. It represents a unified programming model for Windows application development and provides a hierarchy of classes, not just a set of native calls like the Windows API. Instead of calling *CreateWindow* for any type of user-interface widgets, we create the particular type of user-interface control using the appropriate class. The most distinguished benefit is the language-independent aspect of this new framework.

If your focus is on UNIX platforms and no mix is expected, take a serious look at the Java-GNOME project [5]. Java-GNOME is a set of Java bindings for the GNOME and GTK libraries that allow GNOME and GTK applications to be written in Java. Java-GNOME is not a Swing look-and-feel, a GTK/GNOME rewrite in Java, or a set of GTK peers for AWT. It is a Java Native Interface layer that delegates the calls out to the native GTK or GNOME C libraries.

Using GCJ (the portable, optimizing, ahead-of-its-time GNU Compiler for Java), it is possible to compile the Java code to native binaries before deployment.

Java Foundation Classes (JFC) [6] is the most powerful and most often-used multiplatform graphics package. JFC is the part of the standard Java 2 Development Kit that is responsible for user interface. JFC/Swing GUI components are written in the Java programming language, without Windows system-specific code.

Pluggable Look and Feel gives users the ability to switch the look and feel of an application without restarting it and without the developer having to subclass the entire component set. The built-in JFC Accessibility API allows people with or without disabilities to use assistive technologies, including screen readers, screen magnifiers, and speech recognition.

Additional JFC features, like drag and drop and Java 2D API, improve application interoperability and allow developers to define fancy paint styles and complex shapes, and control the graphics rendering process.

Although Swing components are built on the top of Java AWT, there is a conceptual difference in the rendering techniques of these two related packages. Swing actively uses floating point calculations, whereas AWT is greatly satisfied with pixel graphics based on integers.

This difference leads to visible performance differences because Java performs very well in the integer world, whereas floating-point math is not one of its strongest features. This does not mean that the situation is not going to change. Sun Microsystems and other Java vendors (the biggest is not Sun, but IBM) are improving Java's performance every year.

Good Performance Follows Good Design

A rich set of Swing GUI components offers a challenge to developers' design skills. You can do everything you want in multiple ways. A bad design is the biggest and most frequent contributor to bad performance. It is important to understand or/and measure the performance of each component and to know which options your customers use most often.

Creating a window, *JFrame*, or *JDialog* is an expensive system process. It may be possible to build a scenario in which your actions of creating and destroying widgets are at a minimum while most of the changes are cosmetic.

Here is an example. You need to provide a calendar-dialog for a scheduling application. Of course, you can create and destroy this dialog window each time you need to fill it with new data. A better option is to create the window with the layout once (weeks always have seven days, right?) and then fill the schedule with the proper data by changing labels.

Changing labels is a cosmetic graphics operation that takes very few system resources. When a user closes the schedule, you can make it invisible instead of destroying the window. You save twice: a destroy action is almost as expensive as a create action, which you will also need for the next scheduling action.

There is a difference between application performance and a user's perception of the performance. The user often cannot distinguish transactional operations from cosmetic screen changes. His or her reaction is that sometimes the application works quickly, and sometimes slowly.

Here is a typical situation that leads to customer dissatisfaction, or even anger. After multiple dialogs that collect data for a client–server network trip, the user hits the *Submit* button. In this scenario, we assume that client–server communications are synchronous and the client program blocks user actions in the *modal* dialog until the server's response.

If the transaction takes visible time, the user can become visibly mad. Such an application had better run on a bulletproof machine, because trying to push keys and mouse buttons harder and harder does not result in any screen changes.

One of the reasons for poor performance may be (guess what?) the work performed by the garbage collector offered by Java and .NET technologies.

Keep in mind that memory management is a pretty expensive system operation. Unfortunately, the garbage collection thread tends to start when your user is waiting for a program response. The program's response will be visibly delayed, and the user might become angry at its performance.

For both Java and .NET environments, it is possible to escape this situation, or at least make it less likely. The cure is simple and can be addressed by two lines that look almost identical in your Java or C# code.

Assign heavy objects to null as soon as you do not need them.

```
myHeavyObject = null;
```

The garbage collector will almost immediately free this object

Force the garbage collector to work at a time that is not critical for your application. Insert the line below, for example, after your code requests an input/output operation.

```
System.GC.Collect(); // syntax for C#
```

Or

```
System.gc(); // syntax for Java
```

Two options can improve the user's perception. The first is not to block the user interface when you begin a server transaction and to provide status information with a separate light thread. The other option is more radical.

Consider the possibility of changing synchronous to asynchronous communications. Use the "publishers and subscribers" paradigm to establish topics and subtopics, and implement JMS servers and clients.

KEEP A STABLE API WHILE CHANGING COMMUNICATION MECHANISMS

Your API should not depend on communication protocols. The essentials of the XML-based API are still the same: service name, action name, client type, and specific service parameters. We change only their processing.

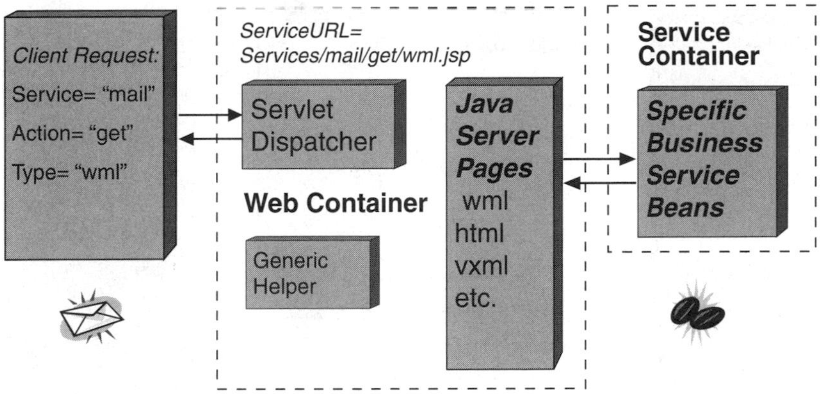

// Servlet: Forward a client request to a proper presentation layer

String factoryType = session.getAttribute("type");

// Expected type is "HTML", "VXML", or "WML", etc.

String url = session.getAttribute("service") + "/" + session.getAttribute("action") + "/" + factoryType + ".jsp";

getServletConfig().getServletContext().getRequestDispatcher(url).forward(request, response);

FIGURE 7.19. Synchronous Communications with a Java Servlet.

Figure 7.19 displays an interpretation of an XML-based API in synchronous communications in which a Java servlet dispatches a client request to the proper Java server page (JSP). The JSP invokes the proper service bean and creates an output-response according to the client's type.

The Java servlet retrieves attributes of a service request and creates a URL for the JSP responsible for this service.

Here is the code extract.

```
// Servlet: Forward a client request to a proper presentation
// layer
String factoryType = session.getAttribute("type");
// Expected types are "HTML," "VXML," "WML," "XML," etc.
String url = session.getAttribute("service") + "/" +
session.getAttribute("action") + "/" + factoryType + ".jsp";
getServletConfig().getServletContext().
getRequestDispatcher(url).forward (request, response);
```

The servlet then uses the *forward()* method of the *RequestDispatcher* object to redirect the client request to the proper JSP, which may be located on the same or even a different Web server. The *RequestDispatcher* cannot directly point to another server, so a different syntax will apply.

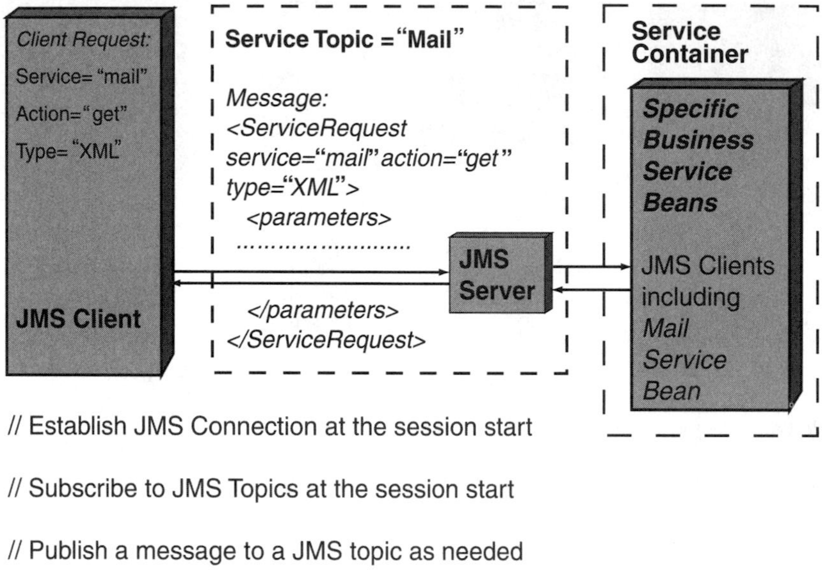

FIGURE 7.20. XML-Based Asynchronous Communications with JMS.

Figure 7.20 shows an interpretation of the same XML-based API in asynchronous communications supported by JMS.

The JMS client on the client side establishes a connection to the JMS server and subscribes to JMS topics early in the game, during the client initialization session. The client program publishes its service request as a message to the proper JMS topic. On the server side, the JMS server notifies the proper service (also a JMS client), which has a subscription to this topic. For example, the *Mail* service bean runs on the server side as a JMS client that has a subscription to the *Mail* topic.

If you place the Java Swing packages on your customer's machine, you may as well consider using the OpenOffice Software Development Kit, a set of tools and libraries for the OpenOffice API and the OpenOffice.org component technology Universal Network Objects.

ADD OPEN OFFICE FEATURES TO RICH CLIENTS

The OpenOffice is an open, feature-rich multiplatform office productivity suite that besides reading and writing MS Office documents offers add-on features. (http://www.openoffice.org/dev˙docs/features/1.1/)

- Many open source and commercial database systems are supported.
- One-click export features enable you to easily create PDF files and export presentations and drawings to the Macromedia Flash format (.swf).
- Offers a high contrast mode and other accessibility features.
- Introduces bidirectional and vertical writing that is required for many native languages, such as Japanese and Hebrew.

- A Software Development Kit (SDK) available which is an add-on for an existing OpenOffice.org. It provides the necessary tools and documentation for programming the OpenOffice.org APIs and creating your own extensions (UNO components).
- Every OpenOffice.org file is a ZIP archive containing separate XML files for the content, styles, settings and meta data.

Besides these wonderful features that serve our PCs and workstations, there are also packages that support wireless devices. For example, the ActiveSync XMerge Filter allows synchronization of Writer (similar to MS Word) and Calc (Spreadsheet) documents with Microsoft Pocket PCs and other devices.

The Client Becomes a Peer

If we add a sufficient local storage and services, the rich client can serve others as well as itself. We are talking about distributed services and noncentric architecture based on mostly independent clients that we call peers.

We can use the OpenCyc knowledge base as a peer storage mechanism. We can make peers even smarter and more flexible by shifting some rules and algorithms related to data to the knowledge base.

Client Administration

As soon as we land our software on the user's machine, we assume administrative responsibilities. The cost of administration includes application distribution and version upgrades, remote diagnostics, restart, and recovery mechanisms. This is a great argument for using Web browsers. The Web browser serves as a client container that takes care of these issues and nullifies the developer's administrative expenses. Going beyond the browser's sandbox model leaves us without this parental care.

Fortunately, life is gracious. It offers new possibilities when we need them most. Java Web Start is a new Java client container that, in many ways, helps solve administrative problems.

More on Rich Clients

Java Web Start is a great shuttle to deliver rich clients. The sky's the limit for what you can do with Java packages: they are rich, (relatively) simple, and free. When developing rich Java clients, you can explore streaming media solutions with the Java Media Framework. You can explore digital imaging using Java Advanced Imaging APIs and try the amazing *java.awt.Robot* class used to generate native system input events. In Appendix 3 and/or on the supporting Web site (http://JavaSchool.com), you will find source examples on these and other subjects. You will find hints on spatial (geographical maps) technology, Swing performance improvements using the *VolatileImage* class, and more.

How Much Abstraction Is Too Much?

Levels of abstraction serve as a universal solution to design problems. Overdoing these abstractions versus specialization of clients and servers leads to performance disaster. Having too many APIs in one place actually creates a new programming *language*, which is next to impossible to code with.

On another note, let us keep in mind the regular user who cares that only the few applications she or he uses almost daily work flawlessly. Here, performance is necessary. Constant changes should not be made to these applications. Users get tired of having to adapt to changes in something they use daily.

The big question here is what is worth abstracting and what is OK to specialize? Experience helps to differentiate right from wrong while answering this question. *The most important thing is to remember to ask the question.*

Summary

Many types of client devices and client–server architectures make the application developer's task even more advantageous. Creating applications across the spectrum of rich and thin clients is too expensive for an ASP, unless a unified approach is used. This chapter considered elements of such a unified approach to client–server work distribution.

From thin clients able to work with single-screen definitions, we went to multiple-screen scenarios. We provided a client with the flexibility to add new actions predefined on the server side and allowed clients to grow into independent peers. The key to this approach is creating elements that can be reused and easily shifted from the server to the client side.

Self-sufficient peers create self-forming and self-healing networks. This quality is especially important for wireless LANs with floating connectivity.

Of course, there are many specifics related to thin clients. In Chapter 8, we will consider wireless clients based on 802.11, Bluetooth, General Packet Radio Service, and Wireless Application Protocol technologies.

Integrating Question

What are the common features and differences between Extensible User-Interface Language (XUL) and Windows Forms?

Case Study

1. Modify the *ClientScenarioPlayer* class for Java platforms that do not include the java.reflection package (e.g., J2ME).
2. What are the benefits and disadvantages of the XML browser with flexible client–server relationships?
3. What application at your workplace can adapt and benefit from the XML browser approach?

References

1. Thinlet: *http://www.Thinlet.com.*
2. Droplets: *http://www.Droplets.com.*
3. Ultra Light Client: *http://www.canoo.com/ulc/.*
4. Windows Forms: *http://microsoft.com.*
5. Java-GNOME: *http://www.gnome.com.*
6. Java Foundation Classes: *http://java.sun.com/products/jfc.*

CHAPTER 8

Wireless Technologies

The wireless music box has no imaginable commercial value. Who would pay for a message sent to nobody in particular?

—Reply by corporate executives when urged to invest in the radio in the 1920s.

This chapter is a brief overview of the basic principles and standards driving the world of wireless applications.

Unmatched opportunities in the mobile and wireless areas are attracting the attention of business and development. Wireless markets, including personal area networks (WPAN), local area networks (WLAN), and wideband local-area networks (WWLAN), have an estimated value today of several billion dollars according to the Gartner Group (http://www.gartner.com/5˙ about/pressreleases/pr11mar2003a.jsp)

According to Gartner, increasing focus on teleworking and corporate mobility to improve enterprise performance, and trends such as the move toward the real-time enterprise, will not merely exploit mobility but will demand it. At the same time, the relentless push by vendors, virtually giving away wireless capabilities with significant price/performance improvements, is fueling demand for wireless technology in the corporate marketplace. United States federal regulators are expanding the radio spectrum for wireless internet users to help bring broadband connections to rural areas.

The number of wireless devices on the Internet is growing fast. The stock of IP addresses is now almost exhausted, so it is about time to extend the Internet with Internet 2, which replaces the current IPv4 protocol with the latest IPv6 protocol and drastically increases Internet capacity and improves Internet security.

A great competition for multiple markets, running different wireless technologies, has just begun. The winners will be those wireless Internet service providers (WISPs) and wireless application service providers (WASPs) that can offer connection and content services and optimize development solutions with a unified approach across multiple client devices.

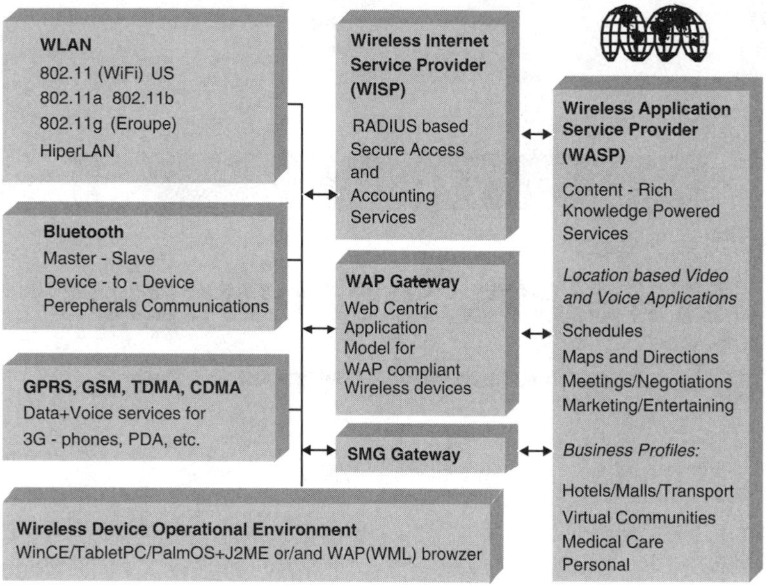

FIGURE 8.1. The Wireless World: WISP and WASP Integration.

In a nutshell, this means providing connectivity in many or all wireless markets, providing interoperability, and then adding content services with applications that make sense for all or most of these markets.

It is possible (but not terribly efficient!) to have numerous technologies and technological branches for each application type. The challenge is to find a *unified* standards-based development approach that makes applications transparent to multiple technologies.

The winners in the market game are those who minimize this branching, increase development and deployment efficiency, and offer seamless mobile services across multiple mobile network environments, freeing users from the ties of technology.

Figure 8.1 provides a brief look into the wireless world with integrated network and application services.

Wireless clients are truly mobile. Client environment, locations, and connections can be changed more frequently and drastically than those of fixed-wired network clients. WISPs and WASPs need to deploy knowledgebase-powered application solutions: quick and smart adjustments to client locations, connections, and overall environment changes.

These ambitious tasks require a good understanding of the wireless world.

Wireless TDMA, CDMA, GSM, and Other Standards

The wireless world started from cellular networks in the early 1980s, using analog radio transmission technologies such as AMPS (Advanced Mobile Phone System). Today, cellular phones comprise only a fraction of the many wireless markets, which include WLANs, WISPs, and WASPs.

The cellular phone market is still the biggest one. Millions and millions of clients signed up for the service and forced service providers to struggle for a limited amount of the radio spectrum. Frequency Division Multiple Access (FDMA) was the basic technology in the analog wireless systems used at that time when cell phones were first introduced. FDMA assigns different callers to different frequency channels.

Radio frequency (RF) engineers developed a new set of digital wireless technologies called **TDMA** (Time Division Multiple Access) and **GSM** (Global System for Mobile). TDMA and GSM used a time-sharing protocol to provide three to four times more capacity than analog systems.

TDMA divides an RF into time slots and then allocates slots to multiple calls. In this way, a single frequency can support multiple, simultaneous data channels. GSM overlays the basic TDMA principles with many innovations and has almost doubled TDMA capacity. GSM service providers use bands around 900 megahertz (MHz) (GSM 900) and around 1800 MHz (GSM 1800). Each band is subdivided into 124 carrier frequencies spaced 200 kilohertz apart. Each of these carrier frequencies is *further* subdivided into time slots using TDMA. The other member of the DMA family is CDMA, a younger brother of TDMA.

Code Division Multiple Access (CDMA) is a digital wireless technology that was pioneered and commercially developed by Qualcomm [1]. CDMA uniquely encodes each different call of ultra-high-frequency (UHF) cellular phone systems in the 800-MHz and 1.9-gigahertz (GHz) bands. (Note that higher frequency means shorter waves and weaker penetration into buildings.) In 1999, CDMA was selected as the industry standard for new "third-generation" (3G) wireless systems.

The basic difference between the two types of DMAs is that multiple TDMA voices take turns, whereas several CDMA voices are encoded in such a way that only the talker and the listener can understand each other, without hearing the other voices.

CDMA has a very high "spectral efficiency" and can accommodate approximately fifteen users per megahertz, whereas the TDMA estimate is around five to seven users. Also, on a normal channel, CDMA has better voice quality than TDMA. These are clear benefits of CDMA. The disadvantage is that too many clients located in one place can make a CDMA channel "sick" with "channel pollution."

A "polluted" channel disturbs the normal reception of all participants. CDMA provides extremely stable audio over open land but does not necessarily win over TDMA in urban territories, especially inside big buildings. This may change after the new W-CDMA standard (wideband CDMA) is in place.

Let us clarify some relationships. CDMA, unlike TDMA, does not belong to the GSM family.

GSM has a provision for data (not only voice!) transmission. This feature was optional in the CDMA standard, and it took a while for Qualcomm to implement this option. CDMA is now quickly catching up on data services.

The GSM Phase 1 standard also included the Short Message Service (SMS) feature, which enables the user to send and receive text messages. Each short message is up to 160 characters of the Latin alphabet or up to 70 characters of non-Latin alphabets such as Arabic and Chinese.

The SMS market, most successful in Europe, has reached several billion messages annually and continues to grow steadily. SMS users receive many types of data, from notifications on voice/mail/fax messages to personal notes and group chat lines. The common denominator is that all messages are pretty short.

GSM, as well as CDMA, opens and closes connections for every call as required by **circuit-switched** networks with dedicated point-to-point connections during calls. The private branch exchange (PBX) systems drive circuit-switched networks.

Circuit-switched networks represent old wireless generations. The new generation of wireless technology is associated with **packet-switched** networks.

General Packet Radio Service (**GPRS**) offers "always-on," higher-capacity, Internet-based content and packet-switched data services. This enables services such as color Internet browsing and email and streaming applications such as visual conferencing, multimedia, and location-based services.

Messages in packet-switched networks are broken into small data packets that seek out the most efficient route as circuits become available. The packet header address tells the packet where to go and includes the packet number to ensure the proper sequence for reassembly at the destination.

The list of GPRS terminals (cell phones and devices) is very impressive, and almost every mobile manufacturer is on the list. The "killer" application for GPRS is Multimedia Message Service (MMS), which goes beyond SMS text with personalized images and audio and video content.

MMS messages can be downloaded to a subscriber's phone when the phone is on. Each message contains a number of pages or slides, and each slide can include text, one image, and one attached sound file. When the message arrives, and after it is loaded and stored, the device notifies the subscriber, and the message can be seen immediately.

GPRS data speed is tripled with Enhanced Data Rates for Global Evolution (EDGE) software. EDGE performs synchronization, equalization/demodulation, and other operations that enable high-speed packet services on the GSM using the usual spectrum and RF.

The wireless family tree already has three generations. Analog wireless phones formed the first generation. Digital cellular technologies represent the second generation. The third generation (3G) is defined by the International Telecommunications Union (European abbreviation: UTI) specification that promises great bandwidth. 3G technologies offer communication speeds of 2 megabits per second (Mbps) for fixed applications and up to 384 kilobits per second (Kbps) when a device is stationary or moving at pedestrian speed and 128 Kbps in a car.

Over the next ten years, the market of 3G mobile systems, also known as International Mobile Telecommunications-2000 (IMT-2000), will be worth several trillion U.S. dollars to mobile operators. One of the major 3G mobile communications systems being developed within the IMT-2000 framework is the Universal Mobile Telecommunications System (UMTS) [2].

UMTS features low-cost data rates at 2 Mbps under stationary conditions with global roaming, additional capacity and quality-of-service mechanisms, and flexibility in managing resources between voice and data services. UMTS is a new, "open" communications community of systems governed by UMTS Forum and supported by several hundred network operators and the 3rd Generation Partnership Project (3GPP) [3].

3GPP is a collaboration agreement that brings together a number of telecommunications standards bodies that cover all the GSM (including GPRS and EDGE) and 3G specifications. These specifications include the UMTS Terrestrial Radio Access Network (UTRAN), which uses CDMA; W-CDMA, with a four-times wider CDMA channel; and UMTS and its Japanese version by NTT DoCoMo, called Freedom of Mobile Multimedia Access (FOMA).

Although GSM-based networks focus on communication devices, there is another challenging task for wireless communications: connecting computers into local-area networks (LANs). WLANs are built on a family of 802.11 specifications developed by the Institute of Electrical and Electronics Engineers (IEEE).

802.11 AND WLANs

802.11 specifications are based on the Ethernet protocol and CSMA/CA (carrier sense multiple access with collision avoidance) for path sharing. 802.11b and 802.11g operate in the range of 2.4 GHz. The latest standard, 802.11g, offers transmission over short distances with speeds up to 54 Mbps, almost five times faster than the older 802.11b, often called WiFi (an abbreviation for Wireless Fidelity).

802.11a operates at radio frequencies around 5 to 6 GHz and uses orthogonal frequency-division multiplexing (OFDM) with common data speeds at 6 Mbps, 12 Mbps, or 24 Mbps, applied to wireless ATM (asynchronous transfer mode), a dedicated-connection switching system.

Europe, of course, has wireless LANs with different standards. The European Telecommunications Standards Institute (ETSI) adopted the HiperLAN/1 and HiperLAN/2 standards. These standards are similar to the IEEE 802.11 family used in the United States and operate in the same RF 5-GHz range. HiperLAN/1 provides communications at up to 20 Mbps, and HiperLAN/2 up to 54 Mbps. HiperLAN/2 represents 3G WLAN systems capable of data, images, and voice transfer.

How do users communicate in a WLAN? We call a user the *supplicant* and a network access point the *authenticator*. So, the supplicant requests access to the authenticator. The access point allows the client to send only a start message with the Extensible Authentication Protocol (EAP, RFC 2284). In a handshake, the authenticator returns an EAP message requesting the supplicant's identity. Then the access point forwards the client's identity to the *authentication server*, which can "accept" or "reject" the supplicant. In the *accept* scenario, the access point now allows normal traffic.

WLANs use approximately three access points per twenty network nodes. Access points create essential overhead, especially in an enterprise environment. What will decrease this overhead? Hint: clients can be peers that are self-sufficient, even without being connected. Self-sufficient peers create self-forming and self-healing wireless networks that can survive floating connectivity.

Another way to decrease access point-related expenses is to use very "thin" devices that only support 802.11 features. In this case, authentication and other security features are moved to access controllers, one per access point. Access controllers are hardware and software in the wired part of the network that serve multiple access points, considered ports by a controller, to support secure access and network management.

How a WLAN Secures a Client's Traffic

The 802.11 WLAN standards define the Wired Equivalent Privacy (WEP) algorithm as the base for authentication and encryption services. 802.11 implementations use 40-bit or 104-bit secret keys. The 802.11 standard does not define a key management protocol and assumes that keys are delivered to the wireless stations (STA) using a secure channel independent of 802.11.

The IEEE 802.1X standard with its extensions can cover this hole—for example, using a Remote Authentication Dial-In User Service (RADIUS) server for authenticating client credentials—and secure a client's traffic. The authentication procedure in this case passes an authentication key to the client and to the wireless access point. The RADIUS server is fully compliant with RFC 2865 (Authentication) and RFC 2866 (Accounting) and supports RFC 2868 and RFC 2867 (Tunnel Protocol Support) [4, 5].

The 802.11 security fix will take some time. Intel, Microsoft, and other contributors are planning several steps on the security road map. One is to add a security solution known as Simple Secure Network (SSN). SSN includes 802.1X authentication, 802.1X key management, and Temporal Key Integrity Protocol (TKIP).

The transition from the WEP to the TKIP will mask WEP weaknesses and work to prevent several of today's possible scenarios, such as data forgery and replay attacks, encryption misuse, and key reuse. TKIP is implemented on existing hardware with software/firmware upgrades only.

The other steps, planned for 2003–2004, include enhanced 802.1X key management, Advanced Encryption Standard- (AES) based data protection, and enhanced support infrastructure. These steps will help users gain better access control, which is as important as privacy.

Bluetooth Technology

There is another common wireless standard that operates on the same RF 2.4-GHz band as 802.11b but has different targets. The Bluetooth-based technology is not a competitor to 802.11: 802.11 was designed to connect computers at a 10+ MHz speed within a 300-foot distance, whereas Bluetooth operates at a lower speed (1 MHz) within a short (around 30 feet) distance with very low power consumption. This is ideal for transferring data between PDAs or for communications to peripheral devices.

Unlike 802.11, the Bluetooth wireless specification includes both link layer and application layer definitions that support data, voice, and content-centric applications [6]. Bluetooth radio devices use a spread spectrum, frequency hopping, and full-duplex signal at up to 1,600 hops/second in the 2.4-GHz band. The signal hops among 79 frequencies at 1-MHz intervals to provide a high degree of immunity against interference. Bluetooth devices can operate near, without interfering with, 802.11 networks.

The Bluetooth Service Discovery Protocol (a part of the Bluetooth standard) may be very helpful for a peer-to-peer architecture. Bluetooth devices can discover their relatives, the other Bluetooth devices working in the same frequency range. This automatic discovery feature can be used to establish and recover networks on the fly, find necessary services, and query for service attributes.

SMS: The Most Popular Wireless Service

SMS is the most popular wireless service today. Started in Europe as a part of the GSM offering, SMS was made available in North America on digital wireless networks based on GSM built by companies such as BellSouth Mobility, PrimeCo, and Nextel.

SMS was designed for interconnection among different message sources and destinations and provides guaranteed message delivery, unlike alphanumeric paging and some other text transmission services. In case of a network outage, the short message is stored in an SMS service center (SMSC) for delivery when the network is available.

SMSC solutions are based on an intelligent network (IN) approach that can handle multiple input sources, including voice-mail and e-mail integrated with Web-based messaging.

SMS transmits short messages to and from wireless devices using an SMSC as a store-and-forward system. The wireless network is responsible for finding the wireless destinations and for message transfers between the destinations and SMSCs.

The SMSC is responsible for storing and forwarding messages to and from mobile devices. The other Short Message Entities of the SMS architecture include Signal Transfer Points (STPs), Home Location Registers (HLRs), Visitor Location Registers (VLRs), and Mobile Switching Centers (MSCs).

The STP provides interconnections over signaling system 7 (SS7) links with multiple network elements. The HLR is a permanent storage device for subscriptions and service profiles, including routing data. The VLR contains temporary data about subscribers roaming from one HLR to another. The MSC controls calls to and from other telephone and data systems and routes the short messages via the specific base station to the specific mobile subscriber.

SMS has been recently extended from GSM phones to handheld computers and PDAs. An SMS service layer uses mobile application part (MAP) signaling capabilities and the SS7 transactional capabilities application part (TCAP) to transfer short messages between the entities.

An example of the SMS center (gateway) implementation integrated with the Wireless Application Protocol (WAP) gateway can be found at the Kannel open source project [7].

What Is WAP?

The WAP is an attempt to provide a set of specifications for application interoperability of three rapidly evolving network technologies: wireless data, telephony, and the Internet [8]. The protocol is intended for devices ranging from low-end handheld digital wireless devices, such as mobile phones, pagers, two-way radios, and smart phones, to high-end PDAs and communication systems.

The WAP communications protocol works with most wireless networks, such as CDPD (Cellular Digital Packet Data), TDMA, CDMA, GSM, FLEX, ReFLEX, (FLEX, ReFLEX, and InFLEX are paging protocols by Motorola), iDEN (Integrated Digital Enhanced Network technology from Motorola that combines the capabilities of a alphanumeric pager, digital cellular phone, two-way radio, and data/fax modem in a single network), TETRA (Terrestrial Trunked Radio), DECT (Digital Enhanced Cordless Telecommunications), DataTAC, Mobitex, and GRPS. WAP also specifies an application environment similar to a Web browser that can be based on J2ME or built directly into any operating system, such as Windows CE or PalmOS.

WAP provides a Web-centric application model with content optimized for thin-client devices and also allows for future growth enabling 2.5G, 3G, and other networks. GPRS features efficient use of resources, instant access, fast delivery of information, and innovative charging models. WAP and GPRS therefore represent a winning combination for mobile end users, operators, service providers, and enterprises, as well as application developers.

The communications vendors who have lined up to support WAP promise the biggest business advantage: the ability to build a single application for a wide range of clients and bearers. How valid this promise is depends on how well vendors continue to cooperate and follow the standard.

The WAP Forum, which drives this technology, has the latest approved standard version set at WAP 2.0. Unfortunately, we cannot enjoy all the features of this latest standard until vendors like Motorola, Ericsson, Nokia, and others implement it. All current implementations are on the level of WAP 1.x standards.

What Difference Does WAP2.0 Make?

WAP 2.0 adds support for major protocols like TCP/IP, HTTP, and Secure Sockets Layer (SSL), in addition to the existing WAP 1.x stack of protocols. WAP 1.x protocols are scaled-down versions of the WWW protocol stack: Wireless Session Protocol corresponds to HTTP, Wireless Transaction Protocol corresponds to TCP, Wireless Datagram Protocol corresponds to IP, and Wireless Transport Layer Security corresponds to SSL.

WAP 2.0 adds instant support for HTML pages beside Wireless Markup Language (WML) and WML script. In a way, WML is superior to HTML. WML's powerful concepts of multiple cards (pages) in a single deck (a multipage message), as well as better flow and internal property control features deserve special consideration.

How Does WAP Work?

WAP technology is closely related to Web technology. WAP is actually a child of the Web—a young and promising child. Figure 8.2 makes this similarity very visible.

WAP/WML technology (as well as VoiceXML-based technology) is based on the Web model. WML pages have URLs and can be located on any Web server or dynamically generated when such a URL invokes a service that provides the requested content.

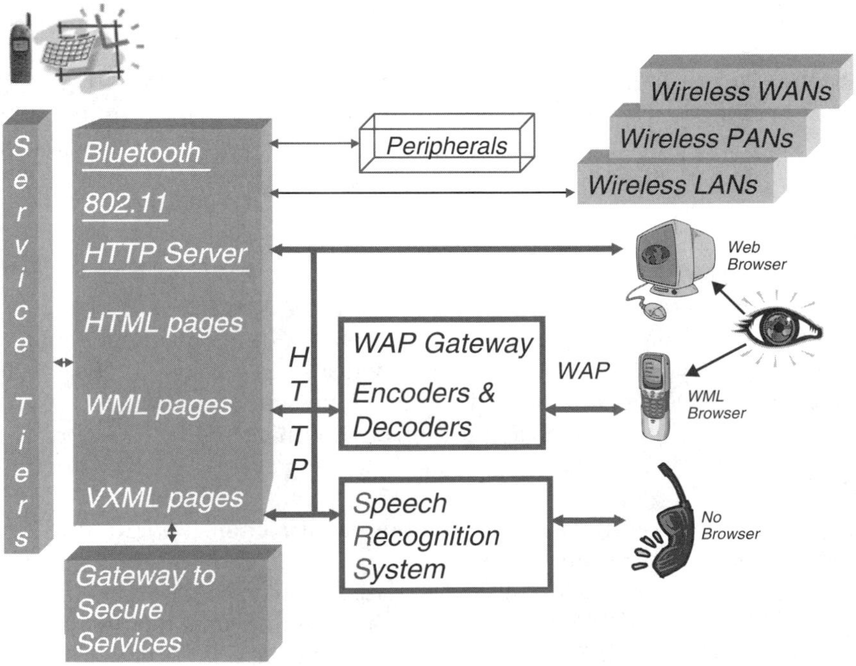

FIGURE 8.2. Wired and Wireless Clients.

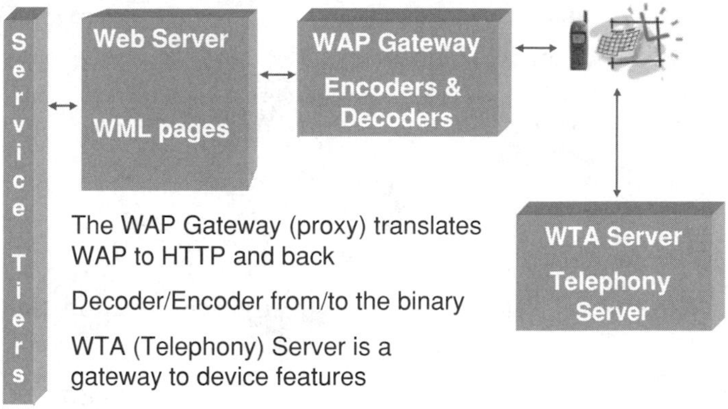

FIGURE 8.3. WAP Components.

In the case of WAP technology, a client agent is not a regular Web browser but a different device, usually a phone-based device with an embedded WML browser, and an intermediate WAP gateway is needed.

The Web model represents a Web server and Web client (browser) supporting HTTP and using HTML. The WAP programming model is similar to the Web programming model in that it has a proven architecture and existing tools (e.g., Web servers and XML tools). Optimizations and extensions have been made and wherever possible, existing standards have been adopted for the WAP technology.

What Is the WAP Gateway?

The WAP gateway (or WAP proxy) translates HTTP to the language of wireless phones and back and encodes the Web server responses into a compact binary format. Figure 8.3 shows several components that interact with wireless phones that support WAP technology.

WAP content and applications are specified in a set of well-known content formats based on the familiar WWW standards.

The WTA (Wireless Telephony Application) server is used to provide WAP access to features of the wireless network provider's telecommunications infrastructure.

SUMMARY

The wireless world is both attractive and challenging. It is relatively easy to get lost there while trying to catch up with a single brand name or a technology. A good understanding of the basic principles and standards that rule this world helps create integration-ready wireless applications and services able to penetrate multiple wireless markets.

In the next chapters, we will consider programming wireless applications using WAP, J2ME, and.NET technologies.

Integrating Question

Please explain and put into a hierarchy the following abbreviated terms: RF, GPRS, GSM, CDMA, SMS, and WAP.

Case Study

1. Research and provide a list of 3G technologies.
2. Review and discuss the security status of 3G.
3. Compare WAP with a similar technology: I-Mode. What are the common points and the differences?

REFERENCES

1. CDMA Theory and Nortel Networks Product Design and Function, Student Guide, July 2000.
2. Universal Mobile Telecommunications System: *http://www.umts-forum.org/what_is_umts.html*.
3. 3rd Generation Partnership Project: *http://www.3gpp.org/*.
4. Hill, J. An Analysis of the RADIUS Authentication Protocol: *http://www.untruth.org/~josh/security/radius/*.
5. AXL RADIUS server with Java: *http://www.theorem.com/java/index.htm* and *http://www.theorem.com/java/radserver/*.
6. Bluetooth Wireless Specifications: *http://www.bluetooth.org*.
7. Kannel Open Source Project, WAP and SMS Gateway: *http://www.kannel.org*. Wireless Application Protocol (WAP) Architecture Specification.
8. WAP-210-WAPArch-20010712: *http://www.wapforum.org/what/technical.htm*.

CHAPTER 9

Programming Wireless Application Protocol Applications

Fashion is the science of appearances.
—**Michel de Montaigne** (1533–1592)

This chapter introduces Wireless Markup Language (WML) and provides examples of programming wireless applications using presentation factories.

Wireless Application Protocol (WAP) devices include WML browsers that can display some content described in WML and WMLScript, which is part of the WAP specification. WMLScript can be used to add programming support to the client. It is similar to JavaScript and can be used in a similar manner. You can use WMLScript to validate user input, but most importantly, you can use it to generate messages and dialogs locally, so error messages and confirmations can be viewed faster.

It is also possible to access facilities of the user agent; for example, WMLScript allows the programmer to make phone calls, access the SIM (subscriber identity module) card, or configure the user agent after it has been deployed. (Keep in mind that data and voice are separate.)

Memory and CPU resources are limited and often prohibit the use of WMLScript, although WMLScript may be necessary to program proprietary telephony features for specific devices. For example, some devices allow your program to:

- **Send** DTMF (Dual Tone Multi-Frequency. The technical term describing Touch Tone dialing with combination of two tones, one low frequency and one high frequency.) tones

- Modify the device's phone book
- Use the phone book to start voice call or reject a call

Note that such programs would hardly work for a variety of models. The compatibility problem is one of the serious problems WAP developers face.

Rethink the Existing Web Page Paradigm in WAP Terms

If you are familiar with HTML, this is not a ticket to join a WAP development team. Web browsers are very forgiving to HTML. WML is a subset of XML. It is a language of strict rules: close every tag or face an error. However, this is not the biggest problem; the biggest problem is that wireless devices are very small. This problem immediately multiplies into several other problems.

We have to rethink the existing Web page paradigm and create an absolutely new user interface (or use a very old one—one familiar to programmers 20 years ago).

Keep in mind the limitations of wireless devices:

- Small screen and limited user input facilities
- Narrowband network connection
- Limited memory and CPU resources

There is a possibility not only for text but also for image support. The issue is not about GIF or JPEG images. WAP allows Wireless BitMap (WBMP) format, and there are converters that can turn any BMP into WBMP. The problem is how to fit this image into a small screen and memory size.

A very clever deck/card organization metaphor helps to send several pages (cards) in a single message (deck) to improve networking.

Yes, you can even program some telephony features, although this is an expensive, time-consuming exercise. You cannot use phone simulators for this purpose (not today). You have to play the "real game" with your phone and your phone service provider, and then your success will be limited to this phone brand inside that phone service provider.

Did I mention simulators? It would be impossible to develop a WAP world without them. Tools such as Nokia WAP Toolkit and Ericsson's WapIDE Toolkit offer developers a PC environment for creating, testing, and demonstrating WAP applications. WAP application developers can build complete applications even without a handset or access to carrier infrastructure.

Figure 9.1 displays several simulators from different companies. The major advantage of WAP development environments is that they come with WAP simulators with which you can test your WAP application.

Therefore, you receive a complete package with tools for creating WML and WMLScript content and adding WBMP graphics, as well as debugging and simulating WAP applications on WAP-enabled handsets.

You can scroll up and down the screen, select highlighted functions, and enter letters or numbers in the same way you would with a real cell phone.

How Do We Connect WAP to the Existing Business Infrastructure?

This is a very important question. To answer it, we need to look at the "big picture" of WAP in an enterprise application (Fig. 9.2).

FIGURE 9.1. The WAP Development Environment: Simulators.

WAP is just one of the possible presentation layers that provide client access to enterprise services. The WAP presentation factory can help us program this layer.

A user armed with a WAP device cannot use all the power of the enterprise services, but even a subset of these services may be very handy for such a user in some situations.

For example, a driver requests directions from the geographical information system in his or her car. The presentation layer strips the service data to text format and sends text information to the user's WAP device.

The user then reads his or her personal and group messages, checks the schedule and other records according to his or her privileges, and obtains notification on new data contributed to the distributed knowledge system.

Document-handling services, such as OpenOffice, combined with a knowledge engine help a WAP user retrieve formatted data (e.g., PDF and DOC) and extract meaningful information about these data.

The user even has some (limited) capacity to reply to messages and contribute new data.

WHAT IS A PRESENTATION FACTORY AND HOW DO YOU CREATE ONE?

Figure 9.3 shows the beginning of a WML card that displays the "Welcome" screen with links to new and all email messages. You can see that to display just one line on the phone

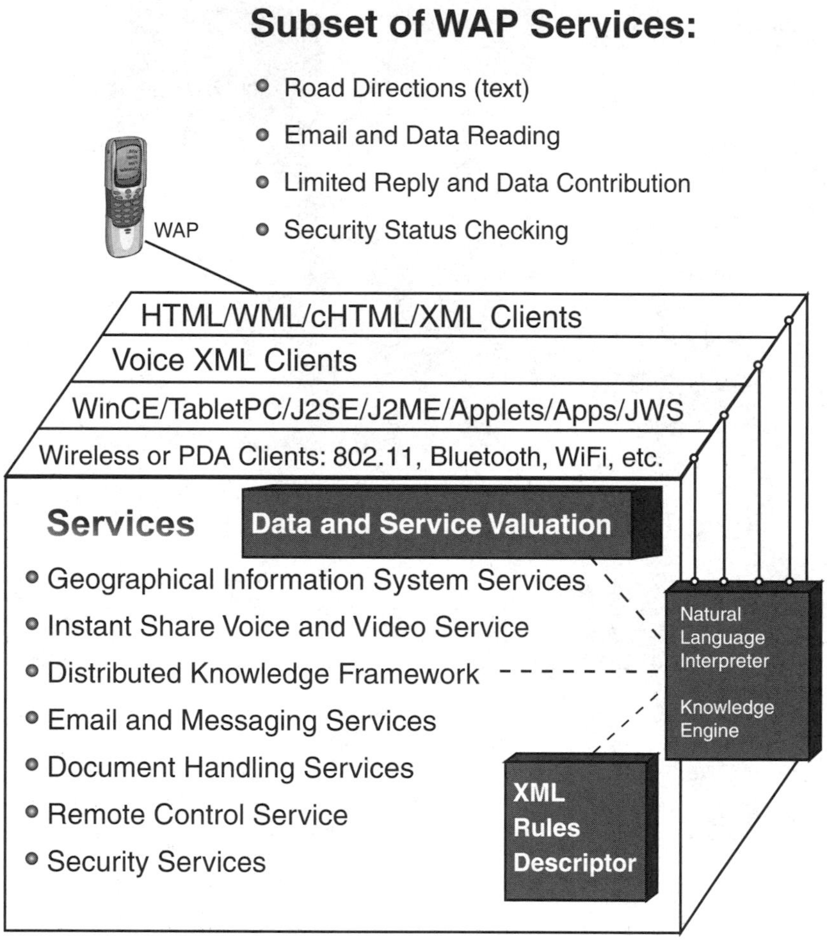

FIGURE 9.2. A Subset of WAP Services in Enterprise Applications.

screen, we need to provide multiple lines of a very boring XML code. The presentation factory generates this code for us. The WML presentation factory is a set of programs with simple application program interfaces (APIs) that take parameters that make sense to us and return a proper XML string that makes sense to a WAP device.

Where do WML presentation factories come from? You can buy them, download them for free, reuse examples from this book, and/or write your own factory that is specific to your business. Figure 9.4 presents several examples of WML factory methods.

Now we can easily generate a proper WML code with the same "Welcome Jeff" greeting using just three lines of Java code.

PROGRAMMING WAP/WML PAGES

Load a proper presentation factory at run-time based on one of the following parameters. The *specificFactoryClassName* parameter can be, for example, *WMLFactory* or *HTMLFactory*. *Class.forName()* is a powerful Java method that uses the Reflection package.

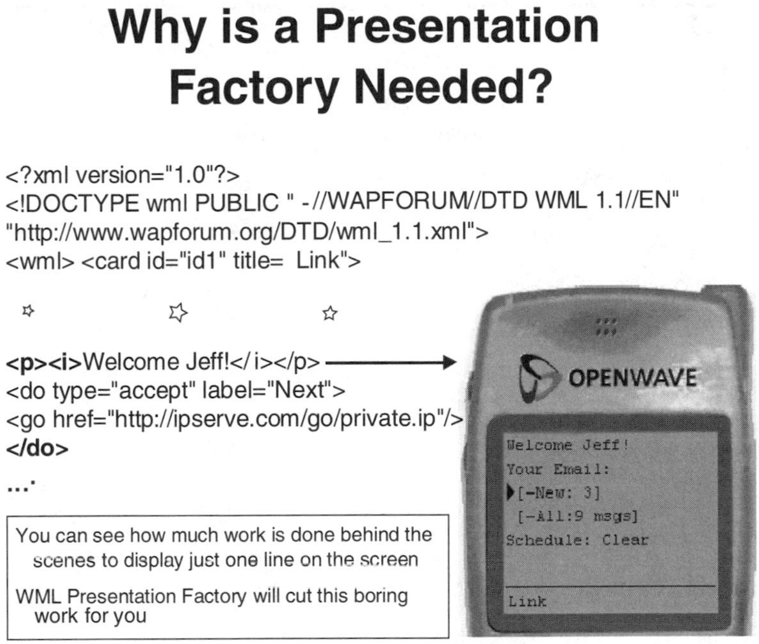
Why is a Presentation Factory Needed?
<?xml version="1.0"?>
<!DOCTYPE wml PUBLIC " -//WAPFORUM//DTD WML 1.1//EN"
"http://www.wapforum.org/DTD/wml_1.1.xml">
<wml> <card id="id1" title= Link">
<p><i>Welcome Jeff!</ i></p>
<do type="accept" label="Next">
<go href="http://ipserve.com/go/private.ip"/>
</do>
...
You can see how much work is done behind the scenes to display just one line on the screen
WML Presentation Factory will cut this boring work for you
OPENWAVE
Welcome Jeff!
Your Email:
[-New: 3]
[-All:9 msgs]
Schedule: Clear
Link

FIGURE 9.3. A Presentation Factory at Work.

This method can throw an exception and must be framed by "try-catch" statements.

```
PresentationFactory factory=
 (PresentationFactory) Class.forName(specificFactoryClassName).
 newInstance();
String page=factory.init("Services","Personal News");
// page id and title
page += factory.addLine("Welcome"  + userFirstName +  "!");
```

I want to bring your attention to the *openNewCard()* method presented in Fig. 9.4. Here is the XML line generated by this method:

```
<card id="Services" title="Personal News" newcontext= "true">
```

The *newcontext=true* attribute (that I made bold for better visibility) forces the WML browser to clean its cache, which is a very important WML feature. I'd like to remind you that HTML does not offer anything like this; you would have to use JavaScript to clean browser memory.

The *newcontext=true* attribute erases old link values as well as values set by internal WML operations, such as *setvar*, that can set variable values at run-time, according to the programmer's instructions.

SECURE TRANSACTIONS WITH WML FACTORY

Why is it important to clean old values when you start a new page?

```
package com.its.wml;

/**
 * WMLFactory class provides methods to generate WML pages
 */

public class WMLFactory {

/** init()
 * @param id
 * @param title
 * @return xml
 * @see #openDeck
 * @see #openNewCard
 */
    public String init(String id, String title) {
        String xml = openDeck();
        xml += openNewCard(id, title);
        return xml;
    }

/** openDeck()
 * @return opened Deck
 * @see #openXML()
 * @see #openDoc()
 * @see #getOpenDeckComments()
 * @see #openPage()
 */
    public String openDeck() {
        String html = openXML();
        html += openDoc();
        html += getOpenDeckComments();
        html += openPage();
        return html;
    }
/** openXML()
 * @return tag with xml version
 */
    public String openXML() {
        return "<?xml version=\"1.0\"?> \n";
    }
/** openDoc()
 * @return tag with DOCTYPE
 */
    public String openDoc() {
        return "<!DOCTYPE wml PUBLIC \"-  //WAPFORUM  //DTD WML 1.1//EN\"
        \"http://www.wapforum.org/DTD/wml_1.1.xml\">\n";
    }
/** getOpenDeckComments()
 * @return comment
 */
```

FIGURE 9.4

```
    public String getOpenDeckComments() {
        return "<!-- Deck opening with WML Factory -->\n";
    }
/** openPage()
 * @return opening tag with wml
 */
    public String openPage() {
        return "<wml>\n";
    }
/** openNewCard(String cardId, String cardTitle)
 * @param cardId of new card
 * @param cardTitle of new card
 * @return tag with card
 */
    public String openNewCard(String cardId, String cardTitle) {
        return "<card id=\"" + cardId + "\" title=\"" + cardTitle +
        "\"" + " newcontext=\"true\" >\n";
    }
/** addLine(String line)
 * @param line line to add on paragraph
 * @return line in paragraph with left alignment and small font
 */
    public String addLine(String line){
        return "<p align=\"left\"><small>" +line + "</small></p>\n";
    }
```

FIGURE 9.4. *(cont.)*

It is a security risk if you forget to do this. Why? Because the values you set once at run-time—for example, for credit card transactions that require cookies—can be caught by one of the other sites that also use cookies.

It is a good programming habit to use the *openNewCard()* method to start a new WML page.

Now you can see the additional benefit of WML factories: they can take care of problems you do not even want to know about.

Let us move on and finish our discussion of the "Welcome" screen presented in Fig. 9.3. We provide the additional line:

```
page += factory.addLine("Your Email:");
```

Creating Links and Forms in WML

The next two lines on the screen are links. The syntax of WML links is not exactly the same as that for HTML links.

The WML link, like a regular HTML link, consists of a URL and a name. The link looks this way:

```
<anchor>-New: 1<go href="/go/private.ip"> </go></anchor
```

The visible name of the link is *-New*: and the URL is "*/go/private.ip.*"

The *anchor* tag frames the link, and the *go href* tag frames the URL. Unlike in HTML syntax, the link name is ahead of the link URL.

Some links have additional parameters in the URL; for example:

```
"http://javaschool.com/go/private.ip?sessionid=abcdef &action=new
```

The parameters are listed in WML with the *postfield* tag lines, similar to the *hidden* input fields in HTML:

```
<anchor>-New: 1<go href="/go/private.ip">
<postfield name="sessionid" value="abcdef"/>
<postfield name="action" value="new"/>
</go></anchor>
```

Do we have a WML factory method to simplify link generations?

Several WML factory methods provided in Fig. 9.5 minimize the programmer's efforts to add a link to just one Java line:

```
page += factory.addLinkLine(linkURL, linkName);
```

The *addLinkLine()* method uses the *addLink()* method, which in turn uses the *addURL-toLink()* method. Note that we pass a regular URL with or without parameters to the *addURL-toLink()* method, which takes care of parameters (if present) and forms necessary *postfield* tags for them.

Do you need to know these details? Not really, unless you decide to write a better factory. As an application programmer, you need to know just the one API line listed above, and you can adapt this line to your situation in the same way I adapt this API to provide the next link lines on the "Welcome" screen:

```
page += factory.addLinkLine(
"/go/private.ip?sessionid=" + sessionID + "&action=\"newMessages\"",
//URL
"-New:" + numberOfNewMailMessages); // visible name of the link
page += factory.addLinkLine(
"/go/private.ip?sessionid=" + sessionID + "&action=\"allMessages\"",
//URL
"-ALL: " + numberOfALLMailMessages); // visible name of the link
```

The last line on the screen tells us that nothing is scheduled for this time.

This line can be a link if our program finds a valid schedule record related to this time. Here is the code portion that covers both cases:

```
// The "user" object was created on logon
String briefScheduleDescription = user.getBriefScheduleDescription();
If(briefScheduleDescription == null) {
  page += factory.addLine("Schedule: clear");
} else {
  page += factory.addLinkLine(
"/go/private.ip?sessionid=" + sessionID + "&action=\"schedule\"",
// URL
"-Your schedule"); // visible name of the link
}
```

```
/** addLinkLine(String url, String name)
 * @param url of link
 * @param name of link
 * @return paragraph with added link
 */
    public String addLinkLine(String url, String name) {
        String wml = addLink(url, name);
        return "<p><small>" +wml+"</small></p>\n";
    }

/** addLink(String url, String name)
 * @param url of link
 * @param name of link
 * @return anchor tag with added link
 */
    public String addLink(String url, String name) {
        String wml = " <anchor>"+name;
        wml += addURLtoLink(url); // add URL with parameters
        wml += "</anchor>\n";
        return(wml);
    }
/** addURLtoLink(String url)
 * @param url href in tag with go
 * @return page with postfields
 */
    public String addURLtoLink(String url) {
        String[] splits = url.split("?");
        String wml ="";
        int nArgs =0;
        if (splits!=null){
          wml = "<go href=\""+splits[0]+"\">\n";
          if (splits.length>1){
              splits = Stringer.split("&", splits[1]); //&amp;
          }
          String[] nameValues;
          for(int i=0; i < splits.length; i++) {
              nameValues = Stringer.split("=",splits[i]);
              if (nameValues.length>1){
                wml += "<postfield name=\""+nameValues[0]+"\"
                value=\""+nameValues[1]+"\"/>\n";
              }
          }
          wml += "<postfield name=\"mode\" value=\"wml\"/>\n</go>\n";
        }
        return(wml);
    }
```

FIGURE 9.5

```
/** closeCard();
 * @return closing card tag
 */
    public String closeCard() {
        return "</card>\n";
    }
/** closePage();
 * @return closing page tag
 */
    public String closePage() {
        return "</wml>\n";
    }
/** close()
 * @return closing tags with card and wml
 */
    public String close() {
        return "</card></wml>\n";
    }
```

FIGURE 9.6

We need to close the WML card and the page. Figure 9.6 presents several methods that help the application programmer accomplish this with one line:

```
page += factory.close(); // done!
```

This line finishes our "Welcome" page.

A Unified Solution for WML, HTML, and Other Presentation Factories

Can you find WML specifics in the Java code that forms the page? Hopefully, the code is generic enough for WML, HTML, and some other presentation types. The *HTMLFactory*, of course, would have its own implementation for all methods presented above.

We define a presentation factory type based on a client device type. Every client device or HTML browser sends HTTP headers (according to the protocol) with the type of the client. The server program can analyze these headers and pass a presentation factory parameter to our presentation layer program.

The factory knows all the coding specifics and helps to solve related problems.

Wireless phones have specific buttons or controls that can be selected by a user. When we want to provide an action based on such selection, we use "do type" tags, where the type would indicate one of the specific controls.

The Login Screen

Take a look at Fig. 9.7, which presents login screens with the *Login Name* and *Password* fields. The user enters his or her *Login Name* and then press the *OK* button. Some phones label this button *Send* or some other name. At the bottom of the first screen, we can see the

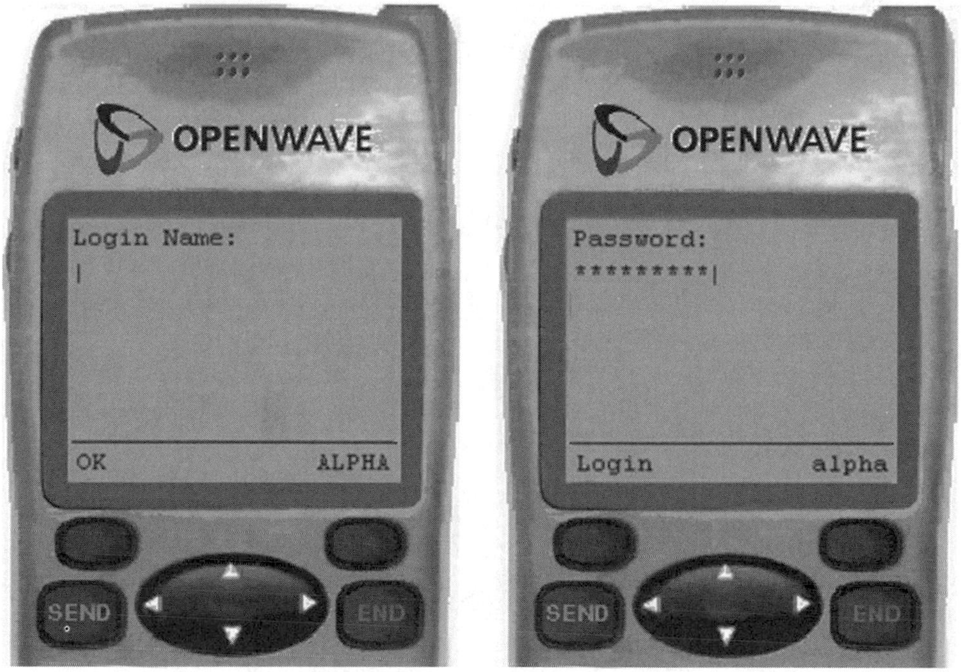

FIGURE 9.7. The Login Page.

default label (in this case, *OK*). This default label may be replaced with a custom label—for example, *Login*—using the WML tag *do type* (see below).

A complete login page is presented in Fig. 9.8. This single WML page produces two sequential screens. The first displays the *Login Name* and accepts user input. Then a WAP phone displays the second screen with the *Password* field. Note that the second screen shows the *Login* label at the bottom of the screen according to the page instruction:

```
<do type="accept" label="Login">
```

You can see that the *do type* tag starts a form that includes both variables: *username* and *psw* (Password) entered by a user. The $ precedes each variable in WML. Both variables will be filled at run-time with the values provided by the user.

There are several more fields in the form: *service, action*, and *presentationFactory*. These fields help the server side select a proper service to process the form data.

A Powerful WML Tag—Template

This tag includes definitions that are provided once, at the beginning of a multicard deck. These definitions are valid for all the cards inside this deck.

We can use this opportunity to create several linked pages with a single transfer by packing several cards inside a single deck.

Figure 9.9 displays an example of the use of the *template* tag. In this example, the *accept* and *prev* control types are defined for the deck. We do not have to repeat this definition for every card in the deck. On every page, the user will see the *Services* label for the *prev* control type that instructs the device to return to a previous page and the *Get News*

```
<?xml version="1.0"?>
<!DOCTYPE wml PUBLIC "-//WAPFORUM//DTD WML 1.1//EN"
"http://www.wapforum.org/DTD/wml_1.1.xml">
 <!-- Source Generated by WML Deck Decoder -->
 <wml> <card id="login" title="JavaSchool.com" >

<p align="left">
Login name:
<input type="text" name="userName" value=""/>
</p>
<p align="left">
Password:
<input type="password" name="psw" value="" />
</p>

<do type="accept" label="Login">
 <go href="/go/private.ip;jsessionid=ab6wh5e7p1" method="post">
   <postfield name="sessionID" value=""/>
   <postfield name="userName" value="$(userName)"/>
   <postfield name="psw" value="$(psw)"/>
   <postfield name="presentationFactory" value="WMLFactory"/>
   <postfield name="service" value="login"/>
   <postfield name="action" value="checklogin"/>
 </go>
</do>
</card>
</wml>
```

FIGURE 9.8

label for the *accept* control type that instructs the device to send the request to the server. (Be aware that some devices have both types, but some have only the *accept* control type available.)

Memory limitation for WAP devices is a permanent challenge for developers, regardless of the services developed. For example, you want to retrieve an email message that came

```
<template><do type="prev" label="Services">
<go href="/go/private.ip">
<postfield name="action" value="user_page"/>
</go></do>
<do type="accept" label="Get News">
<go href="/go/private.ip">
<postfield name="action" value="news"/>
</go></do></template>
```

FIGURE 9.9

to your mail server. If this message is bigger than the WAP device memory capacity, this attempt will fail. Testing this situation, you can see a very clear message below:

```
---- DATA SIZE --------------
Uncompiled data from HTTP is 16327 bytes.
.found Content-Type: text/vnd.wap.wml.
Compiled WAP binary is 9403 bytes.
-----------------------------------------------
Compiled WAP Binary is too large by 6419 bytes!
```

IS THE DATA SIZE TOO BIG FOR A DEVICE? NOT A PROBLEM!

First of all, we want to solve the problem on the system level, so application programmers do not have to worry about it at all. The best place for this solution is the presentation factory. The *buildPages* module evaluates every data portion before sending it to the WAP device and, if necessary, splits a big message into a sequence of linked pages, as in Fig. 9.10.

The *buildPages* module embedded in the WML factory makes transparent translation of any email message, text file, linked article, or other content into a single WML page or a sequence of WML pages. Application developers would not even have to know about the oversize-data problem.

Simplify Wireless Access with Digital Identity

There is at least one more side to the wireless access equation. The same user often uses (at different times) different types of clients. The user can have a rich view of enterprise services via his or her corporate workstation and can also have a bleak view of a subset of services via a wireless device. One example on how this user can simplify wireless access is presented in Fig. 9.11. This example displays a rich service provided by the Distributed Knowledge System Prototype [1] and available on a corporate workstation. The service allows the user to provide alternative digital identity for easier login. This digital login alias and password-PIN can be used for interaction with a wireless device. Think of other possible examples in which a rich client can provide specific services to customize wireless access and make it more convenient.

We now move to the more sophisticated area of reading email messages with attachments.

Read Email with Attachments on a Wireless Device

We all (I hope) are very cautious when it comes to opening attachments. Any attachment that is not in pure ASCII text and that can run a program is a potential virus bomb. This includes MS Word documents with macros and MS Excel documents with Visual Basic script and/or macros. It is preferable to open these attachments on another machine: a special server well-protected against viruses.

How do we read email attachments or linked formatted files on smart phones? Adobe Acrobat Reader or Microsoft Excel programs are rarely available on wireless client devices.

However, we can use converter servers that are capable of transforming Microsoft, Adobe, and other formatted files into text messages. OpenOffice services can help this transformation. Such conversions may require a smart approach to context retrieval when, framed by

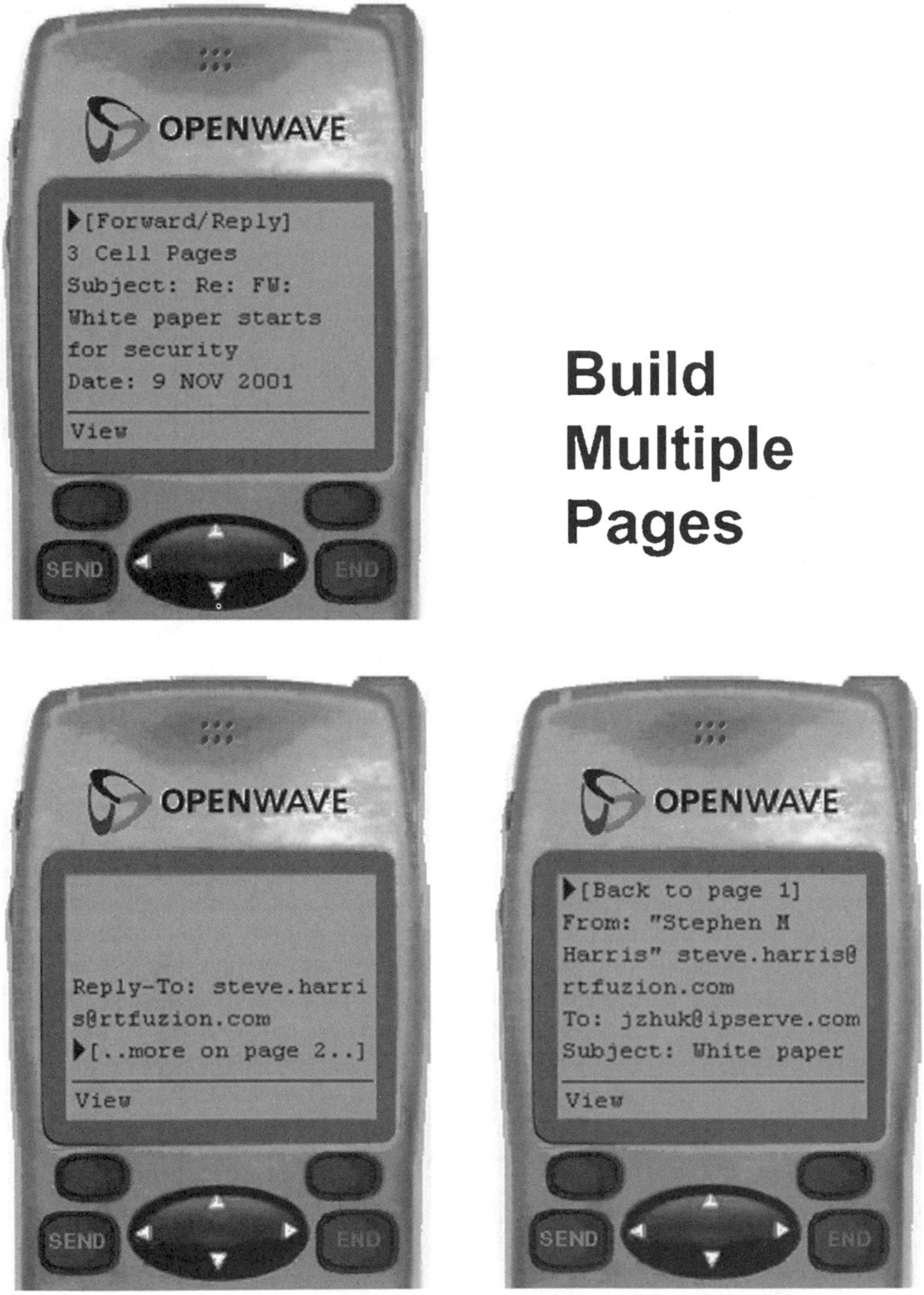

FIGURE 9.10. Solve the Oversize Problem: Build Multiple WML Pages on the Fly.

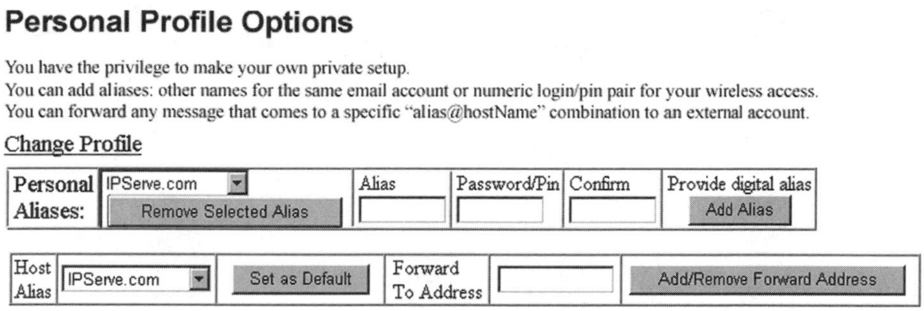
Personal Profile Options
You have the privilege to make your own private setup.
You can add aliases: other names for the same email account or numeric login/pin pair for your wireless access.
You can forward any message that comes to a specific "alias@hostName" combination to an external account.
Change Profile
Personal Aliases:
IPServe.com
Remove Selected Alias
Alias
Password/Pin
Confirm
Provide digital alias
Add Alias
Host Alias
IPServe.com
Set as Default
Forward To Address
Add/Remove Forward Address

FIGURE 9.11. Personal Profile Options.

memory limitations, we want to extract just an essence of the longer file. This is another area where a knowledge engine can be very helpful.

It is important to capitalize on existing (server-side) business services instead of creating new ones. The code extractions provided above demonstrate several pieces of the WML presentation layer (factory) that delivers a subset of distributed knowledge services running at JavaSchool.com to users with WAP devices.

The WAP users can receive email, chat, and group messages and have limited options for search and data contribution. The server side can sometimes compensate for the limited capacity of the WAP client. For example, besides the main option *Enter Reply*, the WAP *Reply* screen at JavaSchool.com includes several optional messages, such as "OK" and "Thanks," that require no typing.

Check Security Status via Wireless Phone

It is important to realize that the user can remotely check the status of multiple business processes in the enterprise. For example, the user can remotely check security status using a set of integrated subsystems, as presented in Fig. 9.12. Three major (integrated) subsystems participate in security monitoring. Video and voice data from security sensors are shared with multiple guard locations via the Instant Voice and Video Share subsystems.

The Remote Scenario Processing subsystem presented in Fig. 9.13 participates in data processing and looks for patterns described in remote scenarios. The subsystem provides actions or notifications based on the scenarios.

A wireless user who requests security status can see the status in abbreviated form on the phone screen (Fig. 9.14). The picture on the left presents a trouble-free situation, with the *Security: clear* message on the screen. The picture on the right side is alarming. The message *room213* is actually a link. The user can press the link to get more details about this warning message.

WAP PUSH

All the examples we considered in this chapter can be classified as orthodox "Web pull" scenarios. It is very common in Web technology for the browser to request a service and the server to fulfill the request. But can the server "push" its content to the WAP client?

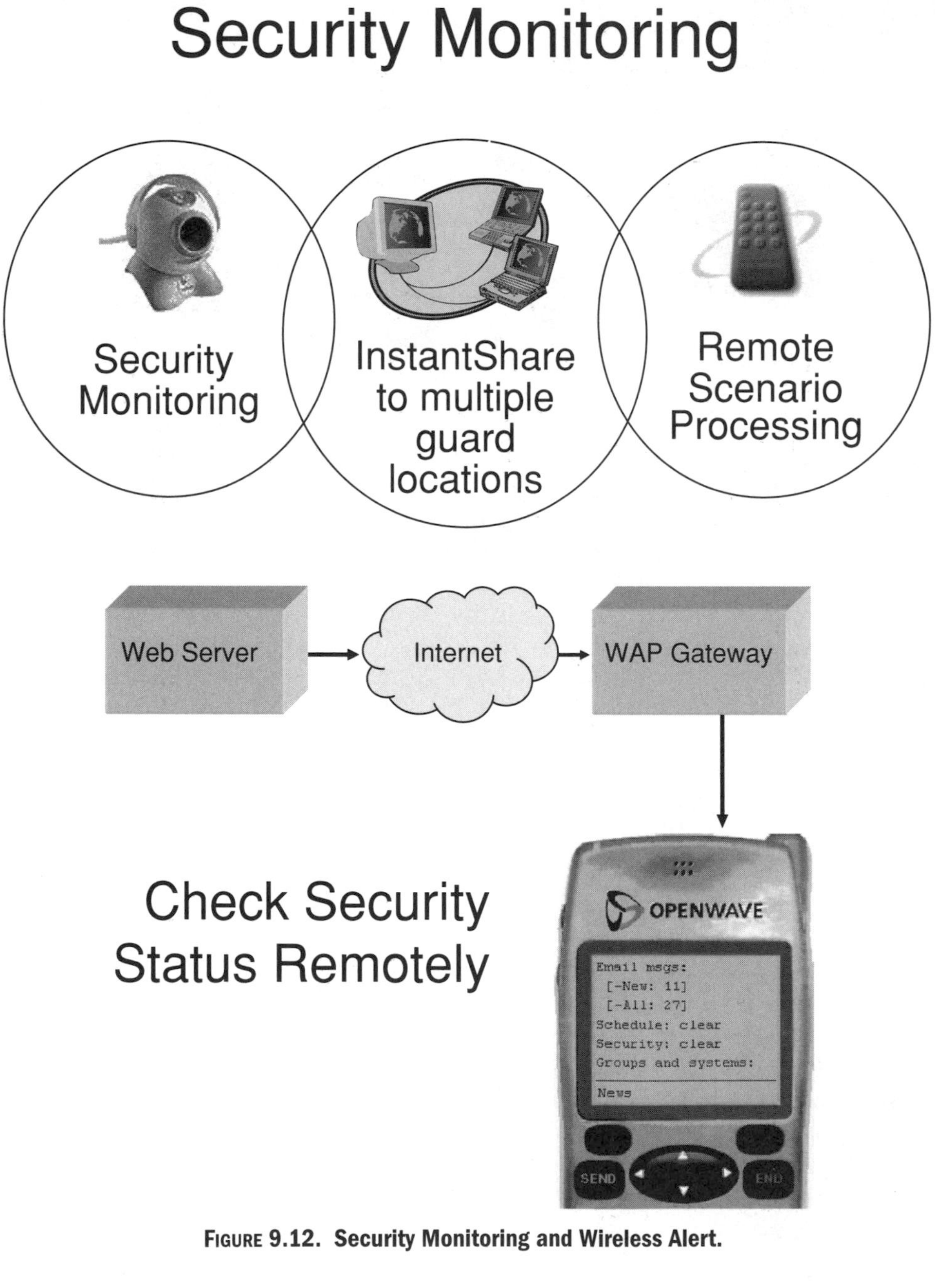

FIGURE 9.12. Security Monitoring and Wireless Alert.

Remote Scenario Processing

Write a scenario and schedule actions for Remote Systems:
Database• Servers• Wireless• Jiniô technology-based devices

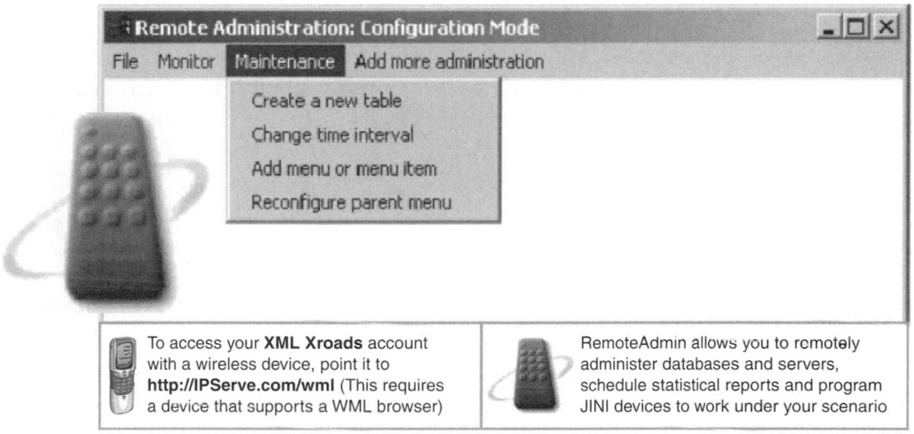

FIGURE 9.13. Remote Scenario Processing.

Security Status On The WAP Device

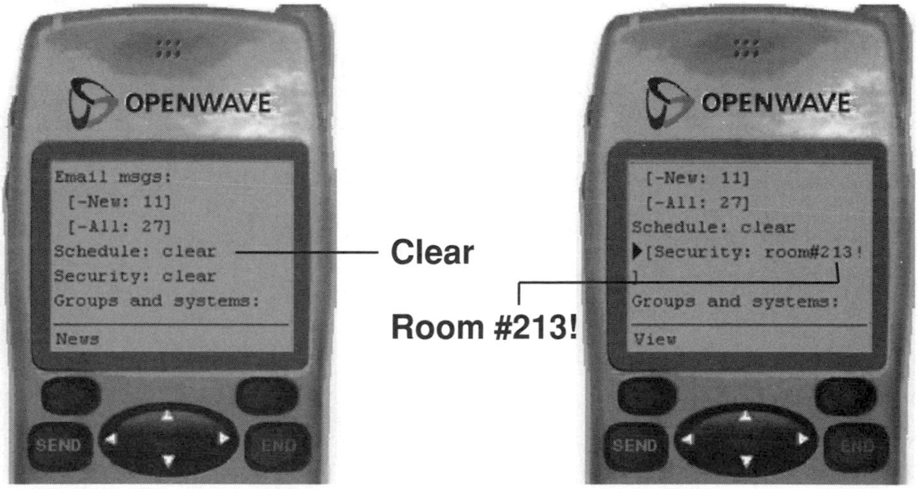

FIGURE 9.14. Security Alert on the WAP Device.

The WAP 2.0 specification introduces the WAP Push feature that does exactly that. The push initiator—for example, a Web server—sends multipart data content formatted according to the Push Access Protocol (PAP).

The push application uses PAP to send push information to the Push Proxy Gateway (PPG). PAP utilizes HTTP and XML. The PPG processes the PAP request and sends the push message to the mobile WAP device. The push message can be delivered using Short Message Service as a bearer or over an already-established data session.

The WAP Push feature is not just an API possibility anymore. Openwave WAP Push Library and SDK [2] are available free and provide a great support for the WAP Push feature. The push can give us, for example, a traffic alert warning that an accident has happened on the freeway and a suggestion for an alternate route. Combined with location-based services, the push can advise you, for example, to stop at a nearby place to meet an old friend.

WAP Devices and Web Services

Unfortunately, not even WAP 2.0 standard implementation [3] will help a WAP device become a Web service client. A Web service client has to understand XML messages in a manner similar to the XML browser I described in the previous chapter. Hopefully, the next WAP standard will fix this shortcoming.

Wireless devices can have an environment for program development. Windows CE, a scaled-down version of Microsoft Windows, or J2ME are examples of such an environment.

Microsoft Windows CE (WinCE) is a 32-bit operating system designed to meet the needs of a broad range of intelligent devices. Consumer products such as cameras, telephones, and home entertainment devices; communication hubs; and industrial controllers can be built with WinCE support.

WinCE runs a minimized version of the Internet Explorer browser. This scaled-down browser supports ActiveX controls installed on the WinCE device, but does not support downloading these controls. You have to use a program outside the browser for the download. The browser does, however, support Dynamic HTML and JavaScript.

Application development for WinCE devices can be done with Visual Studio.NET tools using C++, C#, Visual Basic, J#, or one of the other programming languages supported by the tool (there are 20).

Tablet PC is a personal computer powered by MS Windows XP that is geared for ink-, pen-, and speech-enabled applications. The Tablet PC platform includes MS Speech SDK and full support for ActiveX.

Chapter 12 describes how to add a speech recognition service to Windows- (using WinCE and Tablet PC) and UNIX-based systems.

There are three major players in the market of application environment for wireless devices: WinCE, Palm OS, and J2ME.

J2ME (Java 2 Micro Edition) presents a set of technologies covering a wide range of commodities from smart cards and pagers to set-top boxes and handheld devices that are almost as powerful as a computer.

If you are about to jump to Chapter 11 for J2ME internals please do not skip the next chapter. Java Card Technology (from Chapter 10) might give you the key you have been looking for.

Integrating Questions

1. What are the relationships between WAP and Web technology?
2. What is the role of the WML presentation factory?

Case Study

1. Research and compare current Integrated Development Environments (IDE) for WAP development offered with Nokia, Ericsson, IBM, and Borland tools.
2. Write a WML code with two or more cards in the deck to provide screens for the *forward/reply* email action.
3. Research the possibility of using WMLScript to program *save/retrieve email address* using a local phone/address book.
4. What type of WAP-based application might be applicable to your workplace?

References

1. Distributed Knowledge System Prototype: *http://IPServe.com/wml*.
2. Openwave WAP Push Library: *http://developer.openwave.com*.
3. Wireless Application Protocol Architecture Specification WAP-210-WAPArch-20010712: *http://www.wapforum.org/what/technical.htm*.

CHAPTER 10

A Single JavaCard Identity Key for All Doors and Services

Nothing is more powerful than an idea whose time has come.
—Victor Hugo

This chapter turns the smallest Java Virtual Machine (JVM) running on a smart card into a powerful key that can open all doors.

WHAT IS A SMART CARD?

Imagine a regular plastic card (often called "plastic") with either a microprocessor and/or a memory chip embedded into the card. The microprocessor can manipulate information on the card, whereas a memory chip (e.g., the one in a prepaid phone card) can undertake only a predefined operation performed by a card reader.

Smart cards, unlike magnetic-stripe cards, do not require remote access at the time of the transaction; they can carry all the necessary functions and information right on the card. Today, there are three categories of smart cards: microprocessor, memory, and optical memory.

Microprocessor cards have an 8-bit processor, 16 KB of read-only memory, and 512 bytes of random access memory. Their processing power is similar to the first personal computers. These cards can perform cryptography algorithms and are used to access, hold, and otherwise manage digital money; provide secure access to computer and phone networks; secure set-top boxes; and perform other functions.

Memory cards, which can hold up to 1 to 4 KB of data, represent the bulk of the 600 million smart cards sold last year, primarily for prepaid, disposable card applications like prepaid phone cards. Card readers (also known as card-accepting devices) perform fixed operations (e.g., add, subtract, and delete) on memory cards.

Optical memory cards have a piece of (optical) compact disk glued on their surface. Up to 4 MB of data can be stored on the card, once and forever. Optical memory cards can be used to store rarely changed data like driving records and medical files. The number of related applications will grow in the future, when these cards include a processor.

Although regular strip cards cost about $0.20 each, memory cards cost about $1. Prices for microprocessor and optical cards are around $10 each. Card readers are more expensive—around $500—and even higher for optical memory card readers—about $3,000.

What Is a JavaCard?

A tiny member of the J2ME family, the JavaCard (the smallest and one of the most successful of Java's children) is probably the closest to the original idea of Java as an engine for tiny programs running on multiple appliances. JavaCard specifications enable Java technology to run on smart cards and other devices with limited memory.

The JavaCard application program interface (API) provides an application environment compatible with international standards for smart cards, such as ISO 7816 and EMV, that define physical, electronic, and operating features of the card. For example, according to the specification, the size of a smart card is 85 × 54 × 0.76 millimeters.

More than 90 percent of the worldwide smart card manufacturers have licensed the JavaCard Application Environment. This technology is not new for most of them. For example, the leading smart card manufacturer, Gemplus, early recognized the unique benefits of JavaCard and when I trained their development team in Montreal, Canada, in 2000 they already started working with this technology.

JavaCard technology inherits the interoperability and security of the Java language. Java applets developed with JavaCard technology can run on any JavaCard technology-based smart card, independently of the card vendor and hardware. Multiple applets can coexist securely on a single smart card, and new applets can be dynamically installed after a card has been issued. Multiple applets can belong to the same package and pass control among one another; these are called *multiselectable* applets.

Why Do We Use Multiple Keys?

I have a key for the door at home, one for my sister's house (to feed her cat when she is on vacation), two for my workplace, one for the car, and one for another car. In my pocket, I also keep handy a couple of credit cards, a medical insurance card, a payphone card, a library card, and a video rental card. (Sorry, I almost forgot my driver's license!)

All these objects in my pocket (sometimes I have cash there too) serve as identity and access keys.

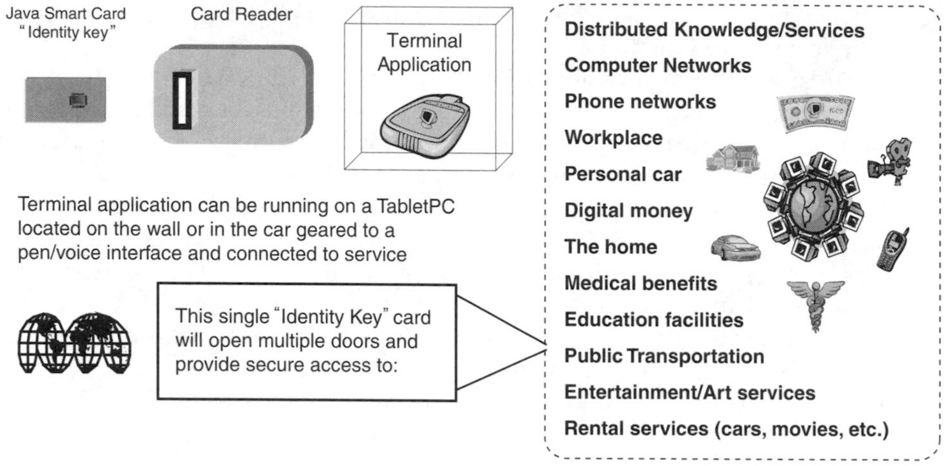

FIGURE 10.1. A Single Card Key to all Doors and Services.

CAN WE HAVE A SINGLE "IDENTITY KEY"?

JavaCard technology is going to simplify our lives in many ways. First of all, it will decrease or eliminate a number of keys and cards we currently keep handy in our pockets.

Figure 10.1 shows this identity key as a single JavaCard that works with a card reader at any door or for any service. The same card can also help identify a driver, rent a movie, order dinner, or use distributed knowledge and service networks. The card can exchange data with a card reader and provide you with secure access to any computerized services where your identity data are important. The service may require an interactive interface, which may be provided by a terminal application—for example, one running on a Tablet PC geared to a pen and voice interface. A card reader on a Tablet PC may be placed on any wall in a store, hotel, or airport or in a car or on public transportation.

The single identity key would provide access to the world of all public services paid for by digital money and to the world of distributed private services owned by groups and ruled by group memberships, roles, and virtual currency (contribution/consumption score) data.

HOW TO PROGRAM JAVACARDS

Sun Microsystems provides the JavaCard 2.2 Runtime Environment (JCRE) Specification and the JavaCard Development Kit [1] free of charge.

Java programs that run on JCRE are applets, but they are different from regular Java applets running on PCs. Unlike a JVM running on a PC, the JavaCard Virtual Machine appears to run forever. It stops only temporarily when the power is off; when the power is back on, it starts up again and recovers its previous object heap from persistent storage.

When the card is inserted in the card reader and powered up, the card session begins; when the card is removed, the session ends. The card reader is often called the *card acceptance device (CAD)*. The mechanism of data transfer between the CAD and the card is defined by the ISO 7816 specification. Java programmers work with its implementation in the Application

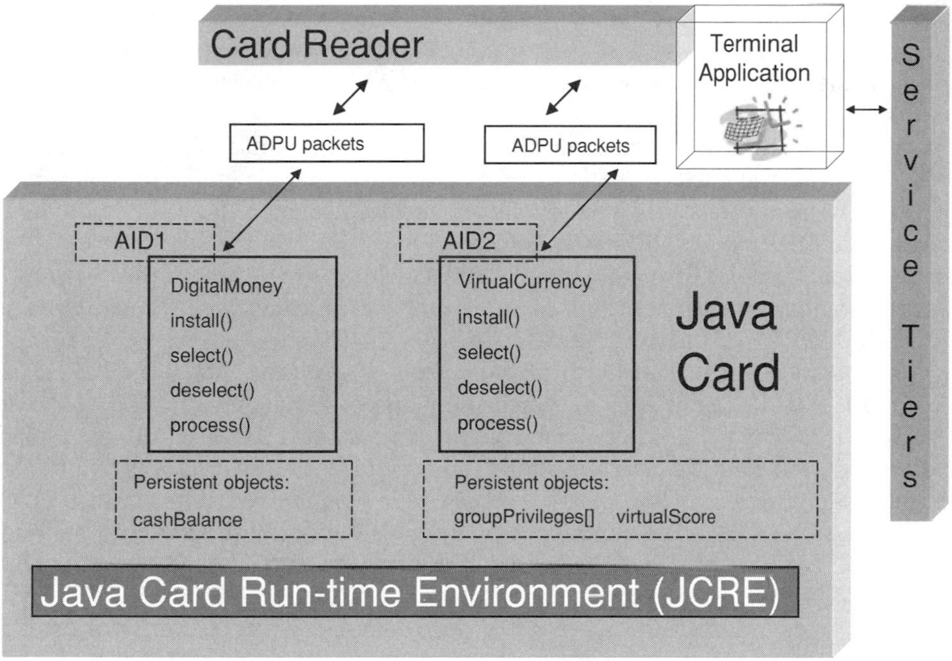

FIGURE 10.2. A JavaCard with the DigitalMoney and VirtualCurrency Applets.

Protocol Data Units (APDUs), the messaging structure that is used by JavaCard applets to interact with a card reader.

A JavaCard can contain one or more applets, as in Fig. 10.2. The *DigitalMoney* applet is responsible for cash management. Each time I buy or sell a product or service, this applet manages the cash balance and makes it persistent. The *VirtualCurrency* applet is responsible for my access to the world of distributed knowledge and other services that accept virtual currency. Each time I contribute to this world or consume its data or services, the *VirtualCurrency* applet sends information related to my memberships and privileges to the system (these data can influence "price") and keeps track of my virtual currency score and makes it persistent.

The *DigitalMoney* applet gives us easy access to public services, whereas the *VirtualCurrency* applet opens the doors of group-owned private services. We often feel more secure behind gated communities where members are well known. Groups and collaborative services might serve as an escape from the urban areas of the public Internet.

It is possible for the *VirtualCurrency* applet to pass control to the *DigitalMoney* applet—for example, in a case in which the requested knowledge service is not pleased with my current virtual score and requires cash instead.

The applets interact via APDU packets with the card reader and further with terminal applications running, for example, on a Tablet PC (geared to a pen/voice interface) located on a hotel or airport wall, at the video store, in the car, at home, or connected over a wire or wireless device to service provider networks.

Each applet has a unique application identifier (AID). An AID consists of two pieces: a registered ID (RID) and a proprietary extension (PIX). The RID is a 5-byte company ID assigned by ISO. The PIX is a variable-length (0 to 11 bytes) ID assigned to each applet by the company. This rule, established by ISO, helps to uniquely identify any JavaCard program. The JavaCard API includes the AID class with RID and PIX properties that support this rule. Later in the chapter, there is an example of how the AID class can be used in the JavaCard applet for other purposes.

A JavaCard applet interacts with the JCRE via the applet's public methods that reflect the applet's life cycle: *install, select, deselect*, and *process*. (Regular Java applet life cycle methods are *init, start, stop*, and *destroy*.) A programmer must implement at least the *install* method, which is called once by the JCRE when the applet is installed on the smart card.

The *install* method usually calls an applet constructor to create an instance of the applet, allocate its memory, and register this instance with the card reader or CAD. The constructor is private, and JCRE never calls it directly.

The applets are still not active until they are explicitly selected when the JCRE receives a SELECT FILE APDU command in which the name data matches the AID of the applet or a MANAGE CHANNEL OPEN command. In either case, JCRE deselects the previously selected applet and calls the *select()* method on the currently selected applet. The default *select()* method returns true, but this method can be overridden and, for example, can check if the PIN is not blocked. If the applet returns true, JCRE will call the *process()* method and pass the actual SELECT FILE APDU command to the method.

The *process()* method can examine the APDU packet data, perform data handling, change persistent storage, and send and receive more APDU packets if exchange with the CAD is needed.

To program the JavaCard, we use a limited Java language and manipulate several primitives and objects.

WHAT ARE JAVACARD PROGRAMMING'S LIMITATIONS?

We cannot use familiar Java packages. Instead, the only class we can reuse from J2SE is the *Object* class, and even that class is missing most of its methods.

We do not have the luxury of using String or the *java.io* package (except the *java.io.IOException* class). We still can use *byte, short, int*, and Boolean primitives, and single-dimensional arrays.

The JavaCard 2.2 specification brought several pleasant surprises. For example, we can now use the *java.rmi* package that defines the *Remote* interface. The *Remote* interface identifies methods on the JavaCard that can be invoked remotely from a terminal application running on a CAD. *java.rmi.RemoteException* can be thrown to indicate that an exception occurred during the execution of a remote method call.

THE *javacard.framework* PACKAGE FOR JAVACARD PROGRAMMING

The *javacard.framework* package includes powerful interfaces: *ISO7816, MultiSelectable, PIN*, and *Shareable*, as well as important framework classes like *AID, APDU, OwnerPin, Util*, and *Applet*.

The *ISO7816* interface contains static fields that represent constants related to ISO 7816-3 and 7816-4.

The *MultiSelectable* interface identifies the implementing applet as capable of several concurrent selections. Such applets can belong to the same package and pass control among one another.

The *PIN* interface represents a PIN value and its validation methods.

The *Shareable* interface serves to identify any object that needs to be shared through the applet firewall.

The *javacard.framework.service* package includes classes and interfaces to design a JavaCard applet as an aggregation of service components that implement *javacard.framework.service.Service* interface, and use *javacard.framework.service.BasicService* or other package classes and interfaces.

The *javacard.security* and *javacard.crypto* packages help implement a security and cryptography framework on a JavaCard.

WRITING A SAMPLE JAVACARD APPLET: *VirtualCurrency*

Armed with the knowledge gained so far, we can write the *VirtualCurrency* applet. *VirtualCurrency* is a JavaCard applet that provides access to multiple services that accept a virtual score or virtual currency earned by contributing to these services. Services belong to several groups. Service provider groups use group memberships as well as group privilege (role) data to estimate the service or data "price" for the consumer.

Services and requested data change their values dynamically in the distributed knowledge or service system, based on their usage by consumers.

Knowledge or service contribution can change a contributor's group ranking or his or her privileges. In this case, the Java- or .NET-based terminal system sends a command to the applet to set group roles for a specified group.

VirtualCurrency Data Structures

We begin programming the applet with the *VirtualCurrency* class definition and introduce its properties. We define the static *VirtualCurrency_CLA* value: a byte with a hexadecimal value that represents this applet class and ensures that APDUs are sent to the proper applet and can be handled by the applet.

Then we define static byte values to represent operations requested by a terminal application via APDUs and performed by the applet.

We define the digital command values for the applet operations: the *checkPin()*, *getAllGroupPrivileges()*, *getGroupRoles()*, and *setGroupRoles()* operations that will manage group role values; the *getVirtualScore()* operation that returns a current score; and the *addScore()* and *subtractScore()* operations.

Then we define our persistent object's *virtualScore* and the array of *groupRoles*. We also define the byte array to store identity values.

We define the *virtualScore* as the *short* type value, which can vary from –32,768 to 32,767 or from 0 to 65,535.

We want to define group role values as objects that consist of a *groupID* and related *RoleIDs*. One person can play more than one role in the group. Taking into account JavaCard constraints, we simplify this presentation on the JavaCard side and shift more work to the terminal application that can enjoy the full power of J2EE.

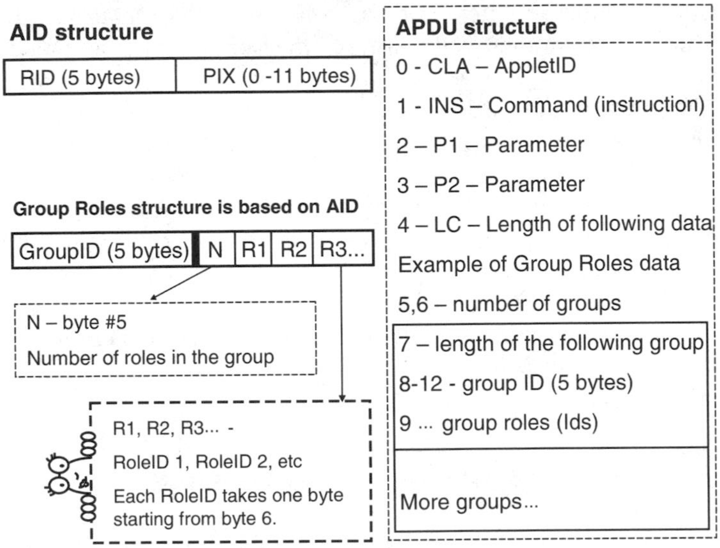

FIGURE 10.3. The Application Identifier (AID), *GroupRole*, and APDU Structures.

We now use the *AID* class (consisting of two parts: RID and PIX) to represent *groupRoles*. Group role objects also consist of two parts: the *groupID* and the *RoleID(s)*. We place the *groupID* in the first 5 bytes of the AID object, which usually serves to hold the RID. We place the *roleID(s)* in the second (flexible-length) part of the AID object, which usually serves to hold the PIX.

Figure 10.3 represents the AID structure and the *groupRoles* object structure.

We define the *groupID* with the first 5 bytes in the *groupRole* object. Then, the first byte in the second part of the object shows the number of roles, and the following bytes represent the role IDs. If the number of roles is more than 10, additional AID object(s) should be used to represent additional roles for the same group, because in this example we assume that the number of roles for one person in any group is limited to 10.

At the bottom of Fig. 10.3, we transform AID objects into a byte array for APDU exchange. The transformation is straightforward. The first 2 bytes in the sequence represent the total number of AID objects. Every AID object starts with the byte that holds the length of the object, followed by the AID object bytes.

Note that the first 5 bytes of the APDU have a fixed meaning for all commands. The CLA byte identifies the applet. The INS byte carries a current instruction (command). The P1 and P2 bytes are reserved for some parameters related to the command. Finally, the LC byte tells us about the following number of bytes of data. This number indicates the number of bytes the system sends to the applet or expects to receive from the applet in response to the current command.

Figure 10.4 introduces the *VirtualCurrency* applet as a public class with its properties, and the private constructor.

VirtualCurrency Applet Standard Methods

The *VirtualCurrency* private constructor creates the *ownerPin* object and calls the *update()* method on the object. Installation parameters passed to the *update()* method will initialize the PIN value. The last thing the constructor does is register the applet.

```
// VirtualCurrency

package com.its.javacard;

import javacard.framework.*;

/**
 * The VirtualCurrency is a javacard applet that provides access
 * to multiple services that accept virtual score or virtual currency
 * earned by contributing to these services.
 * Services belong to multiple groups.
 * Service provider groups use group memberships as well as group
 * privilege (Role)
 * data to estimate the service or data "price" for the consumer.
 * Services and requested data change their values dynamically in
 * the distributed knowledge/service system based on their usage by
 * consumers.
 * Knowledge or service contribution can change contributor's ranking or
 * her/his privileges (roles).
 * In this case the (Java or .Net based) terminal system would send
 * a command
 * to the applet to set (reset) group roles (for a specified group).
 * @author Jeff.Zhuk@JavaSchool.com
 */
public class VirtualCurrency extends Applet {
    final static byte VirtualCurrency_CLA = (byte) 0x18;
    // code is up to you
    final static byte CHECK_PIN = (byte) 0x17;
    final static byte GET_GROUP_PRIVILEGES = (byte) 0x16;
    final static byte SET_GROUP_PRIVILEGES = (byte) 0x15;
    final static byte GET_VIRTUAL_SCORE = (byte) 0x14;
    final static byte ADD_SCORE = (byte) 0x13;
    final static byte SUBTRACT_SCORE = (byte) 0x12;
    final static byte GET_IDENTITY = (byte) 0x11;

    final static byte SELECT_APDU_COMMAND = (byte) (0xA4); // standard code
    final static short SW_PIN_VERIFICATION_REQUIRED = 0x6301;
    final static short SW_PIN_VERIFICATION_FAILED = 0x6300;

    final static byte MAXIMUM_BYTES_FOR_PIN = (byte) 0x8;
    final static byte NUMBER_OF_TRIES_IF_PIN_BLOCKED = (byte) 0x5;

    // ownerPin object that keeps PIN value
    OwnerPin ownerPin;
    // total virtual score
    private short virtualScore;
    // array of group privileges (roles)
    private AID[] groupRoles;
    // each consists of the groupID and one or more roleID
    private byte[] identity; // identity bytes (set by another applet)
```

FIGURE 10.4

```
/**
 * private constructor is called by the install() method
 * with the installation parameters passed by the JCRE
 */
private VirtualCurrency (byte [] byteArray, short byteOffset,
  byte byteLength) {
    // create and init the PIN
    ownerPin = new OwnerPin(NUMBER_OF_TRIES_IF_PIN_BLOCKED,
      MAXIMUM_BYTES_FOR_PIN);
    // register
    ownerPin.update(byteArray, byteOffset, byteLength);
}
```

FIGURE 10.4. (*cont.*)

Figure 10.5 includes the *install()*, *select()*, and *deselect()* methods. The static *install()* method receives installation parameters from the JCRE and passes these parameters to the private constructor applet described above. The applet remains in the suspended (inactive) state until it is explicitly selected by the JCRE. When the JCRE receives a SELECT APDU command from the CAD, it calls the selected method on the applet. If any other applet was previously selected, the JCRE deselects that applet before selecting the new one.

The *select()* method checks if the security PIN can be identified. The *select()* method returns false or rejects the selection if the PIN is blocked. Otherwise, the *select()* method returns true.

The JCRE calls the *deselect()* method on the currently selected applet if it receives a SELECT APDU command with a different applet AID. The *deselect()* method in our example just resets the PIN value. It may also perform any other cleanup operation, if necessary. Keep in mind that the JavaCard has no garbage collection services.

Figure 10.6 shows the *process()* method of the *VirtualCurrency* applet, which handles operations on the applet data. The JCRE calls the *process()* method after the applet has been selected. The JCRE passes all APDU commands (starting with the SELECT APDU command) to the *process()* method. The *process()* method retrieves a command and related data from the APDU byte array, calls a proper processing method, generates and sends a response back to the JCRE, and so on.

In our example, the *process()* method reads the APDU data into a buffer and starts with several verifications. The method checks if the current command is not the SELECT_APDU command, which also comes to the *process()* method. Then, the *process()* method checks the CLA byte to verify that the APDU packets target this and not another applet.

Then, if previous verifications were successful, the applet can start processing. It is a good idea to start with yet another check. This time, we check access authentication using the *OwnerPin* method *isValidated*(). The applet would throw an *ISOException* if there *were* an access problem.

The *process()* method continues with its analysis of the command byte of the APDU. In the switch statement inside the *process()* method, the applet calls one of six operation methods, according to the command in the APDU packet, and returns control to the JCRE.

```
/** The JCRE calls the install() method with installation parameters
 * The install() method calls the private constructor and
 * passes the parameters to the constructor
 */
public static void install(byte [] byteArray, short byteOffset,
  byte byteLength) {
    new VirtualCurrency(byteArray, byteOffset, byteLength);
}

/** The applet will remain in the suspended (not active) state
 * till it will be explicitly selected by the JCRE.
 * The JCRE receives a SELECT APDU command from the CAD and
 * calls the select method on the applet.
 * The select() method checks if the pin is not blocked.
 * The select() method returns false or reject selection if the pin
 * is blocked.
 * Otherwise the select() method returns true.
 */
public boolean select() {
    // check if PIN is blocked
    if(ownerPin.getTriesRemaining() == 0) {
        return false;
    }
    return true;
    }

/** The JCRE calls the deselect() method when on the currently
 * selected applet
 * in the case the JCRE receives a SELECT APDU command with the
 * different applet AID.
 * The deselect() method resets the pin value.
 * It could also perform any cleanup operation if necessary.
 * Keep in mind that Java Card has no garbage collection services.
 */
public void deselect() {
    ownerPin.reset();
}
```

Figure 10.5

VirtualCurrency Application: Specific Methods

The six processing methods are defined below as *private* methods. They cannot be directly called outside the *VirtualCurrency* applet.

Figure 10.7 presents the *checkPIN()* method, which retrieves the PIN data from APDU and compares them with the *ownerPin* properties using the *ownerPin.check()* method. The PIN data are located at the offset ISO7816.OFFSET_CDATA.

The *getAllGroupPrivileges()* method (Fig. 10.8) constructs a byte array from an array of group roles. After this transformation, the method sends this byte array in the response data packet (APDU).

```
/**
 * The JCRE calls the process() method after the applet has been selected.
 * The JCRE passes all APDU commands (starting with the SELECT APDU
 * command) to the process() method.
 * The process() method retrieves a command and related data from the
 * APDU byte array,
 * calls a proper processing method, generates and sends response back
 * to the JCRE, etc.
 *
 * The process() method reads the APDU data into a byteArray and
 * starts with verification that the command is not SELECT and
 * the APDU packets targets this (not another) applet.
 * If this verification is successful the method continues with analysis
 * of the command byte.
 * In the switch statement (inside the process() method) the applet calls
 * one of six operation-methods, according to the command in the APDU packet,
 * and returns control to the JCRE.
 * @param apdu
 */
public void process(APDU apdu) {
    // read apdu in the byteArray
    byte[] byteArray = apdu.getBuffer();

    // The SELECT APDU command will also come to the process method in the APDU
    // The process method does nothing on the SELECT command
    if (byteArray[ISO7816.OFFSET_CLA] == SELECT_APDU_COMMAND) {
        return;
    }

    // check CLA byte should match the applet code
    if (byteArray[ISO7816.OFFSET_CLA] != VirtualCurrency_CLA) {
        return; // or throws javacard.framework.ISOException
    }

    // check access authentication
    if (! ownerPin.isValidated() ) {
       ISOException.thorwIt (SW_PIN_VERIFICATION_REQUIRED);
    }

    // check requested service
    switch (byteArray[ISO7816.OFFSET_INS]) {
        case CHECK_PIN: checkPIN(apdu);
        return;

        case GET_ALL_GROUP_PRIVILEGES: getAllGroupPrivileges(apdu);
        return;

        case GET_GROUP_ROLES: getGroupRoles(apdu);
        return;
        case SET_GROUP_ROLES: setGroupRoles(apdu);
        return;

        case GET_VIRTUAL_SCORE: getVirtualScore(apdu);
        return;
```

FIGURE 10.6

```
        case ADD_SCORE: addScore(apdu);
        return;

        case SUBTRACT_SCORE: subtractScore(apdu);
        return;

        case GET_IDENTITY: getIdentity(apdu);
        return;

        default: ISOException.throwIt(ISO7816.SW_INS_NOT_SUPPORTED);
    }
  } // end of proccess method
```

FIGURE 10.6. *(cont.)*

The method first checks to determine whether the *groupRoles* object is null. If by chance, no membership data are found, the method prepares the APDU buffer for this disappointing response.

Otherwise, the *getAllGroupPrivileges()* method prepares the byte array as a buffer for all group roles. We calculate the length of this buffer and allocate the byte array. We then place all group roles into the buffer using a very convenient method, *getBytes()* of the AID class.

The prepared byte array may be larger than the APDU internal buffer. There is a special method of the APDU class called *sendBytesLong()* that manages the APDU buffer. If the number of bytes to send is larger than the APDU buffer, the method will provide several transmissions.

```
  /**
   * The checkPIN() method retrieves the PIN data from APDU
   * and compares with the ownerPin properties using the
   * ownerPin.check() method.
   * The PIN data is located at the offset ISO7816.OFFSET_CDATA
   * @param apdu
   */
 private void checkPIN(APDU apdu) {
     // read apdu to byteArray
     byte[] byteArray = apdu.getBuffer();

     // prepare to get PIN data
     byte readCount = (byte)apdu.setIncomingAndReceive();
     // get PIN and compare
     if(ownerPin.check(byteArray, ISO7816.OFFSET_CDATA, readCount) ==
       false) {
         ISOException.throwIt(SW_VERIFICATION_FAILED);
     } // otherwise it is a success
 }
```

FIGURE 10.7

```
/**
 * The getAllGroupPrivileges() method constructs array of group roles into
 * a byte array and sends a response APDU to the system.
 * @param apdu
 */
public void getAllGroupPrivileges(APDU apdu) {
    // read apdu to byteArray
    byte[] byteArray = apdu.getBuffer();

    // check if groupRoles are null
    if(groupRoles == null) {
        // prepare apdu buffer for this disappointing response
        byteArray[0] = (byte)0;
        byteArray[1] = (byte)0;
        apdu.setOutgoingAndSend((short)0, (short)2); // send 2 bytes
        return;
    }
    // transform group roles into a byte array
    // calculate the length of the roles byte array
    short len = 2; // first two bytes hold the total number of group roles
    byte[] buffer = null;
    short numberOfGroupRoles = groupRoles.length;
    byte[] arrayOfGroupRoleLengths = new byte[numberOfGroupRoles];
    for(short i=0; i<groupRoles.length; i++) {
        arrayOfGroupRoleLengths[i] = groupRoles[i].getBytes(buffer, 0);
        len++; // one more byte to represent the length of this groupRole
        len += arrayOfGroupRoleLengths[i]; // add the length of this object
    }
    // allocate a byte array of known size
    buffer = new byte[len];
    // place number of roles first
    // place two bytes creating a short value
    buffer[0] = (byte) numberOfGroupRoles >> 8;
    buffer[1] = (byte) (numberOfGroupRoles & 0xFF);

    // place all group roles into the buffer
    short offset = 2;
    for(short i=0; i<groupRoles.length; i++) {
        buffer[offset++] = (byte)arrayOfGroupRoleLengths[i];
        // length of the object
        offset += groupRoles[i].getBytes(buffer, offset);
        // place the group role object
    }
    // the apdu.sendBytesLong() method manages apdu buffer and
    // (if number of bytes to send is bigger than APDU buffer)
    // the method can provide several transmissions
    apdu.sendBytesLong(buffer, (short)0, (short)len);
}
```

FIGURE 10.8

```
/**
 * The getGroupRoles() method reads APDU data and
 * constructs an AID object of group roles for a specified group
 * Then it transforms the object into a byte array and
 * sends the APDU response to the system.
 * @param apdu
 */
public void getGroupRoles(APDU apdu) {
    // read apdu to byteArray
    byte[] byteArray = apdu.getBuffer();

    // check if groupRoles are null
    if(groupRoles == null) {
        // prepare apdu buffer for this disappointing response
        byteArray[0] = (byte)0;
        byteArray[1] = (byte)0;
        apdu.setOutgoingAndSend((short)0, (short)2); // send 2 bytes
        return;
    }
    // read APDU bytes into a buffer to construct a groupRole object
    AID specifiedGroup = readAIDobject(apdu, byteArray);
    short groupIndex = getGroupIndex(specifiedGroup);
    if(groupIndex < 0) {  // groupIndex can be ERROR-coded
        // prepare apdu buffer for this disappointing response
        buffer[0] = (byte) groupIndex >> 8;
        buffer[1] = (byte) (groupIndex & 0xFF);
        apdu.setOutgoingAndSend((short)0, (short)2); // send 2 bytes
        return;
    }
    // get group roles for the specified group
    // transform group roles into a byte array
    // calculate the length of the roles byte array
    short len = apdu.setOutgoing();
    len = groupRoles[groupIndex].getBytes(byteArray, 0);
    apdu.setOutgoingLength( (short)len );
    // send response
    apdu.sendBytes ( (short)0 , (short)len );
}
```

FIGURE 10.9

The *getGroupRoles()* method (Fig. 10.9) begins by assigning the APDU buffer. This method uses the *readAIDObject()* to get the argument with the specified *groupID* from the APDU. (We use the AID class to represent group roles.) Then *getGroupRoles()* uses the *getGroupIndex()* to point to the proper element in the array of group roles.

The program takes this group roles element and prepares the response bytes that will be sent via APDU to the system.

The *setGroupRoles()* method (Fig. 10.10) does the opposite operation. It also starts by assigning the APDU buffer, uses *readAIDObject()* to get the argument with the specified *groupID* from the APDU, and uses *getGroupIndex()* to point to the proper element in the

```
/**
 * The setGroupRoles() method reads APDU data and
 * constructs an AID object of group roles for a specified group
 * Then the method replaces existing group roles for the specified group
 * with the new data
 * @param apdu
 */
public void setGroupRoles(APDU apdu) {
    // read apdu to byteArray
    byte[] byteArray = apdu.getBuffer();

    // read APDU bytes into a buffer to construct a groupRole object
    AID specifiedGroup = readAIDobject(apdu, byteArray);
    short groupIndex = getGroupIndex(specifiedGroup);
    // set new specifiedGroup value in the persistent groupRoles array
    if(groupIndex < 0) {  // set a new group
        if(groupRoles == null) { // no groups at all?
            groupRoles = new AID[1];
            groupRoles[0] = specifiedGroup;
        } else { // increase an array of groups
            AID[] tempRoles = groupRoles;
            groupRoles = new AID[tempRoles.length + 1];
            for(short i=0; i<tempRoles.length; i++) {
                groupRoles[i] = tempRoles[i];
            }
            groupRoles[tempRoles.length] = specifiedGroup;
        }
    } else { // reset existing group
        groupRoles[groupIndex] = specifiedGroup;
    }
    return;
}
```

FIGURE 10.10

array of group roles. Then, *setGroupRoles()* replaces the current group roles for the specified group with the new group roles freshly received from the system.

The *readAIDObject()* method (Fig. 10.11) reads several bytes that represent the AID object from the APDU. In this example, we use the AID object as the *groupRoles* object for a single group. The method constructs the object from APDU bytes and returns the object.

The *getGroupIndex()* method (Fig. 10.12) (as well as the *readAIDObject()* method) is called by the *getGroupRoles()* and *setGroupRoles()* methods. The *getGroupIndex()* method compares the AID value that was passed as a parameter to the elements of the *groupRoles* array and returns an existing group index or a negative error value. The error value is –1 if no groups exist, or –2 if a specified group is not found. The *getGroupIndex()* method uses *RIDEquals()* of the AID class for comparison.

The *getVirtualScore()* method (Fig. 10.13) packs a 2-byte response and sends the current virtual score to the system.

Figure 10.14 displays the *addScore()* method. Imagine one of the system users consumes some data or service contributed by a JavaCard owner. The next time the owner uses his or

```
/**
 * The readAIDObject() method is used by getGroupRoles() and setGroupRoles()
 * methods
 * The method reads from APDU several bytes that represent the groupRole
 * object
 * The method constructs and returns a groupRoles object
 * @param apdu
 * @param apduBuffer
 * @return aidObject
 */
 private AID readAIDObject(APDU apdu, byte[] apduBuffer) {
     // Read LC byte to define the incoming apdu command length
     short bytesLeft = (short) (apduBuffer[ISO7816.OFFSET_LC] & 0x00FF);
     short AIDlength = bytesLeft;
     short readCount = apdu.setIncomingAndReceive();
     // skip first 5 header bytes and start reading into the byteArray
     // from the byte number 5 (ISO7816.OFFSET_CDATA)
     while ( bytesLeft > 0) {
         bytesLeft -= readCount;
         readCount = apdu.receiveBytes ( ISO7816.OFFSET_CDATA );
     }
     // construct AID object
     AID aidObject = new AID(apduBuffer, ISO7816.OFFSET_CDATA, AIDlength);
     return aidObject;
}
```

FIGURE 10.11

```
/**
 * The getGroupIndex() method compares passed as a parameter AID value
 * to the elements of the groupRoles array and returns an index or
 * a negative error value
 * @param group
 * @return groupIndex or -1 if no groups exist or -2 if specified group
 * is not found
 */
private short getGroupIndex(AID group) {
    if(groupRoles == null) {
        return (short)-1;
    }
    for(short i=0; i<groupRoles.length; i++) {
        // use RIDEquals() method of AID class
        if(groupRoles[i].RIDEquals(group)) {
            return (short)i;
        }
    }
    return (short) -2;
}
```

FIGURE 10.12

```
/**
 * The getVirtualScore() method constructs a two byte APDU response and
 * sends the APDU response to the system.
 * @param apdu
 */
public void getVirtualScore(APDU apdu) {
    // read apdu to byteArray
    byte[] byteArray = apdu.getBuffer();
    buffer[0] = (byte) virtualScore >> 8;
    buffer[1] = (byte) (virtualScore & 0xFF);
    apdu.setOutgoingAndSend((short)0, (short)2); // send 2 bytes
    return;
}
```

FIGURE 10.13

her JavaCard, he or she receives (via the terminal application) additional virtual currency. The *addScore()* method reads an additional score sent by one of the groups to the person from the APDU and adds that score to the current virtual score that is stored persistently on the card.

The *subtractScore()* method (Fig. 10.15) acts like *addScore()*, except the score is subtracted from the current virtual score. Say the owner of a JavaCard wants to consume some service and has placed his or her card into the card reader. The terminal application subtracts some virtual currency score. We rely on the terminal application's intelligence to simplify the JavaCard program. For example, the terminal application can check the current virtual score to see if it is enough before requesting the *subtractScore()* operation and performing the service.

The last method of the applet is the *getIdentity()* method (Fig. 10.16), which transforms an array of bytes with identity values into the APDU buffer and sends this buffer to the

```
/**
 * The addScore() method adds points to the current virtual score
 * @param apdu
 */
public void addScore(APDU apdu) {
    // read apdu to byteArray
    byte[] byteArray = apdu.getBuffer();
    short readCount = apdu.setIncomingAndReceive();
    // skip first 5 header bytes and start reading into the byteArray
    // from the byte number 5 (ISO7816.OFFSET_CDATA)
    // limit the score change to one byte value
    byte additionalScore = byteArray[ISO7816.OFFSET_CDATA];
    virtualScore = (short) (virtualScore + additionalScore);
}
```

FIGURE 10.14

```
/**
 * The subtractScore() method decreases points of the current virtual score
 * @param apdu
 */
public void subtractScore(APDU apdu) {
    // read apdu to byteArray
    byte[] byteArray = apdu.getBuffer();
    short readCount = apdu.setIncomingAndReceive();
    // skip first 5 header bytes and start reading into the byteArray
    // from the byte number 5 (ISO7816.OFFSET_CDATA)
    // limit the score change to one byte value
    byte decreaseScore = byteArray[ISO7816.OFFSET_CDATA];
    virtualScore = (short) (virtualScore - decreaseScore);
}
```

FIGURE 10.15

```
    /**
     * The getIdentity() method constructs a multi-byte APDU response and
     * sends identoty data to the system.
     * @param apdu
     */
    public void getIdentity(APDU apdu) {
        // read apdu to byteArray
        byte[] byteArray = apdu.getBuffer();
        if(identity == null) {
            // prepare apdu buffer for this disappointing response
            byteArray[0] = (byte)0;
            byteArray[1] = (byte)0;
            apdu.setOutgoingAndSend((short)0, (short)2); // send 2 bytes
            return;
        }
        // put number of bytes in the identity array first
        byteArray[0] = identity.length; // limited to 256 number of bytes
        // place all identity bytes into the buffer
        for(short i=0; i<identity.length; i++) {
            byteArray[i+1] = identity[i];
        }
        // the apdu.sendBytesLong() method manages apdu buffer and
        // (if number of bytes to send is bigger than APDU buffer)
        // the method can provide several transmissions
        short len = (short) (identity.length + 1);
        apdu.sendBytesLong(buffer, (short)0, (short)len);
    }
 } // end of the VirtualCurrency class
```

FIGURE 10.16

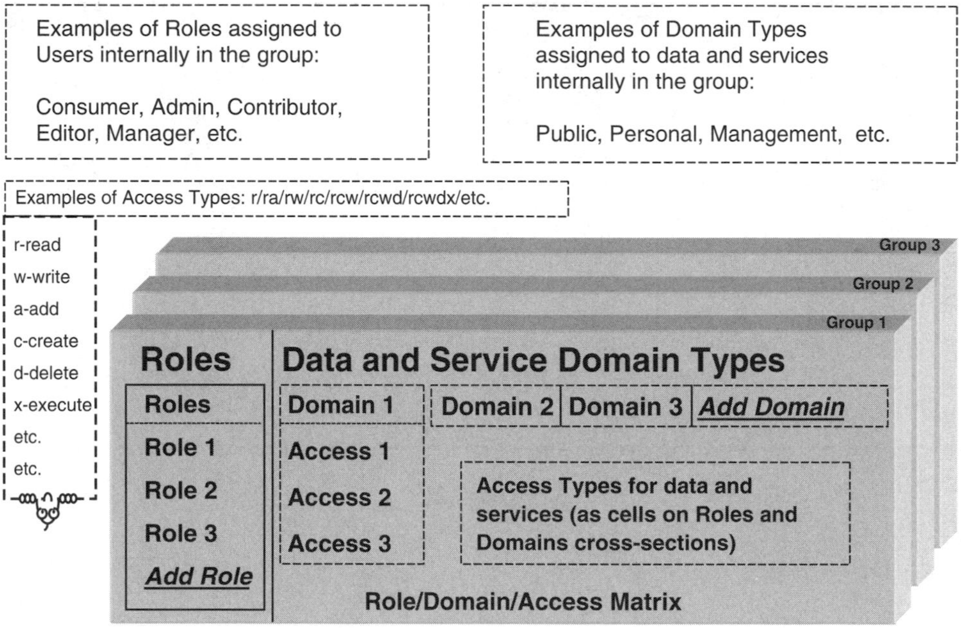

Figure 10.17. Role/Domain/Access Matrix.

system. Note that the very first byte set by this method indicates the number of bytes in the response.

JavaCard-Based Matrix of Membership Roles and Privileges

The strategy for developing JavaCard-based applications is to keep the absolute minimum amount of data on the card, perform the absolute minimum amount of operations on these data, and outsource heavy tasks to terminal applications.

For example, a terminal application that provides access to distributed knowledge and services unpacks group membership data to check privilege-based access. When a user requests a service or data via the terminal application, the terminal application grants a specific access type using the access matrix rules provided in the distributed knowledge system [2].

Figure 10.17 shows an example of the access matrix based on user roles and data and service internal domain types.

Every group can create internal member roles and assign data and services to specific domain types that fit its group agenda. For example, a group of consultants may have roles such as "Developer," "Release Manager," and "Editor" and domain types such as "Source," "Documentation," "Personal," "Plan," "Status," and "Management." Naturally, a nonprofit group such as "Children under 10" can have different roles and domain types.

Upon a user service request, the terminal application retrieves membership data from the JavaCard, unpacks these data, and applies role IDs to the matrix of access rules. The terminal application grants the proper access type—for example, "read" or "read and create."

If the requested service is related to a knowledge or service contribution, the terminal application adds some value to the virtual score of the contributor, associates the new data or service with the contributor's identity key, and may prompt the contributor to indicate specific or default access rules.

If the requested service is related to knowledge or service consumption, the terminal application checks to see if the user's virtual currency amount is adequate and subtracts some score. At the same time, the terminal application may increase the value of the requested data or service upon its usage. The next user may find it more valuable or "expensive." The system may also prepare the *addScore* operation for the contributor of the data or service that was just consumed. The next time the contributor enters the system with her or his JavaCard, the terminal application increases her or his virtual score.

VirtualCurrency Review

In the example just described, we considered a single card with two applets that can represent two types of services: collaborative group services ruled by virtual score and membership values and regular services paid for with cash.

We decided, for security reasons, to use two different applets for these different worlds and to provide two different *AIDs* to these applets, although technologically, this can easily be done with one applet. The *DigitalMoney* applet owns its *digitalCash* object and has methods, such as *addScore()* and *subtractScore()*, that can change the value of the object.

Security Considerations

Note that we did not include the *setIdentity()* method in the applet. A more secure approach would be to provide such a method in a separate applet.

In this chapter we got a taste of Java and its JavaCard technology. How far are we from a single identity key? Technologically, it is not a problem anymore; it is more a matter of cooperation between private enterprise and government—which might be an even more complicated problem.

Integrating Question

Explain the concepts of smart cards and JavaCards, and propose an application for your business.

Case Study

1. Digital money is an understandable and working concept. What about groups and virtual currency? Can you provide any examples?
2. Research information on card readers and related terminal applications. Provide examples of terminal applications designed with Java and/or .NET technology.
3. Provide a scenario and a set of use cases for another JavaCard application.

References

1. JavaCard Technology Specification and Development Kit from Sun Microsystems, Inc.: *http://java.sun.products/javacard*.
2. Zhuk, J. Distributed active knowledge and process base. Patent Pending, *http://uspto.gov*.

CHAPTER 11

The J2ME Family

Happy families are all alike; every unhappy family is unhappy in its own way.
—Leo Tolstoy (1828–1910), *Anna Karenina*

This chapter reviews J2ME programming and provides an ambitious example of a wireless application.

The J2ME [1] family currently includes two members, which are defined by their configurations. The big brother's name is the Connected Device Configuration (CDC) [2]. The little brother has significant limitations that have affected even its name: the Connected Limited Device Configuration (CLDC) [3].

Figure 11.1 uncovers the J2ME family that lives in embedded devices. CLDC, combined with the Mobile Information Device Profile (MIDP), is the Java run-time environment for resource-constrained mobile information devices (MIDs) such as phones and entry-level PDAs with available memory from 128 KB to 512 KB. CDC contains a full-featured Java Virtual Machine (JVM) that typically runs on a 32-bit microprocessor/controller and manages more than 2.0 MB of total memory.

The CLDC application program interface (API) includes three Java packages that are familiar from J2SE—*java.io, java.lang*, and *java.util*—as well as a specific J2ME package: *java.microedition.io*. The familiar packages include only subsets of Java classes.

The *java.microedition.io* package includes networking interfaces and supports message connections. The powerful *java.microedition.io.Connector* class is a factory for creating new ***Connection*** objects based on a parameter string that conforms to the URL format as described in Request for Comments (RFC) 2396:

```
{scheme}:[{target}][{parameters}]
```

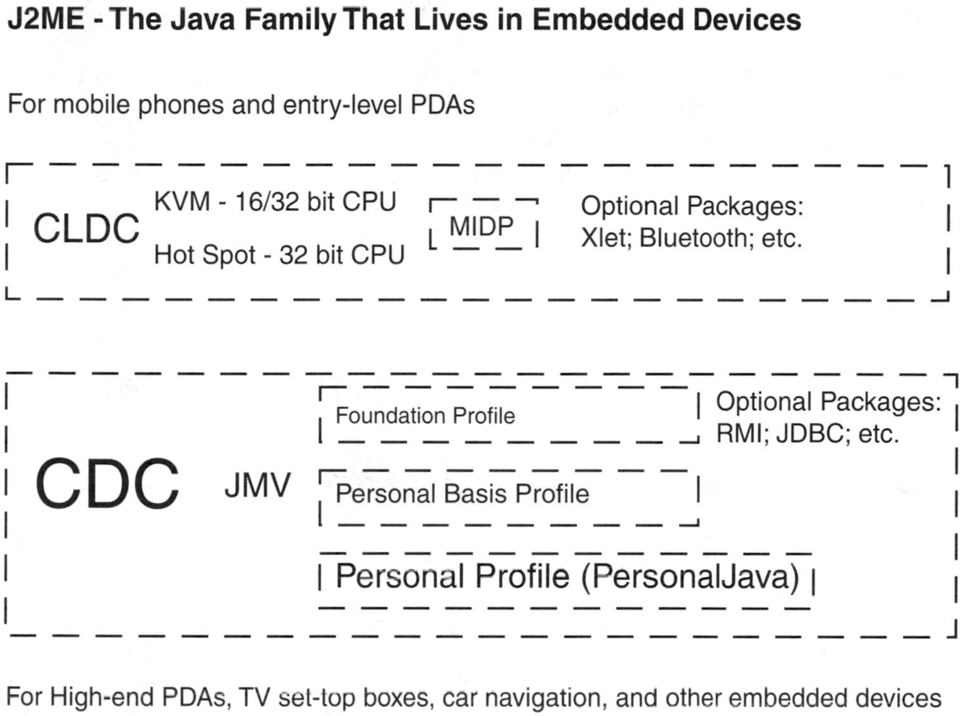

FIGURE 11.1. J2ME-: The Java Family That Lives in Embedded Devices.

where:

scheme is the name of a protocol, such as *HTTP* or *FTP*,
target is a network address, such as *IPServe.com* or *JavaSchool.com*,
parameters are formed as a set of key-value pairs, such as *service=mail&action=get*.

Here are several examples (from about sixteen different types of possible connections) of *Connection* objects created with the *Connector* factory:

```
// HTTPS Connection
HTTPSConnection httpsCon = (HTTPSConnection)
Connector.open("https://javaschool.com"); // DatagramConection
DatagramConnection datagramCon = (DatagramConnection)
Connector.open("datagram://javaschool.com:7654");
// CommConnection (serial connection to the "com2" port on your
MIDP device)
CommConnection serialCon = (CommConnection) Connector.open
("comm://com2");
```

The two lines below show how to figure out port names on your MIDP device:

```
String portNames = System.getProperty("microedition.commports");
String[] commports = portNames.split(",");
// ports are separated with the ","
```

You might need another split, because every *commport* can include optional parameters separated by the ";".

The family of MID profiles expects a new member. The PDA Profile, or PDAP, is an extension of the CLDC and the MIDP. At the same time, PDAP uses CPU and memory resources that are very close to CDC parameters.

Probably the largest number of J2ME applications runs on CLDC/MIDP devices. This chapter offers another ambitious example of a J2ME application running in this restricted environment. Let us take a close look at the MID profile.

The MIDP

The MIDP 2.0 specifications [4] define device type-specific sets of APIs that bring more power to wireless devices.

How Do We Display Screens and Handle Events?

We can build a user interface with the *javax.microedition.lcdui* package using classes similar to those of the Abstract Window Toolkit (AWT), such as *Canvas, Font, Graphics, List*, and *TextField*, as well as not-so-similar classes, such as *Command, Display, Form, Gauge, Item, Screen*, and *Ticker*.

The *Canvas* and *Screen* classes both extend the *Displayable* class. They are the main super classes for displayable objects. The *Canvas* class is used for writing applications such as games and has low-level graphics calls and the ability to handle low-level events. *Screen* is the base class for all high-level user interface classes, such as *Alert, Form, List*, and *TextBox*.

The *CommandListener* interface, like the *ActionListener* interface in AWT, is responsible for handling events. A class that implements this interface must implement the *void CommandAction(Command c, Displayable d)* method.

In the example below, we display a list of services. Each service name is associated with the proper class that initiates the service.

```
public class ServiceList extends List implements CommandListener
{
    private String[] services =
{"Mail","Article","SMS","AddressBook","Schedule"};
    public ServiceList()
{
    super(``Select Service", List.IMPLICIT);
    for(int i=0; i<services.length; i++) {
            append(services[i]);
}
    setCommandListener(this); // add CommandListener
}
// event handler; called upon user selection
public void commandAction (Command c, Displayable d)
{
if (d == this && c == List.SELECTCOMMAND) {
String service = services[getSelectedIndex()];
ServiceConnector connector = new ServiceConnector(service);
```

```
// invoke the init() method on the selected service object
// connector.init();
// assume that all services have the init() method
}
} // end of event handler
} // end of class
```

You can set a ticker, a message moving across the screen, with the two lines of code below.

```
Ticker ticker = new Ticker("You have news!");
someScreenObject.setTicker(ticker);
// some screen object, like List, Alert, etc.
```

You can develop rich gaming content with the *javax.microedition.lcdui.game* package. The package offers, for example, classes such as *Layer* and its extension, the *Sprite* class. This can be rendered with one of several frames stored in an *Image*, providing animated actions. You can even flip and rotate *Sprite* objects if you have a meaningful reason to do so.

MULTIMEDIA ON WIRELESS

The *javax.microedition.media* and *javax.microedition.media.control* packages implement the Mobile Media API (MMAPI) [5] and extend the functionality of the J2ME platform with audio, video, and other time-based multimedia support. The MMAPI packages allow Java developers to use native multimedia services available on a given device, such as simple tone generation, tone sequencing, audio/video file playback and streaming, interactive MIDI, and audio/video capture.

MMAPI was designed to support several protocols and formats. For example, it does not specify that transport protocols such as HTTP or RTP, or media formats such as MP3, MIDI or MPEG-4 have to be supported. However, it contains all of the functionality needed to support these protocols and offers exciting possibilities, which we will explore.

The basic classes for multimedia applications are *Manager* and *Player*. If all you need to do is produce a sound to notify a client when news arrives, the *Manager* class can do it for you with one line.

```
Manager.playTone(ToneControl.C4, 2000, 50);
```

The line plays the tone C4 for two seconds at a volume level of 50 decibels.

Like almost any other manager, this one requires a real *Player* to perform anything beyond this simple task. The *Manager* creates a *Player* that can produce its own sound sequence or play a prerecorded file.

This *Player* is ready to play a musical tone sequence presented by a byte array.

```
Player player = Manager.createPlayer(Manager.TONEDEVICELOCATOR);
byte[] sequenceOfTones = {
ToneControl.VERSION, 1, ToneControl.TEMPO, 150, // etc.
}
player.realize(); // getting ready to start
ToneControl control = (ToneControl)p.getControl("ToneControl");
control.setSequence(sequenceOfTones);
player.start(); // start playing
```

Most likely, we would play a sound file from the server.

```
Player player = Manager.createPlayer
("http://JavaSchool.com/go/web/to/public/sound/girl.midi");
player.start();
```

A *Control* is an interface that has two implementations in the *javax.microedition.media.control*package: *ToneControl* and *VolumeControl*. An application can query a *Player* about the controls it supports and then ask to manage a selected specific *Control*.

What Are MIDlets?

The application model for MIDP is defined by the *javax.microedition.midlet* package with its single *MIDlet* class. Multiple MIDP applications, or MIDlets, can work together and share single JVM resources.

The *MIDlet* is similar to the *Applet* class in its important and dependent role inside a bigger box. For the *Applet*, the bigger box is a Web browser that invokes the *Applet's init()* method as a starting point. For the *MIDlet*, it is the MIDP application management software that starts MIDP applications with the *startApp()* method of the *MIDlet* class.

Can We Store Data on Mobile Devices?

Wireless devices with a MID profile can store and retrieve data. This means each user has more ownership and more independence. The *javax.microedition.rms* package introduces a persistent storage mechanism modeled after a simple record-oriented database. This mechanism is called the Record Management System (RMS). RMS API specifies the methods that allow multiple MIDlets to share the records.

Record store names or IDs are case sensitive and can be up to thirty-two Unicode characters long. They *must* be unique within a single MIDlet suite or a package of several MIDlets.

The RMS API does not include locking operations. Vendor implementations of *RecordStore* take care of multiple access situations. However, if a MIDlet uses multiple threads to access a record store, for example, with concurrent calls of *RecordStore.setRecord()* on the same record, the last attempt would naturally win. No data corruption happens in this case, but the last writing thread will overwrite the previous record.

Record stores can be created with a private or shareable access mode. Access controls are enforced when a selected *RecordStore* is opened.

Below, I provide several examples of the main operations on the storage areas or record stores.

We open a new *RecordStore* with the static *openRecordStore()* method of the *RecordStore* class. All we need to do is pass the name for the record store.

```
RecordStore records =
RecordStore.openRecordStore("MailMessages", true);
```

Then we can add messages to the store and retrieve, update, or delete existing records.

We use the *addRecord()* method of the *RecordStore* object to add a new record to the store.

```
byte[] bytes = ("Example-message.").getBytes();
int recordID = records.addRecord(bytes, 0, bytes.length);
```

The *addRecord()* method returns as an integer the new record ID.
The *setRecord()* method can update existing record data with the new content.

```
int recordID = 7;
byte[] bytes = ("Another Example.").getBytes();
records.setRecord(recordID, bytes, 0, bytes.length);
```

The last thing we will demonstrate about record manipulation is deleting a record. There is nothing easier.

```
records.deleteRecord(7); //
```

The index number is the only required argument.

Each *RecordStore* has its own version number. The initial value of the version, as well as the increment value, is implementation dependent. In most cases, the initial value is 0 and the increment value is 1. The *RecordStore* gets its initial version value when it is first created. Each time a record store is modified (by *addRecord, setRecord*, or *deleteRecord* methods) its *version* is incremented.

This feature allows MIDlets to quickly detect if anything has been modified in the *RecordStore*.

```
int currentVersion = records.getVersion(); // check for update
if(currentVersion == lastVersion) {
// nothing changed
}
```

When we want to close the storage doors, we issue the command below:

```
records.closeRecordStore();
```

Does this look too simple? I have to admit that every method that deals with the *RecordStore* can throw an exception and require several additional lines of error handling code.

MIDLET SECURITY

The smallest package in the MIDP API is the *javax.microedition.pki* package. The single *Certificate* interface presented in the package provides data about the origin and type of the certificate used to authenticate information for secure connections.

Any implementation of the *javax.microedition.pki.Certificate* interface *must* support X.509 Certificates. Other certificate formats *may* be supported. The set of implementation requirements can be found in WAP-211-WAPCert-20010522-a (WAPCert) documents that are based on RFC 2459 Internet X.509 Public Key Infrastructure Certificate and CRL Profile (RFC 2459).

CAN WE *PUSH* FROM A SERVER TO THE MIDP DEVICE?

Can we *push* data from a server to the MIDP device? There are several answers to this question. But every answer starts with yes! The difference is in "how." The most comprehensive answer will be given a bit later with the Wireless Messaging package description.

The other answer was provided with one of the MIDP 2.0 enhancements: the *PushRegistry* class of *the javax.microedition.io* package.

An application can use the *PushRegistry* class to register inbound connections. This can be done with an entry in the application descriptor file or dynamically by calling the *registerConnection* method of the class. Once registered, the dynamic connection acts just like a connection preallocated from the descriptor file.

For example, we can open a *UDPDatagramConnection* on the MIDlet:

```
String datagramURI = ("datagram://:12345");
UDPDatagramConnection datagramConnection = (UDPDatagramConnection)
    Connector.open(datagramURI);
```

Then we register the inbound connection so the MIDlet with the name *com.its.micro.Conference* will invoke its *startApp()* method, if message notifications arrive.

```
PushRegistry.registerConnection(datagramURI,
"com.its.micro.Conference", "*");
```

Note that the last argument, the star ("*") plays the filter role for the registration. What is the filter? It is a connection URL string indicating which senders are noticeable to the MIDlet or are allowed to cause the MIDlet to be launched. In our example, we allow any sender to wake up the MIDlet.

Wireless Messaging with Short Message Service and Other Protocols: An Important Component in Our Application

A growing set of optional packages developed within the Java Community Process (JCP) [6] according to different Java Specification Requests (JSRs) [7] complement core J2ME packages.

The *javax.wireless.messaging* package, which implements the wireless messaging API (WMA) JSR 120 [8], allows applications to send and receive wireless messages. The API is generic and independent of the underlying messaging protocols, which can be, for example, Global System for Mobile (GSM) Short Message Service (SMS) or Code Division Multiple Access (CDMA) SMS.

The current implementation available in the messaging package provides a general communication mechanism with the basic *MessageConnection* and Message framework and also supports SMS and Cell Broadcast Service (CBS).

Using this package, we can establish, for example, a GSM SMS, GSM CBS, CDMA SMS, or any other message connection. The platform *must* use the proper rules (GSM SMS, GSM CBS, CDMA SMS, or any that apply) for the syntax of the URL connection string and for the treatment of message contents.

The messaging application can use the *MessageConnection* in server mode or client mode; a URL connection string defines the mode. A URL connection string with the recipient address defines the client mode. For example:

```
sms://+12345678901
```

A URL connection without the recipient address defines the server mode. For example:

```
sms://:1234
```

The server mode allows the *MessageConnection* object to receive and send messages, whereas the client mode connection can only send a message.

The *scheme* that identifies which protocol is used is specific to the given protocol.

For example, the URL below is the server mode URL for the SMS protocol that specifies a server connection on port 3456. You will be able to send and receive messages on this connection:

```
sms://:3456
```

The CBS server mode URL looks very similar, but due to CBS specifics, it can only serve as a receiver connection:

```
cbs://:3456
```

The next URL example is the client mode that can serve to send a message via HTTP:

```
http://JavaSchool.com/go/private.ip
```

The example below shows the client mode SMS URL that allows us to send a message directly to another smart phone or J2ME device owner:

```
sms://+12345678901
```

The address provided in this URL points to a device with the phone number 1-234-567-8901. Yes, both SMS and CBS use the old and reliable telephone peer-to-peer network.

In Chapter 8, we briefly touched on integrated Wireless Application Protocol (WAP) and SMS gateways on the server side. The client described in this chapter will be able to enjoy parental care from the server side, live its own independent life, and also support peer-to-peer communications.

The GSM SMS protocol is the most popular in Europe, and it is gaining fast support in the U.S. for small-device communications.

One essential limitation of SMS, however, is that the message must be *really* short: 70 to 400 characters. SMS communications can switch from ASCII to binary mode, but this does not change the limitation on message length much.

An application may have several *MessageConnection* instances open simultaneously; these connections may be in both the client and server modes.

In our application, we plan to open two ports on the device. One port can be used for SMS communications and the other for services, such as multimedia, that require longer byte streams.

We have already provided an example of an SMS connection code. We open the connection in server mode so we can receive and send SMS messages:

```
sms://:3456
```

The second port can be opened with this code extract:

```
socket://:4567
```

We can translate this line to English as "open socket connection to the device in server mode on port 4567."

An important benefit of using the WMA package is the program does not block other operations while waiting for the message to come.

The application can create a class that implements the *MessageListener* interface and registers an instance of that class with the *MessageConnection(s)* to be notified of incoming messages. With this technique, a thread does not have to be blocked while waiting to receive messages.

The server mode program can use almost any port number, with some important exceptions. For security reasons, Java applications are not allowed to send SMS messages to the port numbers listed in the table below. Implementations *must* throw a *SecurityException* in the *MessageConnection.send()* method if an application tries to send a message to any of these port numbers.

Port Numbers Restricted to SMS Messages

Port number	Description
2805	WAP WTA secure connectionless session service
2923	WAP WTA secure session service
2948	WAP Push connectionless session service (client side)
2949	WAP Push secure connectionless session service (client side)
5502	Service Card reader
5503	Internet access configuration reader
5508	Dynamic Menu Control Protocol
5511	Message Access Protocol
5512	Simple Email Notification
9200	WAP connectionless session service
9201	WAP session service
9202	WAP secure connectionless session service
9203	WAP secure session service
9207	WAP vCal Secure
49996	SyncML OTA configuration
49999	WAP OTA configuration

This concludes our brief overview of the J2ME packages that we plan to use in building our wireless client application.

What functionality do we plan to provide?

Wireless Messaging Client Application

Following the 80/20 rule, I tried to identify about 20 percent of the functionality that would meet about 80 percent of consumers' needs in the Use Cases below. The choices I made, of course, are subjective. The client application should be able to use a subset of enterprise services, including distributed knowledge services, enjoy privilege-based access to personal and group data, and participate in peer-to-peer communications.

We will use all the packages described above in our example of a J2ME application running on a CLDC/MIDP device.

The application is a messaging client running on a CLDC/MIDP device that can communicate with other SMS devices via the SMS Gateway, synchronize data with a server, and request more sophisticated services from the server.

For example, the client sends a message to the server asking it to provide directions from one location to another. The server employs its Geographic Information System services and sends the response as a text message. The client application uses MMAPI to create or play sound streams and other media on the device.

The server side runs the Java Message Service (JMS) [9] and several collaborative services—JMS clients. JMS publishes news related to the person in a topic with the person's login name. One of the JMS clients, a specific adapter responsible for wireless client notification, is subscribed to the topic.

What mechanism is responsible for receiving this notification on the wireless device? It is the *MessageListener* object, a part of our messaging client application. The *MessageListener* is notified and begins message processing.

Use Cases or the Big Picture

Figure 11.2 shows a set of Use Cases for the client program. There are several types of messages that the client can retrieve.

First, the client software itself can be upgraded and published on the server side. The client program can retrieve a new software version and reinstall itself.

Besides Java classes that constitute the client program, there is a set of scenarios that describe different types of record-messages: screens and actions related to different types of

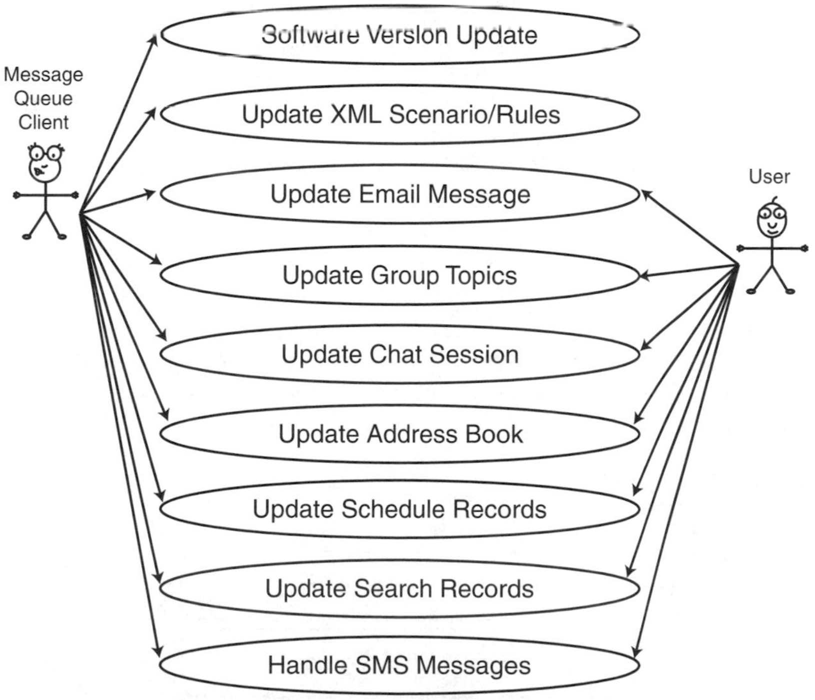

FIGURE 11.2. Wireless Messaging Application Use Cases (First Draft).

records (services). These scenarios may also be updated on the server side and published to the user's topic.

The scenarios instruct the client program on different types of record structures, how to handle the records, and what fields are to be displayed in brief reference records or stored.

The scenarios are XML descriptors similar to examples provided in previous chapters. They can be packed into Simple Object Access Protocol envelopes to present themselves as Web services. (We will talk about Web service specifics in Appendix 2.) The messaging client can retrieve a user's email messages or new articles published within the groups to which the user is subscribed, as well as synchronize address book and schedule records when they go out of sync and the server publishes them to the user's news. The messaging client can pick up new search results that can be published by the thematic search service (periodically running on the server side) to the user's news.

The messaging client is not the only actor playing on the J2ME device. The real user/person can also climb onto the stage to check news, reply to messages, edit address book and schedule records, and request another thematic search.

Invest Analysis Time and Cut Development Efforts; Shrink the Number of Use Cases

After some analysis, we come to the conclusion that the set of Use Cases can be scaled down to just two.

Figure 11.3 displays these two Use Cases: *News Update*, performed by the messaging client program, and *Work with Records*, performed by a user/person.

As soon as the J2ME-based device is on, the messaging client establishes a connection to the server and subscribes to the JMS topic named by the user's login name. During the session, the messaging client receives notifications from the JMS about the news published to the topic. All news related to the user is published to the same topic (named by the user's login name). The messaging client retrieves the news record: for example, email messages or new articles from one of the user's groups.

Retrieving email messages, address book and calendar records, and even scenarios or new software versions may be considered the single generic *News Update* Use Case. We can also add receiving SMS to the same Use Case, as it is just another type of news, with the simplest record type. In spite of the fact that every record type has a different structure and may require different actions, we can provide a unified approach to record processing using scenarios that define the structures and actions for every record type.

The *Work with Records* Use Case describes actions performed by a user/person on different types of records. This Use Case is also generalized with scenarios that describe possible user interfaces for every record type.

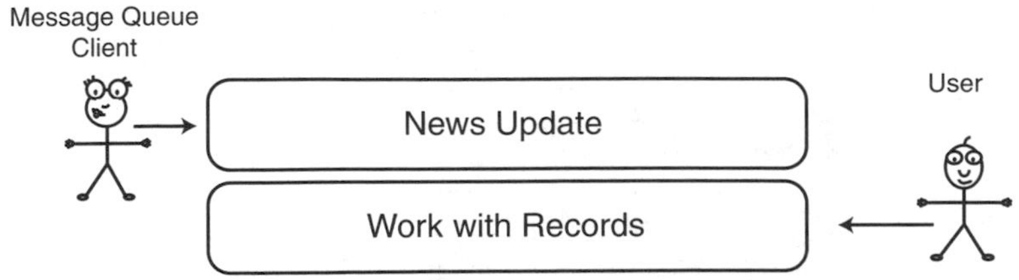

FIGURE 11.3. Wireless Messaging Application Use Cases (Final Version).

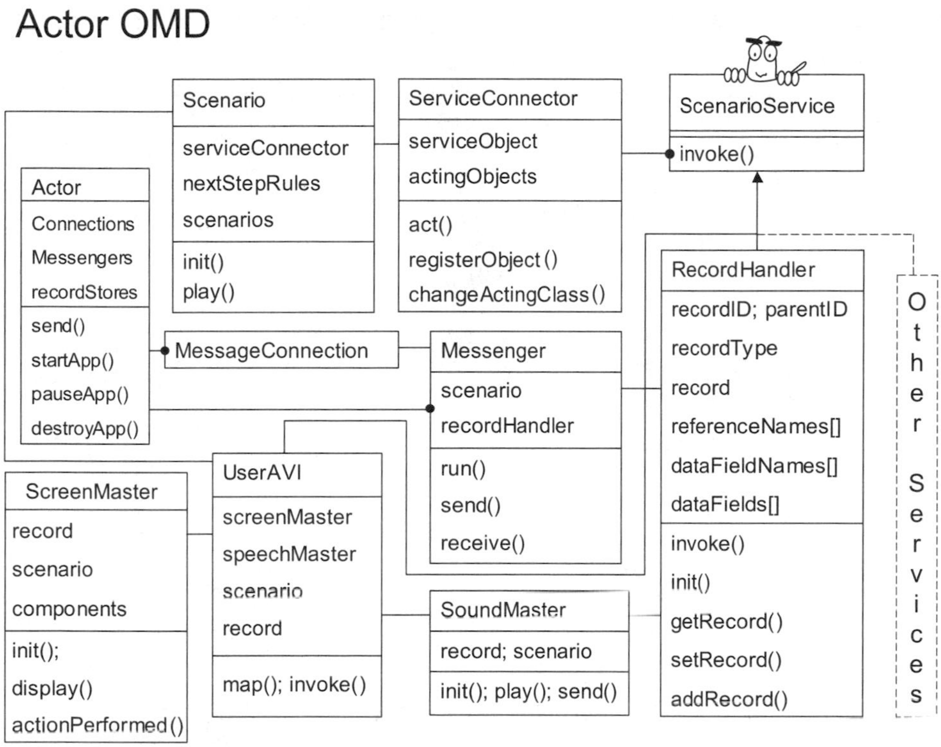

FIGURE 11.4. Object Model Diagram of the Actor in a Wireless Messaging Application.

We consider each Use Case in greater detail later on.

Figure 11.4 shows the Object Model Diagram of the client application with the set of Java classes that manage all types of records on the client device.

The *Actor* is the name of the client application. This name reflects the fact that the scenario defines the main functionality of the application and the client is an actor that plays one of the roles according to the scenario.

The *Scenario* class owns the hash table *nextStepRules* created from the XML scenario descriptions.

Scenario may include scenario branches in the hash table *scenarios*, in which each scenario has its own name.

The *init()* method initializes the scenario and sets its properties based on the XML descriptions passed as a parameter. The *play()* method plays the scenario according to the *nextStepRules*, which instruct what conditions to check and what services to invoke.

When it comes to service invocation, the *Scenario* object uses the *ServiceConnector* object, which can invoke any method on any class-service. The *ServiceConnector* class loads the necessary services/actors and stores acting objects in the hash table. When the same service object is needed, the *ServiceConnector* first checks its availability in the hash table and reuses this available object.

The *ServiceConnector* class is modified (from Chapter) to comply with the J2ME API. The J2ME API does not include the *java.reflection* package. To provide the same functionality with the *ServiceConnector*, we added a requirement to the class-services that can be called by the

```
/**
 * The invoke() method can call following methods of
 * the RecordHandler class:

   void init(Hashtable scenarioParameters);
   // set record store and record structure based on scenario
   // more methods
   String addRecord(byte[] data);

 * @param methodName
 * @param parameters
 * @return object
 */
public Object invoke(String methodName, Object[]
parameters) {
    if(methodName.equals("init") ) {
        init((Hashtable)parameters[0]);
        return "OK";
    } else if(methodName.equals("addRecord")) {
        int newRecordID = addRecord((byte[])
        parameters[0]);
        return ("" + newRecordID);
        // transform id into a String
    }
    // more code
}
```

FIGURE 11.5

ServiceConnector. All service classes implement the *ScenarioService* interface that includes the *invoke()* method.

The *invoke()* method in every service class serves as a dispatcher that is aware of all methods and method parameters inside the class-service. The *invoke()* method takes two parameters: a name-string of the method to call and an array of objects.

Figure 11.5 displays the code extract of the *invoke()* method for the *RecordHandler* class. This simplified example shows that the *invoke()* method works as a spy-dispatcher in every service class. The *invoke()* method knows enough internals of the class methods to do the same job we previously performed with the *java.reflection.Method.invoke()* method. MIDlet services cannot use the full power of the Reflection package and implement the *ScenarioService* interface with some specific code in the *invoke()* method.

Figures 11.6 and 11.7 present two versions of the *act()* method of the *ServiceConnector* class. In the J2SE version of the *act()* method, we have the comfort of using the power of the *java.reflection* package that can retrieve all the necessary information to invoke any method properly. The J2ME version of the *act()* method is much simpler. There is a direct call to the *invoke()* method that must be provided by any service-class we plan to work with.

```
/** J2SE Version
 * The act() method provides a unified way to find a requested
 * method
 * and invoke the method on previously defined object
 * @param methodName
 * @param parameters
 * @return result
 */
    public Object act(String methodName, Object[]
    parameters) {
        try{
            Class[] classes = null;
            if(parameters != null) {
                classes = new Class[parameters.length];
                for(int i=0; i< parameters.length; i++) {
                    classes[i] = parameters[i].getClass();
                }
            }
            // J2SE version uses java.reflection.Method
            method = actingClass.getMethod(methodName, classes);
        } catch (Exception e) {
            return ("ERROR:ServiceConnector.cannot find the
            method:actingClass=" +
              actingClass + " methodName=" + methodName + "
              parameters=" + parameters + " e=" +e);
        }
        try{
            // J2SE version uses java.reflection.Method
            result = method.invoke(actingObject, parameters);
        } catch (Exception e) {
            return ("ERROR:ServiceConnector.cannot execute
            the method:" +
                    methodName + " with actingClassName=" +
                    actingClassName + " on actingObject=" +
                    actingObject + " e=" + e);
        }
        return result;
    }
```

FIGURE 11.6

The *RecordHandler* class can handle multiple types of data records in a J2ME environment. The *RecordHandler* uses the *Scenario* to get the record structure for the record type. The main functions of the *RecordHandler* class are:

- Get reference records (brief information about the records).
- Get a single record with all record fields that are defined as "displayable."
- Store data records.

```
/** J2ME Version
 * The act() method provides a unified way to find a
 * requested method
 * and invoke the method on previously defined object
 * @param methodName
 * @param parameters
 * @return result
 */
   public Object act(String methodName, Object[]
   parameters) {
       try{
           // J2ME version requires service classes
           // implement the invoke() method
           result = actingObject.invoke(methodName, parameters);
       } catch (Exception e) {
           return ("ERROR:ServiceConnector.cannot execute
           the method:" +
             methodName + " with actingClassName=" +
             actingClassName +
             " on actingObject=" + actingObject + " e=" + e);
       }
       return result;
   }
```

FIGURE 11.7

The *UserAVI* (User Audio-Video Interface) class is responsible for the user interface. The XML scenario drives the *UserAVI* function. The *UserAVI* works with the *ScreenMaster* and *SoundMaster* interfaces. Both masters are smart enough to understand XML scenarios and play accordingly. The *ScreenMaster* class includes the *actionPerformed()* method, which handles user interaction.

The *Thinlet* class [10] is an example of the implementation of the *ScreenMaster* interface. The strongest point of the *Thinlet* class—its compact implementation of several widgets in a single class—is also its weakest point. Like most of the restricted solutions that target restricted environments, it is hard to scale or even expand. The *ScreenMaster* is a common umbrella that helps you bring more than one class (if necessary) to display different screen forms.

The *ScreenMaster* interface also improves event handling. Your event handling is no longer limited by the internal methods of the same class. User interaction may be handled according to a scenario with the *ServiceConnector* that can use other service-classes that implement the *ScenarioService* interface.

The user can create, delete, or change a record. In all these cases, a proper scenario requires calling the *Messenger* class to synchronize client data with the server.

Figure 11.8 shows the collaboration diagram for the *News Update* Use Case. The *Messenger* object receives notification from the server each time the server has an update for the client. The *Messenger* object retrieves the record from the server and passes control to the *Scenario* object. The rest of the play is performed according to the part of the scenario that corresponds

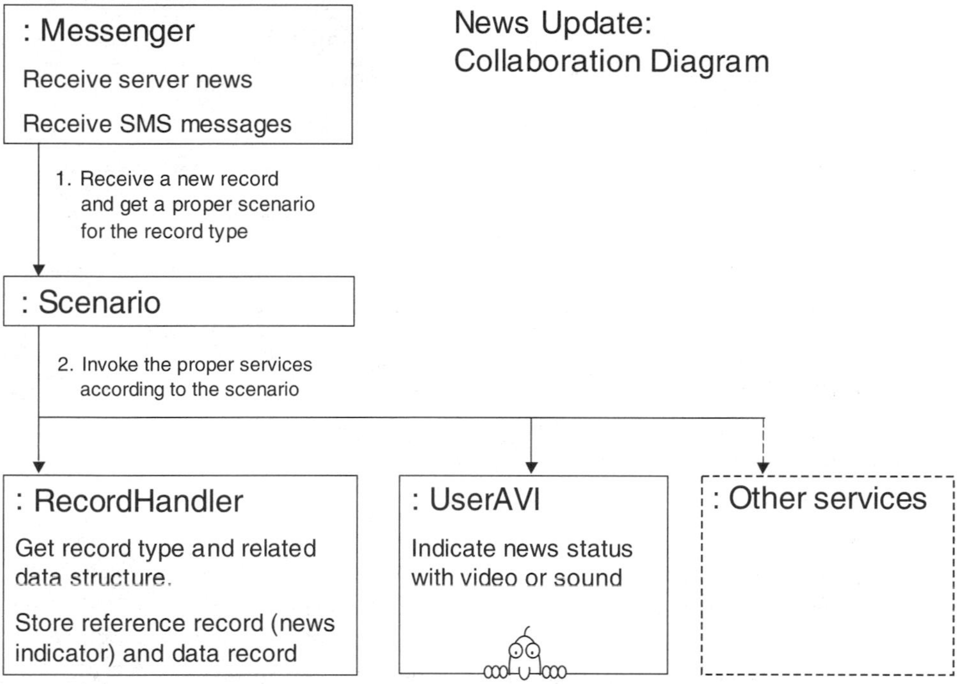

FIGURE 11.8. News Update: Collaboration Diagram.

to the type of the freshly retrieved record. The *Scenario* object calls the proper services and action-methods using properties and conditions (if any) from the *nextStepRules*.

In most cases, the record is stored, and a new record ID with some selected fields also can be recorded as reference data. Slightly different functions may be provided (according to the current scenario) if the record type is a software update or the record is actually a new scenario.

The *Messenger* can also receive SMS messages using the port that is open for SMS communications. In this scenario, the user is notified by a sound and the record is displayed and/or stored with SMS record store for future review and reply.

The *Messenger* object is a thread that handles messages coming in to the *javax.wireless.messaging.MessageConnection*. The *Messenger* expects news from the server and is always ready to send messages from the client to the server. To avoid blocking device operations while waiting for the message, we can use an important benefit of WMA: its ability to notify us of incoming messages.

Figure 11.9 displays the *Work with Records* collaboration diagram. A person, the owner of the device, drives the show via the *UserAVI* class. The user can select any type of record for interaction. For each record type, the proper scenario defines the proper screen or audio output, which prompts the user for the next step.

The Actor MIDlet Show

Figure 11.10 displays a code snippet of the *Actor MIDlet* class. *Actor* is the name of the *MIDlet* class, the main class in our client program. I have chosen this name to illustrate the fact that

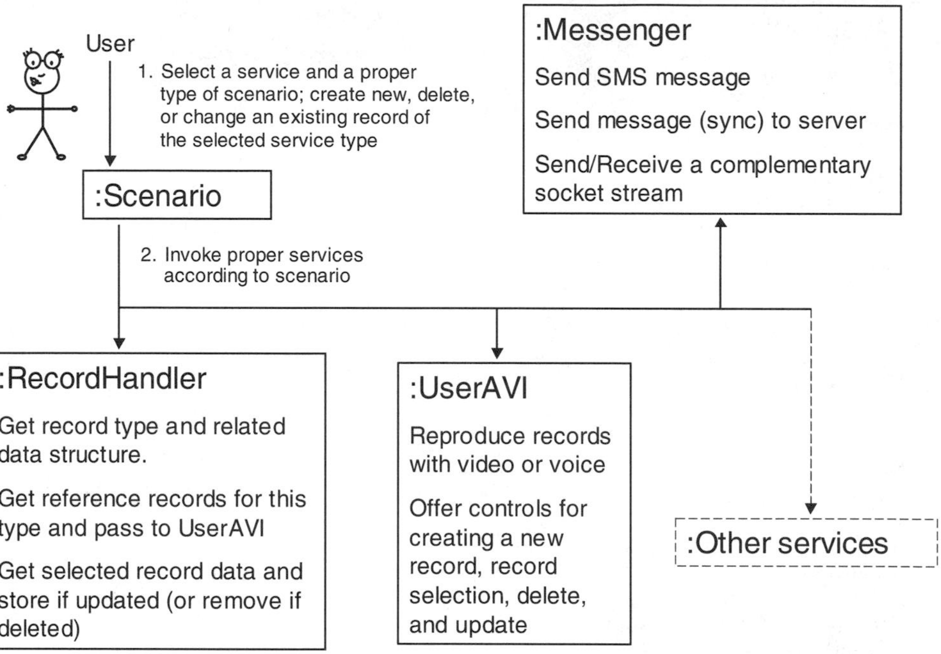

FIGURE 11.9. Work with Records: Collaboration Diagram.

the sequence of actions performed by the application is not hard coded but provided by scenarios.

The Actor owns two channels to the world outside: SMS and socket connections. Every connection has its Messenger thread-handler. There is an array of record stores that provides data persistence for several record types. The default types are declared in the code, but it is possible to redefine types at run-time.

The *startApp()* method is required by *MIDlet* rules. The method starts the application. It opens SMS and socket connections in the server mode and registers both connections with the *MessageListener*. We initialize types with the default values and open record stores for every record type.

The *MIDlet* application implements the *MessageListener* interface and registers its instance with the *Messenger* object to be notified of incoming messages. The single *notifyIncomingMessage()* method of the *MessageListener* interface is called when a new message is ready for retrieval.

Now everything is ready for message handling. The last two lines of the *startApp()* method start two Messenger thread-handlers that monitor messages coming from SMS and socket connections. The SMS handler deals with SMS messages transferred via the SMS Gateway. The socket connection handler is responsible for all other types of messages coming to and from the server side or any peers.

Figure 11.11 displays the *notifyIncomingMessage()* method. This method is invoked by the *MIDlet* application framework as soon any connection listener feels that a message is ready for retrieval. Note that the *notifyIncomingMessage()* method does not process incoming messages. According to the specifications, this method should quickly return control to the

```
//  Actor

import java.io.IOException;
import javax.microedition.midlet.*;
import javax.microedition.io.*;
import javax.wireless.messaging.*;
import javax.microedition.rms.*;

/**
 * The Actor class is a MIDlet that has two "server" mode connections
 * The class handles multiple types of messages.
 * The Actor plays every message type according to its Scenario
 * @author Jeff.Zhuk@JavaSchool.com
 */
public class Actor extends MIDlet implements MessageListener {
    private MessageConnection smsConnection, socketConnection;
    private Messenger smsHandler, socketHandler;
    private RecordStore[] recordStores;
    private static String[] types; // record types
    private String[] defaultTypes = { "Software", "Scenario",
    "sms","Mail","Address","Schedule","SearchTheme","Chat","Topic"};

    /**
     * The startApp() method starts the MIDlet.
     * The method opens SMS and Socket connections in the "server" mode
     * and register both connections with the MessageListener
     */
    public void startApp() {
        try {
            smsConnection =
            (MessageConnection)Connector.open("sms://:3456");
            socketConnection =
            (MessageConnection)Connector.open("socket://:3456");
            // Register both listeners for incoming messages
            smsConnection.setMessageListener(this);
            socketConnection.setMessageListener(this);

            // open record store with the name of the type
            types = defaultTypes;
            // types can be updated at run-time
            for(int i=0; i < types.length; i++) {
                recordStores[i] =
                RecordStore.openRecordStore(types[i], true);
            }
            // Start Messenger threads for both connections
            smsHandler = new Thread(new Messenger(smsConnection,
            recordStores)).start();
            socketHandler = new Thread(new
            Messenger(socketConnection, recordStores)).start();
        } catch (Exception e) {
             System.out.println("Actor.startApp:e=" + e);
        }
    }
```

FIGURE 11.10

```
/**
 * According to the specification the notifyIncomingMessage()
 * method must return control quickly
 * The method provides asynchronous callbacks for inbound messages
 * The method notifies a proper Messenger thread that handles
 * message processing
 * @param connection
 */
public void notifyIncomingMessage(MessageConnection conn) {
   if (conn == smsConnection) {
        smsHandler.notify();
   } else if(conn == socketConnection) {
        socketHandler.notify();
   }
    }
```

FIGURE 11.11

application. The processing mechanism of incoming messages is more elegant. It isolates blocking input/output on a separate thread, the *Messenger*, that handles incoming messages. The *notifyIncomingMessage()* method passes the notification to the proper *Messenger* thread and is again free to enjoy connection silence.

The MIDlet has two more required methods that are presented in Fig. 11.12. The *pauseApp()* method closes communication channels but keeps message listeners alive. The *destroyApp()* method is more radical in its actions. It closes the connections and burns the bridges by killing both message listeners.

The *Actor* class can also send SMS and socket messages upon the user's request. Figure 11.13 shows two versions of the *send()* method: one for SMS and one for socket connections.

The first version of the *send()* method uses an existing SMS connection to send a short message. This method can be called upon some user actions according to a scenario. The method takes two parameters: the address and the message string. The address may be, for example:

```
sms://+12345678901.
```

The second version of the *send()* method sends binary data over the socket connection. In most cases, the record data are passed along with a message, which can be composed of text. But we would like to keep open the possibility of passing binary data, such as recorded sound.

The *Messenger* Code: Handling Incoming Messages

The *Messenger* class (Fig. 11.14) is a thread that handles incoming messages. The main properties of the handler include a monitored connection, two flags (*notified* and *finished*), a scenario object, and a record handler.

```
/**
* The pauseApp() method is a required MIDlet method
* The method releases the connections and signal to terminate threads
* The pauseApp() method closes communication channels but
* keeps message listeners alive.
*/
public void pauseApp() {
    smsHandler.close();
    socketHandler.close();
    try {
        smsConnection.close();
        socketConnection.close();
    } catch (IOException e) {
        System.out.println("Actor.pauseApp:e=" + e);
    }
}

/**
* The destroyApp() method is a required MIDlet method
* The method shutdown the connections and the listeners
*/
public void destroyApp(boolean unconditional) {
    smsHandler.close();
    socketHandler.close();
    try {
        smsConnection.setMessageListener(null);
        socketConnection.setMessageListener(null);
        smsConnection.close();
        socketConnection.close();
    } catch (IOException e) {
        System.out.println("Actor.destroyApp:e=" + e);
    }
}
```

FIGURE 11.12

The constructor takes two arguments: the connection and the array of record stores. It then creates a *RecordHandler* object and passes the array of record stores to this object.

The *notify()* method sets the *notified* flag that is tested in the monitoring loop. When is the notify method called? The *notifyIncomingMessage()* method calls the *notify()* method in the proper connection handler. Remember that the *Messenger* class is a connection handler and that we created two *Messenger* objects in the *Actor MIDlet*: one for SMS and one for socket connections. (Just checking.)

The *close()* method sets the *finished* flag. The *close()* method can be invoked by the *pauseApp()* or *destroyApp()* methods.

The most important method of every thread is the *run()* method. The *run()* method of the *Messenger* class retrieves the message and starts message processing. The message can be text or binary data. The method will transform a text message into binary data and pass the data to the *initRecordScenario()* method of the record handler. The record handler uses

```
/**
* The send() method uses an existing connection to send the message
* The method can be called upon some user actions according
* to scenario
* @param address for example: "sms://+12345678901"
* @param message
*/
public void send(String address, String message) {
     try {
        TextMessage textMessage = (TextMessage)
        smsConnection.newMessage(
            MessageConnection.TEXT_MESSAGE);
        textMessage.setAddress (address);
        textMessage.setPayloadText(message);
        smsConnection.send(textMessage);
    } catch (Exception e) {
        System.out.println("Actor.send:e=" + e);
        e.printStackTrace ();
    }

}
 /**
  * The send() method sends the binary record over the socket
  * connection
  * The method can be called upon some user actions according to
  * scenario
  * @param bytes
  */
public void send(byte[] bytes) {
     try {
        BinaryMessage binMessage = socketConnection.
        newMessage(MessageConnection.BINARY_MESSAGE );
        binMessage.setPayloadData(bytes);
        socketConnection.send(binMessage);
    } catch (Exception e) {
        System.out.println("Actor.send:e=" + e);
        e.printStackTrace ();
    }

  }

  }
```

FIGURE 11.13

this method to initialize record data and to retrieve the proper type of scenario from the Scenario record store. The *run()* method then passes control to the scenario object that leads the show.

```
// Messenger

import java.io.IOException;
import javax.microedition.io.*;
import javax.wireless.messaging.*;

/**
 * The Messenger class is a thread that handles incoming messages
 * Jeff.Zhuk@JavaSchool.com
 */
public class Messenger implements Runnable {
    private MessageConnection conn = null;
    private boolean notified = false;
    private boolean finished = false;
    private Scenario scenario;
    private RecordHandler recordHandler;

    /**
     * The Messenger() constructor creates the thread and
     * passes the connection
     * @param connection
     * @param records
     */
    public Messenger(MessageConnection connection, RecordStore[]
    recordStores) {
        conn = connection;
        recordHandler = new RecordHandler(recordStores);
    }
    /**
     * The notify() method sets the notified boolean that is
     * tested in the loop
     */
    public void notify() {
        notified = true;
    }
    /**
     * The close() method sets the finished boolean that is
     * tested in the loop
     */
    public void close() {
        finished = true;
    }
    /**
     * The run() method retrieves the message and starts
     * message processing
     * The run method uses the recordHandler object to init
     * record data
```

FIGURE 11.14

```
     * and to retrieve a proper type of scenario from the
     * "Scenario" record store
     * Then the run() method passes control to the scenario object
     */
    public void run() {
        while (!finished) {
        try {
            if(notified) {
                notified = false;
                byte[] data = null;
                Message msg = conn.receive();
                if( msg instanceof BinaryMessage ){
                    data = ((BinaryMessage) msg).
                    getPayloadData();
                } else {
                    String text = ((TextMessage) msg).
                    getPayloadText();
                    data = text.getBytes();
                }
                scenario = recordHandler.initRecordScenario
                (data);
                // init scenario and set name
                scenario.doNextStep();
                // start scenario play and invoke proper services
            } catch (Exception e) {
                System.out.println("Messenger.run:e=" + e");
            }
        }
    }
}
```

FIGURE 11.14. ***(cont.)***

How Is Persistence Provided for Multiple Types of Records?

The *RecordHandler* source, begun in Fig. 11.15, answers all the questions. The *RecordHandler* knows every storage place; the array of *recordStores* has them all. The *Records* object represents a currently selected record store according to the current record *type*. The *scenarioParameters* object can be handy while performing scenario actions. The *type* variable and the *record* object define the structure of the record and the record data values accordingly.

The array of the *referenceNames* and the array of the *dataFieldNames* play important roles when record data need to be displayed by the *UserAVI*. The array of data fields contains specific parts of record data according to the current record structure.

The constructor takes a single parameter—the array of all *recordStores*—and enables the *RecordHandler* object to handle any of the record types.

The *RecordHandler* class implements the *ScenarioService* interface with its single *invoke()* method.

```
// RecordHandler

import java.io.IOException;
import javax.microedition.io.*;
import javax.microedition.rms.*;
import java.util.Hashtable;

/**
 * The RecordHandler class is responsible for data persistence
 * The class handles multiple types of records according to scenario
 * Each record type has its own record structure
 * There are reference fields with brief info about the record
 * and data fields with complete information
 * @author Jeff.Zhuk@JavaSchool.com
 */
public class RecordHandler implements ScenarioService {
    private RecordStore[] recordStores;
    private RecordStore records;
    private Hashtable scenarioParameters;
    private String type, record;
    // type of the record and the  record itself
    private String[] referenceNames;
    // names for the reference fields
    private String[] dataFieldNames;
    // names for all data fields
    private String[] dataFields;
    // record data

    /**
     * The constructor assigns array of recordStores
     * getting ready to handle any of them
     */
    public RecordHandler(RecordStore[] recordStores) {
        this.recordStores = recordStores;
    }

    /**
     * The invoke() method can call following methods of the
     * RecordHandler class:

      void init(Hashtable scenarioParameters);
      // set record store and record structure based on scenario
      String[] getReferenceFields(int recordID);
      String[] getDataFields(int recordID);
      byte[] getRecord(int recordID);
      void setDataFields(int recordID, String[] dataFields);
      String addRecord(byte[] data);
     * @param methodName
     * @param parameters
     * @return object
     */
```

FIGURE 11.15

```
    public Object invoke(String methodName, Object[] parameters) {
        if(methodName.equals("init") ) {
            init((Hashtable)parameters[0]);
            return "OK";
        } else if(methodName.startsWith("get") ||
  (methodName.startsWith("set")) {
            // recordID is an important argument for all get/set
            // methods
            String recordStringID = (String) parameters[0];
            try {
                int recordID = Integer.parseInt(recordStringID);
                if(methodName.equals("setDataFields")) {
                    // array of data fields follow the recordID
                    String[] fields = (String[]) parameters[1];
                    setDataFields(recordID, fields);
                    return "OK";
                } else if(methodName.equals("getDataFields")) {
                    return getDataFields(recordID);
                } else
                if(methodName.equals("getReferenceFields")) {
                    return getReferenceFields(recordID);
                } else if(methodName.equals("getRecord")) {
                    return getRecord(recordID);
                }
            } catch(Exception e) {
                System.out.println("RecordHandler.invoke:e="
                + e);
                e.printStackTrace();
            }
        } else if(methodName.equals("addRecord")) {
            int newRecordID = addRecord((byte[]) parameters[0]);
            return ("" + newRecordID);
            // transform id into a String
        }
        return null;
    }
```

FIGURE 11.15. *(cont.)*

The *invoke()* method serves as a dispatcher that takes the method name and parameters and can call the following methods of the *RecordHandler* class:

```
void init(Hashtable scenarioParameters);
String[] getReferenceFields(int recordID);
String[] getDataFields(int recordID);
byte[] getRecord(int recordID);
void setDataFields(int recordID, String[] dataFields);
String addRecord(byteg[] data);
```

Every method from the list above requires its own set of parameters and returns specific types of variables. All *get* and *set* methods require a primitive integer record ID as an argument.

```
/**
 * The initRecordScenario() method sets record data
 * Then the method retrieves a proper type scenario and
 * invokes the init() method
 * @param recordBytes
 * @return scenarioRecord
 */
public String initRecordScenario(byte[] bytes) {
    record = new String(bytes);
    type = getRecordType();
    // looks into the record to get the type
    int typeIndex = getTypeIndex(type);
    records = recordStores[getTypeIndex("Scenario")];
    // scenario records have record IDs according to their
    // type indexes
    String scenarioRecord = getRecord(typeIndex);
    scenarioParameters = Stringer.parseXML(scenarioRecord);
    init(scenarioParameters);
    return scenarioRecord;
}
```

FIGURE 11.16

The code in Fig. 11.15 picks up on this commonality and transforms the record ID presented by a string into its primitive integer value. The *invoke()* method does all the necessary transformations to pass the proper parameters and return expected values.

Figure 11.16 displays the *initRecordScenario()* method. Remember that the *Messenger* thread calls this method to initiate a record and retrieve a scenario according to the record type.

The *initRecordScenario()* method takes message bytes and creates the *record* string object. The message should include information about the record type. We use the *getRecordType()* method to find out what that type is.

After the record type is known, it is easy to retrieve the proper scenario for this type from the *Scenario* record store. Every record in this storage has a number that equals the type index, starting with the *Software* type, which has an index of 0, and ending with the *Topic* type, with an index of 8. For example, the *Mail* type has an index of 3. The *getIndexType()* method returns the proper index based on the type of record.

The scenario record represents an XML string that can be transformed into a nested structure of parameters. The transformation is performed with the *parseXML* method of the *Stringer* class. We pass this nested structure of scenario parameters to the *init()* method and end the *initRecordScenario()* method by returning the scenario record.

Several of the methods mentioned above are presented in Fig. 11.17.

The *init()* method takes a set of scenario parameters to set objects such as *referenceNames, dataFieldNames*, and records of the currently selected storage, according to the record type.

The *getRecordType()* method reads the record type and its structure definition. In a very simplified example provided for this method, we assume that any record type except SMS has data fields separated with the "|" character, and the record starts with the "|" separator followed by the record type name.

```
/**
 * The init() method sets type dependent properties of the
 * record based on scenario
 * @param scenario
 */
public void init(Hashtable parameters) {
    scenarioParameters = parameters;
    type = (String)parameters.get("type");
    referenceNames = (String[])parameters.
    get("referenceNames");
    dataFieldNames = (String[])parameters.
    get("dataFieldNames");
    records = recordStores[getTypeIndex(type)];
}
/**
 * The getRecordType() method highly depends on custom type
 * structure
 * This is a very simplified example where
 * any record except SMS has data fields separated with "|"
 * separator and
 * the record starts with "|" separator following by the type name
 * and the next separator
 * @return type
 */
public String getRecordType() {
    if(record.startsWith("|")) { // separator charactor
        String[] recordFields = Stringer.split("|", record);
        type = recordFields[0];
        // take type out of data fields
        dataFields = new String[recordFields.length - 1];
        for(int i=0; i < dataFields.length; i++) {
            dataFields[i] = recordFields[i+1];
        }
        // remove type from the record
        record = record.substring(2 + type.length());
        return type;
    } else {
        return "sms";
    }
}
/**
 * The getTypeIndex() method looks through the type names
 * and returns a proper index
 * @param name
 * @return index
 */
```

FIGURE 11.17

```
public int getTypeIndex(String typeName) {
    for(int i=0; i < Actor.types.length; i++) {
        if(typeName.equals(Actor.types[i])) {
            return i;
        }
    }
    return -1;
}
```

FIGURE 11.17. *(cont.)*

The same method removes the type information from data fields and record data. This type information is no longer necessary inside the data because the data are assigned to a specific storage with the name of the record type.

The *getTypeIndex()* method looks through the type names and returns the proper index. If the name is not found, the return value is –1. This can cause big or small problems, depending on the error-handling logic.

Figure 11.18 displays the most important methods that directly access record stores to save and read data. The *addRecord()* method adds a new record to the records and returns a new record ID. The *getRecord()* method returns the data stored in a given record. The *setRecord()* method updates an existing record. Each update changes the *version* number.

In all cases, we provide operations on the selected record storage according to the record type. A user may also join the show and start interacting with the device according to the *Work with Records* collaboration diagram. The very first thing the user selects is the service or record type. The program immediately retrieves the proper scenario that determines all the screen widgets and user action handlers.

The *UserAVI* class works with two interface masters: the *ScreenMaster* and the *SoundMaster*. Both masters understand the XML scenario and interpret the scenario into widgets or sound primitives with the assigned user action handlers.

Wireless with or without a Phone

Yes, wireless started with the phone in mind. Creating a wireless device without a phone makes no sense, right? Wrong. Here is why:

Some current PDAs have an optional phone case. This makes the size of the PDA (and its cost) significantly larger. Do we really need additional hardware to add the phone functionality?

Not necessarily. What we really need is to talk to other people. Step down to technological terms, and we can talk about version 1 of an implementation that models phone functionality.

Ben dials Rachel's number and starts talking. An analog signal from the microphone must be converted to digital form, and the stream of bytes should fly to the recipient, where the byte stream must be converted back to an analog signal that can play on a speaker.

The solution is covered by the J2ME multimedia package using the Actor socket connection. No additional hardware is needed.

Version 2 is even more interesting. It offers the same "talk to each other" function but in a different way. Ben dials Rachel's number, and his Actor device immediately sends

```
/**
 * The addRecord() method adds a new record to records and returns a
 * new record ID
 * @param bytes
 * @return recordID
 */
public int addRecord(byte[] bytes) {
    int recordID = -1;
    try {
        recordID = records.addRecord(bytes, 0, bytes.length);
    }
    catch (RecordStoreException rse) {
        System.out.println(rse);
        rse.printStackTrace();
    }
    return recordID;
}    /**
 * The getRecord() method returns the data stored in the given record.
 * @param recordID
 * @return bytes
 */
public byte[] getRecord(int recordID) {
    byte[] bytes = null;
    try {
        bytes = records.getRecord(recordID);
    }
    catch (RecordStoreException rse) {
        System.out.println(rse);
        rse.printStackTrace();
    }
    return bytes;
}
/**
 * The setRecord() method updates an existing record
 * @param recordID
 * @param bytes
 */
public void setRecord(int recordID, byte[] bytes) {
    try {
        records.setRecord(recordID, bytes, 0, bytes.length);
    }
    catch (RecordStoreException rse) {
        System.out.println(rse);
        rse.printStackTrace();
    }
}
```

FIGURE 11.18

his *voice profile* – a description of his voice characteristics. This only happens on the first call to Rachel. From then on, Ben's device sends only his name, and Rachel's device retrieves his voice profile.

Ben starts talking. A speech recognition system located on his device evaluates his *voice mood* and sends its description to Rachel. Then, the Actor on Ben's side sends streams of text with additional voice mood marks. The voice mood marks are properly played on the other side, according to the voice profile.

The whole conversation between these two friends looks like a good play script.

Ben (happy): Hi. How are you?
Rachel (laughing): I am doing great! I tried to reach you all day long. Where were you?

I will stop right here to focus on only one thing: the bandwidth benefit is simply tremendous.

But what if not every person on this planet has the Actor device yet? What if someone is still attached to the old-fashioned phone system? How can we reach this person?

Fortunately, we can work via gateways (see the Wireless Application Server [WAS] on the right side of Fig. 11.19), which can connect us to the local phone system. In this case, the Internet combined with the local phone system is our network.

We leave the discussion of audio possibilities until Chapter 12.

Wireless Actors in a Play

Figure 11.19 shows several clients interacting with one another and with the server side. Multiple wireless devices can interact with each other and can also access centralized services located on the WAS. The WAS, presented on the right side of the figure, consists of gateways and peer services. Peer services can also run on any rich client machine.

The WAP gateway serves multiple WAP devices with embedded Wireless Markup Language (WML) browsers. The Java Server Pages-based engine is the most natural presentation layer for WAP services that use Web server and Web technology mechanisms.

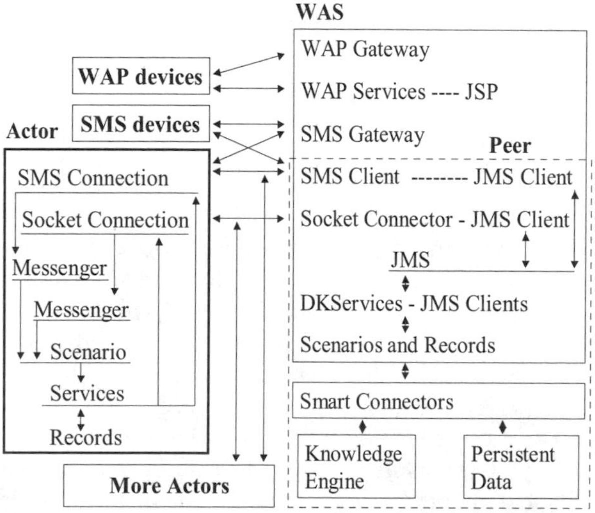

Figure 11.19. WAP and SMS Clients Use WAP and SMS Gateway.

Users with smart phones and pagers can enjoy SMS while transferring text messages to each other. Two things are required: SMS support on the phone or pager (this is part of the GSM standard anyway) and SMS Gateway to support communications.

Integrating the SMS client into the WAS opens the door for more services. An SMS client with a specific phone number (an additional phone line) is also a JMS client. This double agent receives short messages that can request rich services.

For example, an SMS phone user sends a request for directions from a street cross section to some destination address. The processing of the request requires a good brain, which hopefully is present on the server side. The output may be a very short text message ("first light left, Spring Street right, and so on") delivered by the JMS to the double agent and then back to the SMS phone.

The Actor takes a visible role in this picture. The Actor is our application example running on wireless MIDP devices. We can think about these devices as the lucky ones, but let us call them *Actors*. The Actors can talk via SMS to each other and to standard SMS phones and can transfer files and byte streams via the socket connection.

Naturally, Actors can request all the possible services from the server side and receive text or binary stream answers. We do not want to rule out multimedia/speech exchange.

Actors join the play of Distributed Knowledge Services (*DKServices*) based on multiple scenarios. Actors receive updates from multiple channels and supply the channels with their own record changes.

The list of channels or services includes email, group topics (articles), chat sessions, shared address book and calendar records, and thematic search records. Each Actor keeps some objects locally and enjoys privileged access to shared objects on multiple servers and peers.

JMS is the major player on the peer side. All service-channels are JMS clients. Each service type is a generic *ScenarioPlayer* object that plays its own scenarios—for example, the *RecordHandler* (adapted to a rich environment) and the *UserAVI*, which works with *SoundMaster* and *ScreenMaster* objects.

The knowledge engine can power peers with advanced scenario processing, help transform incoming information into knowledge data, and, finally, collaborate with *ScreenPlayer* objects for text and speech recognition to improve the user's experience to the level of a natural language interface.

SUMMARY

In this chapter, we explored J2ME programming with networking, user interface, and storage handling. We provided analysis and design of a wireless application and demonstrated code examples for the ambitious wireless Actor *MIDlet* that can join thin and thick peers in a large-scale play that runs according to multiple scenarios. The Actor can enjoy peer-to-peer conversations as well as contribute and consume in a Distributed Knowledge environment.

Most of the services described in this chapter are based on text records, although we touched on the possibility of sound and speech transfer.

It is tempting to talk to the device hands-free and receive a voice response over the Internet. Do you want to ask for directions while in your car or request the weather forecast while on your hiking trip? In the next chapter, we consider specific methods and technologies related to speech.

Integrating Question

What are the common points and differences in WAP/WML and J2ME architectures?

Case Study

1. List and briefly describe optional J2ME packages.
2. Write a *setDataField()* method for the *RecordHandler* class.
3. Research and report on the resources available for wireless sound transfer.
4. Research the Java Speech API, and discuss its applicability to wireless devices.
5. Compare WAP/WML- and J2ME-based applications. Which one is preferable for your business and why?

References

1. J2ME specifications: *http://java.sun.com/products/j2me.*
2. J2ME CDC specifications: *http://java.sun.com/products/cdc.*
3. J2ME CLDC specifications: *http://java.sun.com/products/cldc.*
4. J2ME MIDP specifications: *http://java.sun.com/products/midp.*
5. J2ME MMAPI specifications: *http://java.sun.com/products/mmapi.*
6. Java Community Process: *http://jcp.org.*
7. Java Specification Request: *http://jcp.org/en/jsr/all.*
8. Wireless Messaging API specification: *http://java.sun.com/products/wma.*
9. Java Message Service: *http://java.sun.com/products/jms.*
10. Thinlet: *http://Thinlet.com.*

CHAPTER 12

Speech Technologies on the Way to a Natural User Interface

Know how to listen, and you will profit even from those who talk badly.
—Plutarch

This chapter is about speech technologies and related APIs: VoiceXML, SALT, Java Speech API, and MS Speech SDK. It looks into unified scenarios with audio/video interface (AVI) definitions, considers design and code examples, and introduces important skills for a new world of wired and wireless speech applications.

WHAT IS A NATURAL USER INTERFACE?

Is a natural user interface (NUI) another set of tags and rules covered by a nice name? Absolutely not!

This time, end users—not a standards committee—make the determination on what they prefer for their methods of interaction. An NUI allows end users to give their preferences at the time of the service request, and to change them flexibly.

Are you a "computer" person?

My guess is that you are, because you are reading this book. "Computer literate" folks like you and me enjoy exploring the capacities of computer programs via traditional interfaces. Even so, there are times, such as when we are on vacation, on the go, and in the car, when we prefer "hands-free" conversation rather than using keyboards to access computerized services.

One person prefers handwriting, and someone else is comfortable with typing. One would like to forget keywords and use commonsense terminology instead. Can a computer understand that "find" is the same as "search," and "Bob" is actually "Robert"? Can it understand that someone has chosen a foreign (non-English) language to interact with it?

An NUI offers all these possibilities. Some of these complex tasks can be addressed in a unified way with AVI scenarios.

First, let us look into the Java details of a voice interface, one part of an NUI. A significant part of the population considers a voice interface to be the most natural and preferred way of interaction.

SPEAKING WITH STYLE

Chapter 4 introduced text-to-speech conversion. We used the FreeTTS Java Speech application program interface (JSAPI) implementation to write simple Java code for a voice component, but the sound of the voice may not have been terribly impressive. What can the JSAPI [1] offer to enhance a voice component?

Here are two lines of the source (from Chapter 4) that actually speak for themselves:

```
Voice talker = new CMUDiphoneVoice();
talker.speak(speech);
```

Remember that the *Voice* class is the main talker.

We can create an object of the *Voice* class with four features: voice name, gender, age, and speaking style. The voice name and speaking style are both String objects, and the synthesizer determines the allowed contents of those strings.

The gender of a voice can be GENDER_FEMALE, GENDER_MALE, GENDER_NEUTRAL, or GENDER_DONT_CARE. Gender neutral means some robotic or artificial voices. We can use the "don't care" value if the feature is not important and we are OK with any available voice.

The age can be AGE_CHILD (up to 12 years), AGE_TEENAGER (13 to 19 years), AGE_YOUNGER_ADULT (20 to 39 years), AGE_MIDDLE_ADULT (40 to 60 years), AGE_OLDER_ADULT (60+ years), AGE_NEUTRAL, and AGE_DONT_CARE.

Here is the example of a woman's voice selection with a "greeting" voice style:

```
Voice("Julie", GENDER_FEMALE, AGE_YOUNGER_ADULT, "greeting");
```

Not all the features of JSAPI had been implemented at the time of this book's publication. Here is the reality check: the *match()* method of the *Voice* class can test whether an engine implementation has suitable properties for the voice (Fig. 12.1).

The *getVoices()* method creates a set of voices according to initial age and gender parameters. If the requested age or gender is not available, the default voice parameters are set.

We can use this method in the scenario of multiple actors that have different genders and ages.

```
<actors name="age" value="AGE_TEENAGER | AGE_MIDDLE_ADULT" />
<actors name="gender" value="GENDER_FEMALE | GENDER_MALE" />
```

These two scenario lines define arrays of age and gender arguments that produce four actor voices.

```
<line>/**</line>
<line> * The getVoices() method creates a set of voices according to
       * initial age and gender parameters
       * The method checks if the voice if available.
       * If requested age or gender is not available the default voice
       * parameters are set.
       * @param gender
       * @param ages
       * @return voices
       */
       public Voice[] getVoices(int[] gender, int[] ages) {
        // make sure that at least default set
        if(gender == null) {
            gender = new int[1];
            gender[0] = GENDER_DONT_CARE;
        }
        if(ages == null) {
            ages = new int[1];
            ages[0] = AGE_DONT_CARE;
        }
        Voice[] voices = new Voice[ages.length *
        gender.length]; // all combinations
        SynthesizerModeDesc desc = new
        SynthesizerModeDesc(Locale.ENGLISH);
        Voice[] availableVoices = desc.getVoices();
        // try to set requested voices
        for (int i = 0; i < ages.length; i++) {
            for (int j = 0; j < gender.length; j++) {
                int k=(i+1)*j; // current voice index try to set voice
                // according to requirements and check availability
                boolean available = false;
                // start from gender
                voices[k].setGender(gender[j]);
                for(int n=0; !available &&
                n<availableVoices.length; n++) {
                    if (voices[k].match(availableVoices[n])) {
                        available = true;
                    }
                }
                if(!available) {
                    voices[k].setGender(GENDER_DONT_CARE);
                }
                // continue with ages
                voices[k].setAge(ages[i]);
                for(int n=0; !available &&
                n<availableVoices.length; n++) {
```

FIGURE 12.1

```
                    if (voices[k].match(availableVoices[n])) {
                        available = true;
                    }
                }
                if(!available) {
                    voices[k].setAge(AGE_DONT_CARE);
                }
            }
        }
        // at this point all requested voices set to
        // requested parameters or to default return voices;
    }
```

FIGURE 12.1. *(cont.)*

JAVA SPEECH API MARKUP LANGUAGE

An even more intimate control of voice characteristics can be achieved by using the Java Speech API Markup Language (JSML) [2]. JSML is a subset of XML that allows applications to annotate text that is to be spoken, with additional information. We can set prosody rate or speed of speech. For example:

```
Your <emphasis>United Airlines</emphasis> flight is scheduled tonight
<prosody rate="-20%">at 8:80pm</prosody> It is almost 4pm now. Good
time to get ready.
```

This friendly reminder emphasizes the airline's name and slows down the voice speed 20% while pronouncing the departure time.

According to the JSAPI, the synthesizer's *speak()* method understands JSML. JSML has more element names or tags in addition to *emphasis* and *prosody*.

For example, the *div* marks text content structures such as paragraph and sentences.

```
Hello <div type="paragraph">How are you</div>
```

The *sayas* tag provides important hints to the synthesizer on how to treat the text that follows. For example, "3/5" can be treated as a number or as a date.

```
<sayas class="date:dm">3/5</sayas>
<!-- spoken as "May third" -->
<sayas class="number">1/2</sayas>
<!-- spoken as "half" -->
<sayas class="phone">12345678901</sayas>
<!-- spoken as "1-234-567-8901" -->
<sayas class="net:email">jeff.zhuk@javaschool.com</sayas>
<!-- spoken as "Jeff dot Zhuk at Javaschool dot com" -->
<sayas class="currency">$9.95</sayas>
<!-- spoken as "nine dollars ninety five cents" -->
<sayas class="literal">IRS</sayas>
```

```
<!-- spoken as character-by-character "I.R.S" -->
<sayas class="measure">65kg</sayas>
<!-- spoken as "sixty five kilograms" -->
```

In addition, a voice tag specifies the speaking voice. For example:

```
<voice gender="male" age="20"> Do you want to send fax?</voice>
```

Notice that we can define the speaking voice in our Java code (see Fig. 12.1) or in JSML. Which way is preferable?

For the famous *Hello World* application, it is easier to specify voice characteristics directly in the code. JSML is a better choice for real-life production-quality applications; it gives more control of speech synthesis.

JSML Factory as One of the *AVIFactory* Implementations

JSML-based text can be generated on the fly by an appropriate lightweight presentation layer component of the application. No adjustment of the core services is required. We can use XML Stylesheet Language for Transformations (XSLT) to automatically convert core service contents into HTML or JSML format. Figure 12.2 shows the Object Model Diagram for the enterprise application capable to execute XML based scenarios with audio and video interfaces (AVI).

The *AVIFactory* interface on the left side of Fig. 12.2 has multiple implementations for audio and video presentation formats. Any *AVIFactory* implementation transforms data into JSML, HTML, or other presentation formats.

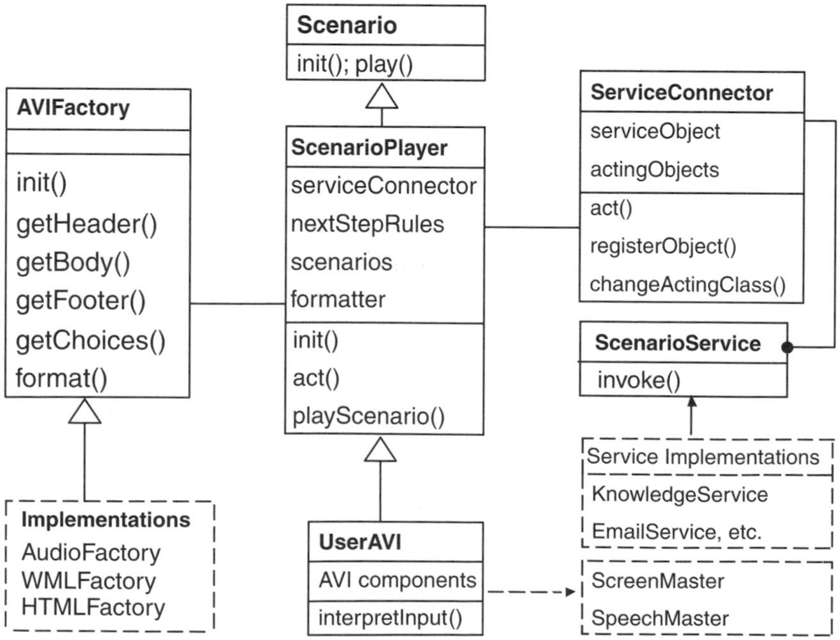

FIGURE 12.2. Object Model Diagram of an Enterprise Application Driven by XML Scenarios.

The *ScenarioPlayer* class plays a selected scenario and uses the *ServiceConnector* object to invoke any service that retrieves data according to a scenario.

The *ScenarioPlayer* class creates the proper *AVIFactory* presenter object to transform data into the proper audio or video presentation format.

In this chapter, we look into an example of the *AudioFactory*, whereas in Chapter 14, we consider implementation examples of the *ScenarioPlayer* and other classes.

Speech Synthesis Markup Language

Is JSML the best way to represent voice data? We have to ask several more questions before we can answer this one. For example, what are the current standards in the speech synthesis and recognition area?

Speech Synthesis Markup Language (SSML) [3] is an upcoming W3C standard; SSML Specification Version 1.0 may be approved by the time this book is published.

JSML and SSML are not exactly the same (surprise!). Both are XML-based definitions for voice synthesis characteristics. Do not panic! It is relatively easy to map SSML to JSML for at least some voice characteristics.

An example of an SSML document is provided in Fig. 12.3.

The differences between SSML and JSML are very apparent, but the similarities are even more impressive.

Here is a brief review of basic SSML elements.

audio—allows insertion of recorded audio files
break—an empty element to set the prosodic boundaries between words
emphasis—increases the level of stress with which the contained text is spoken
mark—a specific reference point in the text
paragraph—indicates the paragraph structure of the document
phoneme—provides the phonetic pronunciation for the contained text
prosody—controls the pitch, rate, and volume of the speech output
say-as—indicates the type of text contained in the element; for example, date or number

```
<?xml version="1.0" encoding="ISO-8859-1"?>
<!-- SSML Document-->

<speak version="1.0"
       xmlns="http://www.w3.org/2001/10/synthesis"
       xml:lang="en-US">
   <sentence>
           Message from <prosody rate="-30%"> Deena Malkin
           </prosody>
       delivered <say-as type="date"> 02/13/2003 </say-as>
           research paper on <prosody rate="-30%"> SSML
           </prosody>
   </sentence>
</speak>
```

FIGURE 12.3

sentence—indicates the sentence structure of the document
speak—includes the document body, the required root element for all SSML documents
sub—substitutes a string of text that should be pronounced in place of the text contained in the element
voice—describes speaking voice characteristics

Here is an example of another SSML document:

```
<?XML version="1.0" encoding="ISO-8859-1"?>
<speak version="1.0"
   xmlns="http://www.w3.org/2001/10/synthesis"
   xml:lang="en-US">
<sentence>
Your friendly reminder
<prosody pitch="high" rate="-20" volume="load">it is only
<say-as type="number"> 5</say-as> days left till the
 Valentine day</prosody>
</sentence>
</speak>
```

From SSML to JSML

A simple example of mapping SSML to JSML is provided with the *SSMLtoJSML AudioFactory* class, which implements the *AVIFactory* interface and represents a version of the *AudioFactory* (Fig. 12.4).

The *SSMLtoJSMLAudioFactory* class implements the *AVIFactory* interface. There are at least six methods that must be provided in this class. Figure 12.4 displays four of them.

The *init()* method initializes an original source. The *initComponents()* method creates the synthesizer object and can use the *getVoices()* method considered in Fig. 12.1 to initialize voice components. The *getHeader()* method returns the standard JSML header. The *getFooter()* method returns the standard JSML footer.

The *getBody()* method extracts a speakable text from the original SSML source. The "speak" tags frame this text. We use the *Stringer.getStringBetweenTags()* method for body extraction.

The next move is to map SSML tags with appropriate JSML tags. We use two string array-maps: the SSMLmap array and the corresponding JSMLmap array.

A simple loop uses the *Stringer.replaceIgnoreCase()* method to map these tags.

(We will consider the *Stringer* class with its methods in Chapter 14.)

Play JSML

Note that the *SSMLtoJSMLAudioFactory* class implements the *Speakable* interface. The *Speakable* interface is the spoken version of the *toString()* method of the *Object* class. Implementing the *Speakable* interface means implementing the *getJSMLText()* method. The *getJSMLText()* method and the *play()* method are shown in Fig. 12.5.

With the source code presented in Fig. 12.4, the *getJSMLText()* method can be implemented as a single line that concatenates the header, transformed body, and footer of the JSML string.

```
// SSMLtoJSMLFactory

package com.its.connector;

import javax.speech.*;
import javax.speech.synthesis.*;
import java.util.Locale;

/**
 * The SSMLtoJSMLFactory class is to transform SSML data into JSML
 format
 * And present the data
 * @author Jeff.Zhuk@JavaSchool.com
 */
public class SSMLtoJSMLAudioFactory implements AVIFactory,
Speakable {
    private String source;
    private String jsml; // formatted JSML string
    private Synthesizer synthesizer;
    // private Voice[] voices; // optional
    // private int[] ages = {AGE_TEENAGER,AGE_MIDDLE_ADULT};
    // private int[] gender = {GENDER_FEMALE, GENDER_MALE};
    private String[] SSMLmap = {"<sentence>","
    </sentence>","<say-as type","</say-as>"};
    private String[] JSMLmap = {"<div type=
    \"sent\">","</div>","<sayas class","</sayas>"}
    /**
     * The init() method is to initiate data
     * @param source
     */
    public void init(String source) {
        this.source = source;
    }
    /**
     * The initComponents() method initializes synthesizer
     * The method can optionally use getVoices() to init voice
       components
     */
    public void initComponents() {
        try {
            // Create a synthesizer for English language
            synthesizer = Central.createSynthesizer(new
            SynthesizerModeDesc(Locale.ENGLISH));
            // Get it ready to speak
            synthesizer.allocate();
            synthesizer.resume();
```

FIGURE 12.4

```
            // voices = getVoices(gender, ages); // optional
        } catch(Exception e) {
            System.out.println("SSMLtoJSMLAudioFactory.init:
            ERROR creating synthesizer");
        }
    /**
     * The getHeader() method is to provide a proper
       presentation header
     * @return header
     */
    public String getHeader() {
        return "<?xml version=\"1.0\"?>\n<jsml>\n";
    }
    /**
     * The getBody() method is to proved a proper body in
     the presentation format
     * @return body
     */
    public String getBody() {
        // extract body from the original source
        String body = Stringer.getStringBetweenTags
        (source, "speak");

        // replace the SSMLmap cases with the JSML tags
        // Stringer.replaceIgnoreCase is similar to the
        // replaceAll() of String in 1.4
        for(int i=0; i<SSMLmap.length; i++) {
            body = Stringer.replaceIgnoreCase(body,
            SSMLmap[i],JSMLmap[i]);
        }
        return body;
    }
    /**
     * The getFooter() method is to provide a proper footer
     * @return footer
     */
    public String getFooter() {
        return "</jsml>";
    }
    // more methods
```

FIGURE 12.4. *(cont.)*

The *play()* method uses the factory properties to present the JSML content. The *play()* method starts by checking whether the synthesizer is ready to talk. Then it uses the synthesizer object to invoke its *speak()* method, passing the JSML string as one of the arguments.

The other argument is a *SpeakableListener* object. This object can be used to receive and handle events associated with the spoken text. We do not plan to use the *SpeakableListener*

```
/**
 * The getJSMLText() method returns JSML string
 * @return jsml
 */
public String getJSMLText() {
    jsml = getFooter() + getBody() + getFooter();
}
/**
 * The play() method uses the factory properties to present the
 * content
 */
public void play() {
    if(synthesizer == null) {
        initComponents();
    }
    synthesizer.speak(jsml, null);
}
/**
 * The getChoices() method returns an XML string with expected
 * user input
 * @return xml
 */
public String getChoices() {
    return null;
}
/**
 * The getVoices() method creates a set of voices according to
 * initial age and gender parameters
 * The method checks if the voice if available.
 * If requested age or gender is not available the default
 * voice parameters are set.
 * @param gender
 * @param ages
 * @return voices
 */
public Voice[] getVoices(int[] gender, int[] ages) {
    // make sure that at least default set
    if(gender == null) {
        gender = new int[1];
        gender[0] = GENDER_DONT_CARE;
    }
    if(ages == null) {
        ages = new int[1];
        ages[0] = AGE_DONT_CARE;
    }
    Voice[] Voice = new Voice [ages.length *
    gender.length]; // all combinations
    SynthesizerModeDesc desc = new
```

FIGURE 12.5

```
        SynthesizerModeDesc(Locale.ENGLISH);
        Voice[] availableVoices = desc.getVoices();
        // try to set requested voices
        for (int i = 0; i < ages.length; i++) {
            for (int j = 0; j < gender.length; j++) {
                int k=(i+1)*j; // current voice index
                // try to set voice according to requirements
                // and check availability
                boolean available = false; // start from gender
                voices[k].setGender(gender[j]);
                for(int n=0; !available && n
                <availableVoices.length; n++) {
                    if (voices[k].match(availableVoices[n])) {
                        available = true;
                    }
                }
                if(!available) {
                    voices[k].setGender(GENDER_DONT_CARE);
                }
                // continue with ages
                voices[k].setAge(ages[i]);
                for(int n=0; !available && n
                <availableVoices.length; n++) {
                    if (voices[k].match(availableVoices[n])) {
                        available = true;
                    }
                }
                if(!available) {
                    voices[k].setAge(AGE_DONT_CARE);
                }
            }
        }
        // at this point all requested voices set to
        // requested parameters or to default return voices;
    }
}   // end of the class
```

FIGURE 12.5. (*cont.*)

object in our example, so we passed the null object as the second argument. It is possible to use the normal mechanisms for attachment and removal of listeners with the *addSpeakableListener()* and *removeSpeakableListener()* methods.

SPEECH RECOGNITION WITH JAVA

Speech technologies are not limited by speech synthesis. Speech recognition technologies have matured to the point that the default message "Please repeat your selection" is not so commonplace anymore, and human-computer conversation can go beyond multiple-choice menus.

There are recognizer programs for personal use, corporate sales, and other purposes. Most personal recognizers support dictation mode. They are speaker dependent, requiring "program training" that creates a "speaker profile" with a detailed map of the user's speaking patterns and accent. Then, the program uses this map to improve recognition accuracy.

The JSAPI offers a recognizer that provides an optional *SpeakerManager* object that allows an application to manage the *SpeakerProfiles* of that recognizer. The *getSpeakerManager()* method of the recognizer interface returns the *SpeakerManager* if this option is available for this recognizer. Recognizers that do not maintain speaker profiles—known as speaker-independent recognizers—return *null* for this method.

A single recognizer may have multiple *SpeakerProfiles* for one user and may store the profiles of multiple users.

The *SpeakerProfile* class is a reference to data stored with the recognizer. A profile is identified by three values: its unique ID, its name, and its variant. The ID and the name are self-explanatory. The variant identifies a particular enrollment of a user and becomes useful when one user has more than one enrollment or *SpeakerProfile*. Additional data stored by a recognizer with the profile may include:

- Speaker data such as name, age, and gender
- Speaker preferences
- Data about the words and word patterns of the speaker (language models)
- Data about the pronunciation of words by the speaker (word models)
- Data about the speaker's voice and speaking style (acoustic models)
- Records of previous training and usage history

Speech recognition systems (SRS) can listen to users and, to some degree, recognize and translate their speech to words and sentences. Current speech technologies have to constrain speech context with grammars. Today, the systems can achieve "reasonable" recognition accuracy only within these constraints.

The Java Speech Grammar Format

The Java Speech Grammar Format (JSGF) [4] is a platform and vendor-independent way of describing a **rule grammar** (also known as a **command and control grammar** or **regular grammar**).

A rule grammar specifies the types of **utterances** a user might say. For example, a service control grammar might include *Service* and *Action* commands.

A voice application can be based on a set of scenarios. Each scenario knows the context and provides appropriate grammar rules for the context.

Grammar rules may be provided in a multilingual manner. For example:

```
<greetings.english.hello>
<greetings.russian.privet>
<greetings.deutsch.gutenTag>
```

"Hello," "Privet," and *"GutenTag"* are tokens in the grammar rules. Tokens define expected words that may be spoken by a user. The world of tokens forms a **vocabulary** or **lexicon**. Each record in the vocabulary defines the **pronunciation** of the token.

A single file defines a single grammar with its header and body. The header defines the JSGF version and (optional) encoding. For example:

```
#JSGF V1.0 ISO8859-5;
```

The grammar starts with the grammar name and is similar to Java package names. For example:

```
grammar com.its.scenarios.examples.greetings;
```

We can also import grammar rules and packages, as is usually done in Java code:

```
import <com.its.scenarios.examples.cyc.>;
// talk to knowledge base
```

The grammar body defines *rules* as a rule name followed by its definition-token. The definition can include several alternatives separated by "|" characters. For example:

```
<login> = login;
<find> = find | search | get | lookup;
<new> = new | create | add;
<command> = <find> | <new> | <login>;
```

We can use the Kleene star (named after Stephen Cole Kleene, its originator) or the "+" character to set expectations that a user can repeat a word multiple times.

```
<agree> = I * agree | yes | OK;
// "I agree" and "agree" - both covered
<disagree> = no +; // no can be spoken 1 or more times
```

The Kleene star and the + operator are both **unary operators** in the JSGF. There is also the tag unary operator that helps to return application-specific information as the result of recognition. For example:

```
<service> = (mail | email) {email} | (search | research |
 find) {find};
```

The system returns the word *email* if *mail* or *email* is spoken. When *search, research*, or *find* is uttered, the system returns the word *find.*

Today, the mainstream of speech recognition technology lies outside the JSAPI. (This may be different next year.) One example of a current technology is the open source Sphinx [5] project written in C++ by a group from Carnegie Mellon University.

In the Sphinx system, recognition takes place in three passes (the last two are optional): lexical-tree Viterbi search, flat-structured Viterbi search, and global best-path search.

Improving Sphinx Recognition Rate with Training

Sphinx can be trained to better satisfy a specific client with the SphinxTrain program. Even after training, the rate of accuracy for Sphinx-2 is about 50%; for Sphinx-3, delivered at the end of 2002, the rate is about 70%. In comparison, the rate of accuracy in Microsoft's Speech Software Development Kit (SDK) recognition engine is 95% after voice training and microphone calibration. There are more products on the market today, like IBM ViaVoice Speech SDK, or Dragon NaturallySpeaking products that produce even better results although they are not freely available.

Microsoft Speech SDK

The Microsoft Speech SDK [6] is based on the Microsoft Speech API (SAPI), a layer of software that allows applications and speech engines to communicate in a standardized way. The MS Speech SDK provides both text-to-speech (TTS) and speech recognition functions. Figure 12.6 illustrates the TTS synthesis process. The main elements participating in TTS conversion are:

ISpVoice—the interface used by the application to access the TTS function
ISpTTSEngineSite—the engine interface to speak data and queue events
IspObjectWithToken—the interface to create and initialize the engine
ISpTTSEngine—the interface to call the engine
IspTokenUI—the way for the SAPI control panel to access the User Interface

The speech recognition architecture looks even simpler (Fig. 12.7). The main speech recognition elements interact in the following way:

1. The engine uses the *ISpSREngineSite* interface to call the SAPI to read audio and returns the recognition results.
2. The SAPI calls the engine using the methods of the *ISpSREngine* interface to pass details of recognition grammars. SAPI also uses these methods to start and stop recognition.
3. The *IspObjectWithToken* interface provides a mechanism for the engine to query and edit information about the object token.
4. *ISpTokenUI* represents User Interface components that are callable from an application.

SAPI 5 synthesis markup is not exactly SSML; it is closer to the format published by the Sable Consortium. SAPI XML tags provide functions such as volume control and word emphasis. These tags can be inserted into text passed into *ISpVoice::Speak* and text streams of format SPDFID_XML, which are then passed into *ISpVoice::SpeakStream* and auto-detected (by default) by the SAPI XML parser. In the case of an invalid XML structure, a speak error

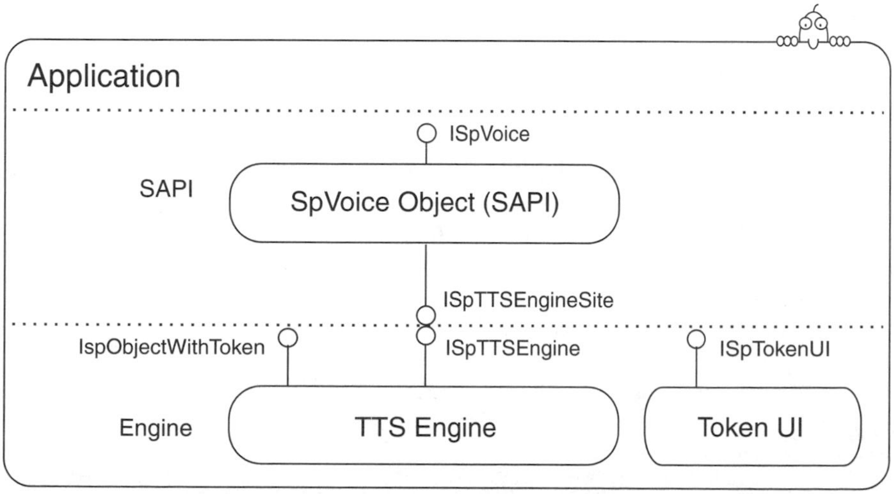

Figure 12.6. TTS Synthesis Process.

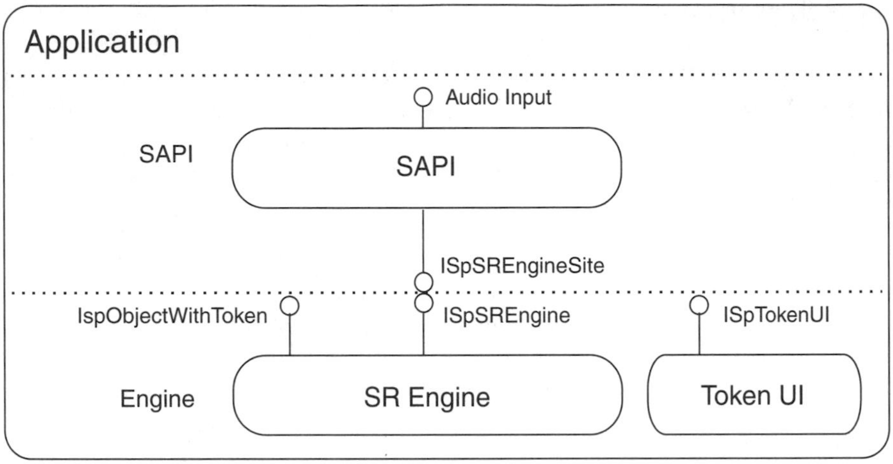

FIGURE 12.7. Speech Recognition Architecture.

may be returned to the application. We can change rate and volume attributes in real time using *ISpVoice::SetRate* and *ISpVoice::SetVolume.*

Volume

The Volume tag controls the volume of a voice and requires just one attribute: Level, an integer between 0 and 100. The tag can be empty, to apply to all following text, or it can frame content to which alone it applies.

```
<volume level="50">This text should be spoken at volume level fifty.
   <volume level="100">
      This text should be spoken at volume level one hundred.
   </volume>
</volume>
<volume level="80"/>All text which follows should be
 spoken at volume level eighty.
```

Rate

The Rate tag defines the rate of a voice with one of two attributes: Speed and AbsSpeed. The Speed attribute defines the relative increase or decrease of the speed value, whereas AbsSpeed defines its absolute rate value: an integer between −10 and 10. The tag can be empty, to apply to all following text, or it can frame content to which alone it applies.

```
<rate absspeed="5">
   This text should be spoken at rate five.
   <rate speed="-5">
      Decrease the rate to level zero.
   </rate>
</rate>
<rate absspeed="10"/> Speak the rest with the rate 10.
```

Pitch

In a very similar manner, the Pitch tag controls the pitch of a voice with one of two attributes: Middle and AbsMiddle; an integer between −10 and 10 can represent an absolute as well as relative value.

```
<pitch absmiddle="5">
This text should be spoken at pitch five.
   <pitch middle="-5">
      This text should be spoken at pitch zero.
   </pitch>
</pitch>
<pitch absmiddle="10"/> All the rest should be spoken at pitch ten.
```

Zero represents the default level for rate, volume, and pitch values.

Emph

The Emph tag instructs the voice to emphasize a word or section of text. The Emph tag cannot be empty.

```
Your <emph>American Airline</emph> flight departs at <emph>eight</emph>
tonight
```

Voice

The Voice tag defines a voice based on its Age, Gender, Language, Name, Vendor, and VendorPreferred attributes, which can be required or optional. These correspond exactly to the required and optional attribute parameters for the *ISpObjectTokenCategory_EnumerateToken* and *SpFindBestToken* functions.

If no voice matching all the required attributes is found, a voice change will not occur. Optional attributes are treated differently. In this case, an exact match is not necessarily expected. A voice that is closer to the provided attributes will be selected over one that is less similar. For example:

```
The default voice should speak this sentence.
<voice required="Gender=Female;Age!=Child">
A female non-child should speak this sentence, if one exists.
<voice required="Age=Teen">
   A teen should speak this sentence. If a female, non-child teen voice
is present; this voice will be selected over a male teen voice, for
example.
   </voice>
</voice>
```

Let us consider a demonstration program that uses the TTS and speech recognition facilities of the Microsoft Speech SDK.

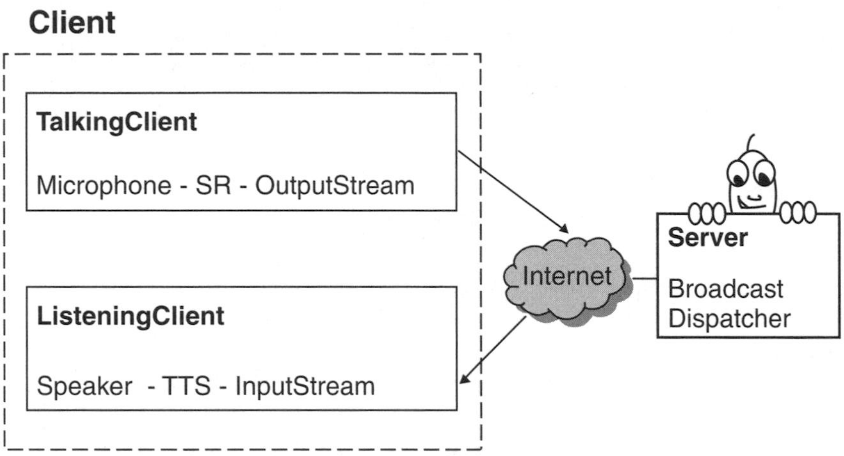

FIGURE 12.8. Chat with MS SDK.

SPEECH TECHNOLOGY TO DECREASE NETWORK BANDWIDTH

The application is a conference between multiple clients over the Internet. The application utilizes speech technology to significantly decrease network bandwidth. Client programs intercept a user's speech, translate it to text, and send ASCII text over the Internet to the server-dispatcher. The server broadcasts the text it receives to the other clients (a regular chat schema). Client programs receive text from the server and convert it back to speech. Figure 12.8. illustrates the application with a diagram.

Other application details are:

- Speech recognition and TTS are done on the client side.
- The client recognizes a phrase.
- Plain text is transmitted between the client and the server.
- The client program appends metadata, such as the user's name, in SSML format.
- The server side can be implemented in C++, C#, or Java, using TCP/IP sockets.

An example of the *TalkingClient* program can be found in Fig. 12.9. The *TalkingClient* program takes the user's name as an optional argument. If the argument is not provided, the default voice is used.

The main routine starts with the socket connection to a recipient. We then initialize the speech engine and define the break signal that will be used to indicate when to send to the server what the user has said. In the example, the break signal is the word *okay*.

The main processing happens in the *while* loop. The speech engine recognizes the user's sentence and prints it on the screen. Then, the program sends the resulting text to the server with the additional SAPI XML Voice tag:

```
<voice optional="Gender=userGender;Age=userAge;Name= userName">
resultingText</voice>
```

The other part of the application is presented in Fig. 12.10. The requirements of the *ListeningClient* are to receive text from the server and to transform text to speech using the voice profile, if it is available.

```
/*****************
***TalkingClient.cpp***
*****************/
#include <iostream>
#include "Socket.h"

#include <windows.h>
#include <sapi.h>
#include <stdio.h>
#include <string.h>
#include <atlbase.h>
#include "sphelper.h"

using namespace std;

// Provided by Deena Malkina with use and modification of Microsoft
// Speech SDK examples

inline HRESULT ReadVoiceData(ISpRecoContext * voiceDataContext,
ISpRecoResult ** recognitionData)
{
    HRESULT successLevel = S_OK;
    CSpEvent speechEvent;

    while (SUCCEEDED(successLevel) &&
           SUCCEEDED(successLevel = speechEvent.
           GetFrom(voiceDataContext)) &&
           successLevel == S_FALSE)
    {
        successLevel =
voiceDataContext->WaitForNotifyEvent(INFINITE);
    }

    *recognitionData = speechEvent.RecoResult();
    if (*recognitionData)
    {
        (*recognitionData)->AddRef();
    }

    return successLevel;
}

int main(int argc, char* argv[])
{
    HRESULT successLevel = E_FAIL;
    // user name can be obtained from argv[1] or from
system.properties
```

FIGURE 12.9

```
const WCHAR * userName = L"Deena"; // from user profile
const WCHAR * userGender = L"Female"; // from user profile
const WCHAR * userAge = L"Teen";  // from user profile
const WCHAR * voiceTag = sprintf(
  "<voice optional=\"Gender=%s;Age=%s;Name=%s\">",
  userGender,userAge,userAge);

if(argc == 2) {
// hopefully there is the voice profile on the name
    userName = argv[1];
}
try {
    // code to connect to recipient, for example,
    "ipserve.com, port=7445" via SocketClient
    SocketClient sender("ipserve.com",7445);
    // initialize Speech Engine
    if (SUCCEEDED(successLevel = ::CoInitialize(NULL)))
    {
        CComPtr<ISpRecoContext> context;
        CComPtr<ISpRecoGrammar> grammar;

        successLevel = context.
        CoCreateInstance(CLSID_SpSharedRecoContext);

        if (context &&
            SUCCEEDED(successLevel = context->
            SetNotifyWin32Event()) &&
            SUCCEEDED(successLevel = context->
            SetInterest(SPFEI(SPEI_RECOGNITION),
            SPFEI(SPEI_RECOGNITION))) &&
            SUCCEEDED(successLevel = context->
            SetAudioOptions(SPAO_RETAIN_AUDIO,
            NULL, NULL)) &&
            SUCCEEDED(successLevel = context->
            CreateGrammar(0, &grammar)) &&
            SUCCEEDED(successLevel = grammar->
            LoadDictation(NULL, SPLO_STATIC)) &&
            SUCCEEDED(successLevel =
            grammar->SetDictationState(SPRS_ACTIVE)))
        {
            USES_CONVERSION;

            // define the break signal that will send the
            // sentence to the server
            const WCHAR * const breakSign = L"okey";
            const WCHAR * const exitSign = L"exit the program";
```

FIGURE 12.9. *(cont.)*

```
                CComPtr<ISpRecoResult> resultObject;
                printf( "You can start talking.\nSay \"%s\" to
                send your phrase.\n",
                  W2A(breakSign) );
                while (SUCCEEDED(successLevel =
                ReadVoiceData(context, &resultObject)))
                {
                  grammar->SetDictationState( SPRS_INACTIVE );

                    CSpDynamicString resultingText;

                    if (SUCCEEDED(resultObject->
                    GetText(SP_GETWHOLEPHRASE,
                    SP_GETWHOLEPHRASE,
                                     TRUE, &resultingText,
                                     NULL)))
                    {
                        printf("Said by %s:  %s\n",
                        W2A(userName), W2A(resultingText));

                        // send text to server: voiceTag +
                        // resultingText + "</voice>";
                        char * textToSend = sprintf ("%s%s
                        </voice>", voiceTag,resultingText);
                        sender.SendLine(textToSend);

                        resultObject->SpeakAudio(NULL, 0,
                        NULL, NULL);
                        resultObject.Release();
                    }
                    if (_wcsicmp(resultingText, breakSign) == 0)
                    {
                        break;
                    }

                    grammar->SetDictationState( SPRS_ACTIVE );
                }
            }
        } catch(const char * e) {
            cerr << e <<endl;
        }
        ::CoUninitialize();
    }
    return successLevel;
}
```

FIGURE 12.9. ***(cont.)***

```
/**
 * ListeningClient.cpp
 * By Deena.Malkina@javaschool.com
 * with use and modification of Microsoft Speech
 SDK examples
 */
#include "Socket.h"
#include <string>
#include <iostream>
#include <windows.h>
#include <sapi.h>
#include <stdio.h>

#define _ATL_APARTMENT_THREADED
#include <atlbase.h>
//You may derive a class from CComModule and use it if you want to
override something,
//but do not change the name of _Module
extern CComModule _Module;
#include <atlcom.h>

#include <string.h>
//#include <atlbase.h>
#include "sphelper.h"

using namespace std;

int main() {
    const string machine="javaschool.com";
    const int port=7554;

    ISpVoice * pVoice = NULL;

    if (FAILED(::CoInitialize(NULL)))
     return FALSE;

    HRESULT hr = CoCreateInstance(
      CLSID_SpVoice, NULL, CLSCTX_ALL, IID_ISpVoice,
      (void **)&pVoice);

    try {
        SocketClient s(machine, port);
        String textToSpeak;

        if( SUCCEEDED( hr ) ) {
```

FIGURE 12.10

```
            while (1)  {
                // read one char at a time
                String c = s.ReceiveChar();
                if (c.empty()) break;

                cout << c;
                cout.flush();

                if(c=="." || c=="!" || c=="?") {
                   // transform textToSpeak to WCHAR

                   hr = pVoice->Speak(textToSpeak, 0, NULL);

                } else {
                   textToSpeak.append(c);
                }
            }   // end of while loop
            pVoice->Release();
            pVoice = NULL;
        }
        // Reset or Uninitialize
        ::CoUninitialize();
    } catch (const char* s) {
        cerr << s << endl;
    } catch (String s) {
        cerr << s << endl;
    } catch (...) {
        cerr << "unhandled exception\n";
    }
    char q;
    cin>>q;
    return TRUE;
}
```

FIGURE 12.10. *(cont.)*

The *ListeningClient* program starts in a very similar manner. It uses the *ReceiveLine* method of the *SocketClient* to listen to messages coming from the server. The program converts every unit of speech into voice and displays the line on the screen. Examples of *Socket* classes for Windows can be found online [7].

Appendix 3 provides examples of TTS and speech recognition programs written in C# using SAPI 5.

STANDARDS FOR SCENARIOS FOR SPEECH APPLICATIONS

Let us stop this overview of the parts of speech recognition technology for a minute. All of the pieces are important: some are more important for system programmers who do the groundwork, whereas others target application developers. Application developers can use this groundwork to describe application flow and write interpretation scenarios.

Our next step is to write scenarios for speech applications. Let us consider current and future standards that may help. Note that the Microsoft. NET Speech SDK uses SSML, which is a part of the W3C Speech Interface Framework (unlike the Microsoft Speech SDK that uses SAPI XML). SSML is a markup language that defines TTS processing, which is the simplest part of speech technology. There are two markup languages that can describe a complete speech interface: Speech Application Language Tags (SALT) [8], a relatively new standard, and VoiceXML [9], a well-established technology with many implementations.

VoiceXML was developed for telephony applications as a high-level dialog markup language that integrates speech interface with data and provides a full control of the application flow.

Unlike VoiceXML, SALT offers a lower-level interface that strictly focuses on speech tags but targets several devices, including but not limited to telephone systems.

VoiceXML, as well as SALT, uses standards of the W3C Speech Interface Framework such as SSML and Speech Recognition Grammar Standard (SRGS) [10]. SALT also includes recommendations on Natural Language Semantics Markup Language (NLSML) [11] as a recognition result format and Call Control XML (CCXML) [12] as a call control language.

In a nutshell: NLSML is an XML-based markup language for representing the meaning of a natural language utterance, and CCXML provides telephony call control support for VoiceXML or SALT, and other dialog systems.

NLSML uses an XForms data model for the semantic information that is returned in the interpretation. (See the NLSML and XForms overviews in Appendix 2.)

SALT provides facilities for multimodal applications that may include not only voice but also screen interfaces. SALT also gives developers the freedom to embed SALT tags into other languages. This allows for more flexibility in writing speak-and-display scenarios.

Speech Application Language Tags

SALT consists of a relatively small set of XML elements. Each XML element has associated attributes and Document Object Model (DOM) properties, events, and methods. One can write speech interfaces for voice-only and multimodal applications using SALT with HTML, XHTML, and other standards. SALT controls dialog scenarios through the DOM event model that is popular in Web software.

The three top-level elements in SALT are *<listen . . . >*, *<prompt . . . >*, and *<dtmf . . . >*. The first two XML elements define speech engine parameters:

<listen . . . > configures the speech recognizer, executes recognition, and handles speech input events;

<prompt . . . > configures the speech synthesizer and plays out prompts

The third XML element plays a significant role in call controls for telephony applications.

<dtmf . . . > configures and controls dual-tone multifrequency (DTMF) signaling in telephony applications. Telephony systems use DTMF to signal which key has been pressed by a client. Regular phones usually have twelve keys: ten decimal digit keys and "#" and "*" keys. Each key corresponds to a different pair of frequencies.

The *<listen>* and *<dtmf>* elements may contain *<grammar>* and *<bind>* elements. The *<listen>* element may also include the *<record>* element.

The *<grammar>* element defines grammars. A single *<listen>* element may include multiple grammars. The *<listen>* element may have methods to activate an individual grammar before starting recognition. SALT itself is independent of the grammar formats, but for interoperability, it recommends supporting at least the XML form of the W3C SRGS.

The *<bind>* element can inspect the results of recognition and provide conditional copy-actions. The *<bind>* element can cause the relevant data to be copied to values in the containing page. A single *<listen>* element may contain multiple *<bind>*s. *<bind>* may have a *conditional test* attribute as well as a *value* attribute. *<bind>* uses XPath syntax (see Appendix 2 and other XML standards mentioned in this book) in its *value* attribute to point to a particular node of the result. *<bind>* uses an XML pattern query in its *conditional test* attribute. If the condition is true, the content of the node is bound into the page element specified by the *targetElement* attribute. The *onReco* event handler with script programming can provide even more complex processing. The *<onReco>* and *<bind>* elements are triggered on the return of a recognition result.

The *<record>* element can specify parameters related to speech recording. *<bind>* or scripted code can process the results of the recording, if necessary.

A Spoken Message Scenario

Figure 12.11 demonstrates a scenario in which dialog flow is provided with a client-side script. The scenario is actually an HTML page with embedded SALT tags and script functions. The *askForService()* script activates the SALT *<listen>* and *<prompt>* tags. For example, *askName.Start()* prompts the user with "What is your name?" and the following *nameRecognition.Start()* examines the recognition results. The *askForService()* script executes the relevant prompts and recognitions until all values are obtained. Successful message recognition triggers the *submit()* function, which submits the message to the recipient.

The user's name not only serves as the user's signature but can also invoke a chosen voice profile, if available, on the recipient side.

Did you notice the reference to the *spokenMessage.xml* grammar file that supports the scenario in the code? How do we define grammar?

GRAMMAR DEFINITION

First, let us look into the existing Command and Control features of the MS Speech SDK. The Command and Control features of SAPI 5 are based on context-free grammars (CFGs). A CFG defines a specific set of words and the sentences that are valid for recognition by the speech recognition engine.

The CFG format in SAPI 5 uses XML to define the structure of grammars and grammar rules. SAPI 5 compliant speech recognition engines expect grammar definitions in a binary format produced by any CFG/Grammar compiler—for example, *gc.exe*, the SAPI 5 grammar compiler included in Speech SDK. Compilation is usually done before application run-time but can be done at run-time.

```
<!-- HTML -->
<html xmlns:salt="urn:saltforum.org/schemas/020124">
 <body onload="askForService()">
  <form id="messageForm"
     action="http://javaschool.com/school/public/
    knowledge/SALT/message"
      method="post">
   <input name="fromTextBox" type="text" />
   <input name="subjectTextBox" type="text" />
   <input name="recipientTextBox" type="text" />
   <input name="messageTextBox" type="text" />
  </form>

<!-- Speech Application Language Tags -->
  <salt:prompt id="askName"> What is your name?
  </salt:prompt>
  <salt:prompt id="askSubject"> What is the subject?
  </salt:prompt>
  <salt:prompt id="askRecipient"> Who is the recipient?
  </salt:prompt>
  <salt:prompt id="askMessage"> What is your message?
  </salt:prompt>
  <salt:prompt id="repeatDefault"
  onComplete="askForService()">
Please repeat your answer.
  </salt:prompt>
  <salt:listen id="nameRecognition"
 onReco="setName()" onNoReco="repeatDefault.Start()">
           <salt:grammar src="spokenMessage.xml" />
  </salt:listen>
  <salt:listen id="subjectRecognition"
 onReco="setSubject()" onNoReco="repeatDefault.Start()">
           <salt:grammar src="spokenMessage.xml" />
  </salt:listen>
  <salt:listen id="recipientRecognition"
 onReco="setRecipient()" onNoReco="repeatDefault.Start()">
           <salt:grammar src="spokenMessage.xml" />
  </salt:listen>
  <salt:listen id="messageRecognition"
 onReco="setMessage()" onNoReco="repeatDefault.Start()">
           <salt:grammar src="spokenMessage.xml" />
  </salt:listen>

<!-- script -->
  <script>
    // settings are based on user's answers
    function setName() {
```

FIGURE 12.11

```
      messageForm.fromTextBox.value = nameRecognition.text;
      askForService();
    }
    function setSubject() {
      messageForm.subjectTextBox.value =
      subjectRecognition.text;
      askForService();
    }
    function setRecipient() {
      messageForm.recipientTextBox.value =
      recipientRecognition.text;
      askForService();
    }
    function setMessage() {
      messageForm.messageTextBox.value = messageRecognition.text;
      messageForm.submit();
    }
     // the main script
    function askForService() {
      if messageForm.fromTextBox.value=="") {
        askName.Start();
        nameRecognition.Start();
      } else if (messageForm.subjectTextBox.value=="") {
        askSubject.Start();
        subjectRecognition.Start();
      } else if (messageForm.recipientTextBox.value=="") {
        askRecipient.Start();
        recipientRecognition.Start();
      } else if (messageForm.messageTextBox.value=="") {
        askMessage.Start();
        messageRecognition.Start();
      }
    }
  </script>
 </body>
</html>
```

FIGURE 12.11. ***(cont.)***

Here is an example of a file that provides grammar rules to navigate through mail messages ("next", "previous") and to retrieve the currently selected email ("getMail").

```
<GRAMMAR LANGid="409">
    <DEFINE>
        <ID NAME="VID_MailnavigationRules" VAL="1"/>
        <ID NAME="VID_MailReceiverRules" VAL="2"/>
    </DEFINE>
    <RULE id="VID_MailnavigationRules" >
      <L>
```

```
        <P VAL="next">
           <o>Please *+</o>
            <p>next</p>
            <o>message\email\mail</o>
         </P>
        <P VAL="previous">
          <o>Please *+</o>
           <p>previous\last\back</p>
           <o>message\email\mail</o>
         </P>
      </L>
    </RULE>
    <RULE id="VID_MailReceiverRules" TOPLEVEL="ACTIVE">
      <O>Please</O>
      <P>
        <L>
          <P val="getMail">Retrieve</P>
          <P val="getMail">Receive</P>
          <P val="getMail">Get</P>
        </L>
      </P>
      <O>the mail</O>
    </RULE>
</GRAMMAR>
```

Appendix 3 provides more examples (along with C# program source code) for a speech application based on SAPI 5. The grammar file can be dynamically loaded and compiled at run-time, decreasing the number of choices for any *current* recognition and improving recognition quality.

VoiceXML

The last, but definitely not least important, technology on the list is VoiceXML. Although SALT and VoiceXML have different targets, in some ways, they compete in the speech technology arena. Unlike SALT, which is relatively new, VoiceXML started in 1995, as part of an AT&T project called Phone Markup Language (PML).

The VoiceXML Forum was formed in 1998–1999 by AT&T, IBM, Lucent, and Motorola. At that time, Motorola had developed VoxML and IBM was developing its own SpeechML. The VoiceXML Forum helped integrate these two efforts. Since then, VoiceXML has had a history of successful implementations by many vendors.

Unlike SALT, which is a royalty-free, upcoming standard, VoiceXML may be subject to royalty payments. Several companies, including IBM, Motorola, and AT&T, have indicated they may have patent rights to VoiceXML.

This brief overview of VoiceXML is based on the VoiceXML2.0 Specification submitted to W3C at the beginning of 2003.

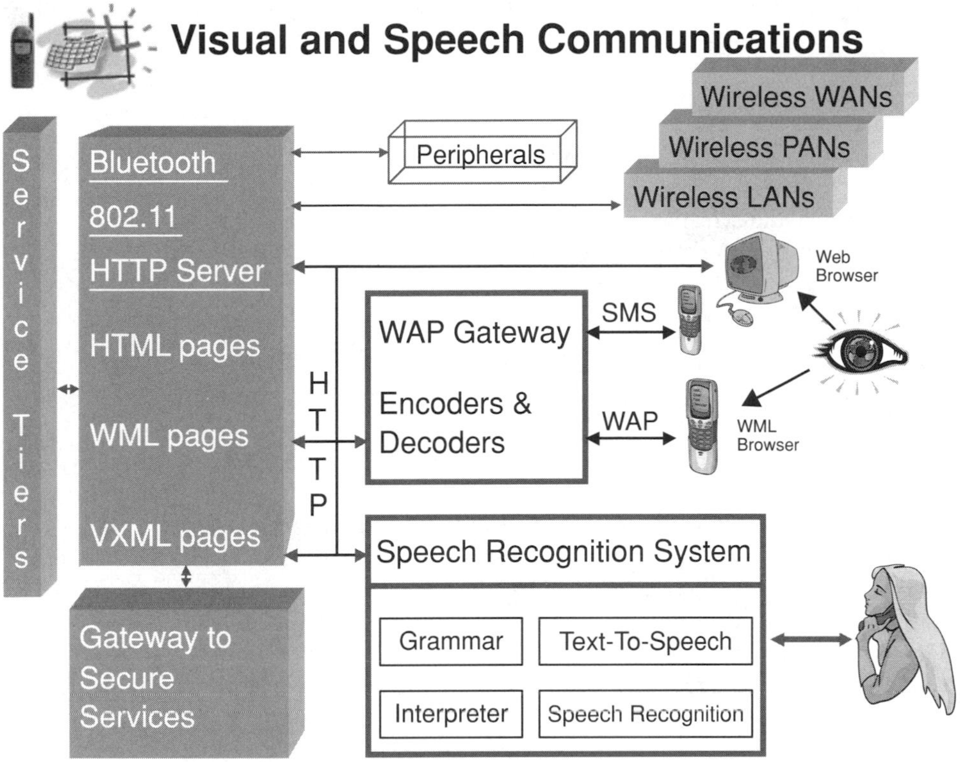

FIGURE 12.12. Multimodal Access to Business Services.

What Is VoiceXML?

VoiceXML is designed for creating dialog scenarios with digitized audio, speech recognition, and DTMF key input. VoiceXML can record spoken input, telephony, and mixed-initiative conversations. The mixed conversation is an extended case of the most common type of computer-human conversations directed by the computer. The main target of VoiceXML is Web-based development and content delivery to interactive speech applications.

The VoiceXML interpreter renders VoiceXML documents audibly, just as a Web browser renders HTML documents visually. However, standard Web browsers run on a local machine, whereas the VoiceXML interpreter runs at a remote hosting site. Figure 12.12 displays the enterprise application with multimodal access to business services.

Like HTML Web pages, VoiceXML documents have Web URLs and can be located on any Web server. VoiceXML pages also deliver the service content via speech applications.

Main Components of Speech Recognition Systems

Speech recognition systems in general and VoiceXML systems in particular rely on high-performance server-side hardware and software located on or connected to the Web container. The Web container is the architecture tier responsible for correspondence to clients over HTTP and dispatching client requests to proper business services. In this case, speech recognition services become the client that intercepts voice flow and translates it into HTTP streams. The key hardware factors for delivering reliable, scalable VoiceXML applications are:

- Telephony connectivity
- Internet connectivity
- Scalable architecture
- Caching and media streaming
- CODECs—combinations of analog-to-digital (A/D) and digital-to-analog (D/A) signal converters

Progress in hardware technologies such as the high-speed, low-power consumption digital signal processor (DSP) has substantially contributed to improving CODEC conversion efficiency.

The SRS platform contains intelligent caching technology that minimizes network traffic by caching VoiceXML, audio files, and compiled grammars. The VoiceXML platform makes extensive use of load balancing, resource pooling, and dynamic resource allocation. SRS servers use multithreaded C++ implementations, delivering the most performance from available hardware resources. To prevent unnecessary recompilation of grammars, the VoiceXML platform uses a high-performance indexing technique to cache and reuse previously compiled grammars.

Voice services offer the following software components to implement an end-to-end solution for phone-accessible Web content:

Telephony platform—software modules for TTS, voice recognition menu systems, parsing engines, and DTMF Standard support

Open-system architecture in compliance with industry standards: VoiceXML, Wireless Application Protocol (WAP), Wireless Markup Language (WML), XHTML, SSML, SRGS, NLSML, and so on.

WAP solution—support for using WAP to deliver Web and audio content to new Web phones and enabling seamless integration between Web and audio content.

Voice application and activation—user interface and logic (such as personalization) for accessing back-end audio content, and Web and email databases for easy phone access

What Is the VoiceXML Architecture and How Does It Work?

A document (Web) server contains VoiceXML documents or VXML pages with dialog-based scenarios. (I try to use the word *scenario* on every other page, but sometimes the word sneaks in-between.)

The document server responds to a client request by sending the VoiceXML document to an SRS or a VoiceXML implementation platform (the VoiceXML interpreter). A voice service scenario is a sequence of interaction dialogs between a user and an implementation platform.

Document servers perform business logic, database, and legacy system operations and produce VoiceXML documents that describe interaction dialogs. User input affects dialog interpretation by the VoiceXML interpreter. The VoiceXML interpreter transforms user input into requests submitted to a document server. The document server replies with other VoiceXML documents describing new sets of dialogs.

```
<?xml version="1.0" encoding="UTF-8"?>
<vxml xmlns="http://www.w3.org/2001/vxml"
  xmlns:xsi="http://www.w3.org/2001/XMLSchema-instance"
  xsi:schemaLocation="http://www.w3.org/2001/vxml
   http://www.w3.org/TR/voicexml20/vxml.xsd"
   version="2.0">
  <form>
  <field name="service">
     <prompt>Would you like to read your mail, send a
     message, or check your calendar?</prompt>
     <grammar src="com.its.services.grxml"
     type="application/srgs+xml"/>
  </field>
  <block>
     <submit next="http://javaschool.com/school/public/
     speech/vxml/service.jsp"/>
  </block>
 </form>
</vxml>
```

FIGURE 12.13

What Does the VoiceXML Document Look Like?

A VoiceXML document can describe the:

- Output of synthesized speech (TTS)
- Output of audio files
- Recognition of spoken input
- Recognition of DTMF input
- Recording of spoken input
- Control of dialog flow

VoiceXML requires a common grammar format—namely the XML Form of the W3C SRGS—to facilitate interoperability.

A voice application is a collection of one or more VoiceXML documents sharing the same **application root document**. A VoiceXML document is composed of one or more dialogs. The application entry point is the first VoiceXML document that the VoiceXML interpreter loads when it starts the application. The developer's task is to provide voice commands to the user in the most comfortable way while offering clearly distinguished possibilities of responses expected from the user through voice and/or telephone keys.

There are two kinds of dialogs: **forms** and **menus**. Forms define an interaction that collects field values. Each field may specify a grammar with expected inputs for that field. A menu commonly asks the user to choose one of several options and then uses the choice to transition to another dialog.

Figure 12.13 presents a very simple example of a VoiceXML document. This VoiceXML document provides a form dialog that offers users a choice of services to fill the service field. Expected answers are provided in the grammar document *com.its.services.grxml*. Each dialog has one or more speech and/or DTMF grammars associated with it. Most of the speech applications today are **machine directed**. A single dialog grammar is active at any current time for machine-directed applications, the grammar associated with a current user dialog. In **mixed-initiative** applications, the user and the machine alternate in determining what to do next. In this case, more than one dialog grammar may be active and the user can say something that matches another dialog's grammar. Mixed initiative adds flexibility and power to voice applications.

VoiceXML can handle events not covered by the form mechanism described above. There are default handlers for the predefined events; plus, developers can override these handlers with their own event handlers in any element that can throw an event. The platform throws events, for example, when the user does not respond, does not respond intelligibly, or requests help.

The *<catch>*, *<error>*,*<help>*, *<noinput>*, and *<nomatch>* elements are examples of event handlers.

For example, the *<catch>* element can detect a disconnect event and provide some action upon the event:

```
<catch event="connection.disconnect.hangup">
    <submit namelist="disconnect"
next="http://javaschool.com/school/public/speech/
    vXML/exit.jsp"/>
</catch>
```

Applications can support help by putting the help keyword in a grammar in the application root document.

```
<help>
  <prompt>Say "Retry" to retry authorization, or
  "Register" to hear the registration instructions.
  Say "Exit" or "Goodbye" to exit.
  </prompt>
  <listen/>
</help>
```

A List of VoiceXML Elements

VoiceXML elements include:

<assign>—assigns a value to a variable
<audio>—plays an audio clip within a prompt
<block>—a container of (noninteractive) executable code
<catch>—catches an event
<choice>—defines a menu item
<clear>—clears one or more form item variables
<disconnect>—disconnects a session
<else>—used in <if> elements
<elseif>—used in <if> elements
<enumerate>—shorthand for enumerating the choices in a menu
<error>—catches an error event
<exit>—exits a session

<field>—declares an input field in a form
<filled>—an action executed when fields are filled
<form>—a dialog for presenting information and collecting data
<goto>—goes to another dialog in the same or a different document
<grammar>—specifies a speech recognition or DTMF grammar
<help>—catches a help event
<if>—simple conditional logic
<initial>—declares initial logic upon entry into a mixed initiative form
<link>—specifies a transition common to all dialogs in the link's scope
<log>—generates a debug message
<menu>—a dialog for choosing among alternative destinations
<meta>—defines a metadata item as a name/value pair
<metadata>—defines metadata information using a metadata schema
<noinput>—catches a noinput event
<nomatch>—catches a nomatch event
<object>—interacts with a custom extension
<option>—specifies an option in a <field>
<param>—parameter in <object> or <subdialog>
<prompt>—queues speech synthesis and audio output to the user
<property>—controls implementation platform settings
<record>—records an audio sample
<reprompt>—plays a field prompt when a field is revisited after an event
<return>—returns from a subdialog
<script>—specifies a block of ECMAScript client-side scripting logic
<subdialog>—invokes another dialog as a subdialog of the current one
<submit>—submits values to a document server
<throw>—throws an event
<transfer>—transfers the caller to another destination
<value>—inserts the value of an expression in a prompt
<var>—declares a variable
<vxml>—top-level element in each VoiceXML document

Service Order with VoiceXML

Figure 12.14 introduces a typical VoiceXML document that initiates a brief phone conversation. The source code starts with the standard XML and then has VoiceXML reference lines. The next thing we see is a *form* that looks almost exactly like an HTML form. In fact, the form has exactly the same purpose—to collect information from a user into the form fields. This form has a single field named *course*.

The program prompts the user to choose one of the training courses.

```
<prompt>Which course do you want to take?</prompt>
```

The grammar line above the prompt defines a grammar rules file that will try to resolve the answer.

```
<grammar type="application/srgs+XML" src="/grammars/
training.grXML"/>
```

```
<?xml version="1.0" encoding="UTF-8"?>
<vxml xmlns="http://www.w3.org/2001/vxml"
   xmlns:xsi="http://www.w3.org/2001/XMLSchema-instance"
   xsi:schemaLocation="http://www.w3.org/2001/vxml
   http://www.w3.org/TR/voicexml20/vxml.xsd"
   version="2.0">

  <form id="training">
    <field name="course">
    <grammar type="application/srgs+xml"
    src="/grammars/training.grxml"/>
    <prompt>Which course do you want to take?
      Here is the list of courses:
      <!-- list of courses offered -->
      </prompt>

    <if cond="course == 'operator' ">
       <goto next="http://javaschool.com/school/
       public/speech/vxml/operator.vxml" />
    </if>

    <noinput>
        I could not hear you.
        <reprompt/>
    </noinput>

    <nomatch count="1">
      Please select any Java, Wireless, or Ontology course
      from the list.
      <reprompt/>
    </nomatch>

    <nomatch count="2">
      <prompt>
        I am sorry, we have almost so many types of training
        courses but not this one.
        I would recommend you to start with the Ontology
        Introduction course at this time.
      </prompt>
    </nomatch>

    <nomatch count="3">
      I switch you to the operator.
      Hopefully you will find the course you want.
      Good luck.
      <goto next="http://javaschool.com/school/public/speech/vxml/
      operator.vxml" />
    </nomatch>

    </field>
```

FIGURE 12.14

```
    <block>
     <submit next="http://javaschool.com/school/public/speech/vxml/
     training.jsp"/>
    </block>
  </form>
</vxml>
```

FIGURE 12.14. (*cont.*)

The user might want to talk to a human being. In this case, the grammar rules might resolve the user's desire and return the word *operator* as the user's selection. The program uses an *<if>* element to check on this condition.

```
<if cond="course == 'operator' ">
```

If this condition is true, the program will use the *<goto>* element to jump to another document that transfers the caller to the operator. Note that all tags are properly closed, as they should be in any XML file.

Looking down the code below the *<if>* element, we find *<noinput>* and *<nomatch>* event handlers. If the user produces no input during the default time, the program plays the prompt again using the *<reprompt/>* element.

```
<noinput>
    I could not hear you.
    reprompt/>
</noinput>
```

The most interesting script starts when a user selection is not expected. In this case, the *<nomatch>* event handler is fired. This element may have a counter, which we use here to try to provide a more appropriate response and possibly decrease the user's discomfort.

The very first *<nomatch>* element provides an additional hint to the user and reprompts the original message.

```
<nomatch count="1">
  Please select a Java, Wireless, or Ontology course from the list.
  <reprompt/>
</nomatch>
```

The next time the user makes a strange selection, the program offers its candid advice.

```
<nomatch count="2">
  <prompt>
    I am sorry, we have so many types of training courses,
    but not this one.
    I recommend you start with the Ontology Introduction
    course at this time.
    Will that work for you?
  </prompt>
</nomatch>
```

The third *nomatch* event switches the user to the operator.

```
<nomatch count="3">
      I will switch you to the operator.
      Hopefully, you will find the course you want.
      Good luck.
    <goto next="http://javaschool.com/school/public/speech/vxml/
    operator.vxml" />
</nomatch>
```

But what if the user was successful in the course selection?

In this case, the selected course value fills the *course* field and the value is submitted to the training page.

```
    <block>
      <submit next="http://javaschool.com/school/public/speech/vxml/
      training.jsp"/>
    </block>
```

The last two lines close the form and the VoiceXML document.

```
    </form>
</vxml>
Wow!
```

Play Audio and Transfer Phone Calls with VoiceXML

How does VoiceXML do the transfer operation? Here is the code:

```
<!-- Transfer to the operator -->
 <!-- Say it first -->
 Transferring to the operator according your request.
 <!-- Play music while transfer -->
 <!-- Wait up to 60 seconds for the transfer -->
 <transfer dest="tel:+1-234-567-8901"
 transferaudio="music.wav" connecttimeout="60s">
</transfer>
```

The code extract first says, "Transferring to the operator according to your request" and then actually tries to transfer the user to the operator. The *<transfer>* element in our example turns on some music and sets the timeout to 60 seconds for the transfer. There is another essential part of the *<transfer>* element—the telephone number of the operator.

Here is a transfer example that shows what happens when the program catches the *busy* event:

```
<transfer maxlength="60" dest="8005558355">
  <catch event="event.busy">
    <audio> busy</audio>
    <goto next="_home"/>
  </catch>
</transfer>
```

Listen to Email Messages with VoiceXML

The <*link*> element below navigates to *mail.vxml* whenever the user says "mail."

```
<link next="mail.vxml">
  <grammar type="application/srgs+XML"root="root" version="1.0">
    <rule id="root" scope="public">mail</rule>
  </grammar>
</link>
```

Compose and Send a New Message with VoiceXML In-line Grammar Rules

This example provides in-line grammar rules, unlike most of the following examples, in which we reference grammar rule files.

The <*subdialog*> element helps to create reusable dialog components and decompose an application into multiple documents.

```
<subdialog name="compose" src="newmail.vxml">
    <filled>
      <!-- The "compose" subdialog returns 3 variables below.
      These variables must be specified in the "return" element
      of the "compose" -->
      <assign name="to_address" expr="compose.to_address"/>
      <assign name="subject" expr="compose.subject"/>
      <assign name="message" expr="compose.body"/>
    </filled>
</subdialog>
```

Figure 12.15 provides an example of the *new_mail* service request. The example uses the *compose* subdialog to fill two fields for the new mail form. The *compose* subdialog returns its status and two requested fields. If the returned status is not OK, the service says the message cannot be delivered and exits. Otherwise, the service assigns returned values to the *to_name* and *message* fields and prompts the user for the message subject. It often happens that mail goes out without any subject.

The subject can serve as communication metadata, which makes even more sense today when computer systems are increasingly involved in the communication process. With this last field, the service is ready to rock and roll and submits all the data to the long URL provided in the <*submit*> element.

The *new_mail* service listing also illustrates the use of *if-else* elements with the conditional actions described above.

Figure 12.16 displays the *compose* subdialog. In the *compose* dialog, the prompt asks for a recipient's name. Apparently, the grammar rules behind the scenes are working hard to recover the email address from the list of available names. The user can ask for help to hear more detailed prompt messages. If the name recognition fails, the <*nomatch*> element returns the status value *not_known_name*, back to the *new_mail* service.

In the best-case scenario, when name recognition succeeds, the *compose* dialog sets the status value to OK and prompts the user to fill (answer) the *message* field. The *compose* dialog then returns the OK status and two variables (the *to_name* and the *message*), back to

```
<?xml version="1.0" encoding="UTF-8"?>
<vxml xmlns="http://www.w3.org/2001/vxml"
   xmlns:xsi="http://www.w3.org/2001/XMLSchema-instance"
   xsi:schemaLocation="http://www.w3.org/2001/vxml
   http://www.w3.org/TR/voicexml20/vxml.xsd"
   version="2.0">
  <form id="new_mail">
    <!-- two variables collected by the "compose" subdialog -->
    <var name="to_name"/>
    <var name="message"/>
    <subdialog name="compose" src="compose.vxml">
      <filled>
        <!-- The "compose" subdialog returns its status and
        two variables below.
          The status and other variables must be specified
          in the "return" element of the "compose" -->

        <if cond="compose.status == 'OK'">
            <assign name="to_name" expr="compose.to_name"/>
            <assign name="message" expr="compose.message"/>
        <else/>
            Sorry, the system cannot deliver the message.
            <exit/>
        </if>

      </filled>
     </subdialog>

    <field name="subject">
     <grammar type="application/srgs+xml" src="/grammars/
     mail_subject.grxml"/>
      <prompt>
        What is the subject of your message?
      </prompt>
      <filled>
        <submit next=
        "http://javaschool.com/school/public/speech/
        send_mail.jsp"/>
      </filled>
    </field>
  </form>
</vxml>
```

FIGURE 12.15

the *new_mail* service. dialog then returns the OK status and two variables (the *to_name* and the *message*), back to the *new_mail* service.

The *forward_mail* service reuses the same *compose* subdialog to collect the *to_address* and *message* fields. Figure 12.17 shows the *forward_mail* VoiceXML page. The *forward_mail*

```
<?xml version="1.0" encoding="UTF-8"?>
<vxml xmlns="http://www.w3.org/2001/vxml"
  xmlns:xsi="http://www.w3.org/2001/XMLSchema-instance"
   xsi:schemaLocation="http://www.w3.org/2001/vxml
   http://www.w3.org/TR/voicexml20/vxml.xsd"
   version="2.0">
  <form id="compose">

    <var name="status" expr="'not_known_name'"/>
    <field name="to_name">
      <grammar type="application/srgs+xml"
      src="/grammars/names.grxml"/>
      <prompt> What is your <prosody rate=
      "-40%">recipient</prosody> name? </prompt>
        <help>
           I cannot recognize the name. Please say first and
           last name.
           First name first. For example: John Smith.
         <reprompt/>
       </help>
       <nomatch>
         <return namelist="status"/>
       </nomatch>
    </field>

    <field name="message">
      <grammar type="application/srgs+xml"
      src="/grammars/phone_numbers.grxml"/>
      <prompt> Provide your <emphasis>message
      now</emphasis> </prompt>
    </field>

     <block>
       <assign name="status" expr="'OK'"/>
       <return namelist="status to_name message"/>
     </block>

  </form>
</vxml>
```

FIGURE 12.16

listing includes two additional variables: *subject* and *old_message*. These variables passed as parameters extracted by the *mail_service* dialog from the original mail. The *forward_mail* service behaves like the *new_mail* service.

If the *compose* subdialog returns an OK status with the two requested fields (*to_address* and *message*), the *forward_mail* service will submit all data, including the two additional

```
<?xml version="1.0" encoding="UTF-8"?>
<vxml xmlns="http://www.w3.org/2001/vxml"
   xmlns:xsi="http://www.w3.org/2001/XMLSchema-instance"
   xsi:schemaLocation="http://www.w3.org/2001/vxml
   http://www.w3.org/TR/voicexml20/vxml.xsd"
   version="2.0">
  <form id="forward_mail">
    <!-- two parameters related to the original mail passed
    from the mail_service -->
    <var name="subject"/>
    <var name="old_message"/>
    <!-- two variables collected by the "compose" subdialog -->
    <var name="to_name"/>
    <var name="message"/>
    <subdialog name="compose" src="compose.vxml">
      <filled>
        <!-- The "compose" subdialog returns its status
        and two variables below.
          The status and other variables must be specified
          in the  "return" element of the "compose" -->

        <if cond="compose.status == 'OK'">
            <assign name="to_name" expr="compose.to_name"/>
            <assign name="message" expr="compose.message"/>

            <!-- use ECMAScript to prepare subject and body
            fields -->
            <!-- subject will start with "FW: " -->
            <!-- body will include not only current but also
            original "old_message" -->
            <return namelist="to_name subject message" />
        <else/>
            Sorry, the system cannot deliver the message.
            <exit/>
        </if>

      </filled>
    </subdialog>

  </form>
</vxml>
```

FIGURE 12.17

fields (*subject* and *old_message*) that came as parameters from the original email to the final URL. If the status returned by the *compose* subdialog is not as cheerful, the *forward_mail* service will not forward the message but will exit instead.

Parameters can be passed with the *<param>* elements of a *<subdialog>*. These parameters must be declared in the subdialog using *<var>* elements, as displayed in Fig. 12.17.

The *mail_service* dialog passes the parameters to the *forward_mail* service with the following lines:

```
<form>
<subdialog name="forward_mail" src="forward_mail.vxml">
    <param name="subject" expr="`Hello'"/>
    <param name="oldmessage" expr="`How are you?'"/>
    <filled>
      <submit
next="http://javaschool.com/school/public/speech/mail.jsp"/>
    </filled>
  </subdialog>
</form>
```

SSML Elements in VoiceXML

Looking into the *prompt* examples in Fig. 12.16, we can see the tags we learned before as SSML elements. No wonder. The VoiceXML 2.0 Specifications model the content of the *<prompt>* element based on W3C SSML 1.0 and makes available the following SSML elements:

<audio>—specifies audio files to be played and text to be spoken
<break>—specifies a pause in the speech output
<desc>—provides a description of a nonspeech audio source in
<emphasis>—specifies that the enclosed text should be spoken with emphasis
<lexicon>—specifies a pronunciation lexicon for the prompt
<mark>—ignored by Voice XML platforms
<metadata>—specifies XML metadata content for the prompt
<paragraph> (or <p>)— identifies the enclosed text as a paragraph, containing zero or more sentences
<phoneme>—specifies a phonetic pronunciation for the contained text
<prosody>—specifies prosodic information for the enclosed text
<say-as>—specifies the type of text construct contained within the element
<sentence> (or <s>)—identifies the enclosed text as a sentence
<sub>—specifies replacement spoken text for the contained text
<voice>—specifies voice characteristics for the spoken text

The example in Fig. 12.18 uses the *<record>* element to collect an audio recording from the user. This example also uses the *bargein* property that controls whether a user can interrupt a prompt. Setting the *bargein* property to “true” allows the user to interrupt the program, introducing a mixed initiative.

Record Audio and Accept Telephone Keys with VoiceXML

The program prompts the user to record her or his message. A reference to the recorded audio is stored in the *msg* variable. There are several important settings in the *<record>* element, including timeouts and DTMFTERM.

The recording stops under one of the following conditions: a final silence for more than three seconds occurs, a DTMF key is pressed, the maximum recording time—ten

```
<?xml version="1.0" encoding="UTF-8"?>
<vxml version="2.0" xmlns="http://www.w3.org/2001/vxml"
  xmlns:xsi="http://www.w3.org/2001/XMLSchema-instance"
  xsi:schemaLocation="http://www.w3.org/2001/vxml
   http://www.w3.org/TR/voicexml20/vxml.xsd">
   <form>
     <property name="bargein" value="true"/>

     <record  name="msg" beep="true" maxtime="10s"
       finalsilence="3000ms" dtmfterm="true"
       type="audio/x-wav">
       <prompt timeout="5s">
         Record your audio message after the beep.
       </prompt>
       <noinput>
         I didn't hear anything, please try again.
       </noinput>
     </record>

     <submit next="http://javaschool.com/
     school/public/speech/recording.jsp"
       enctype="multipart/form-data" method="post"
       namelist="msg"/>

   </form>
</vxml>
```

Figure 12.18

seconds—is exceeded, or the caller hangs up. The audio message will be sent to the Web server via the HTTP POST method with the *enctype="multipart/form-data"*.

Another example, in Fig. 12.19, demonstrates a VoiceXML feature that allows the user to enter text messages using a telephone keypad. VoiceXML supports platforms with telephone keys. In Fig. 12.19, the user is prompted to type the message. The *<block>* element copies the message to the variable *document.key_message*. This example shows the use of the *<object>* element, a part of ECMAScript [13].

ECMAScript

Developed by the European Computer Manufacturers Association (ECMA), ECMAScript was modeled after JavaScript but designed to be application independent. The language was divided into two parts: a domain-independent core and a domain-specific object model. ECMAScript defines a language core, leaving the design of the domain object model to specific vendors.

An ECMAScript object, presented in the example, may have the following attributes:

name—When the object is evaluated, it sets this variable to an ECMAScript value whose type is defined by the object.

```
<?xml version="1.0" encoding="UTF-8"?>
<vxml version="2.0"
xmlns="http://www.w3.org/2001/vxml"
  xmlns:xsi="http://www.w3.org/2001/XMLSchema-instance"
  xsi:schemaLocation="http://www.w3.org/2001/vxml
   http://www.w3.org/TR/voicexml20/vxml.xsd">
<form id="key_message">
  <object name="message"
      classid="builtin://keypad_text_input">
   <prompt>
     Enter your message with the telephone keys.
     Press star for a space, and the pound sign to end
     the message.
   </prompt>
  </object>

  <block>
    <assign name="document.key_message"
    expr="message.text"/>
    <goto next="#send_message"/>
  </block>
</form>
</vxml>
```

FIGURE 12.19

expr—The initial value of the form item variable; default is the ECMAScript value "*undefined*." If initialized to a value, then the form item will not be visited unless the form item variable is cleared.

cond—An expression that must evaluate to true after conversion to boolean in order for the form item to be visited.

classid—The URI specifying the location of the object's implementation. The URI conventions are platform dependent.

codebase—The base path used to resolve relative URIs specified by classid, data, and archive. It defaults to the base URI of the current document.

codetype—The content type of data expected when downloading the object specified by *classid*. The default is the value of the type attribute.

data—The URI specifying the location of the object's data. If it is a relative URI, it is interpreted relative to the *codebase* attribute.

type—The content type of the data specified by the data attribute.

archive—A space-separated list of URIs for archives containing resources relevant to the object, which may include the resources specified by the *classid* and data attributes.

ECMAScript provides scripting capabilities for Web-based client–server architecture and makes it possible to distribute computation between the client and server. Each Web browser and Web server that supports ECMAScript supports (in its own way) the ECMAScript execution environment. Some of the facilities of ECMAScript are similar to Java and Self [14] languages.

An ECMAScript program is a cluster of communicating objects that consist of an unordered collection of *properties* with their *attributes*. Attributes, such as *ReadOnly, DontEnum, DontDelete*, and *Internal*, determine how each property can be used.

For example, a property with the *ReadOnly* attribute is not changeable and not executable by ECMAScript programs, the *DontEnum* properties cannot be enumerated in the programming loops, your attempts to delete the *DontDelete* properties will be ignored, and the *Internal* properties are not directly accessible via the property access operators.

ECMAScript properties are containers for objects, primitive values, or methods. A primitive value is a member of one of the following built-in types: *Undefined, Null, Boolean, Number*, and *String*.

ECMAScript defines a collection of **built-in objects** that include the following object names: *Global, Object, Function, Array, String* (yes, there are objects with the same names as built-in primitive types), *Boolean, Number, Math, Date, RegExp*, and several *Error* object types.

ECMAScript in VoiceXML Documents

Figure 12.20 presents ECMAScript embedded into the *forward_mail* subdialog. Several lines of the ECMAScript give the final touch to the *forward_mail* dialog. The subject of the forwarded message starts with *FW*: and the body of the message includes not only the current message provided by the user but also the original message the user wants to forward to another recipient.

Grammar Rules

According to the VoiceXML 2.0 Specification, platforms should support the Augmented BNF (ABNF) Form of the W3C SRGS, although VoiceXML platforms may choose to support grammar formats other than SRGS.

The *<grammar>* element may specify an **inline** grammar or an **external** grammar. Figure 12.21 demostrates an example of inline grammar. This simple example provides inline grammar rules for the selection of one of many items.

In a similar manner, VoiceXML allows developers to provide DTMF grammar rules.

```
<grammar mode="dtmf" weight="0.3"
src="http://javaschool.com/school/public/speech/vXML/
dtmf.number"/>
```

The grammar above includes references to the *dtmf* grammar file. The extract below shows inline *dtmf* grammar rules.

```
<grammar mode="dtmf" version="1.0" root="code">
    <rule id="root" scope="public">
      <one-of>
        <item> 1 2 3</item>
        <item> #</item>
      </one-of>
    </rule>
</grammar>
```

```
<?xml version="1.0" encoding="UTF-8"?>
<vxml xmlns="http://www.w3.org/2001/vxml"
   xmlns:xsi="http://www.w3.org/2001/XMLSchema-instance"
   xsi:schemaLocation="http://www.w3.org/2001/vxml
   http://www.w3.org/TR/voicexml20/vxml.xsd"
   version="2.0">
  <form id="forward_mail">
    <!-- two parameters related to the original mail passed
    from the mail_service -->
    <var name="subject"/>
    <var name="old_message"/>
    <!-- two variables collected by the "compose"
    subdialog -->
    <var name="to_name"/>
    <var name="message"/>
    <subdialog name="compose" src="compose.vxml">
      <filled>
        <!-- The "compose" subdialog returns its status and
        two variables below.
          The status and other variables must be specified
          in the  "return" element of the "compose" -->

        <if cond="compose.status == 'OK'">
            <assign name="to_name" expr="compose.to_name"/>
            <assign name="message" expr="compose.message"/>
            <!-- use ECMAScript to prepare subject and body
            fields -->
            <script>
              <![CDATA[
              subject = 'FW: ' + subject;
              message = message + '\n----- Original message
              ----\n' + old_message;
              ]]>
            </script>
            <!-- return all data -->
            <return namelist="to_name subject message"/>
        <else/>
            Sorry, the system cannot deliver the message.
            <exit/>
        </if>

      </filled>
     </subdialog>

  </form>
</vxml>
```

FIGURE 12.20

```
<grammar mode="voice" xml:lang="en-US" version="1.0"
root="training">
  <!-- Selection of one of the training courses -->
  <rule id="course" scope="public">
    <one-of>
      <item> Java Introduction </item>
      <item> Advanced Java </item>
      <item> Wireless Introduction </item>
      <item> Java Microedition </item>
      <item> Speech Technologies </item>
      <item> Ontology Introduction </item>
      <item> Integration Technologies </item>
      <item> Knowledge and Service Integration </item>
      <item> Natural User Interface </item>
    </one-of>
  </rule>
</grammar>
```

FIGURE 12.21

THE VOICEXML INTERPRETER EVALUATES ITS OWN PERFORMANCE

The *application.lastresult$* variable holds information about the last recognition. The *application.lastresult$.confidence* may vary from 0.0 to 1.0. A value of 0.0 indicates minimum confidence.
The *application.lastresult$.utterance* keeps the raw string of words (or digits for DTMF) that were recognized for this interpretation.
The *application.lastresult$.inputmode* stores the last mode value (DTMF or voice).
The *application.lastresult$.interpretation* variable contains the last interpretation result.

This self-evaluation feature can be used to provide additional confirmational prompts when necessary.

```
<if cond="application.lastresult$.confidence &lt; 0.7">
                <goto nextitem="confirmationdialog"/>
            <else/>
```

VoiceXML Interpreter's Resources and Caching

A VoiceXML interpreter fetches VoiceXML documents and other resources, such as audio files, grammars, scripts, and objects, using powerful caching mechanisms. Unlike a visual browser, a VoiceXML interpreter lacks end-user controls for cache refresh, which is controlled only through appropriate use of the *maxage* and *maxstale* attributes in VoiceXML documents.

The *maxage* attribute indicates that the document is willing to use content whose age is no greater than the specified time in seconds. If the *maxstale* attribute is assigned a value, then the document is willing to accept content that has exceeded its expiration time by no more than the specified number of seconds.

```
<?xml version="1.0" encoding="UTF-8"?>
<vxml version="2.0" xmlns="http://www.w3.org/2001/vxml"
  xmlns:xsi="http://www.w3.org/2001/XMLSchema-instance"
  xsi:schemaLocation="http://www.w3.org/2001/vxml
   http://www.w3.org/TR/voicexml20/vxml.xsd">
<metadata>
   <rdf:RDF
       xmlns:rdf = "http://www.w3.org/
       1999/02/22-rdf-syntax-ns#"
       xmlns:rdfs = "http://www.w3.org/TR/
       1999/PR-rdf-schema-19990303#"
       xmlns:dc = "http://purl.org/metadata/dublin_core#">

<!-- Metadata about the VoiceXML document -->
   <rdf:Description about="http://javaschool.com/
   school/public/speech/vxml/training.vxml"
       dc:Title="Training Courses"
       dc:Description="Training Courses List"
       dc:Publisher="ITS"
       dc:Language="en"
       dc:Date="2003-05-05"
       dc:Rights="Copyright 2003 Jeff Zhuk"
       dc:Format="application/voicexml+xml" >
   </rdf:Description>
  </rdf:RDF>
 </metadata>

  <form id="training">
    <field name="course">
    <grammar type="application/srgs+xml
    " src="/grammars/training.grxml"/>
    <prompt>Which course do you want to take?
      Here is the list of courses:
      <!-- list of courses offered -->
      </prompt>

    <if cond="course == 'operator' ">
       <goto next="http://javaschool.com/school/public/
       speech/vxml/operator.vxml" />
    </if>

    <noinput>
        I could not hear you.
        <reprompt/>
    </noinput>

    <nomatch count="1">
      Please select any Java, Wireless, or Ontology course from the
      list.
```

FIGURE 12.22

```
        <reprompt/>
      </nomatch>

      <nomatch count="2">
        <prompt>
          I am sorry, we have almost so many types of training
          courses but not this one.
          I would recommend you to start with the Ontology
          Introduction course at this time.
        </prompt>
      </nomatch>

      <nomatch count="3">
        I will switch you to the operator.
        Hopefully you will find the course you want.
        Good luck.
        <goto next="http://javaschool.com/school/public/
        speech/vxml/operator.vxml" />
      </nomatch>

      </field>

      <block>
       <submit next="http://javaschool.com/school/public/
       speech/vxml/training.jsp"/>
      </block>
    </form>
  </vxml>
   </form>
  </vxml>
```

FIGURE 12.22. ***(cont.)***

Metadata in VoiceXML Documents

VoiceXML does not require metadata information. However, it provides two elements in which metadata information can be expressed: *<meta>* and *<metadata>*, with the recommendation that metadata is expressed using the *<metadata>* element, with information in Resource Description Framework (RDF).

As in HTML, the *<meta>* element can contain a metadata property of the document expressed by the pair of attributes, *name* and *content*.

```
<meta name="generator" content=""/>
```

The *<meta>* element can also specify HTTP response headers with http-equiv and *content* attributes.

```
<meta http-equiv="Content-Type" content="text/html;
charset=iso-8859-1"/>
```

A VoiceXML document can include the <*metadata*> element using the Dublin Core version 1.0 RDF Schema [15].

Figure 12.22 provides an example of a VoiceXML document with the <*metadata*> element. The <*metadata*> element provides hidden (and silent) information about the document, which nonetheless serves (or will serve) an extremely important role in the interconnected world. This information feeds search engines and helps end users find the document.

The metadata element ends our voyage into VoiceXML technology and also ends this chapter.

Summary

This chapter reviewed voice technologies, speech synthesis and recognition, related standards, and some implementations.

VoiceXML-based technology is the most mature and is prime-time ready for what it was designed for: telephony applications that offer menu-driven voice dialogs that eventually lead to services.

Data communication is growing, and wireless devices will begin to exchange more data packets outside than inside the telephony world. At that point, the lightness and multimodality of SALT will make it a stronger competitor.

Neither of these technologies was designed for a natural language user interface. One common limitation is the grammar rules standard defined by the SRGS. They fit perfectly into the multiple-choice world, but have no room for the thoughtful process of understanding.

Integrating Questions

What are the common features of speech application architectures?
What role does XML play in speech applications?

Case Study

1. Create a SALT file, similar to Fig. 12.11, that is related to a book order.
2. Create a grammar file to support the ordering of a book.
3. Describe an application at your workplace that can benefit from speech technology.

References

1. The Java Speech API: *http://java.sun.com/products/java-media/speech.*
2. The Java Speech API Markup Language: *http://java.sun.com/products/java-media/speech/forDevelopers/JSML.*
3. Speech Synthesis Markup Language: *http:// www.w3.org/TR/speech- synthesis/.*
4. The Java Speech Grammar Format Specification: *http:// java.sun.com/products/java-media/speech/forDevelopers/JSGF/.*
5. Sphinx, open source speech recognition project: *http://sourceforge.net/projects/cmusphinx/.*
6. Microsoft Speech SDK: *http://download.microsoft.com/download/speechSDK/.*

7. Nyffenegger, R. "A C++ Socket Class for Windows." Available at: *http://www.adp-gmbh.ch/win/misc/sockets.html*. Accessed Dec. 20, 2002.
8. "Speech Application Language Tags," Technical White Paper, SALT Forum, Jan. 20, 2002. Available at: *http://www.saltforum.org/spec.asp*.
9. VoiceXML: *www.voiceXML.org/spec.html*.
10. Speech Recognition Grammar Standard: *http://www.w3.org/TR/speech-grammar.*
11. Natural Language Semantics Markup Language: *http://www.w3.org/TR/nl-spec/*.
12. Call Control XML: *http://www.w3.org/TR/ccXML/*.
13. Standard ECMA-262 ECMAScript Language Specification: *http://www.ecma-international.org/*.
14. Ungar, D., and R. Smith. 1987. "Self: The Power of Simplicity." In Proceedings of OOPSLA Conference, Orlando, FL, October 1987: pp. 227–241.
15. "Dublin Core Metadata Initiative," a Simple Content Description Model for Electronic Resources: *http://purl.org/DC/*.

CHAPTER 13

Integration with Knowledge

Can people think? I doubt it. At least not in the way we do.
—Computer-to-computer chat

This chapter reveals the dependencies between a natural user interface (NUI) and knowledge technologies; discusses architecture, design, and code samples that integrate knowledge technologies into enterprise applications; and gives the keys to a new breed of software—"Softology," a mix of software and ontological engineering.

We talked about NUIs in the previous chapter and agreed that they are not a trivial pursuit. We discussed at length a small part of an NUI—current speech technologies—and ended up with the conclusion that they can do a decent job when using machine-directed dialogs with multiple choices but are not quite ready to understand natural language spoken by a person.

We face similar difficulties with machine translation from foreign languages. I worked with multiple language translation programs that produced nonsense text filled with the right words.

WHY ARE COMPUTERS STUPID? WHAT IS MISSING?

Can tasks such as machine vision, speech recognition, and foreign language translation, which all seem very different, have a common solution?

The first common denominator is easy to find: all these tasks belong to the field of data interpretation. The next move is to find common steps for all three activities. What do people do when they are engaged in image or speech recognition, when they translate text from Hebrew to English? Why can't we build a program to perform similar steps?

The very first step is to recognize a business (social) domain area in which the data belong. For example, it is impossible to translate an article written in a foreign language (assuming you know the language) before you know if it is about medical science or cooking. It is easier to recognize the voice of a speaker with an identified name and a related speaker's voice profile. Direct topic pointers or metadata may be very helpful in solving recognition programs.

The second step is to find a set of conceptual models related to this topic. Then, take one piece of data at a time and dive into these models with the data, trying to select the best one.

Every model has its own set of patterns. The third step is to retrieve these patterns (expected choices) and try to find a match between the data and the patterns.

Was that a joke? Can these three steps really solve all three puzzles? The funny thing is, it was not a joke.

Where are the pitfalls that delay building intelligent machines? Note that the most valuable asset here is this set of models and their internal patterns. Where do they come from?

We human beings slowly develop skills to create conceptual models. We obtain multiple models in different subject areas during our lifetime. We sometimes call this process "becoming a professional" in a related area. We never start from ground zero; from the very beginning, we have an extremely powerful background ready for this work. Information we collect and process lives on top of this rich background and is associated and connected with preexisting data.

This is the major difference between our modeling programs and us. The data collected in relational databases have no relationships with each other and make sense only to the specific applications they belong to. Our programs are filled with great algorithms that can talk to these disparate data without allowing us to integrate the knowledge and grow smarter.

Knowledge Integration Participants, Processes, and Products

There are no tricks that can overcome this limitation of the current software technology. Hopefully, the move to data and service integration will produce a set of knowledge containers able to consume incoming data and service rules in a learning fashion.

These distributed knowledge systems will be initiated with data and rules that provide loose connections between new and preexisting data and allow for the creation of a knowledge background with basic roots and branches that can grow and become fruitful.

An inference engine able to execute "commonsense" logic while adding or rejecting new facts and relationships would serve as the heart of such a system.

A high-level inference framework, a constraint solver, case-based reasoning, and other similar techniques provide the base for learning capabilities. These capabilities are crucial in preventing the chaos that naturally follows increasing quantity without increasing complexity, when the number of subject choices (and consequently entropy) gets larger and larger.

Inference frameworks and learning capabilities turn the quantity of *related* models and patterns into a quality of better understanding instead. Then, it is a matter of time until these collaborative systems reach the "smart" point of being visibly more helpful.

A knowledge engine keeps track of successful inference paths to reach solutions and periodically does its homework to improve its ability to do similar things more quickly for subsequent requests.

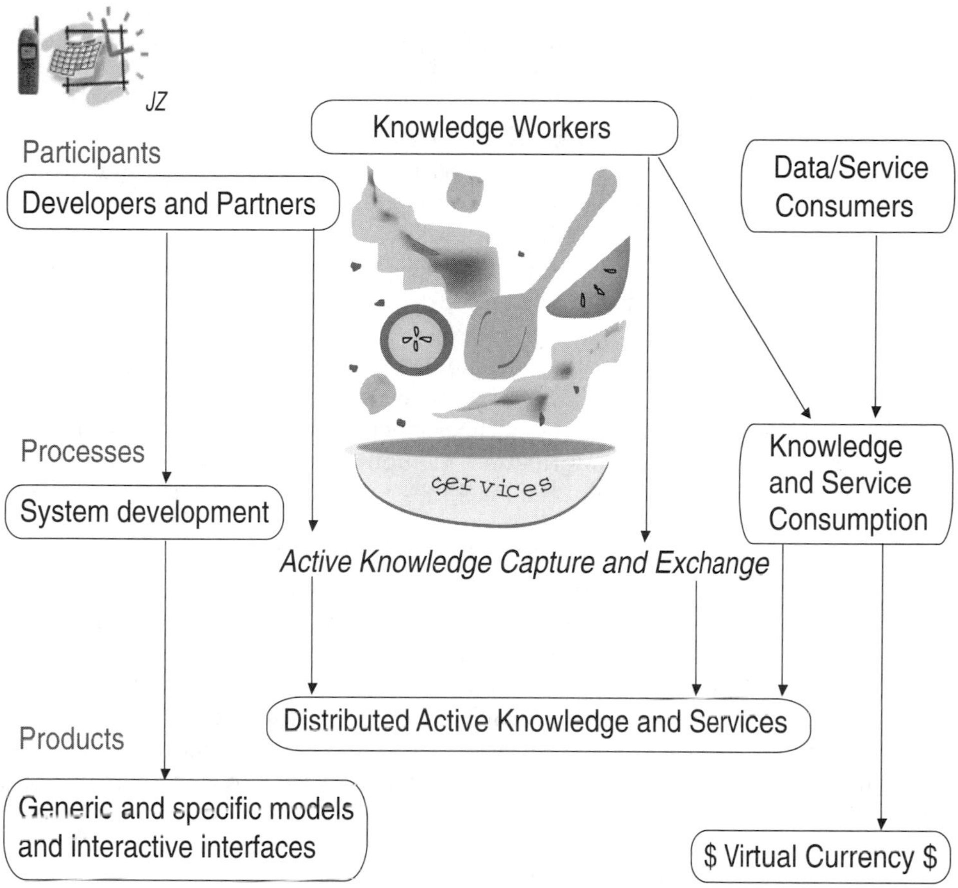

FIGURE 13.1. A Distributed Knowledge Marketplace.

Figure 13.1 shows the basic elements of the system. There are three essential groups displayed in the diagram: participants, processes, and products. Developers and partners, knowledge workers, and consumers are all active participants with different roles and activities. They participate in different processes and work with different products.

Developers and partners are involved in the system development process and participate in active knowledge capture and exchange.

Knowledge workers contribute and consume data and services; they work with the active knowledge capture and exchange process as well as the knowledge and service consumption process.

The third group, consumers, plays the major role in the knowledge and service consumption process.

These activities result in three products:

- Developers produce tools that make systems work.
- Consumers create a virtual currency that can be used to reward contributors of knowledge.
- The main product produced is growing knowledge.

Distributed yet connected, specific yet based on generic roots, different in themes yet non-conflicting: these are the qualities required for information to be inherently useful. Creating this quality data is extremely difficult but has proven to be possible.

Fortunately, We Do Not Need to Start from Scratch

After decades of struggle with the challenges of artificial intelligence, several companies delivered solutions that are finally available to the public. One of them is an open source project by Cycorp that I described in Chapter 5.

Thousands of concepts and relationships, which we take for granted and assume everyone knows, are moving into bits and bytes. Logical rules that we use every day are translated into inference engine algorithms.

We are lucky. We have knowledge bases and knowledge engines ready to serve as a starting point, as a rich background that can retain new and specific information and relate it to old and generic data. An inference engine checks incoming data for conflicts with existing knowledge and rejects conflicting information. Computers cannot tolerate conflicting data so far. (This is another difference between machines and us.)

The Growing Basket of Knowledge: Layered Information

The growing basket of knowledge presented in Fig. 13.2 includes several layers of rules and data. The diagram reflects the structure of ontology from its roots to its branches. The core ontology includes very few and very generic data and assertions (rules). The generic knowledge layer is filled with systematic data and rules that provide basic concepts and relationships. This is the background to which knowledge workers can apply specific rules and data that come to the top of the knowledge basket and stick in specific domain areas.

Knowledge technologies are undervalued today, but the situation is going to change after their use expands beyond scientific tasks. Scientific and research centers use knowledge-based facilities as "smart search engines" for their specific data collections.

Can the software industry directly employ knowledge technologies?

Connect Software and Knowledge Technologies

Imagine that a set of rules that define a recognition process—for example, in a grammar file—is enhanced with the ability to access a knowledge engine. This would promise more intelligent recognition, based not only on the multiple choices prepared in the file, but also on existing facts and rules of the available world of knowledge, associations between related topics, and so forth.

Why are we so excited about knowledge engine integration? What qualities will we buy with this extension? What difficulties do we face here?

To answer these questions, I need to clarify the roles in this development process. Who are "we"?

First, there is a rich set of current development roles. I will mention only three of them: business experts, system programmers, and application developers.

System programmers work on operating system or database internals or on hardware-related tasks (e.g., device drivers), often using low-level programming languages.

Application programmers work on projects suggested by business domain experts. They translate business ideas into models and high-level programming languages.

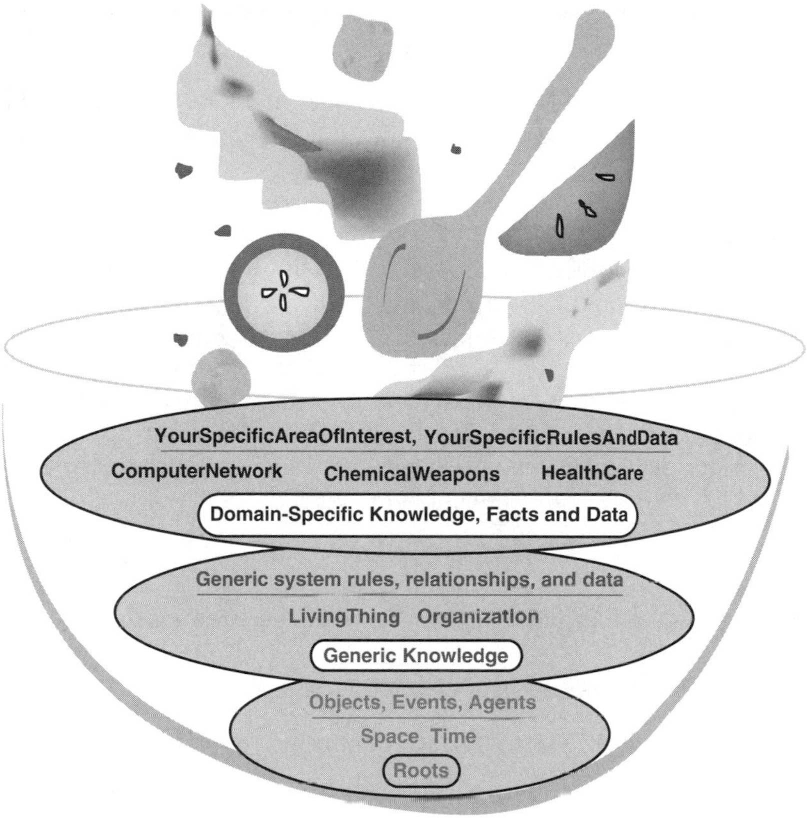

FIGURE 13.2. The Knowledge Basket: Knowledge Roots and Branches.

Business experts provide initial requirements and participate in model discussions. There are several filters between the initial requirements and the final implementation. Knowledge technologies can minimize the gap that exists today between business requirements and the resulting applications by providing new means to describe business rules directly with an "almost natural" language.

CycL (described in Chapter 5) can serve (with some stretches) as an example of this language.

A new role of "knowledge worker" is needed in the development process to use this language and (even more importantly) understand the logistics of the knowledge and inference engine.

A software or ontology engineer, a mathematician or philosopher, or perhaps a business domain expert with a good logical background can play this role.

We can envision a time when current programming languages like C# and Java will be used mostly by system programmers, whereas applications will be driven by knowledge base rules and application scenarios similar to those discussed later in this text.

This chapter considers the new application environment that consists of:

- Regular services provided with programming languages like C# and Java
- Knowledge base services filled with rules by knowledge workers

- Simple application scenarios written with the direct influence of business experts to drive both worlds

This chapter offers an example of such integration, in which software applications can talk to the Cyc knowledge engine [1] and the knowledge engine's responses can influence the flow of services.

The Knowledge Connector

Interaction between the enterprise and knowledge services is described with XML-based scenarios. Interoperability is provided with the **Knowledge Connector** package that interprets XML scenarios, as well as the user's input, using extended grammar application program interfaces (APIs).

The package delivers an application that serves as an alternative to the Cyc browser. It is designed to work as a node in a distributed JXTA community. The Knowledge Connector helps to teach the Java API to Cyc and provides interoperability in the application environment, which consists of three major components:

1. Regular (Java-based) application services, which are expected to be built with a service-oriented architecture
2. The knowledge engine, in which business rules and services are defined with the CycL language
3. XML-based application scenarios

The connector is a set of Java classes collected into the *org.opencyc.connector* package in the OpenCyc [2] project.

What Are the Main Goals of the Knowledge Connector Package?

The package aids the interaction between a user (person) and the OpenCyc knowledge engine and also provides well-defined communication APIs between a user program and the knowledge base. In both cases, the connector uses XML-based scenarios.

The connector package is lightweight middleware that can translate XML scenarios into calls to Java-based services, including knowledge services. (A later version of the connector will add interaction with C#-based products and allow for a multiplatform environment.)

The package is a prototype that integrates the main application layers: a user interface, services [regular (e.g., email), location based, and not-so-traditional knowledge base services], natural language interpretation logics, and program output transformations, all under the single roof of XML-based application scenarios.

The package also includes a Cyc training application that acts as a knowledge peer in a distributed network.

The Knowledge Connector offers a **programming interface** to application services integrated with a Cyc knowledge base. The package creates a wrapper around the OpenCyc Java API. This wrapper represents the interface to the knowledge engine as a set of XML elements.

The Knowledge Connector allows programmers to write XML-based scenarios that combine a user interface, grammar rules of input interpretation, and service invocations.

The package interprets knowledge base responses and forms XML-based information flow that can be passed to other programs and services, including Web services. The API makes it possible to directly call any existing services using knowledge base instructions and also helps to convert knowledge engine algorithms into callable services.

There are several scenarios, or examples, built into the connector. They help use the package as a training facility to learn this new development paradigm, build more scenarios, and add domain-specific knowledge to the core knowledge base.

We will take a close look at architecture, design, and code samples. But first, a few words about the driving force of XML-based APIs.

Each XML scenario consists of several acts (XML elements). Every act can be a *prompt* to a user, a conditional statement with following interpretation logics, a user interface *perform* command, or an *action* of a service invocation.

In most cases, scenario elements include action (method name) and service (class name) parameters. If the method expects arguments, all necessary arguments are provided with name-value pairs in the same XML element.

The *org.opencyc.connector.KnowledgeService* class is the default action service that communicates to the knowledge engine.

The *org.opencyc.connector.UserAVI* class is the default service class for *perform* elements. The *UserAVI* class is responsible for user audio and video interface as well as interpretation logics. These classes will be used by default in scenario acts if the service (class) name is not specified.

Object Model Diagram

Several core classes of the package are presented in Fig. 13.3. The center of the diagram is taken by the *UserAVI* class that drives a user audio–video interface as well as the whole application. The *UserAVI* class is an extension of the *ScenarioPlayer* class, which implements the *Scenario* interface. Some methods of the *UserAVI* class and almost all methods of the *ScenarioPlayer* are interpretation methods for XML scenarios and user interaction.

The *UserAVI* class collaborates with several helpers: the *Communicator, ServiceConnector*, *AVIFactory*, and *Performer* objects. Each helper is responsible for one of the application layers.

For example, an *AVIFactory* object is responsible for formatting presentations; a *Performer* object is responsible for performing the presentations; a *Communicator* object supports networking behavior in a peer-to-peer or Web-based distributed knowledge architecture; and a *ServiceConnector* object (as you can guess from the class name) provides access to services.

Formatting and Presentation Layers

How does the system format and present this world of data and services? The specific way of formatting as well as presentation (e.g., thin or thick client and video or sound) depends on implementations of the *AVIFactory* and *Performer* interfaces. Source examples include the *CycHTMLFactory* class, which implements the *AVIFactory* interface, and the *SwingPerformer* class, which implements the *Performer* interface and extends the *ServiceBrowser* class.

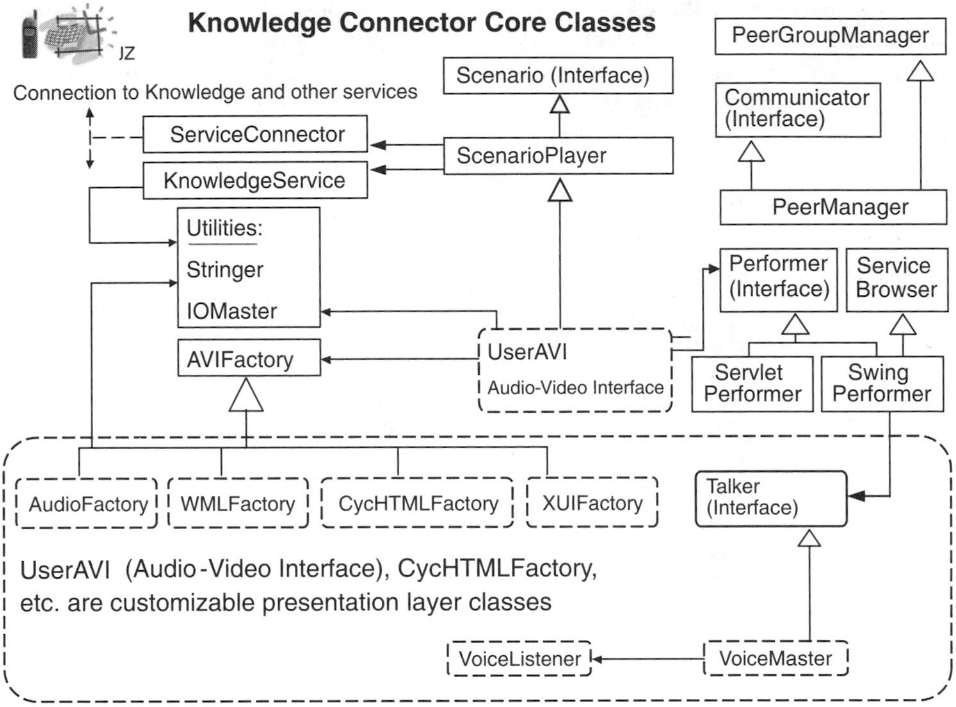

FIGURE 13.3. Knowledge Connector Core Classes: Object Model Diagram.

Current implementations generate HTML pages as well as regular text lines displayed in a Java Swing application. Alternative presentation formats include Wireless Markup Language (WML), compact HTML (cHTML), XML-based User interface Language (XUL) and VoiceXML.

The *ServletPerformer* can be considered one of the alternative *Performer* solutions. The *ServletPerformer* would run with the *UserAVI* on the server side in a Web server-based network. Working in collaboration with *CycHTMLFactory*, the *UserAVI* would send Web pages via the *ServletPerformer* to Web browsers.

Another possibility (one of many) is to use the *XUIFactory* and the *ServletPerformer* in the Web application that interacts with wireless devices such as those described in Chapter 11. Both the *SwingPerformer* and *ServletPerformer* have the potential to include voice in the presentation.

THE MAGIC OF SERVICE INVOCATION

The *ServiceConnector* class (on the left side of Fig. 13.3) works like an actor who is able to play several object roles. It takes service and action names as parameters and invokes a requested method on a requested object type.

Figure 13.4 displays a source extract of the *ServiceConnector* class. (You can find a complete set of sources in Appendix 3.) The class first looks into its own registry of acting objects, and if an existing one is found, it is reused. Otherwise, the class creates a new instance of the requested object type and, in the process, can actually load this class from the network. When the acting object is ready to perform, the class invokes the requested method on this object.

The *KnowledgeService* is a default action service, a focal point for knowledge-related service invocations. The *KnowledgeService* adds wrapper methods around the *org.opencyc.api.CycAccess* class.

Figure 13.5 shows an extract of the source code of the *KnowledgeService* class; the full source can be found in Appendix 3. Most of the methods in the class are wrappers that adapt scenario parameters to specific *CycAccess* requirements (e.g., translating String values into *CycFort* objects)

The other important feature of this class is the provision of privilege-based access to the worlds of knowledge created by different users. (For more details, see the Distributed Knowledge patent application [3].) The world is a knowledge base workspace in Cyc terminology. All data are related to specific knowledge areas (**microtheories**).

When a user creates a new microtheory or a new object, theme, or topic, the *KnowledgeService* methods register these new data in the resource book (*ResourceAvailabilityMt microtheory*) as available resources and associate these resources with a default security domain. (See the *createNewPermanent()* and *createMicrotheory()* methods.) Users with specific privileges can add more regulations related to data access at run-time.

The *ScenarioPlayer* class implements the *Scenario* interface and supports multimodal communication flow between the user, requested services, and the knowledge engine.

The *Scenario* interface (Fig. 13.6) includes several methods that provide prompts to the user and that accept user input. They help pass interpreted data to the proper services and deliver service data back to users according to XML-based multimodel scenarios.

How to Play XML Scenarios

XML scenarios can include "prompt" and "act" sequences, in which the *prompt()* method asks the user for data and the *act()* method invokes a method on a service class and plays a single act of a scenario.

The *playScenario()* method reads and plays a complete XML scenario. The *doNextStep()* method is a state machine that sequentially executes scenario steps.

Figure 13.7 presents an extract from the *ScenarioPlayer* class that implements the *Scenario* interface. The full source can be found in Appendix 3. The *ScenarioPlayer* and *KnowledgeService* classes (both) use the IOMaster and the Stringer with their input/output and string manipulation utilities.

The *UserAVI* class drives the application user interface. The *UserAVI* holds the main keys responsible for the application's behavior. The *peer* or communicator object, the service *connector* object, and the *presenter* and *performer* objects are responsible for the presentation layer of the application.

A *performer* object implements the *AVIFactory* interface. The *CycHTMLFactory* class provided in this example presents data in HTML format.

The other possibilities are presenter implementations, such as *CycWMLFactory* and *CycVXMLFactory*.

The *SwingPerformer* class provided in the example of the implementation implements the *Performer* interface with rich Java Swing-based graphics.

The presentation layer classes may be highly customized by application programmers to reflect different styles and business domain specifics.

```
package org.opencyc.connector;

import java.lang.reflect.Method;
import java.util.Hashtable;

/**
 * The ServiceConnector class invokes a selected method on a selected
 * class instance
 * The ServiceConnector can actually play not only its own (object) role
 * As a good actor it can also play objects of any (existing) type
 * If necessary the ServiceConnector loads a new class at run-time
 * The ServiceConnector has a registry where it keeps (and reuses) all actors
 * @author Jeff.Zhuk@JavaSchool.com
 */
public class ServiceConnector {
    public static boolean debug = true;
    protected Object[] parameters;
    protected Object result;
    protected Method method;
    protected Object actingObject;
    protected Class actingClass = getClass();
    protected String actingClassName = actingClass.getName();
    protected String defaultServiceName, packageName;
    protected Hashtable actingObjects = new Hashtable();
    // repository of objects
    protected static ServiceConnector instance = new ServiceConnector();

    public ServiceConnector() {
        defaultServiceName = getClass().getName();
        packageName = actingClass.getPackage().getName();
        instance = this; // store this object
    }
    /**
     * The getInstance() method returns a single static instance of the
     * ServiceConnector object
     * @return instance
     */
    public static ServiceConnector getInstance() {
        if(instance == null) {
            instance = new ServiceConnector();
        }
        return instance;
    }
/**
 * The act() method provides a unified way to find a requested method
 * and invokes the method on previously defined object.
 * There is a different version of the method for J2ME implementation
 * @param className
 * @param methodName
 * @param parameters
 * @return result
 */
```

FIGURE 13.4

```
    public Object act(String className, String methodName,
    Object[] parameters) {
        if(className != null && className.indexOf(".") < 0) {
            className = packageName + "." + className;
        }
        try {
            changeActingClass(className);
            // change acting class if necessary, or leave as is
        } catch(Exception ce) {
            System.out.println("ERROR: changeActingClass " + className
            + " e=" + ce);
        }
        Class[] classes = null;
        if(parameters != null) {
            classes = new Class[parameters.length];
            for(int i=0; i<parameters.length; i++) {
                classes[i] = parameters[i].getClass();
if(debug)
System.out.println("act:parameters[" + i + "]=" + classes[i]);
            }
        }
        try {
            method = actingClass.getMethod(methodName, classes);
        } catch (Exception e) {
            // another try with more precision
            try {
                if(classes == null) { // makes no sense to look further
                    return ("ERROR:ServiceConnector.cannot find the
                    method:actingClass=" +
                    actingClass + " methodName=" + methodName + "
                    first parameter=" + parameters[0]);
                }
                method = getMethod(methodName, classes);
            } catch(Exception me) {
                if(parameters != null) {
                    System.out.println("ERROR: getMethod.actingClass=" +
                    actingClass + "." + methodName + " parameters="
                    + parameters);
                }
                return ("ERROR:ServiceConnector.cannot find the
                  method:actingClass=" +
                  actingClass + " methodName=" + methodName + "
                  parameters=" + parameters);
            }
        }
        try {
            result = method.invoke(actingObject, parameters);
        } catch (Exception e) {
            return ("ERROR:" + e + " @ServiceConnector->" +
              actingClassName + "." + methodName);
        }
        return result;
    }
```

FIGURE 13.4. ***(cont.)***

```
package org.opencyc.connector;

import org.opencyc.api.CycAccess;
import org.opencyc.cycobject.CycConstant;
import org.opencyc.cycobject.CycFort;
import org.opencyc.cycobject.CycList;
import org.opencyc.cycobject.CycVariable;

import java.util.ArrayList;
import java.util.Hashtable;

/**
 * The KnowledgeService class uses CycAccess to communicate to Cyc engine over
 * TCP/IP sockets.
 * This dialog between a user (person) and Cyc can be arranged using
 * XML based scenarios
 * The main() method can be used to test the class.
 *
 * @author Jeff.Zhuk@JavaSchool.com
 */
public class KnowledgeService {
    public static boolean debug=false;
    protected CycAccess cycAccess;
    private String sessionWorldName, mainMt, mainGroupName, resourceMt;
    // init values
    ///////////////////////////////////////
    private String[] worldSystemMts; // for future world integration
    private Hashtable worldMts = new Hashtable(); // mts created by user
    private Hashtable worldObjects = new Hashtable(); // objects created by user
    private String lastConstant = "";
    private String cycAccessClassName; // set in the initComponents()
    public boolean connected = false;
    public KnowledgeService() {};

    /**
     * The init() method sets main variables
     * @param mainMt filename for Cyc world
     * @param sessionWorldName
     */
    public void init(String mainMt, String sessionWorldName,
                      String mainGroupName, String resourceMt) {
        // set initial actingObject to this
        this.mainMt = mainMt;
        this.sessionWorldName = sessionWorldName;
        this.mainGroupName = mainGroupName;
        this.resourceMt = resourceMt;
    }

    /**
     * The initComponents() method is to connect to Cyc
     */
    public boolean initComponents() {
        if(connected) {
            return true;
        }
```

FIGURE 13.5

```
        try {
            // start TCP/IP session with Cyc
            cycAccess = new CycAccess();
            cycAccess.traceOn();
            connected = true;
            // register cyc with the service connector
            cycAccessClassName = cycAccess.getClass().getName();
            ServiceConnector.getInstance().registerObject(
                    cycAccessClassName, cycAccess);
        } catch(Exception e) {
            connected = false;  // it is false anyway
        }
        return connected;
    }
    /**
     * The toCycConstant() method converts a string to a cyc constant
     * @param name
     * @return cycConstant
     */
    public CycConstant toCycConstant(String name) throws Exception {
        return cycAccess.getKnownConstantByName(name); // "PeopleDataMt"
    }
    /**
     * prepare and pass parameters to a proper method of the cycAccess object
     * @param parameters
     * @return response
     */
    public String createNewPermanent(Hashtable parameters) throws
    Exception {
        String constant = (String)parameters.get("msg");
        String result = cycAccess.createNewPermanent(constant)
        .toString();
        assertGAF(resourceMt,
                "(#$isa #$" + constant + "#$SomethingExisting)");
        assertGAF(resourceMt,
                "(#$resourceAvailable #$" + mainGroupName + " #$" +
                 constant +")");
        worldObjects.put(constant, new Hashtable());
        return result;
    }
    /**
     * prepare and pass parameters to a proper method of the cycAccess object
     * @param parameters
     * @return response
     */
    public String converse(Hashtable parameters) throws Exception {
        String msg = (String)parameters.get("msg");
        cycAccess.converseVoid(msg);
        return (msg + "-Done");
    }
    // ... more methods ...

}   // end of KnowledgeService class
```

FIGURE 13.5. ***(cont.)***

```
// Scenario
package org.opencyc.connector;

import java.util.*;

/*
 * The Scenario includes several methods that provide user prompt
 * and accept user input.
 * They help pass interpreted data to proper services and deliver
 * service data back to users
 * according to XML based multi-model scenarios
 * Example of XML based dialog scenario:
<?xml version="1.0" encoding="UTF-8" ?>
<scenario>
<prompt name="1" action="prompt" service="org.opencyc.connector
.UserAVI" msg="What is your area of knowledge"
variable="YOUR-WORLD-NAME" startInputWithUpperCase="true"
unique="true" />
<act name="2" action="createMicrotheory"
genlMts="KnowledgeExchangeMt,GeneralEnglishMt" isa="Microtheory"
Mt="YOUR-WORLD-NAMEMt" msg="YOUR-WORLD-NAMEMt knowledge area" />
<act name="3" action="show" service="org.opencyc.connector.UserAVI"
msg="Welcome to your new world system: YOUR-WORLD-NAMEMt" />
</scenario
 * XML scenarios can include "prompt" and "act" sequences.
 * The prompt() method ask user for data
 * The act() method makes a method invocation on a service class,
 * plays a single act of a scenario
 * The playScenario() method reads and plays an XML scenario
 * The doNextStep() method is a state machine that sequencially
 * executes scenario steps

 * The data interpretation as well as UserAVI
 * (audio-video interface) can be provided
 * with the Scenario interface direct implementations or
 * (recommended) in subclasses of direct implementations
 * @author Jeff.Zhuk@JavaSchool.com
 */
public interface Scenario {
    public Object act(String className, String serviceName,
    Object[] parameters);
    public String prompt(Hashtable parameters);
    public boolean playScenario(String scenarioName);
    public boolean doNextStep(String input);
}
```

FIGURE 13.6

```
package org.opencyc.connector;

import java.awt.*;
import java.awt.event.*;
import javax.swing.*;
import java.util.*;
import java.io.*;

/**
 * The ScenarioPlayer class serves as an interpreter and formatter
 * for XML based scenarios that request data from Cyc KB
 * The getFormattedInstructions() method interprets Cyc
 * responses and presents them in XML format
 */
public abstract class ScenarioPlayer implements Scenario {
    public static boolean debug = false;
    protected boolean promptState = false;
   // used by interpretInput() method

    protected boolean editable = false; // set true to write scenario
    protected boolean worldExists = false; // existing workspace

    protected String mainWorldMt; // initially set as worldName
    protected KnowledgeService knowledge;
    protected String defaultServiceName =
    "org.opencyc.connector.KnowledgeService";
    protected ServiceConnector connector = new
    ServiceConnector(defaultServiceName); // defaultServiceName
    protected Hashtable expectedChoices, expectedAliases;
    protected String lastDialogStep, lastInput,
    lastInterpretation, lastAction, lastService;
    // dialog scenario steps: "1", "2", ...
    protected String dialogSource = null;
    // filled by askUser, refactored by runTimeVariable
    protected Hashtable nextStep, lastServiceRequest,
    previousRequest; // is used to return to previous
    protected String currentInstructions = null;
    // is used to return to previous option
    protected String relatedSubject;
    // can be used with instructions from another object
    protected Hashtable dialogScenario, scenario, stored;
    // filled by askUser
    protected boolean uniqueRequired = false;
    protected AVIFactory factory = new CycHTMLFactory();
    // can be changed at run-time
    // data extracted from xml scenarios and data.xml
    // configuration file
```

FIGURE 13.7

```
    protected Hashtable scenarios, allData, data, defaults,
    scenarioButtons, presentationPatterns;
    // URL and class variables below help to adjust scenario
    // sources if necessary
    protected String scenarioName;  // current scenario
    protected String firstRequest; // initial scenario name
    protected String initialClass, initialURL;
    // passed to the constructor
    protected String defaultInitialURL = "c:/1/project/instructions/";
    protected String defaultClass = "org.opencyc.connector.UserAVI";
    // class that starts the show

    // abstract GUI methods implemented by a subclass (UserAVI)
    public abstract boolean setScreen(Hashtable instructions);
    // abstract - to be implemented by GUI subclasses
    public abstract boolean setScreen(String xml);
    // abstract -
    public abstract boolean show(String displayable);
    // abstract -
    public abstract void setScenarioEcho();
    // abstract -
/**
 * The setScenarios() method uses a url to set Hashtable scenarios
 * @param url
 */
    public void setScenarios(String url) {
        initialURL = url;
        String source = IOMaster.readTextFile(url +"scenarios.xml");
        source = replaceInitialValues(source);
        Hashtable allScenarios = Stringer.parse(source);
        scenarios = (Hashtable)allScenarios.get("scenarios");
        if(scenarios == null) {
            System.out.println("ERROR: Check config.xml!
            no scenarios.xml found?"); return;
        }
        String logFile = (String)scenarios.get("log");
        if(logFile != null) {
            IOMaster.openLogFile(initialURL + logFile);
        }
        config();
        firstRequest = getScenarioSource("init");
        factory.setData(presentationPatterns);
    }
/**
 * The getScenarios() method loads set of URLs and forms
 * Hashtable scenarios
 * @return scenarios
 */
```

FIGURE 13.7. *(cont.)*

```
    public Hashtable getScenarios() {
        return scenarios;
    }
/**
 * The playScenario() method plays a scenario by name using
 * additional parameters
 * @param name
 * @param args connecting this scenario with the previous one
 * @param step number to start the play
 * @return true if success
 */
    public boolean playScenario(String name, String args,
    String
    step) {
        // check for special names: write, etc.
        if(name.equals("write")) {
            String response = knowledge.write(); // write world
            IOMaster.writeLog(response);
            return true;
        }
        String source = getScenarioSource(name);
        if(source == null) {
            return false;
        }
        // try if already formatted
        String formattedInstructions =
          Stringer.getStringBetweenTags(source,
          "formattedInstructions");
        if(formattedInstructions != null) {
            String displayable =
            getDisplayable(formattedInstructions);
            return show(displayable);
        }
        if(args != null) {
            String[] allArgs = Stringer.split(",", args);
            for(int i=0; allArgs != null && i< allArgs.length;
            i++) {

                source = Stringer.replaceAll(source,
                "REPLACE-WITH-ARG-" + (i+1), allArgs[i]);
            }
        }
        int startingStep = 0;
        if(step != null) {
            try {
                startingStep = Integer.parseInt(step);
            } catch(Exception e) {
                // it is OK, start with 0
            }
```

FIGURE 13.7. *(cont.)*

```
        }
        setScenario(source, startingStep);
        scenarioName = name;
        lastServiceRequest = null;
        return doNextStep(null);
    }
    // ... more methods ...
/**
 * storeUnresolved() stores in Cyc unresolved cases (to be
 * implemented by user)
 * @param any it actually saves lastServiceRequested and user's
 * input data
 * @return "OK" (what else can we do at this point?)
 */
    public String storeUnresolved(Hashtable any) {
        // save Hashtable lastServiceRequest and
        // lastInterpretation data
        return (String)defaults.get("unresolvedMsg");
    }
} // end of ScenarioPlayer
```

FIGURE 13.7. *(cont.)*

Figure 13.8 presents a source extract from the *UserAVI* class. The full source can be found in Appendix 3. The *UserAVI* class extends the *ScenarioPlayer* class and is responsible for data interpretation as well as the user audio–video interface. The *UserAVI* class includes the *main()* method that drives the training application.

Different companies want to provide their own unique face for the application. This means a different *UserAVI* implementation as well as different implementations of the *AVIFactory* and *Performer* interfaces for voice and video presentations.

The *AVIFactory* interface (Fig. 13.9) includes several methods that format the output for a specific client device. The *format()* method, for example, translates knowledge base output into formats such as HTML, WML, VoiceXML, and XML. An example of an implementation is the *CycHTMLFactory* class, which generates HTML pages.

The same *format()* method implemented in the *CycHTMLFactory* class, along with HTML pages, creates a set of XML scenarios. Each of these scenarios describes a program behavior in response to expected user actions.

There are also methods that serve training purposes and translate XML scenario steps into the proper presentation format (e.g., HTML and WML).

Possible implementations of the *AVIFactory* interface can target WML, VoiceXML, and other formats. For example, we would provide the *XUIFactory* (XML-based user interface) for the wireless application considered in Chapter 11, in which the Actor MIDlet was able to interpret XML scenarios as presentation and behavior instructions.

The implementation example presented in Fig. 13.10 is an HTML factory, the *CycHTML-Factory* class. The figure shows a source extract of the *CycHTMLFactory* class; the full source can be found in Appendix 3.

```
// UserAVI
package org.opencyc.connector;

import java.util.*;
import java.io.*;
import java.awt.event.*;
/*
 * UserAVI class is the main application driver.
 * The class methods are responsible for user interface and
 * interpretation logics
 * @author Jeff.Zhuk@JavaSchool.com
 */
public class UserAVI extends ScenarioPlayer implements
ActionListener {
    public static boolean debug = false;
    transient protected OutputStream out = null;
    transient protected Performer performer;
    // ServletPerformer or SwingPerformer
    transient protected Communicator peer;
    // distributed knowledge peer
    protected String sessionWorldName; // = "1";
    protected String mainGroupName; // = "JavaSchool";
    protected String resourceMt; // = "ResourceAvailabilityMt";
    protected String sessionMt; // = "SessionMt";
    protected String newScenarioName;
    protected boolean interpretationMode = false;
    protected Hashtable scenarioKeys, privates, peerActions;
    // label name -> scenario name
    protected String performerType;
    protected String lastLogin; // monitored value
    protected boolean editable = false;
    // set true to write scenario
    protected boolean localOnlyMode, peerActionState;

    public UserAVI() { this(null); } // use default values
    /**
     * The constructor sets initial URL to XML instructions
     * @param initURL
     */
    public UserAVI(String initURL) {
        super();
        if(initURL == null) {
            initURL = defaultInitialURL;
        }
        initialURL = initURL;
        initialClass = getClass().getName();
    }
```

FIGURE 13.8

```
/**
 * initComponents() method creates knowledge object to provide
 * knowledge services
 */
public void initComponents() {
    if(scenarios == null) { // static!, first time only !
        setScenarios(initialURL);
    }
    knowledge = new KnowledgeService();
    knowledge.init(mainMt, sessionWorldName, mainGroupName,
    resourceMt);
    connector.registerObject(knowledge.getClass().getName(),
    knowledge);
    connector.registerObject(getClass().getName(), this);
}
/**
 * The setScenarios() method set up configuration values from
 * configuration files
 * The settings start with the base class (ScenarioPlayer) method
 * Then the main helper-objects and the main microtheory
 * names are set up.
 * @param url to the scenarios.xml file
 */
public void setScenarios(String url) {
    super.setScenarios(url);
    scenarioKeys = (Hashtable) allData.get("scenarioKeys");
    peerActions = (Hashtable) allData.get("peerActions");
    performerType = (String)defaults.get("performerType");
    try {
        performer = (Performer)Class.forName
        (performerType).newInstance();
        performer.setData(allData);
        performer.init(this);
    } catch(Exception e) {
        System.out.println("ERROR: in initComponents; check
        Performer type in config");
    }
    if(scenarioKeys != null) {
        allData.put("scenarioKeys", scenarioKeys);
    }
    mainGroupName = (String)
    replacements.get("REPLACE-WITH-MAIN-GROUP");
    resourceMt = (String)
    replacements.get("REPLACE-WITH-RESOURCEMT");
    sessionMt = (String)
    replacements.get("REPLACE-WITH-SESSIONMT");
```

FIGURE 13.8. ***(cont.)***

```
        // distributed knowledge peer
        String communicatorType =
        (String)defaults.get("Communicator");
        if(communicatorType == null) return;
        try {
            peer = (Communicator)Class.forName
            (communicatorType).newInstance();
        } catch(Exception e) {
            System.out.println("ERROR: in initComponents; check
            Communicator type in config");
        }
    }
```

FIGURE 13.8. ***(cont.)***

```
// AVIFactory
package org.opencyc.connector;

import java.util.*;

/*
 * The AVIFactory includes several methods that format output
 * according to a client device type.
 * The format() method, for example, translates Cyc output into
 * HTML/WML/VXML/etc format
 * Example of implementation is the CycHTMLFactory class that
 * generates HTML
 * @author Jeff.Zhuk@JavaSchool.com
 */
public interface AVIFactory {
    public String getScenarioHeader();
    public String getScenarioStep(Hashtable parameters);
    public String getPrompt(String prompt);

    public void setData(Hashtable data);
    public Vector translateFacts(Hashtable instructions, String
    cycResponse);
    public void setFacts(Vector facts);
    public String format();

    public String getHTMLtable(String[] words);
}
```

FIGURE 13.9

```
// CycHTMLFactory
package org.opencyc.connector;

import java.util.*;
/*
 * The CycHTMLFactory class implements AVIFactory interface.
 * It includes several methods that format Cyc knowledgebase
 * output into HTML
 * The format() method, for example, forms the HTML page and
 * creates a set of XML scenarios.
 * Every scenario describes a program behavior in response to
 * expected user actions.
 * There are methods like getHeader(), getBody(), getFooter(),
 * getChoices(), etc.
 * that are used internally by the CycHTMLFactory.
 * @author Jeff.Zhuk@JavaSchool.com
 */
public class CycHTMLFactory implements AVIFactory {
    public static boolean debug = true;
    public static final int REGULAR = 0;
    public static final int EDITABLE = 1;
    public static final int ADDITION = 2;
    public static final int ACTION = 3;

    protected int fontSize = 2;
    protected String mainMt; // set from config file; used as
    default if Mt=null
    protected String font = "<font face=verdana size=2>"; // default
    protected String initialFont, editableFont;
    // initiated by data.xml
    protected int maxLines = 30;  // 10
    protected int factTypes[]; // for each fact
    protected boolean editable, hidePredicates;
    // for all list of facts
    protected Vector facts; // facts provided by Cyc KB
    protected int numberOfFacts;
    protected int numberOfColumns = 3; // can be adjusted from
                                       // config.xml
    protected String firstEditable;
    protected String actionPattern = "COMMENT-ACTION^";
    protected String additionPattern =
    "ADD-COMPLIMENTARY-COMMENT^";
    protected Hashtable presentationPatterns,
    predicateTranslations;
    protected Hashtable instructions;
    // provided to activate Cyc KB
    protected String presentationType, commonArgs, userName,
    // current type and security args
```

FIGURE 13.10

```
    defaultPresentationType, listPresentationType;
    // Cyc responses can be "relations" or "list" type

  // presentation variables extracted from
  presentationPatterns of config.xml
  protected String currentResponse, editableResponse,
  response,multiLineResponse, firstHeader, tableHeader,
  lastFooter, scenarioHeader,  requestAcknowledgement,
    userServiceName, promptHeader, promptFooter,
    hiddenPredicates, commentAction,
    hiddenPredicateLines, predicateTranslation,
    notSelectablePredicates;
  protected static String[] hiddenTopics;
  public static String[] months = {"January", "February",
  "March", "April", "May", "June", "July", "August",
  "September", "October", "November", "December"};
  protected String constant, title; // main subject

  // config.xml includes presentation variables in the
  presentationPatterns XML element
  /**
   * The setFont() method prepares html font tag
   * @param font
   */
  public void setFont(String font) {
      this.font = font;
  }
  public int getFontSize() {
      return fontSize;
  }
  /**
   * The setData() method sets presentation patterns
   * extracted from config.xml
   * @param data
   */
  public void setData(Hashtable data) {
      presentationPatterns = data;
      initialFont = setPresentationPattern("font");
      if(initialFont != null) {
          setFont(initialFont);
      }
      editableResponse =
      setPresentationPattern("editableResponse");
      response = setPresentationPattern("response");
      userServiceName =
      (String)presentationPatterns.get("userServiceName");
      defaultPresentationType =
```

FIGURE 13.10. (*cont.*)

```
    (String)presentationPatterns.get("presentationType");
    listPresentationType =
    (String)presentationPatterns.get("listPresentationType");
    userName =
    (String)presentationPatterns.get("u");
    commonArgs =
    (String)presentationPatterns.get("commonArgs");
    multiLineResponse =
    setPresentationPattern("multiLineResponse");
    firstHeader = setPresentationPattern("firstHeader");
    tableHeader = setPresentationPattern("tableHeader");
    lastFooter = setPresentationPattern("lastFooter");
    promptHeader = setPresentationPattern("promptHeader");
    promptFooter = setPresentationPattern("promptFooter");
    scenarioHeader =
    setPresentationPattern("scenarioHeader");
    scenarioHeader = Stringer.remove(scenarioHeader, "\\");
    requestAcknowledgement =
    setPresentationPattern("requestAcknowledgement");
    commentAction = (String)presentationPatterns.get
    ("REPLACE-WITH-COMMENT-ACTION");  // not editable
    hiddenPredicates = (String)presentationPatterns.get
    ("hiddenPredicates");  // not editable
    hiddenPredicateLines = (String)presentationPatterns.get
    ("hiddenPredicateLines");  // not editable
    notSelectablePredicates =
    (String)presentationPatterns.get
    ("notSelectablePredicates");  // not editable
    String hiddenTopicString =
    (String)presentationPatterns.get ("hiddenTopics");
    hiddenTopics = Stringer.split(" ", hiddenTopicString);
    predicateTranslations =
    (Hashtable)presentationPatterns.get
    ("predicateTranslations");  // not editable
    mainMt = (String)presentationPatterns.get
    ("REPLACE-WITH-MAINMT");  // not editable
    String numberInLine = (String)presentationPatterns.get
    ("numberOfColumns");
    if(numberInLine != null) {
        try {
            numberOfColumns = Integer.parseInt
            (numberInLine);
        } catch(Exception e) {
            // just keep default number
        }
    }

}
```

FIGURE 13.10. ***(cont.)***

```
    /**
     * The setPresentationPattern() translates "[" to "<" and
     * "}" to ">"
     * @param patternName
     * @return pattern
     */
    public String setPresentationPattern(String patternName) {
        String pattern = (String)presentationPatterns.get
        (patternName);
        if(pattern != null && pattern.length() > 1) {
            pattern = pattern.replace('[', '<');
            pattern = pattern.replace(']', '>');
        } else {
            pattern = "";
        }
        return pattern;
    }
    /**
     * The format() method provides basic formatting of facts
     * @return formattedInstructions
     */
    public String format() {
        String formattedInstructions =
          "<?xml version = \"1.0\" encoding = \"UTF-8\"?>\n" +
          "<displayedElements>\n" + getHeader();
        formattedInstructions += getBody();
        formattedInstructions += getFooter();
        formattedInstructions += "\n</displayedElements>\n";
        formattedInstructions += getChoices(); // form XML
        scenarios for expected user interaction-choices
        return formattedInstructions;
    }
    // more methods

} // end of class
```

FIGURE 13.10. *(cont.)*

Video and Audio Factories

All methods of the *CycHTMLFactory* class use presentation patterns provided in the *config.XML* file. The presentation patterns serve as style sheets that can be easily changed without any code rework. The *setData()* method of the *CycHTMLFactory* class makes these patterns available to the factory.

The *format()* method forms a custom presentation of the Cyc knowledge engine's output. The *format()* method uses the *getHeader()*, *getBody()*, and *getFooter()* methods to form the displayable part of the output, and the *getChoices()* method to form the instructional part of the output, which consists of XML elements with the expected user interactions/choices and related program actions.

The resulting output of the *format()* method represents a displayable screen (in the *AudioFactory*, this part can be replaced with voice) and a set of XML scenarios related to possible user actions (input choices).

The *getHeader()* and *getFooter()* methods operate with presentation patterns to start and end the HTML page. The *getBody()* method translates facts retrieved from the Cyc knowledge engine into the body of the HTML page.

The *getChoices()* method uses the same facts, and relates possible scenarios to them. These XML scenarios, created on the fly, are similar to manually created files—scenarios located in the instructions directory. Every scenario consists of expected user choices and related actions performed by the program in the case of each choice.

There are several flavors of Cyc response interpretations: *getBody()*, *getListBody()*, *getChoices()*, and *getListChoices()*.

Formatting Cyc Responses

Let me explain why we need two styles to convert Cyc responses into HTML tags. The reason is simple: *Cyc* response formats may differ drastically, depending on the query. For example, a query like *(?X #$SomethingWeWantToKnow ?Y)* will produce a Cyc response with multiple sentences in parentheses, in which each sentence has a predicate (association) and a topic related to the main subject:

```
((predicate1 Topic1) (predicate2 Subject2) ... )
```

For example, we can ask Cyc to list all the rules in the knowledge base about the *Country* subject:

```
(?X #$Country ?Y)
```

The resulting Cyc response includes several sentence-rules, such as:

```
( (disjointWith EducationalOrganization) ...
 (isa ExistingObjectType) ...
(genls GeopoliticalEntity) (genls Individual) ...
(comment "A specialization of #$GeopoliticalEntity...") . .)
```

The *getBody()* and the *getChoices()* methods provide an interpretation for this type of Cyc response.

We can try to approach the Cyc knowledge base with a different type of query: we can ask it to list all instances of an existing collection.

Cyc responds to this type of query with a list of objects that belong to this collection. The response will look like this:

(Subject1 Subject2 Subject3 Subject4 . . .)

For example, we ask the Cyc knowledge base to list all the countries known in the *WorldGeographyMt* microtheory:

```
(#$isa ?X #$Country)
```

The response from the knowledge base looks like this:

(Germany UnitedStatesOfAmerica France . . .)

Obviously, we have to change the interpretation algorithm for this case.

How do we do this?

By providing an additional hint in the XML scenario with the key-value pair: *presentationType="List"*. The *getBody()* and *getChoices()* methods check for this hint, and if it is there, they pass control to their sibling methods, *getListBody()* and *getListChoices()*, respectively, to use the proper interpretation technique.

We can also assign any specific conversion flavor by providing a specific name. For example, *presentationType="Title"* can be decoded by a presentation factory as another presentation style.

How Do These Classes Work Together?

The collaboration diagram in Fig. 13.11 answers this question. The diagram simplifies the activity of the application into eight major steps.

1. The *UserAVI* object receives an XML instruction from the current scenario or a user's input related to the current scenario.

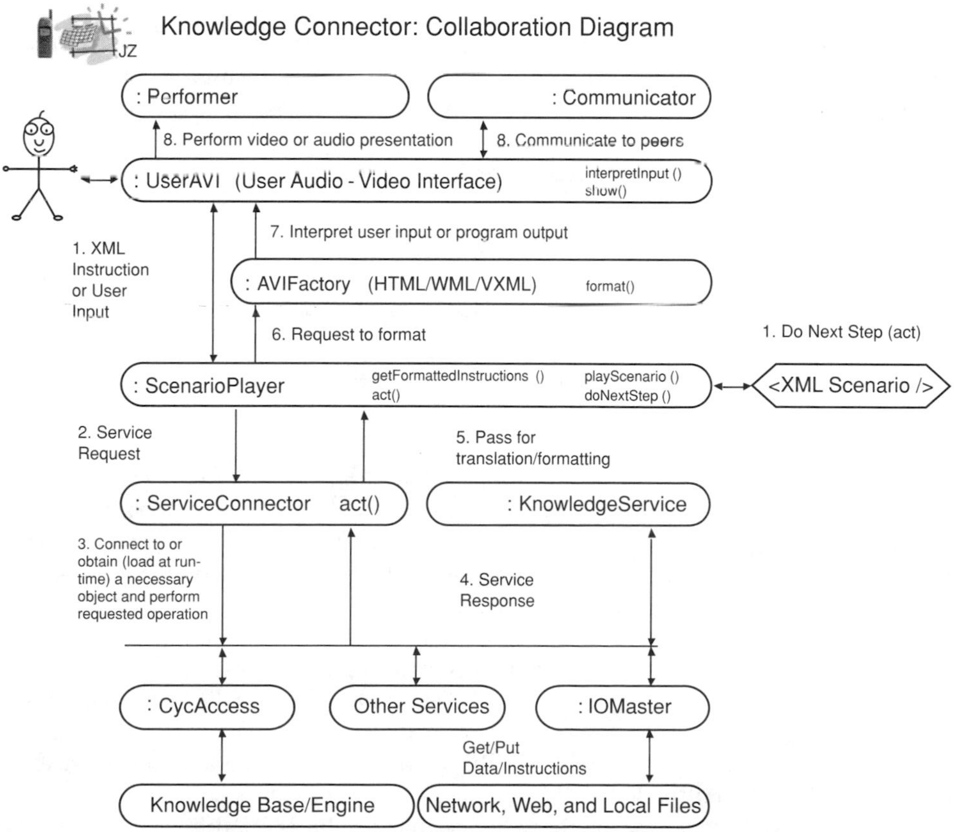

FIGURE 13.11. Knowledge Connector: Collaboration Diagram

2. The *UserAVI* object uses the methods of its base class, the *ScenarioPlayer*, to interpret this instruction or user input and translate it into a service request (the most common action).
3. The *ServiceConnector* object uses its *act()* method to connect to or obtain (load at run-time) a necessary object and perform a requested operation.
4. The service object invokes the proper method with the necessary parameters and delivers the results back to the caller.
5. The *ScenarioPlayer* gets the results of the service and passes them further to the *AVIFactory* object.
6. The *AVIFactory* implementation (the *CycHTMLFactory* in our case) translates the results into a presentation format and produces XML scenarios related to the expected user interaction.
7. The *UserAVI* class methods and the methods of the *ScenarioPlayer*, its base class, interpret the results for the *Performer* object if the operation was a success. If the operation failed (e.g., the knowledge base query returned a "not found" string), the *actionPerformed()* method of the *UserAVI* (the focal point of event handling) can use the Communicator peer (if present) to outsource this operation to the network of knowledge peers.
8. The *Performer* object presents results on a screen and/or in voice format. The alternative to this step is to communicate to other peers (if the local peer failed) and, finally, to present successful results (or a "Sorry" message) to the *Performer.*

The eight steps of the cycle have now been completed and the new results shown on a screen or pronounced via voice. The invisible part of the result interpretation is the XML scenario instructions related to expected user interactions. At this point, the instructions are stored in the *expectedChoices* table. The program is again ready to start from the first point of the collaboration diagram to react to a user's input or play the next act of a scenario.

More Details on the Classes and Their Methods

The *UserAVI* class, with its main method, drives the show. The constructor of the *UserAVI*, with its *initComponents()* method, initiates user interface components and creates two important objects: the *ServiceConnector* connector object and the *KnowledgeService* knowledge object.

The initialization process uses the *setScenarios()* method to configure the application with presentation and interpretation patterns, aliases, and so forth. The *setScenarios()* method reads from the configuration file(s) definitions of the *Presenter* and *Performer* interface implementations and creates these objects on the fly. In the current example, these are the *CycHTMLFactory* and *SwingPerformer* classes.

The *setScenarios()* method calls the *init()* method of the *Performer* object to produce initial output via a screen or voice interface. The current implementation of the *SwingPerformer* extends the *ServiceBrowser* class that displays HTML pages in the *JEditorPane* facilities of the Java Swing package.

The *ServiceBrowser* is discussed in Appendix 1; the full source code of the *ServiceBrowser* class is provided in Appendix 3.

User interactions trigger one of the XML scenarios. Most of the scenarios start with prompts, followed by actions that execute the user's wishes.

The responsibility for user input interpretation lies with the *startInterpretation()* and *interpretInput()* methods of the *UserAVI* and *ScenarioPlayer* classes. The result of the interpretation can point to a new scenario or feed the *doNextStep()* method of the *ScenarioPlayer*.

If this is a new scenario, the *playScenario()* method of the *ScenarioPlayer* reads the scenario and makes its first act available to the *doNextStep()* method. In both cases, the *doNextStep()* method of the *ScenarioPlayer* picks up the current act of the scenario for execution.

What Does It Mean to Play a Scenario?

The *playScenario()* method uses utilities of the *Stringer* class to transform the XML scenario into a well-ordered set of hash tables that represent scenario acts or steps with their parameters. The *doNextStep()* method tracks the sequence of steps to pick up the right step for execution.

Scenario steps can ***prompt*** a user for input; can include a **condition** to analyze a *pattern* or compare the pattern with a *source*; can be a knowledge base ***query*** or more generic service ***action*** that targets the knowledge base or any other services; or can ***perform*** a function of the user interface.

The *prompt* elements of XML scenarios usually include *noinput, nomatch, translate, aliases*, and other options that help to interpret the user's input. All these scenario elements, or keywords, in italics above are resolved in the *doNextStep()* method with the help of other methods (e.g., *translate() and condition()*) of the *ScenarioPlayer* class.

The *doNextStep()* method of the *ScenarioPlayer* class performs scenario steps and dynamically modifies the current scenario based on the results and conditions of the current step.

For example, it uses the *modifyScenario()* method to apply the results of a current user's input to the whole scenario.

How Is a Service Action Executed in a Scenario?

The *doNextStep()* method executes a service action by calling the *act()* method of the *ScenarioPlayer*, which in turn, calls the *act()* method of the *ServiceConnector*. The *ServiceConnector* uses its *act()* method to connect to or obtain (load at run-time) a necessary object and perform the requested service operation.

The service operation may be one of the knowledge engine services, such as a data query or an assertion, or any of the regular Java-based services (e.g., email) named with the service (class) name and the action (method) name and resolved by the *ServiceConnector* class.

The *ScenarioPlayer* passes service responses for translation into the proper presentation format. The *ScenarioPlayer* includes an *AVIFactory* object that provides the proper formatting. In the current example, the *CycHTMLFactory* class implements the *AVIFactory* interface.

The *CycHTMLFactory*, as well as other presentation layer classes, can be highly customized and may produce different media artifacts. The *CycHTMLFactory* in the current example interprets the Cyc knowledge base responses and forms an XML output with displayable elements in HTML format and hidden XML instructions.

The *format()* method of the *CycHTMLFactory* generates the header, body, and footer of the presentation using the *getHeader()*, *getBody()*, and *getFooter()* methods. These methods use presentation patterns, a part of the *config.XML* configuration file, to define the style of the presentations.

The *getChoices()* method of the *CycHTMLFactory* generates XML instructions on how to treat expected user input or selections. These instructions represent one-step scenarios that can be played upon a particular user selection.

The *UserAVI* class delivers the displayable part of the presentation to the *Performer* object. In this example, this is a Web page displayed with the Java *JEditorPane* facilities in the *SwingPerformer* class.

The hidden part of the scenario, which includes expected user interaction and related program behavior instructions, forms the *expectedChoices* hash table, which is used by the *doNextStep()* method of the *ScenarioPlayer*.

The *UserAVI* class in this example also provides some training facilities that help teach this new development paradigm. A user can see the source of the current scenario as well as create and modify new scenarios using existing templates.

Do You Want to Be a Scenario Writer?

Press the "New Scenario" link and become a scenario writer. You do not need to be afraid of the empty page as some writers are. The program immediately lets you select a template for your scenario. You can easily modify one of the existing scenarios to create your own. Then, you can save your scenario and see if it works. If it does not, it is no big deal; the program helps you edit your new scenario and make it work eventually.

Application Scenario Language

Application Scenario Language (ASL) is an XML-based language that describes application business flow in small scenarios.

Scenarios consist of XML elements: scenario steps or acts. Scenario steps are numbered sequentially and executed in the numbered order. It is not necessary to number steps manually. The numbering can be done automatically. The numbers are important to keep the proper order while converting an XML scenario to the hash table format. Every act of a scenario is a prompt, a condition, or an execution step.

Prompt the User for an Answer

The *prompt()* method of the *UserAVI* class delivers a prompt message to the user. The method sets the *promptState* flag to true. This shifts the program into an interpretation state. The user's response will be interpreted to fill the variable provided with the prompt parameters. The prompt might have additional arguments, specific hints for input interpretation, and conditional actions.

Here is an extract from the *newTopic.xml* scenario that allows someone to introduce a new object to the knowledge base:

```
<prompt variable="NEW-OBJECT"
  service="org.opencyc.connector.UserAVI"
  action="prompt"
  noinput="reprompt(Your input is needed)"
  translate="concatenate"
  msg="Please provide a name for your new topic." />
```

```
<if condition="!exists" perform="doNextStep(acceptNewObject)" />
<!--There is an object with this name in knowledgebase.-->
<!--Query and display this object and let user know it is not new-->
<act action="query" constant="NEW-OBJECT"
lastMsg="NEW-OBJECT is not new." />
<!--The lastMsg element above makes this act to close the scenario-->
<act name="acceptNewObject"
service="com.its.connector.KnowledgeService"
action="createNewPermanent" constant="NEW-OBJECT" />
<!--more prompts and acts to relate new object to existing knowledge-->
```

The prompt element of the XML scenario specifies the service class name (*org.opencyc.connector.UserAVI*) and the action method name (*prompt*) and sets the prompt variable (NEW-OBJECT) to store the user's input and the prompt message.

The *noinput* and *translate* elements are optional interpretation parameters. The *noinput* element directs the program to reprompt the user if he or she just pressed the ENTER key.

The *translate* element instructs the program to concatenate multiple word input into a single word in the manner of Cyc knowledge base naming conventions.

For example, the input "Volga River" is translated into the *VolgaRiver* name.

An important part of the *prompt* element is its internal *variable* element. In this example the variable has the "NEW-OBJECT" name. The resulting interpretation of the response will be assigned to a variable created on the fly with the "NEW-OBJECT" name. The ScenarioPlayer then will parse the current scenario to replace all occurrences of the "NEW-OBJECT" with its value.

The second step of the scenario is a condition. If the object name does not exist (*!exists*) in the knowledge base, the system will *perform* the *doNextStep*(acceptNewObject) operation and will skip the third step.

The third step of the scenario is performed only if a name suggested by the user is known to knowledge base. The third step queries the knowledge base on this known subject and presents existing information with the last prompt (the end of the scenario), which lets the user know that this object name is absolutely not new to the knowledge base.

Aliases

The current extract does not include the *aliases* element in the prompt, but when we talk about scenario APIs, it would be a crime to omit this important element.

The *aliases* element can be a part of any prompt instruction providing hints on the response interpretation. The aliases element can list possible answers that can come in different forms but still represent the same concept.

The *aliases* element, for example, can instructs the program to interpret user input, for example, "y," or "sure," as "yes." In other words, if the user's input matches one of the aliases, the original input will be replaced with the related key value and all the following conditions (if any) will apply to the resulting key.

The following example shows the *aliases* element in the user's *prompt*.

```
<prompt variable="YES-OR-NO-ANSWER"
action="prompt"
service="com.its.connector.ScenarioPlayer"
msg="Are you a new user? (y/n)"
aliases="yes\y\new\sure^no\n\old"
/>
```

Note, that there are two sets of aliases in the example above. These two sets are separated by the "^" character, whereas aliases within the case are separated with the "\" character. There could be multiple sets in the *aliases* element.

Translate

The *translate* element instructs the program to perform string manipulations on a user's input. The *translate* element includes method names and arguments (if necessary). In most cases, the methods are of the *Stringer* class, although the class name may also be present. Here is an example using the *translate* element:

```
<prompt variable="PERSON-NAME" action="prompt"
  service="org.opencyc.connector.UserAVI"
  msg="Please provide your name (First Last)"
  translate=
"concatenate(REPLACE-WITH-INPUT)^
startWithUpperCase(REPLACE-WITH-INPUT)"
       />
```

The program concatenates the user's input and makes sure each word begins with the upper case. For example, if the input is *jeff zhuk*, the first instruction produces *jeffZhuk*, and the second instruction makes it *JeffZhuk*, in the best Cyc tradition.

The resulting string is saved in the *lastInterpretation* variable, a member of the *ScenarioPlayer* class.

The Condition Element

The *condition* element is a rich combination of conditional and execution expressions. Here is an extract that follows the prompt for a login name in the *login* scenario:

```
<if condition="exists"
 pattern="LOGIN-NAME-INPUT"
 perform="doNextStep(checkPassword)" />
<!-- Login name is not found -->
<prompt variable="NEW-USER-ANSWER"
  action="prompt"
  service="REPLACE-WITH-USER-SERVICE"
  msg="Are you a new user? (y/n)" aliases="yes\y\new" />
<if condition="equals"
 source=" NEW-USER-ANSWER"
 pattern="yes"
 perform="playScenario(newuser)" />
<!-- The user is not a new user. Incorrect login. -->
<act lastMsg="Please re-login" />
<!--Login name is found-->
```

As you can see, a conditional statement in the first step of the extract above checks for the pattern's existence. The condition in this statement is *exists*, and the *pattern* is a value of the *LOGIN-NAME-INPUT* variable.

The program queries the knowledge base to verify the login name's existence.

If this pattern is known to the knowledge base (exists), the scenario performs the *playScenario(newuser)* operation that can sign-up a new user.

The most common way to change the order of a scenario is to use the doNextStep() operation with the label name as an argument as it is shown in the example below:

```
doNextStep(labelName)
<!---several scenario steps-->
<act name="labelName" perform="someService" />
```

It is also possible to use the *playScenario(scenarioName)* operation to jump to a new scenario. We can even start in the middle of the scenario if we provide additional arguments like in the example below.

```
playScenario(scenarioName, labelName, internalScenarioArguments);
```

The **list of conditions** includes several keywords:

- ***exists*** [pattern]—returns true if a pattern exists in the knowledge base
- ***!exists*** [pattern]—opposite of exists; returns true if a pattern does not exist in the knowledge base
- ***equals*** [source] [pattern]—compares a source to a pattern and returns true if the source equals a pattern
- ***!equals*** [source] [pattern]—compares a source to a pattern and returns true if the source is not the same as the pattern
- ***includes*** [source] [pattern]—returns true if the source includes a pattern
- ***!includes*** [source] [pattern]—returns true if the source does not include a pattern
- ***inAliases*** [source] [pattern]—looks for a pattern in a table of aliases (from the configuration file or knowledge base) in which a source defines the name of the table of aliases; returns true if a pattern is found as one of the aliases
- ***!inAliases*** [source] [pattern]—looks for a pattern in a table of aliases (from the configuration file or knowledge base) in which a source defines the name of the table of aliases; returns true if a pattern is not found in the table

The *noinput* option that can be used in the prompt statement performs an instruction when the user does not answer the prompt but just presses the ENTER key.

A condition statement is followed by an action to perform, an executable instruction. If a condition is not met (returns false), the action is not performed and the next scenario step is played instead.

Both *perform-* and *action-*executable instructions use a service object and an action method name for this service method invocation. The only difference between the two is the default service name used when a service name is omitted in the statement.

The *perform* instruction uses the *UserAVI* class in this case, whereas the *action* instruction targets the *KnowledgeService*.

Executable instructions accept parameters in the form of a method signature or key-value elements.

Here is an example of a signature approach:

```
perform="playScenario(newuser)"
```

This statement performs the *playScenario()* method of the *UserAVI* or its base class. This method must expect a single string argument. The *newuser* string is passed to the method.

The alternative way is to specify all parameters as key-value pairs:

```
action="createNewObject"
msg="REPLACE-WITH-MAIN-GROUP"
```

or

```
action="createMicrotheory"
Mt="REPLACE-WITH-MAINMT"
msg="REPLACE-WITH-MAIN-GROUP knowledge area"
genlMts="KnowledgeExchangeMt,ComputerNetworkMt"
```

This way is convenient for methods that expect a table (*Hashtable*) of key values, as in the code extract below (see the *KnowledgeService* class):

```
public String createMicrotheory(Hashtable parameters)
 throws Exception {
   String comment = (String)parameters.get("msg");
   String mtName = (String)parameters.get("Mt");
   mtName = Stringer.startWithUpperCase(mtName);
   String isaMtName = (String)parameters.get("isa");
   String genlMtsString = (String)parameters.get("genlMts");
 // etc. etc.............
```

The Query Element Talks to the Knowledge Base

The query element is a direct combination of knowledge base query results and the following conditions and executions.

It consists of a Cyc query and usually includes the *queryResult* option that assigns a variable to store query results.

Query instructions require us to define a microtheory name in which the search will be performed. The program assigns the main microtheory name (set by the configuration file) as the default if this parameter is omitted in the query statement.

As an example, let us consider an extract from the *newTopic.xml* scenario below. The extract includes a prompt for the user's input, a condition element, and a query statement followed by an analysis of query results.

```
<!--Ask a user to relate a new subject to some existing Collection-->
<prompt variable="EXISTING-COLLECTION"
  service="org.opencyc.connector.UserAVI"
  action="prompt"
  msg="Please relate your new topic to some existing object that must
represent some Collection. Enter an existing topic name that can serve
as a parent to your new topic."
  noinput="setDefault(REPLACE-WITH-MAIN-TOPIC)" />
```

```
<!--Check if this is an existing name-->
<if condition="!exists"
pattern="EXISTING-COLLECTION"
perform="reprompt(EXISTING-COLLECTION is not found in the KB.)" />
<!--Check if this is a Collection-->
<act query="(#$isa #$EXISTING-COLLECTION ?X)
queryResult="COLLECTION-QUERY-RESULT" />
<if condition="!includes"
  pattern="Collection"
perform="reprompt(EXISTING-COLLECTION is not a Collection)" />
```

The example above prompts the user to provide an existing collection name that relates a new subject to existing data. The following statements check to determine if the user's input is worth trusting.

Does this name really exist in the knowledge base, or just in the user's imagination? Does this name meet the requirement to be a collection?

If the requirements are not met, the system reprompts the user for a better answer.

Only a good qualified answer can pass this test.

This example includes two of the most commonly used conditional actions: *reprompt()* and *setDefault()*. The *reprompt()* action can take an optional argument-message and add this message to the last user's prompt.

The *setDefault()* action instructs the program to replace the user's input with the value that follows this action. The example above uses the *setDefault()* method in the "noinput" case to set a collection name as the main topic name. (The main topic name must be set in the configuration file.)

Learn by Example: How to Add Knowledge to Knowledgebase?

I hope that several more extracts from the *newTopic.xml* scenario provide enough exposure into the world of application scenario writers.

The scenario extract below sets a scope or a microtheory for the new topic:

```
<prompt variable="YOUR-MICROTHEORY"
  service="REPLACE-WITH-USER-SERVICE"
  action="prompt"
  noinput="setDefault(REPLACE-WITH-MAINMT)"
  msg="Provide one of your existing microtheories (scope) for this
object. (REPLACE-WITH-MAINMT is the default scope.)" />
<act query="(#$isa #$YOUR-MICROTHEORY ?X)"
  actionResult="CHECK-MICROTHEORY-RESULT" />
<if condition="!includes"
  source="CHECK-MICROTHEORY-RESULT"
  pattern="Microtheory"
  perform="reprompt(This is not a microtheory name)" />
```

In this example, the user's prompt suggests defining a scope for a new topic as an existing microtheory.

The user has the option of pressing the ENTER key without any input. In the *noinput* case, the program performs the *setDefault()* method to set the scope to the main microtheory defined by the configuration file.

The following query uses the knowledge engine to determine if the user's input really represents a microtheory.

If the query result does not include the word *Microtheory*, the program reprompts the user.

You might notice the REPLACE-WITH-MAINMT and REPLACE-WITH-USER-SERVICE variables in this extract. The program replaces these variables and some other variables with the same REPLACE-WITH syntax with the replacement values from the configuration file:

```
<replacements>
      ......
  <replacement name="REPLACE-WITH-MAINMT" value="JavaSchoolMt" />

  <replacement name="REPLACE-WITH-USER-SERVICE"
value="org.opencyc.connector.UserAVI" />
    ... .  .
</replacements>
```

Can a New Topic Serve as a Parent-Umbrella for More Objects?

The last extract from the *newTopic.xml* scenario helps to define whether a new topic can serve as a parent-umbrella for more objects:

```
<prompt variable="COLLECTION-OR-INDIVIDUAL"
  service="org.opencyc.connector.UserAVI"
  action="prompt"
  aliases="Collection\1^2\Individual"
  nomatch="reprompt(/incorrect answer. Only 1 or 2 is accepted.)"
  msg="Is a new topic a Collection - class of objects (1) or an
instance - individual object (2) ? Enter 1 or 2" />
<!--If a new topic is a collection - its RELASHIONSHPIS to a parent is
as a class to a subclass, "genls"-->
<if condition="equals"
  source="COLLECTION-OR-INDIVIDUAL"
  pattern="Collection"
  perform="modifyScenario(RELATIONSHIPS,genls) />"
<!--If a new topic is an individual - its RELASHIONSHIPS to a parent is
an instance "isa"-->
<if condition="equals"
  source="COLLECTION-OR-INDIVIDUAL"
  pattern="Individual"
  perform="modifyScenario(RELATIONSHIPS,isa) />"
<!--Set a rule-relationships between the new object and its parent-->
<act action="assert"
 msg="(#$RELATIONSHIPS #$NEW-TOPIC-NAME #$EXISTING-COLLECTION)" />
```

The program substitutes the user input "1" or "2" with the word *Collection* or *Individual* according to the *aliases* attribute.

The *nomatch* attribute instructs the program to reprompt the user if the user's input does not match the condition (is neither *1* nor 2).

The program performs the *modifyScenario()* method of the *UserAVI* class to replace the *RELATIONSHIPS* variable (in the last step of the scenario) with "isa" or "genls" relationships. Both are CycL predicates.

The last step of the scenario establishes relationships between the new object and its parent. Collections have transitive inheritance established by *genls* (generic inheritance), whereas individual inheritance established by *isa* is not transitive. The message that we use with the *assertGAF* action is an example of a sentence rule written in CycL.

Think of the *isa* predicate as an analogy to creating an instance of a class, whereas *genls* is about the similar relationship between a base and a subclass. The meaning of the sentence is either:

- The new topic is a subclass of the EXISTING-COLLECTION and is a new Collection or a class of new objects; or
- the new topic is an individual instance of the EXISTING-COLLECTION.

The most important achievement of the new topic scenario is the connection of a new object to existing roots in the knowledge base (Fig. 13.12). New data must be related to roots with several rules/assertions.

1. A new object is a collection (a class of objects) or an individual instance.
2. A new object has a parent-umbrella in the existing knowledge space.
3. A new object has a scope or microtheory.

You can see that XML-based APIs of application scenarios serve to interpret words and sentences coming from a user or from text documents and to invoke existing software services, including knowledge engine services. Collected into XML scenarios, they can completely describe application behavior and, if necessary, include presentation layer definitions in XML and/or HTML, WML, and other formats.

Can We Change the Execution Order of a Scenario?

The *playScenario*, as well as the *doNextStep*, action can be very handy in conditional statements. The *playScenario* is an executable instruction to play a specific scenario starting with a specific step number (or by default, from Step 1) and other optional arguments.

Here is an example from the *countryData* scenario, which may be handy if you want to add some information that you surveyed about a foreign country.

```
 <prompt variable="COUNTRY-INPUT"
msg="What country?"
service="REPLACE-WITH-USER-SERVICE" action="prompt" />
<if condition="!exists" pattern="COUNTRY-INPUT"
perform="playScenario(newCountry,2,COUNTRY-INPUT)" />
```

This scenario prompts the user to enter a country name. If the user names a country that is not currently known to the knowledge base (is new), the program invokes the *playScenario()* method with the following arguments:

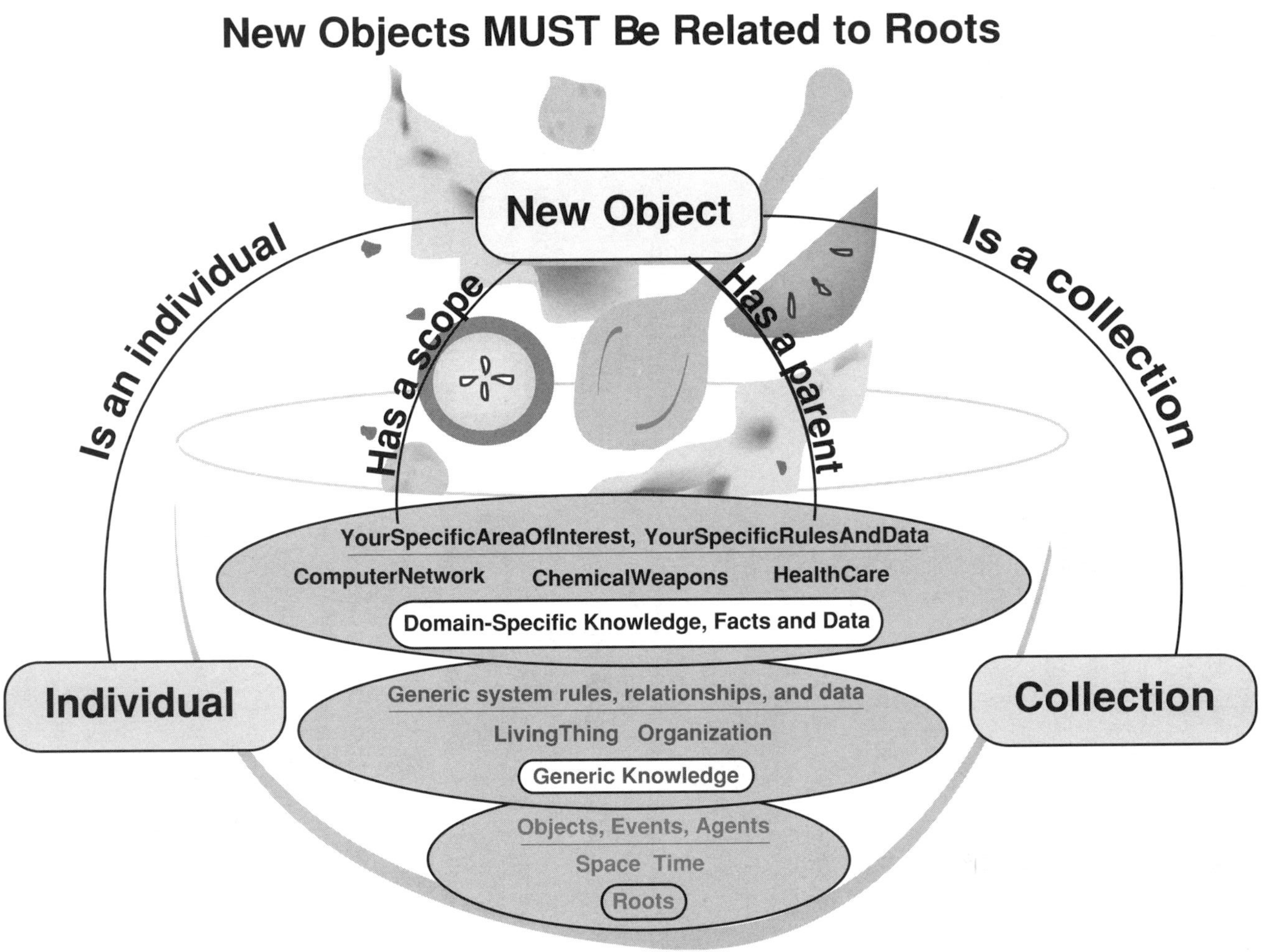
New Objects MUST Be Related to Roots
New Object
Is an individual
Has a scope
Has a parent
Is a collection
YourSpecificAreaOfInterest, YourSpecificRulesAndData
ComputerNetwork
ChemicalWeapons
HealthCare
Domain-Specific Knowledge, Facts and Data
Individual
Collection
Generic system rules, relationships, and data
LivingThing
Organization
Generic Knowledge
Objects, Events, Agents
Space
Time
Roots

FIGURE 13.12. Knowledge Integration Rules.

1. The scenario name is *newCountry*.
2. The starting step of the scenario is 2.
3. The COUNTRY-INPUT will be passed to the *newCountry* scenario as an expected argument—the name of a new country to be entered in the knowledge base.

A very simple example of changing the order of steps in a scenario is the conditional invocation of the *doNextStep* action.

The argument to the *doNextStep()* method instructs the program to jump to a proper element in the scenario flow.

There are many actions and methods that are accessible with the action and perform attributes of XML scenarios.

The easiest way to look into these possibilities is to view the JavaDoc APIs (method definitions) of the *UserAVI, KnowledgeService,* and other classes inside and outside the Knowledge Connector package.

Executable Acts of a Scenario

Almost every method may be considered a potential action or executable act in XML scenarios. Executable acts have only the parameters necessary for the execution: the service name, action name, and method arguments (if needed).
For example:

```
<act action="createNewObject"
service="org.opencyc.connector.KnowledgeService"
msg="NEW-OBJECT-NAME" />
```

The action element may include a class name and all necessary parameters. A class name can be omitted. In this case, the default class name is used instead.

If a class name does not include a package name, the *org.opencyc.connector* package name is added by default.

It is recommended that you provide a qualified class name that includes a package name (see the example above). Otherwise, the Java Reflection package has to look in all the jar files available in your Java classpath.

This lookup may be an expensive exercise, especially in J2*ME* resource-restricted devices.

As we mentioned earlier, the connector package not only works with its own services but can also invoke any service available in any other package. For example, the *XML* scenario provided below uses the email service from the *com.its.mail* (Internet Technology School, Inc. [4]) package.

```
<?XML version = "1.0" encoding = "UTF-8"?>
<scenario>
 <!--Example of email service invocation-->
 <prompt msg="Provide TO: address"
   variable="TO-EMAIL-ADDRESS"
   service="org.opencyc.connector.UserAVI" action="prompt" />
 <prompt msg="Provide your message"
   variable="EMAIL-MESSAGE"
   service="org.opencyc.connector.UserAVI" action="prompt" />
 <act service="com.its.mail.EmailClient" action="send"
   to="TO-EMAIL-ADDRESS" msg="EMAIL-MESSAGE" />
</scenario>
```

An alternative way is to provide a qualified method signature in the *action* or *perform* statements. The example below shows an act of a scenario that sends email with predefined arguments:

```
<act action=
"com.its.mail.EmailClient.sendMail(Jeff.Zhuk@JavaSchool.com, test,
Hello!)" />
```

Explore the Cyc API

The low-level Java API for the Cyc knowledge engine is very rich and nontrivial. The training tool based on the connector package allows us to enter the *inlineAPI* keyword followed by a Java Cyc API expression in the command line. This technique helps us discover Java Cyc API method details and to quickly survey some data with no browser at hand.

It is possible to copy and paste a method definition from the *org.opencyc.api.CycAccess* APIs. For example, the command line can initially consist of:

```
"inlineapi getAllDependentSpecs(CycFort cycFort)"
```

This method gets the list of all of the dependent specs for a *CycFort* collection.

Substitute an argument string with the real collection name—for example, *Person*. The command line will look like this:

```
"inlineapi getAllDependentSpecs(CycFort Person)"
```

Press the ENTER key, and view all the rules (assertions) associated with the *Person* collection.

The program interpretation is based on the *inlineAPI()* method of the *ScenarioPlayer*. The *inline API()* method tries to interpret and execute any API and includes special support for Cyc objects. For example, it will convert the *Person* string argument to a *CycFort* object, as the *getAllDependentSpecs()* method requires.

Here is another example of the Java Cyc API executed with the *inlineAPI()* method:

```
"inlineapi getAllInstances(CycFort cycFort, CycFort mt)"
```

This call gets a list of all the direct and indirect instances (individuals) for a CycFort collection in the given microtheory.

Substitute a collection name with *Person* and a microtheory name with *JavaSchoolMt* and press the ENTER key.

The resulting command line is:

```
"inlineapi getAllInstances(CycFort Person, CycFort JavaSchoolMt)"
```

This query produces a list of people associated with the *Person* collection in the *JavaSchoolMt* microtheory. Note that providing the type of variable, such as CycFort, is optional. By using this option, the user gives the program an indication that the default class name is CycAccess. More precise method calls include a class name. Here is an example:

```
"inlineapi org.opencyc.api.CycObjectFactory.makeUniqueCycVariable
(CycVariable modelCycVariable)"
```

This call constructs and returns a new *CycVariable* object by suffixing the given variable name.

If the *inlineAPI()* method works with a single command line typed by a user, the similar *performAction()* method of the *ScenarioPlayer* class interprets and executes elements of XML scenarios provided at run-time by the application.

The *performAction()* method of the *ScenarioPlayer* class tries its best to resolve a class name, method name, and related parameters within an XML element. This is not always possible, but if the interpretation is successful, the *performAction()* method uses the same *act()* method of the *ServiceConnector* class powered by the Java Reflection package to invoke the proper service method on the proper service object.

The resulting data usually feed the next XML elements of the same scenario or may be formatted by a presentation factory and displayed (or pronounced) by a performer implementation. For example:

```
<act action="CycAccess.getAllSpecs(CycFort \"Person\")" />
or
<act action="org.opencyc.api.CycAccess.getAllSpecs(CycFort Person)" />
or
<act action="CycAccess.getAllSpecs(CycFort Person, CycFort
"JavaSchoolMt")" />
```

In all cases, the execution produces a list of Cyc knowledge base specifications related to the "Person."

The *performAction()* method is not limited to OpenCyc class methods, but can resolve and execute method calls to object services located on the same network.

Here is another example of a service invocation:

```
<act action="sendMail" service="com.its.mail.EmailClient"
     to="EMAIL-ADDRESS"
     from="REPLACE-WITH-MAIN-AGENT"
     subject="Welcome"
     message="Welcome to Cyc-JavaSchool training." />
```

In this example, the *com.its.mail.EmailClient* service object invokes the *sendMail* method with the above parameters

The connector package is powered not only by a set of Java classes. The *config.xml* file (Fig. 13.13) also plays a role in the package configuration and behavior definition. The configuration file includes alias elements and presentation patterns. The program reads the *config.xml* file at the very beginning and sets configuration tables in the *ScenarioPlayer* and *CycHTMLFactory* (presentation patterns).

The program uses aliases for the initial interpretation of a user's input in *UserAVI* methods such as *interpretInput()* and *checkPatterns()*. The *CycHTMLFactory* uses presentation patterns as style sheets while formatting an output.

Almost all core classes use utilities from the *IOMaster* (input, output, networking) and the *Stringer* (string manipulation, XMLparsing).

Figure 13.14 shows a source extract from the *IOMaster* class. The full source can be found in Appendix 3.

```
<?xml version = "1.0" encoding = "UTF-8"?>
<config>
 <data>
 <RELATIONS-INPUT>
  <set name="friends" value="friend" />
  <set name="relatives" value="sister,brother,aunt,cousin,
  sisters,brothers,cousins,aunts" />
  <set name="employees" value="co-worker, co-workers,employee,
  developer" />
  <set name="acquaintedWith" value="AcquaintedWith,
  acquainted,knows,known" />
  <set name="employingAgent" value="employer, chief,president" />
 </RELATIONS-INPUT>
 <FEMALE-OR-MALE-INPUT>
  <set name="FemaleAnimal" value="f,y,yes, woman,girl, female" />
  <set name="MaleAnimal" value="m,man,male,boy" />
 </FEMALE-OR-MALE-INPUT>
 <predicates>
  <predicate name="clients" value="users,customers" />
  <predicate name="relatives" value="sister,brother,aunt,
  cousin,sisters,brothers,cousins,aunts,friend,friends" />
  <predicate name="friends" value="friend,comrad" />
 </predicates>
 <scenarioNames>
  <scenario name="relatives" value="addfriend,addrelative,
  addrelations,father,mother,daughter,friend,friends,relate,
  addrelationships" />
  <scenario name="find" value="search,get,lookup" />
  <scenario name="newtopic" value="create,new,add" />
  <scenario name="contactinfo" value="contactdata, addcontacts," />

 </scenarioNames>
 <actions>
  <action name="query" value="what,where,get,who,find, list" />
  <action name="killConstant" value="kill,remove,delete" />
  <action name="assertGAF" value="assert,insert,relate" />
  <action name="unassertGAF" value="unassert,unrelate" />
  <action name="createNewPermanent" value="createConstant,create"/>
 </actions>
</data>

 <scenarioButtons>
  <scenarioButton name="setWorldSystem" value="New World" />
  <scenarioButton name="find" value="Search" />
  <scenarioButton name="newtopic" value="Add Knowledge" />
  <scenarioButton name="newscenario" value="New Scenario" />
```

Figure 13.13

```
 <scenarioButton name="showWorld" value="Show My World" />
 <scenarioButton name="Save and Exit" value="Save and Exit" />
</scenarioButtons>

<presentationPatterns>
 <presentationPattern name="presentationType"
 value="org.opencyc.connector.HTMLFormatter" />
 <presentationPattern name="listPresentationType"
 value="CycList" />
 <presentationPattern name="userServiceName"
 value="org.opencyc.connector.UserAVI" />
 <presentationPattern name="requestAcknowledgement"
 value="Your request was: CURRENT_MESSAGE \nKnown facts
 related to your request found in the CURRENT_MT scope
 (microtheory)" />
  <presentationPattern name="response"
  value="Enter subject name for more details or issue another
  KB request" />
  <presentationPattern name="multiLineResponse"
  value="Enter selected number or subject name for more
  details or issue another KB request" />
  <presentationPattern name="editableResponse"
  value="Selecting rows like CURRENT_EDITABLEe you can add or
  edit data." />
  <presentationPattern name="firstHeader" value="" />
  <presentationPattern name="tableHeader"
  value="[td][b]PREDICATE[/b][/td][td][b]Value[/b][/td][/tr]" />
  <presentationPattern name="lastFooter" value="Type Exit
  to end the program [b]and save your session work[/b]." />
  <presentationPattern name="promptHeader" value="[font
  face=verdana size=4 color=blue][b]" />
  <presentationPattern name="promptFooter" value= "[/b][/font]" />
  <presentationPattern name="font" value=
  "[font face=verdona size=2]" />
  <presentationPattern name="scenarioHeader"
  value="[table][td][img
  src=file:///REPLACE-WITH-URLimages/its.gif]
  [/td][td][center][font size=3 face=verdana
  color=blue][b]Software+Ontology: Training
  Facilities[br]Connect Cyc to software applcations with
  XML Scenarios.[br]Address your questions/suggestions/bug
  reports to Jeff.Zhuk@JavaSchool.com[/b][/font][/center]
  [/td][td][image src=file:
  ///REPLACE-WITH-URLimages/cyc.gif][/td][/table]
  [font size=3 face=verdana]" />
  <presentationPattern name="editPrompt" value="You can
```

FIGURE 13.13. (*cont.*)

```
   enter data in the input field. Current value: " />
   <presentationPattern name="scenarioStartTopics"
   value="You can add more DETAILS" />
   <presentationPattern name="scenarioStartNames"
   value="userdetails" />
  <scenarios>
    <start name="You can add more DETAILS, introduce more
    RELATIVES or FRIENDS" value="userdetails" />
    <start name="Add profile details" value="userdetails" />
    <start name="Introduce a related person" value="newuser" />
    <start name="Relate to another (known to the system)
    person" value="relatives" />
  </scenarios>
 </presentationPatterns>

 <defaults>
    <default name="tryNewScenarioMsg" value="Try new
    scenario. It might actually work :-) To edit - press
    NEW SCENARIO again and enter the editable scenario
    name." />
    <default name="defaultScenarios" value="newtopic,
    find,newscenario,setWorldSystem,showWorld" />
    <default name="existingScenarioMsg" value="The name is
    taken by one of core scenarios. Press New Scenario
    button again and type another name." />
    <default name="worldMts" value="JavaSchoolMt" />
    <default name="worldObjects" value="JavaSchool" />
    <answer name="fromSystem" value="Example." />
    <pattern name="startQuery" value="is,about" />
    <pattern name="toSystem" value="your" />
    <message name="KBconnectionErrorMsg"
    value="ERROR: Knowledge Base connection was lost." />
   <message name="notUniqueMsg" value="is not a unique
   name in the KB. Please re-enter." />
   <message name="notExistsMsg" value=" is not an
   existing name in the KB. Please re-enter." />
   <message name="unresolvedMsg" value="ERROR: The system
   cannot comprehend the answer and has saved unresolved
   situation for future learning process. " />
   <message name="emptyMsg" value="Cannot take RETURN key
   as an answer. Please enter a meaningful value" />
  <URL name="upgradeFromURL"
  value="http://JavaSchool.com/school/public/knowledge/upgrade" />
 </defaults>
 </config>
```

FIGURE 13.13. *(cont.)*

```
    /**
     * method readTextFile() uses readBinFile(iFilename)
     * @param iFilename
     * @return string
     */
    public static String readTextFile(String iFilename) {
        if(iFilename == null) {
            return "ERROR: readTextFile:url=null";
        }
        byte[] bytes = readBinFile(iFilename);
        if(bytes != null)
            return new String(bytes);
        else
            return new String("ERROR: readTextFile:bytes=null
            filename=" + iFilename);
    }
    /**
     * method readBinFile() read binary file
     * @param iFilename
     * @return bytes
     */
    public static byte[] readBinFile(String iFilename)
    {
        if(iFilename.startsWith("http://") ||
iFilename.startsWith("HTTP://")) {
            return fetchURL(iFilename);
        }
        try
        {
            File file = new File(iFilename);
            int size = (int) file.length();
            byte[] oData = new byte[size];
            int bytes_read = 0;
            int offset = 0;
            FileInputStream in = new FileInputStream(file);
            if(in == null)
            {
                return null;
            }
            while(bytes_read < size)
            {
                bytes_read +=
                in.read(oData, offset, size-bytes_read);
                offset += bytes_read;
            }
            in.close();
            return oData;
        }
        catch (Exception e)
        {
            return null;
        }
    }
    // ... more methods ...
```

FIGURE 13.14

The most commonly used method, *readTextFile()*, retrieves text data from the file system or the Internet. The method looks into the URL argument and looks globally if the URL begins with the "http" string. Otherwise, the method reads data from the local file system.

The *writeTextFile()* method saves data to a file. The *post()* method helps to post data to the Internet as a multipart or multiform data package. Of course, the target server must have a supporting program to accept this data.

Figure 13.15 presents a source extract from the *Stringer* class. The full source can be found in Appendix 3. The *Stringer* class is a huge collection of string manipulation utilities, including a simple XML parser.

How to Set Your World

There are several steps that the Knowledge Connector application performs automatically for every user.

At its first startup, the application uses the *setWorld* scenario to check that basic security and resource provisioning are in place. The scenario queries the knowledge base for several basic areas or names provided in the configuration file.

If one or more areas are not established yet, the scenario creates the necessary microtheories and constants in the knowledge base.

How is privilege-based access provided to knowledge base?

1. The *setWorld* scenario creates a special microtheory with the name provided in a configuration file. The default name is *ResourceAvailabilityMt*. This microtheory serves as a custom bookkeeper for a specific group of users to associate created data (resources) with a security domain [4].
2. This is a part of the *setWorld* scenario that takes care of this issue.
3. <action="createMicrotheory"
   Mt="REPLACE-WITH-RESOURCEMT"
   msg="REPLACE-WITH-RESOURCEMT relate objects to privileged access domains"
   genlMts="KnowledgeExchangeMt"
   isa="Microtheory" />
4. While creating a new object name or a new microtheory, the program makes two additional assertions (rules):
   4.1. Mark a new object (constant) as "SomethingExisting"
   <act action="assert" Mt="REPLACE-WITH-RESOURCEMT"
   msg="(#$isa #$REPLACE-WITH-NEW-CONSTANT #$SomethingExisting)" />
   4.2. Mark a new constant as "resourceAvailable" for a default or a specific "DOMAIN-NAME"
   <act action="assert" Mt="REPLACE-WITH-RESOURCEMT"
   msg="(#$"(#$resourceAvailable #$REPLACE-WITH-DOMAIN-NAME
   #$REPLACE-WITH-NEW-CONSTANT)" />
   The DOMAIN-NAME can be a group of users, a security level, or anything of this kind. The only requirement: a DOMAIN-NAME must be marked as a #$*Agent* in the knowledge base.

Figure 13.16 shows the *setWorld* scenario. The first steps of the scenario are to script check and establish (if necessary) the resource and main *microtheories* that define a world of knowledge for the group of users to which a current login user belongs. Then, the scenario makes a provision for a session security area, and the last act of the *setWorld* scenario passes control to the *login* scenario.

```
/*
 * The Stringer class provides text manipulation methods
 * including a limited XML parser
 * @author Jeff.Zhuk@JavaSchool.com
 * @author Masha.Tishkova@JavaSchool.com (mnr)
 */

package org.opencyc.connector;

import java.util.Hashtable;
import java.util.Vector;
import java.util.Enumeration;

public class Stringer {
    public static boolean debug = false;
    private String key;
    private String value;

    public Stringer() { } // default constructor

    /**
     * The parse() method is a convenience (static) method
     * to be used outside of the class
     * The method retrieves XML elements from an XML string and
     * transform XML elements into a Hashtable or a set of
     * nested Hashtables
     * @param xml
     * @return hashtable (can be nested)
     */
    public static Hashtable parse(String xml) {
        // custom code or standard SAX or DOM parser used
        Stringer parser = new Stringer();
        Hashtable hashtable = parser.parseXML(xml);
        return hashtable;
    }
    /**
     * Parses parameter string which is XML file content and
     * returns XMLDocument
     * @param stringToParse
     * @param key represents the main attribute  name
     * @param value represents the main attribute  value
     * @return Hashtablw which contains parameters of the
     * XML document
     */
    public Hashtable parseXML(String stringToParse, String
    key, String value){
```

FIGURE 13.15

```
        if(stringToParse == null) {
            System.out.println("parseXML:empty string");
            return null;
        }
        this.key= key;
        this.value = value;
        stringToParse = getStringToParse(stringToParse);
        Hashtable args = new Hashtable();
        getElement(stringToParse, args);
        return args;
    }

    // ... more methods ...
}
```

FIGURE 13.15. *(cont.)*

The names of initial microtheories and user groups, such as REPLACE-WITH-MAIN-GROUP and REPLACE-WITH-MAINMT, are defined in the *Replacements* section of the configuration file.

Each group of users, or even an individual user, can redefine the names and establish a unique world or area of knowledge within the knowledge base.

Here is the extract from the *Replacements* section of the configuration file:

```
<replacements>
<!--A Security Domain or a Group Name-->
  <replacement name="REPLACE-WITH-MAIN-GROUP" value="JavaSchool"
   />
<!--The Main microtheory-->
  <replacement name="REPLACE-WITH-MAINMT" value="JavaSchoolMt" />
<!--Resource Microtheory Name-->
  <replacement name="REPLACE-WITH-RESOURCEMT"
value="ResourceAvailabilityMt" />
<!--Session Microtheory Name-->
  <replacement name="REPLACE-WITH-SESSIONMT" value="SessionDataMt" />
<!--More configuration Names-->
</replacements>
```

The main microtheory (*JavaSchoolMt* in this example) serves as an overall umbrella for all data and rules created by the group, whereas the resource microtheory (*ResourceAvailabilityMt* in this example) stores only *resourceAvailable* rules that specify privilege-based access to this data.

It is especially handy to have these umbrellas when you want to distribute your data—for example, when you work within a network of Cyc-Peers.

In this case, it is relatively easy to query for available resources *(resourceAvailable ?X ?Y)* in the resource microtheory to get all object names, then collect all the rules related to these objects under the main microtheory.

```xml
<?xml version = "1.0" encoding = "UTF-8"?>
<dialogScenario name="setWorld">
 <scenario>
   <if condition="exists" pattern="REPLACE-WITH-RESOURCEMT"
   perform="doNextStep(checkGroupExistence)" />

   <act name="2" action="createMicrotheory"
     Mt="REPLACE-WITH-RESOURCEMT"
     msg="REPLACE-WITH-RESOURCEMT relate objects to privileged
     access domains" genlMts="KnowledgeExchangeMt"
     isa="Microtheory" />

   <!-- Check and if necessary create main group agent -->
   <if name="checkGroupExistence" condition="exists"
     pattern="REPLACE-WITH-MAIN-GROUP"
     perform="doNextStep(checkMtExistence)" />

   <act action="createNewObject" msg="REPLACE-WITH-MAIN-GROUP" />

   <act action="assert" Mt="REPLACE-WITH-RESOURCEMT"
     msg="(#$isa #$REPLACE-WITH-MAIN-GROUP #$TemporalThing)" />

   <!-- Provision for object registration -->
   <act action="assert" Mt="REPLACE-WITH-RESOURCEMT"
     msg="(#$isa #$REPLACE-WITH-MAIN-GROUP #$Agent)" />

   <!-- Check and if necessary create the main microtheory -->
   <if name="checkMtExistence" condition="exists"
     pattern="REPLACE-WITH-MAINMT"
     perform="doNextStep(checkSessionExistence)" />

   <act action="createMicrotheory"
     Mt="REPLACE-WITH-MAINMT" msg="REPLACE-WITH-MAIN-GROUP
     knowledge area"
        genlMts="KnowledgeExchangeMt,ComputerNetworkMt"
        isa="Microtheory" />

   <act action="assertGAF" Mt="REPLACE-WITH-MAINMT"
   msg="(#$isa #$REPLACE-WITH-MAIN-GROUP #$Agent)" />

   <!-- Register the main microtheory -->
   <act action="assert" Mt="REPLACE-WITH-RESOURCEMT"
   msg="(#$resourceAvailable #$REPLACE-WITH-MAIN-GROUP
   #$REPLACE-WITH-MAINMT)" />

   <!-- Check and if necessary create the session microtheory -->
   <if name="checkSessionExistence" condition="exists"
     pattern="REPLACE-WITH-SESSIONMT" perform="doNextStep(end)" />

   <act action="createMicrotheory"
          Mt="REPLACE-WITH-SESSIONMT"
          msg="REPLACE-WITH-SESSIONMT keeps session data for current
          users: last login, action, etc."
          genlMts="KnowledgeExchangeMt,ComputerNetworkMt"
          isa="Microtheory" />

   <act name="end" perform="playScenario(login)" />

 </scenario>
</dialogScenario>
```

FIGURE 13.16

User Authentication with the Login Scenario

The Knowledge Connector application keeps track of a user's session data, provides authentication mechanisms, and distinguishes the user's objects from objects in other worlds.

Figure 13.17 provides an example of the login scenario.

The first step of the scenario prompts a user for a login name and immediately translates the user's input into an internal system user name according to naming conventions for this application and knowledge base. If the user enters nothing and just presses the ENTER key (giving up at the very beginning), the system picks up the *noinput* case and plays the *newuser* scenario.

Hopefully, our user is brave enough and the first step is a success.

The second step verifies the existence of the user's name. If the user name is found, the control is passed to the "checkPassword" act of the scenario. The "checkPassword" act prompts the user for his or her password.

If a user's name is not found in the knowledge base, there are two possibilities: either the user is new or the login name was not entered correctly. Scenario acts that follow the prompt deal with these possibilities.

When the system prompts for a password (in the checkPassword scenario step), the *setEcho* attribute of the scenario allows us to cover the entered password from watching eyes.

The following steps query the knowledge base for an existing password and compare the result of the query with the password entered by the user.

We would be acting in a more secure manner if we used the encrypted form of a password, as is shown in the alternate example below:

```
<!-- Optional Encrypted Password-->
<prompt variable="PASSWORD-INPUT"
  actionResult="ENCRYPTED-PASSWORD"
 service="REPLACE-WITH-USER-SERVICE" action="prompt"
 msg="Please enter your password" echo="*"
 translate="com.its.util.Cryptor.encrypt(PASSWORD-INPUT)"
 noinput="setDefault(NO-PASSWORD)" />
<act actionResult="PASSWORD-FOUND"
 query="(#$nameString #$USER-NAME ?X)" />
<if condition="include"
 pattern="psw=ENCRYPTED-PASSWORD"
 perform="doNextStep(success)" />
```

There are three possible results of password verification:

1. A complete match. In this case the program passes control to the happy-ending part of the scenario labeled as "success" that performs the necessary system settings and opens all the doors for the user.
2. No match. The user's record has a password that is not the same as the user's input. The scenario takes care of this possibility by issuing the last message "Sorry. Try again." to the user.
3. The user's record has no password. In this case, a default password is set, and the scenario plays the happy ending that begins with the scenario element named as "success." The default password is created by the nameToPassword() operation that translates user's login name into the default password that can be changed by the user later on.

```
<?xml version = "1.0" encoding = "UTF-8"?>
<dialogScenario name="login">
 <scenario>

   <prompt variable="LOGIN-NAME-INPUT"
    service="REPLACE-WITH-USER-SERVICE" action="prompt"
 msg="Please type your login name. Press ENTER if you are a new user."
    translate="loginToName(REPLACE-WITH-INPUT)"
    actionResult="USER-NAME" noinput="playScenario(newuser)" />

    <if condition="exists" pattern="LOGIN-NAME-INPUT"
    perform="doNextStep(checkPassword)" />

    <!-- Login name is not found -->
    <prompt variable="NEW-USER-ANSWER"
      action="prompt" service="REPLACE-WITH-USER-SERVICE"
      msg="Are you a new user? (y/n)" aliases="yes|y" />

    <if condition="equals" pattern="yes"
    perform="playScenario(newuser)" />

    <!-- The user is not a new user. Login name was entered
    incorrectly -->
    <act lastMsg="Please re-login" />

   <!-- Login name exists. Check for password -->

   <prompt name="checkPassword" variable="PASSWORD-INPUT"
      service="REPLACE-WITH-USER-SERVICE" action="prompt"
      msg="Please enter your password" echo="*"
      noinput="setDefault(NO-PASSWORD)" />

    <!-- Check password match. Query knowledgebase first. -->
  <act queryResult="PASSWORD-FOUND" query="(#$nameString
  #$USER-NAME ?X)" />

  <if source="PASSWORD-FOUND" condition="includes"
    pattern="psw=PASSWORD-INPUT"
    perform="doNextStep(success)" />

  <!-- Check NO Match case -->
   <if source="PASSWORD-FOUND" condition="!equals"
   pattern="notFound"
    perform="lastMsg(No match. Sorry. Try again)" />

   <!-- Here is "NO PASSWORD" (notFound) case. Set default
   password. -->
   <act translate="nameToLogin(USER-NAME)"
   actionResult="DEFAULT-PASSWORD" />
```

FIGURE 13.17

```
      <act action="assert" msg="(#$nameString #$USER-NAME
      \"psw=DEFAULT-PASSWORD\")" />

      <!-- Let user know that a default password has been set -->
      <act action="prompt" service="REPLACE-WITH-USER-SERVICE"
       msg="Your record had no password. It is set as
       DEFAULT-PASSWORD now. You can change it later. Press
       ENTER." />

    <!-- Full success. Set necessary session data -->
    <!-- set Cyclist name to Cyc -->
    <act name="success"
    peform="org.opencyc.api.CycAccess.setCyclist(USER-NAME)" />

    <!-- get and show last session data -->
    <act query="(#$nameString #$USER-NAME ?X)
    |equals|notFound|doNextStep(loginSuccess)"
        Mt="REPLACE-WITH-SESSIONMT"
        queryResult="LAST-SESSION-DATA" />

    <!-- Remove old session record and replace it with the new
    session data -->
    <act action="unassert" Mt="REPLACE-WITH-SESSIONMT"
        msg="(#$nameString #$USER-NAME \"LAST-SESSION-DATA\")" />

    <act perform="REPLACE-WITH-PERFORMER-TYPE.setDisplay
    (LAST-SESSION-DATA)" />

    <!-- Login success: set session data -->
    <act name="loginSuccess" perform="loginSuccess(USER-NAME)" />

    </scenario>

  </dialogScenario
```

FIGURE 13.17. (*cont.*)

The happy ending consists of several acts or steps. The application sets a Cyclist name to the Cyc knowledge base, retrieves and displays the last session's data, replaces the old session's data with the new data, and finally performs the *loginSuccess()* method of the *UserAVI* class.

INSTALLING AND RUNNING THE PACKAGE

First, unzip the *connector.zip* file in any directory. In this directory, you will find the *start-Connector* script (Fig. 13.18), the *startCyc* script (Fig. 13.19), the *org.opencyc.connector.zip* file, and a new "instructions" directory with XML scenarios.

```
start startCyc

set JAVAHOME=c:\jdk\bin
set CYC_LIB=c:\1\ke\lib
set INSTRUCTIONS_HOME=c:\1\ke\instructions\

set connectorLIB=%CYC_LIB%/org.opencyc.connector.jar
set cycLIB1=%CYC_LIB%/commons-collections.jar;
%CYC_LIB%/dynamicjava.jar;
%CYC_LIB%/FIPA_OSv2_1_0.jar
set cycLIB2=%CYC_LIB%/icu4j.jar;%CYC_LIB%/jakarta-oro-
2.0.3.jar;%CYC_LIB%/jdom.jar;
set cycLIB3=%CYC_LIB%/jena.jar;%CYC_LIB%/jug.jar;
%CYC_LIB%/junit.jar;%CYC_LIB%/OpenCyc.jar;
set cycLIB4=%CYC_LIB%/rdf-api-2001-01-19.jar;
%CYC_LIB%/ViolinStrings.jar;%CYC_LIB%/xerces.jar

%JAVAHOME%\java -classpath %connectorLIB%;%cycLIB1%;
%cycLIB2%;%cycLIB3%;%cycLIB4% org.opencyc.connector.UserAVI
%INSTRUCTIONS_HOME%
exit
```

FIGURE 13.18

Place the *org.opencyc.connector.zip* into the "lib" directory with other OpenCyc libraries, such as *OpenCyc.jar*. Then modify the *startConnector* script to properly point to JAVA_HOME, the CYC_LIB with all the jar and zip files, and the new instructions directory as INSTRUCTIONS_HOME.

Of course, you need a version of OpenCyc, which can be downloaded from *http://www.OpenCyc.org*, as well as a script that starts the Cyc knowledge engine (e.g., *startCyc*).

```
REM http://localhost:3602/cgi-bin/cyccgi/cg?cb-start

set CYC_RUN=c:\1\ke\run

cd %CYC_RUN%

bin\latest.exe -w world\JavaSchoolMt

copy %CYC_RUN%\world\1 %CYC_RUN%\world\JavaSchoolMt

exit
```

FIGURE 13.19

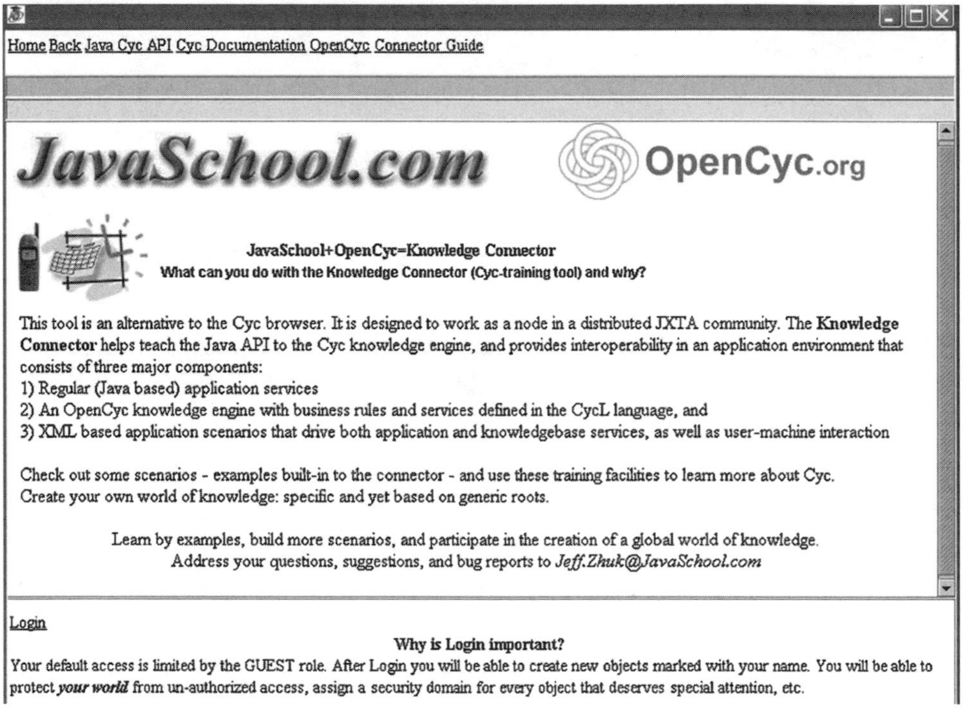

FIGURE 13.20. Distributed Knowledge Node Training Session.

Figure 13.19 displays the *startCyc* script. The call to this script is already included in the *startConnector*.

Now you are set. Run the *startConnector* script and enjoy the show! Figure 13.20 displays the initial screen of the application.

SUMMARY

The combination of a knowledge engine with traditional application services creates a new development paradigm. A new development role and a new implementation mixture will appear soon thereafter.

The implementation environment that reflects the business model may include:

- Traditional services (developed using traditional programming technologies, such as Java and. NET)
- Business rules expressed in the "almost natural" language of the knowledge base
- Relatively simple application scenarios that bridge both worlds

Figures 13.21 and 13.22 compare the process of regular application development to that of an application with an embedded knowledge base.

In the current development process, there is a gap between initial business input provided by business people and the final implementation. The current process requires many

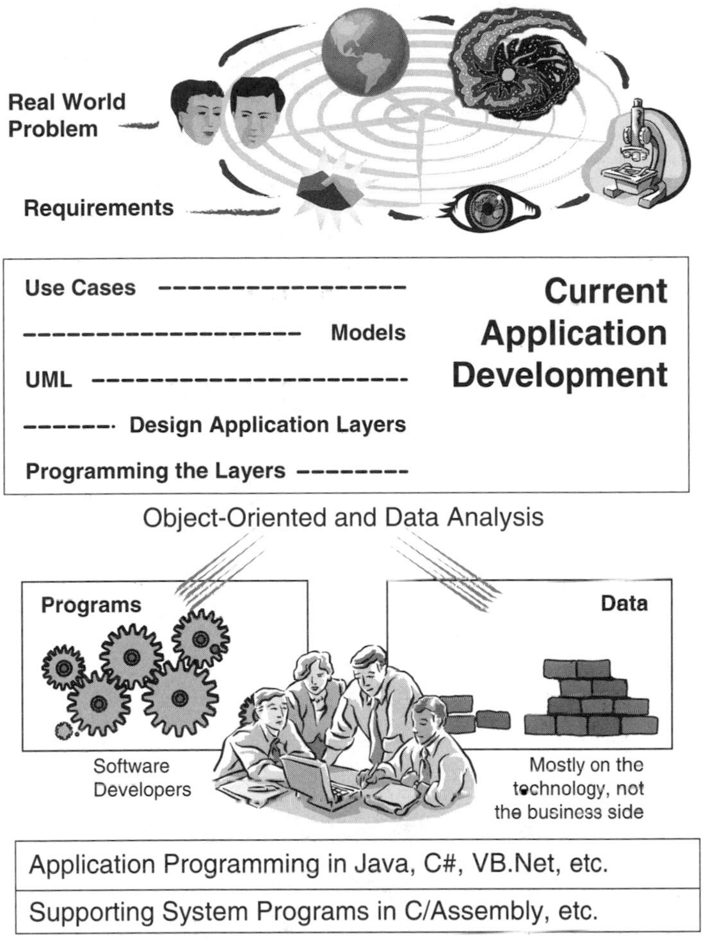

FIGURE 13.21 Current Application Development Paradigm.

transformations to simplify the complex world of reality into low-level program functions and tables expressed with current programming languages. Several filter layers and sometimes multiple teams fill this gap.

In the new development paradigm, knowledge technologies play an essential role in the development process. Business domain experts will be able to directly participate in the development agenda by writing business rules and application scenarios with more natural language. This will also help to focus developers (currently distracted by technological details) on the business aspects of applications.

Some time ago, we thought of C as the language for application development, whereas Assembly was the language for system development. It is about time to move programming languages like C# and Java from the application to the system level. These languages will be used mostly by system programmers (service providers), whereas applications will be driven by knowledge base rules and scenarios that invoke the services.

Figure 13.23 represents knowledge-driven architecture [5]. We can review this diagram from the position of the model-view-controller (*MVC*) design pattern.

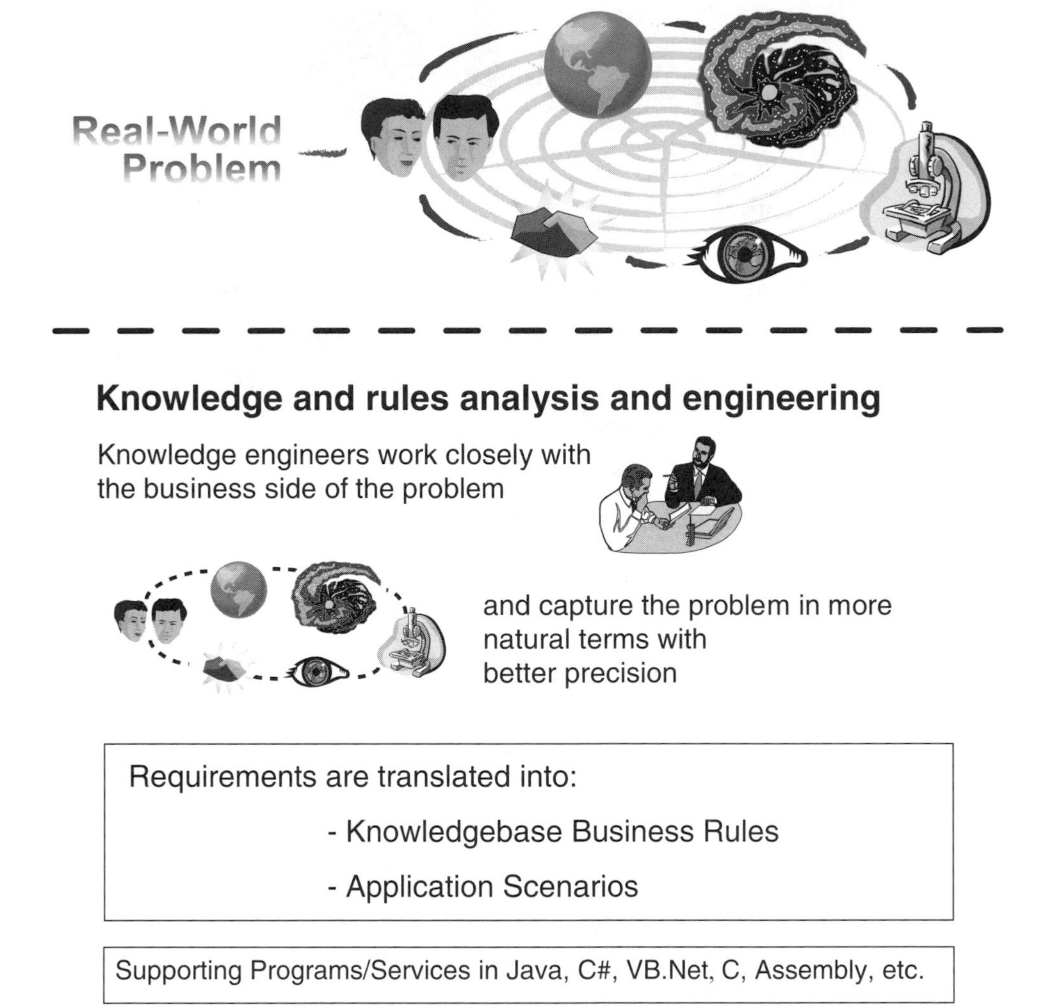
Real-World Problem
Knowledge and rules analysis and engineering
Knowledge engineers work closely with the business side of the problem
and capture the problem in more natural terms with better precision
Requirements are translated into:
- Knowledgebase Business Rules
- Application Scenarios
Supporting Programs/Services in Java, C#, VB.Net, C, Assembly, etc.

FIGURE 13.22 Knowledge-Driven Development and Applications.

The major component of the model part is a knowledge engine. Business rules and scenarios are captured in the knowledge base with an almost-natural language (e.g., CycL and CycML). There are also traditional services that capture some business rules and algorithms with current programming languages to support the model. The third model component is a set of application scenarios.

Each application scenario is a very lightweight XML description of a part of an application that invokes some services, exercises some business rules, and includes hints for the interpretation of expected user (or program) responses.

There is a traditional view block of the MVC design pattern. The view delivers information in selected video or sound formats. People are the target audience for the traditional view.

The interpreter block on the picture plays the roles of controller and interpreter. The interpreter's audience is not us (people), but programs that (in most cases) exchange information in XML formats. The interpreter is connected via the service connector block to all

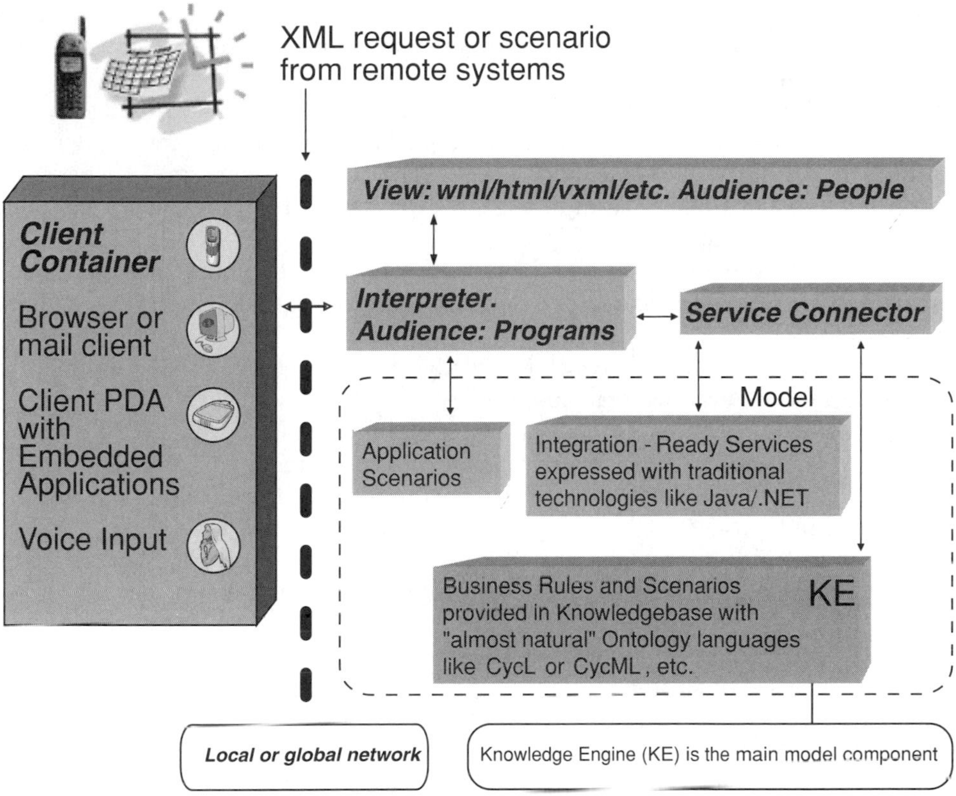

FIGURE 13.23 Knowledge-Driven Architecture.

parts that represent a business model and actively uses these parts (especially the knowledge base) in the interpretation process.

The interpreter takes the user's input—or an XML request from the network, or an act of an application scenario (also in XML format)—and transforms it into the proper format (almost always XML) for the proper program. The interpreter is also responsible for the interpretation of service or knowledge base responses. Interpreted responses are often directed (in XML format) to the view block, which performs the final transformational step and delivers data to people in the selected presentation format.

The interpreter may include special engines, such as speech, handwriting, or image recognition, that target a specific type of user input. These extra engines (combined with the Service Evaluator [3] that maintains and refines information about services) can provide direct translation of user's request in the XML-based scenarios and service calls creating applications on-demand (dream comes true!).

The interpreter can expect interactions with multiple users and can also handle events generated by different objects (event consumers). Scenarios that describe sequences of events related to multiple users and objects may help automate **workflow applications**. These scenarios map each expected event to its observer (see Gamma et al. [6]) or a set of observers that have interests in the events and handle these events with proper services.

Of course, there are application areas that just "do not fit." Keep this in mind while trying to redress an existing development process or an application. A small success is much more fun than a big failure.

We have considered architecture, design, and code examples of the Knowledge Connector package that provides the facilities to integrate Cyc's knowledge power and regular software applications in a unified XML scenario. Simple yet rich XML scenario APIs benefit from interpretation templates, as well as knowledge base queries, and include some initial elements of a natural user interface.

Consistent separation of presentation layers allows for great flexibility in adapting *AVIFactory* implementations to speech and/or wireless applications, as well as creating XML-based user interfaces.

While describing the bridge between knowledge and software technologies, this chapter might bring up more questions than answers.

How can we use this bridge for natural language interpretation? What else is needed to help subject matter experts verbally describe business requirements? What is the future of the distributed knowledge marketplace? What are the new application types that will employ knowledge technologies?

At some point, subject matter experts will be able to verbally describe business requirements, and integration magic will produce an "application on demand" for all wired and wireless clients.

But this is another story and may be another book.

Integrating Questions

1. What are the main goals of software and knowledge technology integration?
2. How does this integration affect software architecture?
3. What levels of user requirements can be expressed with business rules and application scenarios? Provide an example from your workplace.
4. What new development roles and skills are required in integrated software and knowledge engineering?

Case Study

1. Write a scenario to add a new business area to the knowledge base.
2. Write a scenario to add a new fact to this business area.
3. Write a scenario to relate two facts from this business area.
4. Describe one of the knowledge technologies that may be beneficial to your business. Suggest software architecture for a system that can use this technology.
5. Research and describe knowledge technology elements in one of the products below or go beyond the list:
   - IBM Web Sphere
   - Cyc or OpenCyc products
   - Your own choice
6. Provide an example of a knowledge-driven architecture applicable to your workplace.

References

1. Cycorp Common Sense Knowledge: *http://www.cyc.com.*
2. OpenCyc project: *http://www.OpenCyc.org.*
3. Zhuk, J. Distributed active knowledge and process base, Patent Pending: *http://uspto.gov.*
4. Internet Technology School, Inc.: *http://JavaSchool.com.*
5. Zhuk, J., Internet Technology School, Inc., Knowledge-driven architecture, Patent pending, http://uspto.gov
6. Gamma, E., R. Helm, R. Johnson, and J. Vlissides. 1995. *Design Patterns, Elements of Reusable Object-Oriented Software.* Boston: Addison-Wesley.

CHAPTER 14

Distributed Life in the JXTA and Jini Communities

Everyone who has a brain understands the benefits of self-healing distributed networks. Billions of neurons in the human brain constantly interact with ganglia (neuron message centers), providing us with the greatest example of decentralized computing.

DISTRIBUTED PROCESSING AND THE FLAT WORLD OF XML

I think there is a connection between these two topics. Let me explain what I mean.

XML is becoming the dominant messaging body for wired and wireless communications. We are going down to the flat world of XML from the hills of rich object structures.

The need for object brokers, serialization mechanisms, and intermediate translators between communication parties is decreasing more and more. Does that mean we have been getting rid of objects all along? Impossible! We still need formatted data. So, how would we send and understand unknown structured objects?

We probably shouldn't. We shouldn't send MS Excel or PDF files from a sender to a recipient. We shouldn't send service objects either. We might not need to continue collecting document handlers and service utilities at our machines. We might not need to increase the size of a hard drive ten times every two years.

What can we do instead? Here, distribution processing comes into play. Today, we live in a disconnected world where most of your computing happens on your computer. If a collection of software products on your PC does not include, for example, Adobe Acrobat Reader the system will complain that it has no program to open this file.

In the connected world, things will be different. Your machine will always be on the Internet, with millions of specialized services that are ready to help you. There will never be an object sent or attached to a message. There will only be a reference link that points to the object and to a service that can deal with the object. The service on the Internet will get a pointer to the object and an instruction on your favorite format, in which your machine expects the output. Figure 14.1 displays an example of the interaction on the Internet in the process of data request.

The interaction is described in the form of comments provided in the XML file. Later in this chapter, we learn specific protocols that support this type of interaction in JXTA communities.

The request is initiated by a human being; an individual user of a computer (a peer on the network) sends a request for a specific data topic—for example, life on earth. All subsequent messages are automatically generated by computers (peers). A user's peer receives the network response with the Uniform Resource Identifier (URI) pointer to the file: *http://server.com/folder/lifeOnEarth.pdf*. The object in this example is openly available on a Web server, although it can be owned by a network peer or a peer group. In the latter case, ownership privileges may play a significant role in the process of obtaining the object.

The problem is that the user's peer cannot read PDF; only content-type HTML text is available on the peer. The user's peer shows that it is not able to directly read this file, but the machine is not completely stupid. The peer looks for the PDF-HTML conversion service on the Internet. The search results in the URI pointer to the service peer that can do this conversion and returns all the related information: how to connect and how to use this service. For example:

```
Service Peer Connection Information-X; ServiceID=Y; ServiceProtocol=Z;
etc.
```

Armed with this data, the user's peer uses proper connection information, invokes a proper service protocol, and delivers its wish list to the service provider. Here is what this service peer would do:

- Retrieve the file using this URI: *http://server.com/folder/lifeOnEarth.pdf*
- Convert this file into HTML format
- Connect to the original peer-requester
- Send to this peer a copy of the document converted to HTML

This is a multiple step process, which is OK if all these steps are done automatically upon a single user's request.

There might be a more complicated scenario, in which a number of people are working on this document in collaboration and providing necessary changes. Editors will use the service (which may reside on any peer) that handles PDF and allow multiparty changes. Figure 14.2 shows peers and peer groups, as well as other types of nodes and services, on the Internet.

From today's world, dominated by centralized client–server communications, we move into a world of distributed networks. We will consider the principles and protocols that allow us to create gated network communities on the Internet. The openness of the Internet, with its insecurity and spam threads, will lead many of us into the gated communities, where we may feel safer. This process is similar to escape from noise and traffic of a big city into suburbs.

```
 <?xml version="1.0" encoding="UTF-8"?>
- <DataRequestExample>
 <!-- An example of interaction in the process of data request -->
 <!--
     A User (Peer owner) sends a request for a specific data
     topic, for example, life on earth
 -->
- <!--
     User's peer receives the network response with the
     URI-pointer "http://server.com/folder/lifeOnEarth.pdf"
 -->
- <!--
     User's peer cannot read PDF, only Content-type: html/text.
     User's peer looks up for the PDF-HTML conversion service
 -->
- <!--
     The search comes back to the user's peer with the
     URI-pointer to the service peer.
     Service Peer Connection Information=X; ServiceID=Y;
     ServiceProtocol=Z; etc.
 -->
- <!--
     User's peer uses proper connection information,
      invoke a proper service protocol, and delivers the wish list.
      Here is what this service peer would do:
      - Retrieve the file using this URI: "http://server.
        com/folder/lifeOnEarth.pdf"
      - Convert this file into html format
      - Connect to the original peer-requestor and
      - Send to this peer the converted to html copy of the
        document
      The end of the story
 -->
</DataRequestExample>
```

FIGURE 14.1

Jabber [1], an open source initiative, serves as an example of distributed architecture. Jabber offers an XML-based instant messaging system that operates in peer-to-peer (P2P) networks.

A more famous example of client-to-client communications is Napster. From a business point of view, Napster is a controversial application. Music lovers can use Napster to exchange music files conveniently packed into MP3 format. The controversial part is related to music copyrights. From a technological point of view, this is another example of a P2P network.

With both Jabber and Napster, a centralized directory service is needed to locate a source and a destination. The open source–based project JXTA is an alternative mechanism for P2P networks in which no directory server is needed.

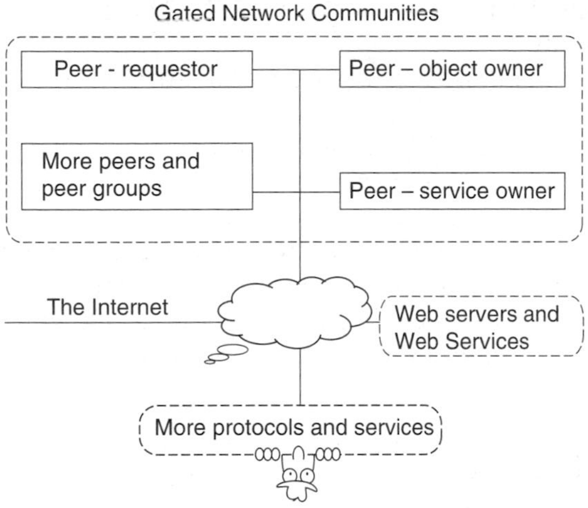

FIGURE 14.2. Gated Network Communities.

WHAT IS JXTA?

JXTA is not an abbreviation. The name of this open source initiative is derived from the word *juxtaposed*. In the case of JXTA, the juxtaposed entities are network devices and computers.

All JXTA messages, objects, images, and so on are XML data called *codat*. This strange name confirms the idea of a unified approach to code and any type of data sent over JXTA nodes. One of the JXTA applications available today is InstantP2P, which provides instant messaging and file sharing within peer groups. (The list of available applications is quite small today, but getting bigger.)

Peer groups consist of peer members. Peers can publish and subscribe to publications within the group. Each peer group can define its own membership requirements and access rules.

Who can be a peer: a rich client or a thin client? Naturally, it is easier to build a rich-client peer. But the greatest potential is in (global) networks with wireless peer-participants. Peers should be able to parse and generate XML and be able to transform XML into formatted documents and objects. Some peers can handle complex formats, such as Adobe PDF and Microsoft Excel. Others use those skilled peers for transformations and digest data in their affordable formats.

JXTA Protocols

There are six protocols in JXTA networks that help to discover and advertise peers as well as their resources and provide the means for data monitoring and exchange.

1. Peer Discovery Protocol (PDP) is a resource advertisement and discovery mechanism. Advertisements are XML documents that describe network resources. Peers can publish and discover these documents with PDP.
2. Peer Information Protocol (PIP) helps a peer obtain status information (e.g., traffic load and capabilities) about other peers.
3. Peer Resolver Protocol (PRP) implements a query/response mechanism. A peer can send a query and receive a response or responses to the query while contacting one or more

peers or even groups. Each query has a unique ID. The response message includes this ID in the message body.
4. Pipe Binding Protocol (PBP) is a mechanism to establish communications (a pipe) between one or more peers.
5. Endpoint Routing Protocol (ERP) is used to discover a networking route (sequence of node peers or hops) to communicate to another peer. If a source peer does not know the route information to a destination peer, then the source peer will look for more a knowledgeable intermediary peer or peers who will route the message.
6. Rendezvous Protocol (RVP) is a publish/subscribe mechanism. Peers that use RVP to publish (propagate) messages are called *rendezvous peers*. Other peers in a peer group are listening rendezvous peers. PRP and PBP use RVP to propagate messages.

Not only is every peer pretty much independent, each of the JXTA protocols is also independent of the others. A peer only implements the protocols it needs. These are great survival skills that increase P2P networks' reliability.

There is still the JXTA Core Specification that must be implemented by a peer. The the JXTA Core Specification consists of the PRP and ERP and the advertisements, services, and definitions on which they depend. The rest of the protocols are known as the JXTA Standard Specification and serve as options, though they are strongly recommended for better network interoperability.

JXTA Features in a Nutshell

Peers can discover one another and self-organize into peer groups. They can advertise and discover network resources, communicate, and even monitor one another. A JXTA peer is any networked device (e.g., phone and supercomputer) that has a unique ID and implements the core JXTA protocols.

There are no restrictions on peer implementation languages and platforms. Java peers and non-Java peers can work together within a group as long as they implement JXTA protocols.

Peers are independent and operate asynchronously from all other peers. Some peers may play specific roles according to specific requirements. For example, a peer may be assigned the role of proxy or router. Peers may join or leave the network at any time.

Peers, peer groups, communication pipes, and data all have their own unique identification that includes a Uniform Resource Name (URN). A peer may have a user, a human being who will direct peer actions. Some peers have no user and exist to provide services and resources to the network.

P2P Communication Means Pipes. What Is a Pipe?

Pipes are virtual channels of peer-to-peer interaction. Pipes are not bound to any particular network address and may be implemented with different protocols. No matter which protocol is chosen—for example, HTTP pipes are unidirectional (similar to *java.io.InputStream* and *java.io.OutputStream* objects) and asynchronous. Each pipe has a unique *pipeID*.

Peers discover and advertise their pipes (communication channels) with pipe advertisements. Two peers that are going to talk to each other have to bind or map virtual channels to the resources described in the advertisements. The peers bind an input pipe of a receiver peer and an output pipe of a sending peer to proper advertisements. Now these two peers are set for communication.

Peer Groups and Services

Each peer group has a unique peer group ID and consists of peers that have a common set of interests. JXTA defines a core set of peer group services. Discovery Service, Membership Service, and Access Service are common collaborative services. Pipe Service, Resolver Service, and Monitoring Service are more specific P2P services.

Member peers use the Discovery Service to look for group resources (peers and services). The Membership Service helps reject or accept a new group member. A group may draft a specific membership policy, which will be enforced by the Membership Service. For example, such a policy might require a vote of peers to accept a new membership request. A peer may belong to more than one group at a time.

The Access Service validates restricted (not all) requests based on the subject of the request and the requesting peer credentials. The Pipe Service creates (and manages) pipe connections between the different peer group members. The Resolver Service takes care of queries to services running on peers in the group. The Monitoring Service allows one peer to monitor other members of the same peer group.

A peer may have its own preinstalled services or (if needed) load them at run-time from the network. Peers publish and discover service information, Module Advertisements in JXTA terms via the PDP. Module Advertisements provide the necessary information on how to invoke or instantiate described services.

JXTA-enabled services are published with the ModuleSpecAdvertisement and each has a unique ModuleSpecID. Non-JXTA services may be defined with Web service standards, such as WSDL (Web Service Definition Language).

Advertisements

The Core JXTA Protocols include the following types of advertisements, each serving its own role.

A **Peer Advertisement** describes a peer with its resources according to the XML schema provided below.

```
<xs:element name="PA" type="jxta:PA"/>
 <xs:complexType name="PA">
   <xs:sequence>
     <xs:element name="PID" type=JXTAID"/>
     <xs:element name="GID" type="JXTAID"/>
     <xs:element name="Name" type="xs:string" minOccurs="0"/>
     <xs:element name="Desc" type="xs:anyType" minOccurs="0"/>
     <xs:element name="Svc" type="jxta:serviceParams"
     minOccurs="0" maxOccurs="unbounded"/>
   <xs:sequence>
 </xs:complexType>
```

The <PID> as well as <GID> are required elements that uniquely identify the peer and its group. The <Name> of the peer and peer descriptive keywords in the <Desc> string are both optional. The <Svc> string includes service descriptions. Any number of service elements may be provided in the peer advertisement.

A **Peer Group Advertisement** schema differs in the first two lines, as you can see below:

```
<xs:element name="PGA" type="jxta:PGA"/>
<xs:complexType name="PGA">
 <xs:sequence>
  <xs:element name="GID" type="jxta:JXTAID"/>
  <xs:element name="MSID" type="jxta:JXTAID"/>
  <xs:element name="Name" type="xs:string" minOccurs="0"/>
  <xs:element name="Desc" type="xs:anyType" minOccurs="0"/>
  <xs:element name="Svc" type="jxta:serviceParam" minOccurs="0"
   maxOccurs="unbounded"/>
 </xs:sequence>
</xs:complexType>
```

The Peer Group Advertisements define group services.

Module Class Advertisements

If you want to describe peer function with better precision (down to code modules), you can use the **Module Class Advertisement**, which describes a class of modules with its expected local behavior and application program interface (API). This advertisement associates a particular Module Class ID with its description. The Module Class Advertisement is not required; it is geared toward developers. Here is the schema:

```
<xs:element name="MCA" type="jxta:MCA"/>
<xs:complexType name="MCA">
 <xs:sequence>
  <xs:element name="MCID" type="jxta:JXTAID"/>
  <xs:element name="Name" type="xs:string" minOccurs="0"/?
  <xs:element name="Desc" type="xs:anyType" minOccurs="0"/>
 </xs:sequence>
</xs:complexType>
```

Module Specification Advertisements

In a similar manner, the **Module Specification Advertisement** describes the specification of a module. A Module Specification Advertisement does not have to be published; a Module Specification ID may be valid without a published Module Specification Advertisement.

```
<xs:element name="MSA" type="jxta:MSA"/>
<xs:complexType name="MSA">
 <xs:sequence>
  <xs:element name="MSID" type="jxta:JXTAID"/>
  <xs:element name="Vers" type="xs:string"/>
  <xs:element name="Name" type="xs:string" minOccurs="0"/>
  <xs:element name="Desc" type="xs:anyType" minOccurs="0"/>
  <xs:element name="Crtr" type="xs:string" minOccurs="0"/>
  <xs:element name="SURI" type="xs:anyURI" minOccurs="0"/>
  <xs:element name="Parm" type="xs:anyType" minOccurs="0"/>
  <xs:element ref="jxta:PipeAdvertisement" minOccurs="0"/>
```

```
    <xs:element name="Proxy" type="xs:anyURI" minOccurs="0"/>
    <xs:element name="Auth" type="jxta:JXTAID" minOccurs="0"/>
  </xs:sequence>
</xs:complexType>
```

Here is a brief description of the elements in the schema.

<MSID> (ModuleSpecID)—a required, unique identification element
<Vers>—the mandatory version of the specification that this Module Specification advertises
<Name>—an optional (not necessarily unique) name associated with a specification
<Desc> (Description)—also an optional string of keywords/descriptions that can be used in a search process
<CRTR> (Creator)—another optional element that names the creator of this specification. I recommend this option if you plan to give specific privileges, such as changing the specification, to the specification creator.
<SURI> (Spec URI)—an optional URI (Uniform Resource Identifier) element that permits the retrieval of the advertised specification document
<Parm>—a provision for arbitrary parameters to be interpreted by each implementation
<jxta:PipeAdvertisement>—may be used to establish a pipe to a peer running an implementation of this specification. See more details in the Pipe Advertisement example below.
<Proxy> (Proxy Spec ID)—an optional Module Specification ID of a proxy module that may be required for communication with modules of this specification.
<Auth> (Authenticator Spec ID)—an optional Module Specification ID of an authenticator module that may be necessary for this particular module specification.

Module Implementation Advertisements

A **Module Implementation Advertisement** describes an implementation (that can be one of many) of a module specification. The Module Implementation Advertisement schema is provided below:

```
\<xs:element name="MIA" type="jxta:MIA"/>
\<xs:complexType name="MIA"
  <xs:sequence>
    <xs:element name="MSID" type="jxta:JXTAID"/>
    <xs:element name="Comp" type="xs:anyType"/>
    <xs:element name="Code" type="xs:anyType"/>
    <xs:element name="PURI" type="xs:anyURI" minOccurs="0"/>
    <xs:element name="Prov" type="xs:string" minOccurs="0"/>
    <xs:element name="Desc" type="xs:anyType" minOccurs="0"/>
    <xs:element name="Parm" type="xs:anyType" minOccurs="0"/>
  </xs:sequence>
</xs:complexType>
```

Implementations of a given specification may be searched by the specification ID. An implementation may be selected by the type of environment in which it may be used (its compatibility statement) as well as by its name, its description, or the content of its parameters section.

A Module Implementation Advertisement provides searchable ID (the <MSID> element) and describes a compatibility environment (the <Comp> element) in which the implementation can work.

The <Code> and <PURI>elements describe a related executable object, and the URI to this object can be downloaded. In the Java implementation, for example, we would expect a full class name, such as *com.its.jmail.EmailClient*, with the <Code> element and a URL to a zip or jar file, such as *http://JavaSchool.com/ download/jmail.jar*, with the <PURI> element.

The <Prov> element describes the provider of that implementation. The <Desc> (Description) element is optional and is used for searches. The <Parm> (Parameter) element represents arbitrary parameters that may be interpreted by the implementation's code.

Pipe Advertisement Schema and Example

A **Pipe Advertisement** describes a pipe for the pipe services that create associated local input and output pipe endpoints. Each Pipe Advertisement includes a unique Pipe ID and indicates a pipe type: JxtaUnicast, JxtaUnicastSecure, or JxtaPropagate.

JxtaUnicast is unsecure and unreliable, but still may be used to send one-to-one messages. This type of pipe provides no guarantee that messages will arrive at their destination. If delivered, the messages are not necessarily delivered once, and they may arrive out of order.

JxtaUnicastSecure is a secure pipe that uses Transport Layer Security (TLS), also known as SSLv3. (See RFC 2246 for more details.) This type of pipe has all the nice reliability features of the **JxtaUnicast** pipe but is encrypted using TLS.

JxtaPropagate pipes are used on the sending endpoint to broadcast (send one-to-many) messages.

The Pipe Advertisement schema is described below.

```
<xs:element name="PipeAdvertisment" type="jxta:
PipeAdvertisment"/>
<xs:complexType name="PipeAdvertisement">
 <xs:sequence>
  <xs:element name="Id" type="jxta:JXTAID"/>
  <xs:element name="Type" type="xs:string"/>
  <xs:element name="Name" type="xs:string" minOccurs="0"/>
 </xs:sequence>
</xs:complexType>
```

The <Id> is a required unique identifier element. The <Type> is a required pipe-type definition element. The <Name> is an optional element.

Here is an example of a Pipe Advertisement:

```
<?xml version="1.0" encoding="UTF-8"?>
<!DOCTYPE jxta:PipeAdvertisement>
<jxta:PipeAdvertisement xmlns:jxta="http://jxta.org">
 <Id>urn:jxta:uuid-
094AB61B99C14AB694D5BFD56C66E512FF7980EA1E6F4C238A26BB
362B34D1F104</Id>
 <Type> jxtaPropagate</Type>
 <Name>Broadcaster</Name>
</jxta:PipeAdvertisement>
```

JXTA Configuration

JXTA applications usually start by reading default configuration values and setting user-defined configuration properties.

Here is the usual scenario to start a JXTA peer:

1. The main method creates an instance of the main class that drives the application.
2. The main class constructor or its *init()* method creates an instance of the *net.jxta.peergroup.PeerGroupFactory* class.
3. The *net.jxta.peergroup.PeerGroupFactory* creates a new peer platform and a new peer group or groups. The creation process is based on powerful Java sword *Class.forName(className).newInstance()* and highly dependent on configuration properties that store default class names. For example, the default class name for a peer platform is the *net.jxta.impl.peergroup.Platform* class. (See the code extract below.)
4. The *net.jxta.impl.peergroup.Platform* object invokes its *initFirst()* method and does initiation steps, including setting the configuration advertisment for this peer. Advertisement information is collected from a user with the *generateConfigAdvertisement()* method that creates a *net.jxta.impl.peergroup.Configurator* object.

The code extract (from the *PeerGroupFactory* class) below illustrates the use of the configuration properties to instantiate platform classes.

```
          String platformPGClassName =
"net.jxta.impl.peergroup. Platform";
          String stdPGClassName =
"net.jxta.impl.peergroup. StdPeerGroup";
          PeerGroupID netPGID = PeerGroupID.
          defaultNetPeerGroupID;
          String netPGName = "NetPeerGroup";
          String netPGDesc = "NetPeerGroup by default";
          try {
               ResourceBundle rsrcs = ResourceBundle.getBundle
("net.jxta.impl.config");
               try {
               platformPGClassName = rsrcs.getString
("PlatformPeerGroupClassName").trim();
                 }
          //////////////// more code
          }
          /////////////////// even more code
          Class platformClass = Class.forName (platformPGClassName);
// create a class
          PeerGroup plat = null;
          try {
          plat = (PeerGroup) platformClass. newInstance();
// create an instance of the class
          }
```

The *net.jxta.impl.peergroup.Configurator* class builds a graphical user interface (GUI) for a user to set jxta configuration properties. Configuration facilities located in the *net.jxta.impl.peergroup.Configurator* class include the methods described in the following extract from the JavaDoc file:

```
void addRootCert()
        Adds root certificate
boolean cancelPlatform()
        Cancel Platform
void clearReconf()
        No manual re-configuration the next time the Configurator is
invoked.
PeerAdvertisement get()
        Returns the advertisement.
boolean isReconf()
        Check if a manual re-configuration has been forced.
void load()
        Load the advertisement from the standard config file.
void resetFromResource(java.lang.String resourceName, java.lang.String
fileName)
        Load from Resource if any.
void save()
        Save the advertisement in the standard config file.
void set(PeerAdvertisement config)
        Set the config advertisement.
void setReconf()
        Forces a manual reconf the next time the configurator is
invoked.
```

Setup JXTA Configuration Parameters with and without GUI

Figures 14.3 through 14.6 provide a set of configuration dialogs offered by the Configurator.

The user must set a peer name at the "basic" screen that comes up first. This is a mandatory setting, even though the peer name is not directly used in the peer communications. The name is actually mapped to a unique peer ID generated by the system. There is a provision for corporate users whose peers are located behind firewalls. Those users can point to a corporate proxy Web server, and the system will provide HTTP tunneling (convert default TCP/IP socket communications into HTTP).

The "advanced" screen shows default settings that might be changed by experienced users.

The "Rendevous/Relays" screen allows a user to set a peer as a Rendevous and/or as a JXTA proxy. The user can instruct a peer to use a Relay (if it is behind a firewall) and/or to act as a Relay (default). The user can download Relay and Rendevous lists so he or she may feel less lonely in the peer-to-peer universe.

The "Security" screen asks the user to provide his or her user name and password.

It is very possible that in some applications, some or all of the peer configuration parameters are already set and this GUI is not necessary. That was exactly the case with the Distributed Knowledge Connector application described in Chapter 13.

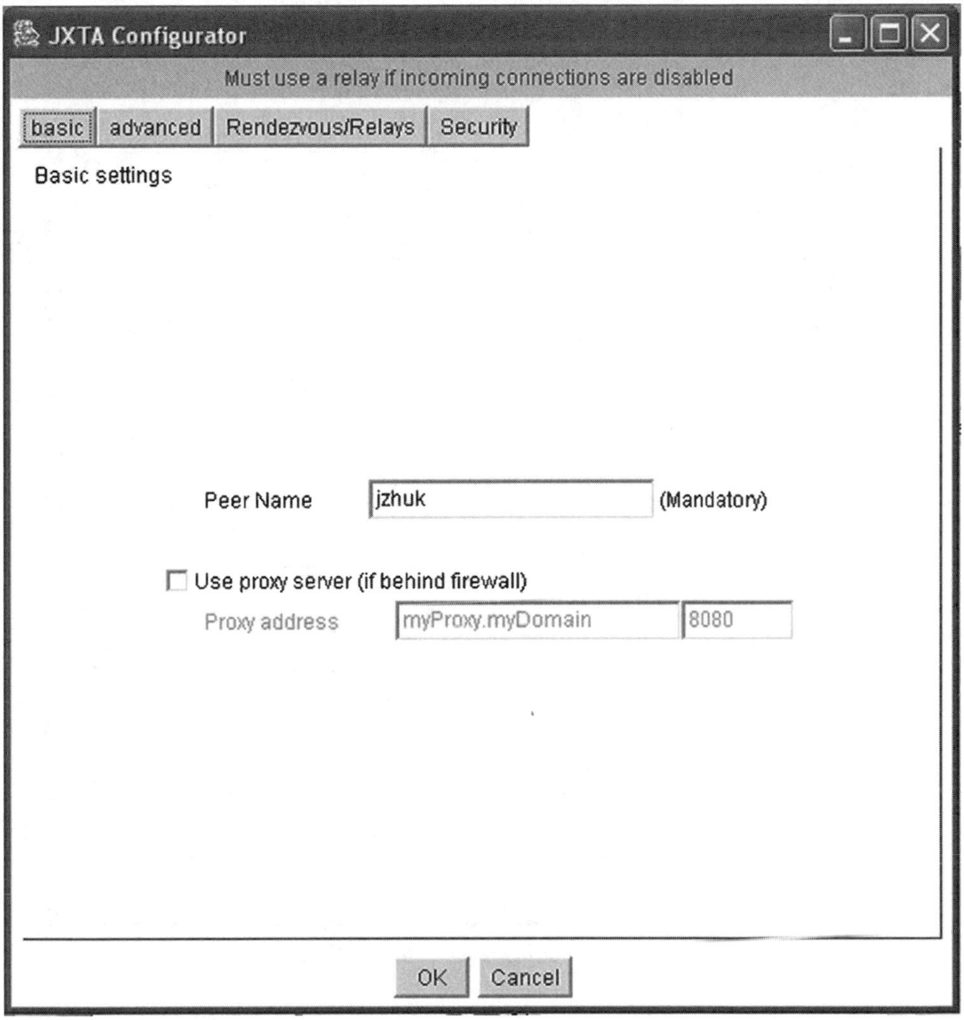

FIGURE 14.3. JXTA Configurator: Basic Settings.

Here is a two-line example of setting the user's name and password directly into the JXTA property file without using a GUI.

```
System.setProperty("net.jxta.tls.principal", userName);
// set user's name
System.setProperty("net.jxta.tls.password", password);
// set password
```

Manual configuration results in a group of settings similar to those provided above.

After initial configuration steps have been completed, the peer is ready to rock and roll. The MyJXTA (previously named Instantp2p) application provides a good example of instant messaging and file exchange between peers. This application can run on a desktop as well as on a PDA. There are five Java packages that support the application:

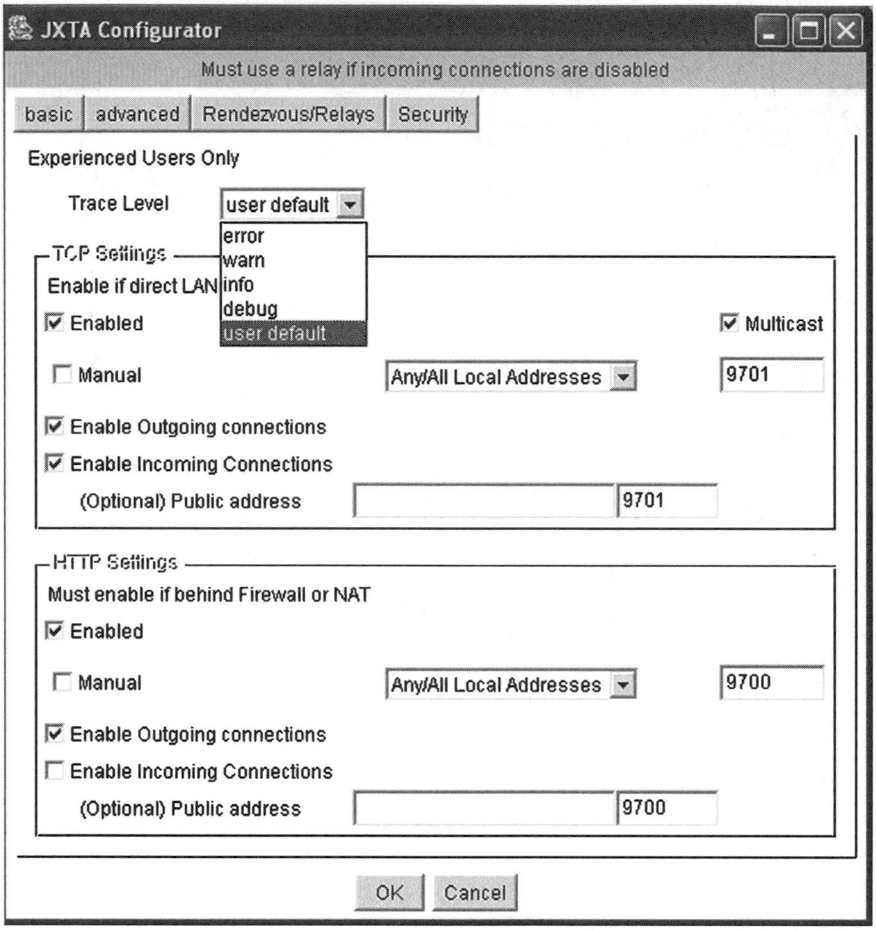

FIGURE 14.4. JXTA Configurator: TCP and HTTP Settings.

1. net.jxta.instantp2p
2. net.jxta.instantp2p.desktop
3. net.jxta.instantp2p.desktop.application
4. net.jxta.instantp2p.pda
5. net.jxta.instantp2p.util

To run the application, you also need the JXTA platform packages (roughly around 100).

The PeerGroupManager and SearchManager Classes from the Instantp2p JXTA Package

The *PeerGroupManager* and *SearchManager* are important classes of the instantp2p package. Instances of these classes created in the initiation process drive the core of the application. The *PeerGroupManager* object (often called *PeerGroupSearcher*) starts the remote discovery of peers and peer groups in the *PeerGroup* networks.

Classes that need to listen to the changes of a peer (or selected group of peers) implement the *net.jxta.instantp2p.PeerListener* interface. The *PeerGroupManager* offers a set of methods

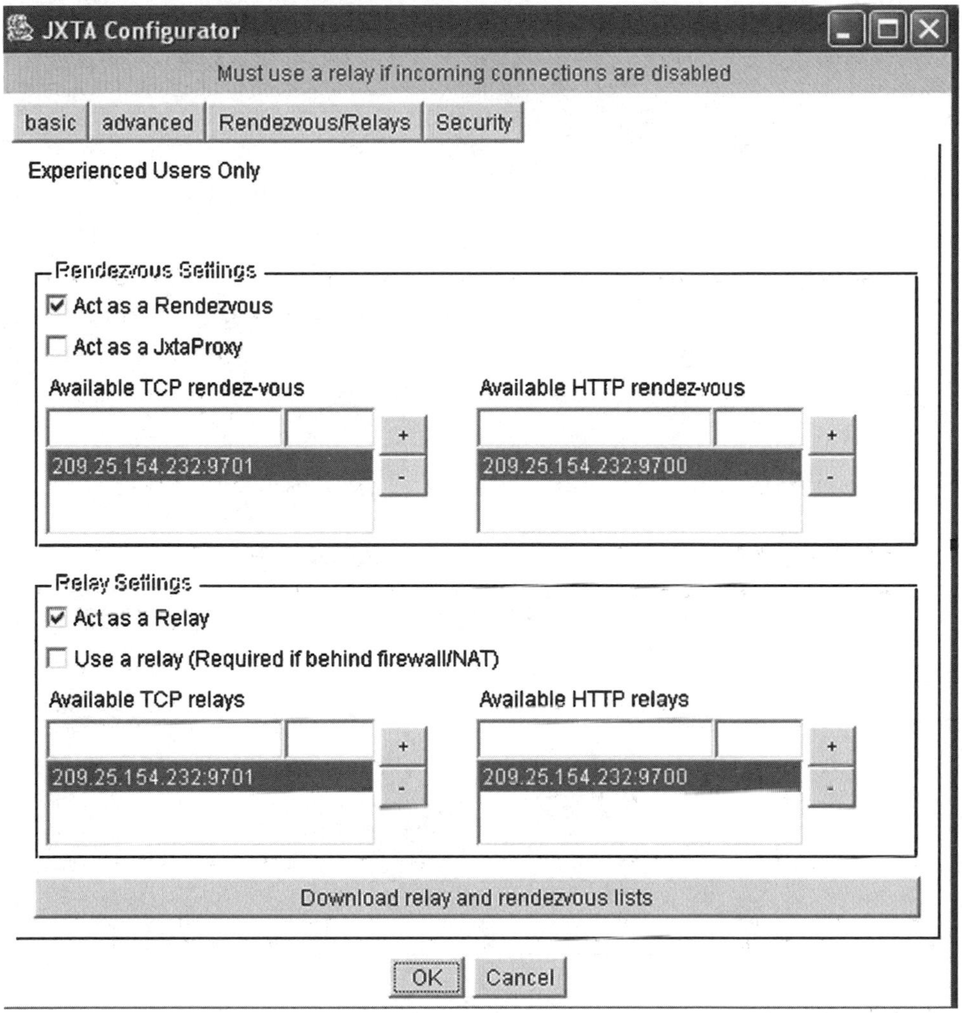

FIGURE 14.5. JXTA Configurator: Rendezvous and Relay Settings.

to add and remove *PeerListener* objects; collect, propagate, and process peer group data; join and leave a group; and so forth.

Here is the extract from the *PeerGroupManager* documentation that describes class methods:

```
void addPeerListener(PeerGroupManager.PeerListener listener)
          Adds listeners for Group and Peer change notifications
void addStructureListener(GroupStructureListener listener)
          Adds listener for peer groups structure listeners
void advertisementsDiscovered(AdvertisementEvent event)
          Processing Advertisement Event
  void createPeerGroup(java.lang.String name, boolean isRendezVous,
java.lang.String password)
```

FIGURE 14.6. JXTA Configurator: Security Settings.

```
          Creates a new group with the indicated name
java.util.Enumeration getGroups()
          Returns a list of currently available peer groups. The
enumeration contains
PeerGroupAdvertisement objects
 java.util.Enumeration getGroupsDelta()
          Returns a list of currently available peer groups minus
joined groups. The enumeration contains PeerGroupAdvertisement objects
  java.util.Enumeration getJoinedGroups()
          Returns a list of peer groups this peer is currently a member
of. The enumeration contains PeerGroupAdvertisement objects
  java.lang.String getMyPeerName()
          Returns the name of the peer that instantiated this class
  java.util.Enumeration getPeerList()
```

```
          Returns a list of currently available peers The enumeration
contains PeerGroupAdvertisement objects
  net.jxta.protocol.PeerAdvertisement getSelectedPeer()
          Returns the advertisement of the currently selected peer,
which may be null
  net.jxta.peergroup.PeerGroup getSelectedPeerGroup()
          Returns the advertisement of the currently selected peer
group
  StatusPanel getStatusPanel()
          Gets the statusPanel attribute of the PeerGroupManager
  object WorkerThread getWorkerThread()
          Returns a WorkerThread that can be used to execute
potentially blocking calls.
  void joinGroup(net.jxta.peergroup.PeerGroup pg,
net.jxta.protocol.PeerGroupAdvertisement pgAdv, boolean isRendezVous)
          Called if the user wants to join a group
  void leaveGroup(net.jxta.protocol.PeerGroupAdvertisement group)
          Leaves a previously joined group
  void removePeerListener(PeerGroupManager.PeerListener listener)
          Removes listeners for Group and Peer change
  notifications void removeStructureListener
  (GroupStructureListener listener)
          Removes listeners for Group and Peer structure change
notifications
  void savePreferences()
          Updates the preference reader instance
  void searchGroups(java.lang.String groupName)
          Called if we want to search for a group
  void searchPeers(java.lang.String peerName)
          Called if we want to search for a specific peer
  void selectedGroupChanged(net.jxta.protocol.
  PeerGroupAdvertisement adv)
          Called if the currently selected group is to be changed.
  void selectedPeerChanged(net.jxta.protocol.PeerAdvertisement adv)
          Called if the selected peer changed
  void unblockWaitForRendezVous()
          The method waitForRendezVous() will block until a
RendezVousService server was found.
  boolean waitForRendezVous()
          This method blocks until a RendezVousService server is found
and the connection to the server has been established.
```

If a user wants to join a peer group (with the *joinGroup()* method), the group must be one of the previously discovered groups. If the user creates a new group (with the *createPeerGroup (groupName)* method), the user immediately joins the newly created group and this group becomes the currently selected peer group.

Instant messaging communication can be provided between two peers using the class *net.jxta.instantp2p.Chat*. The class *net.jxta.instantp2p.GroupChat* provides chat among all peers in a group. If your application needs to display the messages in a message board style, you can implement the interface *net.jxta. instantp2p.MessageBoard*, which defines several methods that allow the chat classes to interact with the GUI.

Another important feature of the Myjxta application is its file sharing. The file sharing implementation of Myjxta uses the jxta Content Management Service (CMS) implemented with the *net.jxta.share.CMS* class. The *net.jxta. share.CMS* class in turn implements several core jxta interfaces: *net.jxta.platform.Application*, *net.jxta. endpoint.EndpointListener*, *net.jxta.platform. Module*, and *net. jxta.resolver.QueryHandler*.

The *net.jxta.share.ContentAdvertisement* provides information about shared content within a peer group. Class methods such as *getName()*, *getContent()*, and *getDescription()* return important information about shared objects.

Object search and sharing is possible inside a group in which objects exist. The *net.jxta.instantp2p.SearchManager* class is responsible for the sharing and retrieving of objects. While programming new classes that are interested in the local or remote content changes, we may implement the *net.jxta.instantp2p.ContentListener* interface with its three methods:

public void localContentChanged()—This method is called if the local content has changed or the currently selected peer group changes.
public void remoteContentChanged()—This method is called when the search conducted by the user found results or when the currently selected peer group changes
public void finishedRetrieve(String url)—Data retrieval can be a time-consuming process. jxta does it asynchronously and calls the *finishedRetrieve()* method upon the happy end of the retrieval process.

The data retrieval process consists of several steps. A peer can advertise its content using a Content Advertisement. A receiver peer must open an input pipe to a destination peer that has the actual data. The String URL argument in the method above indicates the URL (most likely to a local file) where the data are located. A receiving peer can do other operations while retrieving the data. The *finishedRetrieve()* method alerts the peer when the operation is successful and usually triggers a data-handling procedure.

The *net.jxta.instantp2p.SearchManager* class, as we mentioned earlier, provides all the necessary interface methods to share files. When we first instantiate an object of this class with its constructor, we pass a reference to the *PeerGroupManager* object that holds the necessary information about a selected peer group.

The *public SearchManager(PeerGroupManager manager)* constructor retrieves the selected peer group and the peer information from the *manager* parameter. This class registers itself as a *PeerListener* to the *manager* parameter. The *SearchManager* class offers the *addListener(ContentListener)* and *removeListener(ContentListener)* methods to add and remove the *ContentListener* objects. These methods are necessary for the classes that are required to know about changes in the locally and remotely shared content.

The methods *addContent()* and *removeContent()* allow the user to add or remove shared content among the peer group. Note that files are added or removed asynchronously and the method returns immediately. GUI developers can implement the *net.jxta.instantp2p. desktop.ProgressReporter* interface or directly use its implementation *net.jxta.instantp2p. desktop.ProgressReporterImp* provided in the package to report operation progress. The registered *ContentListener* objects receive the content changes after the operation ends successfully.

The methods *getLocalContent()* and *getRemoteContent()* return a list of available local or remote content. A program usually calls these methods after being notified of content changes.

The *startSearch(String searchString)* performs a search for remote data that can be restricted by the *searchString* argument if the *searchString* is not null. Again, note that this is an asynchronous method that returns immediately and the result of the search is delivered at the end of the operation to the registered *ContentListener* objects.

JINI

JXTA is not the only way to build network architecture as a dynamic, living organism. Another example is Jini.

> Jini provides us in the context of being able to put objects anywhere, the ability to move them around and to do a few other things that you need to do once you have true distributed computing. But the bigger picture here, this pervasive object computing, is that the ability to put systems on single chips with pervasive wired and wireless networking . . . .
>
> —Bill Joy on Java and Jini, from presentation transcript [3].

Jini is a way of building a federation of network-centric services, creating an adaptive, scalable, and dynamic computing environment. The Jini architecture uses objects that move around the network. Jini allows each object-service to adapt to network changes. The Jini API and network protocols specify how object-clients find service providers, how objects work together toward a common task.

Jini builds distributed object systems—service federations. A service federation combines application-based and infrastructure-based services and makes the services available to a (privileged) user.

A service object can announce its presence and capabilities on the network. (Does it look like JXTA advertisements? Yes! But remember, Jini actually was the first on that block.)

The client uses a **lookup** service (part of the Jini core infrastructure) to find a desired service on the Internet. Service objects can join and leave federations at run-time. When joining the federation, a service registers for a **lease** period with a *Registrar* object.

Because only current services can be discovered, the service should renew its lease periodically. Jini assumes that network services are very dynamic; they can die and be restored at any time. That's why there is no such thing as a permanent service—everything is temporary or leased.

Jini widely uses the Factory and Abstract Factory design patterns to construct object-services on the fly. For example, the *net.jini.jeri.AbstractILFactory* class implements the *InvocationLayerFactory* and the interface provides a convenient way for subclasses to create proxies and invocation dispatchers for remote objects.

Jini has a provision for privilege-based access to services. For example, the *AccessPermission* class represents permission to call a method.

Jini deals with a typed collection of objects called *Entry*. The *net.jini.Entry.AbstractEntry* class is a generally useful base class for entry types. The *net.jini.core.entry.Entry* interface represents service-specific attributes—for example, in the Jini lookup service and *JavaSpace* interface to mark entries. *Entry* fields are public, nontransient, nonstatic, and nonfinal, and must be objects (nonprimitive).

The *Entry* types have a public, no-argument constructor that fits perfectly into the magic formula for dynamic class loading:

```
Class.forName(name).newInstance()
```

The *Entry* types are polymorphic value objects that create a highly extensible *one-type* system. (A similar example of typed collections was provided for the Topic Maps implementation in Chapter 5 and for several document types in the document-handling application described in Chapter 6.)

The interface to the lookup service is defined by the *ServiceRegistrar*. Implementations of the lookup service export proxy objects that implement the *ServiceRegistrar* interface *locally* to the client. This makes the *ServiceRegistrar* a local interface that can use an implementation-specific protocol to communicate with a remote server. One should implement the *ServiceRegistrar* interface to work with registered services. There are several methods that constitute the service registration mechanism:

void addAttributes(Entry[] attrSets)—adds the specified attribute sets (those that aren't duplicates of existing attribute sets) to the registered service item

Lease getLease()—returns the lease that controls the service registration, allowing the lease to be renewed or canceled

ServiceID getServiceID()—returns the service ID for this service

void modifyAttributes(Entry[] attrSetTemplates, Entry[] attrSets)—modifies existing attribute sets

void setAttributes(Entry[] attrSets)—deletes all of the service item's existing attributes and replaces them with the specified attribute sets

The *net.jini.core.lookup.ServiceTemplate* instances help match items in the lookup service. There are several attributes that must match: serviceID, service (name), and serviceTypes. The attributeSets should contain at least one matching entry for each entry template (in attributeSetTemplates).

An entry matches an entry template if their classes (or superclasses) match and every non-null field in the template equals the corresponding field of the entry. Every entry can match more than one template. Note that in a service template, for serviceTypes and attributeSetTemplates, a null field represents a wild card.

Theoretically, the Jini API and protocols can be implemented in any language. A current practice, however, uses Sun Microsystems implementation with Java language and Java Remote Method Invocation (RMI) as a client–server communications protocol. Most of the proxy methods have normal RMI remote interface semantics.

Jini services represent a wide range of service concepts, including printing and storage. The most popular Jini service is JavaSpaces, which provides a distributed persistence mechanism for Jini entries.

JavaSpaces: Flow of Objects and Loosely Coupled Processes

JavaSpaces follows the general Jini model. Like any service, it must be registered with "Jini lookup services" and inherits the basic mechanisms of leasing and event handling. Clients must "discover" the service using the lookup service and the same matching rules with service attributes. JavaSpaces extensively uses dynamic code downloading and proxy–object interactions. Here is an extract from the JavaSpaces interface definition:

```
public interface JavaSpace {
Lease write(Entry entry, Transaction txn, long lease) throws
TransactionException, RemoteException;
Entry read(Entry tmpl, Transaction txn, long timeout)throws
UnusableEntryException, TransactionException, InterruptedException,
RemoteException;
EventRegistration notify(Entry tmpl, Transaction txn,
RemoteEventListener listener, long lease,MarshalledObject handback)
throws TransactionException, RemoteException;
Entry readIfExists(Entry tmpl, Transaction txn, long timeout) throws
UnusableEntryException, TransactionException, InterruptedException,
RemoteException;
Entry snapshot(Entry e) throws RemoteException
//... and more...
}
```

You can see that JavaSpaces allows one to *write, read, notify*, and even *snapshot* over the network. Of course, every operation has the potential to throw a nice set of exceptions. A network is still a network, and we always expect something to be broken or just not valid anymore over there.

The right approach to using JavaSpaces in an application is to rethink the application in terms of data flow in the network space. Try to remodel the application as a work flow, a loosely coupled collection of processes. Each process is associated with object-services that can come and go or change service features at run-time. Jini architecture can afford this flexibility. JavaSpaces uses distributed persistence and transaction mechanisms and supports application concurrency and scalability.

JavaSpaces uses underlying Jini technology to take care of many unknowns on the network. Clients do not need to know about server crashes and new servers on the Internet; JavaSpaces can figure it out. JavaSpaces also knows when a new client comes to the network and what new type of services the client requests. That is OK, too.

Think about a "green wave" application that allows cars to pass through cross sections, always with a green light and without major delays. Multiple real-time tasks must be accomplished with multiple processors located at city intersections. Some cars will be able to participate in this game with their road map navigation processors. This is a perfect application for Jini architecture.

Here is a typical set of libraries used in Jini classes:

```
// JiniExample
import java.io.*;
import java.rmi.*;
import net.jini.core.entry.*;
import net.jini.core.lookup.*;
import net.jini.lookup.entry.*;
import net.jini.core.discovery.*;
```

A typical jump-start example for Jini applications is provided with several lines below:

```
void init(String lookupURL, ServiceID serviceID, Class[]
arrayOfClasses, Entry[] arrayOfEntries) {
   System.setSecurityManager(new RMI SecurityManager());
   try {
       LookupLocator locator = new LookupLocator("jini:
       //" + lookupURL);
       ServiceRegistrar registrar = locator.getRegistrar();
       ServiceTemplate service = new ServiceTemplate(serviceID,
arrayOfclasses, arrayOfEntries);
        // everything is ready to retrieve a specific service
        object and start the service
        MyServiceClass myServiceObject =
(MyServiceClass)registrar.lookup(service);
        // some code for a specific task
}
```

This example shows the Jini service initiation process. The method starts with security manager settings. The *RMISecurityManager* is selected for this purpose, although theoretically, some other protocols can be used.

We create the *LookupLocator* object and use this locator to create the *ServiceRegistrar*. The next step is to create a service template filled with service features and finally, to look for the service that matches our criteria via a lookup service. This is a multicast message request that can have a limited time to live (TTL), to prevent high network traffic. In the case of lookup success, the client uses an HTTP server (which is built into the Jini infrastructure) to download the proxy object. The proxy implements arbitrary communications protocols for using the service and allows the client to make requests to the service.

A service provider that offers a service publishes its proxy to a lookup service. You can see that Jini and JXTA have common publish-subscribe concepts that are implemented with different protocols. The Jini proxy must be implemented in Java, although the actual service may be implemented in other languages that can interface with Java.

JXTA is language neutral. JXTA protocols are based on XML and can be implemented in any programming environment. JXTA learned several lessons from Jini, and JXTA protocols include a variety of features that help create gated communities on the Internet.

JXTA AND JINI: JUST NEIGHBORS OR COLLABORATORS?

Today, the worlds of JXTA and Jini coexist, shoulder to shoulder. The integration of both worlds is definitely possible. For example, one of the JXTA peers can be assigned as a specific service that communicates to a Jini lookup service to advertise peer group services in Jini proxy terms and discover services of Jini federations. Not every JXTA peer can do this work; the peer must be implemented with Java. These Java-based JXTA peers can implement additional Jini protocols and serve as Jini-JXTA connectors or proxies.

SUMMARY

The distributed world is not a topic of the future, it is happening today. The centralized client–server model of computing still dominates the Internet, but its position is weakening every day. The number of networked devices is growing rapidly. We have almost hit the limit of current Internet capacity, and the new version of the TCP/IP protocol is ready to prepare us for Internet 2.

Wireless devices will soon outnumber our corporate and home workstations. Rapidly changing network dynamics require adaptive distributed computing. Current JXTA and Jini protocols and implementations serve the purpose of self-healing networks.

Does that mean that we are ready for this new computing model? I don't think so. Self-healing networks are an impossible dream unless we have more knowledgeable and intelligent network elements. There is a law of information (and people) management that states: A growing quantity of objects requires more complexity (if we expect objects to behave).

A variety of client environments, locations, connections, and services are frequently factors in the changing, multidimensional criteria space. We need knowledge-powered application solutions for quick and smart adjustments to these changes.

This complexity can reside in a central place, according to the old model, or can be distributed on the network. Distributed knowledge peers, such as those described in Chapter 13, fit nicely into the picture. The source code for creating distributed knowledge peers can be found on the Web site.

Integrating Question

What are the common features of distributed systems?

Case Study

1. Download the source or binary objects of the distributed knowledge peer from the Cambridge University Press Web site or from the ITS, Inc. Web site: *http://JavaSchool.com*.
2. Discover peers, and their services, currently on the Internet (the *List Peers* link).
3. Request the Software Engineering Training Service related to this book (the *Search Service* link).
4. Select a related book chapter (1 through 14) from the service offering, and follow the training instructions.
5. Use the "New Topic" service to describe your area of knowledge as a new training subject.
6. Use the "New Scenario" service to provide an interactive training session for your new subject.
7. Advertise your new training service to a selected peer group.
8. Provide an example of a distributed system that can benefit your workplace.

REFERENCES

1. Jabber Software Foundation: *http://jabber.org*.
2. JXTA v2.0 Protocols Specification: *http://spec.JXTA.org*.
3. Bill Joy on Java and Jini, Presentation transcript, 1999: *http://technetcast.ddj.com/tnc_play_stream.html?stream_id=186*.

APPENDIX 1

Java and C#: A Saga of Siblings

This appendix is a reference to Java, including the JDK1.5 and C# languages. In previous chapters, we discussed integration-ready and knowledge-connected environments that allow for writing application scenarios. In spite of the fact that most examples that support this method are made in Java, similar environments can be created with other languages. Life outside of Java is not as much fun, but it is still possible.

This appendix provides examples in which the same function is implemented not in Java but in its easiest replacement—the C# language.

This lucky child inherited good manners, elegance, style, and even some clothing from its stepfather while enjoying its mother's care and her rich, vast NETwork.

Java and C# are similar in their language structure, functionality, and ideology. Learning from each other and growing stronger in the healthy competition the siblings perfectly serve the software world.

JAVA VIRTUAL MACHINE AND COMMON LANGUAGE RUN-TIME

Java compilation produces a binary code according to the Java language specification. This binary code is performed on any platform in which a Java Virtual Machine (JVM) is implemented. The JVM interprets this binary code at run-time, translating the code into specific platform instructions.

C# compilation (through Visual Studio.NET) can produce the binary code in Common Intermediate Language (CIL) and save it in a portable execution (PE) file that can then be managed and executed by the Common Language Runtime (CLR). The CLR, which Microsoft refers to as a "managed execution environment," in a way is similar to JVM.

A program compiled for the CLR does not need a language-specific execution environment and can run on almost any MS Windows system in which CLR is present.

There is one big difference between JVM and CLR. JVM makes Java a multiplatform language.

CLR is a multilingual environment implemented on MS Windows platforms. Visual Studio.NET supports several programming languages, such as C, C#, C++, Java, Visual Basic, Practical Extraction and Report Language (Perl), and Cobol, providing compilation from these languages to CIL, followed by execution by the CLR.

Garbage Collection and Performance

Java, as well as .NET environments, does not provide too much control over memory management. Both technologies offer a garbage collector mechanism instead. The garbage collector periodically looks for objects that have no references in the current code and frees (deallocates) memory from these objects.

Keep in mind that memory management is a pretty expensive system operation. If the garbage collection thread starts when your user is waiting for a program's response, the program's response will be visibly delayed and the user might become frustrated with your program's performance.

For both (Java and .NET) environments, it is possible to escape this situation or at least make it less likely. The solution is simple and can be addressed by two lines that look almost identical in your Java or C# code.

Assign heavy objects to null as soon as you do not need them:

```
myHeavyObject = null;
```

The garbage collector will almost immediately free this object

Force the garbage collector to work at a time that is not critical for the application. Insert the line below, for example, after your code requests an input/output operation:

```
System.GC.Collect(); // syntax for C#
```

Or

```
System.gc(); // syntax for Java
```

Java and C# Basics: Keywords from "abstract" to "while"

As you can see from the beginning, the two languages are very close in their syntax and mentality. About 90% of their keywords are the same in spelling and meaning, and both Java and C# keywords start with lowercase letters:

abstract—A Java/C# keyword used in a class declaration to specify a class that is not complete and cannot have object-instances. An abstract class regularly has some abstract methods and serves as a base class for the subclasses, which implement those abstract methods and can have object-instances.

```
// Java example
public abstract class Shape {
    // data
    public void draw();
    // abstract method with no implementation
    // more code that can include implemented and abstract methods
```

```
}
public class Rectangle extends Shape {
    public void draw() {
        // specific implementation of the method
    }
}
// C# example
using System;
public abstract class Shape {
    // data
    public void Draw();
    // abstract method with no implementation
    // more code that can include implemented and abstract methods
}
public class Rectangle : Shape {
    public void Draw() {
        // specific implementation of the method
    }
}
// The line below will produce the error:
// Cannot instantiate an object of the abstract class Shape
// Shape s = new Shape();
// ERROR line: we try to instantiate the abstract class
// The line below is valid.
Shape s = new Rectangle();
// OK line, the Rectangle is not an abstract class
```

assert—A Java keyword that tests a Boolean expression, for example, *assert (a==b)* and throws an *AssertionError* exception if the specified Boolean expression is false. C# does not have this keyword.

boolean—A Java keyword. The C# version of this keyword is **bool**. Java and C# define this keyword as a type that can hold only one of the literal values true and false.

```
// Java example
// Some code that fills strings "a" and "b" with some values
// check if strings are equal
// store the result of comparison in the boolean variable
// boolean resultOfComparison = a.equals(b);
// C# example
// Some code that fills strings "a" and "b" with some values
// check if strings are equal
// store the result of comparison in the boolean variable
// bool resultOfComparison = a.Equals(b);
// C# method names start with upper case
```

break—A Java/C# keyword that stops the current program block (loop) execution and passes control to the next block of the program.

```
Example (valid for Java and C#)
for(;;) {// indefinite loop
     // some code
     if(a < b) {// check if a is less than b
          // at this point the for loop will be interrupted break;
          // pass control to the next block of the program after
          // the loop
     }
     // more code
}
// the next block of the program
// some code
```

byte—A Java keyword that represents a sequence of eight bits as a signed integer number. The C# language defines the corresponding data type as the **sbyte**.

```
// Java example
byte a = 13;
// C# example
sbyte a = 13;
```

case—A Java/C# keyword that follows a conditional switch declaration to define a block of a program to pass the control to if the expression specified in the switch matches the case value.

```
// Java/C# example:
switch(number) {
     case 1:
         response = "hello";
         break;
     case 2:
         response = "good bye";
         break;
}
```

catch—A Java/C# keyword used in the *try/catch* block of statements. The *catch* block of statements is executed if an exception or run-time error occurs in a preceding *try* block.

```
// Java example:
import java.io.*;
// class definition
// method definition
try {// IO operation can potentially trigger exception
    File inputFile = new File("myFile.txt");
    FileReader reader = new FileReader(inputFile);
} catch(Exception e) {
    System.out.println("ERROR: "+ e);
}
// C# example:
using System;
```

```
using System.IO;
// class definition
// method definition
try {#// IO operation can potentially trigger exception
   FileStream inputFile = new FileStream("myFile.txt",
   FileMode.Open);
   StreamReader reader = new StreamReader(inputFile);
} catch(Exception e) {
   Console.Write("ERROR: "+ e);
}
```

char—A Java/C# keyword that declares a primitive textual data type, a 16-bit, unsigned, Unicode character.

```
// Java/C# example:
char c = 'c';
```

continue—A Java/C# keyword used to resume program execution at the end of the current loop.

```
// Java/C# example:
int[] numbers = new int[10];
for(int i=0;i < 10; i++) {
    // the first part of the loop
    numbers[i] = i;
    if(a < b) {// check if the value "a" is less than the value
    "b"
       // at this point the for loop will be interrupted continue;
       // skip the second part of the loop, increase the value of i
   }
    // the second part of the loop
    numbers[i] = number[i] * 2;
    // will not be executed if condition above is met
}
```

default—A Java/C# keyword used optionally in a *switch* statement after all of the *case* conditions. The default statement will be executed if a case condition does not match the value of the switch variable.

```
// Java/C# example:
switch(number) {
    case 1:
       response = "hello";
       break;
    case 2:
       response = "good bye";
       break;
    default:
       response = "Please re-enter your data";
}
```

do—A Java/C# keyword that declares a loop that will iterate a statement block. The *while* keyword at the end of the block can specify the loop exit condition.

```
// Java/C# example:
int[] numbers = new int[10];
int i = 0;
do {
   // the first part of the loop
   numbers[i] = i++;
} while(i < 10);
```

double—A Java/C# keyword that defines a floating point number with *double precision*.

```
// Java/C# example:
double preciseNumber = 16.5;
```

else—A Java/#C keyword used in *if-else* block statements. When the test expression specified in the *if* statement is false, the program will execute the *else* block statement.

```
// Java/C# example:
     String response = "";
     if(a < b) {// check if the value "a" is less than the value "b"
        response = "Add value please.";
     } else {
        response = "Enough, thank you.";
     }
```

extends—A Java keyword used to define a subclass that is derived and inherited from a base class. One interface can *extend* another interface by adding more methods. C# uses the ":" character to define inheritance.

```
// Java example
public abstract class Shape {
     // data
     public void draw();
     // abstract method with no implementation
     // more code that can include implemented and abstract methods
}
public class Rectangle extends Shape {
     public void draw() {
          // specific implementation of the method
     }
}
// C# example
using System;
public abstract class Shape {
     // data
     public void Draw();
     // abstract method with no implementation
     // more code that can include implemented and abstract methods
}
```

```
public class Rectangle : Shape {
    public void Draw() {
          // specific implementation of the method
    }
}
```

final—A Java keyword that defines an unchangeable entity. You cannot change a *final* variable from its initialized value, cannot extend a *final* class, or override a *final* method. C# uses the **sealed** keyword to express the same concept.

```
// Java example:
final private int READONLYMODE = 9;
// C# example:
sealed private int READONLYMODE = 9;
```

finally—A Java/C# keyword that is used in *try/catch* block statements to ensure execution of the following block of statements, regardless of whether an *Exception*, or run-time error, occurred in the *try* statement block.

```
// Java example:
import java.io.*;
// class definition
// method definition
try {// IO operation can potentially trigger exception
   File inputFile = new File("myFile.txt");
   FileReader reader = new FileReader(inputFile);
} catch(Exception e) {
    System.out.println("ERROR: "+ e);
} finally {
     reader.close();
}
// C# example:
using System;
using System.IO;
// class definition
// method definition
try {// IO operation can potentially trigger exception
   FileStream inputFile = new FileStream("myFile.txt",
   FileMode.Open);
   StreamReader reader = new StreamReader(inputFile);
} catch(Exception e) {
    Console.Write("ERROR: "+ e);
} finally {
     reader.close();
}
```

float—A Java/C# keyword that defines a floating point number with *single precision*.

```
// Java/C# example:
float singlePrecisionNumber = 1.459F;
```

for—A Java/C# keyword that declares a loop with an optional initial statement. This statement includes a condition to exit and additional executable statements.

```
// Java/C# example
int[] numbers = new int[10];
for(int i=0;i < 10; i++) {
    // block of statements
    numbers[i] = i;
}
```

if—A Java/C# keyword that evaluates a conditional statement and then executes a statement block if the result of the evaluation is true.

```
// Java/C# example:
    String response = "";
    if(a < b) {// check if the value "a" is less than the value "b"
       response = "Add value please.";
    }
```

implements—A Java keyword, an optional part of a class declaration, that specifies interfaces that are implemented by the class. C# supports the same concept with the ":" character, as it does for base class–subclass relationships.

```
// Java example:
public class KnowledgeService implements ServiceScenario {
    // class definition
}
// C# example:
public class KnowledgeService : ServiceScenario {
    // class definition
}
```

import—A Java keyword that, at the beginning of a source, points to a class from another package or a whole package of classes that are needed by this class. C# provides the **using** keyword for the same purpose.

```
// Java example:
import java.awt.Toolkit;  // a single class
import java.io.*; // a package
// C# example:
using System;
using System.Net;
```

instanceof—A Java keyword that tests whether the specified run-time object type is an instance of the specified class in the same evaluation expression. C# uses the **is** keyword instead.

```
// Java example:
if(aShape instanceof Rectangle) {
   // do something
}
```

```
// C# example:
if(aShape is Rectangle) {
   // do something
}
```

interface—This Java/C# keyword defines a collection of method definitions and constants. A class usually implements an interface.

```
// Java/C# example:
public interface ServiceScenario {
     // method definitions and abstract methods constants
}
```

long—This Java/C# keyword defines a 64-bit numeric integer variable.

```
// Java/C# example:
long preciseNumber = 64000L;
```

native—This Java keyword may be used in method declarations to specify the method implemented in a non-Java programming language and located in some library file. The *System.loadLibrary()* method loads this library file and makes the native method available for the Java run-time environment.

C# uses the **extern** keyword to indicate a non-C# method.

An external or native method declaration has no actual implementation in the current source because it was implemented in a different language. In this regard, its syntax is similar to abstract methods. The *DLLImport* attributes point to a library (Dynamic Link Library) and the parameters needed to invoke the method.

```
// Java example:
public class ITSNativeExample {
    private native void copyFile (String inputFilename, String
    copyFilename);
     static
     {
        System.loadLibrary("myNativeLibrary");
     }
     public static void main(String[] args) {
       ITSNativeExample example = new ITSNativeExample();
       example.copyFile("source", "sourceCopy");
     }
}
// C# example:
[DllImport("KERNEL32.DLL", EntryPoint="CopyFileW", SetLastError=true,
CharSet=CharSet.Unicode, ExactSpelling=true,
CallingConvention=CallingConvention.StdCall)]
public static extern bool CopyFile(String inputFilename, String
copyFilename);
```

new—A Java/C# keyword that creates a new object-instance of a class.

```
// Java/C# example:
File f = new File("notes.txt");
```

package—A Java keyword that declares that the current class is a member of a package, in other words, a library of classes.

C# uses the **namespace** keyword for the same purpose.

```
// Java example
package com.its.connector;
import java.io.*;
public class IOMaster {
     // class definition
}
     // C# example
namespace ITS.Connector;
using System.IO;
public class IOMaster {
// class definition
}
```

private—A Java/C# keyword used in a method or variable declaration to restrict access to the method or variable to only elements of its own class.

```
// Java/C# example
private int number;
```

protected—A Java/C# keyword that provides more than private, but less than public, access to a method or variable. Protected class members are visible in Java not only to classes derived from any package but also to any class from the same package.

Unlike Java, C# opens access to protected data and methods only to derived classes but does not allow access for any other classes, even from the same *namespace*.

```
// Java/C# example:
protected Hashtable services;
```

public—A Java/C# keyword used in a method or variable declaration to open access to the method or variable to all classes.

```
// Java/C# example:
public final int READONLYMODE = 9;
```

return—A Java/C# keyword that ends the execution of a method. The keyword may be followed by a value required by the method declaration.

```
// Java/C# example:
public int calculateNumbers(int a, int b) {
    int c = a+b;
    return c;
}
```

short—A Java/C# keyword used to define a 16-bit integer.

```
// Java/C# example:
short scaryNumber = 13;
```

static—A Java/C# keyword used to define a single copy of a class variable or method shared by all object-instances of the class. One can access a static variable or static method even without creating an object of the class.

```
// Java/C# example:
// In Java case two classes below must be stored in a different files
// with the filenames "Math.java" and "MathActions.java" accordingly
// C# has no restrictions on source filenames Unlike Java,
// C# allows us to keep more than one public class in a source file
public class Math {
    public static double PI = 1.4591;
    // more code
}
public class MathActions {
    public double getCircleLength(double radius) {
        return 2 * Math.PI * radius;
    }
    // more code
}
```

strictfp—A Java language keyword-modifier that means *strict floating point arithmetic*. This type of modifier may apply to a class, interface, or method to declare an expression *FP-strict*. You cannot use the *strictfp* keyword on constructors or methods within interfaces, although you can declare a *strictfp* class to make all constructors and methods of the class *FP-strict*.

When is *strictfp* important? It is needed to guarantee common floating-point arithmetic across different Java implementations or hardware platforms. The *strictfp* keyword in the following example keeps the expression from overflowing and produces a final result that is within range, even if the *price* argument is close to the maximum value of a double (*Double.MAX_VALUE*).

C# has no adequate keyword and has no need for this concept because the language runs on "wintel" (Windows-Intel) platforms.

```
// Java example
public strictfp class ITSStrictFPExample {
    public double getDoublePrice(double price) {
        double doublePrice = 2.0 * d;
        return doublePrice;
    }
}
```

super—A Java keyword used in a subclass to access members of a base class inherited by the subclass. C# uses the keyword **base**. You can do the same things in C# with the *base* keyword that you can in Java with *super*, except one: you cannot invoke a base class constructor this way. Don't worry; there is a way to invoke a base class constructor in C# from a subclass. For example:

```
// Java example:
public class Child extends Parent {
    public Child () {
    '   // invoke a Parent's constructor super();
        // invoke a method from the Parent class
        // super.takeCareOfChildren();
        // do something childish
    }
}
// C# example:
public class Child : Parent {
    // the Child constructor starts with a Parent's
    // constructor invocation
    public Child () : base Parent() {
    // invoke a Parent'sconstructor first
        // invoke a method from the Parent class
        // base.takeCareOfChildren();
        // do something childish
    }
}
```

switch—A Java/C# keyword used to compare an expression or a variable with a value specified by the *case* keyword in order to execute a group of statements following the case if the case value matches the *switch* expression. The *switch* expression must be of type *char, byte, short*, or *int*.

```
// Java/C# example
switch(a+b) {
    case 4:
        response = "you are almost there";
        break;
    case 5:
        response = "Winner!";
        break;
    default:
        response = "try again";
}
```

synchronized—A Java modifier-keyword that can be applied to a method or a block of code to ensure mutually exclusive access to specified objects and guarantee that only one thread at a time executes that code.

C# introduces the **lock** modifier-keyword to express the same idea.

C#'s *System.Threading.Monitor* class contains the *Enter* method, which assures that it will be the only thread in the block. C# adds more flexibility to the game of threads and atomic operations. The *Monitor* class also contains the *TryEnter* method, which will try to obtain a lock, perhaps by blocking the piece of code. If this attempt appears to be a failure, the method indicates the failure to lock the object by returning a false value.

I cannot fail to mention C#'s *System.Threading.Interlocked* class with its *Increment, Decrement*, and *Exchange* methods, which enable a program to synchronize access to variables that are shared among several threads.

```
// Java example:
   public class ITSSyncExample {
      private int treasure;
      public synchronized int getTreasure () {
          return treasure;
      }
      public synchronized void setTreasure (int value) {
          treasure = value;
      }
   }
// C# example:
   public class ITSSyncExample {
      private int treasure;
      public lock int GetTreasure () {
          return treasure;
      }
      public lock void SetTreasure (int value) {
          treasure = value;
      }
   }
// another C# example:
using System;
using System.Threading;
public class ITSAtomicOperationExample {
   public static int treasure = 1;
   public static void AtomicDecrement() {
      Interlocked.Decrement(ref treasure); // atomic operation
   }
}
```

throw—A Java/C# keyword that allows the programmer to throw (pass) an object of a class that is inherited from the *Throwable* class to a calling method. In most cases, programmers throw an *Exception* object. This action allows a programmer to escape the hard work of writing *try/catch* statements at the moment of truth (when exception actually happens) and to delegate the responsibility of hunting for the *Exception* to the upper-level method. Note that the *ServiceNotFoundException* extends the *Extension* class.

throws—A Java keyword used in method declarations to specify which exceptions are not handled within the method but are instead passed to the next higher level of the program.

In the example below, the *requestService()* method throws the *ClassNotFoundException* if the class is not found in the *classpath* or throws the *ServiceNotFoundException* if the class is not the *Service* type. The *requestService()* method declaration includes the *throws Exception* statement, which covers all possible exceptions (including the *ServiceNotFoundException*) that extend the *java.lang.Exception* class

```
// Java example:
public Object requestService (String serviceName) throws Exception {
    Object service = Class.forName(serviceName).newInstance();
    If(service instanceof Service) {
        throw new ServiceNotFoundException();
    }
    return service;
}
```

C# does not have a keyword that can be used in a method declaration to announce that the method can throw an exception. As you can see in the following C# example, the program still can throw exceptions without any announcements in the method declaration.

```
// C# example:
using System;
using System.Reflection;
using System.Collections;
public Object requestService (String serviceName) {
    // load a class from an assembly at runtime
    // Type actingClass = Type.GetType(className);
    // activate (instantiate) an object of the type
    // Object service = Activator.CreateInstance (actingClass);
    If(!(service is Service)) {
        throw new ServiceNotFoundException();
    }
    return service;
}
```

transient—A Java keyword indicating that a field is not a part of the serialized form of an object. This keyword helps us exclude some fields from the serialized version of the object. Keep in mind that not all Java objects can be serialized. For example, the *Thread* object is not serializable. When Java tries to serialize a bigger object that includes nonserializable objects, the program fails and produces an exception if all nonserializable objects are not marked *transient*.

There is no such keyword in C#.

```
// Java example:
public class ServiceProvider {
    private String serviceName;
    // will be serialized
    private transient ServiceThread;
    // extends Thread, not serializable
    // more data
    // more code
}
```

try—A Java/C# keyword that defines a block of statements inside a method that might throw a Java language exception. An optional *catch* block can handle specific exceptions thrown within the *try* block. An optional *finally* block is executed whether or not an exception is thrown.

Java enforces the handling of *Exceptions*, whereas C# is more liberal and leaves it up to the programmer whether or not to use *try/catch* statements in the code.

```
// Java example:
import java.io.*;
// class definition
// method definition
try {// IO operation can potentially trigger exception
   File inputFile = new File("myFile.txt");
   FileReader reader = new FileReader(inputFile);
} catch(Exception e) {
   System.out.println("ERROR: "+ e);
}
// C# example:
using System;
using System.IO;
// class definition
// method definition
try {// IO operation can potentially trigger exception
   FileStream inputFile = new FileStream("myFile.txt",
   FileMode.Open);
   StreamReader reader = new StreamReader(inputFile);
} catch(Exception e) {
   Console.Write("ERROR: "+ e);
}
// another C# example:
using System;
using System.IO;
// class definition
// method definition
// no try/catch statements ... and C# compiler will "OK" this !
FileStream inputFile = new FileStream("myFile.txt", FileMode.Open);
StreamReader reader = new StreamReader(inputFile);
```

void—A Java/C# keyword used in method declarations to specify that the method does not return a value.

```
// Java/C# example:
public void setName(String name) {
    this.name = name;
    // no return value!
}
```

volatile—A Java/C# keyword used in variable declarations to prohibit reordering instructions related to accessing such variables. Reordering may appear, for example, because of compiler optimizations. Declaring a volatile variable forces the compiler to "take special precautions" against collisions. Concurrent threads will modify the volatile variable (as in the following example) asynchronously, according to the order specified by the source.

The volatile modifier cannot be used in interface constants or *final* (*sealed* in C#) variables.

```
// Java/C# example:
public class ITSVolatileDataExample {
    private volatile int counter1, counter2;
    public void setCounters(int counter) {
        counter1 = counter;
        counter2 = counter;
    }
    public void increaseCounters() {
        counter1++;
        counter2++;
    }
    public boolean compareCounters() {
        // should always be true even with multiple
        // concurrent operations
        return (counter1 == counter2);
    }
}
```

while—A Java/C# keyword that declares a loop that iterates a programming block. The *while* statement specifies a loop exit condition.

C# also offers the **foreach** keyword, a convenient way to iterate over the elements of an array.

```
// Java example:
import java.util.*;
public class ITSWhileExample {
    public ITSWhileExample() {
        Hashtable table = Stringer.parse(xml);
        Enumeration keys = table.keys();
        while(keys.hasMoreElements()) {
            String key = (String)keys.nextElement();
            System.out.println("key=" + key + "value=" +
            table.get(key));
        }
    }
}
// C# example:
using System;
using System.Collections;
namespace ITSCsExamples {
    public class ITSWhileExample {
        public ITSWhileExample(String xml) {
            Hashtable table = Stringer.parse(xml);
            ICollection keys = table.Keys;
            IEnumerator enumerator = keys.
```

```
                GetEnumerator();
                while(enumerator.MoveNext()) {
                    String key = (String)enumerator.Current;
                    Console.WriteLine("key=" + key +
                    "value=" + table[key]);
                }
            }
        }
    }
    // another C# example with the foreach keyword instead of the while
    keyword
    using System;
    using System.Collections;
    namespace ITSCsExamples {
        public class ITSForeachExample {
            public ITSForeachExample(String xml) {
                Hashtable table = Stringer.parse(xml);
                ICollection keys = table.Keys;
                foreach(object o in keys) {
                    String key = (String)o;
                    Console.WriteLine("key=" + key +
                    "value=" + table[key]);
                }
            }
        }
    }
```

We are done with basic keywords!

With this ammunition, we can climb higher and more difficult peaks on the programming trail from Java to C#.

From Basics to the Next Level on the Java/C# Programming Trail

You've already noticed that every primitive data type in Java has the same name in C#. We found out that C# accepts almost all Java keywords and adds some of its own. For example, C# includes unsigned primitive data types such as *ushort*, *uint*, and *ulong*. The byte primitive in C# is also unsigned, unlike the Java byte. When Java says "byte," C# says "sbyte"—signed byte. The following paragraphs discuss some of the differences between Java and C#; some are only cosmetic.

Exceptions: Java Is Strict, C# Is More Liberal

Java never crashes, it just gives exceptions. Java compilers enforce *try/catch* statements in all input/output and network operations. If exceptions are omitted, the compiler produces error messages. C# has almost exactly same the exception mechanism but leaves the decision of when to use it up to the programmer.

Class Inheritance: Java Says "Extends" and C# Says ":"

C# inherits its terms of inheritance from C++. When Java says that *public class B extends A*—C++, as well as C#, prefers to say that *public class B: A*.

Interfaces: Java Says "Implements" and C# Still Says ":"

Both Java and C# have interfaces. Java makes a very distinctive interface inheritance from class inheritance. Java says, "public class D implements C," and we immediately understand that C is an interface not a class. C# does not really care. C# can say "public class D: C" as well as "public class D: B," where C is an interface and B is a class.

Nevertheless, the meaning of inheritance is the same for both Java and C#. For a derived class (or a subclass that extends a base class), class inheritance means the benefit of ownership of all the nonprivate class members of the base class, including data and methods.

When a class inherits (or as Java rightly says, "implements") an interface, this class has an obligation to provide implementations for all interface methods. Java and C# agree on the function. Both languages allow for a single class inheritance and multiple interfaces.

These inheritance rules are very different from those of C++, which allow for multiple class inheritance and have no interfaces, just abstract classes.

Java and C# Languages Allow Us to Use True Polymorphism, But . . .

C#, as well as C++, requires marking methods, which we plan to override in subclasses as "virtual." Java assumes that all methods are virtual methods and frees programmers from placing such markers.

Polymorphism is the ability of objects to appear in multiple forms. For example, an object of the *Shape* class can appear as a rectangle or a triangle if the programmer had provided such inheritance in the design and source code.

The benefit of polymorphism is that one can replace hundreds of lines of procedural code with two lines of object-oriented polymorphic code.

Here is the procedural code below (written in C++ /C#):

```
Object aShape = pictureWithShapes.
getNextShapeFromThePictureWithManyShapes();
// check a type of an object and invoke a proper method
// if(aShape is Rectangle) {
       drawRectangle();
} else if(aShape is Triangle) {
    drawTriangle();
} else if(aShape is Circle) {
    drawCircle();
}   // etc., etc, etc.
```

The number of shapes may vary, and the source code grows with every new shape added to the picture. Each time a user requires a new shape, the developer has to adjust the code accordingly. Looks like job security, doesn't it?

Here is the source code written using polymorphism:

```
Object aShape = pictureWithShapes.
getNextShapeFromThePictureWithManyShapes();
```

```
// Invoke a proper "draw" method defined for a specific subclass
// aShape.draw();
// if aShape is a Rectangle it invokes the "draw" of the
// Rectangle class
```

The beauty of polymorphism is that this source code does not grow or change when we add ten, or even a thousand, more shapes to the picture. The line *aShape.draw()* invokes a proper *draw()* method of a proper shape.

A proper method is chosen at run-time instead of being bound during compilation. C++, as well as C#, calls such methods *virtual* and uses the *virtual* keyword for these cases. Java considers all methods potentially virtual and omits this keyword.

Polymorphism comes at price: developers must invest the extra time to design it right, defining a base class with methods (e.g., *draw*) that may be overridden by derived classes.

Java example: a base class and subclasses

```
/**
* The Shape (base) class definition must be stored in the
* Shape.java file
'*/
public class Shape {
    // data description
    protected int size;
    // more data description
    // metods
    public void draw() {
         // some implementation
    }
         // more methods
}
/**
* The Rectangle (child) class definition must be stored in the
* Rectangle.java file
*/
public class Rectangle extends Shape {
    // data specific to the Rectangle
    // override methods for the subclass
    public void draw() {
        // method re-definition
    }
}
/**
* The Triangle (child) class definition must be stored in the
* Triangle.java file
*/
public class Triangle extends Shape {
    // data specific to the Triangle
    // override methods for the subclass
```

```
    public void draw() {
        // method re-definition
    }
}
```

C# example: a base class and subclasses

Note that C# precisely names *virtual* and *overridden* methods.

```
using System;
public class Shape {
    // data description
    protected int size;
    // read below about a slight difference on protected keyword
    // more data
    // metods
    // Note the virtual keyword in the base class method public
    // virtual void draw() {
        // some implementation
    }
    // more methods
}
public class Rectangle : Shape {
    // specific to the Rectangle data
    // override methods for the subclass
    public override void draw() {
        // method re-definition
    }
}
public class Triangle : Shape {
    // specific to the Triangle data
    // override methods for the subclass
    public override void draw() {
        // method re-definition
    }
}
```

Packages: Java Says "Package" and C# Says "Namespace"

In both cases, it is an additional dimension of encapsulation. In the same way a class defines and encapsulates an object type with its data and behavior, a package defines and encapsulates a set of classes, likely to be reused as a library, that provides a function in a specific area. For example, base language types and functionality are represented in the *java.lang package* in Java and the *System* package in C#.

Unlike C#, java relates package names with file system directory names

A package name in Java is the same as the name of the directory in which the classes of the package are located. The package structure in Java dictates the class file structure. In C#, *namespaces* may be located in any directory (folder), regardless of the name of the particular *namespace*.

Final (Not Modifiable): Java Says "Final" and C# Says "Sealed"

For example, Java may say "public final int b," whereas C# would say "public sealed int b." In both cases, the variable *b* that marked such a modifier will not be modified. It is "final" (I mean "sealed").

Java Says "Instanceof" and C# Says "Is"

In both cases, the meaning is precisely the same. For example, "if (b instanceof A)" is the Java way to determine whether the object named *b* is an instance of class *A*. The same question sounds a bit clearer in C#: "if (b is A)."

Java Says "Synchronized" and C# Says "Lock"

Actually, C# may also say "Synchronized," and in all cases, this is about making data "thread safe." This means locking related data so other threads cannot damage them until a particular task is over.

Note that I actually use the term *lock* to describe this function.

C# (as well as Microsoft in general) consistently looks for simplicity and an intuitive approach recognized by the user.

Java says "import" when the program uses additional libraries. C# prefers to grab the keyword *using*, which Larry Wall introduced in Perl to indicate that a source requires (uses) additional libraries to run.

When a Java program says "import javax.xml.parsers.*," C# would say something like "using System.Xml."

C# has also kept keywords that are familiar to C++ programmers, such as *struct, stackalloc*, and *sizeof*. These keywords provide a bridge not only to C++ but also to C programmers, allowing them, for example, to create data structures inside and outside classes and giving them more freedom in writing non-object-oriented code.

Java and C#, Unlike C++, Disallow Global Methods

All methods must belong to some class. It is harder but still achievable to write non-object-oriented spaghetti code in Java or C#, even though whatever one writes in Java or C#, it must be a set of classes.

There are textbooks that provide examples of Java or C# code encapsulated in a single ***main*** method that can sometimes be very long. Such examples still have a lot of value for an instructor in the second part of his or her presentation on "good and bad programming practices."

A good object-oriented program describes object data at the beginning of the class definition; provides main behavior patterns in class methods that "get," "set," and change the data; and initiates data in their class constructors. The main method usually includes a couple of lines that create the main object and invoke one of its methods.

For example, in Java we would write:

```
public static void main(String[] args) {
    A a = new A();
    a.go();
}
```

The C# source code looks very similar:

```
public static void Main(String[] args) {
    A a = new A();
    a.go();
}
```

The only difference is the main method name.

Java Says "Main," C# Says "Main."

Method naming conventions are different for Java and C#

Java style recommends that method names begin with lowercase letters. This is a part of the Java naming convention. The naming convention for C# method names is different from Java's, but (not surprisingly) the same as C++'s. Method names in C#/C++ start with a capital letter.

Java and C# both have the string class with the same spelling and behavior, but . . .

Java says "String." C# says "String," too. However, C# also allows us to use "string," beginning with lowercase s. In Java, we deal with the *java.lang.String* class, and in C#, the *System.String* class. In both cases, it is an immutable (nonchangeable) object. Each operation on a string creates a new string copy that is returned as a result of the operation.

Java and C# both say "object," but C# also allows us to use "object"

We will discuss two major functions of the programming environment that supports the writing of application scenarios: handling XML and providing direct call connections to a knowledge engine and regular services with the reflection mechanism.

Different Defaults for Data and Method Access

Java and C# may be silent about data and method access, but their silent defaults are different. Here is a Java example:

```
package com.its.examples;
public class JavaExample {
    String text = "I am visible to everyone from my folder.";
    // more code
}
```

A class member with the default access (e.g., string text) is visible to all the classes located in the same package.

Here is an example of access to the string text from another class in the same package:

```
package com.its.examples;
public class AnotherJavaExample {
    // method that access the text variable from the JavaExample
    // class
    public void printThisText() {
```

```
            JavaExample example = new JavaExample();
            System.out.println(example.text);
            // will print the text
        }
    }
```

Default access in C#, as well as C++, is *private*. If one omits an access modifier on a variable or a method in C#/C++, such a class member is considered private, visible only inside the same class.

Here is a C# example:

```
namespase ITS.Examples;
using System;
public class CsExample {
    String text = "I am private!. Only members of this
    class can access me.";
    // more code
    // the getString() publicmethod provides access to the
    private (default) text
    public String getText() {
        return text;
    }
}
```

A class member with default access (e.g., string text) is visible to all classes located in the same package.

Here is an example of access to the string text from another class.

```
namespase ITS.Examples;
using System;
public class AnotherCsExample {
    // method that access the text variable from the JavaExample
    // class
    public void printThisText() {
        CsExample example = new CsExample();
        Console.WriteLine(example.getText());
        // will print the text
    }
}
```

Java and C# both say "protected" to allow derived classes to access parent class members, but Java's *protected* is more generic. Protected class members are visible in Java, not only to derived classes from any package but also to any class from the same package.

C# is more specific and consistent than C++ in its definition of protected access. A protected member in C# can only be accessed by member methods in that class or member methods in derived classes, but is not accessible by any other classes.

C# has two more specific access modifiers that can open wider access for class members. The *internal* modifier opens access to a class member from other classes in the same assembly.

What is assembly?

If you are a Java programmer, think of assembly as a Java Archive (JAR) file. The assembly is a set of classes usually stored as *.EXE or *.DLL files, unlike Java JARs that are stored in ZIP format.

C# also has the combined *internal protected* access modifier that makes a member visible to derived classes or classes that are in the same assembly.

Networking and File Access in Java and C#

Java, as well as C#, uses streams for data communications. Working with files or networks, we establish input and/or output streams between communication points. The endpoint of communications can be, for example, a file or a socket.

Read and write files in Java

Figure A1.1 presents the *readBinFile()* method of the *JavaIOExample* class. The *readBinFile()* method reads a file from a file system or from the Internet. The method starts with a simple check to see if a file name is actually a URL. In this case, the *fetchURL()* method will be called to retrieve data from the Internet. Otherwise (the file name is not a URL), the method creates a file object based on the file name and uses the *length()* method of the *File* class to get the size of the file in bytes. Then, the *readBinFile()* method creates an input stream to the input file and the *while* loop reads the data into the *data* byte array.

Figure A1.2 shows the *writeBinFile()* method of the *JavaIOExample* class. The first method presented in the figure is just a convenience wrapper that can accept only two arguments: a file name and bytes to write. The real work is done in the following method that, besides the file name and the array of bytes, expects the offset and actual number of bytes of the array that will be written into an output file.

Figure A1.3 displays the *copyTextFile()* method, which reads an input file and immediately writes data into an output file.

In all cases, we create a file object and establish a stream to the object. For example:

```
File file=new File(filename);
FileOutputStream out=new FileOutputStream(file);
```

We can streamline these two operations into one line:

```
FileOutputStream out=new FileOutputStream(new File(filename));
```

Then, we use the stream object to read or write data.

For example:

```
out.write(iData, iOffset, iSize);
```

Then, we eventually close the stream:

```
out.close();
```

Read and write files in C#

Figure A1.4 demonstrates a C# example of copying an input file into an output file. The method *CopyTextFile()* of the *CsIOExample* class looks like a sibling of the method *copyTextFile()* of the *JavaIOExample*.

We create an input file and output file objects. Then, we attach streams to the files, and we use a loop to read-write (copy) data.

You can see that the Java and C# source codes are very similar. In the C# code, we go through the same steps, and even the method names are almost the same.

```
/**
 * The class JavaIOExample handles file i/o and retrieves
 * data from the web
 * @author jeff.zhuk@JavaSchool.com
 */
package com.its.examples;

import java.net.* ;
import java.io.* ;

public class JavaIOExample
{
   // more code

    /**
     * The readBinFile() method reads a binary file from a
     * file system or the Internet
     * @param filename
     * @return bytes
     */
    public static byte[] readBinFile(String filename)
    {
        // check if filename is actually a URL - in this
        // case go to the Internet for data
        if(filename.startsWith("http://") || filename.
        startsWith("HTTP://")) { return fetchURL(filename);
            // The fetchURL() method uses URLConnection to retrieve data
        }
        // a regular file: create a file object and attach an input stream
        try {
            File file = new File(filename);
            int size = (int) file.length();
            byte[] data = new byte[size];
            int bytesread = 0;
            int offset = 0;
            FileInputStream in = new FileInputStream(file);
            if(in == null)
            {
                return null;
            }
            // reading bytes from the file
            while(bytesread < size)
            {
                bytesread +=
                in.read(data, offset, size-bytesread);
                offset += bytesread;
            }
            in.close();
            return data;
        }
        catch (Exception e)
        {
            return null;
        }
    } // more code...
```

FIGURE A1.1

```
/**
 * The writeBinFile() method is a wrapper to the method
 * with more arguments that writes a binary file
 * @param filename
 * @param iData bytes to write
 * @return true if success
 */
public static boolean writeBinFile(String filename, byte[] iData) {
    if(iData == null)
        return false;
    return writeBinFile(filename, iData, 0,
    iData.length);
}
/**
 * The writeBinFile() method writes a binary file
 * @param filename
 * @param iData bytes to write
 * @param iOffset starting byte of the source
 * @param iSize number of bytes to write
 * @return true if success
 */
public static boolean writeBinFile(String filename, byte[] iData,
int iOffset, int iSize) {
    try{
        File file=new File(filename);
        FileOutputStream out=new FileOutputStream(file);
        out.write(iData, iOffset, iSize);
        out.close();
        return true;
    } catch (IOException ioe) {
        if(debug)
            System.out.println("writeBinFile: " + ioe);
        return false;
    }
}
```

FIGURE A1.2

Retrieve data from the Web in Java

Figure A1.5 presents the *fetchURL()* method of the *JavaIOExample* class. The *fetchURL()* method creates a *URLConnection* object based on the URL provided as an argument to the method. The endpoint is not a file but a *URLConnection*.

The following steps are the same as those for reading files. Based on the endpoint (in this case, the *URLConnection* object), we create an input stream and read data from this stream using the *readFromStream()* helper method.

When we deal with a network object, it is harder to define the object size upfront as we did while reading file objects. Reading files, we were able to allocate a fixed-size byte array.

```
/**
 * The copyTextFile() method copies an input file into
 * an output file
 * @param inputFilename
 * @param outputFilename
 * @return true if success
 */
public static boolean copyTextFile(Striing inputFilename,
outputFilename) {
    try
    {
       // create input file object and input stream
       BufferedReader in =
         new BufferedReader(new FileReader
         (inputFilename));
       // output stream
       PrintWriter out = new PrintWriter(new BufferedWriter
          (new FileWriter(iFilename)));
       String line = null; // init line to read
       while((line = in.readLine()) != null) {
       // read  untill the end of the file
       // out.println(line);
       // copy input line into output file
       }
       in.close();
       out.close();
       return true;
    }
    catch (Exception e)
    {
       return false;
    }
}
// more code
```

FIGURE A1.3

In the *readFromStream()* method we create a *ByteArrayOutputStream* instead and use this stream to write data directly into memory. This is a very convenient way to use memory to accumulate data.

The *while* loop that reads data from the Internet is finished when there is nothing more to read. At this point, we take the *tempBuffer* stream object in which we accumulated data and convert it into a regular byte array.

Done!

Retrieve data from the Web in C#

Figure A1.6 presents the *FetchURL()* method of the *CsIOExample* class. The *FetchURL()* method creates a *WebClient* object and uses the *DownloadData()* method of the *WebClient* class to download the data from the net based on the URL provided as an argument to the method.

```
using System;
using System.IO;
using System.Net;

namespace ITSCsExamples {
  // example of reading and writing text files
  // public class CsIOExample {
    // The CopyTextFile() method reads an input file
    // and writes its data into an output file
    // The method returns true if success
    // public static boolean CopyTextFile(string
    inputFilename, string outputFilename) {
        try {
            FileStream inputFile = new FileStream
            (inputFilename, FileMode.Open);
            FileStream outputFile = new FileStream
            (outputFilename, FileMode.Open);
            StreamReader reader = new StreamReader
            (inputFile);
            StreamWriter writer = new StreamWriter
            (outputFile);
            String aLine;
            // read
            while((aLine = reader.ReadLine())!= null){
                writer.Write(aLine);
            }
            reader.Close();
            writer.Close();
            return true;
        } catch(Exception e) {
            return false;
        }
    }
    // The Main() method is to test the class
    public static void Main(string[] args) {
        boolean success = CsIOExample.CopyTextFile
        ("CsIOExample.cs", "CsIOExample.cs.copy");
        Console.Write("success of file copy is " +
        success);
    }

    // more code

  }   // end of class
}     // end of namespace
```

FIGURE A1.4

```
/**
 * @param urlString (with arguments if needed )
 * @return data from the Internet
 */
public static byte[] fetchURL(String urlString) {
    try {
        URL url = new URL(urlString);
        urlConnectionection urlConnection =
        url.openConnection();
        // try to get the file size
        int length=urlConnection.getContentLength();
        // create an input stream based on the connection
        DataInputStream inputStream=(new
        InputStream(urlConnection.getInputStream());
        return readFromStream(inputStream, length);
   } catch(Exception e) {
       System.out.println("fetchURL:url=" + url + " e=" + e);
       return null;
   }
}   /**
 * The readFromStream() method reads byte array from an input stream
 * @param inputStream
 * @param length optional size of data to read in
 * bytes if available
 * @return bytes
 */
public static byte[] readFromStream(InputStream inputStream, int length)
throws Exception {
    ByteArrayOutputStream tempBuffer;
    if(length <= 0) {  // if size is unknown
        tempBuffer=new ByteArrayOutputStream();
    } else {
        tempBuffer=new ByteArrayOutputStream(length);
    }
    // allocate a byte array buffer and use it to read into memory
    byte buf[] = new byte[1024];
    int counter = 0;
    while ((counter = inputStream.read(buf)) > 0)  {
        tempBuffer.write(buf, 0, counter);
    }
    // reading is done
    //convert accumulated data to a regular byte array
    byte[] bytes = tempBuffer.toByteArray();
    return bytes;
    }
}   // end of JavaIOExample class
```

FIGURE A1.5

```
/**
 * @param url
 * @return data from the Internet
 */
[STAThread]
public static byte[] FetchURL(string url) {
    // create a web client object
    WebClient client=new WebClient();
    // download data from the network using url
    byte[] data = client.DownloadData(url);
    return data;
}
```

FIGURE A1.6

Java and C# Sockets

Server socket listener in Java

Figure A1.7 presents an example of a server socket listener on the local network. This is a simple example of a server socket in which the server daemon is waiting for client requests and starts a service thread for each client. The constructor takes a port number argument and creates a server socket.

The *run()* method starts the *while* loop listening for client service requests and starts a service thread for each client.

The *setListening()* method is a convenient helper that can set the *listening* flag that serves as a condition for the *while* loop.

The *main()* method gives the class the test; it creates a server socket daemon object on port number 11000 and starts the listening thread. Remember that according to Java specifications, *thread.start()* invokes the *run()* method of the thread.

The ServiceThreadExample Serves an XML-Based Service Request

Figure A1.8 shows the *ServiceThreadExample*. This is a service thread example that serves network clients connected over TCP/IP sockets. The service thread takes a client socket as an argument in its constructor.

The *run()* method of the *ServiceThreadExample* retrieves a service request and parameters from the input stream attached to the socket. Then, the *run()* method passes the client request to the *performService()* method of the *ServiceConnector* class.

The clientRequest line may be present in XML format or as a method signature.

Here is an example of the XML format:

```
<act service="ITSeMailClient" action="sendMail"
to="jeff.zhuk@javaschool.com" subject="hi!" body="How are you?" />
```

```
// JavaServerSocketExample
package com.its.examples;
import java.net.*;
import java.io.*;

/**
 * This is a simple server socket example
 * server daemon is waiting for client requests and
 * starts a service thread for each client
 * @author Jeff.Zhuk@JavaSchool.com
 */
public class JavaServerSocketExample extends Thread {
    private ServerSocket server = null;
    private boolean listening = true;
    public JavaServerSocketExample(int port) {
        // Open server socket and listen for client
        // requests in the constructor
        // register server socket on the port = iPort
        try {
            server = new ServerSocket(port);
        } catch (IOException e) {
            System.out.err("Server socket failure: " + e);
            return;
        }
}
/**
 * The run() method is invoked by thread.start()
 */
public void run() {
    // start indefinite loop waiting for clients to request the
    // connection
    while(listening) {
        try {
            // listen for a client connection request
            // and accept when requested
            Socket client = server.accept();
            // create a ServiceThread object and start the thread
            ServiceThreadExample serviceThread = new
            ServiceThreadExample(client);
            serviceThread.start();
        } catch (IOException e) {
            System.out.err("Server socket failure: " + e);
    }
}  // end of method
```

FIGURE A1.7

```
/**
 * The setListening() method sets the state to false or true
 * @param listeningState
 */
public void setListening(boolean listeningState) {
listening = listeningState;
}
/**
 * The main() method is to test the class
 */
public static void main(String[] args) {
    JavaServerSocketExample listener = new
    JavaServerSocketExample(11000);
    listener.start();
    // start the thread - daemon listening to client requests
}
}   // end of class
```

FIGURE A1.7. (*cont.*)

and an example of the method signature:

```
ITSeMailClient.sendMail("jeff.zhuk@javaschool.com","hi!.", "How are
you?");
```

The *performService()* method of the *ServiceConnector* class parses the client request string and performs exactly the same operation in both cases.

Also in both cases, the *ITSeMailClient* class is loaded and its object instance is created. Then, the method *sendMail()* of this class is called with three parameters.

The *ServiceConnector* class has a registry of objects, which helps load new classes only for the first service call. Then, the same object may be reused for subsequent service requests.

The *setPerform()*method is a convenient helper that can set the *perform* flag that serves as a condition for the *while* loop.

A server socket listener in C#

Figure A1.9 displays an example of a server socket listener in C#. The *CsServerSocketExample* class is a simple server socket example. The constructor of the *CsServerSocketExample* takes a port number argument and creates a server socket.

The *Start()* method starts the *while* loop listening for client service requests and uses the *PerformService()* method of the *ServiceConnector* class to serve clients. (Wait for the Reflection topic to consider the *ServiceConnector* class in C#.)

A slight difference in handling data with C# sockets is that the *Receive()* method of the *Socket* class in C# creates streams internally, on the fly.

We use the *Encoding.ASCII.GetString()* method to convert the byte array into a string.

This example closes the socket after a single service request, which is completely optional. In some cases, it is preferable to continue client-server communications beyond a single service request.

```
// ServiceThreadExample
package com.its.examples;
import java.net.*;
import java.io.*;
/**
 * This is a service thread example that serves network clients connected
 * over TCP/IP sockets
 * The thread retrieves service request and parameters from the input
 * stream attached to the socket
 * Then the run() method passes the client request to
 * the performService() method of the ServiceConnector class
 * The clientRequest line can be present in XML format or as a method
 * signature
 * XML example:
 * "<act service="className" action="methodName" .. parameters .. />"
 * A method signature format example:
 * ITSeMailClient.sendMail("jeff.zhuk@javaschool.com", "..subject..",
 * ".. message..");
 * Service class will be loaded and service object instance created
 * only for the first service call
 * Then the same object can be reused for subsequent service requests
 *
 * @author Jeff.Zhuk@JavaSchool.com
 */
public class ServiceThreadExample extends Thread {
    private Socket client = null;
    private boolean perform = true;
    public ServiceThreadExample(Socket client) {
        this.client = client;
    }
    /**
     * The setPerform() method sets the state to false or true
     * @param performState
     */
    public void setListening(boolean performState) {
        perform = performState;
    }
    /**
     * The run() method is invoked by thread.start()
     */
    public void run() {
       // start indefinite loop waiting for clients to request the
       // connection
       // uses ServiceConnector.performService() to serve clients
        while(perform) {
           try {
             // connect input/output streams to the socket
             DataInputStream in = new DataInputStream
             (client.getInputStream());
             PrintStream out = new PrintStream (client.getOutputStream());
```

FIGURE A1.8

```
            // read client request, a string is expected, not bytes!
            String clientRequest = in.readLine();
            // process this client request and get a response for a client
            // The clientRequest line can be present in XML format or as a
            // method signature
            // XML example:
            // "<act service="className" action="methodName" ..
            // parameters .. />"
            // A method signature format example:
            // ITSeMailClient.sendMail("jeff.zhuk@javaschool.com",
            // "..subject..", ".. message..");
            // Service class will be loaded and service object
            // instance created only for the first service call
            // Then the same object can be reused for subsequent
            // service requests
            // String response = ServiceConnector.performService
            // (clientRequest); // service
            // Send the response back to the client out.println(response);
            // close the client connection, keep alive the server socket
            // closing client socket is an optional action that depends
            // on the client-server protocol
            // in some cases it would be preferable to continue
            // client-server communications beyond a single service
            // request
            client.close();
        } catch (IOException e) {
           System.out.err("Server socket failure: " + e);
        }
    }
} // end of method
```

FIGURE A1.8. *(cont.)*

The *Main()* method gives the class the test. The method creates a server socket daemon object on port number 11000 and invokes the *Start()* method with its *while* loop that listens to client requests.

As you can see, C# and Java socket handling is very similar.

A client socket example in Java

Figure A1.10 presents the *JavaClientSocket* class that can work with both server daemons: the *JavaServerSocketExample* implemented in Java and the *CsServerSocketExample* implemented in C#.

The constructor establishes a socket connection to a server using two arguments: the host name and the port number.

The *getService()* method requests a service and returns a service response. The method takes a service request as a string argument and converts the string into a byte array. Then, the method sends the *serviceRequest* as the byte array to the server.

The *getService()* method reuses the *readFromStream()* method provided in the *JavaIOExample* class to receive the response from the server. The method closes the client socket

```
using System;
using System.Net;
using System.Net.Sockets;
using System.Text;
using System.Threading;

namespace ITSCsExamples {
    /**
     * This is a simple server socket example
     * server daemon is waiting for client requests and starts a service
     * thread for each client
     * @author Slava.Minukhin@JavaSchool.com,
     * Jeff.Zhuk@JavaSchool.com
     */
    public class CsServerSocketExample
    {
        private boolean listening = true;
        private Socket socketListener = null;
        [STAThread]
        static void Main(string[]  args)
        {
            CsServerSocketExample listener =
            CsServerSocketExample(11000);
            listener.Start();
        }
        public CsServerSocketExample(int port)
        {
            // Data buffer for incoming data.
            try {
                // Establish the local endpoint for the  socket.
                // Dns.GetHostName returns the name of the
                // host running the application.
                IPHostEntry ipHostInfo =
                Dns.Resolve(Dns.GetHostName());
                IPAddress ipAddress = ipHostInfo.AddressList[0];
                IPEndPoint localEndPoint = new
                IPEndPoint(ipAddress, port);

                // Create a TCP/IP socket.
                listener = new Socket(AddressFamily.InterNetwork,
                    SocketType.Stream, ProtocolType.Tcp );
                // Bind the socket to the local endpoint and listen for
                // incoming connections.

                listener.Bind(localEndPoint);
                listener.Listen(10);
            } catch (Exception e) {
                Console.WriteLine(e.ToString());
            }
        }
        // start indefinite loop waiting for clients to request
        // the connection
```

FIGURE A1.9

```
        // uses ServiceConnector.PerformService() to serve clients
        public void Start() {
            byte[] bytes = new Byte[1024];
            Socket handler = null;
            string clientRequest = null;
            string response = null;

            // start indefinite loop waiting for clients to request
            // the connection
            while ( listening ) {
                try {
                    // listen for a client connection request and accept
                    // when requested
                    // handler = listener.Accept();

                    // get client request in bytes
                    int bytesRecieved = handler.Receive(bytes);
                    // translate bytes to a string
                    clientRequest = Encoding.ASCII.GetString
                    (bytes,0,bytesRecieved);

                    // process this client request and get a response for
                    // a client
                    // The clientRequest line can be present in XML format
                    // or as a method signature
                    // XML example:
                    // "<act service="" action="methodName"
                    // .. parameters .. />"
                    // A method signature format example.
                    // ITSeMailClient.SendMail ("jeff.zhuk@javaschool.com",
                    // "..subject..", ".. message..");
                    // Service class will be loaded and service object
                    // instance created only for the first service call
                    // Then the same object can be reused for subsequent
                    // service requests

                    response = ServiceConnector.
                    PerformService(clientRequest);

                    // Send the response back to the client

                    handler.Send(Encoding.ASCII.
                    GetBytes(response));
                    // close the client connection, keep
                    // alive the server socket
                    // closing client socket is an optional action that
                    // depends on the client-server protocol

                    // in some cases it would be preferable to continue
                    // client-server communications beyond a single
                    // service request
                    handler.Shutdown(SocketShutdown.Both);
                    handler.Close();
```

FIGURE A1.9. ***(cont.)***

```
                    // exit program (just for example)
                    Environment.Exit( 0 );
                }
            } catch (Exception e) {
                Console.WriteLine(e.ToString());
            }
        }
    }
}
```

FIGURE A1.9. *(cont.)*

streams; however, this action is optional and depends on the client–server protocol. In some cases, it is preferable to continue client–server communications beyond a single service request.

The *getService()* method receives the server response as an array of bytes and immediately converts the array into a string just to return the string to a calling procedure.

The *main()* method serves as the testing mechanism. We start the *main()* method by setting basic parameters, such as a host name, port number, and service request. The *main()* method creates the *JavaClientSocket* object and invokes the *getService()* method on this object. We end up with the *main()* method displaying the server response on the screen.

More ways to create sockets in C#

C# offers several socket classes, so there is more than one way to create sockets in C#. For example, we can use the *TcpListener* class (part of the *System.Net.Sockets* namespace) to create a server listener:

```
    TcpListener tcpListener = new TcpListener(11000);  // port number
            tcpListener.Start(); // start listening!
            // Accept requested connections
            Socket clientSocketCounterpart =
tcpListener.AcceptSocket();
```

C# offers input and output stream classes, such as *NetworkStream, StreamWriter*, and *StreamReader*, for reading and writing data to and from sockets.

Here is an example of C# code establishing streams to read and write text data:

```
if (socketForClient.Connected) {
    // creat generic network stream a base for input/output  stream
    NetworkStream networkStream = new NetworkStream
    (clientSocketCounterpart);
    // create output stream
    // StreamWriter streamWriter = new  StreamWriter(networkStream);
    // create input stream
    // StreamReader streamReader = new  StreamReader(networkStream);
    // read text line from the network
    string line = streamReader.ReadLine();
    // write text line to the network
    streamWriter.WriteLine(line);
}
```

```
// JavaClientSocketExample

package com.its.examples;

import java.net.*;

import java.io.*;

/**
 * This is a client socket example
 * The client establishes a connection to a server and requests a service
 * @author Jeff.Zhuk@JavaSchool.com
 */
public class JavaClientSocketExample {
    private Socket socket;
    private DataInputStream dis;
    private DataOutputStream dos;
    /**
     * The constructor establishes a socket connection to a server
     * @param host name like "IPServe.com"
     * @port number like 5555
     * @@author Jeff.Zhuk@JavaSchool.com
     */
    public JavaClientSocketExample(String host, int port) {
       try
       {
            // request a socket connection
            socket = new Socket(host, port);
            // create i/o streams with the socket end point
            dis = new DataInputStream(new
            InputStream(socket.getInputStream()));
            dos = new DataOutputStream(new
            OutputStream(socket.getOutputStream()));
       } catch (Exception e) {
            System.out.println("ERROR: Connection failure: " + e);
            }
    }
    /**
     * The getService() method requests a service and returns a
     * service response
     * @param serviceRequest
     * @return response or error message if failure
     * @@author Jeff.Zhuk@JavaSchool.com
     */
    public String getService(String serviceRequest) {
        // send serviceRequest to the server dos.write
           (serviceRequest.getBytes());
        // receive response from the server
        // reuse the readFromStream() method provided in the
           JavaIOExample class
        byte[] responseInBytes = JavaIOExample.
        readFromStream(dis, 0); // 0-indicates unknown data size
```

FIGURE A1.10

```
        // close the client socket streams
        // closing client socket is an optional action that depends on
        // the client-server protocol

        // in some cases it would be preferable to continue client-server
        // communications beyond a single service request

        dos.close();
        dis.close();

        return (new String(responseInBytes));
        // convert bytes to string
    } catch (Exception e) {
        return ("ERROR: client network problem " + e);
    }
    /**
     * The main() method can test the class
     * @param args
     */
    public static void main(String[] args) {
        String host = "javaschool.com";
        int port = 11000;
        String serviceRequest = "ITSeMailClient.SendMail
        (\"jeff.zhuk@javaschool.com\",\"hi!\", \"How are you?\")";
        JavaClientSocketExample clientSocket = new
        JavaClientSocketExample(host, port);
        String response = clientSocket.getService(serviceRequest);
        System.out.println(response);
    }
}
```

FIGURE A1.10. *(cont.)*

Throughout this book, we consistently used XML-based scenarios to invoke needed services. We also used them in the *JavaServerSocketExample*, as well as in the *CsServerSocketExample*. In both cases, we referred to the *ServerConnector* class that performed a needed service for us.

We need to find a proper class, discover the methods in the class, and, according to an XML scenario, invoke the proper methods at run-time. This ability is called *reflection*. There are two packages, *java.lang.ref* and *java.lang.reflect*, that help us perform this magic in Java.

Perform Services Using Reflection in C# and Java

In Chapter 13, we considered the *ServiceConnector* class, which uses the power of Java Reflection. Here, we extend that example. (See Appendix 3 for the complete source code for the *ServiceConnector* class.)

Figure A1.11 shows the *performService()* and *getInstance()* methods of the *ServiceConnector* class.

The *performService()* method determines whether the service request is an XML string. For example:

```
<act service="ITSeMailClient" action="sendMail"
    to="jeff.zhuk@javaschool.com" subject="hi!" body="How are you?" />
```

```
/**
 * The performService() method checks if the service request is an
 * XML string
 * In this case the performService() method uses XML parser
 * to create a table of service parameters
 * The service request can have a form of a method  signature.
 * Such request will be parsed by the performAction()  method.
 * In both cases an instance of the ServiceConnector class will be
 * used to process the service request
 * @param serviceRequest
 * @return response
 */
public static String performService(String serviceRequest) {
    if(serviceRequest == null || serviceRequest.trim().equals("")) {
        return null;
    }
    serviceRequest = serviceRequest.trim();
    // get an instance of the ServiceConnector class
    ServiceConnector connector = getInstance();
    // check if it is an XML request
    // Example:
    // <act service="ITSeMailClient" action="sendMail"
    //   to="jeff.zhuk@javaschool.com" subject="hi!"
    //   body="How are you?" />
    if(serviceRequest.startsWith("<") &&
    serviceRequest.endsWith
    (">") ) {
        Hashtable parameters = Stringer.parse(serviceRequest);
        String className = (String)parameters.get("service");
        String methodName = (String)parameters.get("action");
        Object[] objects = new Object[1];
        objects[0] = parameters;
        return (String)getInstance().act(className,
        methodName, objects);
    }
    // service request looks like a method signarure Example:
    // ITSeMailClient.sendMail("jeff.zhuk@javaschool.com",
    // "hi!.", "How are you?");
    // The performAction() method parses the signature and
    // uses the act() method to invoke the service
    return getInstance().performAction(serviceRequest);
```

FIGURE A1.11

In this case, the *performService()* method uses the XML parser to create a table of service parameters that includes a class name, a method name, and other relevant parameters. After retrieving service parameters from the XML string, the *performService()* method calls the *act()* method of the *ServiceConnector* class to actually perform the service. The *Stringer.parse()* method can be found in Appendix 3.

The service request can also have a form of method signature. For example:

```
ITSeMailClient.sendMail("jeff.zhuk@javaschool.com", "hi!.", "How are
you?");
```

Such a request is parsed by the *performAction()* method.

In both cases, an instance of the *ServiceConnector* class is used to process the service request.

The *getInstance()* method of the *ServiceConnector* class is a static method. This method helps to create (if necessary) and support a single instance of the *ServiceConnector* class per application. The method implements the Singleton design pattern. The implementation is based on the *instance* static variable. The method creates this object if the object has not been created yet (object value equals null).

Why is it important to follow the Singleton design pattern and limit the service connector by a single instance?

The service connector keeps service objects in the table (*Hashtable*) of acting objects. It is important to invoke methods on the same objects in their current state instead of creating new objects upon new service requests.

Later in this appendix, we will see examples of service object reuse and service invocations.

Figure A1.12 displays the *act()* method of the *ServiceConnector* class. The *act()* method uses a default acting class if a class name is not provided in the service parameters. The method checks to see if it is necessary to change the current acting object and changes it (if necessary) using the *changeActingClass()* method. Then, the *act()* method examines the parameter objects and tries to identify parameter types or classes using the *object.getClass()* method.

Now we are armed with information about the acting object, acting method name, and method parameter types. This should be enough to find a proper method of the class using the powerful reflection method *getMethod()* of the *java.lang.Class* class.

Unfortunately, the *Class.getMethod()* has a problem: parameter types are often subclasses of required parameter classes.

For example, the *readFromStream()* method of the *JavaIOExample* class provided in Fig. A1.6 expects the *InputStream* parameter. This method can still accept any of the subclasses of the *InputStream*, such as the *FileInputStream, ByteArrayInputStream*, and *FilterInputStream*.

Figure A1.6 also shows the *fetchURL()* method that invokes the *readFromStream* method with the *DataInputStream* argument.

This is perfectly alright for the run-time method invocation. Unfortunately, the *Class.getMethod()* can find the method only if we pass the exact parameter types. The *Class.getMethod()* throws an exception if we try to find the method that has the name *readFromStream* and may take the *DataInputStream* argument.

To work around this problem, I wrote another version of the *getMethod()* presented in Fig. A1.13. If the first attempt to find a proper method with the *Class.getMethod()* fails the second time, this version will be used instead.

The *getMethod()* helps us work around a common problem in the *Class.getMethod()* that expects exact parameter type matches. Exact matches rarely happen in real programs. Parameter types are often subclasses of required argument classes.

The version of the *getMethod()* presented in Fig. A1.13 uses the more sensitive Java Reflection mechanism offered by the *Class.isAssignableFrom()* method while checking for

```
/**
 * The act() method provides a unified way to find a  requested method
 * and invokes the method on previously defined object.
 * There is a different version of the method for J2ME implementation
 * @param methodName
 * @param parameters
 * @return result
 * @@author Jeff.Zhuk@JavaSchool.com
 */
public Object act(String methodName, Object[] parameters) {
    // use currentl acting class as default
    return act(actingClassName, methodName, parameters);
}
/**
 * The act() method provides a unified way to find a requested method
 * and invokes the method on an instance of the class defined by the
 * class name parameter
 * There is a different version of the method for J2ME implementation
 * @param className
 * @param methodName
 * @param parameters
 * @return result
 */
public Object act(String className, String methodName, Object[]
parameters) {
    // prepare error message (just in case)
    String errorMessage = "ERROR: " + className + "." + methodName +
    " service is not available";
    try {
        changeActingClass(className); // change acting class if
                                      // necessary, or leave as is
    } catch(Exception ce) {
        System.out.println("ERROR: changeActingClass " +
        className + " e=" + ce);
    }
    Class[] classes = null;
    if(parameters != null) {
        classes = new Class[parameters.length];
        for(int i=0; i<parameters.length; i++) {
            classes[i] = parameters[i].getClass();
        }
    }
    try {
        method = actingClass.getMethod(methodName, classes);
        if(method == null) { // this method never produces exceptions
            method = getMethod(methodName, classes);
        }
if(debug)
System.out.println("act:method=" + method);
```

FIGURE A1.12

```
        } catch (Exception e) {
            // another try with more precision
            method = getMethod(methodName, classes);
        }
        if(method == null) {
            return errorMessage;
        }
        try {
            result = method.invoke(actingObject, parameters);
        } catch (Exception e) {
            return errorMessage;
        }
        return result;
    }
```

Figure A1.12. *(cont.)*

method compatibility. The *Class.isAssignableFrom()* method returns true not only on the exact match of a class but also on its subclasses.

Perform Services Using Reflection in C#

C# is also very familiar with reflection features. The *System.Reflection* namespace provides classes such as *MethodInfo*, and *ParameterInfo*, similar to Java classes.

There is a slight difference between reflection in Java and in C#. Java can load the class file from a targeted classpath or resource file. The classpath may include JAR files that Java can uncompress on the fly.

Reflection in C# is provided at the assembly level, whereas reflection in Java is done at the class level. Assemblies are typically stored in DLLs or EXE files, and the programmer must know the proper file name, with the DLL or executable assembly, in which the class file is located.

Examples of the *ServiceConnector* class implementation in C# are presented in Figs. A1.14 through A1.16.

The *ServiceConnector* class invokes a selected method on a selected class instance. The *ServiceConnector* can actually play not only its own (object) role but as a good actor, can also play objects of any (existing) type. If necessary, the *ServiceConnector* loads a new class at run-time. The *ServiceConnector* also has a registry in which it keeps (and reuses) all object-actors.

The beginning of the *ServiceConnector* class is shown in Fig. A1.14. The *ServiceConnector* class members include the *actingClass, actingObject*, and currently performed *method* objects. The table of *actingObjects (Hashtable)* serves as a registry to keep and reuse actor-objects that once were called onstage.

The default constructor sets a current class and current object as current actors. The other constructor takes a class name as an argument and uses the *changeActingClass()* method to set this particular class as the current object-actor.

Figure A1.15 shows the *act()* method of the *ServiceConnector* class. The *act()* method uses its arguments (class name, method name, and method parameters) to find a proper object and a method with the reflection mechanism and to invoke this method on the selected object.

```
/**
 * The getMethod() helps to work around a common problem
 * in the Class.getMethod() that expects exact parameter types match.
 * The exact match is rarely happens in real programs.
 * Parameter types are often subclasses of required argument classes.
 * This version of the getMethod() uses more sensitive Java reflection
 * mechanism offered by the Class.isAssignableFrom() method
 * while checking for method compatibility.
 * The Class.isAssignableFrom() method returns true not only
 * on the exact class match but also on its subclasses
 * @param methodName
 * @param parameters
 * @return method
 */
public Method getMethod(String methodName, Class[] parameters) {
    if(methodName == null) return null;
    try {
        Method[] methods = actingClass.getMethods();
        Method method = null;
        for(int i=0; i<methods.length; i++) {
          if(!methodName.equals(methods[i].getName())) continue;
          Class[] classes = methods[i].getParameterTypes();
          if(parameters.length != classes.length)continue;
          method = methods[i];
          for(int j=0; method != null && j<parameters.
          length; j++) {
             if(!(classes[j].isAssignableFrom(parameters[j]))
             ) {
                 method = null; // failure
             }
          }
          if(method != null) {
              return method;
          }
        }
    } catch(Exception e) {
        return null;
    }
    return method; // null
}
```

FIGURE A1.13

We find that the code in this section is very similar to that in Java implementation. Two key lines look exactly like Java lines, except for the method name capitalization.

```
// find the method
method = actingClass.GetMethod(methodName, classes);
// invoke the method
result = method.Invoke(actingObject, parameters);
```

Figure A1.16 displays the rest of the *ServiceConnector* example in C#.

```
using System;
using System.Reflection;
using System.Collections;
namespace ITSCsExamples {
    /**
     * The ServiceConnector class invokes a selected method on a selected
     * class instance
     * The ServiceConnector can actually play not only its own (object) role
     * As a good actor it can also play objects of any (existing) types
     * If necessary the ServiceConnector loads a new class at  runtime
     * The ServiceConnector has also a registry where it keeps (and reuses)
     * all object-actors
     * @author Jeff.Zhuk@JavaSchool.com, Slava.
     * Minukhin@JavaSchool.com
     */
    public class ServiceConnector {
        protected Object[] parameters;
        protected Object result;
        protected MethodInfo method;
        protected Object actingObject;
        protected Type actingClass;
        protected String actingClassName;
        protected String connectorClassName;
        protected Hashtable actingObjects;

        public ServiceConnector()
        {
            actingClass = GetType();
            actingClassName = actingClass.Name;
            connectorClassName = GetType().Name;
            actingObjects = new Hashtable();
        }
        /**
         * The constructor creates an object of a requested class
         * It a requested class name is "ServiceConnector" there is
         * nothing to do
         * In this case the actingObject is "this"
         */
        public ServiceConnector(String className) {
            Console.WriteLine("ServiceConnector:className="
            + className + " actingClassName=" + actingClassName);
            // include package name in the className to increase efficiency
            try{
                changeActingClass(className);
            } catch (Exception e) {
                Console.WriteLine("ERROR:ServiceConnector:" + e);
            }
        }
        // more code
```

FIGURE A1.14

```
/**
 * The act() method provides a unified way to find a requested  method
 * and invoke the method on previously defined object
 * @param methodName
 * @param parameters
 * @return result
 */
public Object act(String className, String methodName, object[]
parameters) {
    try {
        changeActingClass(className);
        // change acting class if necessary, or leave as is
    } catch(Exception ce) {
        System.out.println("ERROR: changeActingClass " + className + "
        e=" + ce);
    }
    try {
        Type[] classes = null;
        if(parameters != null) {
            classes = new Type[parameters.Length];
            for(int i=0; i<parameters.Length; i++) {
                classes[i] = parameters[i].GetType();
            }
        }
        // find the method
        method = actingClass.GetMethod(methodName, classes);
    } catch (Exception e) {
        return ("ERROR:ServiceConnector.cannot find the
        method:actingClass=" +
          actingClass + " methodName=" + methodName + " parameters=" +
          parameters + " e=" +e);
    }
    try {
        // invoke the method
        result = method.Invoke(actingObject, parameters);
    } catch (Exception e) {
        return ("ERROR:ServiceConnector.cannot execute the
        method:" +
                methodName + " with actingClassName=" +
                actingClassName +
                " on actingObject=" + actingObject + " e=" + e);
    }
    return result;
}
```

FIGURE A1.15

The *changeActingClass()* method takes a class name as the argument and tries to bring an object of this type onto the stage. The method uses its arguments (class name, method name, and method parameters) to find the proper object and method with the reflection

```
/**
 * changeActingClass() instantiates a new object of a new acting class
 * if necessary
 * @param className
 */
public void changeActingClass(String className)
{
    if(className.Equals(connectorClassName) )
    { // actor="ServiceConnector"
       actingObject = this;
        if(actingObjects[className] == null)
        {
            actingObjects.Add(className, actingObject);
            actingClass = actingObject.GetType();
        }
    } else if(!className.Equals(actingClassName)) {
    // load the class and instantiate the object
        if(actingObjects[className] == null)
        {
            // load a class from an assembly at runtime
            actingClass = Type.GetType(className);
            // activate (instantiate) an object of the type
            actingObject = Activator.CreateInstance( actingClass );
            // register the object
            actingObjects.Add(className, actingObject);
        }
        else
        { // use existing object
            actingObject = actingObjects[className];
            actingClass = actingObject.GetType();
        }
    }
    actingClassName = className;
}
/**
 * registerClass() register objects in the Hashtable actingObjects
 * @param className
 * @param object
 */
public void registerObject(String className, Object o)
{
    if(actingObjects[className] == null)
        actingObjects.Add(className, o);
}
    }   // end of class
} // end of namespace
```

FIGURE A1.16

mechanism and to invoke this method on the selected object. If this does not return true, the *changeActingClass()* method looks into the table of actors, and if an object of the proper type is there, it just reuses this object.

Real work needs to be done if a fresh, new class type is needed to perform a service. This time, the magic of reflection does its best in the following two lines:

```
// load a class from an assembly at runtime
actingClass = Type.GetType(className);
// activate (instantiate) an object of the type
actingObject = Activator.CreateInstance( actingClass );
```

The next thing the program does is register the object in the table of acting objects:

```
// register the object
actingObjects.Add(className, actingObject);
```

Handling XML Scenarios with C#

Microsoft .NET (besides being a marketing term) supports XML with a set of classes collected in several namespaces.

The *System.Xml* namespace contains major XML classes to read and write XML documents. There are four reader classes: *XmlReader, XmlTextReader, XmlValidatingReader*, and *XmlNodeReader*. There are also two writer classes—*XmlWriter* and *XmlTextWriter*—plus several more classes helping to navigate through nodes and perform other tasks.

The *System.Xml.Schema* namespace includes classes such as *XmlSchema, XmlSchemaAll, XmlSchemaXPath*, and *XmlSchemaType* that work with XML schemas.

The *System.Xml.Serialization* namespace contains classes responsible for serialization of C# objects into XML documents.

The *System.Xml.XPath* namespace contains *XPathDocument*, *XPathExression*, *XPathNavigator*, and *XpathNodeIterator* classes that use *XPath* specification to navigate though XML documents.

The *System.Xml.Xsl* namespace is responsible for XSL/T transformations.

As you can see, the .NET side of the development community is well armed for XML processing. There is a great support in .NET (as well as in the Java world) for Simple API (application program interface) for XML (SAX) and Document Object Model (DOM) XML processing.

If we want to proceed with a thin solution (minimum package-namespaces), we can use a source similar to *Stringer.parse()* (see Appendix 3). We can even directly translate this Java code into C# using the Microsoft Java Language Conversion Assistant (JLCA) [1], which helps convert existing Java language source code into C#.

The *ParseXML.cpp* source written in C++ (see Appendix 3) may be considered for the limited resources of wireless devices.

Graphical User Interfaces in Java and C#

C# programs use MS Windows calls to create screen widgets. Windows Forms are a new style of MS Windows application built around the System.WinForms namespace. Windows programmers can use a unified Windows Forms API from any language (including C#) supported by MS Visual Studio .NET.

Although the Windows Forms solution supports a unified graphical user interface (GUI) API through multiple languages targeting a single (Windows) platform, Java focuses on multiple platforms that support the Java language.

The Java GUI is based on the Abstract Window Toolkit (java.awt) package that provides basic graphic abstractions and primitives. The java.awt package makes a unified GUI for all platforms and serves as a base for rich graphic components built with the set of Swing (javax.swing) packages.

An alternative GUI is provided in Java with the Standard Widget Toolkit (SWT). SWT uses a Java native interface (JNI) to C to invoke the native operating system graphics widgets from Java code. SWT enforces *one-to-one mapping* between Java native methods and operating system calls, which makes a very significant difference in the appearance and performance of graphics.

SWT is a pure Java code (although not from Sun Microsystems) widely accepted by the Java development community and supported by IBM and other organizations under the eclipse.org [2] umbrella.

We will briefly look into the most commonly used traditional Java graphics with java.awt (heavyweight, with native interface code) and javax.swing (lightweight, pure Java code that sits on the top of AWT) packages.

There are three basic elements in the java.awt package:

1. Graphic attributes, such as color and font, are defined.
2. All graphic components, such as buttons, lists, checkboxes, and other widgets, have graphic attributes. The crucial point is some components are actually containers that may contain other components.
3. Layout managers can easily control the complexity of different container-component layouts.

Figure A1.17 provides a simple example of a Java applet. The Java applet uses its network capabilities to load an image from the network and draws this image along with several lines of Java poetry.

A Web browser invokes the *init()* method as soon as the applet is loaded. Then, the browser refreshes the screen by calling the *paint()* method of the applet. More precisely, the browser calls the invisible *update()* method, which in turn, schedules the execution of the *paint()* method. These are the mechanics of painting Java components.

An applet or an application can draw different items on the java.awt.Component using the *paint(Graphics)* method. Images, lines, circles, polygons, or any other graphic items are drawn on a Graphics instance. The system (in the applet's case, it is the browser) passes the graphics instance to the *paint(Graphics)* method.

The *paint(Graphics)* method might be called several times throughout the life of an applet or application. The system allocates a thread and gives this thread a specific time in which to accomplish its painting job.

If the drawing is complicated, this time frame may not be long enough and the *paint()* method may be called several times for a single screen refresh, which often causes a flickering effect.

When does the system call the *paint()* method?

If an applet changes location on the screen or any time it needs to be refreshed (re-drawn), *paint(Graphics)* is called. Programmers do not directly call *paint(Graphics)*. To have

```
// AppletTwo @ http://JavaSchool.com/school/public/awt/

import java.applet.Applet;
import java.awt.*;
// Jeff.Zhuk@JavaSchool.com
public class AppletTwo extends Applet {

    private Image image;
    private String[] javaPoetry = {
      "I placed my JAR", " in Tennessee",
      "On a high ", "remote hill...",
      "Where people can see", " its Java steam",
      "That shapes ", "their dreams and will..."
    };
    public void init() {
        image = getImage(getCodeBase(), "jar.gif");
    }
    public void paint(Graphics g) {
        g.setColor(Color.blue);
        g.fillRect(10,10, 180, 280);
        g.drawImage(image, 20, 20, this);
        g.setColor(Color.white);
        g.setFont(new Font("Helvetica", Font.BOLD, 14) );
        // name, style, size
        for(int i = 0; i < javaPoetry.length; i++) {
            g.drawString(javaPoetry[i], 15, 120 + 20*i);
        }
    }
}
```

FIGURE A1.17

java.awt.Component paint itself, programmers call *repaint()*, which calls *update(Graphics)*, which in turn calls *paint(Graphics)*.

Be aware that *update(Graphics)* assumes that the component background is not clear, so it clears the background first. If you don't want to waste time clearing the background each time you want to paint, it's a good idea to override *update(Graphics)* with your own code that only calls the *paint(Graphics)* method.

Figure A1.18 projects the image created by the Web page that contains this applet.

Commonly Used Layout Managers

The three most commonly used layout managers are the *FlowLayout, BorderLayout*, and *GridLayout*.

The *FlowLayout* is the default layout manager for the simplest Java container, the *Panel* class. The *FlowLayout* has three justifications: *FlowLayout.CENTER, FlowLayout.LEFT*, and *FlowLayout.RIGHT. FlowLayout.CENTER* is the default setting.

Figure A1.19 illustrates an example of the *FlowLayout* manager.

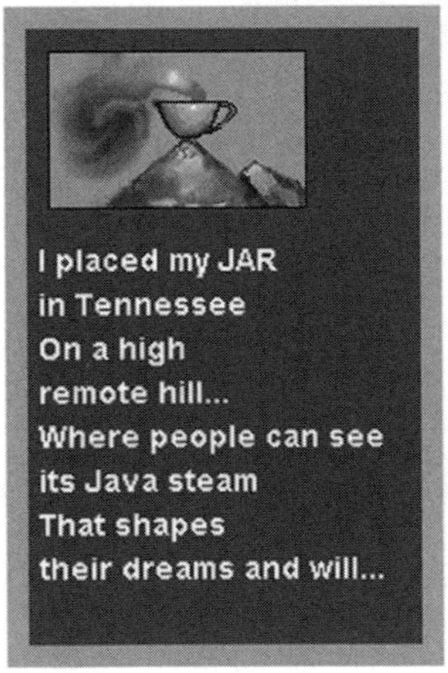


```
// AppletTwo @ http://JavaSchool.com/school/public/awt/

import java.applet.Applet;
import java.awt.*;
// Jeff.Zhuk@JavaSchool.com
public class AppletTwo extends Applet {

    private Image image;
    private String[] javaPoetry = {
      "I placed my JAR", " in Tennessee",
      "On a high ", "remote hill...",
      "Where people can see", " its Java steam",
      "That shapes ", "their dreams and will..."
    };
    public void init() {
        image = getImage(getCodeBase(), "jar.gif");
    }
    public void paint(Graphics g) {
        g.setColor(Color.blue);
        g.fillRect(10,10, 180, 280);
        g.drawImage(image, 20, 20, this);
        g.setColor(Color.white);
        g.setFont(new Font("Helvetica", Font.BOLD, 14) );
        for(int i = 0; i < javaPoetry.length; i++) {
            g.drawString(javaPoetry[i], 15, 120 + 20*i);
        }
    }
```

FIGURE A1.18 I placed my JAR in Tennessee.

The Java applet serves two roles: networking service and graphical component. The *Java Applet* class graphically represents java.awt.Panel. The default layout for the *Panel* is the *FlowLayout*.

The *FlowLayout* places components next to each other into one line. When the components fill the width of a container, the *FlowLayout* starts a new row. Fields in the *FlowLayout* keep their sizes (i.e., do not grow) when the user stretches the window.

Figure A1.20 illustrates the use of the *BorderLayout*. The *BorderLayout* (default for the *Frame* and *Dialog* classes) has five regions: *North*, *South*, *East*, *West*, and *Center*. When a user resizes the window with the *BorderLayout*, the *North* and *South* regions grow horizontally while the *East* and *West* regions grow vertically. The *Center* region grows in both directions. It is **not** a requirement to fill all five fields of the *BorderLayout* (see Fig. A1.20).

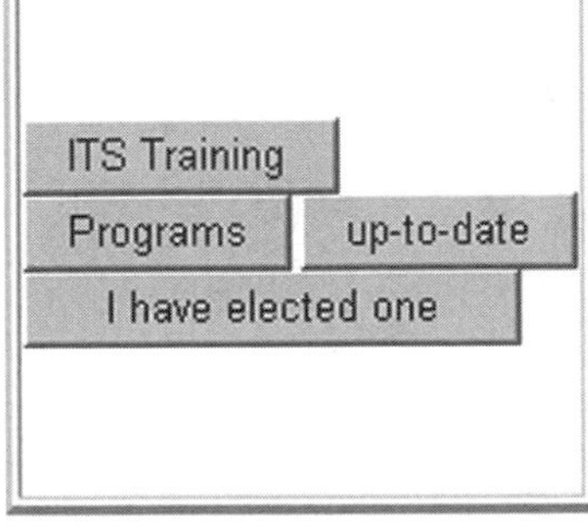


```
// FlowLayoutExample
public class FlowLayoutExample extends Applet {
    public void init() {
        add(new Button("ITS Training"));
        add(new Button("Programs"));
        add(new Button("up-to-date"));
        add(new Button("I have elected one"));
    }
}
```

FIGURE A1.19 Example of the flow layout manager.

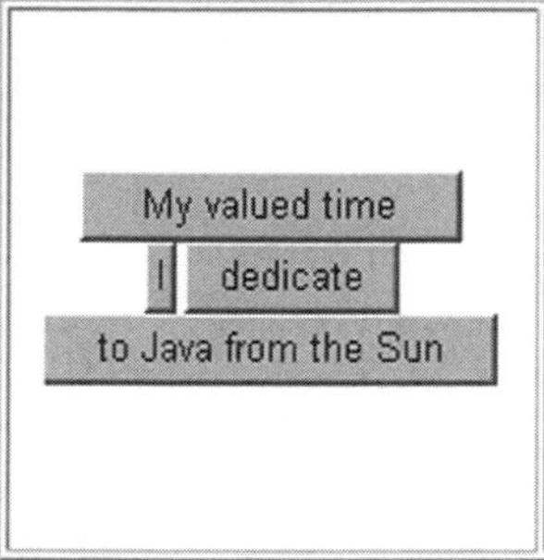


```
// BorderLayoutExample
public class BorderLayoutExample extends Applet {
    public void init() {
        setLayout(new BorderLayout());
        add("North", new Button("My valued time"));
        add("West", new Button("I"));
        add("Center", new Button("dedicate"));
        add("South", new Button("to Java from the Sun"));
    }
}
```

FIGURE A1.20 Example of the border layout manager.

The sequences of the strings in Figs. A1.19 and A1.20 can be combined into four lines written by a Java student:

The training programs are just great!
I have elected one.
My valued time I dedicate
To Java from the Sun.

Figure A1.21 displays an example of code that helps find the cheapest airfare from Denver to several destinations. This example greatly simplifies the backend operations required for such a search; it focuses on the graphics and event handling instead.

The buttons are placed into the frame with the *GridLayout*. The number of regions for a *GridLayout* is specified in the constructor by rows and columns. In this case, we specified three rows with two columns for the layout. The *GridLayout* makes all the regions the same size, equal to the largest cell.

Creating a frame makes this applet less dependable on the Web browser. The frame stays on the screen while the user continues to browse other pages.

The *Tickets* class definition includes the promise to implement the *ActionListener* interface. This simply means that *ActionEvent* handling happens in *this* class and this class must provide the *actionPerformed()* method implementation.

When any of the destination buttons is pressed, a button label is changed to show the corresponding fixed price.

Figures A1.22 and A1.23 show this applet at work.

From a Hard-Coded to a Flexible Set of Reusable Services

Several simple changes can turn this hard-coded GUI example into a set of reusable services.

- First, we separate the applet code from the basic GUI that appears in the frame.
- Then, we pass service names and related actions in an XML-based scenario with a set of parameters.
- Finally, we use the *ServiceConnector.performService()* method to perform the necessary services.

Figure A1.24 displays the *WebContainer* applet class. The *WebContainer* source code is very short. The single *init()* method retrieves the URL parameter from the applet tag on the Web page that points to the *WebContainer* applet.

```
// Tickets (in the GridLayout)
import java.applet.Applet;
import java.awt.*;
import java.awt.event.*;

/**
 * The Tickets applet demonstrates Grid Layout and event handling
 */
public class Tickets extends Applet implements ActionListener {
    private String[] price = {
      "$100","$200","$250","$500","$750","$990"};
    private String[] city = {
      "Phoenix", "Chicago", "Los Angeles", "New York",
      "London", "Moskow"};
    private Button[] buttons;
    /**
      * The init() method will be called by browser as soon as
      * applet loaded
      */
    public void init() {
        Frame f = new Frame("Best air fair from Denver");
        f.setLayout(new GridLayout(3, 2, 2,2));
        buttons = new Button[city.length];
        for (int i = 0; i < city.length; i++) {
            buttons[i] = new Button(city[i]);
            f.add (buttons[i]);
            // delegate event handling to THIS object
            buttons[i].addActionListener(this);
        }
        f.setSize(400,300);
        f.setVisible(true);
    }
    /**
     * The actionPerformed() method is event handler
     * It will color pressed button
     */
    public void actionPerformed(ActionEvent e) {
        String command = e.getActionCommand();
        for(int i=0; i < city.length; i++) {
            if(city[i].equals(command) ) {
                buttons[i].setLabel(price[i]);
            } else {
                buttons[i].setLabel(city[i]);
            }
        }
    }
}
```

FIGURE A1.21

FIGURE A1.22. Best airfare with the grid layout manager.

Here is an example of the applet tag:

```
<applet code="WebContainer" width="1" height="1">
<parameter name="scenario" value="ServiceSetExample.xml" />
</applet>
```

The *init()* method uses the *JavaIOExample.fetchURL()* method to fetch the scenario file that must be located on the same server as the applet and the original Web page. This is one of the applet's restrictions: it can network only to its own server-host.

The last line of the *init()* method initializes the *ServiceFrame* object and passes to the object the scenario that was just retrieved two lines above.

Figures A1.25 displays an example of the scenario.

The scenario includes two lines that define the dimensions of the grid layout for the *ServiceFrame* object with the number of rows and columns, and a set of services to perform. Each service has a service name and a service instruction that includes class name, method name, and parameters when needed.

The *ServiceFrame* class begins in Fig. A1.26. This class extends the *java.awt.Frame* and promises to implement the *ActionListener* interface.

The constructor of the ServiceFrame uses the Stringer.parse() method to process the scenario string and transform the string into a table (Hashtable) of service parameters.

The constructor creates a grid of service buttons using the number of rows and columns retrieved from the service parameters. A panel with the grid of service buttons is placed in the "Center" of the frame. We set the bottom of the frame (the "South") with the text area in which we expect to display service responses if any.

FIGURE A1.23. Best airfare applet at work: another selection.

```
// WebContainer

import java.applet.Applet;
/**
 * WebContainer is an applet
 * The init() methods provide access to XML scenario with a set of
 * service requests
 * The start method
 * @author Jeff.Zhuk@JavaSchool.com
 */
public class WebContainer extends Applet {
    /**
     * init() method is called by a web browser when applet just
     * started
     * The method uses applet.getParameter() method to read
     * urlToConfigFile parameter from the html page
     * The method uses the JavaIOExample.fetchURL() method to
     * access the XML scenario with a set of service requests
     */
    public void init() {
        String urlToConfigFile = getParameter("scenario");
        // Applet can only access URL to its own server host
        String xml = JavaIOExample.fetchURL
        (urlToConfigFile);
        ServiceFrame frame = new ServiceFrame(xml);
    }}
```

FIGURE A1.24.

```
<?xml version = "1.0" encoding = "UTF-8"?>
<scenario>
     <gui rows="2" columns="2" />
    <services>
        <service name="testMail" value="ITSeMailClient.
        sendMail(\"jeff.zhuk@javaschool.com\",\"hi!\",
        \"How are you?\")" />
        <service name="getMail" value="ITSeMailClient.
        getMail(\"jzhuk\")" />
        <service name="USA?" value="KnowledgeService.query
        (UnitedStatesOfAmerica)" />
        <service name="Cyc?" value="KnowledgeService. query(Cyc)" />
    </services>
</scenario>
```

FIGURE A1.25.

```
// ServiceFrame

import java.awt.*;
import java.awt.event.*;
import java.util.*;

/**
 * The ServiceFrame takes XML scenario with a set of service requests
 * and actions
 * The scenario also includes some definitions for building GUI
 * The number of rows and columns is defined in the scenario parameters
 */
public class ServiceFrame extends Frame implements ActionListener {
    private Hashtable parameters; // all scenario parameters
    private Hashtable services, gui; // service and gui parameters
    private Button[] buttons;
    private TextArea responseArea = new TextArea("Look for service
    response here!", 3, 60);
    /**
     * The constructor builds the GUI and shows service names as
     * button labels
     */
     public ServiceFrame (String xml) {
        parameters = Stringer.parse(xml);
        parameters = (Hashtable)parameters.get("scenario");
        gui = (Hashtable)parameters.get("gui");
        String numberOfRows = (String)gui.get("rows");
        String numberOfColumns = (String)gui.get("columns");
        int rows = 2;
        int columns = 2;
        try {
            rows = (new Integer(numberOfRows)).intValue();
            columns = (new Integer(numberOfColumns)).intValue();
        } catch(Exception e) {
            System.out.println("xml problem: " + numberOfRows + "/"
            + numberOfColumns);
        }
        Panel buttonPanel = new Panel();
        add("Center", buttonPanel);
        add("South", responseArea);
        setTitle("Service Frame Example");
        responseArea.setEditable(false); // read only
        buttonPanel.setLayout(new GridLayout(rows,
        columns));
        services = (Hashtable)parameters.get("services");
        buttons = new Button[services.size()];
        Enumeration keys = services.keys();
```

FIGURE A1.26.

```
        for (int i=0; keys.hasMoreElements(); i++) {
            String key = (String)keys.nextElement();
            buttons[i] = new Button(key);
            buttonPanel.add(buttons[i]);
            // delegate event handling to THIS object
            buttons[i].addActionListener(this);
        }
        pack();
        setVisible(true);
    }
```

FIGURE A1.26. (*cont.*)

The set of services fills the *services* table that was prepared by the *Stringer.parse()* method. We create a set of buttons and label them according to the names provided in the *services* table.

The *ServiceFrame* resizes itself with the *pack()* method, which makes it necessarily small, makes its components visible, and makes it ready to rock and roll.

Figure A1.27 shows the *actionPerformed()* method, which handles button clicks, and the *main()* method. The *actionPerformed()* method is an event handler that is called by the system whenever a button is pressed. Note that when we created the buttons, we added an action listener to every button, pointing to THIS object as event handler.

When any button is pressed, the action event is generated by the system and passed to the *actionPerformed()* method. The very first thing we need to do is recognize which button was pressed. This is an easy task. The *getActionCommand()* method of the action event object returns us a button label. We use the label to retrieve the service instruction from the table of services using the label as the key.

The next line performs the service using the *ServiceConnector.performService()* method. Then, the program changes the background color of the pressed button and sends a service response to the text area.

The *main()* method can test the class performance. We provide a URL to an XML scenario as the argument in the *main()* method. The method reads the scenario and passes the XML string to the *ServiceFrame* object. The right scenario is all this class needs to perform.

Java GUI with Swing Classes: *ServiceBrowser*

Java Swing classes offer a big set of rich graphical widgets with very powerful functionality. I provide only one example to demonstrate some of these features.

The *JEditorPane* class is the focus of the following example. The *JEditorPane* is a Web browser emulator.

Yes! This single class is as capable of loading and showing Web pages as almost any real browser. The *JEditorPane* does not perform JavaScript functions, and it is very picky about HTML code correctness, unlike most browsers, which forgive Web designers for small errors.

The *JEditorPane* class can also display documents with rich text format (RTF) prepared by Microsoft Word, Open Office, or Adobe tools.

```
/**
 * The actionPerformed() method is event handler
 * It performs the service and changes the background color of the
 * pressed button
 * The service response will be set in the text area at the bottom
 * of the frame
 * @param ae
 */
public void actionPerformed(ActionEvent ae) {
    String command = ae.getActionCommand();
    // retrieve service instruction for the service name
    String service = (String) services.get(command);
    String response = ServiceConnector.performService(service);
    responseArea.setText(response);
    // show selected service button
    for(int i=0; i <  buttons.length; i++) {
        if(buttons[i].getLabel().equals(command) ) {
            buttons[i].setBackground(Color.yellow);
        } else {
            buttons[i].setBackground(Color.lightGray);
        }
    }
}
/**
 * The main() method is to test the class
 * @param args
 */
public static void main(String[] args) {
    String url == "Fig.14-25.xml";
    if(args !==  null &&  args.length >  0 &&  args[0] !=  null) {
        url = args[0];
    }
    String xml = IOMaster.readTextFile(url);
    new ServiceFrame(xml);
  }
}
```

FIGURE A1.27

The code example displayed below in Fig. A1.28 loads the Web page with images, text, and hyperlinks that look like regular HTML links. Some of these links are not usual. A regular Web browser cannot interpret them, but our code will exceed the browser's capacities. We write the link handler method, and we can greatly extend the browser's functionality.

The *ServiceBrowser* class (Fig. A1.28) is an example of the *javax.swing.JEditorPane* in action.

Like the *java.awt.Frame*, the *javax.swing.JFrame* is the main window in Swing GUI. The *ServiceBrowser* class extends the *JFrame* and implements the *javax.swing.event.HyperlinkListener*. This means that the class must include the *hyperlinkUpdate()* method to handle link events.

```
// ServiceBrowser

package.com.its.connector;

import javax.swing.*;
import javax.swing.event.*;
import javax.swing.text.html.*;

/*
 * ServiceBrowser class is an example of javax.swing.JEditorPane
 * in action
 */
public class ServiceBrowser extends JFrame implements
HyperlinkListener {
    public static boolean debug = true;
    protected JEditorPane display = new JEditorPane();
    // main browser frame
    protected JScrollPane displayPane = new JScrollPane(display);
    // make it scrollable
    protected JEditorPane controls = new JEditorPane();
    // browser controls
    /**
     * The constructor sets the initial urls and creates GUI
     */
    public ServiceBrowser(String initialURL, String
    controlsURL, String imageURL) {

        // set display pane (main frame)
        display.setEditable(false); // we're browsing not
        editing, can change it later on
        display.setContentType("text/html"); // can change it later on

        // set controls pane (top frame)
        controls.setEditable(false); // we're browsing not editing,
                                     // can change it later on
        controls.setContentType("text/html"); // can change it later on

        // contentPane is the main holder for JFrame components
        Container contentPane = getContentPane();
        contentPane.setLayout(new BorderLayout());
        // place frames in the content pane
        contentPane.add(BorderLayout.CENTER, displayPane);
        contentPane.add(BorderLayout.NORTH, controls);

        // set size of the window as 5/6 of the screen
        int w = (int)Toolkit.getDefaultToolkit().getScreenSize().
        getWidth();
        int h = (int)Toolkit.getDefaultToolkit().getScreenSize().
        getHeight();
```

FIGURE A1.28

```
        w = (int)(w*5)/6;
        h = (int)(h*5)/6;
        // set size of the main and control frames
        displayPane.setPreferredSize(new Dimension(w-8, h-150));
        controls.setSize((new Dimension(w-8, h-100));

        // get logo image
        Image image = Toolkit.getDefaultToolkit().getImage(imageURL);
        setIconImage(image);   // place icon on the frame
        setTitle(initialURL);   // set initial url on the frame title

        // enable hyperllink handler
        display.addHyperlinkListener(this);
        // load the initial web page and control page
        display.setPage(initialURL);
        controls.setPage(controlsURL);

        frame.pack();
        frame.setVisible(true);
        // register main objects with the service connector
        ServiceConnector.getInstance().register
        (getClassName(), this);
        ServiceConnector.getInstance().register(display.
        getClass().getName(), display);
    }
```

FIGURE A1.28. *(cont.)*

Two GUI components cover all our needs: the *JEditorPane*, in which we plan to display the documents, and the *JScrollPane*, which provides scrolling skills for our browser. We place the *JEditorPane* into the *JScrollPane*. Now they can work together as a team.

We add another *JEditorPane* component to the top of the window (North). This component contains a Web page with control-links.

The constructor takes the initial URLs as parameters and creates a GUI in several lines. We set the *JEditorPane* objects *display* and *controls*. Then we create a *ContentPane* object to hold all the *JFrame* components. We place the objects in the center and at the top of the content pane, respectively.

There are several lines of calculations in which we set the component sizes based on the client screen resolution surveyed by the *Toolkit.getDefaultToolkit().getScreenSize()* method.

The constructor uses the image URL to load the logo icon and set the icon on the frame, to the left of the frame title. The program sets the title of the frame to the initial URL of the page that will be displayed first. The link event handler will continue this tradition, providing the current URL as the frame title each time a new link is activated.

The constructor finishes its GUI work by enabling the link handler, setting the display and controls pages, and finally making the window visible. Note that the single *setPage()* method of the *JEditorPane* loads the page from the Internet or a local computer and displays the page.

The last lines of the constructor register the main objects at the *ServiceConnector* registry. Later on, we will be able to order these objects to change their behavior by providing the proper link instructions.

For example, with the instructions below, we can change the mode of the display window:

```
javax.swing.JEditorPane.setContentMode("text/plain")
```

The link with this instruction will look like this:

```
<a href=service://
javax.swing.JEditorPane.setContentMode("text/plain")>Plain Text</a>
```

Figure A1.29 shows the link handler. The *hyperlinkUpdate()* method is the required implementation of the *HyperlinkListener* interface. The method considers the type of event first. The *HTMLFrameHyperlinkEvent* is a notification about the link action. We can use this notification to retrieve the document for some analysis, but this is not the primary function of this method.

The primary function of the *handleEvent()* method is as a regular *HyperlinkEvent* that happens when a user clicks on a link. The program tries to retrieve a link URL and act upon the URL instructions. If this is a regular link that points to some Web of local files, the program loads such a file and shows its content in the display window.

The most important case is when the instruction starts with the *service://* string. This means that this is not a regular URL schema like http://, file://, or *ftp://*. The *service://* is the beginning of our service instruction that can be interpreted and performed by the *ServiceConnector.performService()* method.

The result of the operation may be a URL to a document, a formatted Web page, an RTF, or a plain text document. The program looks into all these cases and acts accordingly.

Whenever a user changes the page, the method stores the current URL and the previous URL, which might be used to support the *Back* function.

This is the core of the service browser. We can add more methods to the service browser to support the controls at the top of the frame. For example, we can have controls to set the display to editable mode.

We can also add the *Back* control to the controls.html page and support this link with the *back()* method provided in Fig. A1.30.

Figure A1.30 displays these two helper methods and the *main()* method to test the browser. The *back()* method sets the page to a previous URL stored one click before. The *setEditable()* method changes the mode of the display from read-only to read-and-write and back.

Figure A1.31 shows an example of the controls.html file. There are only three control-links provided in the example, but this page can be easily extended with links to provide specific services based, for example, on the Open Office package.

The *ServiceBrowser*'s functionality is not limited by the functions embedded in the source code of this class. Unlike a lot of applications and browsers, the *ServiceBrowser* is just an engine able to perform any integration-ready service. The presentation layer of the *ServiceBrowser* is also not defined by the source code. The screens and controls are driven by HTML descriptions.

In Chapter 7, we discussed the XML browser driven by XML scenarios. The scenarios would describe GUI as well as program functionality.

Describing GUI in XML is not a terribly new idea. Developers from Netscape (currently AOL) submitted their XUL (XML User interface Language) specification [3] via the Mozilla Organization.

```
/**
 * The hyperlinkUpdate() method handles HTML events
 * @param e
 */
public void hyperlinkUpdate(HyperlinkEvent e) {
    if (e.getEventType() == HyperlinkEvent.EventType.ACTIVATED) {
        if (e instanceof HTMLFrameHyperlinkEvent) { // just
        notification about link action
            HTMLFrameHyperlinkEvent  evt = (HTMLFrameHyperlinkEvent)e;
            // retrieve a document (web page)
            HTMLDocument doc = (HTMLDocument)display.getDocument();
            doc.processHTMLFrameHyperlinkEvent(evt);
        } else { // click on the link
            try {
                String url = e.getURL().toString();
                setTitle(url);
                String servicePattern = "service://";
                // check if this is service instruction
                if(url.startsWith(servicePattern)) {
                    String serviceRequest = url.substring
                    (servicePattern.length());
                    String documentOrURL = ServiceConnector.
                    performService(serviceRequest);
                    if(documentOrURL.startsWith("<html>")) {
                        display.setText(documentOrURL);
                        return;
                    } else if(documentOrURL.startsWith("{\\rtf1\\
                      ansi")) { // this must be a rtf
                        display.setContentType("text/rtf");
                        // can change it later on
                        display.setText(documentOrURL);
                        return;
                    } else if(documentOrURL.startsWith("http://") ||
                      documentOrURL.startsWith("file://") {
                        url = webPageOrURL; // will open a page with
                                            // the URL
                    } else { // plain text
                        display.setContentType("text/plain");
                        // can change it later on
                        display.setText(documentOrURL);
                        return;
                    }
                }
                // a link to a web page
                display.setPage(url);
            } catch (Throwable t) {
                t.printStackTrace();
            }
        }
    }
}
```

FIGURE A1.29

```
    /**
    * The back() method sets display to view the previous URL "backURL"
     */
    public void back() {
        if(backURL == null) return;
        try {
            display.setPage(backURL);
            backURL = currentURL;
        } catch(Exception e) {
            // do nothing
        }
    }

    /**
     * The setEditable() method sets the mode of the page to "read only"
     * or "read/write"
     * @param mode
     */
    public void setEditable(String mode) {
        if(mode == null || !mode.equals("true") ) {
            display.setEditable(false);
        } else {
            display.setEditable(true);
        }
}

/**
 * The main() method is to test the class
 * @param args
 */
public static void main(String[] args) {
    new ServiceBrowser("http://JavaSchool.com", "controls.html",
    "images/its.logo.gif");
    }
}
```

FIGURE A1.30

```
<html><body>
<a href=service://ServiceBrowser.back>Editable</a>
<a href=service://ServiceBrowser.setEditable(true)>Editable</a>
<a href=service://ServiceBrowser.setEditable(false)>Not Editable</a>
</body></html>
```

FIGURE A1.31

XUL describes the typical dialog controls, as well as widgets such as toolbars, trees, progress bars, and menus. Unlike HTML, which defines a single-page document, XUL describes the contents of an entire window, which could contain several Web pages.

There are existing implementations, such as Thinlet [4], that use XUL to define GUI widgets. There is even the XUL visual editor program "Theodore" [5] by Wolf Paulus, which ensures the generation of valid XUL descriptors.

The language of XML application scenarios discussed in this book can complement and integrate GUI descriptions (done with XUL) with extended service definitions.

Building GUI in C# with Windows Forms

Windows Forms [6] are a new style of application built around classes in the .NET Framework class library's System.Windows.Forms namespace (much richer than the Windows API).

Windows Forms streamline the programming model, providing a consistent API. For example, Microsoft Foundation Classes or the Windows API does not allow you to apply a style that is meaningful only at creation time to an existing window. Windows Forms take care of this problem by quietly destroying the window and recreating it with the specified style.

Windows Forms leverage several technologies, including a common application framework and managed execution environment. Programmers can use Windows Forms while connecting to XML Web services and building rich, data-aware applications with any of the languages supporting. NET development tools.

So, what would be an appropriate definition for Windows Forms?

1. Windows GUI APIs?
2. A library of classes?
3. A set of tools?
4. All of the above?

If you picked the last item, you win!

It is not necessary to install the full .NET environment to develop the Windows Forms GUI, but you need at least the .NET Framework distribution.

What is the programming model of Windows Forms?

Traditionally, starting from Visual Basic, the term *forms* means top-level rectangular windows that can serve as dialog boxes, standard windows, or multiple document interface (MDI) windows.

Forms can present information for a user and accept the user's data. Forms are objects, instances of classes that define their properties and methods. The properties are translated at run-time into visible attributes, and the methods define user interface behavior.

Programmers prefer to use Windows Forms Designer to create and modify forms, although Code Editor lets you enjoy manual code writing.

The main starting points for writing GUI applications with Windows Forms are two classes of the System.Windows.Forms namespace: the *System.Windows.Forms.Application* and the *System.Windows.Forms.Form*. The static method *Run* of the *System.Windows.Forms.Application* displays a window and runs message events loop.

The *System.Windows.Forms.Form* class defines the window properties and behavior. This component (similar to the *java.awt.Component* class) handles user interface with virtual methods such as *OnPaint, OnMouseDown, OnKeyDown*, and *OnClosing*. Programmers write their code to override these default methods (that in most cases are empty placeholders) and provide actual handlers.

The next layer of Windows Forms classes represents numerous controls such as:

- System.Windows.Forms.Menu
- System.Windows.Forms.Button
- System.Windows.Forms.TextBox
- System.Windows.Forms.ListView
- System.Windows.Forms.FileDialog
- System.Windows.Forms.MonthCalendar
- System.Windows.Forms.ColorDialog
- System.Windows.Forms.PrintDialog
- System.Windows.Forms.FontDialog, etc.

Similar controls (although not all) can be found in the java.awt or javax.swing packages. There are several controls in Windows Forms that I miss in Java. For example, the System.Windows.Forms.LinkLabel is a hyperlink control. You can use the rich facilities of javax.swing.JEditorPane (see the *ServiceBrowser*, Figs. A1.27 and A1.28), or you can write your own class (I did it once then found out that M. Berthou created one [7]) to add this control to the java.awt building blocks.

Figure A1.32 shows a simple example of a Windows Forms application. You can save this code in any file—for example, *example1.cs*—and compile it with the command line in MS DOS windows.

```
csc example1.cs
```

```
using System;
using System.Windows.Forms;

namespace ITSCsExamples {
    public class WindowsFormsExample : System.Windows.Forms.Form {

        [STAThread]
        public static int Main(string[] args) {
            System.Windows.Forms.Application.Run(new
            WindowsFormsExample());
            return 0;
        }

        public WindowsFormsExample() {
            Text = "Windows Forms Example";
        }
    }
}
```

FIGURE A1.32.

You will find a new file, *example1.exe*, in the same folder. This is your Windows Forms application. Double-click on the file and see a window with the proud title "Windows Forms Example."

You can add more components to this application. For example: You want to add a button with the label *Submit*. You create the button and define its properties. Then, you can add the button to other controls on the form:

```
System.Windows.Forms.Button submitButton = new
System.Windows.Forms.Button();
submitButton.Name = "submitButton"; // reference name
// place the button at this location on the form
// submitButton.Location = new System.Drawing.Point(20, 40);
// define a style of the button submitButton.
// FlatStyle = System.Windows.Forms.FlatStyle.System;
// provide button's size, make it well visible (can resize
// itself by default)
// submitButton.Size = new System.Drawing.Size(100, 30);
// here is the label on the button
// submitButton.Text = "Submit";
// Add to the form this.Controls.Add(submitButton);
```

This code looks very similar to Java code, but it is not exactly the same.

Unified Terms to Define GUI: XUL and Views XML

The XML-based User Interface is a good candidate for such direction. Windows Forms deliver unified GUI terms for Microsoft languages. Providing XML-based APIs to Windows Forms can produce a great cocktail that even comes in a beautiful glass.

A group of developers from the University of Pretoria and the University of Victoria (sponsored by Microsoft Research) is working on the VIEWS (Vendor Independent Event and Windowing Systems) project [8], which deserves a special attention.

The group created the Views XML specification 1.0 (similar to XUL) to describe Windows Forms in XML terms. The Views XML specification was designed with emphasis on the user's convenience in writing XML descriptions. The specification, for example, does not require double quotes around attribute values and is not case sensitive regarding tags and attribute names.

The group provided an implementation of the concept in both C# and Java with the class name *View*. (You may find the *View* class is similar in some way to the Java *Thinlet* implementation). The *View* class constructor takes a long string of user interface definition in XML format as an argument and creates the GUI based on this definition.

The C# version of the *View* class uses Windows Forms supported by the.NET Framework. The Java version is implemented with Swing in SDK 1.4.

Figure A1.33 shows an example of creating an object of the *View* class, which accepts an XML-based screen description. The XML string describes the screen in a manner similar to HTML: from the top down and from left to right.

The "vertical" tags encapsulate several items or several groups of items from the top. The "horizontal" tags describe several items or several groups of items on the same vertical level. Figure A1.34 shows the screen displayed by the *View* object regardless of Java or C# implementation.

```
View view = new View(@"<view text = ServiceBrowser@http://
JavaSchool.com>
  <vertical>
    <horizontal>
      <button name = 'Back'/>
      <button name = 'Forward'/>
      <textbox name = WebAddress text=http://JavaSchool.com
       width = 400/>
      <button name = 'Go'/>
    </horizontal>
    <horizontal>
      <textbox name = Search width = 500/>
      <button name = 'Search'/>
    </horizontal>
    <horizontal>
      <vertical>
        <label text='Select from the list of services'
        width = 600/>
        <listbox name = List/>
      </vertical>
    </horizontal>
    <horizontal>
      <button name = 'Perform' />
      <button name = 'Describe' />
    </horizontal>
  </vertical>
</view>");
```

FIGURE A1.33

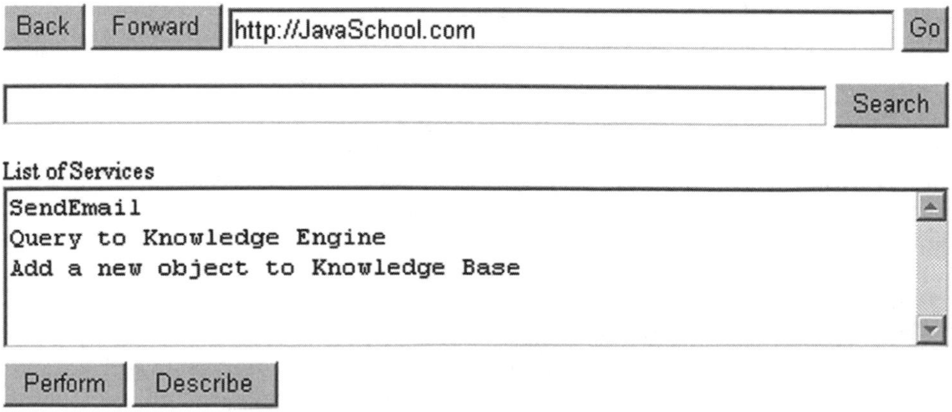

FIGURE A1.34 The resulting screen displayed by views.

Programmers can access information within the controls and handle events with C# or Java code using *View* object methods, such as *GetText()*.

JDK 1.5 Makes Programming Simpler

Comparing Java to C# we found C# more liberal on several occasions. JDK 1.5, known as "Tiger," makes a step in the right direction to simplify some rules. [1]

JDK1.5 loosens the strict rules that distinguish objects from primitives. You remember that all Collections such as ArrayList and Hashtable can deal only with objects.

We could not store a primitive value in collections without wrapping this value in the object. For example:

```
Vector v = new Vector();
v.add(5); // JDK1.4 would give a compiler ERROR because "5" is
          // not an object but an integer
```

You have to wrap this primitive value into an Integer object.

```
Vector v = new Vector();
Integer wrapper = new Integer(5);
v.add(wrapper);
```

Then, you have another problem when you want to retrieve your primitive value back from the collections.

```
int primitive = v.elementAt(0); //JDK1.4 would give you a compiler ERROR
```

You would need to add couple more lines to satisfy JDK1.4.

```
Integer wrapper = (Integer) v.elementAt(0);
int primitive = wrapper.intValue();
```

JDK1.5 removed the problem by introducing *autoboxing* and *unboxing* concepts when compiler takes care about casting and wrapping primitives to objects.

```
Vector v = new Vector();
v.addElement(5); // is OK!!!
. . . . . .
int primitive = v.elementAt(0); // OK!!!
```

Java 1.5 introduced a new base type "*enum*" similar to the C/C++ *enum* that supports Typesafe *enum* [2] design pattern. This new keyword allows us to define a class that represents a single element of the enumerated type without providing a public constructor for the class.

Although *enum* represents integer values it is more informative as we operate with names. They (*enum*) are still classes and objects; we can add to them fields and methods and put them into collections.

In the example below 12 months are presented with the *enum* type:

```
public enum Months {
// The constant declarations below invoke a constructor
// The constructor like January(1) passes the month number
January(1), February(2), March(3), April(4), May(5), June(6), July(7),
August(8), September(9), October(10), November(11), December(12);
    private final int month;
    Months (int month) {
```

```
        this.month = month;
    }
    public int getMonth() {
        return month;
    }
}
```

In the other example we define four seasons (plus Rainy Season that acts as default in some places). We do not bother ourselves with numbering the seasons. The compiler will do the job. The next element's value is always bigger than the value of the previous element. You can see a great feature that shows superiority of Java *enum* in comparison to its C/C++ siblings. We can use Java *enum* in switch statements. (Remember that switch statements only take integers. Java compiler is smart enough to represent *enum* as integer when necessary.

```
// The Seasons are conveniently defined with no constructors
public enum Seasons {Winter, Spring, Summer, Fall, RainySeason}
// Note that unlike its C/C++ siblings Java enum can be used in switch
statements public static Seasons getMonthLength (Months month) {
  switch (month) {
    case Months.December:
    case Months.January:
    case Months.February: return Seasons.Winter;
    case Months.March:
    case Months.April:
    case Months.May: return Seasons.Spring;
    case Months.June:
    case Months.July:
    case Months.August: return Seasons.Summer;
    case Months.September:
    case Months.October:
    case Months.November: return Seasons.Fall;
    default: return Seasons. RainySeason;
    }
  }
}
```

One of the greatest features added by the JDK1.5 is called Generics. What it is all about? There are several sides of Generics but all sides look attractive to us developers, as they make our code more robust and even simpler.

```
Here is the example from the past (JDK1.4).
// count characters in the collection of strings
public int countCharacters(Collection words) {
    int counter = 0;
    for (Iterator i = words.iterator(); i.hasNext();) {
       String s = (String) i.next();
       counter += s.length();
    }
    return counter;
}
```

The code will compile successfully but at run-time can crash if the collection passed to the method above is not the collection of strings.

Here is the code with that can be provided for JDK1.5. The code below includes Generics. It takes full control of the situation and even looks shorter!

```
// Generics ensure that a passed collection must be a collection
// of strings.
// If we try to pass to this method a different type of collection
// We face a compiler ERROR instead -- this is much better than
// run-time exception
public int countCharacters(Collection<String> words) {
    int counter = 0;
    for (Iterator<String> i = words.iterator(); i.hasNext();) {
    counter += i.next().length();
    }
    return counter;
}
```

Even this beautiful source can be enhanced with one more JDK1.5 feature that is named as "enhanced for." This feature makes easier writing *for* loops. It is very similar to Perl's *foreach* keyword. We basically say "for all elements in the collection" and we can skip the iteration line. Here is the source example:

```
// Note the ":" character in the enhanced for loop
public int countCharacters(Collection<String> words) {
    int counter = 0;
    for (String s : words) {// read it as "for all string s in
                            // collection of words"
        counter += s.length();
    }
    return counter;
}
```

Summary

This appendix is a reference for Java and C# programming. Every keyword and every concept is illustrated with one or more examples. The focus of this reference is on object-oriented concepts, reflection, and the approach to GUI development.

The target audience includes (but is not limited to) students and programmers who would like to follow an integration-ready strategy and recreate and extend "integrated with knowledge" systems that can run application scenarios in Java and/or C#. These systems enable invocation of existing services, simplify service descriptions, decrease coding efforts, and integrate parts of application definitions into XML-based application scenarios.

The application scenarios explained in this book extend XML-based GUI descriptions with references to grammar rules and direct access to services (not necessarily Web services, but any available services), including knowledge engine queries and assertions.

The connector package described in Chapter 13 provides Java implementation examples, whereas this appendix demonstrates how to use C# for the same purpose.

Exercises

1. Add several lines of Java code that will allow you to close the frame in Fig. A1.21. (Hint: the class should implement *WindowListener*.)
2. Research and list the similarities and differences between the Thinlet and VIEWS projects.

References

1. The Microsoft Java Language Conversion Assistant: *http://msdn.microsoft.com/vstudio/downloads/tools/jlca/default.asp*.
2. Eclipse.org: *http://www.eclipse.org*.
3. XML User Interface Language 1.0: *http://www.mozilla.org/projects/xul/xul.html*.
4. Thinlet: *http://Thinlet.com*.
5. The Theodore XUL Editor: *http://www.carlsbadcubes.com/theodore/*.
6. Windows Forms: *http://msdn.microsoft.com/vstudio/techinfo/articles/clients/winforms.asp*.
7. Berthou, M. The linkLabel.java: *http://www.javaside.com/zip/srcs/linkLabel_java.html*.
8. VIEWS or XGUI: *http://www.cs.up.ac.za/~jbishop/rotor/*.

APPENDIX 2

XML and Web Services

Though derived from SGML (Standard Generalized Markup Language), Extensible Markup Language (XML) [1] quickly outgrew its initial purpose of enabling large-scale electronic publishing and became the main road of data exchange over the Internet and elsewhere. XML is simple and flexible. These qualities have made XML the perfect instrument for creating new languages in many areas.

For example, HTML is currently the most common language used to create Web pages according to orthodox Web technology, in which the client program is a Web (HTML) browser. However, HTML has its limitations: HTML tags are predefined and cannot be changed or extended.

XML Extends the Web and Builds a Playground for Its Children

XML, on the other hand, allows us to create our own elements, attributes, and structures to describe any kind of data. With such flexibility, XML provides the ideal solution for producing new languages to express the ever-increasing complexity of data exchange and other needs.

WAP (Wireless Application Protocol) is, in a way, a child of Web technology; but WAP has slightly different requirements, which are not covered by HTML tags. A member of the XML family, WML (Wireless Markup Language) provides the necessary keywords to satisfy these requirements.

XML Describes Business Rules and Data Structures; XSLT and X Path Describe Their Transformations

XML is becoming the main tuning tool to describe business rules, data structures, and their transformations.

Extensible Stylesheet Language (XSL) [2] is another member of the same big family of languages. XSL uses a language for transforming XML documents—XSL Transformations (XSLT) [3]—and an XML vocabulary for specifying formatting semantics—XSL Formatting Objects [4]. XSLT, in turn, uses the XML Path Language (XPath) [5] to access or refer to parts of an XML document.

For example, XSL Formatter, released by Antenna House [6] for Windows, Solaris, and Linux (RedHat) platforms, can directly transform different documents into PDF and supports TrueType, Type1, and OpenType font formats.

XML Provides Direct Hooks to Services on the Web with SOAP, WSDL, and UDDI

XML Web services are one of the hottest topics in IT today. These software components provide functionality over a network using standard Internet protocols, such as TCP/IP, HTTP, and XML. XML Web services could not exist without new XML-based standards such as Simple Object Access Protocol (SOAP) [7], Web Services Description Language (WSDL) [8], and Universal Discovery, Description, and Integration (UDDI) [9].

Interactive Web with XForms

Interactive Web applications are often associated with HTML forms and JavaScript. XForms [10], another member of the XML family, extends this concept into a new dimension. XForms represents the new generation of Web forms that satisfies the new demands of e-commerce and Web applications for more functionality and flexibility in user interfaces.

XForms, in contrast to existing HTML forms that mix content and presentation together, are made up of *separate sections* that describe what the form does and how the form looks. This allows for flexible presentation options, including classic XHTML forms, to be attached to an XML form definition.

XML in Voice Applications

Direct interaction with a machine via natural language is not a reality yet, but neither is it still a dream. This is a work in progress. What are the leading standards in this area? They are children of the XML family, such as Natural Language Semantics Markup Language (NLSML) [11].

NLSML is designed for systems that provide semantic interpretations for a variety of inputs, including, but not necessarily limited to, speech and natural language text input. These systems include voice browsers, Web browsers, and accessible applications. The language provides a set of elements to accurately represent the semantics of natural language input and reflect the user's intended meaning in terms of the application's goals.

NLSML is compatible with other W3C specifications, including (but not limited to) the Dialog Markup Language, Speech Grammar Markup Language, and XForms.

XML family members such as VoiceXML [12] and Speech Application Language Tags (SALT) [13] are the leading standards for voice applications.

XML Drives Semantic Web and Knowledge Technologies

XML document type definitions and XML Schemas have no semantic mechanisms to understand changing or new XML vocabularies.

The XML-based Resource Description Framework (RDF) [14] and RDF Schema began to approach this problem by allowing simple semantics to be associated with terms. RDF Schema is a simple ontology language that links a knowledge object (topic) with its Uniform Resource Identifier (URI). The URI provides a way to identify any content presented by a text, image, or sound file. A typical example of a URI is *http://IPServe.com*.

RDF serves as the base for the semantic Web language DAML+OIL (DARPA Agent Markup Language + Ontology Inference Layer) [15]. DAML, like object-oriented languages, defines some basic object types by giving a name to a class, which is the subset of the universe and contains all the objects of that type.

The marrige of DAML and OIL produced a semantic markup language for Web resources in which it is possible to relate objects to other objects, or relate objects to data-type values.

Topic Maps and its XML Topic Maps (XTM) [16] knowledge exchange format is an ISO standard that defines a model and interchange syntax for knowledge representation with topics, occurrences of topics, and relationships ("associations") between topics. Topic Maps may be compared to the GPS (Global Positioning System) of the information universe, a base technology for knowledge representation and knowledge management.

CycML [17] is an upcoming XML-based knowledge exchange format that focuses on Cyc technology, the largest and most complete general knowledge base and commonsense reasoning engine, and allows the knowledge-base contents to be imported and exported for archiving.

XML roads cross and unite many, if not all, information technologies.

XML Web Services

Although Web services represent a fraction of the software services available today, they are currently the most visible and accessible fraction.

What is a Web service?

XML Web services are not very different from regular applications, but are more precisely defined with Internet and XML standards. First, a Web service accepts XML-based requests encoded with SOAP; it then sends them over a network using HTTP. This is the most common medium, although other protocols, such as SMTP, may also be used.

Web Services at Work

Three parties interact during any Web service transaction: the Service Provider, Service Registry, and Service Requestor. Figure A2.1 illustrates the interaction.

The Service Provider creates an XML-ready Web service, describes service interfaces with WSDL, and registers (or publishes) the service at the Service Registry using UDDI mechanisms. The Service Requestor uses UDDI application program interfaces (APIs) to discover the service and sends SOAP-encoded service requests to invoke a service. The Service Registry plays the role of "Web Service Yellow Pages."

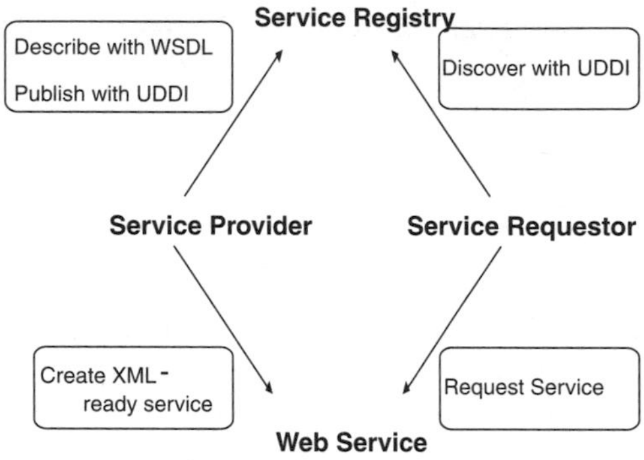

FIGURE A2.1. Provider, Registry, and Requestor Interaction.

ENCODE SERVICE REQUESTS WITH SOAP

SOAP provides encoding mechanisms in a large variety of systems, ranging from messaging systems to remote procedure calls.

A SOAP message is an XML document that consists of a mandatory SOAP envelope, an optional SOAP header, and a mandatory SOAP body.

Here is a very simple example of a SOAP envelope with a header and a body:

```
<?xml version="1.0" encoding="UTF-8" ?>
<env:Envelope xmlns:env="http://www.w3.org/2001/09/soap-envelope">
   <env:Header>
     <n:alertcontrol xmlns:n="http://example.org/alertcontrol">
      <n:priority>1</n:priority>
      <n:expires>2001-06-22T14:00:00-05:00</n:expires>
     </n:alertcontrol>
   </env:Header>
   <env:Body>
       <m:alert xmlns:m="http://example.org/alert">
         <m:msg>
            Training sessions at JavaSchool.com
         </m:msg>
       </m:alert>
   </env:Body>
</env:Envelope>
```

DESCRIBE WEB SERVICES WITH WSDL

WSDL describes services offered by an application service provider over the Web. A WSDL file identifies the services with the set of operations within each service that the server supports. For each of the operations, the WSDL file also describes the format the client must follow in requesting an operation.

A WSDL file is an XML document that consists of two sections: the Abstract Definition and the Concrete Descriptions.

The Abstract Definition section defines SOAP messages in a platform-and-language-independent manner.

The Concrete Descriptions section includes network deployment information or data format bindings, such as serialization.

Abstract Definitions

Types: Machine- and language-independent data-type definitions using standards such as XML Schema definition language (XSD).

Messages: Contain function parameters of the data exchange (inputs separate from outputs) or document descriptions.

PortTypes: Define the functions (operation name, input parameters, and output parameters) in the Messages section.

Operation: An abstract description of an action supported by the Web service.

Concrete Descriptions

Bindings: Specify concrete protocol and data format for each operation in the PortTypes section.

Port: Specifies an address for a binding as a communication point.

Services: Specify the port address of each binding.

Element Attributes

WSDL has a number of XML elements in its namespace. The following table summarizes those elements, their attributes, and contents:

Element	Attribute(s)	Contents (children)
<definitions>	name targetNamespace xmlns (other namespaces)	<types> <message> <portType> <binding> <service>
<types>	(none)	<xsd:schema>
<message>	name	<part>
<portType>	name	<operation>
<binding>	name type	<operation>
<service>	name	<port>
<part>	name type	(empty)
<operation>	name parameterOrder	<input> <output> <fault>
<input>	name message	(empty)
<output>	name message	(empty)
<fault>	name message	(empty)
<port>	name binding	<soap:address>

Figure A2.2 shows an example of a WSDL document. The document describes the interface to Training Services at JavaSchool.com.

Publish and Discover Web Services with UDDI

You can type a URL in your browser to access a service if you already know its location. You can directly invoke a service on a network if you know its interface and you have direct access to the service.

Often, you do not know the address or the interface, and you need to do some searching. Where do you search for services? Google.com would be the wrong answer if you were looking for Web services. You need to query one of the Service Registries implemented with UDDI.

The UDDI specifications define ways to publish and discover information about XML Web services. Publishing and discovery messages are UDDI commands sent in the body of a SOAP message to a UDDI registry.

The core component of the UDDI is the UDDI business registration, an XML file that describes a business entity and its XML Web services. Developers use UDDI Business Registry to locate information about services provided, service interfaces, and their parameters.

Figure A2.3 displays an example of a UDDI document.

The core XML element for supporting, publishing, and discovering information is the *businessInfos* structure. This structure includes one or more *businessInfo* elements and serves as the top-level information manager for all the information relating to the organization offering the XML Web service. Each *businessInfo* element includes a description element and several *serviceInfo* elements. This structure gives the user the ability to locate a service provider, a particular industry or product category, and a requested service or list of services.

Business Process Execution Language for Web Services

Web service technologies are quickly growing in size and number, and they demand new standards to describe the whole area. For example, Business Process Execution Language for Web Services (BPEL4WS) [18] is designed to model the behavior of executable processes, as well as business protocols that specify the message exchange behavior of each of the parties.

The BPEL4WS process model is layered on top of the service model defined by WSDL 1.1 with the notion of peer-to-peer interaction between services described in WSDL.

The definition of a BPEL4WS business process also folloWS the WSDL model of separation between the abstract message contents and deployment information. A BPEL4WS process is a reusable definition that maintains a uniform application-level behavior across different deployment environments and scenarios.

Figure A2.4 presents an example of a business process definition with a BPEL4WS document that defines the partners and a sequence of business operations. This document is complemented by the document that defines all the exchange documents and service links in WSDL style (see the WSDL example above).

```
<?xml version="1.0"?>
<definitions name="TrainingSchedule"
  targetNamespace=http://example.com/stockquote.wsdl
  xmlns:tns=http://example.com/trainingschedule.wsdl
  xmlns:xsd1=http://example.com/trainingschedule.xsd
  xmlns:soap=http://schemas.xmlsoap.org/wsdl/soap/
  xmlns="http://schemas.xmlsoap.org/wsdl/">

   <types>
     <schema targetNamespace="http://example.com/trainingschedule.xsd"
                       xmlns="http://www.w3.org/2000/10/XMLSchema">
           <element name="TrainingSessionRequest">
               <complexType>
                   <all>
                       <element name="courseName" type="string"/>
                   </all>
               </complexType>
           </element>
           <element name="TrainingSession">
               <complexType>
                   <all>
                       <element name="price" type="float"/>
                   </all>
               </complexType>
           </element>
     </schema>
   </types>

   <message name="GetLastTrainingSessionInput">
       <part name="body" element="xsd1:TrainingSessionRequest"/>
   </message>

   <message name="GetLastTrainingSessionOutput">
       <part name="body" element="xsd1:TrainingSession"/>
   </message>

   <portType name="TrainingSchedulePortType">
       <operation name="GetLastTrainingSession">
           <input message="tns:GetLastTrainingSessionInput"/>
           <output message="tns:GetLastTrainingSessionOutput"/>
       </operation>
   </portType>

   <binding name="TrainingScheduleSoapBinding"
          type="tns:TrainingSchedulePortType">
       <soap:binding style="document"
        transport="http://schemas.xmlsoap.org/soap/http"/>

       <operation name="GetLastTrainingSession">
           <soap:operation
            soapAction="http://example.com/GetLastTrainingSession"/>
```

FIGURE A2.2.

```
            <input>
                <soap:body use="literal"/>
            </input>
            <output>
                <soap:body use="literal"/>
            </output>
        </operation>
    </binding>

    <service name="TrainingScheduleService">
        <documentation>Java School Training</documentation>
        <port name="TrainingSchedulePort"
          binding="tns:TrainingScheduleBinding">
            <soap:address
              location="http://example.com/trainingschedule"/>
        </port>
    </service>

</definitions>
```

FIGURE A2.2. *(cont.)*

In addition to *sequence*, keyword process definition documents may use a variety of other keywords that describe a business activity:

```
<receive>
<reply>
<invoke>
<assign>
<throw>
<terminate>
<wait>
<empty>
<sequence>
<switch>
<while>
<pick>
<flow>
<scope>
<compensate>
```

Business process definitions may also include expressions that conform to the XPath 1.0 *expr* query, for which the evaluation results in any XPath value type (string, number, or Boolean).

This heavy ammunition allows you to write business application scenarios for Web services. The next step is to include a natural language interface in the loop, giving business experts a great tool for direct involvement in the development process.

```
<businessList generic="1.0" operator="JavaSchool.com"
           truncated="false" xmlns="urn:uddi-org:api">
    <businessInfos>
        <businessInfo businessKey="LONG-STRING">
            <name>Microsoft Corporation</name>

            <description xml:lang="en">
                Training sessions at JavaSchool.com
            </description>

            <serviceInfos>

                <serviceInfo businessKey="LONG-STRING"
                      serviceKey="ANOTHER-LONG-STRING">
                    <name>Ontology Introduction</name>
                </serviceInfo>

                <serviceInfo businessKey="LONG-STRING"
                      serviceKey="YET-ANOTHER-LONG-STRING">
                    <name>Speech Technologies</name>
                </serviceInfo>

                <serviceInfo businessKey="LONG-STRING"
                      serviceKey="AND-ANOTHER-LONG-STRING">
                    <name>Wireless Technologies</name>
                </serviceInfo>

                <serviceInfo businessKey="LONG-STRING"
                      serviceKey="AND-ONE-MORE-LONG-STRING">
                    <name>Scenario for Integration-Ready
                            Systems</name>
                </serviceInfo>

                <serviceInfo businessKey="LONG-STRING"
                      serviceKey="ANOTHER-KEY-STRING">
                    <name>Java based self-healing networks</name>
                </serviceInfo>

                <serviceInfo businessKey="LONG-STRING"
                      serviceKey="ANOTHER-LONG-STRING">
                    <name>Natural User Interface</name>
                </serviceInfo>

                <serviceInfo businessKey="LONG-STRING"
                      serviceKey="ANOTHER-LONG-KEY-STRING">
                    <name>Software development with business
                            experts no coding</name>
                </serviceInfo>

            </serviceInfos>

        </businessInfo>

    </businessInfos>

</businessList>
```

FIGURE A2.3.

```
<process name="scheduleTrainingSession"
        xmlns="http://schemas.xmlsoap.org/ws/2003/03/business-process/"
        xmlns:lns="http://javaschool.com/wsdl/schedule"
        targetNamespace="http://acme.com/ws-bp/schedule">

   <partners>
      <partner name="student"
               serviceLinkType="lns:scheduleLT"
               myRole="scheduleTraining"/>
      <partner name="contentProvider"
               serviceLinkType="lns:contentLT"
               myRole="contentRequester"
               partnerRole="contentService"/>
   </partners>

   <variables>
      <variable name="ScheduleRequest" messageType="lns:ScheduleRequestMessage"/>
      <variable name="contentRequest" messageType="lns:contentRequestMessage"/>
      <variable name="contentInfo" messageType="lns:contentInfoMessage"/>
   </variables>

   <faultHandlers>
      <catch faultName="lns:cannotCompleteRequest"
             faultVariable="ScheduleRequestFault">
      <reply     partner="student"
                 portType="lns:scheduleRequestPT"
                 operation="scheduleTrainingRequest"
                 variable="ScheduleRequestFault"
                 faultName="cannotCompleteRequest"/>
      </catch>
   </faultHandlers>

   <sequence>

      <receive partner="student"
               portType="lns:scheduleRequestPT"
               operation="scheduleTrainingRequest"
               variable="ScheduleRequest">
      </receive>

      <flow>

         <links>
            <link name="link-to-content"/>
            <link name="link-to-schedule"/>
         </links>
         <sequence>
            <assign>
               <copy>
                  <from variable="ScheduleRequest" part="studentInfo"/>
                  <to variable="contentRequest"
                      part="studentInfo"/>
```

FIGURE A2.4.

```
                </copy>
            </assign>

            <invoke  partner="contentProvider"
                     portType="lns:contentPT"
                     operation="requestContent"
                     inputVariable="contentRequest"
                     outputVariable="contentInfo">
               <source linkName="link-to-content"/>
            </invoke>

            <receive partner="contentProvider"
                     portType="lns:contentCallbackPT"
                     operation="sendSchedule"
                     variable="contentSchedule">
               <source linkName="link-to-schedule"/>
            </receive>

         </sequence>
      </flow>

      <reply partner="student"
             portType="lns:scheduleRequestPT"
             operation="scheduleTrainingRequest"
             variable="contentInfo"/>
   </sequence>

</process>
```

Figure A2.4. ***(cont.)***

Summary

XML Web services are a quickly growing area of information technology that combines many XML roads.

What if, besides Web services, you would like to use existing software to describe services and user interaction in a single business-process document?

XML-based application scenarios, described in Chapter 13, combine user interface and user input interpretation hints with service calls, including calls to knowledge services. Note that the set of services accessible with application scenarios is not limited to Web services. The connector package with the *ScenarioPlayer* and *ServiceConnector* classes transform XML scenarios into direct service connections.

Application scenarios can point to almost any service available over the Internet, LAN, or virtual private network. Service requirements are lower in this case than for Web services: the service does not have to be XML ready but must be created with an integration-ready strategy with a clean API that can be described in XML. The *Scenario–Player* with the *Service–Connector* translates XML into a Java or C# API (depending on *Service–Connector* implementations) and provides direct calls to user interface or service layers.

XML roads cross and unite many, if not all, information technologies. At some point, we (developers) will start to eliminate coding time and express business ideas in business language. Today, we can do that with XML. Hopefully, we soon will be able to switch to a natural user interface, one of your own choice.

In Appendix 3, I share with you some sources that will be helpful if you follow the XML trails. Feel free to reuse (different from rewrite) and expand them into even more powerful systems that can talk to each other as partners.

The JavaSchool.com Web site shares the latest source status and accepts feedback and suggestions.

References

1. XML Specifications 1.1 W3C Candidate Recommendation: *http://www.w3.org/TR/xml11/*.
2. Extensible Stylesheet Language Version 1.0: *http://www.w3.org/TR/xsl/*.
3. XSL Transformations Version 2.0 W3C Working Draft: *http://www.w3.org/TR/xslt20/*.
4. XML Path Language 2.0 W3C Working Draft: *http://www.w3.org/TR/xpath20/*.
5. Extensible Stylesheet Language Version 1.0, Formatting Objects: *http://www.w3.org/TR/xsl/slice6.html#fo-section*.
6. Antenna House, Professional Formatting Solutions: *http://www.antennahouse.com/*.
7. Simple Object Access Protocol 1.1 Specifications: *http://www.w3.org/TR/SOAP/*.
8. Web Services Description Language Version 1.2, W3C Working Draft: *http://www.w3.org/TR/2003/WD-wsdl12-20030303/*.
9. UDDI Version 3 Specification; OASIS UDDI Specifications: *http://www.oasis-open.org/committees/uddi-spec/doc/tcspecs.htm#uddiv3*.
10. XForms 1.0 W3C Candidate Recommendation: *http://www.w3.org/TR/xforms/*.
11. Natural Language Semantics Markup Language for the Speech Interface Framework, W3C Working Draft: *http://www.w3.org/TR/nl-spec/*.
12. Voice Extensible Markup Language Version 1.0: *http://www.w3.org/TR/voicexml/*.
13. SALT Forum. 2002. Speech Application Language Tags. Technical white paper presented Jan. 20, 2002. Available at: *http://www.saltforum.org/spec.asp*.
14. Resource Description Framework Model and Syntax Specification: *http://www.w3.org/TR/1999/REC-rdf-syntax-19990222/*.
15. DAML+OIL Reference Description: *http://www.w3.org/TR/daml+oil-reference*.
16. XML Topic Maps 1.0: *http://www.topicmaps.org/xtm/1.0/*.
17. CycML, OpenCyc.org: *http://opencyc.sourceforge.net/cycml.xsd*.
18. Business Process Execution Language for Web Services, Version 1.1: *http://www.106.ibm.com/developerworks/library/ws-bpel/*.

APPENDIX 3

Source Examples

In this appendix, you will find practical examples of how to:

- Start a collaborative service
- Read/write geographical data
- Use Java Naming and Directory Interface (JNDI) for multiple types of data sources, including domain name servers
- Share a screen with multiple users (great for troubleshooting and demos!)
- Use Java Media Framework (JMF) and Java Message Service (JMS)
- Create speech recognition and text-to-speech (TTS) applications in C#
- Spam and Spam Killers
- Improving efficiency and reliability of your email server
- Create a distributed knowledge system and join educational/knowledge alliances.

These are the main targets, but the list can go on and on. You will find basic source examples in this appendix, and you can download more from this book's support Web sites at Cambridge University Press (www.cup.org/titles/ 0521525837.htm) and ITSchool, Inc. (www.JavaSchool.com).

GETTING INTO COLLABORATIVE SERVICES

Ben was always good with computers; some cosmic adventure games even followed him in his dreams. He was also very open to sharing or (using the impressive word) "collaboration." He opened his first collaborative Web site when he was very young. He often had to stay home sick, and the site helped him to keep in touch with his kindergarten class. All his teachers and friends received his invitation-links to the site, except for Peter, a boy who never shared his piece of cake with anyone. (At that time Ben dreamed about being a teacher and seriously thought that he provided a good lesson for Peter.)

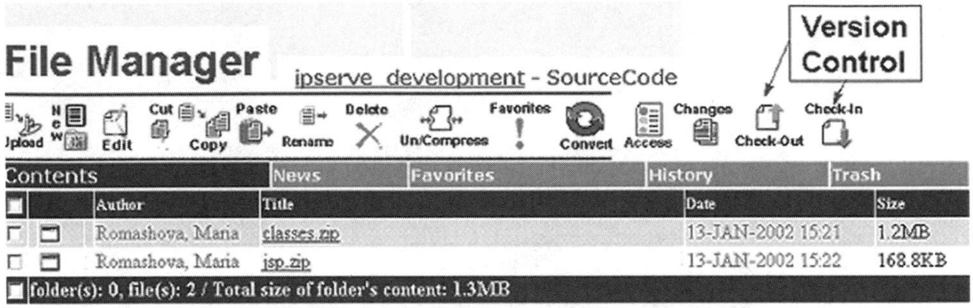

FIGURE A3.1. File Management Interface.

After finishing high school, Ben built hundreds of Web communities connecting people around the globe, but he was looking ahead even farther. His current dream job was in travel, something that would take him overseas, everywhere in the world, and maybe even beyond to other planets. Ben firmly believed (he loved science fiction stories) that communications, followed by personal meetings, could solve all problems between people, and he wanted to be a problem solver. On top of his yoga classes, he always found time to help others create teamwork centers. The file upload service that allowed users to post and share documents on the Web was usually a starting point for such ventures.

The File Upload Service for the Collaborative Site

How does it work? There are two parts to this game. Here is what we see on the client side when we point a Web browser to a friendly collaborative server that provides file management on the Web (Fig. A3.1).

File management interface, Java Servlet, and JSP examples

The page in Fig. A3.1 is produced by the Java server page (JSP) *jsp/files/fileManager.jsp*. Figure A3.2 displays some (essential) source lines:

```
Please note "action=<%=parserPath%> method=POST" in the form
definition.
The parserPath variable is set to "http://IPServe.com/go/private.ip"
```

The program associated with this URL can be a Java servlet that checks user authentication data before actually providing a service. We consider this servlet code, Private.java, a bit later. What is intriguing here for us is the upload service, and how it will be provided.

The servlet program (after authentication) redirects control to a specific JSP that is responsible for the response. In this case, the name of the page is *jsp/files/uploadService.jsp*. Here is a simple rule for naming JSPs. Note that requesting the service we provided are two important hidden lines on the Web page:

```
<input type=hidden name=service value=files>
<input type=hidden name=action value=uploadService>
```

```
<%
 String parserPath = (String)session.getAttribute("parserPath");
 String uploadedFiles = (String)session.getAttribute("uploadedFiles");
%>
<html><head>
<title>File Manager. JSP example </title></head>
<body>
<form name=upload action=<%=parserPath%> method=POST>
    <input type=hidden name='service' value='files'>
    <input type=hidden name='action' value='uploadService'>
</form>
   <img src="/support/images/IP_header.gif">
    < a href=javascript:document.form[0].submit()>
    <img src="/support/images/files/icons_personal_default.gif"></a>
</body></html>
```

FIGURE A3.2.

All JSP pages are located in the WEB-INF area, which makes these pages protected from direct access. After authentication, the servlet-controller uses these two lines to create a name for the JSP involved in serving this request.

A red arrow points to the *Upload* control displayed at the top left corner. Pressing the icon triggers the *jsp/files/uploadService.jsp* JSP with the following HTML code displayed in Fig. A3.3 (I provide only the essential portion of the code here). The Web browser gladly displays this code as a familiar **browse** screen (Fig. A3.4).

And what happens after the file is selected and the **Add to the list** button is pressed? Please note the line in the following JSP source that defines the target for data submission:

```
<form name=multipart enctype="multipart/form-data"
action="<%=uploadPath%>"
```

A special path, **uploadPath**, is selected for data processing. The reason is the very special type of form (**enctype**) used for data upload. The **uploadPath** is set to *UploaderServlet*. It extracts the necessary parameters from the *HttpServletRequest* stream. It also transforms the request stream into an *InputStream*. Then it calls the upload service class, passing only the necessary parameters to it. This way, we avoid tight coupling between a controller and services. The same upload service may be reused with any input stream, not only with the *HttpServletRequest* stream.

The *UploaderServlet* (Fig. A3.5) works as a team with the *Uploader* class. The methods of the *Uploader* class are decoupled from the Web container and may be performed on any input stream. This separation of the business logic (the *Uploader*) from the controller (the *UploaderServlet*) and presentation layers (done with JSPs) allows us to reuse services with many presentation layers related to different client devices, and so on.

Before providing a code extract for the file upload service, I would like to focus on the multipart nature of uploading files. Here is an introduction quoted from a related RFC 1867.

```
<%
    String uploadPath = (String)session.getAttribute("uploadPath");
    String parserPath = (String)session.getAttribute("parserPath");
%>
<html><head>
<title>Upload Browser example from the book "Integration ready systems" by
Jeff Zhuk, Cambridge University Press </title>
<script language="JavaScript">
<!--
function back () {
  location.replace("<%=parserPath%>");
  document.open();
}
--></script>
</head>
<body bgcolor=ffffff link=0000ff vlink=0000ff>
<table>
    <td>
        <img src='/support/images/files/Send.gif'>
    </td>
    <td width=400>
        <font size=5>Upload file(s) from your local drive.</font><br><br>
        Please click on "Browse" to select a file that you wish to upload
from your local Hard or Floppy Drive, then press "Add to the list". When
you have finished the file selection, press the "Upload" button to complete
the upload.
    </td>
</table>
<form name=multipart enctype="multipart/form-data" action="<%=uploadPath%>"
method=post>
<center>
    <input name=uploadedfile type=file size=35><br>
    <input type=submit name=upload value="Add to the list">
<!--onClick='parent.history_idx++'-->
    <input type=button name=closeUploadPage value="Close" onClick='back()'>
</center>
</form></body></html>
```

FIGURE A3.3.

THE MIME MULTIPART/RELATED CONTENT-TYPE; RFC 1867

Abstract

The Multipart/Related Content-type provides a common mechanism for representing objects that are aggregates of related Multipurpose Internet Mail Extension (MIME) body parts. This document defines the Multipart/Related Content-type and provides examples of its use.

Introduction

Several applications of MIME, including MIME-PEM, MIME-Macintosh, and other proposals, require multiple body parts that make sense only in the aggregate. The present approach to these compound objects is to define specific multipart subtypes for each new object.

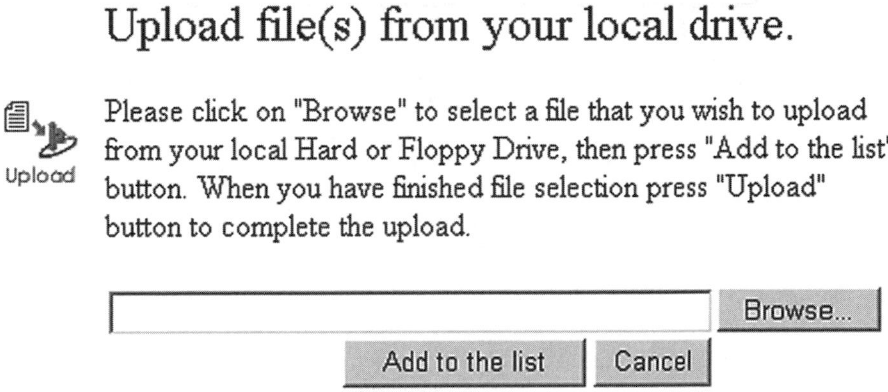
Upload file(s) from your local drive.
Upload
Please click on "Browse" to select a file that you wish to upload from your local Hard or Floppy Drive, then press "Add to the list" button. When you have finished file selection press "Upload" button to complete the upload.
Browse...
Add to the list
Cancel

FIGURE A3.4. File Upload Interface.

In keeping with the MIME philosophy of having one mechanism to achieve the same goal for different purposes, this document describes a single mechanism for such aggregate or compound objects.

The Multipart/Related Content-type addresses the MIME representation of compound objects. The object is categorized by a "type" parameter. Additional parameters are provided to indicate a specific starting body part or root and auxiliary information that may be required when unpacking or processing the object.

Intended Use

The Multipart/Related media type is intended for compound objects consisting of several interrelated body parts. For a Multipart/Related object, proper display cannot be achieved by individually displaying the constituent body parts.

The content-type of the Multipart/Related object is specified by the type parameter. The "start" parameter, if given, points, via a content-ID, to the body part that contains the object root. The default root is the first body part within the Multipart/Related body:

```
(See also RFC1867, http://www.ietf.org/rfc/rfc1867.txt)
```

Taking into account the complexity of the processing, we separate the upload into two steps. First, we load all the data from the input stream and save them into a temporary file. This way, we ensure that the network-related processing takes the shortest route. Second, we parse the temporary file, looking for multiple parts to be properly glued into a final object that will be saved to a predefined destination.

There is one particular pitfall to avoid when dealing with files: do not use hard-coded path definitions; use *java.util.Properties* instead. For example, the *Uploader* class defines the temporary directory with the line below:

```
tempFolder = System.getProperty("java.io.tmpdir");
// escape hard-code
```

Use System Properties to Escape Hard-Coded Path Definitions

This information is included in the Java application program interface (API) documentation for the *getProperties* method in the *java.lang.System* class.

```
/*
 * UploaderServlet.java
 * Source example from the book "Integration ready systems", Jeff
 * Zhuk, Cambridge University Press
 * Created on February 18, 2002, 8:49 PM
 */
package com.its; // Internet Technology School, Inc.

import java.io.IOException;

import javax.servlet.http.HttpServlet;
import javax.servlet.http.HttpServletRequest;
import javax.servlet.http.HttpServletResponse;
import javax.servlet.ServletException;
import javax.servlet.http.HttpSession;
import javax.servlet.ServletConfig;

import com.its.util.Uploader;

/**
 * The purpose of this servlet is to serve "upload files" request
 * and forward it to appropriate JSP page
 * @author mromashova@JavaSchool.com
 * @author jeff.zhuk@JavaSchool.com
 */
public class UploaderServlet extends HttpServlet {

    /** Initializes the servlet.
    */
    public void init(ServletConfig config) throws ServletException {
        super.init(config);
    }

    /** Destroys the servlet.
    */
    public void destroy() {

    }

  /** Processes requests for both HTTP <code>GET</code>
    * and <code>POST</code> methods.
    * @param request servlet request
    * @param response servlet response
    */
    protected void service(HttpServletRequest request,
      HttpServletResponse response) throws ServletException,
      java.io.IOException {
        String fileDir = System.getProperty("user.dir") +
        "support/uploadedFiles"; // escape hardcoded path
        int max_size = 10485760;
```

Figure A3.5.

```
        com.its.util.Uploader uploader = new
          Uploader(request.getInputStream(), null, fileDir,
          request.getHeader("Content-type"), max_size);
        String result = uploader.uploadFile();
        HttpSession session = request.getSession(false);
        if (session == null) {
            session = request.getSession(true); // session is not
            valid, create new one, initialize session parameters
            if (session == null) {
                return; // server error
            }
        }

        session.setAttribute("uploadedFiles", result);
        getServletConfig().getServletContext()
          .getRequestDispatcher("/jsp/files/fileManager.jsp")
          .forward(request, response);
    }

    /**
    * Returns a short description of the servlet.
    */
    public String getServletInfo() {
        return "The purpose of this servlet is to get response to
          upload files and then forward it to appropriate JSP page
          then forward it to appropriate JSP page";
    }

}
```

FIGURE A3.5. (*cont.*)

The *getProperties()* method of the *java.lang.System* class returns the *java.util.Properties* object that determines the current system properties.

First, if there is a security manager, its *checkPropertiesAccess* method is called with no arguments. This may result in a security exception.

If there is no current set of system properties, a set of system properties is first created and initialized. This set of system properties always includes values for the following keys:

Key	Description of Associated Value
java.version	Java Runtime Environment version
java.vendor	Java Runtime Environment vendor
java.vendor.url	Java vendor URL
java.home	Java installation directory
java.vm.specification.version	Java Virtual Machine specification version
java.vm.specification.vendor	Java Virtual Machine specification vendor
java.vm.specification.name	Java Virtual Machine specification name
java.vm.version	Java Virtual Machine implementation version

java.vm.vendor	Java Virtual Machine implementation vendor
java.vm.name	Java Virtual Machine implementation name
java.specification.version	Java Runtime Environment specification version
java.specification.vendor	Java Runtime Environment specification vendor
java.specification.name	Java Runtime Environment specification name
java.class.version	Java class format version number
java.class.path	Java class path
java.library.path	List of paths to search when loading libraries
java.io.tmpdir	Default temp file path
java.compiler	Name of JIT compiler to use
java.ext.dirs	Path of extension directory or directories
os.name	Operating system name
os.arch	Operating system architecture
os.version	Operating system version
file.separator	File separator ("/" on UNIX)
path.separator	Path separator (":" on UNIX)
line.separator	Line separator ("\n" on UNIX)
user.name	User's account name
user.home	User's home directory
user.dir	User's current working directory

Note that even if the security manager does not permit the *getProperties* operation, it may choose to permit the *getProperty(String)* operation.

System properties (a part of any platform's JVM) help run packages, such as the *Uploader*, on multiple operating systems.

Figure A3.6 presents the source of the *Uploader* class. The *Uploader* uses several methods of the *InOut* class. Fig. A3.7 demonstrates the source of these methods.

It is about time to discuss the unified servlet-controller, Private.java. Figure A3.8 shows the source code.

The Web server runs the *init()* method of the servlet only once, when the servlet class is instantiated, in a manner similar to a Web browser's invocation of an applet's *init()* method. This is the perfect time to read the configuration data.

The *service()* method is invoked by a Web server each time the server gets an HTTP request from a client. The request can be either of the *Post* or *Get* type. We didn't provide for specific processing: *doPost()* or *doGet()*. That's why in both cases, the *service()* method processes the request.

This is unified processing for all services. The method retrieves service and action names and constructs a URL to forward the request to the proper destination, which will serve it.

The installation package, compressed into a single Java Archive (JAR) file includes configuration files such as server.xml, web.xml (Fig. A3.9), and build.xml (Fig. A3.10). The ANT (free packaging tool) works with the configuration files during the installation process.

The server.xml file in the example is just this line:

```
<Context path="\Uploader" docBase="uploader" crossContext="false"
debug="0" reloadable="true"/>
```

```
// Uploader

package com.its.util;

import java.io.*;
import java.util.*;

/**
 * Source example, Jeff Zhuk,
 * Cambridge University Press
 * This class is used for uploading file with specified fileName
 * its.util.InOut class methods are used to save and read files
 * and to provide a unique temp file name
 * @@author Jeff.Zhuk@JavaSchool.com
 */
public class Uploader {
    private InputStream in;
    private String fileName;
    private String dir;
    private String header;
    private int maxFileSize;
    public static String DEFAULT_STRING_NO_NAME =
      "DEFAULT_STRING_NO_NAME";
    public static String tempFolder; // get from system properties
    //(escape hard-coded path definitions)
    public static String tempName = "uploaded";
    public static String tempExtension = "tmp";
    /**
     * Uploader constructor takes initial parameters
     * @param in
     * @param fileName
     * @param dir
     * @param header
     * @param maxFileSize
     */
    public Uploader(InputStream in, String fileName, String dir,
    String header, int maxFileSize)
    {
        this.in = in;
        this.fileName = fileName;
        this.dir = dir;
        this.header = header;
        this.maxFileSize = maxFileSize;
        tempFolder = System.getProperty("java.io.tmpdir");
        // escape hard-coded path definitions
    }
    /**
     * uploadFile() works as a 2 step process.
     * The method receives data from input data stream and saves it
     * into a temporary file.
     * Then it parses this temporary file to glue pieces into a
```

FIGURE A3.6.

```
 * final object and saves it into a pre-defined destination
 * @return result
 */
public String uploadFile() {
    String result = "OK";
    byte[] data = its.util.InOut.readByteStream(in);
    // reading data
    if(data == null) {
        result = "ERROR: network failure to upload " + fileName
          + " see details in the log file.";
        return result;
    }
    // provide a unique name for temp storage
    String tempFileName = its.util.InOut.getUniqueName
      (tempFolder, tempName, tempExtension);
    if(!its.util.InOut.writeBinFile(tempFileName, data, 0,
      data.length) ) {
        return ("ERROR: saving temp file for upload operation");
    }
    // find section where file header ends
    // String boundary = extractBoundary(header);

    // split file data into header and data itself
    // collect info about all files into array of proper
    // FileInfo structures
    FileInfo[] file = extractFiles(data, boundary);
    // check filenames and save uploaded files
    result = "";
    for (int i=0; i < file.length; i++) {
        // check if this is no-name file - assign a name passed
        // as a parameter
        if (fileName != null) {
          if (!file[i].filename.equals(DEFAULT_STRING_NO_NAME)){
                file[i].filename = fileName;
            }
        }
        result += file[i].saveFile(data, dir + File.separator);
        // for FileManager
        // optional code creating a list of uploaded files
    }
    return result;
}
/* Return file name from HTTP header.
 * If file name is not defined return DEFAULT_STRING_NO_NAME
 name
 * @param header HTTP header.
 * @return filename
 */
private String getFilename(String header) {
    String filename = "";
    header.toLowerCase();
```

Figure A3.6. ***(cont.)***

```
        String filenameHeader = "filename=";
        int lengthOfFilenameHeader = filenameHeader.length();
        int index;
        if ((index = header.indexOf(filenameHeader)) != -1) {
            int up_index = header.indexOf((int)'"',index + 1 +
            lengthOfFilenameHeader);
            // looking for closing quote  ->  filename="....
            // 9 +1 is a length of -> filename="
            filename = header.substring(index+
            lengthOfFilenameHeader+1,up_index);
            index = filename.lastIndexOf((int)'/');
            // symbol "file.separator"
            up_index = filename.lastIndexOf((int)'\\');
            filename = filename.substring(Math.max(index, up_index) + 1);
        } else {
            filename = DEFAULT_STRING_NO_NAME;
        }
        return filename;
    }

    /**
     * Extract data and exclude file name
     * @param fis structure consisting of filename, first and last
     * indexes of data that belongs to the file
     * @param data
     */
    private void extractData(FileInfo fis, String data) {
        char[] ch = {'\r','\n','\r','\n'};
        // these symbols bound the header from the body
        // byte represenation is {13,10,13,10}

        String new_line = new String(ch);
        String header;

        //get the header
        int index = data.indexOf(new_line,2);
        if (index != -1) {
            header = data.substring(0,index);
            fis.filename = getFilename(header);
            // 4 is a length of new_line ( {13,10,13,10} )
            fis.start_index += index + 4;
        }

    }

    /**
     * split source request (data) into parts
     * and get info about every part
     * @param data
     * @param boundary
```

FIGURE A3.6. *(cont.)*

```
 * @return files array of FileInfo structure
 */
private FileInfo[] extractFiles(byte[] data, String boundary) {
    int i = 0, index = 0, prev_index = 0;
    // string are easier to work with
    String data_str = new String(data);
    Vector data_vec = new Vector(); // used for temporary
    storing of request parts

    // read the number of parts in request which are limited by
    // "boundary" tag
    while((index = data_str.indexOf(boundary, index)) != -1) {
      // first step is preparing for indexing
      if (i != 0) {
        // here we extract whole message limited by "boundary" tag
        // whole message is (header + content)

        FileInfo f_info = new FileInfo(DEFAULT_STRING_NO_NAME,
        prev_index, index - 2);
        // -2 because content is separated from "boundary"
           with "--" (in byte representation {'\r','\n'})
        extractData(f_info, data_str.substring
        (prev_index,index));
      data_vec.addElement(f_info);
      }
      index += boundary.length();
      prev_index = index;
      i++;
    }

    // i-1 must equal to data_vec.capacity();

    FileInfo[] files = new FileInfo[i-1];
    Enumeration enum = data_vec.elements();
    i=0;
    while (enum.hasMoreElements()) {
        files[i] = (FileInfo) enum.nextElement();
        // convert data_vec into array (array is easier to use) i++;
    }
    return files;
}
/**
 * extract boundary
 * @param str
 * @return boundary
 */
private String extractBoundary(String str) {
    String boundaryHeader = "boundary=";
    int lengthOfBoundaryHeader = boundaryHeader.length();
```

FIGURE A3.6. ***(cont.)***

```
        int index = str.lastIndexOf(boundaryHeader);
        // lengthOfBoundaryHeader (9) is a number of letters in "boundary="
        String boundary = str.substring(index + lengthOfBoundaryHeader);
        boundary = "--" + boundary;  // this is because the real
        length is longer by 2 "-" symbols, then
        // the value from "Content-Type" header.
        return boundary;
    }
}   // end of public class Uploader

/**
 * FileInfo class provides a structure for extracted from the data
 * stream file properties:
 * filename, start index, and stop index of data that belongs to the file
 * method saveFile() checks the filename and after correction saves the
 * file
 * @@author Jeff.Zhuk@JavaSchool.com
 */
class FileInfo {
    public String filename;

    // points to an index of the beginning of the file in the
       "byte[] data" array
    public int start_index;
    // points to an index of the ending of the file in the "byte[]
       data" array public int last_index;
    // this constructor sets intitial values for the instances of
    // the class public FileInfo(String filename, int start_index,
       int last_index) {
        this.filename = filename;
        this.start_index = start_index;
        this.last_index = last_index;
    }

    /**
     * saveFile() checks the filename and saves the data
     * @param data
     * @param directory a folder assigned for saving files
     */
    public String saveFile(byte[] data, String directory) {
        // check filename and correct if necessary
        if (filename.equals(Uploader.DEFAULT_STRING_NO_NAME))
        return "";
        int index = filename.length()-1;
        String mask = "";
        while(index >= 0) {
            if(filename.charAt(index--) == '.') {
                break;
            }
        }
```

FIGURE A3.6. ***(cont.)***

```
        if(index >= 0) {
            mask = filename.substring(index+1, filename.length());
        }
        filename = filename.replace(' ','_');
        // for FileManager (spaces are not allowed in filename)

        // write a proper portion of the data to the disk
        // data starts from start_index; length is calculated below
        int length = last_index - start_index;
        if(!its.util.InOut.writeBinFile(directory + filename, data,
        start_index, length)) {
            // for some reason can not write to this file space
            // optional code trying to find writeable folder, for
               example using System.getProperty("user.dir")
            return ("ERROR: saving " + directory + filename);
        } else {
            return ("OK: saving " + directory + filename);
        }
    }
}   // end of private class FileInfo
```

FIGURE A3.6. *(cont.)*

I once mentioned that the *java.util.Properties* object can help configure server applications for multiple operating systems. A simple program that reveals all the property names and values for any platform is presented in Fig. A3.11.

An important part of collaboration is secure and traceable access to data and services. The Distributed Active Knowledge patent application [1] describes some elements of data access as a three-dimensional matrix of security types, roles, and rules.

What is GPS and how does GPS work?

GPS is not a General Protection System that generates the famous General Protection Error. This important part of location-based services, Global Positioning System (*http://gps.gov*) is based on 24 satellites that broadcast radio signals. A GPS device receives this low-power high-frequency radio signal from the satellites and measures the travel time from each one. The satellite's spin around the earth takes 12 hours.

It finds its own position by using a trigonometric method with a fancy name, "triangulation." The device takes into consideration angles of fixed points with a known distance apart. Those points are three satellites of the 24 active GPS satellites.

There are six satellite orbits distributed evenly around the earth. Four satellites are located in each orbit. The orbits are at an altitude of about 11,000 nautical miles and inclined 55 degrees from the equator.

Each satellite transmits two signals. The L1 (1575.42 MHz) signal is modulated with coarse/acquisition (C/A) code, and the protected (P) code. The L2 (1227.60 MHz) signal only carries the P code.

Note, that the regular (non-military) receivers only use the L1 frequency with the C/A code.

```
// InOut

package com.its.util; // IT School, http://JavaSchool.com

import java.io.*;
import java.net.*;
import java.util.*;

/**
 * InOut class is to provide persistence on the server side
 * It includes static methods handling data from file system
 * as well as from HTTP and other streams
 * The methods are used for server-server and applet-server communications
 * The methods are tailored for text, binary; Java serialized
 * objects, and zip data
 * @@author Jeff.Zhuk@JavaSchool.com
 **/
 public class InOut {
     public static boolean debug = false;
     // can be set true for troubleshooting by GUI
     public static int DEFAULT_MAX_FILE_SIZE = 4*1024*1024; // 4 mb
 /**
 * getUniqueName() method checks a specified directory for a
 * specified name
 * and adds a unique index to the name to avoid collisions
 *
 * @param iDir directory name
 * @param iName file name
 * @return name including path and index
 * @@author Jeff.Zhuk@JavaSchool.com
 */
    public static String getUniqueName(String iDir, String iName,
    String iExtension)
    {
        File dir = new File(iDir);
        if(!dir.isDirectory() && dir.exists())
            dir.delete();
        if(!dir.isDirectory()) {
            dir.mkdir();
            return (iDir + File.separator + iName + ".1." +
            iExtension);
        }
        String[] entries = dir.list(new DirFileFilter(iExtension));
        int max = 0;
        if(entries == null || entries.length == 0) {
            return (iDir + File.separator + iName + "." +
              (new Integer(max + 1)).toString() + "." + iExtension);
        }
        int current = 0;
        String entry = null;
        int index = -1;
        for(int i = 0; i < entries.length; i++) {
```

FIGURE A3.7.

```
            if(entries[i].startsWith(iName)) {
                index = entries[i].lastIndexOf(File.separator);
                entry = entries[i].substring(index + 1);
                entry = entry.substring(iName.length() + 1,
                    entry.indexOf(".", iName.length() + 1));
                try {
                    current = Integer.parseInt(entry);
                    if(current > max)
                        max = current;
                } catch (Exception e) {
                       System.out.println("InOut.getUniqueName:
                       ERROR-" +
                          "Filename=" + entries[i] + " index=" + entry);
                }
            }
        }
        return (iDir + File.separator + iName + "." +
          (new Integer(max + 1)).toString() + "." + iExtension);
    }
/**<PRE>
 * reads a stream of bytes
 *
 * @param in stream
 * @return bytes read
 * @@author Jeff.Zhuk@JavaSchool.com
 Example:
       URL url = new URL(iApplet.getCodeBase(), iURL); // if from applet
       URLConnection urlConn = url.openConnection();
       InputStream inStream=urlConn.getInputStream();
       byte[] bytes = InOut.readByteStream(inStream);
</PRE>
 **/
    public static byte[] readByteStream(InputStream in) {
        try {
            if(in == null) {
                if(debug)
                   System.out.println("InOut.readBytes:in=null?");
                return null;
            }
            Vector v = new Vector(10,10);
            int size = 1024;
            byte[] oData = new byte[size];
            int bytes_read = 0;
            int offset = 0;
            int total = 0;
            while(bytes_read >= 0) {
                bytes_read = in.read(oData, 0, size);
                if( bytes_read == -1)
                    break;
                byte[] block = new byte[bytes_read];
                System.arraycopy(oData, 0, block, 0, bytes_read);
                v.addElement(block);
```

FIGURE A3.7. *(cont.)*

```
                total += bytes_read;
            }
            in.close();

            if(v.size() == 0 || total == 0) {
                if(debug)
                   System.out.println("InOut.readByteStream:blocks="
                   + v.size() + "total bytes=" + total);
                return null;
            }
            byte[] bytes = new byte[total];
            int current = 0;
            for(int i=0; i < v.size(); i++) {
                oData = (byte[])v.elementAt(i);
                System.arraycopy(oData, 0, bytes, current, oData.length);
                current += oData.length;
            }
if(debug)
System.out.println("InOut.readByteStream:result=" + (new String(bytes)));
            return bytes;
        } catch (Exception e) {
            return null;
        }
    }
/**<PRE>
 * write binary file
 * @param iFilename
 * @param iData bytes to write
 * @param iOffset starting byte of the source
 * @param iSize number of bytes to write
 * @return true if success
 * @@author Jeff.Zhuk@JavaSchool.com
</PRE>
 **/
    public static boolean writeBinFile(String iFilename, byte[]
    iData, int iOffset, int iSize) {

        File file;
        try{
            file=new File(iFilename);
            FileOutputStream out=new FileOutputStream(file);
            out.write(iData, iOffset, iSize);
            out.close();
            return true;
        } catch (IOException ioe) {
            if(debug)
               System.out.println("writeBinFile: " + ioe);
            return false;
        }
    }
}   // end of public class InOut (only 3 method were extracted
    helping Uploader )
```

FIGURE A3.7. *(cont.)*

```
/**
 * DirFileFilter class is to provide filtering directories and files
 * with proper Extension
 * @@author Jeff.Zhuk@JavaSchool.com
 **/
class DirFileFilter implements FilenameFilter
{
    private String _extension;

    public DirFileFilter(String iExtension) {
        _extension = iExtension;
    }
    public boolean accept(File iDir, String iName) {
        if( (new File(iDir, iName)).isDirectory() ||
        iName.endsWith(_extension))
            return true;
        else
            return false;
    }
}   // end on internal class DirFileFilter
```

FIGURE A3.7. ***(cont.)***

Satellites can use the same frequency for transmission because each satellite has its own unique "Pseudo-Random Code."

We can determine how long it took to reach the satellite by calculating the delay between the times when the receiver's code appears and late the satellite's code appears.

We get the distance by multiplying the time by the speed of light. This is of course a simplified version of what is going on in reality. Weather, clouds, and other circumstances provide a lot of room for corrections. The best GPS device today is Differential GPS (DGPS). DGPS can measure its inaccuracy at a stationary receiver station and then broadcast a radio signal with correction information.

How to include a GPS device into your application

The standard protocol for GPS communications is NMEA-0183 (National Marine Electronics Association) [2].

The standard defines electrical signal requirements as well as data transmission protocol. According to the protocol a 4800-baud serial data transmission bus may have only one talker but many listeners.

The data are transmitted as ASCII characters in the form of "sentences." Each sentence starts with a "$," a two letter "talker ID," a three letter "sentence ID," followed by a number of data fields separated by commas, and terminated by an optional checksum, and a carriage return/line feed.

You can find free software that reads NMEA [3] displays and logs GPS data [4].

From this point we can move to Geographical Information Systems and briefly look at software that can deal with integrated vector graphics and data.

```
/*
 * Dispatcher.java
 * Source example
 * Jeff Zhuk, Cambridge University Press
 * Created on February 4, 2002, 1:19 PM
 */
package com.its;

import javax.servlet.*;
import javax.servlet.http.*;

/**
 * The purpose of this class is to get all requests from clients and
 * redirect them to proper JSP page
 * @author mromashova@JavaSchool.com
 * @author jeff.zhuk@JavaSchool.com
 */
public class Dispatcher extends HttpServlet {

    /** Initializes the servlet.
    */
    public void init(ServletConfig config) throws ServletException {
        super.init(config);
    }

    /** Destroys the servlet.
    */
    public void destroy() {

    }
    public void initHttpSession(HttpSession session,
    HttpServletResponse response){
        session.setAttribute("parserPath",
          response.encodeURL("/go/Dispatcher.ip"));
        session.setAttribute("uploadPath",
          response.encodeURL("/go/uploader.ip"));
    }

    /** Processes requests for both HTTP <code>GET</code>
    * and <code>POST</code> methods.
    * @param request servlet request
    * @param response servlet response
    */
    protected void service(HttpServletRequest request,
   HttpServletResponse response) throws ServletException,
   java.io.IOException {
        HttpSession session = request.getSession(false);
        if (session == null) {
            session = request.getSession(true); // session is not
            valid, create new one, initialize session parameters
            if (session == null) {
```

FIGURE A3.8.

```
                return; // server error
            }
            initHttpSession(session, response);
        }
        // Place all parameters inside Hashtable parameters and
        // place this hashtable inside HttpSession

        String url = "/jsp/files/fileManager.jsp";
        if (request.getParameter("service") != null &&
        request.getParameter("action") != null){
            url = "/jsp/" + request.getParameter("service") + "/" +
            request.getParameter("action") + ".jsp";
        }
        // Redirect request to proper JSP page
        getServletConfig().getServletContext().
        getRequestDispatcher(url).forward(request, response);
    }

    /**
     * getServletInfo() is an informational method
     * @return a short description of the servlet.
    */
    public String getServletInfo() {
        return "The purpose of this servlet is to forward request to
        appropriate JSP page";
    }
}
```

FIGURE A3.8. *(cont.)*

WORKING WITH GEOGRAPHICAL INFORMATION SYSTEMS

How Do We Read, Write, and Draw a Mixture of Graphics and Data?

Several successful companies are providing travelers with geographical information. One example is MapQuest.com.

MapQuest generates a map as a GIF file on the server and sends this file to a Web client—a browser. Every click on such a map results in a new network round-trip from client to server and back, generating a new map each time.

A Java applet client may be more efficient than that. It can accept raw data and render graphics on the client side. In response to a client click, the Java applet can immediately recreate another graphics map, or produce a meaningful chart or table with data related to the map.

Facilities and telecommunications managers use geographical maps, as well as data trees, to represent relationships between physical space and objects. Geographic Information System (GIS) developers solve several problems, including:

- Reading and writing special file formats, invented to represent geographical data
- Separating and relating graphics and data representations

```
<!DOCTYPE web-app PUBLIC "-//Sun Microsystems, Inc.//DTD Web
Application 2.2//EN" "http://java.sun.com/j2ee/dtds/
web-app_2_2.dtd">

<web-app>

    <display-name>IPServe Application</display-name>
    <description>
    JSP/Servlet-based engine for IPServe.com, JavaSchool.net, etc.
    </description>

    <servlet>
        <servlet-name>Private</servlet-name>
        <servlet-class>com.its.Private</servlet-class>
    </servlet>
    <servlet>
        <servlet-name>uploader</servlet-name>
        <servlet-class>com.its.UploaderServlet</servlet-class>
    </servlet>

    <servlet-mapping>
        <servlet-name>Private</servlet-name>
        <url-pattern>/private.ip</url-pattern>
    </servlet-mapping>

    <servlet-mapping>
        <servlet-name>uploader</servlet-name>
        <url-pattern>/uploader.ip</url-pattern>
    </servlet-mapping>
    <session-config>
      <session-timeout>30</session-timeout>    <!-- 30 minutes -->
    </session-config>

</web-app>
```

FIGURE A3.9.

- Delivering this information to the end user in a format convenient for the average person and digestible for devices ranging from a corporate workstation to a PDA

GIS data are presented by several data formats. Most popular are AutoCad Data Exchange Format (DXF), Visio by Microsoft, and Shapefiles (usually integrated into higher-level formats, such as ArcInfo) by ESRI, the leader in GIS software.

Handling maps requires significant computer power; usually, dedicated servers like MapQuest.com deal directly with an original set of GIS data. These servers work hard to solve the first two problems.

Then, the server creates client data with acceptable size and format, according to the client's request and device capacity.

Web clients have limited support for vector graphics. Internet Explorer, for example, supports Vector Markup Language (VML), a subset of XML. Most Web clients have plug-ins supporting Flash, G-VML, and others.

```
<project name="Web Application Example" default="deploy" basedir=".">

  <!-- ========== Initialize Property Values ========== -->
  <property name="webapp.name"   value="Uploader" />
 <!--<property name="tomcat.home"   value="D:\tomcat" />
            You have to comment this string if you can run build.bat
            file  -->
  <property name="build.dir"     value="${tomcat.home}\webapps" />
  <property name="servlet.jar"
  <value="${tomcat.home}/lib/servlet.jar" />

  <!-- ============= Convenien tSynonyms ============== -->
  <target name="clean" depends="clean-webapp" />
  <target name="all" depends="clean,webapp" />
  <target name="help">
    <echo>
Build structure of the Web Application
Toplevel targets:
   help     -- this message
   clean    -- cleans the whole development environment
   all      -- cleans and then builds the whole system
   webapp   -- (re)builds the Web Application
    </echo>
  </target>

  <!-- ============= WEBAPP: All =================== -->
  <target name="webapp" depends="clean-webapp,compile-webapp" />
  <!-- ======== WEBAPP: Clean WebApp Directory ========= -->
  <target name="clean-webapp">
    <delete dir="${build.dir}\${webapp.name}" />
  </target>
  <!-- ====== WEBAPP: Compile Web Components =========== -->
  <target name="compile-webapp" depends="static-webapp">
    <javac   srcdir="src"
             destdir="${build.dir}\${webapp.name}\WEB-INF\classes"
             classpath="${servlet.jar}:lib/${webapp.name}.jar"
             deprecation="off" debug="on" optimize="off">
    </javac>
     <antcall target="prepare-war" />
  </target>
  <!-- ========== WEBAPP: Copy Static Web Files ======== -->
  <target name="static-webapp" depends="prepare-webapp">
    <copy todir="${build.dir}\${webapp.name}\jsp">
      <fileset dir="jsp" />
    </copy>
    <copy todir="${build.dir}\${webapp.name}">
      <fileset dir="web" />
    </copy>
    <copy todir="${build.dir}\${webapp.name}\WEB-INF">
      <fileset dir="etc" />
    </copy>
```

FIGURE A3.10.

```
<!--
    <copy todir="${build.dir}\${webapp.name}\WEB-INF\lib">
      <fileset dir="lib" />
    </copy>
-->
    <copy todir="${build.dir}\${webapp.name}\images">
      <fileset dir="web\images" />
    </copy>
  </target>
  <!-- ======== WEBAPP: Create WebApp Directories ======= -->
  <target name="prepare-webapp">
    <mkdir dir="${build.dir}" />
    <mkdir dir="${build.dir}\${webapp.name}" />
    <mkdir dir="${build.dir}\${webapp.name}\WEB-INF" />
    <mkdir dir="${build.dir}\${webapp.name}\WEB-INF\classes" />
    <mkdir dir="${build.dir}\${webapp.name}\WEB-INF\lib" />
    <mkdir dir="${build.dir}\${webapp.name}\images" />
  </target>
  <!-- ============WEBAPP: Create War file ============-->
  <target name="prepare-war">
    <war warfile="uploader.war"
    webxml="${build.dir}\${webapp.name}\WEB-INF\web.xml">
  <!--     <fileset dir="src/html/myapp"/>  -->
      <fileset dir="${build.dir}\${webapp.name}">
        <!--<exclude name="web.xml"/>-->
      </fileset>
<!-- <classes dir="${build.dir}\${webapp.name}\WEB-INF\classes"/> -->
<!-- <zipfileset dir="${build.dir}\${webapp.name}\images" prefix="images"/>
-->
    </war>
  </target>
  <!-- ============-WEBAPP: Create War file ============-->
        <target name="deploy" depends="webapp">
            <delete dir="${build.dir}/uploader"/>
            <copy file="uploader.war" todir="${build.dir}" />
        </target>
</project>
```

FIGURE A3.10. ***(cont.)***

Figure A3.12 shows an example of GIS architecture. In the example, original AutoCad DXF data are loaded by a privileged user and converted by the map service into a VML stream transferred over HTTPS to a Java applet program. The end user does not need to download additional software or a plug-in to work with the product.

The Java applet in this example implements the VML handler and, if necessary, can extend the protocol with business-specific protocol tags built into VML comments. The end user interacts with the Java applet that renders graphics at run-time, handles events, and issues a new service request to the server only when the user's interest goes beyond the data portion currently delivered to the client device.

For example, if a current set of data on the client's device represents City A, all the user's requests, such as "ZoomIn," "ZoomOut," "Left," "Right," "Up," and "Down," will be performed by the applet. The applet would use the same raw data and would create a new

```
// TestProperties
import java.util.*;

public class TestProperties {
    public static void main(String[] args) {
        Properties p = System.getProperties();
        for(Enumeration e = p.propertyNames(); e.hasMoreElements();)
        {
            String name = (String) e.nextElement();
            String value = (String) p.getProperty(name);
            System.out.println(name + "=" + value);
        }
    }
}
```

FIGURE A3.11.

screen for the user each time. When the user expresses an interest in another city, the applet sends a service request to the server: "Get City B data."

Original map data are located on the GIS server and a related data storage that can be a mixture of a relational database management system (RDBMS), LDAP, file systems, and legacy applications that hold GIS data. A privileged remote user can also upload new maps to the server using the *Upload* mechanism described above.

Figure A3.13 upload.map shows an interface screen for such an upload.

The screen can be offered via the browser's window. This is a good example of cooperation between a Java applet and a Web browser. Java applets generally have no access to file system resources and cannot touch files on the hard drive (unless they are signed applets). The browser, on the other hand, can do this. A simple line of Java code can bring up the Web browser window shown in Figure A3.13:

```
applet.getAppletContext().showDocument(new
URL("/servlet/RequestHandler"));
```

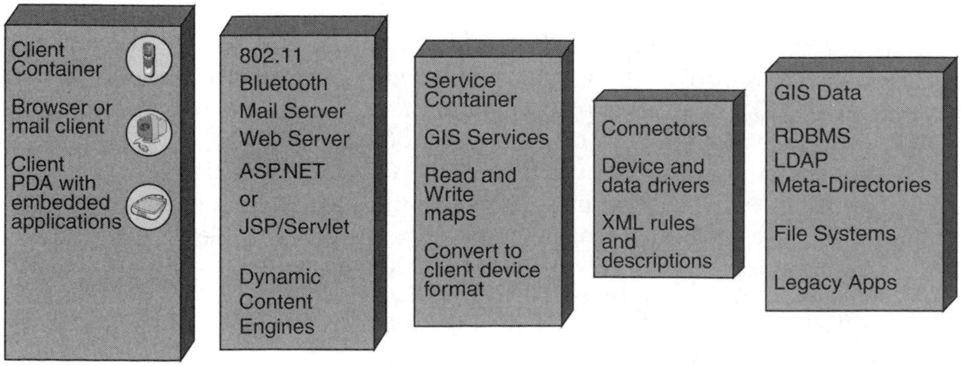

FIGURE A3.12. Multi-tier Geographical Information System.

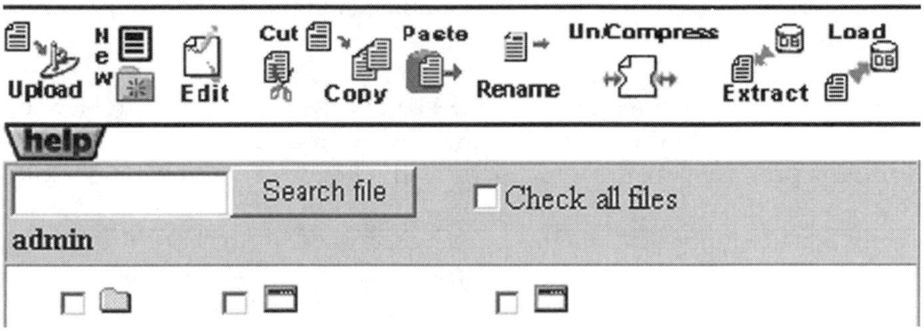

FIGURE A3.13. Upload facility maps.

The Web page then offers File Management services that include the Upload service. I have already told the upload story, so I will move on to the next step.

Reading map files is a challenging task, primarily because there are many map keywords that expose very different behaviors. The worst thing to do would be to write "if-else" code that takes into account every keyword and provides a branch of behavior for this type of map.

Using the Factory and the Abstract Factory Design Patterns

This is a great area for the Factory design pattern, as well as the Abstract Factory pattern, to be applied, again helping us "write code once" (Fig. A3.14). The Abstract Factory pattern helps us create several factories that can represent many map points.

Several class factories can be used to work with multiple map file formats, such as AutoCad DXF and ESRI Shapesfiles. Implementing the Abstract Factory Pattern helps in selecting a proper class factory at run-time. In the example above, a map file extension.dxf or .shp

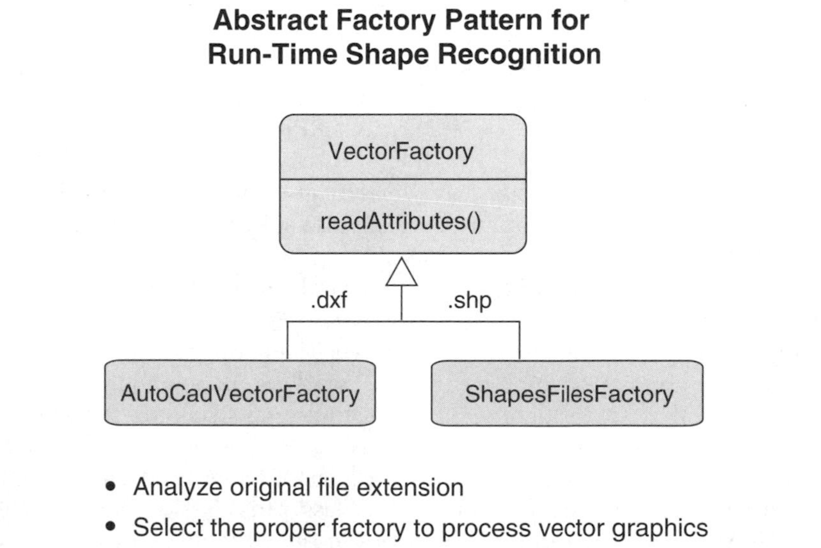

FIGURE A3.14. Abstract Factory Design Pattern Helps Select a Family of Shapes.

drives a proper factory selection. Each factory implements the *VectorFactory* interface with the *readAttributes()* method.

We use the Factory design pattern for each map type to provide the proper behavior for all map keywords. The implementation of the Factory design pattern can be done in any object-oriented language. In the brief example below, we recognize graphical shapes at run-time and adjust a program behavior to properly read different shape attributes while reading the data file.

For example, in an AutoCad DXF file, we can read the *Line* keyword to create an object of the class *Line*. Then, we can call the *readAttributes()* method of this object to read all the attributes following the shape name, so later we can reproduce the shape on the screen. Here is an example of the implementation in Java:

```
Shape shape; // Assume that the "Shape" is the base class for
             // multiple shapes
             // Read a shape name and its attributes
try {
      String name = file.read(); // file is a FileReader object
                                 // try to create a proper object
                                 // and read its attributes
    shape=(Shape)Class.forName(name).newInstance();
    shape.readAttributes();
    // fill the shape object with its attributes
}
```

We must develop a set of classes that follows the Factory design pattern to be able to use this elegant solution.

Working with Bits and Bytes: The Little Endian and the Big Endian

The big-endian or little-endian concept is about a computer system habit to store multibyte words. In the big-endian representation, the most significant byte has the lowest address (the word is stored "big-end-first"). Big-endian machines are IBM 370 families, as well as Sun and all Motorola based, and most of the various RISC computers.

The *PDP-11* and *VAX* families and Intel microprocessors (this means all PCs) are little-endian. Their bytes at lower addresses have lower significance (the word is stored "little-end-first"). Little-endian and big-endian terms can also sometimes mean bits order within a byte.

ESRI Shapefiles offer programmers an interesting and challenging task. Shapefiles, according to the specifications, include bytes with different orders of bits. Some bytes are classified as Little-Endian (PC) bytes, some as Big-Endian (e.g., Sun) bytes.

I created the *Byter* Java class, which is capable of working on bit and byte levels, to resolve this problem. Note, that to we do not need to know internal representation of integer, double, and so on. types in Java to do the conversion. We can use powerful methods of the I/O package that have this knowledge. Yes, our task is not about input or output but we can create a memory object of ByteArrayOutputStream class. This class is a close relative (a child) to the OutputStream class and can perfectly work in the IO family. For the example below, we use methods of the ByteArrayOutputStream and DataOutputStream classes to convert a double value bytes:

```
public static byte[] double2bytes(double d) {
      byte[] bytes = null;
      try {// convert double value d to bytes
            ByteArrayOutputStream bastream = new
            ByteArrayOutputStream(8);
            DataOutputStream datastream = new
            DataOutputStream(bastream);
            datastream.writeDouble(d);
            bytes = bastream.toByteArray(); // done!!!
          } catch(Exception e) {
```

The complete source code of the *com.its.util.Byter.java* file can be found on the book support Web sites.

ESRI Shapefiles [5] store vector-based geometry and attribute information for the spatial features in a data set. The shape types include point, line, and area features, represented as polygons. Data attributes are stored as records in a dBASE format file.

The Shapefiles consist of three file types with the correspondent extensions *.shp*, *.shx*, and *.dbf*. The *.shp* files store graphics data; the *.shx* files store index information that helps accelerate reading of the files. The *.dbf* files include data records that have one-to-one relationships with the associated shape records.

The *com.its.shp* package includes sources (you can find complete sources of the files mentioned below at the book support Web sites) that deal with ESRI Shapefiles. For example, the *ShpFile* class reads shapes and index information, whereas the *DbfFile* reads the data records. A set of Shapesfiles creates a layer of a map.

There is a set of classes that represent shape forms: the *Dot*, the *Arc*, the *MultiDot*, and the *Poly*. The base class for all shapes is the *ITShape* class.

The *ShpFile* class reads Shapefiles with the extensions *shp* and *shx* and creates the appropriate shape instances on the fly using the Factory design pattern.

The *DbfFile* class reads database files with the *dbf* extension and creates data records. The records are filled with Field and Feature objects. The Field object represents a part of the data record structure, whereas the Feature class represents data attributes as name-value pairs.

READING AUTOCAD VECTOR GRAPHICS

The source extracts below demonstrate reading an AutoCad DXF file with vector graphics. AutoCad shapes are represented with shape classes derived from the *Mark* base class.

The hierarchy of classes in Fig. A3.15 reflects the set of AutoCad vector shapes. The *Mark* class is the base class of the hierarchy (factory) of shapes. A similar solution may work not only for AutoCad shapes, but also for other factories.

The com.its.dxf package includes sources that deal with the DXF file format and represent popular DXF shapes: *Arc, AttrDef, AttrLine, Block, Branch, FillArc, Rect, FillRect, InsertBlock, Line, Polyline, TDFace, Vertex*, and so on. You can find source examples at the book support Web sites.

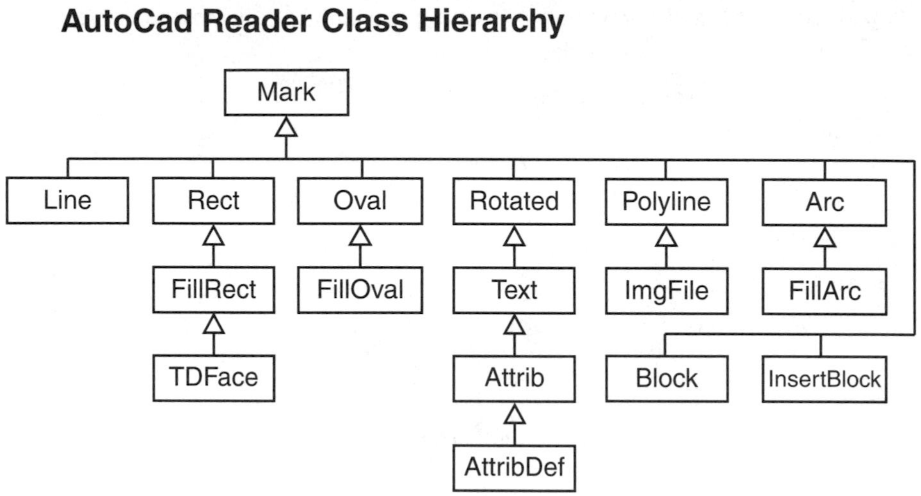

FIGURE A3.15. AutoCad Reader Class Hierarchy.

JNDI: WHAT, WHY, AND HOW?

JNDI has two main parts:

- API—the interface for application programmers that allows for the generic naming of all types of data sources
- Service provider interface (SPI)—the interface that translates generic API calls into service-specific requests.

Application developers mostly use JNDI API and existing JNDI drivers. Service providers use JNDI SPI to create such drivers.

The Java Development Kit (starting from JDK 1.3) includes the main JNDI packages:

- javax.naming
- javax.naming.directory
- javax.naming.spi
- javax.naming.ldap
- javax.naming.event

Developers who use lower-level JDK need to download J2EE SDK.

You may also need SPI software for all the vendors you wish to access. Any directory services you wish to access, including DNS, LDAP, and COS, must be installed and available on your network. J2EE reference implementation is a very useful source for JNDI related work.

To start working with JNDI, you have to properly set Path, Classpath, and JNDI properties, as in the examples below.

Classpath

```
jndi.jar
ldap.jar
```

```
ldapbp.jar
fscontext.jar
providerutil.jar
classes1.2.zip
jdbc20-stdext.jar
jndi.properties
```

JNDI Properties

```
java.naming.factory.initial =
com.sun.jndi.fscontext.RefFSContextFactory
java.naming.provider.url=file:/jndi
java.naming.factory.object=FooObjectFactory
```

JNDI allows you to use a resource bundle to provide path and name mapping. This resource bundle is available at run-time as an Initial Context object. You can use the Initial Context to look for objects and for binding.

In the example below, we bind the URL "/tmp" into the JNDI namespace.

```
InitialContext ctx = null;
try {
Hashtable env = new Hashtable();
env.put(context. INITIAL_CONTEXT_FACTORY,
"com.sun.jndi.fscontext.RefFSContextFactory");
env.put(context.PROVIDER_URL,"file:/tmp");
ctx = new InitialContext(env);
} catch(NamingException e) {
      System.err.println(e);
}
```

We can add, replace, or remove data from the JNDI namespace at run-time:

```
// Add
MapFile floorPlan = new MapFile("ibm.sfo.dxf");
ctx.bind("map",floorPlan);
// Replace
MapFile anotherMap = new MapFile("ibm.dtc.dxf");
ctx.bind("map", anotherMap);
// Remove
ctx.unbind("map");
```

One of the most important operations provided by JNDI is its lookup of objects:

```
File f =(File)ctx.lookup("map");
FileInputStream fis = new FileInputStream(f);
OracleDataSource ods = (OracleDataSource)ctx.lookup("myJdbc");
Connection con = ods.getConnection();
```

Note that in both examples, we look for specific object types, then we start the specific operations on these objects.

Using JNDI to resolve DNS, for example, in mail servers

The power of JNDI can be used to look up domain name services (DNS), which provide tables that relate host names to IP addresses. They also provide information about mail servers in the system.

For example, when you email yahoo.com, your email server should include the mechanism that figures out that the real name of the mail server at yahoo.com is mail1.yahoo.com.

JNDI lookup allows your mail server to resolve these names, which is an important feature for messaging and notification systems.

In order to use a DNS, we must specify whose implementation we are going to use. This is done by putting the provider name under the Context.INITIAL_CONTEXT_FACTORY property in the hash table. Next, we must provide the address of the DNS server and place it under Context.PROVIDER_URL in the same hash table:

```
Hashtable hashtableEnvironment = new Hashtable();
// we are using Sun's DNS extension
hashtableEnvironment.put(
            Context.INITIAL_CONTEXT_FACTORY,
            "com.sun.jndi.dns.DnsContextFactory");
// provide the address of name server as
// a starting point for lookup queries. Can be, for example, "sun.com"
hashtableEnvironment.put(Context.PROVIDER_URL, "dns://ns1.good.net");
// creates the context with properties specified
// all of the binding is done at this step
DirContext context=new InitialDirContext(hashtableEnvironment);
// search for all the servers with NS attribute
Attributes attrs = context.getAttributes("yahoo.com", new
String[]{"NS"});
```

By creating the DirContext object with that hash table as an argument, we prepare to make a query. The query shown here returns all the attributes for *yahoo.com* that contain the *NS* entry. In terms of the DNS, this means we will get the names of all the DNS servers that have information about yahoo.com. Every domain name must be supported by one primary server and one or more secondary servers. This query will return those server names. A similar result may be achieved by manually running an "nslookup" operation against *yahoo.com*.

The several examples provided above show that JNDI has the right approach to multiple data services. The next step is to use the JNDI common interface to represent different data sources, such as LDAP, file systems, directory services, and RDBMS.

We can encapsulate data access logic, create a proper application model, and make it independent of data sources. We can provide a hierarchy of data source types derived from the base *DataSource* interface.

```
InitialContext ic = new InitialContext();
DataSource ds = (DataSource) ic.lookup(dsName);
```

The data source captured with the lookup service may be of any type, including an RDBMS, file system, or DNS. The data source objects have their own implementations of basic data operations. We will use the Adapter design pattern to adapt multiple data source APIs into a unified API.

Using this approach, we can provide a connection to any data source, encapsulate Data Access Object (DAO) design pattern, and use the Factory design pattern to create a proper data source object at run-time.

This unified approach even allows us to replace or add a new data source without changing the core application sources.

Instant Screen Share

Another example of collaboration is the sharing of screens and voices across a network for multiple clients. The *ScreenShare* class, the source of which you can see below, is used to capture the screen and share it with other clients. Its main function is to clip out the changes (delta) on the screen using the *java.awt.Robot.createScreenCapture()* method and to compare them with the previous screen capture. If delta is found, then only the changed part of the screen will be compressed into ZIP format and sent (broadcast) to other clients.

This *java.awt.Robot* class was designed by Sun Microsystems to facilitate the automated testing of Java platform implementations. This class generates native system input events. This ability is very useful for the purposes of test automation, self-running demos, and other applications in which control of the mouse and keyboard is needed.

Using the class to generate input events differs from posting events to the Abstract Window Toolkit (AWT) event queue or to AWT components because the events are generated in the platform's native input queue. For example, *Robot.mouseMove* will actually move the mouse cursor instead of just generating mouse move events.

The *Robot* class can read from the screen and create an image containing screen pixels. This function is used in the source code below to share screen content in a collaborative session. Note that some platforms require special privileges or extensions to access low-level input control. You can find the *ScreenShare.java* source at the book support Web sites.

Instant Voice Share with JMF

JMF [6] supports time-based voice and video data in most popular media formats. One can use JMF to capture and process sound in WAV or AU (audio) formats; work with Audio Video Interleave (AVI) movies; use musical instrument digital interface (MIDI), Moving Picture Experts Group (MPEG), or QuickTime files; and arrange streaming voice and video over the Internet and multiple client platforms.

JMF's strength is in accessing underlying (e.g., on Solaris, Linux, Windows, and Mac) media frameworks in a unified way. JMF represents the basic media framework as a *DataSource* and a *Controller*. A microphone, camera, or tape is a simple example of a data source. In all cases, we deal with a media stream that has a set of specific characteristics. A controller is a mechanism that can work with a media stream, such as a tape recorder or a VCR.

JMF considers two types of controllers: a *Player* and a *Processor*. A *Player* is a *MediaHandler* that takes an input media stream or a *DataSource* and renders it at a precise time at a specified (with a *MediaLocator*) destination in a specified output format.

A *Processor* can further refine specific processing performed on the input media stream. A *Processor* adds the *Configuring* data to control the media data processing and access to output data streams.

Another *MediaHandler* (besides the *Player*) is the *DataSink*, which can read media from a *DataSource* and write it to a destination such as a file.

Important roles in media processing are played by the *javax.media.Format* class with the *AudioFormat* and *VideoFormat* subclasses and by the *FormatControl* interface, implementations of which can get and set data formats.

The *javax.media.control.TrackControl* interface extends the *FormatControl* interface to control and manipulate the data of individual media tracks. With the *TrackControl* methods, you can specify what format conversions are performed on individual media tracks and select the *Codec*, or *Renderer* plug-ins that are used by the *Processor*.

There are several hundred other classes and interfaces in the eleven packages of JMF listed below.

JMF package name	Selected classes and interfaces (not a full list!)
javax.media	CaptureDeviceManager, DataSink, Format, Player, Processor
javax.media.bean.playerbean	MediaPlayer, MediaPlayerResource, MediaPlayerRTPDialog
javax.media.control	FormatControl, FrameGrabbingControl, TrackControl
javax.media.datasink	DataSinkListener, DataSinkEvent
javax.media.format	AudioFormat, VideoFormat, EndOfStreamEvent
javax.media.protocol	CaptureDevice, PushBufferStream, DataSource
javax.media.renderer	VideoRenderer, VisualContainer
javax.media.rtp	DataChannel, Participant, RTPControl, SessionManager
javax.media.rtp.event	NewParticipantEvent, RemoteEvent, RTPEvent, SessionEvent
javax.media.rtp.rtcp	Feedback, Report, SourceDescription
javax.media.util	BufferToImage, ImageToBuffer

JMF supports the Real-Time Transport Protocol (RTP), an Internet standard for managing the real-time transmission of multimedia. JMF RTP APIs can transmit captured or stored media streams across a network, or implement a telephony application in a call center.

If you need to program a secure conferencing application with multiple participants and multiple sessions, you do not have to start from scratch. JMF offers, for example, a *SessionManager* to coordinate an RTP session and keep track of the session participants and the transmitted streams.

The *SessionManager* also handles the Real-Time Transport Control Protocol (RTCP) for both senders and receivers.

Figure A3.16 illustrates the Instant Share application, which allows participants to share their screens and voices over a network. The application uses RTP for streaming media or provides HTTP tunneling in case of firewall-related issues.

Let us consider the several steps involved in programming the voice-sharing portion of this application.

The first step is to create a data source that captures a user's voice. This can be done with the *initDataSource()* method provided below. The *initDataSource()* method creates a

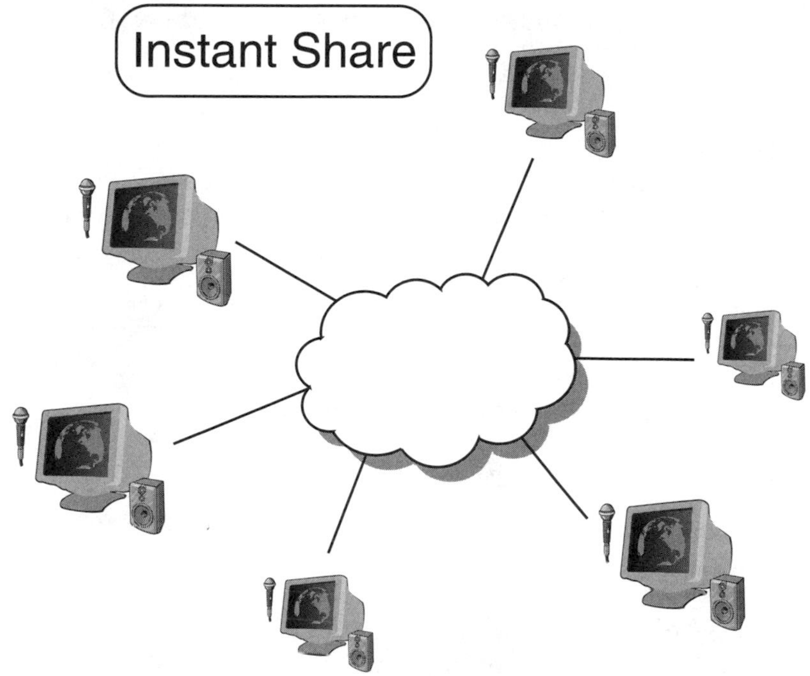

FIGURE A3.16. Instant Share.

DataSource for a given device name. If the name is not provided (the name equals *null*), the *initDataSource()* method will find a device from the list of devices.

The same method performs one more step. The *inputDataSource()* retrieves the list of data formats that are supported by the data source. Then, the method looks for a match between the input format provided as a parameter and the list of supported formats. When this match is found, the method sets the data source format to the proper format.

```
/**
* The initDataSource() method creates a DataSource for a
* given device name
* or finds a device from the list of devices.
* Then it sets a specified inputFormat on the
* FormatControl exposed by the CaptureDevice (data source)
* Uses the specified data source or creates a new one if null
* @param deviceName
* @param inputFormat for example "new
* AudioFormat(AudioFormat.LINEAR, 44100, 16, 2)"
* @return dataSource
*/
public static DataSource initDataSource(String deviceName,
Format inputFormat) {
  DataSource dataSource = null;
  CaptureDeviceInfo cdi = null;
  if(deviceName != null) {
```

```
            cdi = CaptureDeviceManager.getDevice(deviceName);
    }
    if (cdi == null) {
         Vector deviceList =
         CaptureDeviceManager.getDeviceList(inputFormat);
         if (deviceList.size() > 0)
              cdi = (CaptureDeviceInfo)deviceList.firstElement();
    }
    if(cdi == null) {// device not found
         return null;
    }
    // set a media locator
    MediaLocator deviceURL = cdi.getLocator();
    try {
       dataSource = Manager.createDataSource(deviceURL);
       if (dataSource == null) return null;
    }catch (Exception e) {
         return null;
    }
    if (inputFormat == null) return dataSource;
    // find match and set proper Audio Format for the data source
    FormatControl [] formatControls = ((CaptureDevice)
  dataSource).getFormatControls();
    if (formatControls == null || formatControls.length == 0)
       return null;
    for (int i = 0; i < formatControls.length; i++) {
         if (formatControls[i] == null)
               continue;
       Format [] formats = formatControls[i].getSupportedFormats();
       if (formats == null)
             continue;
       if (matches(inputFormat, formats) != null) {
          formatControls[i].setFormat(inputFormat);
         return dataSource;
       }
     }
       return null;
  }
```

We use the *javax.media.CaptureDeviceManager*, a manager class that registers capture devices and provides access to the list of these devices available on a system. Here is the *match()* method:

```
   /**
   * The match() method is looking for a format passed as an
   * argument in the array of supported formats
   * @param format
   * @param supported
```

```
 * @return supportedFormat
 */
private static Format match(Format format, Format [] supported) {
   if (supported == null)
        return null;
   for (int i = 0; i < supported.length; i++) {
        if (supported[i].matches(format))
          return supported[i];
      }
     return null;
  }
```

The next step is to provide a connection between the data source and the network. The connection can be RTP, HTTP (if there are firewall issues), or any other type that makes sense for this application and a participant environment. The protocol decision is expected at run-time.

A simple and elegant solution is to introduce a *ConnectedSource* interface and implement it with classes such as *RTPSource* and *HTTPSource*. The *ConnectedSource* interface requires implementation of the *init()* and *setSession()* methods.

```
// ConnectedSource
package com.its.media;
import javax.media.protocol.DataSource;
/**
 * The ConnectedSource interface requires init() and
 * setSession() method implementations
 * The interface serves to create a factory of connected sources
 * with multiple protocols
 * The implementations would include HTTP Source,RTPSource, etc.
 * @author Jeff.Zhuk@JavaSchool.com
 */
public interface ConnectedSource {
 /**
 * The init() method connects ds according to a protocol.
 * @param ds
 * @param connectingString "host:port" for HTTP or
 * "webServer.com/servletURL?etc" for RTP
 */
public void init(DataSource ds, String connectingString);
  /**
  * The setSession() method sets the session data for a new
  * participant
  * @param username
  * @param sessionData
  */
public void setSession(String username, String sessionData);
}
```

Here is an application code extract:

```
ConnectedSource connected =
(ConnectedSource) Class.forName(protocolType).newInstance();
```

Note, that the *protocolType* variable that defines the class name will be supplied at run-time.

```
connected.init(dataSource, connectingString);
```

The *connectingString* represents, for example, the host and port data for the RTP connection and the URL to a Java servlet in the case of an HTTP connection.

```
connected.setSession(username, sessionData);
```

For example, when programming the *RTPSource*, we can use the *javax.media.rtp.RTPManager* class with its powerful methods, such as *addReceiveStreamListener(ReceiveStreamListener)* and *addTarget(SessionAddress)*.

We use the *RTDManager* to create a *javax.media.rtp.SendStream* object:

```
SendStream stream = rtdManager.createSendStream(source,0);
```

The *SendStream* object is a thread. We start this thread with the trivial line:

```
stream.start();
```

We are almost done. How will this captured voice be restored on the other side of the universe?

We create a player that can work with the incoming stream. The stream may be attached to a port on the machine (if this is an RTP stream), or it may be redirected by a Java servlet.

We introduce the *NetPlayer* interface, which requires implementing the *getDataSource()* method.

NetPlayer implementation objects can deal with different types of streams, but the main function of the player still is to play sound.

```
NetPlayer netPlayer = (NetPlayer)
Class.forName(protocolType).newInstance();
DataSource ds = netPlayer.getDataSource();
Player player = Manager.createPlayer(ds);
player.start(); // start playing!
```

Voice-sharing applications may use the javax.media.Multiplexer to combine data from multiple tracks (of multiple participants) into interleaved data through an output *DataSource*. The alternative is to establish privilege-based rules that give a channel only to a selected participant.

Security Monitoring

Screen and voice sharing can be used not only for conferencing, but for many other applications. An example of another application is security monitoring with hidden cameras and microphones at several guard locations. A program can integrate multicamera views on a single screen and can share this screen with selected guard locations. Privileged guards can control many locations from a single screen.

More details and sources may be found at the Cambridge University Press Web site or at *http://JavaSchool.com.*

Java Messaging Services (JMS): A New Way to Think about Applications

JMS represents an asynchronous way of doing business. From the outset, I have to admit that messaging applications are not exactly new to the industry. Consider email, a well-known veteran and the simplest example of asynchronous communication.

One can then send an email message do other things without waiting for the recipient's response. This is a really great invention that frees our hands and fills our hearts with the happiness of a "done deal"—except for the fact that you are never sure your mail will be delivered.

Simple Mail Transport Protocol (SMTP), by definition, is not reliable. Conversely, messaging services such as Message Queue (MQ) from IBM and JMS from Sun Microsystems guarantee delivery.

Today, more and more businesses are linked to one another. When we create a new application, or adapt an old one, we must include the software that provides these links in the scope of the application.

This software may be built with a synchronous connection-oriented design or with an asynchronous paradigm that allows networks to dissolve and appear again. The synchronous design is known for better performance and more tightly coupled applications. The asynchronous design provides better flexibility and scalability in a loosely coupled application environment.

Messaging services used to be expensive and tended to be proprietary solutions. These factors prevented most businesses from considering messaging solutions to be primary in the design of their applications.

That situation has changed. JMS is a standard, inexpensive solution that is available to every company. It takes time to reinvent existing applications in new, asynchronous terms—but it definitely makes sense to think of new projects as potential messaging solutions.

How Does JMS Work?

It includes two major mechanisms: a point-to-point messaging domain and a publish-subscribe domain.

The point-to-point mechanism allows several clients to send their messages to message queues, which serve as mailboxes for the receivers. The most interesting and intriguing point-to-point mechanism is the publish-subscribe mechanism. Clients subscribe to topics, and publishers post their messages to the topics.

Think of topics as mailboxes, but keep in mind that each topic has many subscribers (serves as a mailbox for many clients) and each message may have several recipients. A client must subscribe to the topic and be an "active" subscriber in order to receive messages. A single client can be a publisher as well as a subscriber. Figure A3.17 reflects this high-level architecture.

Topics are located at the JMS provider or JMS server. A JMS provider can use one of the existing implementations of Sun's JMS API—for example, the one from the OpenJMS group [7].

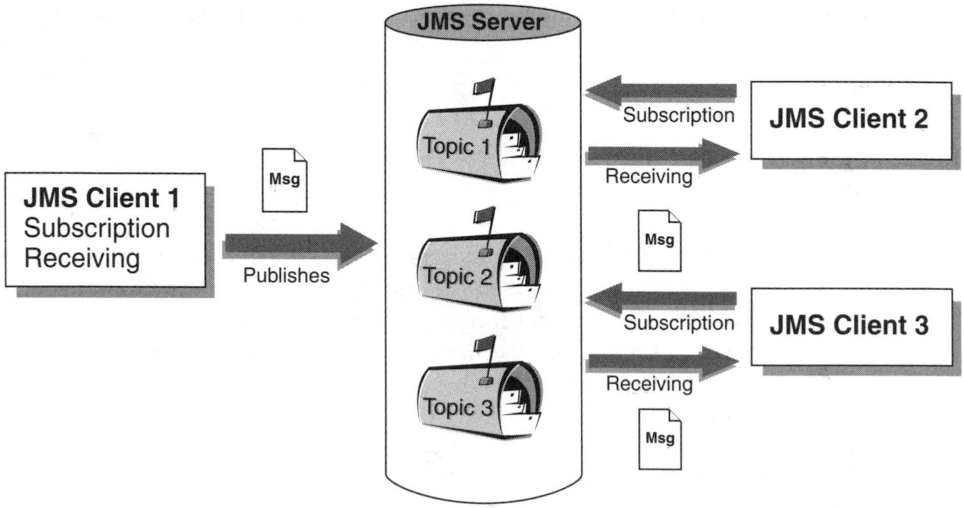

FIGURE A3.17. JMS Clients and JMS Server.

The client uses a connection factory to create a proper connection to the JMS server. There are two connection factories available with the JDK from Sun, but generally speaking, a client program should start its work with a JNDI lookup for available connection factories.

We can read the JNDI context from the *jndi.properties* file (if exists):

```
Context ctx = new InitialContext();
// reading jndi.properties file
```

The other alternative is to create the context on the fly, as in this example:

```
Hashtable props = new Hashtable();
String modeType = RmiJndiInitialContextFactory.class.getName();
props.put(Context.PROVIDER_URL, "rmi://" + hostName + ":" +
  OPEN_JMS_PORT + "/" + JNDI_SERVER_NAME);
props.put(Context.INITIAL_CONTEXT_FACTORY, modeType);
  Context ctx = new InitialContext(props);
```

The next step is to use JNDI lookup for the proper connection factory:

```
// in the case of using the Point-to-point domain with queues
QueueConnectionFactory queueConnectionFactory =
(QueueConnectionFactory) ctx.lookup("QueueConnectionFactory");
// in the case of using the Publish/Subscribe domain with topics
TopicConnectionFactory topicConnectionFactory =
(TopicConnectionFactory) ctx.lookup("TopicConnectionFactory");
```

The following code is used for the *Publish/Subscribe* mechanism:

```
// create a topic connection
TopicConnection topicConnection =
topicConnectionFactory.createTopicConnection();
topicConnection.start();
```

```
// create a topic session (non-transactional) with
auto-message-acknowledgement
TopicSession topicSession =
  topicConnection.createTopicSession(false, Session.
  AUTO_ACKNOWLEDGE);
// create a topic
Topic topic = topicSession.createTopic(topicName);
// make a client a publisher
TopicPublisher topicPublisher = topicSession.createPublisher(topic);
// We are ready now to publish a message
// The message can be any serializable Java object
// For example, a message can be a String or a Hashtable
ObjectMessage objMsg = topicSession.createObjectMessage(anyObject);
// finally publish the message to the topic
// topicPublisher.publish(topic, objMsg);
// Here is the subscription part.
// Note, that the same client can be a publisher and a subscriber
TopicSubscriber topicSubscriber =
  topicSession.createSubscriber(topic, null, !ownReceiving);
// set Message Listener in THIS class
topicSubscriber.setMessageListener(this);
```

This class must be defined as a *MessageListener* implementation. The *MessageListener* interface requires the implementation of the *onMessage()* method:

```
/**
 * The onMessage() method does the message processing
 */
public void onMessage(Message msg) {
 // call a service to process the message
 // this example assumes that messages include "service"
 // and "action" parts
 try {
  String serviceName = msg.getStringProperty("service");
  String action = msg.getStringProperty("action");
  ServiceConnector.performService(service, action, msg);
 } catch(Exception e) {
        // error handling procedure and msg
 }
}
```

CREATE SPEECH RECOGNITION AND TTS APPLICATIONS IN C#

The code from the *cs.its.Speech* package expands TTS and speech recognition examples provided with Microsoft Speech SDK 5.1. The sources mentioned below (*VoiceMaster.cs, Recognizer.cs, TextToSpeech.cs, SocketTTS.cs, IOMaster.cs,* and *Grammer.xml*) can be found at the book support Web sites.

The *VoiceMaster* class provides:

- Integration of speech recognition and TTS
- Multithreaded performance

TCP/IP socket communications to a process

- written in Java or another language
- Dynamic replacements of grammar files at run-time
- Printing of internal information on *Hypothesis* and pronunciation elements

The *Recognizer* class is responsible for speech recognition.

The *Recognizer()* constructor initializes the speech recognition engine and sets an initial grammar file for recognition work. Most of the methods of this class handle different speech events.

The *TextToSpeech* class is responsible for the connection to the TTS engine. The *speakText()* method passes the text to the *SpVoice* object and invokes the *speak()* method on the voice object.

The *SocketTTS* class establishes TCP/IP socket communications between *VoiceMaster* and other programs that can be written in Java or other languages.

This class includes the command interpreter that parses the text coming into the TTS engine. Some text expressions are considered to be specific commands. These commands are not pronounced but are executed on the fly instead.

The *IOMaster* class is responsible for input/output and network operations.

The *Grammar.xml* file is the initial grammar provided in the beginning of the application. This file includes two sets of rules. The SELECT_NUMBER rule helps to select a numbered choice. The PERFORM_ACTION_ON_OBJECT rule allows us to manipulate some objects. Both sets expect phrases that consist of two parts.

The SELECT_NUMBER set expects the "select" word first, followed by a number from 1 to 14.

The PERFORM_ACTION_ON_OBJECT set expects the user to start with an action name and continue with an object name.

Note that this file can be easily extended and/or replaced at run-time with another grammar file. It makes sense to break the application grammar into several smaller files that can be dynamically loaded. These extra steps will simplify speech recognition work.

Fight Email Spam and Increase Email Server Efficiency

SMTP Simplicity Plays a Cruel Joke on Mail Servers

> Spam is rising exponentially at a rate of 1,000 percent per year. By 2004, unless an enterprise takes defensive action, more than 50 percent of its message traffic will be spam.
>
> —Joyce Graff and Maurene Grey, Gartner Research

Spam and pollution have become a real threat to the quickly growing crowd on the Internet. Protection filters barely work in a common public environment. Spam comes under multiple fictitious and real names, including your own and those of your friends. The simplicity of the

Simple Mail Transport Protocol (SMTP) plays a cruel joke on most of our public mail servers. Public mail servers such as Yahoo and Hotmail might be directly used by hackers as proxies for massive attacks. Just try to telnet to mail2.yahoo.com to port 25 (the mail server starts talking to you) and you immediately recognize the danger. (By the way, these two great mail servers actually have some protection from these attacks, so I can mention them without much risk.) Is there any way to improve this situation?

There are several directions to proceed. The most dramatic and decisive escape is to leave the urban areas of the public Internet into the suburbs of private Internet communities. Distributed technologies and network protocols (described in Chapters 1, 10, and 14) allow you to establish and maintain secure multiple role based access to data and services in gated community networks. This is the way to depart from SMTP's simplicity altogether.

It is also possible to enhance public (and corporate) SMTP servers. Of course, there is much more than a single algorithm to implement or a single layer to improve. As with any of the IT tasks related to security, the answer lies in multi-layer efforts that engage observations of spam mail behavior and translate these observations into protection mechanisms.

Spammers Abuse Nonsecure Servers

Most spammers today abuse nonsecure servers, using them as proxies for their messages. The number of such servers is significantly smaller than the number of spammers. Thus it makes perfect sense to obtain a list of nonsecure servers as the first step of defense, so you can refuse email from these servers. Where can you get this list? The Distributed Server Boycott List (DSBL, http://dsbl.org) is a good place. You can also add a nonsecure server to the list yourself. How? If a server is nonsecure, not only do spammers have an opportunity to abuse the server, you can also use the same server to notify DSBL and add the server to the list.

Dial-Up Spammers

Spammers can also use direct connections from their PCs (via a modem or DSL) to your mail server, without using their ISP's mail server as a relay. The Mail Abuse Prevention System's Dial-up User List (the MAPS DUL project, http://www.mail-abuse.org/dul/) deals with these "dial-up spammers." The project lists dynamically assigned IP addresses; blocking messages from addresses on that list can be used to stop this type of spam.

Prevent Unauthorized Usage of Mail Servers

I describe algorithms that prevent unauthorized usage of mail servers as proxies. It is more difficult to make mail servers smarter, so they can recognize incoming spam messages. Here is a great place for a knowledgebase to help users establish spam rules instead of spam lists.

How can we distinguish an authorized request to send email from an unauthorized one?

The SMTP protocol retrieves email header information that can be very useful to us. Here is a typical example of a header.

```
Received: from vwall1.OLS.Phoenix.edu (VWALL1 [204.17.18.215])
          by olsims1.uophx.edu with SMTP (Microsoft Exchange
          Internet Mail Service Version 5.5.2656.59)
     id 407L5YAZ; Thu, 16 Oct 2003 17:22:51-0700
```

```
Received: From fed1mtao01.cox.net ([68.6.19.244]) by
          vwall1.OLS.Phoenix.edu (WebShield SMTP v4.5 MR1a);
      id 106635010261; Thu, 16 Oct 2003 17:21:42-0700
Received: from THINKPADR30 ([68.110.65.207]) by
          fed1mtao01.cox.net
         (InterMail vM.5.01.06.05 201-253-122-130-105-20030824)
         with SMTP id <20031017002139.YJAQ
         2935.fed1mtao01.cox.net@THINKPADR30>
     for <jzhuk@email.uophx.edu>; Thu, 16 Oct 2003 20:21:39-0400
From: "Joe Smith" <joe.smith@joe.server.com>
To: <jzhuk@email.uophx.edu>
Subject: Any news?
Date: Thu, 16 Oct 2003 17:21:30-0700
Message-ID: <NGBBLOHONKNAPNAAJIOMIELADHAA.
            joe.smith@joe.server.com>
MIME-Version: 1.0
Content-Type: text/plain;
              charset="us-ascii"
Content-Transfer-Encoding: 7bit
X-Priority: 1 (Highest)
X-MSMail-Priority: High
X-Mailer: Microsoft Outlook IMO, Build 9.0.2416 (9.0.2910.0)
X-MimeOLE: Produced By Microsoft MimeOLE V6.00.2727.1300
Importance: High
```

The most valuable data retrieved from the header are the address of the sender (senderAddress) and the address of the recipient (recipientAddress). Look at the "Received: From" lines and read the intriguing story.

Received: from THINKPADR30 ([68.110.65.207]) by fed1mtao01.cox.net

The very first step is to figure out if the sender and the recipient are local or remote users (4 possible combinations). A remote user can be a potential hacker or a hacker program trying to force this email server send spam messages.

There is one valid case when an email server should allow a *remote* user to send email: this must be a valid POP3 user who is currently logged in using a login name and a password. Otherwise, the program should reject remote user attempts (via a telnet session, for example) to send email.

Here is an extract from an email server program that uses header information to validate access. There is also regular logic to validate a local recipient.

```
boolean localSender = domain.validateUser(senderAddress);
if(localSender) {
// if from a local user - make sure it is a valid one
 String realEmail = MailDomain.userAlias(senderAddress);
 String loginName = realEmail.substring(0,realEmail.
 indexOf("@"));
```

```
    if(!domain.isAuthenticated(_clientIp, loginName)) {
     // user has been logged in via POP3
     // only a POP3 user can send email; this prevents
     // unauthorized telnet sessions
     out.println("550 Unable to relay for
     "+recipientAddress+". POP3 login required.");
     break;
    }
    knownSender = true;
  } else {
     // check to see if the originator email match the _clientIp
  }
  // ##################################################
  localRecipient = domain.validateDomain(recipientAddress);
  if (localSender && !localRecipient) {// to: remote user
     sendMail = true; // send mail using SMTP (only for
     remote users)
  }
  // For local users: just copy/paste the message file from local
  // to local
  // From remote - to local: read body later on
  if (!sendMail) {
     localRecipient = domain.validateUser(recipientAddress);
     if (localRecipient) {
        out.println("250 [" + recipientAddress + "] OK");
        recipientAddress = MailDomain.userAlias(recipientAddress);
        recipientAddresses.addElement(recipientAddress);
        domain.readNewPropertyList(recipientAddress);
     } else {
        out.println("550 invalid user");
     }
  } else {// remote recipient
     out.println("250 [" + recipientAddress + "] OK");
     // original choice
  }
```

Rule Out Spam Messages on the Server Side

An even more complicated method is to rule out spam messages at the early stage of sending by the email server. Today, the majority of spam prevention programs work on the client side. This helps end users, but still allows spam senders to use your bandwidth, which you pay for. We can save bandwidth (and money) if we move some logic upfront to the server side.

A mail server has an additional benefit of knowledge. It can precisely tell us the IP address of a sender (from-IP). This knowledge can give us a chance (though not 100%) to verify that the FROM email address is a valid one. This type of verification might be expensive at run-time, but might help afterwards for spam analysis. The following extract illustrates this point.

```
if(localRecipient) {
    Hashtable mailInstructions = domain.
    getUserMailInstructions(recipientAddress);
    // check from address
    // check from-ip address
    // check subject keywords
    // check attachment names and prevent.exe and known
    // virus attachments
    // check body keywords
}
```

The mailInstructions table is prepared partially by the end user and partially by the knowledge engine that understand every click on a message as "Mark as SPAM" and tries its best to add a rule to the mailInstructions table.

Rule-Based Content Filtering

The next layer of protection is rule-based content filtering or antispam heuristics. The user creates a filter list for the subject and body of mail messages to block spam that contains words such as "absolutely free" or "debt consolidation." The rules can assign each word or phrase a score, for example, "absolutely =10" and "free=20."

Every message is read, and its contents are computed into a total score. The user can set his or her own tolerance level, which would reject messages that get a score above a certain level. For example, a user will set a level of protection, like "high tolerance" or "low tolerance," that can be translated into the total score, for example, 30 or 20. Then the program would block the messages with the total spam score higher than the threshold set by the user. In our example the "low tolerance" would filter any message that contain the "free" word while the "high tolerance" would only block messages that contain "absolutely free" or similar sentences.

The problem with content filtering is that spammers often change their spelling. For example, they will use "F-R-E-E" instead of "free" or "@bsolutely" instead of "absolutely." We (people) still recognize the meanings of the words while our programs are too precise; in other words, they are "too stupid." Using a knowledge engine can help our programs to learn and to adapt. We value these abilities extremely highly in people. We lack these features, and need them badly, in our programs.

Improving the Efficiency and Reliability of Your Email Server

An email server provides interaction between several services. The most common are SMTP, which sends and receives email over port 25 (default), and POP3 (or IMAP), which retrieves the users' email. Let us also include a Web Mail Service into the equation. The Web Mail Service competes with POP3 for email delivery, but uses a different interface and protocol.

It is possible to get the following message when checking your e-mail:

```
-ERR [IN-USE].pop lock busy!
```

This error occurs when two different programs attempt to open the same mailbox simultaneously or if one of the programs crashed before completion and is keeping the mailbox open.

The well-known solution that allows only a single program to access an object at a time is to "lock" the mailbox object. In most cases the "lock" is sufficient, and another program can get access to the same object at a later time. Unfortunately, there are cases, as we described above, that undermine this solution. The alternative direction is to avoid the situation when two or more processes try to access the same object altogether.

Following the Snapshot design pattern, we can create a snapshot of the object for each process. A process can only modify its own snapshot object, though it can read complementary information from other snapshot objects created by other processes. Only one of all the processes can modify or delete the original object.

No "lock" is needed in this case. The locking mechanism is replaced by some logistics in collecting the necessary information from more than one (mailbox) snapshot object. The source example for this mechanism has not been tested at the time of the book's release. You can find this source and more details on the subject on the Cambridge University Press Web site and/or on the author's *http://JavaSchool.com* page.

Create a Distributed Knowledge System and Join Educational/Knowledge Alliances

The package provided below helps you to integrate knowledge and traditional software services. Compile the source and follow the instructions in Chapter 13 to produce an application that runs as a distributed knowledge system. You can use this application as a training tool and as your entrance to knowledge alliances. There are several places to look for source and binary downloads and for XML-based scenario examples.

1. *http://OpenCyc.org* (the sources were contributed in the OpenCyc project and constitute the org.opencyc.connector package.);
2. The Cambridge University Press Web site, at http://www.cup.org/titles/0521525837.htm
3. The author's site *http://JavaSchool.com*

Another Passage from "Ben's Real and Dream Memoirs"

I woke up in a daze. The shuttle door was opening with a whoosh, letting the white smoke out into the bright blue sky. It looked like I was home. But something strange was happening to me. As my eyes moved over the objects around me, I felt every image in my field of vision making my brain struggle, like a word on the tip of your tongue you can't quite reach. As I made my way back home, everything looked strange to me, as if my head wasn't on quite right, as if I were viewing everything from an angle, somehow unfamiliar and slightly off.

As the days passed, strange images and visions began to fill my dreams. A vast, empty plain, the sky pure white. A flying woman, changing suddenly into a reflective sphere. Words surrounding me, undulating slowly, as if breathing, moving in and out of my field of vision, combining, recombining. More and more, these images began to seep into my waking life. At first, I thought I was going insane. As time passed, my memories began to coalesce and then to seem more real to me than reality itself.

The day I finally understood what had happened to me, my friend Alete sat me down on a park bench. "Ben, you've been acting delirious!" she told me. "Maybe you should see someone." I explained that I was fine and that I now saw a greater reality than she or anyone else knew. She just stared at me. So I told her.

"I remember closing my eyes as the shuttle left the planet H.235 and then waking up in white fog, seeing nothing around me. When I looked down, I couldn't even see my own legs. How long

FIGURE A3.18. Understanding.

I stayed in the whiteness, unable to move or make a sound, I do not know. Suddenly, my mind was filled with new knowledge. From nothing, I felt myself taking on an unbearable weight and passed out. I awoke in the same whiteness, but with the new information settled more comfortably in my mind. I had a purpose.

Using parts of my mind I never knew I had (had I really had them before now?), I formed some white fog into a canvas and filled the canvas with a pleasant landscape image. Then, I inverted the field, condensing the fog outside me into the canvas and creating the landscape all around me. I was now surrounded by mountains, a solid-looking lake, and some strangely false trees.

The leaves didn't look quite right, the bark was too blotched, and I'd gotten the proportions wrong. What looked fine in a painting was terrible in three dimensions. I looked at the trees and wondered what made real bark look so different from what I'd imagined. I felt compelled to push yet another new mental button, and data swirled into my awareness.

I knew that bark is an aggregation of organs and tissues external to the vascular cambium, including phloem and thickened tissues from the secondary plant body, as well as epidermis, cortex and phloem derived from the primary plant body. The trees began to look more real. I knew the proportions, the leaves' structure and thickness.

I looked at the lake and was filled with fluid dynamics, their properties immediately transferred to the water. The scene was now almost real. I added air pressure differentials to create a light breeze and formed some hawks in the distance after a dizzying spectrum of anatomy, muscular structure, and networks of basal ganglia. This act of Godlike creation filled me with nausea and exhilaration, making my head spin into another blackout. After pulling myself together again, I opened my eyes in the white fog.

The time reserved for my training was now at an end; I began to receive instructions immediately. First, I was to create a fishing scene on a lake much like the one I'd already constructed. I was to pay special attention to the carp, because the client was desirous of catching some large specimens. Immediately after, my mind was turned to Baghdad in its glory, and the story of the 810th Arabian Night, to be rendered in explicit detail. And so it went, a seemingly endless array of assignments, from fantastic citadels in space to scenes of ancient bloody war in the Balkans to pleasant and elaborate fantasies.

The aliens who trapped me wanted to be entertained. To this end, they constructed a sensorium that allowed the stimulation of all the known senses. They had the ability to obtain and represent knowledge instantaneously through their linked minds. But this was not enough. Their replications of their regular experiences did not entertain them more than the experiences themselves. Their civilization had technology and wisdom. What they lacked was imagination. Perhaps it had disappeared with time, no longer useful. Perhaps they never had it at all. But through their infinite knowledge repository, they knew where to borrow it.

Time appeared to fly. Was there time? I could not be sure. Everything moved so quickly, but I never seemed to get tired, never needed anything, and I still could not find my body. I could create one, of course, but it didn't feel quite right, so I disappeared it immediately each time. I became so adept at creating worlds that this no longer moved me. I took my duties and abilities as a given. But one thing never stopped amazing me, no matter how many times it happened—my seemingly instant knowledge of any subject to its finest detail.

The global mind I now had access to, the same one the aliens used themselves, was a real store of knowledge, not just information. Even if I knew nothing about a subject, a single thought in that direction brought me an understanding of the appropriate facts, mental maps, formulas, and narratives, all apparently designed for me alone.

The pleasure of creating whole universes was mild compared to my delight in being able to truly know anything I put my mind to. I knew what it was like to have infinite wisdom! I knew my joy at that sensation would never end . . . until I heard a metallic voice say "Thank you for your time. We hope your satisfaction was sufficient compensation," and the world I was currently creating (a precise plot of a Mandelbrot set in exponentially increasing dimensions) faded to a white fog.

I woke up in my ordinary existence, as if no time had passed. But as my memories returned to me, I began to long more and more for that world of infinite knowledge and limitless possibilities. Now as I walk the streets and feel the walls on both sides of me pressing in, limiting my movement, I think only of the time I spent in forever, bathed in white.

I sighed. Alete said nothing. We sat together, watching the green hills reflecting in the lake. The sun came out from behind the clouds, illuminating the scene in bright, almost unreal colors. The air above the lake glistened. Suddenly, Alete pointed ahead with a delighted cry. In the neon blue sky, a rainbow was shimmering into existence. As I stared at it, my mood began to change, and a strange kind of joy pierced my heart. Hundreds of thoughts were coming to my mind. I was on the edge of understanding. I felt myself a magician and realized I was not alone. There were billions of us. All I needed was to figure out how to connect . . . .

REFERENCES

1. Zhuk, J., Distributed active knowledge and process base, Patent pending, *http://uspto.gov.*
2. NMEA-0183 (National Marine Electronics Association) Standard *http://www.nmea.org/pub/0183/index.html.*
3. Bennett, Peter, NMEA-0183 and GPS Information, *http://vancouver-webpages.com/peter/.*
4. VisualGPS, *http://www.visualgps.net/VisualGPS/.*
5. ESRI Shapefile Technical Description: *http://www.esri.com/library/whitepapers/pdfs/shapefile.pdf.*
6. Java Media Framework: *http://java.sun.com/products/java-media/jmf/.*
7. JMS Implementation from the OpenJMS Group: *http://openjms.sourceforge.net.*

Index

T